Listening
TOP

3

Stephen Poirier

Stephen Poirier is from Canada and has a Master of Arts in History.
He has been teaching English in Korea, Russia, and Canada since 1992.
He was also a professor of history at St. Mary's University in Canada from 2003 to
2005. He currently works as an English conversation instructor at a college.

Listening TOP 3

Publisher Kyudo Chung
Editorial Director Juyon Choi
Editors Yoonyoung Hur, Jiyeon Min
Proofreader Michael A. Putlack
Designers Hwayoun Cho, Joowon Jin

First published in January 2010
By Darakwon, Inc.
Darakwon Bldg., 211, Munbal-ro, Paju-si,
Gyeonggi-do 10881 Republic of Korea
Tel: 82-2-736-2031(Ext. 250)
Fax: 82-2-732-2037

Price ₩18,000
ISBN 978-89-5995-217-5 58740
 978-89-5995-877-1 58740 (set)

www.darakwon.co.kr

Components Main Book / Answer Book / 1 MP3 CD
10 9 8 7 6 5 4   22 23 24 25 26

Reach for Excellence!

Listening
TOP

3

DARAKWON

To the **Students**

●

Listening TOP is an advanced listening book series for English learners with a high level of ability. This series is suitable for students who are preparing for any English tests that have a listening section, such as TOEFL or TEPS. The listening exercises are designed to test students' abilities to absorb knowledge quickly and to answer questions based on this knowledge. The information presented may be familiar or may be new to students. As students progress from the first to the last book, their listening skills will improve, and their confidence will grow. The goal is for students to have proficient listening skills when they finish the series.

●●

There are three books in the advanced series, and each book has 12 units. Each unit consists of 19 listening passages, with a mix of dialogs and monologs that are 170-280 words in length. Following each listening passage, there are questions for the students to answer. Topics for the listening passages include everyday situations and more academic-style lessons that are similar to what students would expect to find on a TOEFL exam.

●●●

Each unit has five main parts. The first section of the unit has vocabulary, which prepares the students for the unit. Next come listening drills to help introduce the students to the main topics of the unit. After this come more listening exercises and questions. Then there is a practice test that the students can use to see how well their skills are progressing. Most of the questions are in multiple choice format. Sometimes the questions and answer choices will not be written, but the students must listen for them instead. Question types include listening for the main idea, picking the best title, finding the purpose, listening for details, making inferences, selecting pictures, completing tables, drawing graphs, and making calculations. Included in each unit is an integrated question where the students must both read a passage and then listen to a lecture. Finally, at the end of each unit, there are dictation exercises, so students can practice their listening and note-taking skills.

How to Use **This Book**

Each unit follows the same pattern.

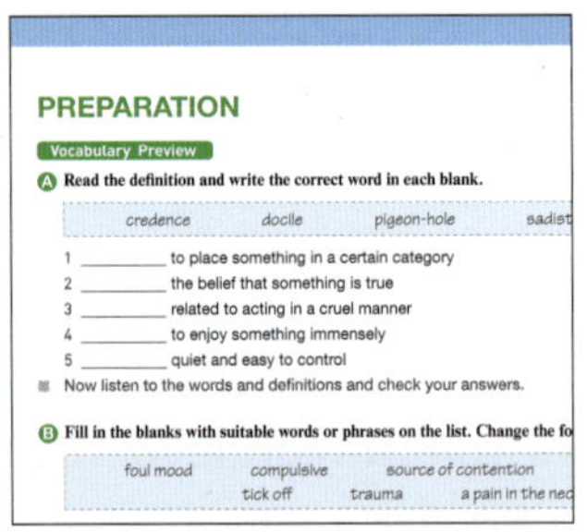

Preparation

Vocabulary Preview

Two vocabulary preview exercises have challenging vocabulary words that students must match with their meanings or fill into sentences.

Expressions and Meanings

In this exercise, students must match seven unique English expressions with their meanings.

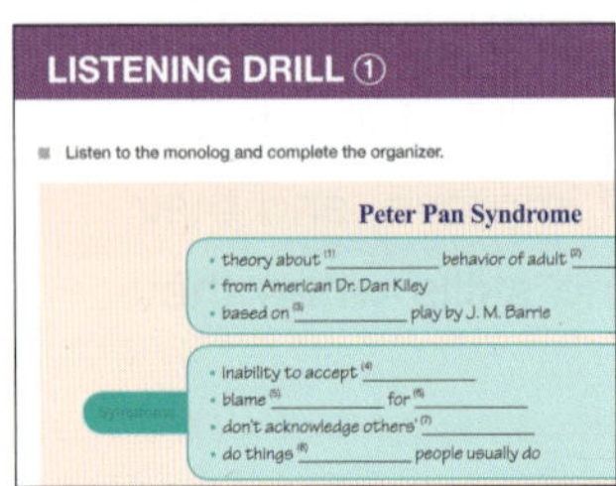

Listening Drill 1, 2

Two monologs and a dialog introduce the main subject of the unit. Students first fill in the blanks on a mind map while listening. Then, they must use the notes from the mind maps to answer questions that deal with general aspects of the listening and also answer questions that deal with specific details.

Exercise

There are nine listening passages in this section. Each is followed by one or two questions, making for a total of twelve questions. Most questions are multiple choice while others may ask students to select a picture, complete a table, draw a graph, or make a calculation. For two listening exercises, students must also listen for the question and the answer choices.

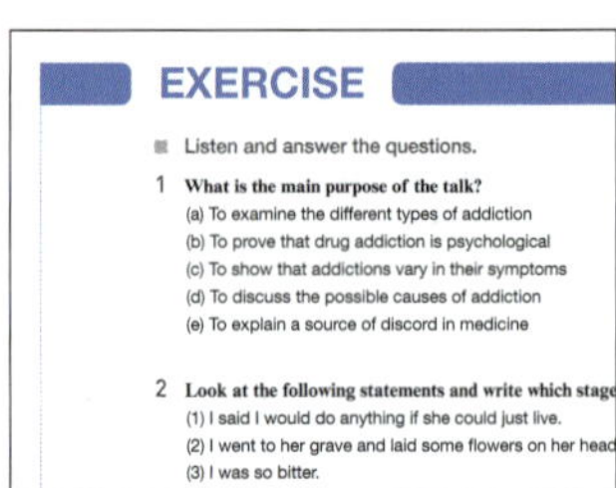

Practice Test

The practice test consists of seven listening passages and ten questions. The final exercise is an integrated selection consisting of a reading passage and a listening exercise. Students must read the passage, then listen to the exercise, and finally answer the questions.

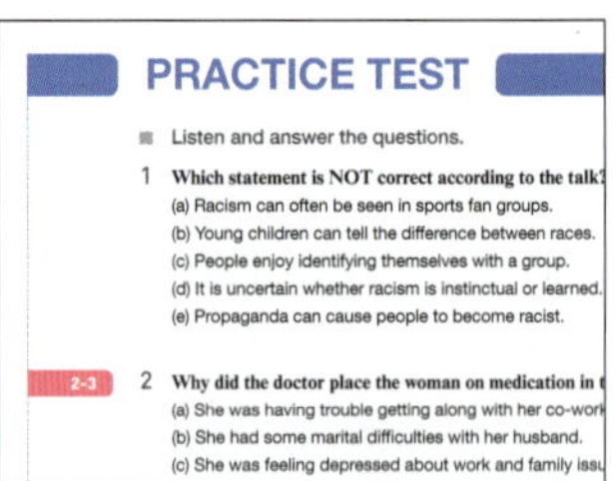

Dictation

At the end of the unit, students listen to the passages in Exercise and fill in the blanks.

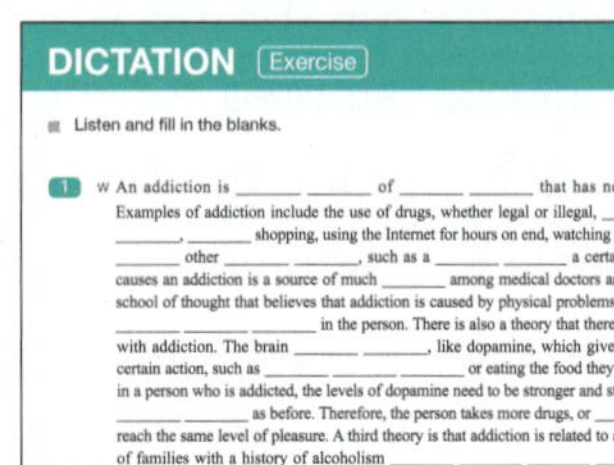

• Dictation exercise for Practice Test & Vocabulary Quiz: Free download from **www.darakwon.co.kr**

Contents

Psychology

PREPARATION

1-1

A Read the definition and write the correct word in each blank.

credence	docile	pigeon-hole	sadistic	relish

1 ___________ to place something in a certain category
2 ___________ the belief that something is true
3 ___________ related to acting in a cruel manner
4 ___________ to enjoy something immensely
5 ___________ quiet and easy to control

▪ Now listen to the words and definitions and check your answers.

B Fill in the blanks with suitable words or phrases on the list. Change the forms if needed.

foul mood	compulsive	source of contention	get out of hand
tick off	trauma	a pain in the neck	

1 An addiction is a form of _____________ behavior in which a person cannot control his or her actions.
2 The game _____________, and the referees could no longer control the violent play of the two teams.
3 The boss has been in a _____________ all day and is shouting at people for the smallest of reasons.
4 I got really _____________ on the bus today when a man kept talking loudly on his cellphone.
5 Dealing with problems all day can be _____________ and cause a lot of stress.
6 The cause of some psychological disorders is a _____________ among experts, who often have strong disagreements.
7 People under severe psychological stress can suffer emotional _____________.

▪ Now listen to the sentences and check your answers.

▪ **Match each expression with its proper meaning.**

1 Everybody was in my face all day.
2 He doesn't want to let go of his youth.
3 The nerve of some people!
4 It's a matter of debate among experts.
5 I'd be letting everyone down.
6 I just want to get it off my chest.
7 It's not too far off base.

ⓐ He wants to remain young forever.
ⓑ Some people say things they shouldn't.
ⓒ I'd disappoint a lot of people.
ⓓ It is very close to being correct.
ⓔ I only want to discuss my problems.
ⓕ People were bothering me a lot today.
ⓖ Not everyone agrees on the answer.

▪ Now listen to the sentences and check your answers.

■ Listen to the monolog and complete the organizer.

1-2

Peter Pan Syndrome

- theory about (1)_____________ behavior of adult (2)_____________
- from American Dr. Dan Kiley
- based on (3)_____________ play by J. M. Barrie

Symptoms

- inability to accept (4)_____________
- blame (5)_____________ for (6)_____________
- don't acknowledge others' (7)_____________
- do things (8)_____________ people usually do

▼

- **women:** believe it explains why men act like (9)_____________
- **men:** claim it has no basis in (10)_____________ - men act childish to escape from too much (11)_____________ of social (12)_____________

General Questions Based on the organizer, answer the questions.

1 What is the main topic of the talk?

(a) The relationships between immature men and women

(b) The use of a literary metaphor for a serious problem

(c) The controversy surrounding a psychological theory

(d) The ways men behave as they try not to grow old

2 Choose the best summary.

(a) The Peter Pan syndrome is an unproven theory which is related to the ways that people try to keep their youth as they get older.

(b) Men and women have widely different opinions on the validity of the Peter Pan syndrome as it relates to adult men who act immaturely.

Specific Questions Listen again. Mark T for true statements and F for false statements.

(1) Dr. Kiley's Peter Pan syndrome theory has some connection to J. M. Barrie's work.   _____

(2) Accepting responsibilities is a sign of the Peter Pan syndrome in men.   _____

(3) Many women were skeptical about the truthfulness of the Peter Pan syndrome theory.   _____

(4) Men blame their occasional childish behavior on society placing too many responsibilities on them.   _____

■ **Listen to the dialog and complete the notes.** ● 1-3

Boy: feels (☐ comfortable / ☐ nervous) now
- has to act in a play → has (1)________ fright
- feels like it is making him (2)________
- worries he will (3)________ everyone (4)________
→ (☐ becomes ready for the show / ☐ asks the girl to act in the play instead of him)

Girl: (☐ agrees to act for the boy / ☐ cheers up the boy)
- is natural to get (5)________ before a performance
- gives him some advice: • look at the other (6)________, not the (7)________
  • think of it like practice
  • imagine the audience in their (8)________

General Questions Based on the notes, answer the questions.

1 What is the main reason the girl talks to the boy?

(a) To help him overcome his nervousness

(b) To make sure that he knows his lines

(c) To discuss ways to become a better actor

(d) To make sure that he is not too sick to act

2 Choose the best summary.

(a) A boy gets a serious case of stage fright before a play, but his fears are calmed by some good advice from a friend.

(b) A girl has to take over a role for a boy when he gets such a serious case of stage fright that he wants to quit a play.

Specific Questions Listen again. Mark T for true statements and F for false statements.

(1) The girl wants to replace the boy in the play. _____

(2) The boy does not want to disappoint the other actors or the audience. _____

(3) The girl suggests that the boy use humor to calm down. _____

(4) The boy gets ill, so he does not want to perform in the play. _____

■ Listen to the lecture and complete the organizer.

A New Area of Psychological Research

Background

- famous murder case of Kitty Genovese in New York
  - (1) ___________ newspaper story that 38 witnesses (2) ___________ to help her

⬇

started research on how people react when they witness a life-threatening event

Crowds

- people often do (3) ___________
- assume (4) ___________ will call the police

⬇

- do not want to accept (5) ___________
- do not want to place themselves (6) ___________

Individuals

- individuals or small groups are more likely to (7) ___________ the victims

⬇

- responsibility is (8) ___________ and not (9) ___________ among others

---

1 What is the main topic of the lecture?

(a) The reasons why a new area of psychology first started

(b) The reactions of people who witness life-threatening situations

(c) The differences between crowds and people who are alone

(d) The nature of crowds and how they react to different situations

2 Choose the best summary.

(a) A murder in 1964 was the catalyst for the beginning of some new research into human reactions when people are a part of a life-threatening situation.

(b) A murder in 1964 led to some new studies that investigated how crowds and individuals react when they see someone in a dangerous situation.

3   Mark T for true statements and F for false statements.

(1) The newspaper that reported the Kitty Genovese story got the facts straight.   _____

(2) Individuals in a crowd feel the responsibility to act is shared among many people.   _____

(3) It is less likely that a person in a crowd will call the police for help than an individual will.   _____

(4) Crowds offer a better chance for a person to survive a life-threatening situation.   _____

4   Why is there a difference in how crowds and individuals react when seeing a life-threatening situation?

(a) Sharing the danger is easier when in a crowd than alone.

(b) Calling the police causes more problems for individuals.

(c) Crowds tend to feel more responsible than individuals.

(d) Individuals have no one to share responsibility with.

Dictation

■ Listen again and fill in the blanks.

M There is a ________ ________ in American ________ ________ that helped start an area of ________ ________ ________ why people help or don't help people in ________ .
On the night of March 13, 1964, Kitty Genovese ________ ________ ________ her apartment building in New York. A ________ ________ that 38 people had ________ the crime but ________ ________ ________ ________ the woman. This report was later ________ ________ , but it caused an ________ and ________ ________ a deeper study of the way ________ ________ ________ when they are ________ in a large crowd and ________ ________ where people are in distress. First, people in crowds often do not ________ ________ when they witness a life-threatening event. When ________ ________ , many thought someone else had already called the police. This ________ ________ they did not want to ________ ________ for calling the police, so ________ ________ someone else had already done so. Therefore, there was no ________ ________ ________ them. Second, when asked why they did not ________ ________ ________ in these life-threatening situations, many people said that no one else was helping, so they ________ ________ ________ to get involved themselves. ________ ________ would only ________ ________ ________ also. The ________ ________ by the researchers was that when in a group, people are ________ ________ ________ ________ someone ________ ________ even if that trouble is life-threatening. However, studies done on ________ ________ where only one or a few people were ________ showed that they almost always help the victims. ________ ________ or in a small group, the ________ is all theirs to do something, and it is ________ ________ so many, so they act.

■ Listen and answer the questions.

1-5

1 What is the main purpose of the talk?
(a) To examine the different types of addiction
(b) To prove that drug addiction is psychological
(c) To show that addictions vary in their symptoms
(d) To discuss the possible causes of addiction
(e) To explain a source of discord in medicine

2 Look at the following statements and write which stage of grief each statement belongs to.
(1) I said I would do anything if she could just live.   ____________
(2) I went to her grave and laid some flowers on her headstone.   ____________
(3) I was so bitter.   ____________
(4) I fell into a deep, black despair.   ____________
(5) I couldn't believe it because she was so young.   __denial__

3-4

3 Why do people find it difficult to talk to strangers?
(a) Most strangers do not look like they will help you.
(b) Sometimes, strangers ignore a request for help.
(c) Strangers feel awkward when people ask questions.
(d) Feelings of shyness are present in most people.
(e) Strangers can be very rude to people they do not know.

4 Based on the talk, which person would a young, white man most likely ask for directions?
(a) A young, white woman   (b) An elderly, white woman
(c) An elderly, black man   (d) A young, black woman
(e) An elderly, white man

5-6
Level up

5 Which is NOT a reason the man is upset?
(a) People kept calling him on his cellphone.
(b) The elevator at work was too crowded.
(c) A man on the subway was very rude to him.
(d) He had to share his desk with someone at work.
(e) He wants to have more privacy in his life.

6 Choose the statement that best summarizes the dialog.
(a) A man complains about the people he meets every day and how they are so rude to him.
(b) A man and women comment on how it is so hard to find a place where they can be alone and not bothered by other people.
(c) A man is angry because his personal space at work is being intruded upon by a co-worker whom he does not even know.

7 **Listen to the question and answer choices and choose the correct answer.**

(a)   (b)   (c)   (d)   (e)

8 **Listen to the question and answer choices and choose the correct answer.**

(a)   (b)   (c)   (d)   (e)

9 **What is NOT true according to the talk?**

(a) Laughter can help expand the body's veins and arteries.

(b) Norman Cousins's laughter therapy included watching TV.

(c) Pain can be lessened when laughter releases a hormone.

(d) Norman Cousins died due to an incurable form of arthritis.

(e) Norman Cousins had many afflictions through his life.

10 **Complete the table with information from the dialog.**

Category	Amount
People Currently with Depression	20 million
- Number of Women	_________ million
- Number of Men	_________ million
Percentage of Americans Who Will Get Depression in Their Lifetime	
Age Group Most Affected by Depression	
Number of Prescriptions for Depression Medication Last Year	_________ million

11 **What can be inferred from the lecture?**

(a) Synesthesia only affects people who have another mental problem.

(b) People who see colors for letters see do not different colors for numbers.

(c) There are a lot of people with synesthesia who are undiagnosed.

(d) All chidren who say strange things have synesthesia.

(e) It is rare for more than one family member to have synesthesia.

12 **Choose the statement that best summarizes the lecture.**

(a) Synesthesia is a rare, incurable mental illness that affects how its sufferers' senses perceive the world.

(b) Synesthesia is a mental condition in which color replaces the function of most of the senses.

(c) Synesthesia is an unusual condition in which the person perceives color when the senses are stimulated.

■ Listen and answer the questions.

`1-6`

1 Which statement is NOT correct according to the talk?
(a) Racism can often be seen in sports fan groups.
(b) Young children can tell the difference between races.
(c) People enjoy identifying themselves with a group.
(d) It is uncertain whether racism is instinctual or learned.
(e) Propaganda can cause people to become racist.

`2-3`

2 Why did the doctor place the woman on medication in the first place?
(a) She was having trouble getting along with her co-workers.
(b) She had some marital difficulties with her husband.
(c) She was feeling depressed about work and family issues.
(d) She wanted to try the medication to reduce nervousness.
(e) She was stressed out and getting angry at people around her.

3 What would the doctor most likely say next?
(a) Then I don't think you'll need any more medication.
(b) I want to see your husband and children next week.
(c) But today I want to prescribe some new medication.
(d) Then in a few weeks we'll see how you are feeling.
(e) Don't forget to fill your prescription before you leave.

`4-5`

4 Why is it necessary for the id to be present from birth?
(a) To allow it time to develop to contend with the ego
(b) To give a person a way to cope with life's reality
(c) To pass on the morals of the mother and father of the baby
(d) To give a baby the instincts it needs in order to survive
(e) To provide a way for people to feel pleasure as well as pain

5 What can be inferred from the talk?
(a) The id cannot overcome the control of the ego or superego.
(b) Freud believed the psyche was a physical part of the brain.
(c) The id is represented by a part of the human brain.
(d) The superego is the last part of the psyche to develop.
(e) Freud proved the reason babies are born with a psyche.

`Level up`

6 Listen to the question and answer choices and choose the correct answer.
(a)   (b)   (c)   (d)   (e)

`Level up`

7 Listen to the question and answer choices and choose the correct answer.
(a)   (b)   (c)   (d)   (e)

8   **Match the characteristics with the four temperaments. Each temperament has two characteristics.**

Characteristic
a. impulsive
b. depressed
c. rational
d. ambitious
e. perfectionist
f. consistent
g. lighthearted
h. short-tempered

(1) sanguine   ______
(2) choleric   ______
(3) melancholic   ______
(4) phlegmatic   ______

9-10

【Integrated Questions】

■ Read the following passage and listen to the lecture.

In April 1971, at Stanford University in the United States, psychology professor Philip Zimbardo devised an experiment to judge what would happen when some people were given a position of authority and others were subjected to this authority. Zimbardo used the idea of a mock prison that was built in the basement of a building at the university, and he assigned some students as guards and others as prisoners. The experiment was supposed to last two weeks, but it had to be ended after six days when the situation got out of hand. The students playing guards had rapidly become very cruel, even sadistic, and subjected the student prisoners to humiliating mental and physical abuse. The prisoners, while at first somewhat rebellious, became very docile and compliant at the end. Two of the student prisoners even suffered severe emotional trauma, and the rest of the prisoners showed some signs of emotional distress. The student guards seemed to relish their role, and some even showed disappointment when the experiment ended early. Zimbardo had observed everything and quickly had to end the experiment when it was obvious that it was beyond his control.

■ Now answer the following questions based on what you read and heard.

9 **What is NOT true according to the reading and listening?**
(a) The guards were allowed to use physical means to punish the prisoners.
(b) Each prisoner was assigned a number, and their names were never used.
(c) The abuse of the prisoners started on the very first day of the experiment.
(d) Each guard had no previous history of acting in a sadistic manner.
(e) The prisoners had some plans to rebel but did not carry them out.

10 **What can be inferred from the reading and listening?**
(a) The professor was absent for some of the experiment.
(b) The students belonged to the Psychology Department.
(c) Some of the guards felt angry when the experiment was over.
(d) The students were carefully selected for the experiment.
(e) Some of the prisoners wanted the experiment to continue.

■ Listen and fill in the blanks.　　　　　　　　　　　　　　　　　　● 1-7

1　W　An addiction is ________ ________ of ________ ________ that has negative ________ ________.
Examples of addiction include the use of drugs, whether legal or illegal, ________ ________, gambling,
________, ________ shopping, using the Internet for hours on end, watching too much TV, and a ________
________ other ________ ________, such as a ________ ________ a certain food like chocolate. What
causes an addiction is a source of much ________ among medical doctors and psychologists. There is one
school of thought that believes that addiction is caused by physical problems in the brain, which ________
________ ________ ________ in the person. There is also a theory that there is a reward system associated
with addiction. The brain ________ ________, like dopamine, which give pleasure to a person when a
certain action, such as ________ ________ ________ or eating the food they enjoy, is ________. However,
in a person who is addicted, the levels of dopamine need to be stronger and stronger to ________ ________
________ ________ as before. Therefore, the person takes more drugs, or ________ or shops more often, to
reach the same level of pleasure. A third theory is that addiction is related to a ________ ________. Studies
of families with a history of alcoholism ________ ________ ________ ________ to this theory. Finally,
there is a moral theory of addiction; according to it, the person does not have a physical or psychological
problem but ________ the moral character needed to ________ ________.

2　B　This magazine article ________ ________ ________ to me.
　G　What's it about?
　B　It says that when someone we love dies, there are ________ ________ ________ ________: denial, anger,
　　　________, depression, and acceptance.
　G　That sounds about right to me. I ________ ________ all of that when my mother died two years ago.
　B　Really? I didn't know you then. Do you want to talk about it?
　G　She had cancer, and the doctors only gave her a ________ ________ ________ ________. At first, I couldn't
　　　believe it because she was so young. She was only 41.
　B　That is a young age to ________ ________ cancer.
　G　Then, I realized that the cancer wasn't ________ ________, so I got angry, ________, and mad at the world.
　　　I was mad at my father, the doctors, and everyone.
　B　It seems like you all had a hard time.
　G　It was so hard. And then I ________ ________ to God, going to church, and asking him to save her. I said I
　　　would do anything if she could just live.
　B　But she didn't.
　G　No, it ________ ________ each day. And then I ________ ________ a deep, ________ ________. I didn't
　　　go to school. I ________ ________ or talked to anyone. And then she died.
　B　Have you finally accepted it?
　G　Yes. Just last week, I went to her grave, laid some flowers on ________ ________, and had a long talk with
　　　her.
　B　It sounds just like what the writer of this article describes. I guess the magazine article was not ________
　　　________ ________ ________.

3-4   M   For most people, one of the ________ ________ to do is talk to a ________ stranger. People may be shy and ________ ________ when ________ with someone they don't know. Sometimes, it is necessary to ________ ________ ________, such as when you need some important information. For example, I need to know the time a bus arrives, so I ask someone who is waiting at the bus stop. The person answers, and, from this ________ ________, we could possibly have a longer conversation. By asking for ________ ________ someone, you can ________ ________ ________ ________ that many people feel when talking to strangers. Who a person approaches to ask for help or information is ________ ________ some ________ ________. We typically ask people of ________ ________ ________ due to the unconscious belief that they will speak the same language and be more willing to talk to a stranger who ________ ________ ________ them. We also ________ ________ ________ women more than men since women are ________ ________ ________ and more ________ of strangers' questions. Finally, we tend to ask ________ ________ more than younger ones since we unconsciously ________ older people ________ ________ and perhaps patience and kindness. Fortunately, most of our fears of strangers are ________. While some people may ignore you and some may be rude, most of the time, strangers will help and respond with kindness.

5-6   M   ________ ________ ________ ________!

W   I'm sorry to hear that. What happened?

M   Everybody was ________ ________ ________ all day. I had no personal space whatsoever.

W   I know what you mean. It's so hard ________ ________ ________ these days. So what exactly ________ ________ ________?

M   First, on the subway, the guy ________ ________ ________ me just had to read his newspaper, and it was ________ ________ ________ ________ the whole time.

W   I hate when people do that. Why couldn't he just ________ ________ ________ so it was smaller?

M   I know! I said that to him, but he just ________ ________ me and told me to mind my own business.

W   The ________ ________ some people! I bet that ________ ________ in a ________ ________ all day.

M   It sure did. And then on the elevator, it was so crowded I could smell what people had for breakfast ________ ________ ________.

W   That's disgusting!

M   It gets worse. They put a new person ________ ________ ________ at work today, and I have to share my desk and computer with him until they find him a ________. I just need more ________ ________, you know? I don't want anyone around me and I don't need anyone ________ me.

W   It's hard to have any personal space these days. The world is so crowded, and technology ________ ________ ________. Cellphones, as useful as they are, can be a real ________ ________ ________ ________ when you want to avoid people or just relax for a little while.

M   It's getting too hard just ________ ________ ________ anymore.

7   G   I have a problem at school, Dad.

M   What's the matter?

G   I don't know. I think the teacher doesn't like me. I ________ ________ on all of my work and usually answered questions in class, but she still only gave me a B in the class.

M   I'll have a talk with her.

G No, no. Don't do that.

M What? I _________ _________ _________ a problem you wanted me to take care of.

G Why do men always want to take care of problems?

M Ah... because they are problems. That's what we _________ _________ _________: We take care of them.

G I just wanted to talk about this. I don't expect you do anything about it.

M Now I'm _________.

G It's not your fault. You're a man. _________ _________ _________ think with your head and to _________ _________ _________. I'm a woman, and we sometimes just want to talk about things to _________ _________ _________ our _________.

M That sounds _________. There I go again, thinking like a man. You know, you're _________ _________ _________ a high school student.

G I know. That still won't change a B into an A. I guess I'll just have to _________ _________.

8

W In psychology, there are many _________ _________ _________ in how people _________ _________ _________. One such school is the Gestalt school, which originated in Berlin, Germany, in the early 20th century. This school believes the _________ _________ our _________ based on the ability of the _________ _________ _________ _________. The _________ _________ of Gestalt psychology is that something must be seen as a whole and not just in its individual parts. An _________ _________ used to describe Gestalt is "the whole is greater than the _________ _________ its parts." Gestalt psychology often uses _________ and _________ _________ to allow people to use their brain in different ways to see the _________ _________ rather than its smaller parts. Gestalt psychology also _________ _________ _________ problem solving. With problem solving, Gestalt psychology divides it into two types: productive and reproductive thinking. Productive thinking uses an insight to solve a problem while reproductive thinking uses _________ _________ to solve a problem.

9

M You may have heard the saying "Laughter is the _________ _________." What it means is that _________ _________ _________ _________ an illness. This may not be _________ _________ _________ it seems at first glance. Laughter causes the body to _________ endorphins, a type of hormone that helps to _________ _________. In addition, laughter can _________ the _________ _________, allowing blood to flow more freely and _________ blood pressure. Laughter is also known to reduce stress, and some studies even show it _________ _________ _________ _________. But can laughter actually cure an illness? There are some _________ in medical history, and none is as famous as the story of Norman Cousins. He was an American journalist who _________ _________ a _________ of illnesses _________ his life. At one point, he was _________ _________ a form of very painful arthritis that not many people survive. Cousins decided to try laughter as a therapy for his _________ _________. He watched hours of comedy movies and TV shows every day while he lay in bed and was _________ _________ _________ move. After a few weeks, he found his pain _________ _________, and he was able to move more. After many months of this therapy, Cousins was able to walk around and _________ _________ like he had before. He lived many years longer than others who had the _________ _________ _________ arthritis. Cousins finally died of a _________ _________ _________ _________ 75 in 1990.

10

M Tonight on *Cross Talk*, we will examine a ________ ________ ________ from the American Psychological Association. Here is Sue Delaney ________ ________ ________ from the report.

W Thanks, Harry. First, what is depression? The ________ ________ is that it is feelings and thoughts which ________ ________ one's ability to function in everyday life. The most ________ ________ from the report is that about ________ ________ Americans currently suffer from depression.

M That's around 7 percent of the population, isn't it?

W Yes, Harry. And about ________ ________ of all Americans will suffer depression ________ ________ ________ in their lives.

M What age groups suffer depression the most?

W The report ________ that the age group from ________ ________ ________ suffers from depression more than any other age group.

M Who suffers from depression more, men or women?

W Nearly ________ ________ many women have depression as men. So of those ________ ________ people who have depression, about ________ are women.

M What are the ________ ________ ________ according to the report?

W The report states that ________ ________ and a lack of interest in activities a person used to enjoy are ________ ________ ________ of depression.

M What are the best ways to treat depression?

W There are two common ways: using ________ and ________. In fact, more anti-depressants are prescribed each year than any other kind of medicine in America. Around ________ ________ prescriptions for anti-depressant drugs were given by doctors to patients in America last year.

M Those are some ________ ________. When we come back from a commercial break, we'll discuss the report with our ________ ________ ________.

11-12

W There is a ________ ________ synesthesia in which people see color when they hear music or when they smell something, or they ________ ________ ________ or numbers with a certain color. For example, "C" has to be red, and the number five has to be green. This ________ ________ more often in women than men, and there is a growing belief that it can be ________. The majority of people with synesthesia ________ ________ ________ ________ and letters. Many others see sounds, including music and voices, producing colors. A few people see colors when they feel pain or ________ certain ________. Much of the research done on synesthesia is recent. Some experts believe that perhaps one in 2,000 people experience ________ ________ ________ of some type, but many of these people do not know what to call their condition, and others ________ ________ ________ ________ ________ ________ that music had color or the number five was green. Perhaps in some cases, people feared they were ________ ________ and did not ________ ________ ________ because they believed that they would be ________. However, there is ________ ________ ________ synesthesia and mental illness. Perhaps all people ________ some ________ of synesthesia as babies. Babies respond very ________ ________ music, bright colors, and lights. There is a theory that a baby's ________ ________ ________ differently from an adult's, and, as we grow older, most of us ________ ________ ________ between the parts of the brain that ________ ________ to see music as color. But not all do, and they are the ones who ________ ________ to have synesthesia as adults.

Art and Culture

PREPARATION

A **Read the definitions and write the correct word in each blank.**

| vilify | conventional | commission | innovative | perspective |

1 ___________ funds given to an artist to do a work of art
2 ___________ the art of creating an effect of distance in a painting
3 ___________ to make malicious or abusive statements about someone
4 ___________ tending to follow what is considered the norm
5 ___________ new and creative, especially in the way something is done

Now listen to the words and definitions and check your answers.

B **Fill in the blanks with suitable words or phrases on the list. Change the forms if needed.**

| astounding | laud | obscure | acceptance rate |
| refer to | pay dividends | conductor | |

1 The _____________ at some art and music schools is very low due to their high standards.
2 Some art and music forms are so _____________ that few people know about them.
3 I'm _____________ the painting with the man on horseback in the forest.
4 The images Michelangelo painted in the Sistine Chapel are quite _____________.
5 Investing in art can _____________ in the future.
6 The _____________ raised his baton, and the orchestra began to play.
7 Mozart was _____________ as a child prodigy when he was just 6 years old.

Now listen to the sentences and check your answers.

Match each expression with its proper meaning.

1 I want to catch a glimpse of her.
2 You've found your calling.
3 I need to touch up my painting.
4 You need to keep up your grades.
5 It'll take a miracle.
6 He is an up-and-coming artist.
7 It fetched a great return on its investment.

a You know what career you want to follow.
b You have to do well in school.
c He'll be famous in the future.
d I want to see her.
e A large profit was made.
f The chance of success is low.
g I have to fix some minor problems.

Now listen to the sentences and check your answers.

Monolog

■ Listen to the monolog and complete the organizer.

2-2

Lascaux Cave

- located in Southwestern France
- has (1) __________ paintings on the walls of the cave : around (2) _________ figures
  - over (3) _________ years old

Painting Skills and Methods

- used (4) __________________
- showed the animals (5) ______________
- used (6) ___________
- used black charcoal
- painted in (7) ___________ colors
- made paints by (8) ________________ with other materials
- used hollowed tubes from (9) ___________ for an airbrushed effect

Purpose's of the Painting

- not for (10) ______________
  - in (11) ______________ locations
  - far from living areas
- used for (12) ______________ or (13) ______________ purposes
- used as instruction for (14) ___________

General Questions Based on the organizer, answer the questions.

1 What is the best title for the talk?

(a) The Meaning of the Lascaux Paintings
(b) The Discovery of the Lascaux Paintings
(c) Lascaux Cave Art Methods and Purpose
(d) Some Methods of Ancient Cave Painting

2 Choose the best summary.

(a) While the ultimate purpose of cave art in Lascaux, France, is unknown, the materials and methods the artists used have been determined.

(b) Cave art in Lascaux, France, dates from prehistoric times and may have been designed to instruct people in hunting methods.

Specific Questions Listen again. Mark T for true statements and F for false statements.

(1) The skill of the Lascaux cave artist was very amateurish. _____

(2) The paint that cave artists used came from a variety of sources. _____

(3) The Lascaux cave paintings may have been decorations. _____

(4) Cave paintings in Lascaux, France, date from more than 10,000 years ago. _____

■ Listen to the dialog and complete the notes.

2-3

Mona Lisa

▶ **Basic Facts:**
- created by Leonardo da Vinci
- believed to be modeled on Lisa Del Giocondo, a rich [1] ________________
  - → discovered by [2] __________ researchers recently
- hangs in the Louvre in [3] __________

▶ **Other Facts:**
- was admired by French kings and emperor Napoleon
- was stolen in [4] __________ and disappeared for [5] ______ years

General Questions Based on the notes, answer the questions.

1 What is the main topic of the dialog?

(a) An artist's most famous work of art

(b) French kings' love for a painting

(c) The reasons a painting is so famous

(d) The location of a famous painting

2 Choose the best summary.

(a) The mystery of the *Mona Lisa*'s model was recently solved, which has led to renewed interest in and fame for the painting.

(b) The *Mona Lisa*'s fame rests on several factors, including the mystery of who the model was and the intrigue of the painting's theft.

Specific Questions Listen again. Mark T for true statements and F for false statements.

(1) The Louvre seems to be a major tourist attraction in Paris. _____

(2) French researchers discovered the name of the model for the *Mona Lisa*. _____

(3) The *Mona Lisa* was stolen in 1902 and disappeared for 13 years. _____

(4) The couple gets in to see the *Mona Lisa* right away. _____

Listen to the lecture and complete the organizer.

`2-4`

William Shakespeare (1564 - (1)________)

Early Life

- born in Stratford-upon-Avon, England
- attended the local school and studied the classics
- got married at age (2)______
- had three children: two daughters and a <u>son</u>

↓

died at age 11 for an (3)________ reason

Career

- wrote (4)______ plays and (5)______ sonnets, some poems
- in London by 1592 (6)________ and writing plays
- (7)___________ of a playing company in 1594
- very (8)________ in his lifetime
- compiled his (9)______ and published them in book form after (10)__________

1 What is the purpose of the lecture?

(a) To give a biographical account of Shakespeare

(b) To explain why Shakespeare became so famous

(c) To show the success of Shakespeare after his death

(d) To discuss where Shakespeare's inspiration came from

2 Choose the best summary.

(a) William Shakespeare wrote both plays and sonnets during his successful life, and his plays are still performed today.

(b) William Shakespeare's life was centered on two places: Stratford-upon-Avon in his early years and London in his remaining years.

3 **Mark T for true statements and F for false statements.**

(1) Shakespeare's works were published in book form during his life.   ____

(2) Shakespeare achieved fame and wealth while he was still alive.   ____

(3) Shakespeare's son died during a deadly epidemic.   ____

(4) Shakespeare was the sole owner of the *Lord Chamberlain's Men*.   ____

4 **When did Shakespeare begin to write plays?**

(a) He began to write when he moved to London.

(b) Shortly after his marriage, he began to write.

(c) It is still uncertain when he began to write.

(d) He started writing plays after losing his son.

Dictation

■ Listen again and fill in the blanks.

w In this term's English ____________ ____________ , we will be ____________ the works of William Shakespeare. Today, we'll start with a ____________ ____________ of his life before ____________ ____________ ____________ . Shakespeare is considered the ____________ ____________ in English literature. His ____________ ____________ ____________ his ____________ ____________ of 38 plays and 154 sonnets as well as some other poems. Shakespeare's plays have been ____________ ____________ ____________ than any other ____________ and have been ____________ ____________ almost ____________ ____________ ____________ . He was ____________ ____________ Stratford-upon-Avon, England, in 1564 and died 52 years later in 1616. ____________ ____________ ____________ about his childhood, but he most ____________ ____________ the local school in Stratford and ____________ ____________ ____________ . He married a local woman, Anne Hathaway, at the age of 18, and she ____________ ____________ ____________ ____________ — two daughters and a son. His son died at age 11, but the ____________ ____________ his death is ____________ . Not much else is known of Shakespeare's life ____________ ____________ ____________ and ____________ ____________ his start in the London theater world. Even when or why he ____________ ____________ is ____________ . He was in London ____________ ____________ ____________ , and some of his plays were ____________ ____________ on London stages. In 1594, Shakespeare was a ____________ ____________ in a ____________ ____________ called the *Lord Chamberlain's Men*, which soon became the ____________ ____________ ____________ in London. Shakespeare became very ____________ over the next 20 years, and he ____________ ____________ ____________ ____________ and bought a large home in Stratford. It was only after Shakespeare's death that two of his company partners ____________ his plays into a book. Of course, these plays ____________ ____________ ____________ ____________ ever since, and Shakespeare's ____________ has only grown in the centuries since his death.

EXERCISE

2-5

1 What is the main idea of the talk?

(a) Frescos give an understanding of life in the past.

(b) There are a lot of historical examples of frescos.

(c) Ancient Rome was home to many great frescos.

(d) Frescos are one of the oldest art forms ever created.

(e) Many civilizations developed their own fresco techniques.

2 Which painting did the man select?

(a)  (b) 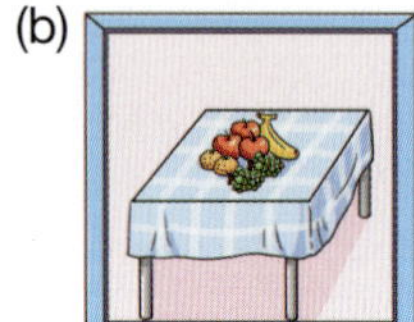 (c)  (d)  (e) 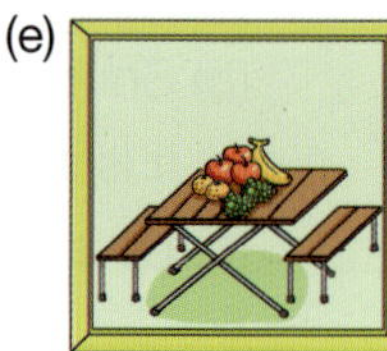

3-4

3 What was the greatest influence on Pavarotti becoming a full time opera singer?

(a) The inspiration his father gave him   (b) His success at an international contest

(c) His failure to become a soccer player   (d) The beginning of his stage career

(e) The praise he received from fans

4 What can be inferred from the talk?

(a) Pavarotti's father learned singing at a local church.

(b) Pavarotti's mother was not a big fan of soccer.

(c) Pavarotti was the leader of a singing chorus.

(d) Pavarotti's talent was inherited from his mother.

(e) Pavarotti's mother had a lot of influence on him.

5-6
Level up

5 Why does the girl feel she will have a hard time getting accepted into Julliard?

(a) She feels she is not qualified for this school.

(b) Applicants must be able to dance and act.

(c) She might not be able to pay the tuition.

(d) She needs to make a video for her application.

(e) There is too much competition for a few spots.

6 Choose the statement that best summarizes the dialog.

(a) A male student offers to help a female student make a film of her dancing to help her get into a famous school.

(b) Two students discuss their plans to move to New York after graduation in order to further their education in the arts.

(c) Two students talk about the chances they have of getting into some famous schools in New York.

7 **Listen to the question and answer choices and choose the correct answer.**

(a)　　(b)　　(c)　　(d)　　(e)

8 **Listen to the question and answer choices and choose the correct answer.**

(a)　　(b)　　(c)　　(d)　　(e)

9 **What is NOT mentioned as an aspect of photography?**

(a) Sports photography is a part of photojournalism.

(b) Some news photos are staged for the photographer.

(c) A goal of fine art photographers is to sell their photos.

(d) Photography can be considered a form of art.

(e) Commercial photos often do not look like the original.

10 **Complete the graph for Broadway ticket sales revenue for the years 1960, 1970, 1980, 1990, 2000, and 2008.**

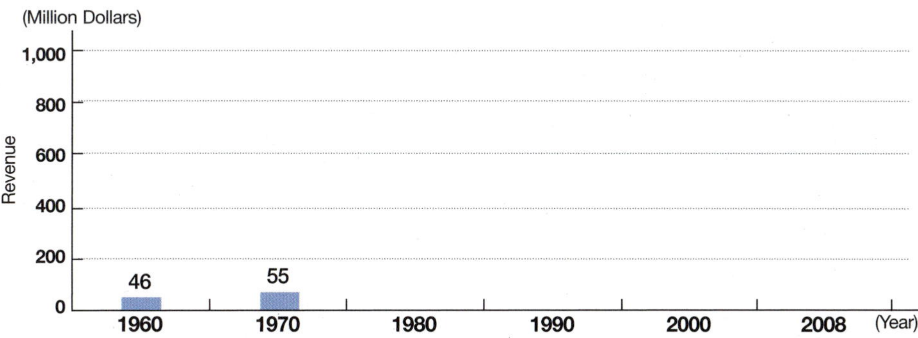

11 **Why did the French royal family leave the Louvre Palace in 1674?**

(a) The palace became a museum.

(b) The French Revolution occurred.

(c) They moved to a different palace.

(d) They turned it into an art school.

(e) The palace was turned into a fortress.

12 **Choose the statement that best summarizes the lecture.**

(a) The famous Louvre is a museum with an impressive collection, but it also has a long history as a fortress, palace, and art school.

(b) The Louvre Museum's large collection is the legacy of hundreds of years as the center of French royal life.

(c) The large collection in the Louvre Museum in France comes from such places as Greece, Rome, and Egypt.

PRACTICE TEST

■ Listen and answer the questions.

2-6

1 Which statement is correct according to the talk?
(a) Renaissance artists studied the works of the Humanists.
(b) Pre-Renaissance paintings mainly used religion as a topic.
(c) Shadow and detail were common in pre-Renaissance art.
(d) Renaissance artists learned perspective from Greek art.
(e) The Renaissance was centered in the southern Italian cities.

2-3

2 What is the main reason the man was confused over what an Oscar party was?
(a) He has no interest in the movie industry or its awards.
(b) He has not spent a lot of time living in the United States.
(c) He had never heard of the Academy Awards until now.
(d) He did not know that Oscar was the name of an award.
(e) He does not get invited to a lot of parties in America.

3 What will the man probably say next?
(a) It doesn't seem to be too difficult to become a member.
(b) What should I bring to your Oscar party?
(c) It sounds like it's tough to become a member.
(d) I'd like to go to the real Oscar ceremony.
(e) I wonder who the members will pick this year.

4-5

4 What is the major criticism of the Grammy Awards from the musician's point of view?
(a) There are too many categories of music that receive awards.
(b) The musicians are not allowed to vote for the awards.
(c) The voting group is too small and needs more members.
(d) The voting is held in secret when it should be more public.
(e) The voters select those musicians which they personally like.

5 What would probably happen if the Grammies were voted for by the public?
(a) Other awards shows, like the People's Choice Awards, would fold.
(b) The number of Grammies would be reduced to only popular categories.
(c) There would be no need for the National Academy of Recording Arts and Sciences.
(d) The most popular musicians of the day would receive many awards.
(e) There would be more criticism of the Grammy's voting process.

Level up

6 Listen to the question and answer choices and choose the correct answer.
(a)   (b)   (c)   (d)   (e)

Level up

7 Listen to the question and answer choices and choose the correct answer.
(a)   (b)   (c)   (d)   (e)

8 **Fill in the blanks in this drawing of an orchestra with the correct instruments.**

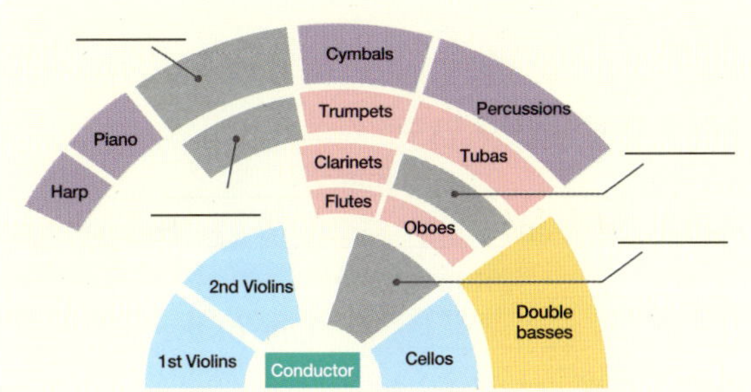

 【**Integrated Questions**】

Read the following passage and listen to the lecture.

What is art? This question has been raised many times since the beginning of the 20th century, when schools of art such as Dadaism and Surrealism, along with such innovative artists such as Pablo Picasso, shattered conventional ideas of what art was. Prior to the 20th century, most art was of religious themes or of everyday life, and people and nature were the main topics. Now almost anything can be a topic of art. Technology has also had a major impact on the arts. First photography, and later film, challenged the accepted boundaries of what constitutes art. Is photography art? Is a movie a piece of art? Some people say yes, and some say no. Even more disturbing to traditionalists is the video and computer age, where, with the use of a few simple software tools, almost anyone can produce a work of quality. Can these people be called "artists" in the same mold as Leonardo da Vinci, Picasso, or Jackson Pollack? Perhaps not, but there needs to be room made for the exploding forms of art that the technological revolution has made possible. Perhaps some day the canvas, easel, and paintbrush will be permanently replaced by the computer screen, the mousepad, and the mouse, and digital screens hanging on walls will show multiple digitalized paintings at the click of a button.

Now answer the following questions based on what you read and heard.

9 **What is the main point of the information presented in both the reading and listening?**

(a) Traditional art is being replaced by technology.

(b) Schools are using technology to teach art.

(c) The computer is replacing traditional art tools.

(d) Art is changing in many ways due to technology.

(e) Technology and art cannot go hand in hand.

10 **What can be inferred from the information presented?**

(a) South Korea is the largest consumer of video art.

(b) The nature of what art is constantly changes.

(c) Art schools will no longer teach drawing by hand.

(d) Many traditional artists refuse to use computers.

(e) Computers have made traditional art tools obsolete.

DICTATION [Exercise]

■ Listen and fill in the blanks. ● 2-7

1 M We can ________ ________ ________ about the history and daily lives of ________ ________ through their art. For example, ________ can be found in the ________ ________ many ________ ________. A fresco is a type of ________ ________ or ________ usually done in ________ ________. The paint is ________ ________ the wet plaster, and, ________ ________ ________, it creates a ________ ________. Under the ________ ________, a fresco can ________ ________ ________ ________. One of the ________ ________ of this type of ________ is found on the island of Crete in Greece and ________ ________ the Minoan civilization. It ________ ________ 1,500 B.C. and shows a ________ ________ over a ________ ________. Frescos have also been found in ________ ________ ________ and in ________ in India. The Indian frescos show the ________ ________ ________ and have been of great ________ to ________. The greatest ________ ________ Roman frescos was found at Pompeii. The city ________ ________ under ________ ________ in 79 A.D., which ________ ________ the frescos for over fifteen hundred years. These frescos have given ________ ________ ________ great ________ ________ the daily lives of Romans. Frescos became a very ________ ________ ________ during the Renaissance. Michelangelo's *The Creation of Adam*, in which ________ ________ ________ to the first man, Adam, is found on the ________ of the Sistine Chapel and is considered the most famous ________ ________ ________.

2 W Welcome to my ________ ________. If anything ________ ________ ________, maybe we can ________ ________ ________ it.

M ________ ________. Say, these look nice. What do you ________ ________?

W These are ________ ________ still life. It's a very old ________ ________ ________ in which the artist takes some ________ ________, such as fruit, ________ ________, and then ________ ________ ________. It is a ________ ________ work for ________ artists. In fact, these ________ ________ by some students at a local art school.

M I like that one there. It seems to be ________ ________ ________.

W Ah, excuse me, sir. Which one?

M The one with the apples and oranges.

W Sir, some of them have green apples, and some have red apples. Which is it?

M Three red apples and ________ ________. I think there is a ________ ________ ________... are those grapes?

W Yes, sir. Some of the ________ ________ ________ ________, and some have green grapes. Which are you ________ ________?

M I want to ________ ________ ________ ________ at the painting with the red apples, oranges, one banana, and the ________ ________ ________ ________.

W There are ________ ________ ________ ones. One has the fruit on a table in the ________, and the other has the fruit on a ________ ________ ________.

M The one in the kitchen. That's the one. How much is it?

W It was done by an ________ ________ ________ ________, so it's just 50 dollars.

M Okay, I'll ________ ________. Oh, I'm hungry. Maybe ________ ________ I like this painting so much.

W Luciano Pavarotti ________ ________ ________ a world-class ________ ________, but he didn't always
________ ________ ________ ________ ________. Pavarotti was ________ ________ a poor Italian family
in 1935 in Modena. His father was a ________ and amateur singer and ________ ________ ________ for
his family. Pavarotti ________ ________ to his father's ________ and ________ ________ with his father
in the ________ ________ when he was 9 years old. When Pavarotti was young, his ________ ________
was ________, and he ________ ________ ________ a soccer player, but his mother ________ ________
that teaching was a ________ ________ ________. He wasn't happy as a teacher, so at the age of 19, he
________ ________ ________ some ________ ________ ________ with a local singing teacher. Pavarotti
became ________ ________ ________ his father's singing ________ from his hometown. In 1955, the
group ________ ________ Wales and ________ ________ ________ in an ________ ________ ________.
After this, Pavarotti ________ ________ and ________ ________ full time to becoming a professional opera
singer. He ________ ________ ________ in 1961 in Italy in the opera *La Boheme*, where he played the
________ ________ Rodolfo, and he made his ________ ________ playing the same part in London. Over
the years, he was ________ ________ one of the greatest voices ever to ________ ________ ________.
His death at age 71 in 2007 ________ ________ was a ________ for music lovers everywhere.

B You're really an ________ ________, Katherine. ________ ________ have you been ________ ________?
G I started ________ ________ when I was five. Since then, I've taken lessons in ________, ________, and
________ ________. I really love dancing.
B Are you planning to be a ________ ________?
G I hope so. When I ________, I plan to ________ ________ Julliard.
B I've ________ ________ ________. It's in New York City, right? I thought it was ________ a ________
________.
G It ________ ________ just a music school when it ________ ________, but it has since ________ ________
dance and acting.
B I guess it'll be tough to ________ ________ ________.
G Yeah. The ________ ________ is around 6 percent. Some people say it's ________ ________ to ________
________ than Harvard. It'll ________ ________ ________ to get accepted.
B You're really ________ though, so I'm sure ________ ________ ________.
G Thanks. But it's also very expensive, so I might not even be ________ ________ ________ ________. So,
what are you ________ ________ ________ ________ ________?
B I'm also planning to go to New York City.
G Oh, which university? Columbia?
B Nope. I'm going to the New York ________ ________. I'm going to be a ________ ________ ________
like Steven Spielberg and Martin Scorsese.
G I didn't know you ________ ________ ________ ________.
B I really ________ ________ ________ over the summer after my dad bought a new video camera. I've been
making some ________ ________ ________ ________. I got some ________ ________ and ________
________ ________ on my computer at home. It's really great.
G It sounds like you've ________ ________ ________.
B I think so. If ________ ________, I could ________ ________ ________ of you dancing. Maybe it will help
you get into Julliard.
G That would be great!

7

G Dad, where does the money _________ _________ to _________ for museums and _________?

M Most of the money comes from the _________ or _________ _________. They also make some money from _________ _________ and _________ _________.

G How much money does the government give?

M Money for the arts comes from city, _________, and _________ _________, so it is hard to _________ _________ _________. In Canada, we have the Canada Council for the Arts, which had a _________ of over 300 million dollars in 2008.

G That's a lot of money. What do they _________ _________ _________?

M The money is given as _________ in _________ _________, and it _________ _________ young _________, dancers, and artists as _________ to _________ _________ _________. It also goes toward paying all of the people who work in national museums and for _________, _________, _________, and _________.

G I think they could use that money to _________ _________ _________ or people who are sick.

M Maybe, but others feel that _________ _________ the world a _________ _________ and can help to _________ _________ to help others.

8

M Art as an _________ is a _________ _________. Paintings go _________ _________ _________ in _________ and are also _________ _________ _________ and _________. It is not something that everyone can do since the most _________ _________ _________ _________ millions of dollars. Although it is _________ _________ for certain what the _________ _________ _________, it is believed that the _________ _________ _________ _________ for a painting was an _________ 140 million dollars in a _________ _________ made by media mogul David Geffen to an _________ _________. The painting was by American artist Jackson Pollack, and it is _________ _________ _No. 5, 1948_. It is an _________ _________ _________ which _________ _________ of yellow and brown paint on a large piece of _________. While not everyone can _________ _________ _________, a small _________ in an up-and-coming artist may _________ _________ in the future. The early works of artists who later _________ _________ often _________ _________ _________ on the investments.

9

M Photography has many _________ and can be used in _________ _________ and _________ _________. Photography _________ _________ _________ three categories: fine art photography, _________, and _________ _________. The purpose of _________ _________ photography is to _________ _________ _________ which _________ the _________ _________ _________. Photojournalism is used to _________ a _________ _________ and to _________ _________ while commercial photography is used to _________ _________ _________ or a service. Fine art photography is _________ _________ by black-and-white or color photography. In addition, _________ _________ _________ _________ or can be _________ and _________ _________ as they happen. Photojournalism, on the other hand, almost always _________ _________ _________ _________ photographs _________ _________ those _________ when someone such as a _________ _________ or an _________ _________ poses for a _________. Photojournalism has many _________ such as sports photography and _________ _________. A further subcategory of entertainment photography is the _________, those _________ that _________ _________ and wait outside their homes _________ hoping for a _________ _________ _________ an embarrassing photo. In the world of commercial photography, most work is done with _________ in _________ _________, and the _________ _________ _________ for _________ or Internet sites. The _________ _________ of commercial photography is to _________ _________, so therefore most commercial photography is _________ and _________ _________ by using _________ _________ or computer software.

10 W Our topic for tonight's show is Broadway, and __________ ________ is Charles Cabbage, who ________
________ Broadway over the years. His ________ ________, *Broadway's Rising Fortunes*, is ________
________ ________. Welcome, Mr. Cabbage.

M Thank you.

W What is the ________ ________ ________ Broadway in the past and today?

M Today it is a ________ ________ ________, which was not ________ ________ ________ in the past.

W Yes, your book gives a lot of ________ ________ how much money was ________ ________ ________
________. In 1960, sales were just ________ ________ dollars, and ________ at the ________ was 7.9
million people.

M Yes. Now ________ ________ 2008. 12.3 million tickets ________ ________, which earned 939 million
dollars. Clearly, the ________ ________ is the ________ ________ ________ today. Of course, in 1960, 46
million dollars was a lot of money.

W When did Broadway ________ ________ this ________ ________?

M The change was ________. In 1970, there were 7.4 million tickets sold and 55 million dollars in ________
________. Things ________ ________ for a while in the mid-1970s, but Broadway ________ in the 1980s.
In 1980, there were 11 million tickets sold and 197 million dollars ________ ________ ________.

W That is a big change. ________ ________ in the 1990s?

M By 1990, ________ ________ ________ a bit to 8 million people, but ________ ________ ________ 282
million dollars. In 2000, attendance ________ ________ ________ ________ as 12 million tickets were
sold, and there were 660 million dollars in ________ ________.

W I guess there is ________ ________ that the bright lights of Broadway will be ________ ________ ________.

11-12 W Students, when we visit France next week, we will be ________ ________ the ________ ________
________ ________, the Louvre. Today, I ________ ________ ________ ________ you a little
more about this ________ ________ ________ museum. The Louvre was ________ ________ as
a ________ in Paris in the 12th century. Only a ________ ________ of the ________ ________
still ________ because the French ________ ________ ________ to become the Louvre Palace,
which became the home of the ________ ________ ________. In 1674, however, King Louis
XIV ________ ________ ________ the Palace of Versailles his ________ ________, so the
Louvre Palace was then ________ ________ ________ ________ ________ of art and ________.
During the next hundred years, the palace was used as a ________ ________ ________ ________.
When King Louis XV ________, he ________ ________ ________ in the Louvre Palace and ________ it.
During the ________ ________, the government made the ________ ________ ________ ________ for
the arts and sciences. It ________ ________ on August 10, 1793. The museum's collection has ________
________ over the years and now ________ ________ ________ ________. The collection is ________
________ eight categories: Egyptian ________, Near Eastern artifacts, ________, Etruscan, and Roman
artifacts, Islamic art, ________, ________ ________, paintings, and prints and ________. Throughout the
year, the museum also ________ ________ ________ ________ resulting from ________ ________. The
museum also holds ________ ________ ________, shows films, and holds ________ ________ ________
in its ________ ________. Last year, 8.5 million people visited the museum. They came to see ________
________ ________ of art as the *Mona Lisa* by Leonardo da Vinci and the *Venus de Milo*.

Economics

PREPARATION

3-1

A Read the definitions and write the correct word in each blank.

eye-catching	gravitate	monetary	fluctuation	investment

1 __________ relating to money, especially the total amount of money in a country
2 __________ able to attract one's attention
3 __________ change that occurs in an unpredictable way
4 __________ money used in a way that may make more money
5 __________ to move steadily towards something

■ Now listen to the words and definitions and check your answers.

B Fill in the blanks with suitable words or phrases on the list. Change the forms if needed.

currency	rip-off	low-yield	boom	recession	mint	government bond

1 From 1941 to 1970, America experienced an economic ____________ during which there was great prosperity for all.
2 ____________ markets are where people can exchange one type of money for another.
3 A wise investment is ____________ because they are protected from loss by the government.
4 Don't eat in that restaurant because it is a real ____________. The prices are high, and the quality is poor.
5 A government ____________ is where coins and paper currency are made.
6 ____________ investments include savings accounts that have low interest rates.
7 At times, an economy may go into a ____________, which is a period of slow economic growth.

■ Now listen to the sentences and check your answers.

■ **Match each expression with its proper meaning.**

1 I'm ready and raring to go.   ⓐ It's too expensive.
2 It costs an arm and a leg.   ⓑ It will be an important factor.
3 That's it in a nutshell.   ⓒ It's the way things usually work.
4 Let's have a gander.   ⓓ That's a good summary.
5 It'll come into play.   ⓔ I'm very excited to begin.
6 It's a typical rule of thumb.   ⓕ They sold a lot of products.
7 Sales went through the roof.   ⓖ Let's take a look at it.

■ Now listen to the sentences and check your answers.

■ Listen to the monolog and complete the organizer.

3-2

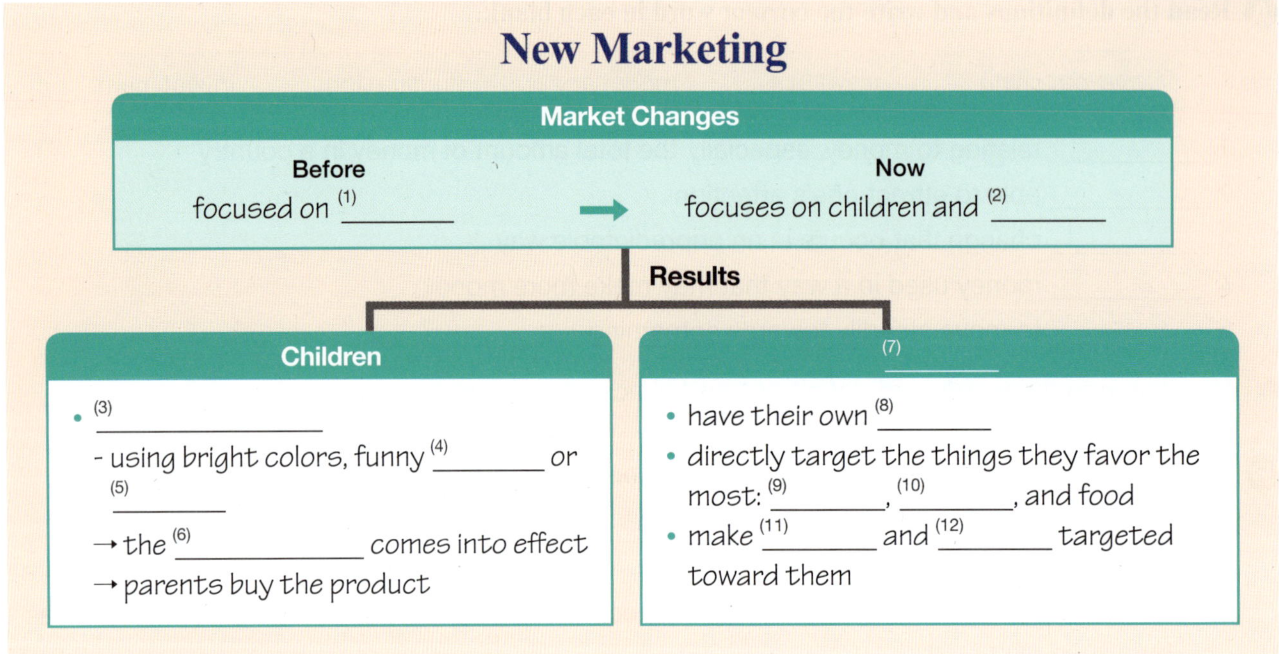

General Questions Based on the organizer, answer the questions.

1 What is the best title for the talk?

(a) The Buying Power of Children and Teens

(b) The Effective Marketing Strategy: Nag Factor

(c) Marketing Strategies for Children and Teens

(d) Children's and Teens' Favorite Products

2 Choose the best summary.

(a) Children and teenagers enjoy certain products that marketers are now focusing on.

(b) Children and teens are a new target of marketers as they have a lot of influence on their parents.

Specific Questions Listen again. Mark T for true statements and F for false statements.

(1) In the past, money-earning adults were the main targets of marketing. _____

(2) Marketers use funny characters on a product to attract children. _____

(3) Teens often have a source of money besides their parents. _____

(4) Marketers use similar designs and brands for all demographics. _____

■ Listen to the dialog and complete the notes. 　3-3

Adam Smith
- the founding father of economics
- born in the (1)__________ century in (2)______________
- wrote a book *The Wealth of Nations* - explains why and how nations become (3)__________

   • people act in own (4)______________ : to make money
    → helping (5)__________ as a whole: doing something of (6)__________ to someone
   - paid based on the (7)__________ of the work
  • (8)______________ - workers doing (9)__________ tasks → help produce more
    → basis of modern (10)______________

General Questions　Based on the notes, answer the questions.

1　What is the purpose of the dialog?
(a) To discuss the life of a famous economist
(b) To examine the ideas of a famous economist
(c) To look at the impact of a famous economist
(d) To refute the theories of a famous economist

2　Choose the best summary.
(a) Adam Smith's economic ideas have helped many nations become prosperous by following his theories.
(b) Adam Smith's theories discuss the relationship between people's interests and economics and the value of a division of labor.

Specific Questions　Listen again. Mark T for true statements and F for false statements.

(1) *The Wealth of Nations* tried to explain why and how countries become wealthy. ______

(2) Adam Smith's main economic theory is that when people act in their own self-interest, it benefits society as a whole. ______

(3) Adam Smith believed people should be paid the same for doing different jobs. ______

(4) An assembly line follows Adam Smith's ideas on the division of labor. ______

■ Listen to the lecture and complete the organizer. 

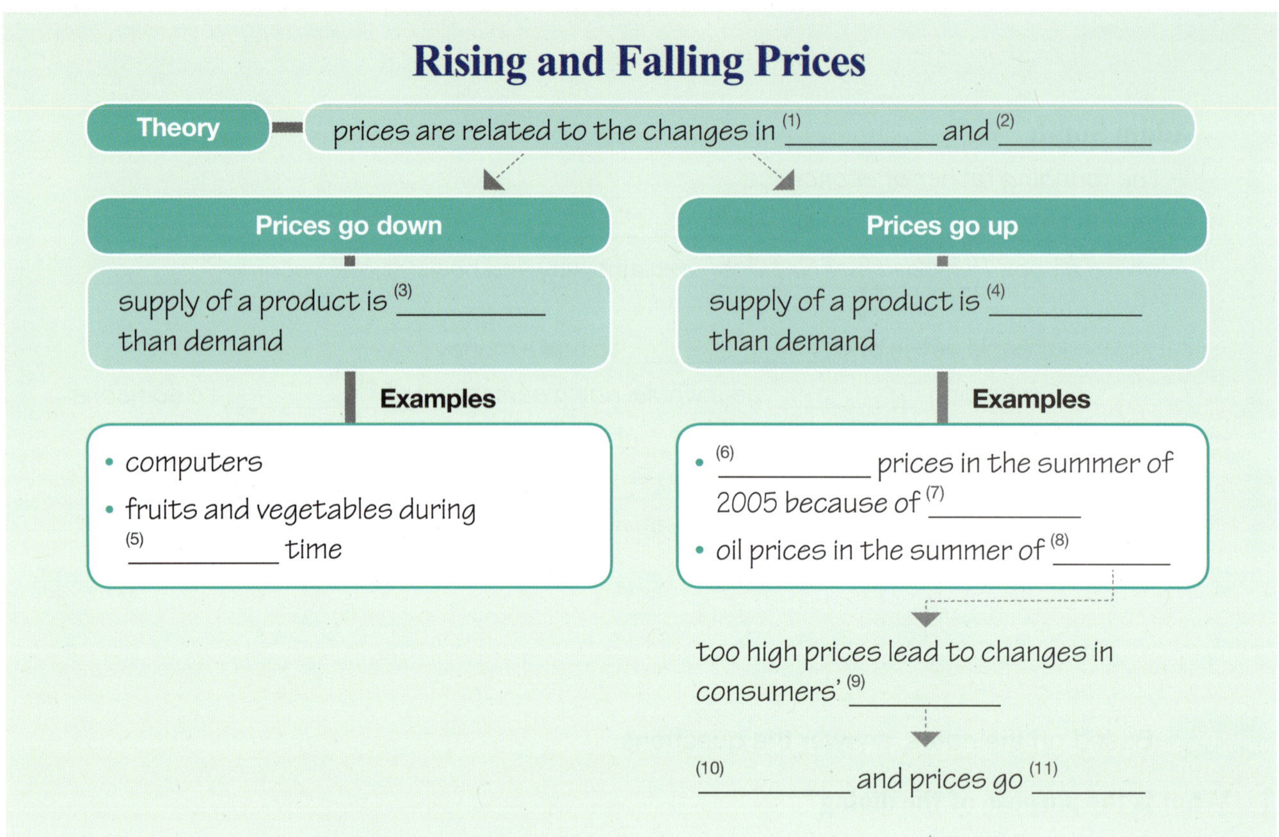

1 **What is the main topic of the lecture?**

(a) The consequences of natural disasters on the prices of products

(b) The relationship between supply and demand for some products

(c) The relationship between prices and supply and demand

(d) The changes in prices of consumers changing their habits

2 **Choose the best summary.**

(a) Product pricing is related to many factors, including seasonal changes, disasters, and the quality of the product.

(b) The price of a product is influenced by the availability of the product and the desire of the consumer for that product.

3 **Mark T for true statements and F for false statements.**

(1) At certain times of the year, food products become much cheaper. _____

(2) Scarcity of a product often affects the price of it. _____

(3) A natural disaster can have a dramatic impact on the price of some products. _____

(4) Consumers have a minor impact on the prices of products. _____

4 **According to the lecture, why did the price of oil drop after rising so high in the summer of 2008?**

(a) Oil companies increased the supply of oil.

(b) Consumers cut back on their use of oil products.

(c) There were no natural disasters after the summer of 2008.

(d) An alternative product for oil has been developed.

Dictation

■ Listen again and fill in the blanks.

W You may ___________ ___________ about the price you pay for ___________ ___________ ___________ . How is the price ___________ ? You've probably heard people ___________ ___________ ___________ for food and gas. You've also ___________ ___________ that computer products ___________ ___________ ___________ over time. Why does this happen? A lot of it ___________ ___________ ___________ ___________ ___________ and demand. When the supply of something is greater than the ___________ by the public for this product—like computers, for example—then the price of that product will ___________ ___________ . If ___________ have too much of a ___________ , they ___________ ___________ ___________ ___________ , and they will ___________ ___________ ___________ to get ___________ to ___________ ___________ . For instance, at ___________ ___________ , markets and shops are ___________ ___________ fresh fruits and vegetables, so the ___________ ___________ ___________ . On the other hand, when there is not enough of a product and the ___________ ___________ ___________ , prices rise. In the summer of 2005, ___________ ___________ in the Gulf of Mexico ___________ oil production there. ___________ ___________ ___________ , oil prices in North America rose almost 50 percent ___________ ___________ ___________ ___________ ___________ . The demand for oil hadn't changed, yet the ___________ ___________ . This caused prices to rise. Still speaking of oil, in the summer of 2008, prices ___________ ___________ for a variety of reasons. This time, the prices were so high that people ___________ ___________ ___________ their ___________ to use ___________ ___________ ___________ . As a consequence, ___________ ___________ . Soon, prices also began to drop. These changes and ___________ ___________ ___________ were the ___________ ___________ ___________ in supply and demand.

■ Listen and answer the questions.  3-5

1 What is the main idea of the talk?

(a) People buy luxury goods because they want to have high-quality goods and show their social status.

(b) Luxury goods are perceived as an important status symbol among upper-class people.

(c) Wealthy people buy luxury goods as a way to invest their money for the future.

(d) In spite of their high prices, luxury goods attract people with their reliable quality.

(e) After working hard for their money, people want luxury goods as a reward for their efforts.

2 Draw the demand curve graph using the price and demand for soda as an example.

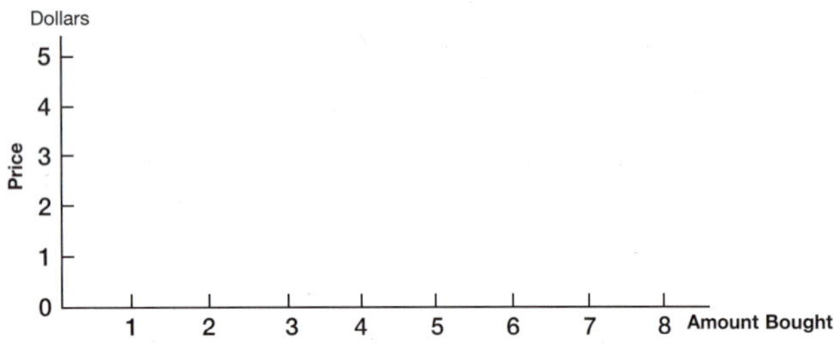

3-4

3 What does the speaker mean by referring to money as a "unit of account"?

(a) Money has value and can be used to buy things.

(b) Money is held in bank accounts in order to save it.

(c) Money is used to measure the value of things.

(d) Money serves as a way to store the value of something.

(e) Money has value that depends on people trusting it.

4 What will probably happen in a situation where the store of value of money is drastically reduced?

(a) People will continue to trust money as a medium of exchange.

(b) People could run to the banks and withdraw all their money.

(c) People would likely ask for more money to be printed.

(d) People may return to the old barter system of exchange.

(e) People might start saving all of their money at home.

5-6
Level up

5 What main reason is given in the talk for consumers switching to a substitute?

(a) A difference in the cost of the regularly used product

(b) A desire to switch from the regularly used product

(c) The increased availability of the regularly used product

(d) A reduction in the demand of the regularly used product

(e) A change in a complement affects the regularly used product.

6 Choose the statement that best summarizes the dialog.

(a) Substitutes and compliments control the rate of supply and demand.

(b) Complements replace substitutes when prices increase a great deal.

(c) The use of substitutes and complements is influenced by price changes.

7 **Listen to the question and answer choices and choose the correct answer.**

(a)   (b)   (c)   (d)   (e)

8 **Listen to the question and answer choices and choose the correct answer.**

(a)   (b)   (c)   (d)   (e)

9 **What is NOT true about GDP according to the talk?**

(a) It is of great concern to governments.

(b) It is compared to past GDP measurements.

(c) It is a sign of economic prosperity or decline.

(d) It is a monthly measurement of goods and services.

(e) It is adjusted for changes in currency values.

10 **Complete the graph for America's unemployment rate from 1930 to 2008.**

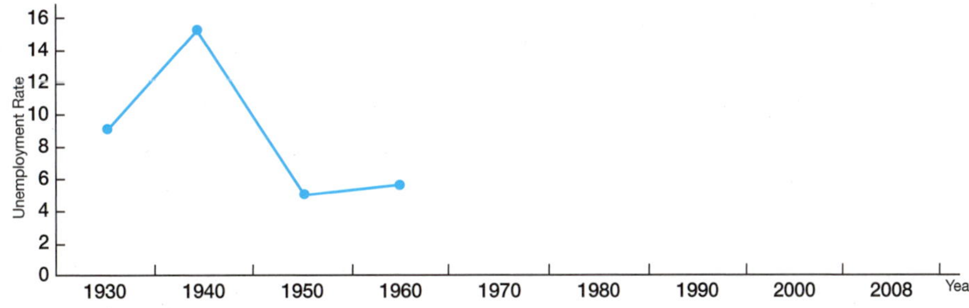

11 **What is the main purpose of the lecture?**

(a) To describe what happens when the money supply increases

(b) To explain how banks count the money on time deposits

(c) To discuss the role of the government in regulating money

(d) To view the ways that the money supply can go up or down

(e) To examine how governments calculate a nation's money supply

12 **What is one possible consequence of an increase in the M3 money supply of a nation?**

(a) Banks will increase the interest rates on loans.

(b) Depositors will spend more of their money.

(c) People will be more likely to borrow money.

(d) Time deposits will become less attractive.

(e) People will probably keep their money at home.

■ Listen and answer the questions.

3-6

1 **What is the main purpose of a country's central bank?**
(a) To maintain the country's gold reserves
(b) To stabilize the nation's currency
(c) To issue and sell government bonds
(d) To lend money to banks in trouble
(e) To do business with other countries

2-3

2 **What will probably happen once the economy improves again?**
(a) Fewer people will borrow money.
(b) People will save more money for the future.
(c) Interest rates on car loans will go down.
(d) Banks will offer better deals on home loans.
(e) Interest rates will likely go up again.

3 **What will the woman probably say next?**
(a) I think I will wait for the economy to improve.
(b) One loan to pay off is enough for me right now.
(c) I do not have enough cash saved to buy a house now.
(d) Maybe since I do not have any outstanding loans.
(e) No one will lend me money because of my poor credit.

4-5

4 **What is the purpose of the lecture?**
(a) To explain why competition occurs   (b) To discuss the importance of competition
(c) To describe how competition works   (d) To show how to get good deals
(e) To explain the idea of the market

5 **Which statement is true about the three types of competition described in the lecture?**
(a) Substitute competition is related to consumers having a limited amount of money.
(b) Direct competition deals with replacing one product with another.
(c) Budget competition is related to similar products for similar wants.
(d) Direct competition deals with products that are of the same kind.
(e) Substitute competition involves a lot of advertising campaigns.

Level up

6 **Listen to the question and answer choices and choose the correct answer.**
(a)   (b)   (c)   (d)   (e)

Level up

7 **Listen to the question and answer choices and choose the correct answer.**
(a)   (b)   (c)   (d)   (e)

8 **Complete the bar graph comparing the number of men and women employed in the five categories of jobs mentioned.**

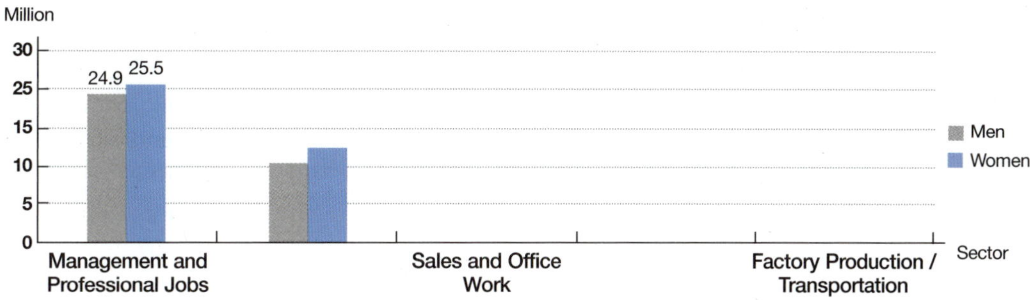

 【Integrated Questions】

Read the following passage and listen to the lecture.

A very important aspect to any country's economy, and one of keen interest to economists, is the capital market. Capital is, of course, another word for money. In this case, it is money used to invest in existing companies or to start new companies. Within the capital market, there are the stock market and the bond market. By selling stocks and bonds, corporations and governments can raise the money they need to expand or to complete public projects such as building roads, bridges, and highways. A stock is a share of a company that gives the buyer partial ownership of a company. Bonds are quite different. When someone buys a bond, it is as if he or she is lending money to the company or government. The government or company agrees to pay the person back the money plus interest at a fixed point in time, such as five or ten years. Within the capital market, there is also some kind of regulator whose job is to make sure nobody cheats or manipulates the market illegally. Most countries have some form of a capital market where investors and companies can come together to buy, sell, and trade stocks and bonds. The most famous capital market is the New York Stock Exchange.

Now answer the following questions based on what you read and heard.

9 **What are the main differences between a stock and a bond according to the information presented in the reading and listening? Choose ALL that apply.**

(a) Stocks offer a high risk and a high return on a person's investment while bonds have a lower risk but offer a lower rate of return on the investment.

(b) Buying bonds is a way to guarantee that an investment is completely secure while with stocks, there are no security guarantees.

(c) Investing in stocks can only be done through a secure money market exchange while bonds can be invested in from anywhere.

(d) Bonds provide an investor a way directly to deal with money markets while stocks are handled by someone else, such as a fund manager.

(e) Investing in stocks gives someone partial ownership of a company while investing in bonds is just like lending money to a company.

10 **According to the information presented, how much return would a Canadian mutual fund investor receive back on an $8,000 investment if the mutual fund failed?**

(a) $8,000   (b) $7,500   (c) $6,000

DICTATION [Exercise]

■ Listen and fill in the blanks.　　　　　　　　　　　　　　　　　　　　　　　　　🔵 3-7

1　M A _______ _______ _______ _______ any high-priced, high-quality good that people want. Such items can _______ almost any _______ _______ _______, such as _______, food, hotels, and _______. Why do people _______ _______ _______ _______ for these products and services? _______ _______ tells us that people will buy the _______ _______ they can for the _______ _______ _______. But with luxury items, there are _______ _______ _______ at work. The first factor is the _______ that high price means _______ _______. Of course, this is not _______ _______ _______, and there are _______ _______ _______ out there, but when a _______ _______ becomes _______ _______ a _______ for quality, people know that they are _______ _______ _______ for their money. This _______ the _______ _______ that is _______ _______ almost any _______. Second, there is the _______ _______ _______. People want to _______ _______ _______ high-quality products. If they have _______ _______ and have _______ _______ _______ _______, they want to show the world that they are _______. By having the best car, watch, and clothes, by _______ _______ the best hotels, by taking a _______ instead of a taxi, and by flying first class _______ _______ _______, they show the world that they are among the _______. As long as there are people with money _______ _______ _______ these products and services, luxury items will _______ _______ _______.

2　M Welcome to *Business Week*. Our guest today is Susan Radcliff, a _______ _______, and our topic is _______ _______. Susan, what are some _______ _______ _______ how much or how many of a product a person will buy?

W One of the _______ _______ is the price of the product.

M Can you _______ _______ _______ of this?

W Certainly. If a can of soda _______ _______ _______, you wouldn't buy it since you would think it costs _______ _______ _______ _______ _______. If the price were three dollars, you might buy one as a _______ _______. If the price _______ to one dollar and 50 cents, you'd _______ _______ _______, and if it were fifty cents, you might buy a lot.

M It sounds very _______. How do _______ _______ these _______?

W We can _______ _______ _______ on a graph to show the _______ _______.

M Can you explain that _______?

W First, we put the price on the _______ _______ and the amount bought on the _______ _______. Let's use the soda example.

M Okay, so at five dollars, a person _______ _______ _______ _______, and at 3 dollars, the person would buy one, right?

W Yes, and when the price _______ to one dollar and 50 cents, we'll say the person would buy three, and then _______ _______ _______, the person would buy eight. When we _______ _______ _______, you can see that we have a _______ _______ which _______ _______ from the left to the right.

M So, _______ _______ the price of a good, the more people will buy, and the _______ _______ _______ _______ _______, the less of it you buy.

W Correct. Generally, demand goes down as prices rise and vice versa.

W One of the ________ ________ of ________ is money. In fact, money is something that ________ ________ ________, but economists look at money ________ ________ ________ ________ than most people. Economists think of money ________ ________ ________ ________—what it does— and to an ________, money has three functions. First, money is used as a ________ ________ ________. This means that with money, we can ________ ________ ________ of different goods and services and ________ ________. This also means that businesses have a ________ ________ ________ if their ________ ________ are ________ ________ ________. The second function of money is as a ________ ________ ________. This is perhaps its ________ ________ ________. Money ________ ________ ________ or the exchange of ________ ________ ________. When we trade for goods or services without using money, it is ________ ________. This ________ that ________ ________ need what the ________ ________ ________, which is not always the case. Money is ________ ________ than ________ because it is ________ ________ ________ for goods and services. This ________ to the third function of money, which is the ________ ________ ________ function. People believe money is ________ ________ and that it has value. People will ________ ________ money as a ________ of exchange if it does not ________ ________ ________. As a ________, money is anything which is accepted as a unit of account, a medium of exchange, and a store of value.

W When economists talk about ________ ________ ________, they must also ________ the concepts of ________ and ________. Does anyone know what a ________ is?

B It's when you ________ ________ ________ with another, such as when the good is in ________ ________ or there is a ________ problem.

W ________ ________ ________ ________ ________. For example, every morning you drink orange juice because it's healthy and ________ ________ ________. Then there is a ________ ________ in the great orange-growing ________ of Florida, and many orange trees are ________ or ________ ________ by the ________ ________. What happens to the price of orange juice?

B The price of orange juice will ________ ________ because there is ________ ________.

W Right. So will your family ________ ________ ________ orange juice ________ ________ it's now very expensive?

B It ________ ________ ________ ________ it is. If it gets really expensive, we probably ________ ________ ________ orange juice.

W So that's when ________ ________ ________ ________. What do you think is a ________ ________ ________ orange juice?

B Apple juice?

W Good choice. Apple juice is a substitute for orange juice. It ________ ________ ________ ________ as orange juice. When the price of one good ________, people ________ ________ to a substitute if it's ________.

B I understand. You also ________ ________. What are they?

W A complement is when ________ ________ ________ ________. This means that they complement ________ ________. A good example is ________ ________ ________. When gas is cheap, people will buy large ________ ________ ________ which use a lot of gas. When gas prices go up, people want to buy ________ ________ which use less gas.

B So, ________ ________ ________ of each other when a change in the price of one good ________ ________ ________ for another good.

W Exactly.

7

G Dad, how do ________ ________?

M Banks use other people's money to ________ ________. That's about ________ ________ ________ I can make it.

G Do you mean they ________ ________ ________ people ________ in the bank?

M Right. Banks ________ ________ a ________ ________ ________ ________ their money. They pay you to keep your money with them ________ ________ ________, which are usually two or three percent per year.

G So then how do they make money?

M Banks ________ ________ ________ to people ________ ________ money to buy a house or a car or to ________ ________ ________. Banks ________ these people a ________ ________ ________, which is usually between five and ten percent. This is the banks' ________, and it's how they make money.

G Can they lend all of their money? ________ ________ I want to ________ ________ ________ ________ and it's not there because they lent it?

M The ________ has ________ ________ that banks must ________ ________ ________ ________ of their money ________ ________ in the banks ________ ________ ________. This is usually about 10 percent of ________ ________ ________.

8

W I'd like to speak a little about one of the ________ ________ ________ and most ________ ________, Milton Friedman. He ________ ________ ________ New York in 1912. He is ________ ________ ________ his work at the University of Chicago, where ________ ________ for 30 years. While there, he ________ ________ ________ a group of ________ who would ________ ________ ________ the Chicago School of Economics. Many of the ________ ________ would be ________ ________ ________ in the United States, Britain, and Canada in the 1980s. Freidman's ________ ________ was that a government should not become ________ ________ ________ ________ a nation's economy. He ________ and ________ ________ ________ on ________ history and theory. In 1976, he won the ________ ________ for Economics. In addition, he won ________ ________ ________ for economics in the United States ________ ________ ________. After his ________ in 1977, he traveled to many countries, ________ Eastern Europe and China, where he ________ ________ and advice on economics. He was also an ________ ________ to President Ronald Reagan from 1980 to 1988. Milton Friedman died in 2006 at the age of 94 in San Francisco.

9

M Economics is very ________ ________ ________ how economies perform, and one of the most ________ ________ is ________ ________ ________, or GDP. This is a topic of ________ ________ for newspapers, ________, and ________, and these ________ are usually ________ ________ a ________ ________. Simply put, GDP is a measurement of the ________ ________ of the ________. With this ________, economists can ________ whether the economy is ________ ________ and people's lives are ________ ________ or whether there is a problem and people may need to ________ ________. The ________ ________ to do this is to ________ the ________ ________ of all final goods and services a ________ ________ ________ a period of time, ________ ________ ________. This is then ________ ________ the ________ ________, and then economists can see if the economy has ________ ________ ________. The value of the dollar ________ ________ ________, and prices ________ ________ ________ ________, so it is important to ________ ________ for these factors. The adjusted GDP is called the real GDP. When it is ________ ________, it is called the ________ GDP. One ________ ________ for calculating GDP is the ________ ________ ________. In this method, GDP ________ ________ ________ investment plus government purchases plus ________ ________ ________. In the end, ________ ________ which method is used, a strong GDP means a strong economy and ________ ________.

10

W The ________ ________ are in on the 2008 ________ ________ in America. I guess we need to do an ________ ________ ________ for next month's magazine.

M You're right. Let's go to the ________ and see how we are doing ________ ________ the past.

W Compared to the ________ ________, I am sure the unemployment rate is ________ ________.

M Let's have a ________. Ah, yes. In 1930, just as the ________ ________ ________, the ________ ________ was 8.9 percent, and 4.3 million people in a ________ of 44 million people were ________ ________ ________.

W Let's just ________ ________ the percentage and ________ ________ ________ for the article ________ ________ ________.

M Sounds like a plan. So we have 1930. Then, in 1940, it ________ ________ as 14.9 percent were ________.

W That was just before World War II started. I'm sure the ________ ________ ________ ________.

M Yes, there was only 5 percent ________ ________ ________. Then, in 1960, it was 5.5 percent, and, in 1970, it was even lower at ________ ________.

W Those were some ________ ________ in America. Now look at 1980. Unemployment ________ ________ 7.1 percent.

M Yes, but, by 1990, it was down to 5.6 percent, and, in 2000, it was the ________ ________ ________ ________ at 4 percent.

W Those were the ________ ________ ________ in 2000. And the ________ ________ for 2008 show it climbed to 6.1 percent.

M That's the result of the ________ ________ ________. I'm sure the figures for the ________ ________ of 2009 are also going to be high.

11-12

W Today, we are ________ ________ ________ the ________ ________. Quite simply, the money supply ________ ________ the ________ ________ ________ ________ in the economy at any point in time. It is ________ ________ ________ the money supply because it can have a ________ ________ ________ ________ on an economy. ________ ________, it can ________ ________ ________ people pay for goods and services and the ________ ________ which banks ________ ________ ________. The money supply is ________ ________ ________, usually through their central bank or other ________ like the Federal Reserve in the United States. The money supply ________ ________ ________ in three different ways. The ________ ________ of the money supply is called M1. This is the ________ of definitions and ________ ________ ________, which is ________ ________ and coins, plus ________ ________ and ________ ________. Checkable deposits are money held in ________ ________ which are easy for people to ________ by ________ ________. The second definition of the money supply is M2. This includes all of the money in M1 plus money in savings accounts and time deposits of less than 100,000 dollars. ________ ________ are savings which ________ ________ ________ for a certain period of time. The ________ ________ is called M3, which includes M1 and M2 plus time deposits ________ ________ dollars. When there is a ________ in the money supply, it means that there is ________ ________ ________ for ________ and ________. In this case, banks can charge ________ ________ ________. When there is an ________ in the money supply, it means that there is more money available, so banks ________ ________ their interest rates to ________ ________.

Biology

PREPARATION

4-1

Ⓐ Read the definitions and write the correct word in each blank.

metabolic	foliage	nocturnal	buoyancy	vertebrate

1 ___________ the leaves of a tree
2 ___________ the ability to float in liquids
3 ___________ related to the burning of food for energy in organisms
4 ___________ an organism with a bony structure and spine
5 ___________ active in the nighttime

■ Now listen to the words and definitions and check your answers.

Ⓑ Fill in the blanks with suitable words or phrases on the list. Change the forms if needed.

creep up on	coniferous	slimy	pesky	diurnal	predator	feline

1 ___________ trees can be recognized by their needle-like leaves and large cone-shaped seeds.
2 ___________ animals are active in the daytime and rest at night.
3 Most ___________ have eyes that look forward so that they can focus on their intended prey.
4 Predators often ___________ prey and use stealth to surprise them.
5 Earthworms digest soil, and then it comes out with a ___________ substance that helps bind the soil.
6 The ___________ animal family includes both domestic and wild cats.
7 Bees can be a ___________ irritation if they get close enough to sting.

■ Now listen to the sentences and check your answers.

■ **Match each expression with its proper meaning.**

1 I've always had a green thumb.
2 It runs in the family.
3 That goes with the territory.
4 There's no need to nag me.
5 It's better to be safe than sorry.
6 Does anything strike your fancy?
7 A small amount goes a long way.

ⓐ It's common in our family.
ⓑ Stop bothering me about that.
ⓒ Is there anything you like?
ⓓ I know a lot about gardening.
ⓔ Not much is needed.
ⓕ It's common for this activity.
ⓖ Be prepared for the worst.

■ Now listen to the sentences and check your answers.

■ Listen to the monolog and complete the organizer.

An Insect's Body

The Head

- antennae, the eyes, the mouth, and the brain
- (1) ___________ : sensory organs - for (2) ___________ or (3) ___________
- mouth - for chewing or (4) ___________

The Thorax

- the (5) ___________ section of the insect's body
- has (6) ___________ segments: each has a pair of legs
- (7) ___________ in one or two pairs - not all have

The Abdomen

- (8) ___________ portion has the (9) ___________ organs
- final stage of (10) ___________
- may have a (11) ___________

General Questions Based on the organizer, answer the questions.

1 What is the main purpose of the talk?

(a) To discuss the function of an insect's abdomen

(b) To explain the components of an insect's body

(c) To describe different types of insect mouths

(d) To examine the bodily functions of insects

2 Choose the best summary.

(a) Insects have three distinct body sections, which have various body parts, such as antennae, wings, legs, and the digestive system.

(b) Insects are distinguished from other small creatures by their three body sections, six legs, and two pairs of wings.

Specific Questions Listen again. Mark T for true statements and F for false statements.

(1) Antennae on insects are used for touching and hearing. _____

(2) A lack of wings does not mean a creature is not an insect. _____

(3) The legs of an insect are attached to the abdomen in three pairs. _____

(4) Insects' mouths have adapted to the type of food each species eats. _____

■ **Listen to the dialog and complete the notes.**　　4-3

Situation: A boy helping his grandmother to take care of her garden

About grandmother - teaches him about the role of (1)__________ in gardening
　　　　　→ knows well about gardening

About the boy - (□ knows / □ doesn't know) much about gardening

Facts about (2)__________ : good for (3)__________ health
　　　　└ eat (4)__________ to help digest food

• leave (5)__________ by plowing through soil → allow (6)__________ and (7)__________ to
reach (8)__________ levels of soil → plant (9)__________ can grow

• slime helps (10)__________ stick together → prevents soil from being (11)__________ by
(12)__________ and (13)__________

 Based on the notes, answer the questions.

1 **What is the main topic of the dialog?**
　(a) The reasons the boy does not like earthworms　　(b) The role of earthworms in the health of soil
　(c) The digestive mechanism of the earthworm　　(d) The best way to use earthworms in gardening

2 **Choose the best summary.**
　(a) Earthworms are necessary for a garden because they help the soil to have more nutrients and allow plants to grow better.
　(b) Earthworms are of great help to gardening since they open up space for air and water in soil and prevent soil erosion.

 Listen again. Mark T for true statements and F for false statements.

(1) The boy knows a lot about why earthworms are good for gardens.　　　　____
(2) Earthworms eat soil and produce slime, which help plants stick to the soil better.　　____
(3) The earthworm tunnels make the soil loose enough for water to get to lower soil levels.　　____
(4) The soil that earthworms ingest helps them digest food.　　　　____

Listen to the lecture and complete the organizer.

Hibernation and Aestivation

Hibernation

When	during the (1)_______ when it gets too (2)_______
Who	typical of (3)_______ animals
	Ex. squirrel
Why	lack of (6)_______ supply in (7)_______
Principle	metabolic rate of the animals is (8)_______
	→ energy consumption becomes slower
What	① eat (9)_______ food before hibernate
	② get fatter
	→ survive the long period of (10)_______

regulate (4)_______ by (5)_______ and burning energy

Aestivation

When	in (11)_______ climates when it gets too hot
Who	typical of (12)_______ creatures
	Ex. frog, snake, crocodile, turtle,
	(14)_______ → climb fence posts, trees, or buildings
What	try to find a (15)_______ spot or cool places such as
	(16)_______ or under (17)_______
Why	to escape extreme (18)_______ and remain mostly inactive

(13)_______ affects their bodies

---

1 What is the main idea of the lecture?

(a) Animals react to temperature changes by becoming inactive for some time.

(b) Hibernation and aestivation are the same thing but affect different animals.

(c) Warm-blooded and cold-blooded animals react to temperatures differently.

(d) Animals hibernate or aestivate due to a lack of food at certain times of the year.

2 Choose the best summary.

(a) Temperature changes and a lack of food result in aestivation in reptiles in hot desert climates while food supply problems are the main reason why mammals hibernate in winter climates.

(b) Hibernation and aestivation are ways that some animals protect themselves from external factors beyond their control, such as extreme temperatures and a lack of food supplies.

3 Mark T for true statements and F for false statements.

(1) A lack of food resources is a major reason why some animals aestivate.   _____

(2) Animals that cannot control their body temperature are more likely to aestivate.   _____

(3) Some snails go underground when the temperature is too hot.   _____

(4) During hibernation, a small amount of food goes a long way.   _____

4 How are hibernation and aestivation similar?

(a) The season in which each occurs   (b) The duration of each period

(c) The activity levels of the animals   (d) The location where each occurs

Dictation

■ Listen again and fill in the blanks.

M Now I'm sure everyone knows that _____ during the winter. Many other _____ , such as _____ , also do the same. However, it may surprise you that some _____ in _____ also become _____ .

The _____ for this action, I mean, when creatures in hot climates "_____ ," is called aestivation. Okay then. Why do creatures _____ or _____ when it gets too cold or too hot? Most animals are _____ or _____ . Mammals are warm-blooded and _____ by consuming food and _____ . In cold weather, however, there is sometimes _____ , so some species, like the squirrel, hibernate. During hibernation, the _____ of the animals is _____ , allowing them to _____ . Hibernating animals consume a lot of food _____ , so they _____ and can survive the _____ . Meanwhile, other creatures are cold-blooded, meaning their body temperature _____ the _____ . Cold-blooded animals living in a _____ , for example, usually _____ a _____ when it gets hot. When the temperature is _____ , they aestivate. In many _____ , species such as _____ , _____ , _____ , and turtles find cool places—typically _____ or _____ —where they can _____ and _____ . Some species of _____ aestivate by _____ , trees, and buildings. They do this to _____ in order to escape the extreme heat of the ground _____ . How long a creature _____ or _____ depends on the species. Some sleep or _____ for many months while others do that for shorter periods of time.

■ Listen and answer the questions.

4-5

1 **What is the main purpose of the talk?**

(a) To discuss the location of modern and ancient marsupials

(b) To explain the extraordinary birthing methods of marsupials

(c) To examine the reasons that marsupials thrive in Australia

(d) To prove that marsupials once lived on every continent

(e) To show how marsupials are the same as other mammals

2 **Complete the table with the correct level of pain for each insect on the pain index.**

Insect	Pain Level on the Pain Index Scale
Paper Wasp	
Paper Wasp	
Bee	2
Hornet	
Harvester Ant	
Fire Ant	

3-4

3 **What physical feature of the albatross helps when it glides?**

(a) The hollow structure of its bones

(b) The large surface area of its wings

(c) The immobility of its large wings

(d) The special tendons in its wings

(e) The overall light weight of its body

4 **What can be inferred about albatrosses from the talk?**

(a) They are not able to float on the ocean water.

(b) They return to their homes after long flights.

(c) They barely flap their wings during flight.

(d) They feed mainly on food from land.

(e) They have special feathers to help them fly.

5-6
Level up

5 **What is NOT true according to the dialog?**

(a) Some types of mushrooms can be fatal if ingested.

(b) It is rather easy to distinguish different mushrooms.

(c) "Toadstool" is just a name given to some mushrooms.

(d) There have been some tragic incidents with mushrooms.

(e) Different types of mushrooms can be similar in appearance.

6 **Choose the statement that best summarizes the dialog.**

(a) While many mushrooms are safe to eat, toadstools are not; therefore, someone should not collect wild mushrooms without an expert guide.

(b) Wild mushrooms are safe to collect as long as you have a special mushroom guidebook to distinguish the safe ones from the dangerous ones.

(c) Mushrooms and toadstools are the same thing as "toadstool" is just a name given to many types of inedible mushrooms.

Level up

7 **Listen to the question and answer choices and choose the correct answer.**

(a)　　(b)　　(c)　　(d)　　(e)

Level up

8 **Listen to the question and answer choices and choose the correct answer.**

(a)　　(b)　　(c)　　(d)　　(e)

9 **Which is NOT true according to the talk?**

(a) Hyenas kill prey but then sometimes lose it to lions.

(b) Territorial fights are usually over possession of females.

(c) Male lions fight other male lions to take over their pride.

(d) Animals mark their territories with secretions that smell.

(e) A territory's food supply cannot support many predators.

10 **Make a graph showing the gestation period for dogs, cats, elephants, rabbits, and mice.**

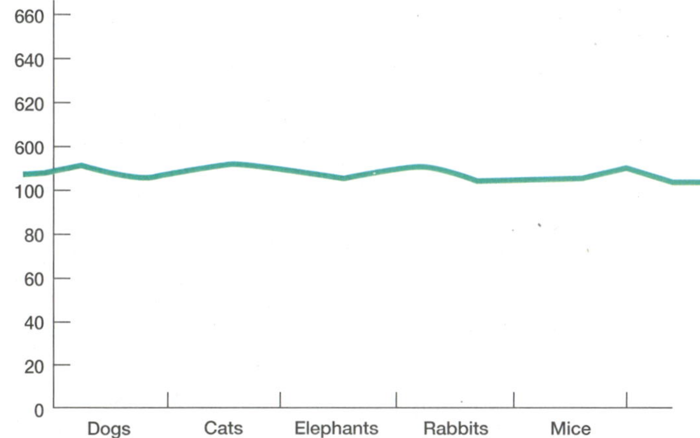

11-12
Level up

11 **What is the main purpose of the lecture?**

(a) To discuss different types of plants and their functions

(b) To show how plants are classified with scientific names

(c) To examine some different ways that plants are classified

(d) To develop a better scientific system of plant classification

(e) To explain how plants are able to spread to new areas

12 **What is the major difference between angiosperms and gymnosperms?**

(a) The nature of their internal vein systems

(b) The heights which they can eventually reach

(c) The number of seeds that they have inside

(d) The method they use to spread their seeds

(e) The nature of their seeds' coverings

PRACTICE TEST

■ Listen and answer the questions.

1 **Which statement is true according to the talk?**

(a) Hormones dictate the circadian and circannian cycles in animals.

(b) Circadian cycles are related to hibernating, migrating, and mating.

(c) The birth of offspring in the spring is an example of a circannian cycle.

(d) Nocturnal animals sleep during the nighttime and hunt during the day.

(e) The sun's movement is key in the triggering of circannian cycles.

2-3

2 **What can be inferred from the dialog?**

(a) The two speakers are brother and sister.

(b) Coniferous trees are taller than deciduous trees.

(c) The girl gets better school grades than the boy.

(d) The boy did well on his last biology test.

(e) There is going to be a bonus question on the test.

3 **What will the boy probably say next?**

(a) Thanks for helping me study for this test.

(b) Why don't you just take the test for me?

(c) It was 379 feet, or 115 meters, high.

(d) That's it! It's my turn to ask the questions.

(e) You have gone completely nuts, you know?

4-5

4 **Why is the ant-aphid relationship called facultative mutualism?**

(a) Both ants and aphids would not survive if the relationship between them were severed.

(b) It is a classic sign of facultative mutualism for ants to protect aphids from beetle attacks.

(c) While both species achieve some benefits from the relationship, both can survive without the other.

(d) Ants and aphids have a common enemy, so it is necessary for them to join forces.

(e) Their relationship has continued for so long that it is almost impossible to end it.

5 **What can be inferred from the talk?**

(a) Ants are rewarded with aphid nectar only after a successful battle with beetles.

(b) When coral turns white, it will definitely die within a short time.

(c) Mutualism involves relationships between animals and is not present in plants.

(d) Zooxanthellae sometimes return to their coral hosts before the coral dies.

(e) Aphids do not have any defensive mechanisms to fight attacking beetles.

Level up

6 **Listen to the question and answer choices and choose the correct answer.**

(a)   (b)   (c)   (d)   (e)

Level up

7 **Listen to the question and answer choices and choose the correct answer.**

(a)   (b)   (c)   (d)   (e)

8 Complete the table with the hearing range of the animals mentioned.

Animal	Hearing Range (Hertz)
Mouse	
Dog	
Cat	
Bat	
Porpoise	

【Integrated Questions】

■ Read the following passage and listen to the lecture.

Primates are the closest link connecting humans to the animal world. For this reason, primates have been studied extensively. Most primates are herbivores, meaning they eat plants. A few species, the common chimpanzee in particular, are carnivores. In West Africa, common chimpanzees have been seen actively hunting, killing, and eating the red colobus monkey. More recently, experts have observed a colony of common chimpanzees in Senegal in West Africa making and using spear-like sticks as weapons while hunting for small game. While tool use among primates was not unknown, the reason for making the tools was. After spending a great deal of time observing the chimps, the researchers had their answer. The chimps took small tree branches, pulled off the leaves, sharpened one of the ends with their teeth, and then used this spear–like weapon to stick into holes in tree trunks where a small species called the bush baby often sleeps in the daytime. On at least 40 occasions, the observers noticed this activity. When news of chimps actively making tools to kill other animals reached the rest of the world, it made headlines and also raised a controversy over what the use of these tools by chimps meant and why it had happened.

■ Now answer the following questions based on what you read and heard.

9 **What is NOT correct according to the reading and listening?**

(a) Chimps in West Africa have been observed killing small animals with weapons.

(b) Adult chimps are usually the ones that do the hunting and act in an aggressive manner.

(c) Sometimes chimps attack and kill other species of monkeys to eat them.

(d) The reports that chimps use spear-like tools have received wide academic support.

(e) Primate researchers must not think of chimps as too human since that attitude can distort their research.

10 **What can be inferred from the reading and listening?**

(a) Chimps had never been observed using spears before 2007.

(b) West Africa is home to a high proportion of living chimps.

(c) Bush babies usually defend themselves when attacked.

(d) Chimps sometimes actively hunt and attack larger animals.

(e) Female chimps hide their aggressive nature from observers.

DICTATION (Exercise)

■ Listen and fill in the blanks.

4-7

1   W Okay, today I __________ __________ __________ the __________ __________ __________ called __________. The most well-known of these animals is the __________, and other well-known __________ __________ the koala bear and the opossum. There are over 300 species of __________ __________ __________, and __________ of them are __________ __________ __________. What __________ __________ from most other __________ is the way their __________ __________ __________. In most mammals, the __________ has a placenta in its __________, which __________ the __________ __________ __________ the mother's __________ __________ to __________ __________. However, in marsupials, the womb is __________ __________ the __________ of a bird's egg and only __________ __________ for a short time. Therefore, the mother carries the offspring __________ __________ for only a __________ __________ of time—about a month—and then the __________ __________ __________. The offspring climbs into a __________ on the front of the __________ __________ __________. Here it may remain for __________ __________ __________ as it develops and __________ __________. Inside the pouch are the female marsupial's nipples, which the offspring __________ __________ and __________ __________ __________ milk and nutrition. __________ __________ of marsupials have been found on all __________, but the __________ __________ __________ marsupials today live in South America and Australia. It is believed marsupials __________ __________ __________ of these two continents because placenta-born mammals __________ them. The hot climates of South America and Australia seem to have made the __________ __________ of birth an __________, and therefore marsupials have __________ in these lands.

2   W Thanks for __________ __________ to your __________ __________, David. I'm really __________ __________ __________ seeing how you __________ __________.

   M First, we have to __________ __________ these __________ __________ so the bees can't __________ us.

   W I've been __________ __________, and __________ __________ __________. That's for sure.

   M I think I've been stung by __________ __________ __________ bee, __________, and hornet. I guess that __________ __________ __________ __________ when you collect honey __________ __________ __________.

   W Which stings __________ __________ __________: bees, wasps, or hornets?

   M It's hard to say since everyone __________ __________ a little __________. An American __________ made a __________ __________ which shows __________ __________ a sting can get. It just has numbers from one to four, with one being __________ pain and four being __________ pain. It's in this __________. Ah, here it is.

   W It looks like __________ __________ the worst pain. The paper wasp __________ __________ __________, and the pepsis wasp rates a four on the __________ __________.

   M Yeah, those can be __________ __________ if you __________ __________. In __________, __________ and bees usually rate only a two. But __________ __________ can have painful stings.

   W Oh, this is the harvester ant! It __________ __________ the ants I had in my ant farm when I was in school.

   M Most likely. It's __________ __________, but it has a sting __________ __________ __________ paper wasps.

   W Do all ants cause such pain?

   M Oh, no. The fire ant rates even __________ __________ __________ and bees on the chart. But they attack in __________, so they can be dangerous.

3-4   W The __________ is one of the __________ __________ among birds. The __________ __________ of the Indian, __________, and __________ oceans, and the __________ __________, are home to these large birds. Albatrosses

can fly ________ ________ ________ of water for ________ ________ kilometers ________ ________
________. They have a ________ ________ ________ that ________ this long-range flight and also have
________ ________ that they use to ________ ________. First off, the ________ has an almost ________
________ ________, which makes it ________ ________ its size would suggest. There is also a ________
in its wings that ________ ________ in place so the wings are ________ and do not ________ ________
from being ________ ________ with just the bird's ________. The wings are large and have a ________
________ ________ for catching more lift while the ________ ________. For flight, the albatross ________
________ its special ________ ________ and the use of the winds and the waves. The albatross ________
________ the ocean, ________ ________ ________, and then ________ ________ and ________ this speed
to ________ and ________. For every 30 centimeters it ________ ________ the ocean, it can move six
meters ________ and then ________ ________ ________ for hundreds of kilometers ________ ________
the ocean. A second technique of flight relies on the ________ ________. The albatross will ________
________—just above wave height—and will ________ ________ from the wind that is ________
________ the waves. As each ________ ________, the albatross gains more lift and ________ ________ its
long journey.

M It's a nice day for a ________ ________ ________ ________.

W Thanks for helping me ________ ________ ________. There should be lots of them ________ ________.
This was the ________ ________ last year.

M I think I see some now.

W No, ________ ________ those. They are not very ________, and some are very ________.

M That's some information I ________ ________ ________ a bit earlier. How can I tell a ________ mushroom
________ ________ ________ mushroom?

W It's hard. That's why I have ________ ________ this mushroom ________ ________. The ones to ________
are the little brown ones because they are the ________ ________ ________. Even a small ________
________ ________ a different species, and some are ________.

M Do you mean I could die ________ ________ a mushroom?

W Yes, it has happened. A ________ ________ in Canada died after eating a type of mushroom ________
________ was safe, but it was ________ ________.

M Now you've ________ ________ ________. Is that type of mushroom around here?

W No, and the mushrooms that ________ ________ are not very poisonous. Some types will ________
________ ________ ________.

M What about ________? Are they around here?

W There is no such thing as a toadstool. That's just a ________ ________ ________ dangerous mushrooms a
long time ago in Europe.

M So, ________ ________ ________ bad mushrooms could be what people call toadstools?

W ________. Oh, stop! You just about ________ ________ those mushrooms. Now those are ________
________ ________.

M Are you sure?

W Yes. Why? Don't you ________ ________?

M Maybe I'll just have a sandwich for lunch.

7

W That's a cute cat. What's its name?

M Bubbles. She's a _________ _________.

W Oh, I think she _________ _________ _________ _________. It looks like she's _________ _________ _________.

M Yeah, she does that when she sees a bird. Cats are _________ _________ at night though. They have _________ _________ _________.

W I _________ _________ when I see a _________ _________ _________ in the dark.

M Yeah, it is _________ _________ _________. Have you ever _________ that some animals have eyes _________ _________ _________ of their heads _________ _________ have them in the _________?

W Yeah, I _________ _________ _________. I imagine it _________ _________ _________ _________ _________ the type of animal. For instance, I think most _________ have forward-facing eyes. Look at your cat, other cats, like lions and tigers, and even dogs.

M That's all the _________ _________ _________ _________. Forward-facing eyes _________ them to _________ _________ _________ in sight.

W And _________ _________ have eyes on the sides of their heads.

M Now that _________ _________. So the prey animals can see if a predator is coming from the _________ to _________ them.

W That sounds _________.

8

M Most plants _________ _________ _________ from soil and _________ _________ _________. However, there are a few plants that _________ _________ from eating other _________ _________—usually _________ and sometimes small animals, _________ _________. These are _________ _________. They are usually found in _________ with _________ _________, such as _________ _________ or _________, which may _________ _________ these plants have _________ _________ _________ other life forms. Carnivorous plants _________ _________ in several ways. The Venus flytrap, for example, _________ _________ _________ on an insect very quickly—just _________ _________ _________—and then uses _________ _________ to consume it. The _________ _________ has a long, _________, _________ _________ that has digestive enzymes _________ _________ _________. Insects _________ _________ and can't _________ _________, so they are _________ _________ the plant. Other carnivorous plants have _________ _________ that trap insects, they have traps like _________ _________ where the insects _________ _________ _________ but can't get out, or they have a _________ that _________ _________ in like a _________ _________ _________ _________.

9

W In the animal kingdom, _________ _________ _________ is one of the _________ _________ of daily life. Many _________, such as lions and _________, choose a _________ and _________ _________ _________ all outsiders. The food _________ within this territory can _________ a certain number of _________ but _________ _________ _________ that number, so it is _________ for the _________ to _________ _________ _________ their territory. They _________ _________ other members of the same species by _________ _________ _________ of their territory _________ _________ or _________ _________ from the body. These secretions _________ _________ _________ _________ that _________ _________ _________ that this territory has been _________. However, this does not _________ _________ _________ _________. Members of _________ _________ may not _________ the stay-away _________ or may be _________ _________ _________ _________ the territory. Hyenas, for example, _________ _________ through lion territories. There is even some _________ that the lions allow this so that the hyenas can _________ _________ _________. Then the _________ _________ the hyenas away so they can _________ the dead animal. But when other lions enter a _________ _________ _________, the occupying lions are not _________ _________. A prime reason for _________ lions to _________ _________ _________ is to fight those male lions that have claimed it. This _________ _________ _________ to _________ a food supply as well as to _________ _________ the _________ _________ and to make a claim on the female lions. In this way, these _________ may kill or _________ _________ the males and take their place.

10

G Hello, Dr. Hibbert.

M Hello, Sally. Hello, Pookie. What can I do for you?

G Pookie is sick.

M ________ ________ ________ ________ your dog is sick, Sally?

G She is very ________ ________. She doesn't want to ________ ________ as much. And she's ________ ________ ________ and is ________ ________ ________. Look at her.

M Well, let me do a ________ ________, and we'll see what the trouble is. Okay... oh, I see ________ ________ ________ now.

G What's wrong with Pookie, Dr. Hibbert?

M Sally, Pookie is going to be a ________ ________ ________.

G Oh, wow. Puppies! ________ ________ ________?

M It's ________ ________ ________. We'll ________ ________ in a few weeks.

G How long do I have to wait?

M The ________ ________ ________ for dogs is about 63 days. I'd say Pookie has about ________ ________ ________ to go.

G Gestation? What does that mean?

M The time it takes an animal to ________ ________. Cats are about the ________ ________ dogs. Their ________ ________ is around 61 days.

G Which animal ________ ________ ________ ________ to have babies?

M ________ ________ the ________. Its gestation period is about 2 years, which is ________ ________ days.

G Wow, that's a long time. Which animal takes the shortest time to have babies then?

M I'm not ________ ________, but mice usually ________ ________ ________ 21 days of ________ ________.

G What about rabbits? I had a ________ ________ ________.

M I remember. A rabbit's gestation is very short; it's only 31 days.

11-12

M There are almost ________ ________ ________ of plants ________ ________ by ________, and there may be many more. So, ________ ________ ________ ________ plants? The ________ ________—without ________ ________ all of the ________ ________ ________—is by ________ the plant's ________ ________, its seed structure, and its ________. There are two types of tissue structures: ________ and ________. Most plants are vascular plants. They have leaves, stems, and root systems. Nonvascular plants don't have ________, ________, or ________ ________. Mosses are a good ________ ________ nonvascular plants. Next, plants ________ ________ by their ________ ________ ________. There are three types of seeds: spores, ________ seeds, and ________ seeds. Mosses and several types of ________ ________ ________. They are ________ ________ by the wind and ________ ________ ________ ________. Plants with naked seeds usually have ________ and they are called gymnosperms. ________, ________, and ________ ________ are some examples of this type. Covered-seed plants are called angiosperms. They have their seeds ________ ________ ________ or ________. Almost all ________ ________ ________ are angiosperms. Angiosperms are ________ ________ ________ two types, depending on their ________ ________ and the number of seeds they bear. Some have ________ internal veins for the ________ ________ ________ and also have one-seed leaves. ________ ________ ________ are in this group. The second type has internal veins ________ ________ ________ and two-seed leaves. Cherry trees and coffee plants ________ ________ ________ ________. Finally, plants are ________ by their height. ________ ________ ________ are the mosses and the ________ ________ ________, flowers, and bushes, and, finally, there are the trees at ________ ________.

Social Issues

PREPARATION

5-1

A **Read the definition and write the correct word in each blank.**

| conscience | counterfeiting | hypocrite | purging | self-esteem |

1 ___________ someone who does the opposite of what he or she believes in
2 ___________ how a person feels about himself or herself
3 ___________ one's sense of right and wrong
4 ___________ the act of copying something to deceive
5 ___________ expelling something

■ Now listen to the words and definitions and check your answers.

B **Fill in the blanks with suitable words or phrases on the list. Change the forms if needed.**

| knockoff | lethal force | alimony | copycat |
| terminally ill | defamation | give in | |

1 Sometimes, the police must use ____________ to detain dangerous criminals.
2 Bloggers can be accused of ____________ if they write lies about people on their blogs.
3 When a famous person kills himself or herself, there is often a rash of ____________ suicides
   by obsessed fans who want to join the star in death.
4 When people are ____________, they may ask a doctor to assist them with suicide.
5 ____________ products cost manufacturers billions in lost profits every year.
6 Although he knew it was wrong, John ____________ to the pressure from his friends and
   smoked a cigarette.
7 She had a hard time after her divorce because her ex-husband did not always pay
   ____________ on time.

■ Now listen to the sentences and check your answers.

■ **Match each expression with its proper meaning.**

1 I'm right as rain.
2 You looked bummed out.
3 We're both in the same boat.
4 You can't fight city hall.
5 Face the facts.
6 It's out of proportion to its importance.
7 Big Brother is watching you.

ⓐ You seem sad.
ⓑ It's hard to go against the government.
ⓒ Accept the reality of the situation.
ⓓ The government is spying on its citizens.
ⓔ It seems more vital than it really is.
ⓕ I'm in good health.
ⓖ We are in a similar situation.

■ Now listen to the sentences and check your answers.

Listen to the monolog and complete the organizer.

5-2

Eating Disorders

Anorexia

- believes he or she is (1) _______
- is obsessed with his or her (2) _______
- is constantly (3) _______; counts calories; is always (4) _______; stops eating; does strenuous (5) _______; smokes cigarettes and (6) _______ gum to control urge to (7) _______

Bulimia

- eats (8) _______ amounts of food in a short time → afterwards feels extreme (9) _______ about (10) _______
- tries to (11) _______ food by self-inducing (12) _______ or taking laxatives

- a symptom of a serious (13) _______ problem
- has low (14) _______
- needs to be (15) _______ life

General Questions Based on the organizer, answer the questions.

1 What is the main purpose of the talk?

(a) To explain the reasons teenage girls go on diets

(b) To describe eating problems among young people

(c) To examine the psychology of eating too much

(d) To warn against some dangerous ways to lose weight

2 Choose the best summary.

(a) While eating disorders center on problems with food, the real cause may be an untreated psychological condition.

(b) Many young people, especially women, obsess about their body image so much that they suffer eating disorders.

Specific Questions Listen again. Mark T for true statements and F for false statements.

(1) People who suffer from anorexia nervosa are overweight. _______

(2) Low self-esteem is one problem associated with eating disorders. _______

(3) People who suffer from bulimia feel guilty about eating so much. _______

(4) The purging of food is common for those who have anorexia nervosa. _______

■ **Listen to the dialog and complete the notes.**　　5-3

Girl

- worries about the boy - hasn't seen him in a $^{(1)}$__________ - he looks sick
  - concludes that he is feeling $^{(2)}$__________
- offers to go with him to talk with the $^{(3)}$__________ about his problem
  - the girl was helped by her $^{(4)}$__________ when the $^{(5)}$__________ was sick

Boy

- tries to (☐ avoid / ☐ answer) the girl's questions
- says only old people get $^{(6)}$__________
- finally (☐ agrees / ☐ refuses) to seek help
  - (☐ convinced by girl's persuasion / ☐ tries to solve his problem by himself)

General Questions　Based on the notes, answer the questions.

1　What is the main idea of the dialog?

(a) A boy describes the symptoms of an illness that is affecting him.

(b) A girl tries to help a friend who has an emotional problem.

(c) A boy goes to see the school nurse because he is not feeling well.

(d) A girl feels strange talking to a friend about her depression.

2　Choose the best summary.

(a) A boy rejects a friend's suggestion to help him overcome a problem because he thinks it is not serious.

(b) A boy's friend notices he has not been himself lately, so she then offers to help him get some aid.

Specific Questions　Listen again. Mark T for true statements and F for false statements.

(1) The boy is eager to join the girl and her friends at the park.　　_____

(2) The girl persists in talking to the boy until he admits he needs help.　　_____

(3) The girl thinks that the school nurse is qualified to help the boy.　　_____

(4) In the past, the girl felt depressed just like the boy feels now.　　_____

■ Listen to the lecture and complete the organizer.

5-4

Steroids

Basic Information

- What: (1) __________ hormones
  - have same effect as (2) __________ hormone testosterone
- Usage: - take in (3) __________ form
  - inject with a needle
  - use (4) __________ and (5) __________
- Effects: - increase (6) __________ and strength
  - cause serious side effects to both men and woman

Effects on Males

- increased (7) __________ behavior
- more (8) __________
- liver damage
- (9) __________
- (10) __________ in breast size
- (11) __________
- stop producing (12) __________ hormones
- bad breath and body odor

Effects on Females

- a (13) __________ of the voice
- more (14) __________ appearance
- (15) __________ of the breasts
- (16) __________
- bad breath and body odor

1 What is the main topic of the lecture?

(a) How to use steroids properly

(b) The side effects of steroids in teens

(c) Why young people use steroids

(d) Steroid abuse among young athletes

2 Choose the best summary.

(a) Steroids enhance a person's athletic ability but should be taken with caution and in small doses.

(b) Although steroids have some positive effects, their possible side effects make them dangerous for anyone to use.

3   Mark T for true statements and F for false statements.

(1) Some American teens believe taking steroids is a very effective way for them to make the grade on sports teams.

_____

(2) Steroids are natural hormone which work like the male hormone testosterone.

_____

(3) Steroids help a user grow taller than he or she is naturally supposed to be.

_____

(4) Young women who take steroids can get a more masculine appearance.

_____

4   Which side effect of steroids is NOT mentioned as one that affects boys?

(a) Their personality can become very aggressive.

(b) Steroids can make them go bald at an early age.

(c) It can be hard for them to have a baby in the future.

(d) Their breasts may shrink after taking steroids.

Dictation

Listen again and fill in the blanks.

M Some recent studies ________________ that there has been an increase in the use of ________ by teenagers in America. Many teenage ________ are ________ a lot of ________ to ________ ________ and to perform well. Instead of taking the time to ________ ________, eat well, and ________ ________, a lot of these amateur athletes ________ ________ ________. Steroids are ________ ________ that have the ________ ________ the natural male hormone testosterone. Users take steroids in ________ ________, ________ with a needle, or use skin gels and creams that ________. Steroids aid in the development of ________ and ________, but they also have a lot of ________ ________, which many young people ________ ________ or just ________. The most common side effects in teenage boys are an increase in ________ ________, the development of ________ ________, ________ ________, possible ________, an increase in breast size, and early ________. There is also the ________ that the ________ ________ ________ ________. The increased amount of testosterone may ________ ________ ________ the user is an adult, so it will stop ________ ________ ________. It's not just teenage boys using steroids though. Some teenage girls use them because they want the ________, ________ common with the ________ they see in magazines. For teenage girls, the side effects of ________ ________ are a ________ of the voice, a more ________ ________, ________, and ________ of the breasts. ________ ________ and ________ ________ are also possible side effects for both men and women.

■ Listen and answer the questions.

5-5

1   What is the best title for the talk?

(a) Who Your Real Friends Are

(b) Peers Break All of the Rules

(c) Peer Pressure in School

(d) All About Peer Pressure

(e) When to Say Yes or No

2   Complete the table with the missing information.

Percentage of Obese American Children - Current	20%
Percentage of Obese American Children - 1970s	
Number of Obese Children Under 5 - Worldwide	
Total Number of Obese Children 12 and Under - Worldwide	
Percentage of Obese Children Who Become Obese Adults	
Total Number of Obese People Worldwide	

3-4

3   What did the South African law attempt to do according to the talk? Choose ALL that apply.

(a) Force the drug companies to reduce AIDS drug prices

(b) Copy and produce major AIDS drugs in South Africa

(c) Design and produce new AIDS drugs in South Africa

(d) Legalize experimenting with new AIDS drugs directly on humans

(e) Purchase cheaper AIDS drugs from other nations

4   What can be inferred from the talk?

(a) African nations outside of South Africa do not have as many AIDS-related deaths as South Africa.

(b) Some of the major pharmaceutical companies making AIDS drugs are originally from South Africa.

(c) Countries that wanted to sell cheaper AIDS drugs to South Africa were also sued by the drug companies.

(d) Domestic drug companies in South Africa are preparing to manufacture cheaper major AIDS drugs.

(e) The South African drug companies received permission to make AIDS drugs from the original drug companies.

5-6
Level up

5   Why does the man call himself a "hypocrite" at one point in the dialog?

(a) He berated the woman for buying counterfeit products, but he also buys clothing in the same manner.

(b) He told the woman that it is wrong to download music and video games and that he was going to stop doing it.

(c) He admonished the woman for buying a knockoff product while he illegally downloads music and video games.

(d) He feels that since everyone is getting expensive games and music for free, he would be stupid not to do the same thing.

(e) He thinks that getting things for free or at a cheaper price is wrong but does not have enough money to pay the full price.

6 **Choose the statement that best summarizes the dialog.**

(a) Buying knockoff products and downloading things are different because the first method takes money from the original producers.

(b) High prices make people buy counterfeit goods, but it is wrong since the original producers receive no money.

(c) Desire for good products drives people to purchase counterfeit goods; however, since everyone is doing it, it can be excused.

7 **Listen to the question and answer choices and choose the correct answer.**

(a)   (b)   (c)   (d)   (e)

8 **Listen to the question and answer choices and choose the correct answer.**

(a)   (b)   (c)   (d)   (e)

9 **Which is NOT mentioned as a reason that divorce has increased in South Korea?**

(a) Korean women have more financial security these days.

(b) Divorce is not as taboo a subject as it was in the past.

(c) Divorce laws that gave men more rights have changed.

(d) Korean women have a stronger political voice than before.

(e) Obtaining a divorce is not as difficult as it used to be.

10 **Complete the table with the missing information on the death penalty.**

Category	197 Countries in Total
Death Penalty Abolished	
Death Penalty Legal and in Use for Special Circumstances (Terrorism)	
Death Penalty Legal But Not Used in More than 10 Years	
Death Penalty Carried Out in 2008	

11 **What role do the media play in people making a final decision to commit a copycat suicide?**

(a) The media often sensationalize the suicide so that people can easily copy the method.

(b) Reporting on a famous suicide goes on and on to the point where people want to kill themselves.

(c) People who commit copycat suicides believe they will get an equal amount of media coverage.

(d) Excessive reporting of a celebrity's suicide may be the catalyst some people need to kill themselves.

(e) Continuing coverage of a celebrity's suicide reminds people how bleak life is if even celebrities kill themselves.

12 **Choose the statement that best summarizes the lecture.**

(a) Copycat suicides have been going on for centuries and will continue because of the cult of celebrity.

(b) Obsessive fans of celebrities who commit suicide like their idol did may already be suicidal before the celebrity's death.

(c) Famous people have a strong influence on young people, but only those with mental problems follow celebrities into death.

■ Listen and answer the questions.

1 What is NOT true about the Yoshiro Hattori incident according to the talk?
(a) Rodney Peairs warned Yoshiro Hattori to stop moving.
(b) Yoshiro Hattori was studying at a university in America.
(c) A Louisiana court acquitted Rodney Peairs in the case.
(d) Yoshiro Hattori was not alone when he was shot to death.
(e) Rodney Peairs was charged with murder in the case.

2-3

2 What can be inferred from the dialog?
(a) The declining birthrate is a result of the increasing number of elderly people.
(b) Income taxes are a major source of government income for the elderly.
(c) Medical costs for the elderly are more expensive than for the young.
(d) Older people are saving up to help pay for their own medical costs.
(e) People having smaller families means there will be fewer older people in the near future.

3 What will the woman probably say next after the boy's last question?
(a) Young people are going to have to think more about saving money for retirement.
(b) Young people don't really care if there is enough money for them after retirement.
(c) Young people think the next generation should provide enough taxes to solve these problems.
(d) Young people believe their retirement pensions will cover the burdens of future expenses.
(e) Young people think they will be able to retire just like their parents and grandparents did.

4-5

4 Why is there still confusion over what is allowed and not allowed on the Internet?
(a) There are not enough police to check the whole Internet.
(b) Laws are different in every country, which causes confusion.
(c) Many people are ignorant of the new Internet regulations.
(d) Quite a few Internet users believe there should be no rules.
(e) The rules for regulating the Internet are not yet set in stone.

5 Which example may be a breach of the media rules as explained in the talk if they also applied to the Internet?
(a) A student says he hates a certain video game in a chat room.
(b) A professor argues in class that Internet rules are unconstitutional.
(c) A citizen uses her computer to write a threatening letter to the president.
(d) A blogger writes a malicious attack on an entertainer he dislikes.
(e) A web designer uses a famous brand name in his new project.

Level up

6 Listen to the question and answer choices and choose the correct answer.
(a)   (b)   (c)   (d)   (e)

Level up

7 Listen to the question and answer choices and choose the correct answer.
(a)   (b)   (c)   (d)   (e)

8 **Complete the table with the missing information on child labor.**

Category	Number
Child Laborers: Worldwide	246 million
Child Laborers: Under 10 Years Old	
Child Laborers: 10-15 Years Old	
Child Laborers: Asia-Pacific Region	
Child Laborers: The Rest of the World	

9-10 【**Integrated Questions**】

■ Read the following passage and listen to the lecture.

International adoption is increasing around the world. While the welfare of the orphan is of great concern, some unintentional harm may be done. There are many case studies of children who have had a negative reaction to being adopted by families not of their culture or race. Usually, it depends on the age these children are adopted. If very young, the child may readily adapt, easily fitting in with the adopted parents' culture and learning its language and customs. However, if the adopted child is older and already identifies with his or her real parents' culture, race, and language, adapting may be more difficult. Adopted children may also wonder who their real parents are and why they abandoned them. For those children adopted by overseas families, finding out who their parents are is much more difficult. In addition to the distance from their home country, there may be language problems when communicating with government agencies in their home country. Even if these adopted children find out who their real parents are, the sad truth is that not all of these birth parents want to meet their children. And if they do, sometimes the language and cultural barriers are so great that such meetings are awkward and painful, making it seem perhaps better for the children not to know at all who their real parents are.

■ Now answer the following questions based on what you read and heard.

9 **What is NOT true about international adoption according to the reading and listening?**

(a) One concern of international adoption is the lack of background checks on adopting parents in some nations.

(b) Adapting to being adopted varies from child to child and depends a great deal on how old the child is when adopted.

(c) Language and cultural barriers may prevent bonding between very young adopted children and their new parents.

(d) It is more difficult for internationally adopted children to find out who their birth parents are.

(e) Relatives of internationally adopted children worry that they will lose touch when the child is adopted.

10 **What is mentioned in both the listening and reading as a main concern about international adoption?**

(a) Many celebrities are focusing too much attention on international adoption, which is giving it a bad name.

(b) An international adopted child may never see or hear from his or her original family again, which may cause harm on both sides.

(c) Searching for his or her real parents may cause great disappointment for an adopted child whether he or she finds the parents or not.

(d) Some nations have weak adoption laws, which make the process too easy since they do not give enough concern for the children involved.

(e) The adopted child will lose his or her sense of identity, especially if adopted by parents of a different race and/or culture.

DICTATION [Exercise]

■ Listen and fill in the blanks.   ● 5-7

1 W An important issue facing children and teens everywhere is ________ ________. It's ________ for young people to understand what peer pressure is and ________ ________ ________ ________. Firstly, your peers are the people who are your friends, the people ________ ________ ________, and the people who are ________ ________ ________ ________ as you. Peer pressure occurs when these people ________ ________ to do something that you ________ ________ ________ to do. It could also be something you think you would like to do or are ________ ________ but that your ________ ________ you is wrong. It may also be some ________ ________ ________ which ________ ________ ________ of the school or the rules ________ ________ ________ ________. There are many reasons why you may want to ________ ________ to peer pressure. Most young people want to ________ ________, to ________ ________, to have friends, and to ________ ________ by other people. These are very ________ ________. You may also worry that people will ________ ________ or ________ ________ if you don't ________ ________ ________ them. It's very difficult to say "no" in the ________ ________ ________ ________, but you need to be able to do it. You should ________ ________ ________ and the opinions and rules of your parents. It also helps if you have a friend who ________ ________ ________ and beliefs so that you can say "no" together.

2 W I read an ________ ________ about ________ and kids in the library this morning. There were some really ________ ________.

  M What was so surprising?

  W It said that in today's America, ________ ________ ________, or 20 percent, of kids are ________. That's four times higher than the number in the 1970s.

  M That is a big change.

  W I was also surprised that it wasn't just in America. The article said that ________ ________ 22 million kids under the age of five were ________ ________ ________ ________ and that it was a problem in ________ ________ also.

  M With everything we know about ________ ________ ________, it's really surprising. I think parents ________ ________ ________ their kids better, especially kids so young.

  W That's where the problem begins. It's up to parents to give kids ________ ________ ________ and to ________ them to be ________. Anyway, the article said that 80% of ________ ________ ________ ________ to be overweight adults. I checked the World Health Organization website, and it said that more than 1 ________ ________ ________ were overweight. About 300 million of them are children 12 and under.

  M That's really ________. There are so many ________ ________ that obese people can get, like heart disease and ________. What's the difference between ________ ________ and ________ anyway?

  W You're overweight if you ________ ________ than you should for your body type and ________. You're ________ ________ if that amount is ________ ________ 10 percent higher than it should be.

3-4 W AIDS is a very ________ ________ which has killed ________ ________ ________ around the world every year. Since AIDS ________ ________ in the 1980s, there have been ________ ________ ________ in the development of drugs to ________ AIDS. This ________ ________ AIDS patients now to live 10 or 20 years ________ ________ they had in the past. The problem is that these drugs are very expensive. The drug companies which ________ ________ ________ can ________ ________ ________ because they ________ ________ ________ for them. Africa has the largest numbers of AIDS cases but also some of the poorest countries in the world, ________ ________ ________ to ________ AIDS drugs for all of those who are ill. To ________ the drug companies, one African nation, South Africa, ________ ________ ________ a law which would ________ ________ drug companies to ________ the same AIDS drugs and to sell them ________ ________ ________. In addition, the law ________ South Africa to ________ AIDS drugs from other countries where they were ________. However, these actions were ________ international law due to ________ ________ ________ ________, and South Africa needed permission from the drug companies to do this. The South African government ________ that millions of people ________ ________ and that life was ________ ________ than the drug companies' profits. The drug companies ________ the South African government, ________ they needed the money to pay for the development of new drugs. Many Africans ________ ________ the drug companies, and the companies eventually ________ ________ ________.

M That's a really nice bag. It must have been very expensive.

W Well, actually, it's not real. It's a ________. I only paid 75 dollars for it. I think a lot of companies ________ ________ ________ ________ for their products just because of their ________ ________. Why shouldn't I be able to get a ________ ________ at a ________ ________?

M Lots of reasons. For instance, ________ ________ companies of millions of dollars every year. When the companies ________ ________, they have to ________ ________ and move to ________ ________. That means thousands of people here could lose their jobs.

W I hadn't ________ ________ ________. But I still think the prices they charge are just way too high, especially for things like ________ and ________. A lot of the clothing is already made in countries with ________ ________.

M Maybe, but the clothing companies spend a lot of money on ________ and ________. They also have to ________ ________ ________ and ideas, which ________ ________ and money.

W Okay. Maybe you're right about that, too. But you ________ ________ and music all the time, and you don't pay for them.

M Oh, ah, yeah, well, you ________ ________ ________. I guess I look like a ________ ________, right? But you know games and CDs are also really expensive. If the prices were cheaper, I ________ ________ ________ from the store.

W It's the same thing with me and my bag. I guess we are both in the ________ ________.

M It looks like it. But it's not like we're alone. Everyone is doing it, so we'd be stupid to ________ ________ ________ ________ for something, right?

W ________, what you just said ________ ________.

M Hey, Sharon. Do you ever ________ ________ the government in Washington ________ ________ ________?

W What are you talking about? Why would the government want to spy on me?

M Well, maybe not you but your parents or your older brother. I read in the paper that recently the government has been ________ ________ a lot on ________ ________ while ________ ________ ________.

They're listening to people's phone calls, _______ _______ _______ _______, and even _______ what library books they borrow.

W How can they _______ all of that?

M It's really easy with _______ _______. They use _______ _______ _______ for key words like "_______" or "blow-up" that people might say on the phone or _______ _______ on the Internet. Also, if someone _______ _______ books about _______ _______, the government starts watching them _______ _______.

W It's like George Orwell's book *1984*. Big Brother is _______ _______. What about my _______ _______ _______?

M They _______ that _______ _______ from _______ is more important than your privacy.

W We have to _______ _______ _______ against this.

M _______ _______ _______. You know you can't fight city hall.

8 W _______ _______ is a serious problem which _______ _______ of a nation should _______ _______ _______. It is when a _______ _______ uses his or her _______ _______ for _______ _______ _______. The most _______ _______ of political corruption is _______, which happens when an official _______ _______ or gifts to do a _______ _______ _______. Another type is called _______, which is when government officials help someone who helped them in the past _______ _______ that person a _______ _______. Nepotism is another form of corruption and is when an official uses his or her power to help a _______ get a job or _______ _______. Government officials may also be _______ _______ _______, which is the _______ of government money or _______. Some officials _______ _______ _______ government projects _______ _______ who then _______ _______ some of their salary to the official _______ _______ _______. This is called a _______. Finally, some government officials have worked closely with _______ _______ to help these groups _______ _______ _______ and to _______ _______ _______ _______.

9 M In today's _______ _______ _______, we're going to look at how families can change due to changes in _______ _______ and the _______. One of the biggest changes is an _______ _______ _______ in different nations. A good example of this is South Korea. For a long time, South Korea had a very _______ _______ _______, and families were seen as very _______ _______ _______. This has changed _______ in the last 10 years, and there are _______ _______ and _______ _______ which _______ _______ _______. Socially, divorce laws have changed in South Korea. Many _______ _______ have helped to _______ _______ _______, which used to be _______ to men. The current laws are _______ _______ and also make getting a divorce _______ _______ it once was. Another change has been the _______ _______ _______ of women. Modern Korean women _______ _______ be very _______ _______ and make a good living, giving them an economic base even if they _______ _______. This is very different from just a _______ _______, when Korean women tended to be stay-at-home wives. In the past, women who wanted to get divorced were _______ _______ _______ so since they had _______ _______ _______ if their husband refused to _______ _______. With the _______ _______ of women to make money, the _______ _______ to divorce is _______.

10

M What do you think about _______ _______, Lena?

W I really think it's wrong. I don't see why we have to _______ _______ as a _______ _______ _______. _______ _______ _______ _______ for life is punishment enough.

M Most people _______ that the main reason for capital punishment is to _______ _______ from _______ _______ _______.

W I've heard that, too, but I don't think it's true. Most states in America have the _______ _______, but they still have more serious crime than Canada, which _______ the death penalty years ago.

M That's interesting. I _______ how many countries _______ _______ the death penalty.

W It should be _______ _______ _______ on the Internet. Just a sec... (pause) Right. These are the 2008 _______. There are 197 countries _______ on this website. It says here that 92 countries have _______ _______ the death penalty. The _______ 105 countries still have the death penalty as law, but 10 of those countries _______ _______ _______ in very _______ _______, such as in cases _______ _______. The _______ _______ the death penalty _______ _______ _______ _______ such as _______.

M But of those countries, 36 of them still have it as a law but _______ _______ _______ in more than 10 years. In 2008, only 25 countries _______ _______ a criminal.

W I really wish that no country would use the death penalty. _______ _______ they _______ _______ _______ and they _______ someone to death who didn't commit a crime?

M Unfortunately, it has happened. Recent DNA _______ has proven that some _______ _______ have been executed.

11-12

W In the modern media-frenzied world, _______ _______ _______ out of proportion to their importance. Businesses have _______ _______ this power of celebrity by _______ _______ _______ to _______ _______ _______ and services in order to _______ _______ _______ _______ them. Sometimes, however, the power of celebrities _______ _______ _______. Many young people like to _______ _______ _______ of their favorite star, even to the _______ _______ _______. This is _______ _______ the Werther effect. It is _______ _______ a character in the novel *The Sorrows of Young Werther*, which _______ _______ _______ Goethe over 200 years ago in Germany. The story ends with the _______ _______ Werther _______ _______ by _______ _______ while dressed in boots, a yellow vest, and a blue jacket as he was sitting at a desk. Over the next few years, so many young men _______ _______ in the _______ _______ that the book _______ _______ in parts of Europe. In a _______ _______ case in the United States, the famous singer Kurt Cobain _______ _______ in 1994. During the following year, an _______ _______ _______ _______ killed themselves while listening to his music. _______ have been aware of this _______ for some time, but it has only recently _______ _______ _______. They _______ _______ _______ for their role in _______ _______ _______ of famous people _______ _______ _______, with the stories lasting for days and weeks. Many experts believe this may give people the _______ _______ _______ _______ if they are already thinking about suicide. Young people are _______ _______, according to the experts, because of their strong _______ _______ _______.

History

PREPARATION

A **Read the definition and write the correct word in each blank.**

intermittent	espouse	procrastinate	revitalize	disseminate

1 ___________ to support a belief, policy, or point of view
2 ___________ to give renewed energy to something
3 ___________ to distribute something, especially information
4 ___________ not happening regularly or continuously
5 ___________ to postpone doing something

■ Now listen to the words and definitions and check your answers.

B **Fill in the blanks with suitable words or phrases on the list. Change the forms if needed.**

humanoid	eke out	put forth	sect	etch	incursion	foster

1 Archaeologists _____________ the theory that modern humans originated in Africa.
2 _____________ with a heated bronze pin on bones was an early method of Chinese writing.
3 He was _____________ a living as a teacher before his famous historical novel was published.
4 The Macedonian conquerors _____________ their culture on the defeated Persian Empire.
5 The skulls, teeth, and jawbones of early _____________ were found at sites in eastern Africa.
6 A _____________ of Egyptian priests prayed to the Nile River god for the annual floods.
7 The 13th century Mongol _____________ into Europe was stopped in Hungary in 1242.

■ Now listen to the sentences and check your answers.

■ **Match each expression with its proper meaning.**

1 They bought it fair and square.
2 I'm a real history buff.
3 Let's jump to it.
4 Don't bite off more than you can chew.
5 What a howler!
6 I'm a bit foggy on that.
7 It threw off their timetable.

ⓐ Don't do more than you can handle.
ⓑ Why don't we get started?
ⓒ That's a funny story, but it's not true.
ⓓ I'm not sure what it is.
ⓔ It upset their schedule.
ⓕ There was no dishonesty involved.
ⓖ I love to study history.

■ Now listen to the sentences and check your answers.

■ Listen to the monolog and complete the organizer.

6-2

The Olduvai Gorge

- **Location**: a valley located in Tanzania in eastern [1]__________
- **Physical Features**: long, narrow valley with [2]__________ layers of exposed rock and soil of [3]__________ origin
  → enables use of [4]__________ dating method
- **Discovery**: early [5]__________ remains and their [6]__________
    - found skeletal remains from [7]__________
    - one skeleton dated to [8]__________ years ago

Louis & Mary Leakey

- most famous researchers who studied and wrote about the gorge
- theorized that humans [9]__________ from these early [10]__________

believed to be the [11]__________ of all [12]__________

General Questions — Based on the organizer, answer the questions.

1 What is the main idea of the talk?

(a) Volcanic rocks are needed to date very old objects.

(b) Modern humans originated in the Olduvai Gorge.

(c) The famous Leakey family studied the Olduvai Gorge.

(d) The Olduvai Gorge is one of many sites of human remains.

2 Choose the best summary.

(a) Anthropologists have unearthed well-preserved human remains in the Olduvai Gorge in Africa, which was formed by volcanic activity.

(b) The Olduvai Gorge in Africa has revealed the remains of the earliest human settlements and is most likely the cradle for all humanity.

Specific Questions — Listen again. Mark T for true statements and F for false statements.

(1) The Olduvai Gorge archaeological site is in seven different layers of soil and rock.   _____

(2) Through the use of the carbon-14 dating method, archaeologists have determined the age of the remains.   _____

(3) Louis and Mary Leakey claimed that the Olduvai Gorge was where the earliest humans lived.   _____

(4) Archaeologists found the remains of different types of early man in the Olduvai Gorge.   _____

■ Listen to the dialog and complete the notes. 6-3

Topic: authenticity of the story about the purchase of Manhattan Island

└— Peter Minuit bought it on May 24, (1)________

- Girl - teacher said the Dutch bought Manhattan for 24 dollars
  - thinks it is a (☐ myth / ☐ true story)
  - later, thinks it was bought (☐ unfairly / ☐ fair and square)
- Boy - it's mostly a (☐ myth / true story)
  - the story changed a little: the actual price was (2)________ guilders
    → the price changed to (3)________ dollars and then to
    (4)______________ and other supplies
  - an old letter confirms the story that the price of the land was (5)________ guilders
  - natives did not realize what they had done
  - area remained Dutch until the (6)________ defeated them in (7)________

General Questions Based on the notes, answer the questions.

1 What is the boy's intention in the dialog?

(a) To disprove a story about early American history

(b) To relate a historical tale that is mostly not true

(c) To give a true account of an event in American history

(d) To convince someone that there is some truth to a story

2 Choose the best summary.

(a) The deal that occurred when the Dutch purchased Manhattan Island for 24 dollars from the natives in 1626 was fair.

(b) The story that the Dutch purchased Manhattan is based on true events, but the details have been changed over the years.

Specific Questions Listen again. Mark T for true statements and F for false statements.

(1) The girl felt that her history teacher's story was too unbelievable to be true. ______

(2) The Dutch West India Company paid Peter Minuit for the rights to Manhattan. ______

(3) The price paid for Manhattan has changed over the years as the story has been retold. ______

(4) The Dutch eventually lost control of Manhattan to the English in 1664. ______

■ Listen to the lecture and complete the organizer.

`6-4`

The Nile River and Ancient Egypt

Facts about the Nile River

- once semi-arid (1)______________ → became desert
- most Egyptians lived and live near Nile or in its (2)______________
- (3)______________: main method to make a living
- the (4)______________ of the Nile brought (5)______________ silt
- getting the right amount of (6)______________ was important
- Egyptian priests: prayed to the Nile River God Hapy to bring (7)______________ every year in (8)______________ or (9)______________

Benefits

- water supply
- important for farming
- a means of (10)______________ - allowed to keep control of the (11)______________
- a (12)______________ to invaders

⬇

made (13)______________ last for thousands of years

---

1 What is the main purpose of the lecture?

(a) To examine the advantages of the Nile River to Egypt

(b) To discuss the religious worship of the Nile River

(c) To describe the nature of the annual Nile River floods

(d) To look at how the Nile protected Egyptian civilization

2 Choose the best summary.

(a) The Nile River provided many benefits to the ancient Egyptians, and, without it, their civilization may never have existed.

(b) The Nile River provided water for the Egyptians to farm the land, so their civilization grew.

3 Mark T for true statements and F for false statements.

(1) Egyptian Pharaohs were responsible for controlling the Nile floods. _____

(2) The annual floods of the Nile were of the same intensity year after year. _____

(3) The Nile allowed the Egyptian pharaohs to rule their people with greater ease. _____

(4) Egypt suffered many invasions and was occupied by its enemies very often. _____

4 What aspect of ancient Egypt is still true today as mentioned in the lecture?

(a) Egyptians depend on the floods to help them with agriculture.

(b) The worship of gods like Hapy is a common practice.

(c) Occasional Nile floods cause great destruction in Egypt.

(d) Most Egyptians live near the Nile River and in its delta.

Dictation

■ Listen again and fill in the blanks.

w Without the Nile River, the ____________ ____________ in Egypt would most likely never have developed. The Nile ____________ several things for the people of ancient Egypt, including a ____________ ____________ ____________ ____________ , a ____________ of ____________ , and a method to ____________ the soil of ____________ during the ____________ ____________ ____________ . Some ____________ ____________ to the land around the Nile being ____________ ____________ in the past, but, by about 8,000 B.C., the land in Egypt ____________ the Nile was ____________ . The Egyptian people ____________ ____________ ____________ ____________ of the Nile and in the ____________ ____________ that forms at ____________ ____________ , where it ____________ into the Mediterranean Sea. Even today, almost all of Egypt's people live along or near the Nile River and its delta. In ancient Egypt, farming was the ____________ ____________ people used to ____________ ____________ an ____________ , and the ____________ of the Nile helped farmers by ____________ ____________ ____________ to their farmland. Some years, the Nile floods were ____________ ____________ and ____________ a ____________ ____________ ____________ ____________ , and other years they were ____________ . In order to get the ____________ ____________ ____________ flooding, the ancient Egyptians ____________ ____________ the Nile River god to ____________ ____________ ____________ each year, which usually ____________ in late August or early September by our ____________ ____________ . The god was called Hapy, and a ____________ ____________ ____________ Egyptian ____________ ____________ ____________ ____________ this god and the ____________ of the ____________ Nile floods. Besides providing rich soil for farming, the Nile River provided an ____________ ____________ of transportation and ____________ ____________ ____________ of the ____________ . Finally, the deserts surrounding the ____________ Nile River provided a ____________ to ____________ ____________ . The ____________ of the Egyptian civilization, which ____________ for thousands of years, is mostly due to these facts.

■ Listen and answer the questions.

6-5

1 What is the best title for the talk?
(a) The Origin of the Sumerian People
(b) The World's First Civilization: Sumer
(c) The Rise and Fall of Ancient Sumer
(d) The Development of the Sumerian City
(e) Sumerian Contributions to Humanity

2 Complete the table with the missing information about the Battle of Thermopylae.

People	Number
Greeks (Total)	7,000
- Spartans	
- Thebans	400
- Thespians	
Greek Dead	
Persians (Total)	
Persian Dead	20,000

3-4

3 What was the main use of Shang oracle bone script?
(a) To make agricultural records of the times
(b) To record questions for divination purposes
(c) To provide a base for later Chinese writing
(d) To show the divinity of the royal family
(e) To keep a record of earlier forms of writing

4 What can be inferred about oracle bone script from the talk?
(a) It was easier to make on turtle shells than on bones.
(b) It was engraved deeply, making it long-lasting.
(c) It was one of many methods of writing in use.
(d) It continued to be used after the Shang Dynasty.
(e) It was replaced by printing with wooden blocks.

5-6
Level up

5 What does the girl think she has some trouble with?
(a) Deciding on a topic for a school history project
(b) Clarifying some details on the Mongol Empire
(c) Using the Internet to do historical research
(d) Memorizing the dates of the Mongol conquests
(e) Finding the time to sit down and write her report

6 **Choose the statement that best summarizes the dialog.**

(a) A student and her tutor finish writing a paper based on the reasons why the Mongol invasion of Europe in the 13th century failed.

(b) A tutor advises a student on how to use a textbook to do research and gives her some advice for a project on the Mongol invasion of Europe.

(c) A student has trouble understanding some aspects of the Mongol invasion of Europe and, with a tutor's help, looks up some details in a textbook.

Level up

7 **Listen to the question and answer choices and choose the correct answer.**

(a)   (b)   (c)   (d)   (e)

Level up

8 **Listen to the question and answer choices and choose the correct answer.**

(a)   (b)   (c)   (d)   (e)

9 **Which is NOT true according to the talk?**

(a) The spread of Hellenism influenced all classes of people.

(b) The Greeks also learned much from the lands they had conquered.

(c) Alexander was the founder of the city of Alexandria in Egypt.

(d) The Library of Alexandria had a vast collection of knowledge.

(e) The Greek conquerors sometimes wedded non-Greeks.

10 **Complete the table with the missing information about inventions from China.**

Invention	First Evidence (Date)	Definite Evidence (Date)
Printing	200 A.D.	
Paper		105 A.D.
Compass		
Gunpowder	9th century A.D.	

11-12
Level up

11 **Why was the Byzantine Empire able to outlast the Western Roman Empire?**

(a) It went on the offensive and re-conquered the Western Roman Empire.

(b) It successfully defeated the enemies that attempted to invade it.

(c) It used money and military skill to provide protection for its lands.

(d) It did not face as many barbarian invasions as the western empire did.

(e) It made deals with invaders by giving them great areas of land.

12 **Choose the statement that best summarizes the talk.**

(a) The Byzantine Empire was the final legacy of the Roman Empire, and it perished when Constantinople was conquered by the Muslims in 1453.

(b) Although the Byzantine Empire was a part of the Roman Empire, it became independent and lasted longer than Rome until it was defeated by the Muslims.

(c) The Byzantine Empire was the product of troubles within the Roman Empire, which forced Byzantine to become independent for 1,000 years.

Listen and answer the questions.

1 **What is the main reason why there is some uncertainty about Marco Polo's account of his travels to the east?**
(a) He did not write the book himself but dictated it to another person.
(b) Many people added their own travel stories when copying the book.
(c) Mistakes were made in the first copies made with printing presses.
(d) The first manuscript was lost for some time and has only recently been found.
(e) Copying and translating led to errors, and many versions now exist.

2-3

2 **What can be inferred from the dialog?**
(a) Tourism is the highest revenue earner for the Angkor region.
(b) The Thai people failed to conquer the city of Angkor.
(c) Some damage has been done to Angkor Wat by tourists.
(d) Sandstone was a common building material for temples.
(e) The Khmer people once ruled Cambodia from Angkor.

3 **What will the boy probably say to the girl next?**
(a) I'll see what I can do about it.
(b) It sounds like you've been there before.
(c) I can make some promises to you.
(d) Maybe you should come with us.
(e) I bet my summer is better than yours.

4-5

4 **Why is Quirigua an important site of the ancient Mayan civilization?**
(a) Its historical record of kings and wars is well known.
(b) It has the largest, most well-preserved Mayan ruins.
(c) It was the center of Mayan civilization for many decades.
(d) It contains a wealth of well-preserved tall monuments.
(e) It is the only site where sandstone was used extensively.

5 **What can be inferred from the talk?**
(a) The Mayans used granite in many of their cities.
(b) Mayan civilization had a complex political structure.
(c) Warfare was common among the Mayan city-states.
(d) Beheading was the normal fate for Mayan enemies.
(e) Quirigua is a famous tourist spot because of its ruins.

Level up

6 **Listen to the question and answer choices and choose the correct answer.**
(a)　　(b)　　(c)　　(d)　　(e)

Level up

7 **Listen to the question and answer choices and choose the correct answer.**
(a)　　(b)　　(c)　　(d)　　(e)

8 **Complete the chart with information about the British and Spanish fleets.**

Category	Number
English Fleet Total	200
Spanish Fleet Total	
English Losses	None
Spanish Losses	
- From English Attacks	
- From Weather and Rocky Shores	

【Integrated Questions】

■ Read the following passage and listen to the lecture.

Pompeii was an ancient town in the Roman Empire and was located near Naples. On August 24, 79 A.D., the nearby volcano Mount Vesuvius erupted. At first, the inhabitants of Pompeii attempted to wait out the eruption in that hope that it would be minor. But, the next day, a violent cloud of ash and hot gases erupted, and the town of Pompeii was buried under a layer of rock and ash while most of its inhabitants were killed. For almost 1,700 years, Pompeii and the nearby town of Herculaneum, which was also buried by the eruption, were lost to the world. Then, in the mid-18th century, both towns were rediscovered. The volcanic ash had preserved the towns to such an extent that even paintings on walls were intact. The towns became major tourist destinations and a source for the study of life in ancient Rome. One of the main accounts of the destruction caused by Vesuvius comes from the letters of the Roman administrator Pliny the Younger, who watched the event from across the Bay of Naples. His uncle Pliny the Elder was in charge of the naval forces in the area, and he died while leading ships to the rescue of the people trying to flee from the destruction. Based on accounts from the time and archaeological evidence, an estimated 16,000 people out of about 20,000 inhabitants died.

■ Now answer the following questions based on what you read and heard.

9 **Which is NOT true according to the reading and listening?**
(a) Vesuvius erupted suddenly and caught the people of Pompeii unaware.
(b) Pompeii had been forgotten until it was rediscovered in the 18th century.
(c) Pliny the Elder died as a result of the eruption of Vesuvius.
(d) Not everyone in Pompeii died during the eruption of Vesuvius.
(e) Pompeii's art and architecture were preserved by volcanic ash.

10 **What aspect do the reading and listening disagree on?**
(a) The number of people killed in the towns destroyed by Vesuvius
(b) The account of Pliny the Elder and his naval rescue of survivors
(c) The exact date that Mount Vesuvius erupted and destroyed Pompeii
(d) The nature of the ruins and their value to historical studies
(e) The influence Pompeii's rediscovery had on art and architecture

DICTATION (Exercise)

■ Listen and fill in the blanks.

1

M The ________ ________ known as Sumer was the first place where ________ ________ in great numbers, developed ________ ________, and created ________ of civilization similar to what we have today. Sumer was ________ ________ the region ________ ________ Mesopotamia, the land between the Tigris and Euphrates rivers in what is now southern Iraq. ________, the evidence shows that ________ ________ of Sumer ________ ________ the northern region of modern Iraq. The first cities, which were really more like small towns, ________ ________ 5,300 B.C. The ________ ________ of the Tigris and Euphrates rivers ________ the early Sumerians to grow a ________ ________ ________ through ________ ________ and ________ ________ based on the waters of the two rivers. This enabled the people to ________ in one place and to ________ ________. By 4,000 B.C., many cities ________ ________, and elements such as ________, military forces, ________, government, and ________ had been established. The ________ ________ ________ human writing, called cuneiform, was ________ ________ in the region around 3,500 B.C., which gives us the ________ ________ ________ from any civilization of the past. These records show ________ ________ between the various Sumerian city-states. Different city-states on occasion ________ ________ ________ themselves as the ________ ________. The ________ of Sumer ________ ________ 2,000 B.C., when a ________ ________ of the soil led to ________ ________ ________, which in turn ________ ________ many people leaving the area. Around 1,700 B.C., the Babylonians ________ the area, effectively ending the Sumer period of Mesopotamia's history.

2

W Today on *History Speaks*, we are ________ the Battle of Thermopylae from ________ ________ ________ with Professor Higgins from the local university. First, Professor, ________ ________ ________ the battle?

M Yes. To ________ ________ ________, the Persians ________ Greece in 480 B.C. A force of Greeks ________ ________ the Spartans ________ the Persian advance in a ________ ________ ________ called Thermopylae. After three days of ________ ________, the Persians ________ ________ ________ the Greek force.

W Now, this action by the Greeks is ________ ________ because so few men ________ ________ tens of thousands of Persians. Is that correct?

M Yes, but there is some ________ ________ the ________ ________ on both sides. ________, it was said that only 300 Spartans ________ ________ 200,000 Persians.

W But there were some other Greeks ________ the Spartans.

M Correct. There were ________ ________ 7,000 Greeks at the battle. There were 4,000 from the Peloponnesian Peninsula, where Sparta was located. That ________ ________ the 300 Spartans. And there were about 3,000 other Greeks, including 400 Thebans and 700 Thespians, ________ ________ ________ to the last man.

W And what about the ________ ________ ________?

M This is ________ ________ ________ ________. Confusion ________ because perhaps ________ ________ ________ Persians came to Greece, but only around 200,000 Persians ________ ________ Thermopylae.

W What were the ________ ________ on each side?

M The best guess is that in ________ ________ ________ ________, the Persians lost about ten percent of their men while the ________ ________ all of the Spartans, Thebans, and Thespians. Most of the rest of the Greek force ________.

3-4

W Many details about _______ _______ _______ come from a form of writing called _______ _______ _______. This type of writing was done with a _______ _______ pin _______ _______ animal bones or sometimes on the _______ of _______ _______. The _______ _______ of oracle bone script _______ _______ the Shang Dynasty, in about 1,400 B.C. The _______ _______ _______ on bones or turtle shells _______ _______ around 1,100 B.C., when the Shang Dynasty ended. At the time, oracle bone script _______ _______ for _______ _______ _______, which I guess we would call _______ _______ _______. The bones or turtle shells were _______ _______ a question and then _______ _______ a fire. An _______ _______ the _______ _______ in the bone or turtle shell as an answer to the question. _______ _______ the divination questions _______ _______ like _______, _______, the health of the royal family, and the weather as it _______ _______ _______. Oracle bone writing was also used to _______ _______ about the Shang Dynasty and its events. These are the earliest examples of historical records in China. However, where exactly the oracle bone script _______ _______ _______ _______. There are examples of _______ _______ to be writing from early times, but there are _______ _______ _______ over these samples. There has as yet been _______ _______ _______ between them and oracle bone script. Therefore, it is _______ _______ that oracle bone script is the _______ _______ all modern Chinese writing.

5-6

M Hi, Joanna, I'm Eric. I'm going to be your _______ _______.

G Hi. I have a _______ _______ _______, so _______ _______ to it, okay? Do you know anything about Mongolia?

M Yes. _______ _______ of Mongolia are you doing _______ _______ _______?

G Its empire. I know the Mongols _______ _______ _______ Europe in the 13th century, but I'm a little _______ _______ _______ _______.

M Let's do some _______ in the textbook.

G Okay. Let's see... page 342... the _______ _______ of Europe. Mongol leader Genghis Khan died in 1227, and the first Mongol _______ _______ European Russia began in the 1230s.

M What was the extent of the Mongol _______ _______ _______?

G They _______ _______ modern-day Russia and then _______ _______ _______ Poland and Hungary. Then they _______ in 1242.

M Right so far. Now, why didn't the Mongols conquer all of Europe, and why did they withdraw?

G Give me a minute. Ah. Here it is. The _______ to Genghis Kahn was his son Ogedei, who died in 1241. Ogedei's wife _______ _______ _______ _______ and was _______ _______ many nobles. As a result, there was a four-year period of _______. This led to the _______ _______ _______ _______ of the Mongol Empire.

M It _______ _______ you know more than _______ _______. I think you have _______ _______ without _______ _______ the _______ of the later Mongol Empire. You don't want to _______ _______ more than _______ _______ _______.

G That sounds like a good idea. Now I need to _______ _______ _______ on it.

M _______ _______ _______.

G Now? I mean, it's not due for another three days.

M It's better to get started now than to _______ and have to _______ _______ _______ the last day.

7

M I'm doing a __________ __________. What's a five-letter word for an __________ __________?

W I bet the answer is China.

M No, it __________ __________. Wait. There was Egypt... No, it doesn't fit either.

W Then it has to be the __________ __________.

M You mean India, right?

W No, Indus. I-N-D-U-S. __________ __________ __________?

M Yeah, __________. What was the Indus civilization?

W One of the __________ __________ __________. It was located __________ the __________ __________ __________ in the area of Pakistan and India today. It __________ __________ about 5,000 to 1,700 B.C.

M Oh, now I remember. I think we learned about it in school. Didn't it have a lot of cities?

W Yes, but there are no __________ __________ or __________ like in Egypt and no Great Wall like in China. Maybe that's why the Indus is __________ __________ __________ __________ other civilizations.

M __________ __________ __________ the Indus civilization?

W No one knows for sure. By 1,700 B.C., most of its people __________ __________ __________ __________. Some researchers think there was a change in the __________ that __________ __________ __________ or that the __________ __________ may have been __________ __________ __________.

8

M In ancient Korea for a time, there were __________ __________ __________: the Silla, the Baekje, and the Goguryeo. The Silla kingdom __________ an __________ __________ of __________ __________ called the *Hwarang*, or "Flower Youths," who __________ __________ __________ the kingdom. Information about the __________ of this group is __________, but __________ __________ seem to agree that sometime in the early 6th century A.D., after the Silla kingdom __________ __________, the *Hwarang* __________ __________. The members __________ __________ __________ the best young males of __________ __________. At first, it is believed it was __________ __________ __________ __________ __________, but, __________, the *Hwarang* __________ __________ a __________ __________. Its members learned hand-to-hand __________ __________, __________, horsemanship, and other necessary military skills. They __________ Buddhist principles and also followed a __________ __________ __________ to the state, to their families, and to __________ __________. Stories of the *Hwarang* being at the __________ __________ __________ to __________ the three kingdoms are legion, and they may have been __________ in the __________ __________ of ancient Korea in 688 A.D.

9

W The term Hellenism is __________ __________ __________ the __________ of Greek culture in the Mediterranean world and the Middle East after the __________ __________ Alexander the Great's __________ in the __________ __________ __________ B.C. Alexander was a king of Macedonia, a land to the north of modern-day Greece. He __________ the Persian Empire and __________ India __________ __________ __________ in 323 B.C. As he __________, Alexander __________ __________, and his __________ __________ __________ Greek kingdoms in the __________ __________ of the Persian Empire. They __________ __________ __________ and __________ Greek ideas on their new subjects. This __________ __________ was not a totally one-way street as the Greeks __________ __________ from the locals, and there was much __________. However much the __________ __________ __________ with the Greeks, there was probably __________ __________ __________ in the lives and cultures of the __________ __________ of the __________ __________. One of the __________ __________ to the __________ of Hellenism was the library in the city of Alexandria in Egypt. Alexander __________ __________ __________ for the city, which became the main seat of __________ __________ in the known world and the __________ __________ __________ for hundreds of years. Scholars from all over the Mediterranean world __________ __________ __________ to Alexandria and its famous museum, which is more like what we __________ __________ a library today. Through its __________ __________ of __________ __________ __________, the Library of Alexandria __________ and __________ knowledge from all corners of the known world.

B All we ________ ________ ________ ________ for our project on ancient China is to ________ ________ what it has ________ ________ the world.

G I found an ________ about the four ________ ________ of ancient China. They were paper, ________, the ________, and ________.

B I think you're wrong about printing. Some people say the Koreans ________ ________ before the Chinese.

G Well, then we can ________ the Koreans in the paper, but we still have to ________ ________ ________ in China.

B Okay, so what's the date for the ________ ________ ________ of printing in China?

G Well, no one knows the ________ ________. Some ________ ________ as early as 200 A.D., but the first book is from 868 A.D.

B We'll ________ ________ ________. Now, what about paper? When was it invented?

G The article gives a date of 105 A.D., but there is a ________ ________ ________ the 8th century B.C. No wait... Sorry. That's 8 B.C.

B Let's go with the ________ ________ ________, which is 105 A.D.

G Okay. Now, ________ ________ ________, there is also some ________. There is a ________ to it in a book from the 4th century A.D., but I'm not sure if that is ________ ________ ________ a compass today. A ________ ________ would be a ________ in a book from 1088.

B Then 1088 it is. Finally, ________ ________ ________?

G Gunpowder was known in the 9th century A.D., but the ________ ________ ________ of it is from 1044. So I guess we should ________ ________ ________ ________.

W All right, the Byzantine Empire is our ________ ________. It ________ ________ ________ the Roman Empire, and, in fact, the Byzantine Empire was ________ ________ ________ the Eastern Roman Empire. In 285 A.D., the Roman Emperor Diocletian ________ ________ ________ the ________ ________ into two parts for ________ ________ ________. He created a system where ________ ________ would ________ ________—one from the east and the other from the west. Then, in 330 A.D., the Emperor Constantine ________ ________ ________ of the Roman Empire to the city of Byzantium, which he renamed Constantinople. This is now the ________ ________ of Istanbul in Turkey. In 395 A.D., the Emperor Theodosius the Great ________ ________ ________ the ________ ________ of the empire to two different sons. ________, the two halves ________ ________ ________. The western empire ________ ________ Germanic ________ ________ by 476 A.D. The Byzantine Empire, I mean the Eastern Roman Empire, ________ ________ by almost a thousand years. Much of this was ________ ________ ________ ________, which it used to ________ ________ ________ ________ like Attila the Hun as well as to ________ its ________ ________ and to ________ its capital city. While the western empire fell to the ________ ________, the Byzantine Empire ________ and even for a time reconquered the ________ ________. However, a ________ ________ ________ in the form of Islam. For many centuries, the Byzantines ________ ________ the Muslims. Gradually, the empire ________. It lost ________ and even had its capital ________ ________ a band of ________ in 1204. During the empire's last days, only the city of Constantinople ________, and when it fell to the Muslims in 1453, the ________ ________ of the Roman Empire was gone.

Physical Sciences

PREPARATION

7-1

(A) Read the definitions and write the correct word in each blank.

| condescending | spatial | discredit | equilibrium | synthetic |

1 ___________ to create a negative feeling about someone or something
2 ___________ a state of balance; equality
3 ___________ acting in a superior manner towards others
4 ___________ not natural; artificial
5 ___________ related to physical space

■ Now listen to the words and definitions and check your answers.

(B) Fill in the blanks with suitable words or phrases on the list. Change the forms if needed.

| dissolve | electrode | circuit | bonding | optical illusion | particle | fortuitous |

1 The molecular _____________ of billions of water molecules creates each snowflake.
2 Many scientific discoveries have been made because of _____________ accidents.
3 Acid will _____________ most things that it comes in contact with.
4 The picture was a(n) _____________ that showed different images depending on how one looked at it.
5 The student connected the wire to the _____________, and the bulb lit up.
6 The search for a small atomic _____________ called the Higgs boson is the subject of a massive experiment.
7 A completed _____________ is necessary for electricity to operate devices.

■ Now listen to the sentences and check your answers.

■ **Match each expression with its proper meaning.**

1 Quit whining.
2 I'm in stitches.
3 Don't be such a jerk.
4 Let's crack the books.
5 It was a blast.
6 Hold your horses.
7 I'm with you so far.

ⓐ We had a great time.
ⓑ Stop complaining.
ⓒ Let's start studying.
ⓓ That's very funny.
ⓔ Wait a moment.
ⓕ I understand up to this point.
ⓖ Stop acting so foolishly.

■ Now listen to the sentences and check your answers.

■ Listen to the monolog and complete the organizer.

7-2

Basic Facts of Antoine-Laurent de Lavoisier	• the Frenchman who lived in the late 18th century • one of the fathers of modern (1) __________ • was also a (2) __________ for the royal regime • (3) __________ during the French Revolution
His Works & Contributions	• the theory of the (4) __________ of mass: (5) __________ of an object in an only (6) __________ system will not (7) __________ if (8) __________ change • proved that (9) __________ is made up of different gases • named (10) __________ the part of air that is breathed • discovered the composition of (11) __________ : (12) __________ and oxygen • created a system to name (13) __________

General Questions Based on the organizer, answer the questions.

1 What is the main purpose of the talk?

(a) To examine the life and death of a great chemist

(b) To explain a scientific theory related to mass

(c) To discuss the scientific work of a great chemist

(d) To describe how some chemical names were created

2 Choose the best summary.

(a) Antoine-Laurent de Lavoisier's theories on the conservation of mass and the composition of water could not save him from being executed for his crimes against the people of France.

(b) Antoine-Laurent de Lavoisier was responsible for many breakthroughs in the field of chemistry, but his life was cut short during the French Revolution.

Specific Questions Listen again. Mark T for true statements and F for false statements.

(1) Lavoisier's theory on the conservation of mass only applies to closed systems. _____

(2) Lavoisier is credited with naming the part of the air humans breathe. _____

(3) Lavoisier used a system of chemical names developed by other scientists. _____

(4) Lavoisier was executed because he had worked for the royal regime of France before the revolution. _____

■ Listen to the dialog and complete the notes.　7-3

Experiment: proving that (1)__________ can be (2)__________ through a person
  - needs a complete (3)______________ to light the light bulb
  - the students must hold hands to complete the circuit

Girl: (☐ passively / ☐ actively) involved in the class
  - (☐ prepared / ☐ not prepared) for class
  - asks the boy to (☐ read the lab instruction manual / ☐ set up the apparatus)
  - is eager to get a good (4)__________
  - is a little upset with her lab partner

Boy: (☐ prepared / ☐ not prepared) for class
  - is late in lab class
  - was practicing (5)__________ until late last night

General Questions　Based on the notes, answer the questions.

1 What is the dialog mainly about?
(a) Fixing an electric circuit in a school lab
(b) Why the boy was late for an experiment
(c) Lighting a light bulb by human conduction
(d) How to perform a scientific experiment

2 Choose the best summary.
(a) Two lab partners do not get along very well, but they work together to successfully complete a scientific experiment in class.
(b) During a lab experiment about electricity, two partners realize that they do not have much in common except for this lab class.

Specific Questions　Listen again. Mark T for true statements and F for false statements.

(1) The boy thinks the girl is not serious about the experiment.　_____
(2) The experiment was designed to prove the human body can withstand an electric shock.　_____
(3) The students were supposed to prepare for the experiment before class.　_____
(4) The girl was very confident that the experiment would work.　_____

■ Listen to the lecture and complete the organizer.

Solids

<Nature>
• form is fixed and (1)________ : molecules in a fixed (2)__________________

<Transformation >
① become liquids through melting
② become (3)________ through sublimation
  Ex. (4)________ turns into gas; does not become a (5)________ first

(6)
____

<Nature>
• molecules (7)________ but not fixed
• (8)________ stays same but (9)________ changes

<Transformation>
① turn solid by freezing
② turn gaseous by (10)____________

States of Matter

(11)
____

<Nature>
• molecules (12)________ move
• will (13)________ unless contained

<Transformation >
① become (14)________ by ionization
② become solid by (15)________
③ becomes liquid by (16)________

Plasma

<Nature>
• created by a partially (17)____________
  : (18)______________ needed to turn (19)________ into plasma
• will (20)________ unless contained

1 What is the main purpose of the lecture?

(a) To explain the way states of matter change

(b) To argue for the need for a fourth state of matter

(c) To describe the most stable state of matter

(d) To give an overview of the nature of the states of matter

2 Choose the best summary.

(a) The stability of the molecules in an object determines its state of matter, and most of the states can be changed to the others.

(b) The four states of matter have different properties, and all four can change from one state of matter to the others.

3 Mark T for true statements and F for false statements.

(1) Solids have molecules with the most fixed spatial relationship. ____

(2) Only gases can become the other three states of matter. ____

(3) Matter retains its volume as a liquid and a gas. ____

(4) Plasma needs a container to prevent its expansion. ____

4 Which of the following is sublimation?

(a) A gas becomes plasma without being a liquid first.

(b) A liquid becomes a gas without being a solid first.

(c) A solid becomes a gas without being a liquid first.

(d) A gas becomes a liquid without being a solid first.

Dictation

■ Listen again and fill in the blanks.

w Traditionally, there are three __________ __________ __________ : solid, liquid, and gas. A fourth, plasma, may also __________ __________ __________ this list. A state of matter __________ the form that matter takes. The __________ of matter is __________ and __________ . The __________ in a solid are in a __________ __________ __________ , meaning that the molecules do not __________ __________ __________ unless an __________ __________ like heat is __________ . A liquid is a state of matter where the molecules of the matter are still in a __________ __________ , but the relationship is __________ __________ __________ . The __________ of the matter __________ __________ __________ , but the shape changes. Thus, in the __________ __________ , the matter will __________ __________ __________ of any __________ it is in. A gas is a state of matter where the __________ __________ __________ and will __________ as far as they can if they are not contained. Meanwhile, __________ is created from a __________ __________ __________ . Only gases can become plasma, and this happens only at __________ __________ __________ . Plasma has __________ __________ as gases and can expand __________ __________ . The states of matter can change from one to another. Solids become liquids __________ when heat is used. A solid can also go directly to a __________ __________ through a process called __________ . For example, the solid form of carbon dioxide, often called dry ice, will __________ __________ a gaseous form under __________ __________ without becoming a liquid first. Liquids become solids by __________ and become gases by __________ . Gases become liquids by __________ and become solids by __________ . An example of deposition is when water vapor __________ __________ to ice if the temperature is low enough.

EXERCISE

■ Listen and answer the questions.

7-5

1 Why are no two snowflakes alike?

(a) The moisture content must be exactly right.　　(b) Snow is only created at certain temperatures.

(c) Different nuclei are in each individual snowflake.　　(d) Too many variables are involved in their creation.

(e) Some are from cold clouds while others are from warm clouds.

2 Write the correct element on each blank beside each picture of the flame.

(1)  __________

(2)  __________

(3)  Magnesium

(4) 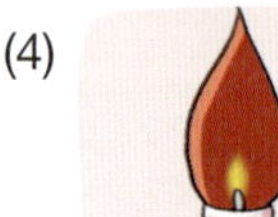 __________

(5)  __________

Copper
Iron
Calcium
Barium

3-4

3 What would happen if two objects of equal force were directly opposed to each other, according to Newton's laws of motion?

(a) The heavier object would very easily repel the lighter object.

(b) They would remain stationary as long as the forces remain equal.

(c) The force in both objects would be expended after a long time.

(d) The larger object would push the smaller object in a new direction.

(e) The acceleration of both objects would be increased a great amount.

4 What can be inferred from the talk?

(a) Newton's laws of motion do not apply to many practical problems.

(b) The first law of motion applies to stationary objects, not moving ones.

(c) A great force is needed to push a moving object from its current path.

(d) It took a few centuries for the laws of motion to be widely accepted.

(e) Heavier objects strike other objects with more force than lighter objects.

5-6
Level up

5 What is the main difference between Edison's DC system and Tesla's AC system?

(a) DC flows back and forth while AC only goes in one direction.

(b) AC has a higher voltage, allowing it to be sent longer distances.

(c) DC has a higher voltage, allowing it to be used for light bulbs.

(d) AC and DC both flow back and forth, but AC has a higher voltage.

(e) DC needs transformers to reduce its power for small motors.

6 Choose the statement that best summarizes the dialog.

(a) Thomas Edison fought a long battle to prevent his system of direct current from being replaced by alternating current systems.

(b) Thomas Edison and Nikola Tesla developed practical electrical systems, but Tesla's system was easier to install and to use.

(c) Nikola Tesla's system of alternating current surpassed Thomas Edison's system of direct current because it was more practical.

Level up

7 **Listen to the question and answer choices and choose the correct answer.**

(a)   (b)   (c)   (d)   (e)

Level up

8 **Listen to the question and answer choices and choose the correct answer.**

(a)   (b)   (c)   (d)   (e)

9 **What is NOT true according to the talk?**

(a) The Large Hadron Collider lies under France and Switzerland.

(b) The first test with the Large Hadron Collider was unsuccessful.

(c) The Higgs boson particle was first discovered three decades ago.

(d) The reason for the existence of mass in the universe is unknown.

(e) The Large Hadron Collider uses proton beams in its experiments.

10 **Complete the table with the atomic number of each noble gas.**

Noble Gas	Atomic Number
Helium	
Neon	
Argon	
Krypton	
Xenon	
Radon	86

11-12
Level up

11 **What is the main purpose of the lecture?**

(a) To describe the ways that ions and isotopes are made

(b) To give some details on the nature of atomic attraction

(c) To show the parts of atoms and how they are measured

(d) To explain the parts of atoms and the ways they behave

(e) To examine the electronic attraction in the structure of atoms

12 **What can be inferred from the lecture?**

(a) An atom with more protons than electrons is negatively charged.

(b) A hydrogen atom needs no neutron because it has one proton.

(c) Isotopes can be formed from ions of neutral atoms like helium.

(d) The atomic number of an atom changes if it becomes an ion.

(e) The atomic mass remains the same in neutral atoms and isotopes.

PRACTICE TEST

■ Listen and answer the questions.   `7-6`

1 What is NOT true according to the talk?
(a) The compass was the first practical use of magnetism.
(b) A Danish researcher discovered electromagnetism by accident.
(c) Magnetism was thought to be found in metals such as copper.
(d) Magnetism is created by the alignment of electrons in atoms.
(e) Some types of matter are unable to create a magnetic field.

2-3

2 What can be inferred from the dialog?
(a) The man is very confident in his memory.
(b) The man has studied physics in the past.
(c) They are walking nearby their home.
(d) The Doppler effect is an unproven theory.
(e) A sound's pitch is related to its volume.

3 What will the woman probably say next?
(a) But why do they call it the Doppler effect?
(b) That wasn't so hard to explain, was it?
(c) We should test the theory in other ways.
(d) I sure hope no one was hurt too badly.
(e) Does it only work with ambulance sirens?

4-5

4 Which of the following is NOT true about neutrinos?
(a) They can change from one type of neutrino to another.
(b) They have an electrical charge and a small mass.
(c) They move in a straight line without stopping.
(d) They are the most numerous particles in the universe.
(e) They move at incredibly high rates of speed.

5 What can be inferred about neutrinos according to the talk?
(a) The weight of a neutrino is so small that it cannot be measured.
(b) Neutrinos are used in many different applications.
(c) A neutrino can change its direction once it begins its journey.
(d) Some neutrinos come from nuclear reactions in nuclear plants.
(e) Neutrinos that enter the body can cause medical problems.

Level up

6 Listen to the question and answer choices and choose the correct answer.
(a)   (b)   (c)   (d)   (e)

Level up

7 Listen to the question and answer choices and choose the correct answer.
(a)   (b)   (c)   (d)   (e)

8 **Fill in the missing information related to diamonds.**

Category	Number/Date
Annual Amount of Natural Diamonds Mined	
Natural Diamonds from Africa	
Natural Diamonds from Russia	5,200 kg
Annual Amount of Synthetic Diamonds Created	
Year First Synthetic Diamonds Created	

9-10 【Integrated Questions】

■ Read the following passage and listen to the lecture.

Chemicals provide a lot of benefits for humans, but, at the same time, they can be dangerous and even fatal. This was never so tragically obvious than in Bhopal, India, when on the night of December 2 and 3, 1984, a chemical disaster eventually led to the deaths of almost 25,000 people. Near the densely populated area of Bhopal was located a chemical plant owned by the American company Union Carbide. The plant made a pesticide and used hazardous chemicals in its manufacture. Later investigations revealed that water entered a large tank containing some chemicals and caused the temperature inside to rise to the point of explosion. Deadly gas fumes were released and spread throughout the area. People breathed in the gas, and some died immediately while many others died days, months, and even years later. Others were killed in the panic that started when the gas caused a rush to escape the area. Eventually, blame was shared between Union Carbide and the government of India. The plant was too close to an urban area, and safety standards were poor. To this day, there is still a dispute over whether the disaster was an accident or deliberate sabotage by a disgruntled worker.

■ Now answer the following questions based on what you read and heard.

9 **What is correct according to the reading and listening?**
(a) The plant was a great distance from any populated areas.
(b) The victims of the disaster were well taken care of.
(c) The plant workers had been through extensive training.
(d) The victims of the disaster died over an extended period.
(e) The company used the usual method of chemical storage.

10 **What can be inferred from the reading and listening?**
(a) There were enough hospital beds for victims in the Bhopal area.
(b) The company supervisors were not at the plant when disaster struck.
(c) The government of India contributed to the compensation fund.
(d) The accident was the result of a deliberate act of sabotage.
(e) There was no warning system set up to inform people of a gas leak.

DICTATION [Exercise]

■ Listen and fill in the blanks. ● 7-7

1 M Have you ever heard the story about no two _________ being _________ _________ _________? Well, it _________ _________ not to be a story but an _________ _________. The reason _________ _________ how snowflakes are formed in the first place. Snowflakes _________ _________ _________ and start as _________ _________ which form around a nucleus. In very cold air—about minus 35 degrees Celsius—the _________ is several _________ _________ _________. In warmer air—about minus 18 degrees Celsius—the nucleus must be a _________ _________ _________ since the temperature is too warm for an ice nucleus to _________ _________ _________ _________. After the nucleus forms, then it grows as _________ _________ in the _________ _________ around the nucleus. Billions of tiny water molecules _________ _________ _________ _________ and _________ _________ the nucleus. Exactly how this bonding _________ _________ is still unclear. As the snowflake _________ _________, it falls and _________ _________ different _________ _________ _________ and temperature in clouds before it reaches the ground. _________ such as the _________ _________ of the air and the temperature at _________ _________, plus the nature of the water _________ _________, all play roles in producing a _________ snowflake each and every time. _________ _________ _________ snowflakes can be the same shape have produced some _________ _________ in labs, but, as yet, no _________ _________ snowflakes have been found in nature.

2 G Sorry I was _________ _________ lab class. What did I miss?

B Oh, it was a _________ today. We got to use the Bunsen burners to test the _________ _________ of _________.

G Before you explain the experiment, _________ _________ _________ _________.

B Metals _________ _________ _________ by _________ _________ certain colors. This way, we can _________ if a metal is _________ in a sample of ore or another mixed sample of _________ _________ _________.

G Okay. What are some _________ of some flame tests you did in class? And speak slowly so I can _________ _________.

B Sure. First, we checked for _________, which gives off a blue-colored flame.

G Copper is blue. Got it. Okay, what was next?

B Then we _________ _________ _________, which is a really _________ _________. I guess you could say it is the color of a _________.

G Did the teacher say that, or are you _________ _________ _________?

B The teacher said, "Brick red," so, no, I'm not making it up.

G Sorry. What was next?

B Magnesium, which was a yellowish green. We were lucky we had on our _________ _________ because it _________ _________ _________.

G It's often used in _________. Any more?

B Barium, which was kind of like an apple green. And, yes, that's how the _________ _________ _________, too.

G So there were only four tests.

B No, there was one more. The last one was iron, which had a kind of _________ _________.

3-4 W Now that you ________ ________ and Sir Isaac Newton's role in ________ it, I want to look at Newton's three ________ ________ ________. They were first ________ in his ________ ________ *The Mathematical Principles of Natural Philosophy* in 1687. I will put the three laws ________ ________ ________ I can and then ________ ________ ________. The first law of motion is that a body will ________ ________ ________ or will move in a ________ ________ at a ________ ________ unless an ________ ________ is placed on that body. For example, a ball on a ________ ________ is not moving. But ________ ________ ________ the white cue ball and the cue ball hits another ball, that second ball is ________ ________ ________ ________ but is moving. The second of Newton's laws of motion tells us how much force ________ ________ when an ________ ________ another object. The second law ________ that the force is ________ to the mass of the object plus its ________. Now, what about the third law? The third law of motion states that for every action, there is an ________ ________ ________ ________. For example, you and a friend ________ ________ ________ ________ with the palms of your hands. You push one way while your friend pushes the other way, and ________ ________ ________ ________. Of course, one person may be ________ and push the other person ________. Newton's law doesn't ________ this result could happen but ________ ________ that forces of motion work in both directions.

5-6 M Welcome to the Nikola Tesla Museum of Electrical History. Before we ________ ________ ________, are there any questions?

G Yes. Who was Nikola Tesla?

M Nikola Tesla was one of the ________ ________ of the ________ ________. He is ________ ________ ________ the creation of the system of ________ ________, or AC, that is used in most ________ ________ ________ today.

G I thought Thomas Edison created the ________ ________ ________ we use today.

M Actually, Edison and Tesla had a long-running ________ ________ which system of electricity was better, DC or AC.

G DC is ________ ________, and AC is alternating current, right?

M Yes. Direct current ________ ________ one direction while alternating current moves ________ ________ ________, first going one way and then going another.

G So, why do we use Tesla's alternating current ________ ________ Edison's direct current system?

M Direct current was used in the late 19th century when electrical systems ________ ________ ________. But DC ________ ________ ________. First, it couldn't be sent ________ ________ ________ since its ________ ________ due to ________ in ________ ________. Second, it had a ________ ________, which was fine for things such as ________ ________ and small motors but was ________ ________ ________ that needed a higher voltage. AC power used high voltage to ________ ________ ________, and it used ________ ________ ________ ________ for light bulbs and small motors.

G It ________ ________ that a man as smart as Thomas Edison would not see that AC was the ________ ________.

M Edison had a lot of time and ________ ________ in DC systems. So, he fought to have AC systems ________. In the end, he lost, and AC systems ________ ________ almost everywhere in the world.

7

W Your hands are so dirty, and so ________ ________ ________. What were you doing?

B Playing soccer, Mom. We won three to two. I ________ ________ ________.

W Congratulations. Now, dinner is almost ready. ________ ________ and put your clothes in the ________ ________ and then ________ ________ ________ before eating.

B I don't think any ________ ________ can get these clothes clean again.

W Don't ________ the power of a good soap or detergent.

B I've always wondered ________ ________ ________ to clean things.

W It has something to do with the ________ ________ of soap. The soap molecules ________ the ________ ________ ________ ________ on your skin or clothing. This then ________ the soap molecules ________ ________ the grease or dirt molecules in water.

B Really? That sounds a bit ________. I'm sure it's ________ ________ ________ than that.

W Of course it is. But that ________ ________ ________ for now. I ________ ________ at my university years ago, but I have forgotten a lot of it.

B I'll just ________ ________ ________ online later.

8

W ________ ________ from a hotter object to a cooler object in an attempt to ________ ________ ________. Heat is ________ in three main ways: ________, ________, and ________. Conduction can ________ in solids, liquids, and gases. It is the result of the ________ ________ ________ and the ________ ________ ________ by ________ ________. It ________ ________ faster in solids than in ________ ________ ________ ________. Heat conduction ________ ________ ________ ________ because the ________ ________ of metals allows a ________ ________ ________ of heat. Convection is the ________ ________ ________ in a gas or liquid by the ________ ________ of the gas or liquid. For example, in water, warm water will ________, and cooler water will ________, causing a heat transfer ________ ________ ________ ________ a contained space to the top. ________ is the transfer of heat ________ ________ ________ by ________ ________. The sun's heat is the ________ ________ ________ of radiation heat transfer.

9

W Deep beneath the Franco-Swiss ________ ________ a device that may change how the ________ ________ ________. This is the Large Hadron Collider, the ________ ________ ________ ever built. A particle accelerator is a device ________ ________ ________ ________ the smallest elements in the universe. This search is done by ________ ________ ________ and parts of atoms, like ________ and ________, and then using ________ ________ of computers to ________ ________ ________. The atoms must be ________ ________ to collide head on, and thus the collider must be very large. The Large Hadron Collider is 27 kilometers long, ________ ________ a great circle, and is about 100 meters ________ ________. Proton beams ________ ________ the circle and are ________ ________ ________ and turned by ________ ________ ________. By colliding protons, the scientists hope to ________ ________ that a ________ ________ called the Higgs boson ________ ________. The Higgs boson may ________ ________ ________ to many ________ ________ about the universe, such as how ________ ________ ________ in the first place. The existence of the Higgs boson ________ ________ over 30 years ago, but, as yet, no one has seen ________ for such a particle. Some scientists call it the God particle since it may ________ ________ ________ to many ________ of the universe. Unfortunately, the first ________ ________ ________ the Large Hadron Collider in 2008 failed. The device ________ ________ ________ in late 2009, with more positive results, but, as yet, the Higgs boson remains elusive.

10

B It's time to study chemistry. Mr. Wilkes is _________ _________ _________ _________ _________ on Fridays.

G Let's _________ the books then. What's first?

B Chapter 6, the noble gases. Why are they called "noble"?

G Wait. Here it is. The noble gases are called "noble" because they have _________ _________ valences of electrons and therefore do not _________ _________ with other _________. Okay, so what are the noble gases?

B There are helium, neon, argon, krypton, xenon, and radon.

G Krypton? As in Superman's _________?

B That's just a _________ _________. Come on. This is serious.

G Okay. So now we need to know the _________ _________. Helium is 2, neon 10, argon 18, krypton 36, xenon 54, and radon 86.

B I'll _________ _________ all that by tomorrow.

G Wait a second. We can use a _________ _________. Start with helium, whose atomic number is 2. _________ _________ 8, and you get 10 for the _________ _________ _________ _________. Then add 8 again and you have the atomic number of argon, 18. Then add 8... No, wait. _________ _________ _________.

B Close, but no cigar. Hey, _________ _________ _________. If we then double 18, we get 36 the atomic number of krypton. Then _________ _________ _________ and we have 54, the atomic number of xenon.

G But the last one is radon, whose atomic number is 86. _________ _________ _________ _________ up to 86.

B We'll just have to remember it, like helium. So, helium is 2, plus 8 _________ _________ for neon, plus 8 equals 18 for argon, plus 18 equals 36 for krypton, plus 18 equals 54 for xenon, and the final one, radon, is... I can't remember!

G 86!

11-12

M The _________ _________ _________ of an _________ are _________, protons, and neutrons. Protons are _________ _________, and neutrons _________ _________ _________. They both _________ _________ the _________ _________ _________ _________, which is _________ _________ _________. Electrons are negatively charged, _________ _________ the nucleus very _________, and form what is called the _________ _________. Let's use a few _________ _________ _________ to explain this _________ _________ _________. Hydrogen is the _________ _________ because it has one electron, one proton, and no neutrons. The _________ _________ _________ of the proton and the electron are what _________ _________ _________. The second simplest atom is the _________ _________. It has two protons and two electrons. It also has two neutrons, which are _________ _________ _________ the _________ of the atom. The two positively charged protons _________ _________ _________ _________ if there were no neutrons, which _________ _________ _________ like a _________ that keeps the helium atom together. These types of atoms, which are _________ _________ _________ _________ charged, are called neutral atoms. In each neutral atom, there are an _________ _________ of protons and electrons. Atoms are _________ _________ their atomic number or atomic mass. The atomic number _________ the _________ _________ _________ in an atom. The atomic mass equals the mass of the electrons, protons, and neutrons in an atom. Sometimes, an atom can have _________ _________ _________ _________ than protons. Positively charged atoms have fewer electrons than protons, and _________ _________ _________ have more electrons than protons. These charged atoms _________ _________ _________. Sometimes, atoms can also have more neutrons than protons. These atoms are called isotopes of the atom.

Politics

PREPARATION

A Read the definitions and write the correct word in each blank.

legislature	entrenched	platform	affiliated	abstain

1 ___________ policies and promises that a political party or a candidate announces just before an election

2 ___________ a group of people who have the power to make or change laws, such as Parliament

3 ___________ not to vote on an issue

4 ___________ firmly established; difficult to change

5 ___________ to be associated with someone or something

■ Now listen to the words and definitions and check your answers.

B Fill in the blanks with the suitable words or phrases on the list. Change the forms if needed.

representative	follow the party line	wait with bated breath
referendum	landslide	concede	turn of events

1 The ______________ on whether to allow gambling in the city was defeated by a large margin.

2 The defeated mayor will ______________ the election to his opponent.

3 Ronald Reagan won 49 out of 50 states in the 1984 election in one of the biggest ______________ victories in American history.

4 The candidates will ______________ for the final election results in this very close contest.

5 Our local government ______________ failed to win the last election and is now out of office.

6 A strange ______________ led to a scandal that saw the leading candidate drop out of the election race.

7 Despite their personal views, politicians must often ______________ or face being kicked out of their political party.

■ Now listen to the sentences and check your answers.

Expressions and Meanings

■ **Match each expression with its proper meaning.**

1 Something is brewing.   ⓐ I had really hoped for something, but it didn't happen.

2 They had someone on the inside. ⓑ I am not going to give up.

3 It was just wishful thinking.   ⓒ The issue involved is important.

4 He was tarred with the scandal brush. ⓓ A person working at the place helped the criminals.

5 It's the principle of the matter.   ⓔ Interesting things are happening.

6 I will fight to the bitter end.   ⓕ He is trying to remain positive.

7 He is putting on a brave face.   ⓖ He was associated with some misdeeds.

■ Now listen to the sentences and check your answers.

■ Listen to the monolog and complete the organizer.   ● 8-2

Types of Elections

Federal Elections	Provincial Elections	Local Elections
• for the whole (1) __________ • decide which (2) __________ party will have (3) __________ • all (4) __________ can vote	• held in (5) __________ • decide the same things as the federal election at the (6) __________ level • those who (7) __________ in the (8) __________ can vote	• decide the (9) __________ of power in (10) __________ and (11) __________ • residents in the (12) __________ or (13) __________ can vote

• main three types of elections in the world though the names may (14) __________
• when elections held: at a fixed time or anytime

By-elections   held when a government representative (15) __________ or (16) __________ in office during a (17) __________ period

General Questions   Based on the organizer, answer the questions.

1   **What is the main purpose of the talk?**

(a) To describe different Canadian elections   (b) To discuss elections at different levels

(c) To examine different types of elections   (d) To show elections in different nations

2   **Choose the best summary.**

(a) There are some common kinds of elections, but how the election system works varies from country to country.

(b) Elections are different in many nations, with things such as the type and time of the election varying from place to place.

Specific Questions   Listen again. Mark T for true statements and F for false statements.

(1) Everyone who is a citizen can vote in Canadian federal elections.   _____

(2) By-elections usually decide who will be the mayor of a city or town.   _____

(3) Presidential elections in America are held every five years.   _____

(4) Residency is an issue when voting in provincial or local elections in Canada.   _____

■ **Listen to the dialog and complete the notes.** ● 8-3

Topic: Discussion about (1)__________ for (2)__________ for student government
   - Candidates: Timmy Parsons - wants to have more junk food (3)__________ in the school
                 Tammy Miller - wants to raise more money for the (4)__________
                              - wants to make the school relax the (5)__________

Girl: voted for (☐ Timmy Parsons / ☐ Tammy Miller)
   - wants to know who the boy will vote for
   - believes the student president has no (6)__________
      → the (7)__________ let the students feel like they are taking part in something
        (8)__________

Boy: doesn't want to say whom he will vote for in the election
   - thinks the (9)__________ issue is very important - students (☐ can / ☐ can't)
     wear what they want now
   - thinks the student election is important - students get a chance to use their
     (10)__________ power

General Questions Based on the notes, answer the questions.

1 What is the main reason the girl talks to the boy?
   (a) To discuss the election candidates   (b) To talk about the election issues
   (c) To go over some school rules   (d) To discover who he will vote for

2 Choose the best summary.
   (a) A student election has two candidates for president, and both of them agree on the important issues facing students.
   (b) A student election causes a disagreement between two students over the value of secret ballots and the merits of the candidates.

Specific Questions Listen again. Mark T for true statements and F for false statements.

   (1) The student election voting place closed before lunchtime.   ____
   (2) Tammy Miller wants more vending machines in the school.   ____
   (3) The students are not allowed to wear certain clothes to school.   ____
   (4) The teachers gave their permission to hold the student election.   ____

LISTENING DRILL ②

Listen to the lecture and complete the organizer.  8-4

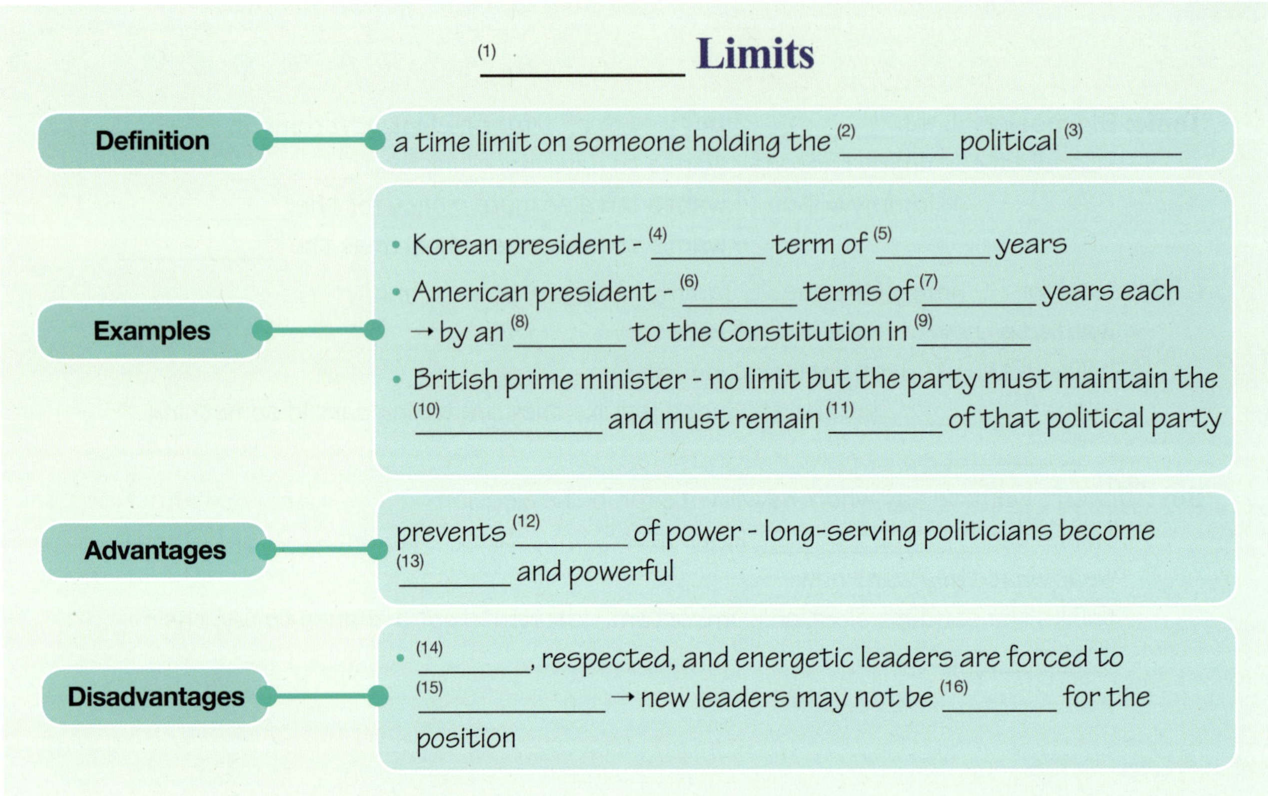

---

1 What is the best title for the lecture?

(a) Political Office Term Limits: Good or Bad? (b) American Presidential Term Limits

(c) Leadership Term Limits around the World (d) The Limits on Holding Political Office

2 Choose the best summary.

(a) Limiting terms on political office is often based on whether certain leaders have proven themselves able or unable to handle the office well for a long time.

(b) The term limits on political office vary around the world; however, the advantage or disadvantage of term limits depends on the individual politician.

3 Mark T for true statements and F for false statements.

(1) The American president was limited to two terms from the beginning of the nation's history.   _____

(2) British prime ministers have no legal limits on how long they can hold office.   _____

(3) Political office term limits are designed to prevent a politician from becoming too powerful.   _____

(4) The Korean president is limited to two terms of five years.   _____

4 What is one disadvantage of political office term limits?

(a) One party may hold power for a long time.

(b) Some office terms are too short.

(c) Good politicians must leave office.

(d) Some leaders may never leave office.

Dictation

■ Listen again and fill in the blanks.

M How long should a   be allowed to   ? In the case of a   , many countries   . However,   the highest office, which is usually   or   , most nations have   . For instance, the president of Korea is limited to one term of five years, and no one   to the office of president of the United States for   of four years each. This wasn't   in America. President Franklin Roosevelt   for 12 years from 1933 to his death in 1945, and he   four times. However, the government   to the   in 1951 limiting the American president to   . In some nations, there is no limit to   someone can hold the highest office. In the British   , which is used in many countries, the   is the   of a   . He or she can be the leader   his or her party   the most seats in the   and as long as that person is the   of his or her political party. The   of having a limit on   is that it   a check on the   . The longer a   , the more   and   he or she can become. On the other hand, a   to presidential term limits is that a popular,   , and   leader is forced to   and may be   by someone not as   for the position.

EXERCISE

■ Listen and answer the questions.

8-5

1 What is the purpose of the talk?
(a) To look at election poll margins of errors
(b) To examine how election polls are done
(c) To discuss election polls and their uses
(d) To explain how election predictions are made
(e) To show the advantages of election polls

2 Complete the table with the information about the Electoral College.

Category	Number
Electoral College Electors	
Electors from States	
Electors from the District of Columbia	
Electoral College Votes for Bush in 2000	
Electoral College Votes for Gore in 2000	

3-4

3 What is one possible advantage of direct representation voting over proportional representation voting?
(a) There are more choices on the ballot.
(b) Only a few candidates run in every district.
(c) People know exactly who they are voting for.
(d) The same party can govern for a long time.
(e) The election results are easier to determine.

4 Which of the following can be inferred from the talk?
(a) Those elected by direct representation voting represent the wishes of all of the voters in a nation.
(b) A coalition of parties forming a government is a regular result of proportional representation voting systems.
(c) Proportional representation is the common form of selecting representatives in Britain.
(d) Candidates in direct representation voting systems do not have to come from the district they run in.
(e) Proportional representation is a better system of voting since each political party can have a seat in government.

5-6
Level up

5 How was election fraud committed according to the newspaper account?
(a) The names of dead people were used on false registration cards.
(b) Someone who works in the election system made some changes.
(c) People with false registration cards managed to vote ten times.
(d) The mayor was caught putting extra votes in the ballot boxes.
(e) The system set up to check identification did not work properly.

6 **Choose the statement that best summarizes the dialog.**

(a) A mayoral election is in dispute because the losing candidate claims fraud, which the winner states is an accusation without merit.

(b) A scandal surrounding a mayoral election will cause harm to all involved even if they are innocent of taking part in any misdeeds.

(c) A mayor may be forced out of office because of an accusation that the recent election results were tampered with.

7 **Listen to the question and answer choices and choose the correct answer.**

(a)　　(b)　　(c)　　(d)　　(e)

8 **Listen to the question and answer choices and choose the correct answer.**

(a)　　(b)　　(c)　　(d)　　(e)

9 **What is NOT true about political parties according to the talk?**

(a) Working-class people tend to vote for more leftist political parties.

(b) Centrist political parties make promises to all classes of people.

(c) Political parties on the right tend to cater to the desires of the wealthy.

(d) Political parties were created during the 18th century French Revolution.

(e) Even in non-democratic nations, political parties may exist.

10 **Fill in the missing numbers in the table for the voting results for governor.**

Candidate	Results Before Last District	Final Results
Joseph Mellon		
Governor Walker	34,310	
Stella Hawking		

11 **What is an issue facing many elderly people on election day according to the lecture?**

(a) They have trouble making it to the location where voting takes place.

(b) They cannot make up their minds on whom to vote for in an election.

(c) They mostly live in rural areas with no public transportation available.

(d) They want to vote but often forget to register for the next election.

(e) They live overseas and do not resister to vote on time for the election.

12 **Choose the statement that best summarizes the lecture.**

(a) Voting is a right that some people do not use either because they do not know how to vote or they are too busy on election day.

(b) Most people try to vote on election day though some others do not because they are indifferent to the issues or mistrust the available candidates.

(c) Failure to vote in an election has many causes, including apathy about elections, trouble with the election process, or difficulties on election day.

PRACTICE TEST

■ Listen and answer the questions.

1 **Which statement is correct according to the talk?**
(a) The Supreme Court can veto any laws passed by the legislature.
(b) The president can order troops into battle without a declaration of war.
(c) The American government system is based on the British system.
(d) The three branches of the American government are under the president's control.
(e) The president has few checks on his authority to run the country.

2-3

2 **What can be inferred from the dialog?**
(a) The election monitors are working for the United Nations in Africa.
(b) The teacher has been an election monitor in the past in Africa.
(c) The election monitors were invited by an African country to come there.
(d) The students will learn about African elections from the substitute.
(e) The adding of extra votes is a common practice in African elections.

3 **What will the girl probably say after the boy's last comment?**
(a) I think the UN might have some trouble in this election.
(b) I guess they want to be recognized as a legal government.
(c) I hope our teacher has lots of fun while she is there.
(d) I believe that we should also have election monitors here.
(e) I figured Africa would have no problems with elections.

4-5

4 **What is the major weakness of referendums according to the talk?**
(a) A lot of money is spent on campaigns to convince people to vote for or against an issue.
(b) Even if a referendum passes with a majority, quite a lot of people may still be against the issue.
(c) Politicians just use referendums to avoid facing up to their responsibilities to make a decision.
(d) Most people think referendum issues are unimportant, so they do not bother to vote on them.
(e) Due to voter influence, most people will vote yes to a referendum even if they are against it.

5 **What can be inferred from the talk?**
(a) All Native American tribes in California wanted to build casinos on their land.
(b) Supporters of both sides to a referendum issue attempt to influence voters by spending money.
(c) Voters who do not choose yes or no on a referendum have ruined their ballots.
(d) Government leaders who use referendums stay in power longer than those who do not.
(e) There is usually a better solution to some issues than to have a referendum.

Level up

6 **Listen to the question and answer choices and choose the correct answer.**
(a)   (b)   (c)   (d)   (e)

Level up

7 **Listen to the question and answer choices and choose the correct answer.**
(a)   (b)   (c)   (d)   (e)

8 **Complete the chart with information about the American legislature.**

Category	Amount
Number of Senators	
Number of Members in the House of Representatives	
Percentage of Senators up for Election Each Year	about _________ %

【Integrated Questions】

■ Read the following passage and listen to the lecture.

In politics, members of the government and political parties use various tactics to achieve their political aims. Most parties vote as a bloc, with all members voting for or against an issue. Each party has members whose job is to keep the other members in line and to ensure they vote the way the party wants them to vote. Sometimes, party members do not follow the party line, but they generally do. When a vote is called for, sometimes not enough party members are present to ensure the vote will go the way they want. When this happens, there are tactics to delay a vote. In America, one such tactic is the filibuster, in which a member gives a long speech in order to kill time. In other countries, legislature members try to prevent a vote by physically stopping those who want to announce a vote from making such an announcement. Or, if they want a vote to go a certain way, they will prevent members of the opposition from entering the legislature building. This has led to physical confrontations in places like Taiwan and South Korea as the supposedly dignified representatives of the people brawl in front of the legislature building and sometimes even inside the building.

■ Now answer the following questions based on what you read and heard.

9 **What is one point mentioned about political tactics in both the reading and listening?**
(a) Members of the legislature vote as they want to.
(b) Physical fighting is a common tactic to prevent a vote.
(c) Fighting between parties leads to a weak government.
(d) Some governments can fall from power at any time.
(e) The government locks the doors during crucial votes.

10 **What can be inferred from the reading and listening?**
(a) Political party members who do not vote the party way can be dismissed from the party.
(b) Governments in Britain frequently fall due to a vote of no confidence in the legislature.
(c) Laws wanted by the people can fail due to political infighting in the legislature.
(d) The party with the second-highest number of seats in the legislature replaces a fallen government.
(e) Delaying tactics, even those involving physical fighting in the legislature, are legal.

DICTATION (Exercise)

Listen and fill in the blanks. 8-7

1 W During an ________ ________, there are many ________ ________ ________ ________ who is most likely to ________ ________ ________. Polls are ________ done by ________ ________ ________ or companies that ________ ________ such matters. The survey companies ask a ________ ________ ________ ________, either ________ ________ or by telephone, or sometimes by the Internet these days, what they think of the major issues or who they would most likely ________ ________ ________ ________ ________. These polls ________ ________ ________ ________, but they are often a good ________ ________ ________ who the winner will be on election day. Even on election day, polls are taken of people ________ ________ ________ ________. Predictions on who the winner will be are done based on these polls even before the voting is finished or the ________ ________. Candidates use the polls to ________ ________ and to see ________ ________ ________ ________ ________. A candidate might ________ his or her ________ in an area where he or she ________ ________ ________ ________ ________ if that area is ________ to the election result. The candidate may also find out that people do not like his or her ________ ________ ________ ________ ________. Therefore, the candidate may ________ ________ the more popular opinion on the issue. For example, abortion is always a controversial issue in American elections, and candidates must be careful to know where the people ________ ________ such an issue.

2 G This is so ________!

M What's the matter, dear?

G I'm studying politics, Dad, and we have to ________ ________ ________ ________ the 2000 election campaign. I can't understand why George Bush won when Al Gore had more votes than him.

M It's the Electoral College system.

G I found that out, but I really don't understand it.

M Each state has ________ ________ ________ Electoral College voters called "electors," and they decide who the ________ will be. There are 538 electors, and ________ ________ wins the majority of them wins the ________ ________.

G How does the government determine ________ ________ ________ ________?

M The number in each state ________ ________ the number of members in the Senate and House of Representatives from that state. There are also three electors from the District of Columbia.

G And these electors ________ ________ ________?

M Yes. They ________ ________ ________ the major political parties. The ________ have the name of the ________ ________, but, in reality, people are voting for the electors that are from these parties.

G So, what's the point of the ________ ________ ________ ________?

M To know which party's electors ________ ________ ________ ________ ________. In 2000, Bush won Florida by only a ________ ________ ________ ________ ________, but that was enough to win the votes of the 25 electors who were Republicans and give him a majority of 271 Electoral College votes. Gore got the rest ________ ________ one elector who ________ ________ ________.

G But Gore had more popular votes across the country! More people wanted him as president.

M But he didn't have enough Electoral College electors and their votes.

3-4

M In politics, there are several ways the people of a country can have their ________ ________ in the government. Two common types are ________ ________ and ________ ________. In direct representation, the people ________ ________ ________ the political candidates in their ________ ________. These candidates usually ________ ________ ________ ________, but they can also be ________. They campaign in their district, and, on election day, the people vote for them. When the votes ________ ________, the candidate with the most votes wins the district and will ________ ________ ________ ________ ________ ________. Proportional representation is different. There are many forms, but very often in countries that use the system, the people ________ ________ ________ for political parties, not ________. When all of the votes are counted, a certain percentage of votes ________ each party's number of seats ________ ________ ________. If a party gets 50% of the vote, for instance, it gets 50% of the seats. Even the smallest party with the fewest votes can ________ ________ ________ ________ if that party gained a large enough percentage to get a seat. The party with the most votes, and therefore the most seats, can ________ ________ ________ and ________ ________ ________. This type of voting is common in ________ Europe. However, it is often ________ ________ ________ ________ ________ as too many parties ________ the voting pool, so no party can ________ ________ ________ ________ and ________ the government successfully without help from other parties.

5-6

W What's in the newspaper today?

M It looks like ________ ________ ________ ________ in City Hall. The newspaper says there are ________ ________ ________ ________ into the recent ________ ________.

W Did some people ________ ________ ________ ________ ________ in the ballot box?

M It seems so. The losing candidate is claming ________ ________ ________ ________ ________. She says she wants a ________ and an ________ of certain voters who registered at the last minute.

W ________ ________ ________. My father said that in the old days, they ________ people ________ the street, gave them a bit of cash, and handed them a voter registration card with some ________ ________ ________ ________ ________. Some guys voted ten times in one election.

M Things are a bit more ________ now. Everyone has to ________ ________ ________ ________ and also show proper ID at the voting station.

W If the ________ really happened, I wonder how they did it.

M The paper says the only way was to have someone on the inside changing the ________ ________ ________. That's where the investigation will begin.

W It doesn't matter if it's true or not. The ________ will be ________ ________ the ________ ________, and he'll never win another election. It's probably best if he resigns now.

M He says it's all ________ ________ and that he will fight to the ________ ________.

7

B My father was really ________ last night.

G What did you do wrong this time?

B Nothing! He ________ ________ ________ some politician who ________ ________.

G Oh, I heard about that. They say he stole some money. My mom said you can't ________ ________ ________ these days.

B My dad said that, too. He even helped when that politician came to town, and he asked people to vote for him. Now my dad ________ really ________.

G I'd be too if I had supported someone who ________ ________ ________ ________ ________ ________.

B He said he's never going to ________ ________ ________ an election or vote the rest of his life.

G I think that's a little silly. Just because of ________ ________ ________, you can't say all politicians are bad.

B I don't know. You only hear about politicians when something bad happens.

G That's partly the ________ ________, too. They are always looking for some ________.

B Maybe the media should be ________ ________. People trust politicians to do ________ ________ ________ ________ ________ them. Instead, we have ones like this guy who was just trying to get rich.

8 W During an election campaign, each ________ presents his or her ________ ________ to the ________ ________. The voters then often use the ________ ________ ________ ________ on these issues to help them decide whom to vote for during the election. Issues can be national ones, which ________ ________ ________ ________, or they can be local ones, which affect one state or city. Some typical issues of a candidate's platform include ________ ________, ________, education, ________, the environment, and ________. Often, candidates follow the ________ ________, which means they follow the opinions of their ________ ________. A common part of any election campaign is a ________ between the candidates. These ________ are important as they show the public what the candidates' platforms are and how well they can ________ ________ ________ ________. These debates ________ ________ ________ in front of an audience and are typically ________ on TV, radio, and the Internet. A ________ and/or audience members ask the candidates questions, and each candidate ________ ________ some time to answer.

9 M In most ________ ________, and even in some not-so-democratic ones, political parties are a ________ ________ of politics. Some ________ ________ ________ are the Republican and Democratic parties in America, the Conservative and Labor parties in Britain, the Green Party in Germany, and the Communist Party in Russia and in many other nations. Political parties are often called left, right, or ________ ________ ________ ________ ________. These ________ ________ ________ the period of the French Revolution in the late 18th century. The ________ of the French representatives to government ________ ________ ________ ________, with those most ________ on the far left, those most ________ on the right, and those neither very radical nor very conservative ________ ________ ________. In modern terms, the Communist Party is very much a ________ ________ while the British Conservative and American Republican parties are ________ ________ ________. Leftist parties are often popular with the poor and the ________ ________ since leftist platforms ________ ________ more ________ ________ for the people, such as free education, medical care, and ________ ________. Parties on the right ________ ________ ________ the wealthy and businesspeople, who do not want the ________ ________ that come with more ________ to the common people. Many parties have more ________ ________ and try to attract both the wealthy and working classes with promises to help both sides with their issues.

10 M Welcome back to *Election Night 2009* at RKO Radio. We'll have all of the results in the state elections in just a few moments. Now let's ________ ________ ________ ________ ________, Debbie Taylor, who is at the ________ ________ ________. Debbie?

W Jake, there is a lot of ________ ________ over here as the vote for governor is ________ ________ ________ ________ ________ ________ yet. At present, Governor Walker is 250 votes ________ the leading challenger, Joseph Mellon, who has 34,560 votes. ________ ________ _______ is Stella Hawking with 24,678 votes. There is just one more ________ ________ _______, and we are waiting for this result.

M Governor Walker was expected to win in a _______. How is he _______ this _______ _______ _______?

W He is _______ _______ _______ _______ _______ and _______ _______, but word is that his advisors are _______ _______ _______ trying to figure out what went wrong. All the polls showed the governor ahead, but... wait. Yes, the final results are coming in now.

M All of our listeners are _______ _______ _______ _______, Debbie.

W And it's _______. The new governor of the state will be Joseph Mellon. He _______ _______ _______ _______ in the last district while Governor Walker only _______ _______, and Stella Hawking received 1,030 votes. That was not enough for either Hawking or Walker to _______ _______ _______ _______ Joseph Mellon.

M I must say this is _______ _______ _______. Can we _______ _______ _______ _______ Governor Walker?

W Perhaps soon, but right now I think we _______ _______ _______ hear Governor Walker _______ _______ _______ _______ Joseph Mellon. _______ _______ for the _______ _______.

11-12

W While voting in an election is a right that many people have, sometimes they don't _______ _______ _______. This is _______ in _______ _______, such as with the less than 50 percent of _______ _______ coming to the polls in America in 1996 and _______ _______ _______ 50 percent in 2000. There are many reasons why people don't vote. These include _______ _______ the _______ _______, problems _______ _______ following the _______ _______, and the person's _______ _______ _______ on election day. Many people feel that their vote has no _______ _______ _______ _______ or simply believe that the choice of candidates is so bad that it is not _______ _______. The second reason people don't vote is that they can't _______ _______ _______ they make following election rules. Usually, a person must register to vote before the election. _______ _______ _______ means a person can't vote. In some cases, such as in Canada, if a person moves to a new _______ _______ less than six months before an election, that individual can't vote in any elections. Sometimes, people are _______ and fail to register or vote _______ _______. The final issue with failing to vote is trouble actually voting on election day. Many _______ _______ have _______ _______ and cannot easily _______ _______ _______ _______ the voting station. Other people have no car or _______ _______ _______ public transportation. If the weather is bad, many people will decide to stay home and not vote. Other people have to work even if the election is on a _______ _______. _______ _______ _______, many people fail to vote, and this can _______ _______ _______ _______ the outcome of an election.

Earth Sciences

PREPARATION

9-1

A **Read the definitions and write the correct word in each blank.**

| moraine | retrograde | depression | distortion | encroachment |

1 ____________ an area of ground lower than its surroundings
2 ____________ the action of taking over more and more of an area
3 ____________ a low ridge created by a glacier
4 ____________ returning to an earlier and worse situation
5 ____________ a change in something from its original shape

■ Now listen to the words and definitions and check your answers.

B **Fill in the blanks with suitable words or phrases on the list. Change the forms if needed.**

| dubbed | humus | infertile | protrude |
| fossil index | decompose | take exception | |

1 Stony, barren land is usually ______________ and unsuitable for agriculture.
2 Dead plants and animals ______________ and make the soil much more fertile.
3 The Everglades in Florida contain many small tree-coverd islands which ______________ from the swampy water.
4 Scientists sometimes get angry and ______________ to their theories being disputed.
5 The supercontinent was ______________ Pangaea by a German scientist.
6 The ______________ is the record of the remains of ancient animals and plants in different layers of the earth's rocky crust.
7 The farmland was very fertile because the topsoil was mostly ______________.

■ Now listen to the sentences and check your answers.

■ **Match each expression with its proper meaning.**

1 Hit me with your best shot.
2 I'll get right on it.
3 He always has his nose stuck in a book.
4 Your explanations always go over my head.
5 You hit the nail on the head.
6 You are no slouch when it comes to that topic.
7 Let me surmise the rest.

ⓐ It's too difficult to understand.
ⓑ You sure know a lot about it.
ⓒ I think I can guess what happened.
ⓓ I'm going to do it now.
ⓔ Go ahead. I'm ready.
ⓕ You are correct.
ⓖ He's always studying.

■ Now listen to the sentences and check your answers.

LISTENING DRILL ①

■ Listen to the monolog and complete the organizer.

9-2

Pangaea

Theory

- based on the theory of (1)__________ → the way in which the Earth's (2)__________ obtained their present (3)__________ and (4)__________
- term credited to a German scientist in (5)__________
- a (6)__________ with all land joined together
- formed about (7)__________ million years ago
- Pangaea has formed and (8)__________ (9)__________ times during 4 billion years

Evidence

- (10)__________ found in one area are the same as those in distant areas
- similar (11)__________ in both places
- ※ Brazil and West Africa provide two examples of evidence

General Questions   Based on the organizer, answer the questions.

1   **What is the purpose of the talk?**

(a) To explain a scientific theory and the evidence that supports it

(b) To prove that a theory is correct by discussing its scientific origins

(c) To describe evidence that supports and refutes a scientific theory

(d) To show that a scientific theory has yet to be proven satisfactorily

2   **Choose the best summary.**

(a) The fossil and geological evidence supports the theory of continental drift, which suggests that the Earth's land was once a large landmass.

(b) The theory that the Earth's land was once a single large landmass was first suggested in 1920 by a German scientist, but it has yet to be proven.

Specific Questions   Listen again. Mark T for true statements and F for false statements.

(1) It is believed that the Earth has gone through cycles where the land was joined and then separated several times.   _____

(2) Pangaea is a word coined to describe the movement of the continents.   _____

(3) Fossils found on both sides of the Atlantic Ocean resemble each other.   _____

(4) The geological evidence for continental drift is rather scanty.   _____

■ Listen to the dialog and complete the notes. 9-3

Woman: a (☐ tourist / ☐ tour guide)
- will show him a slide show of the (1)__________ of the island
- will take a trip around the island to see some various (2)__________
- describes 1. the parasite cones: small volcanoes made when the lava tubes for
   (3)__________ were (4)__________
   2. the lava tube tunnel
   3. the pillar-shaped joints: cracking of the (5)__________ when it was
   (6)__________

Man: a (☐ tourist / ☐ tour guide)
- is interested in (7)__________
- seems to know something about geology

General Questions Based on the notes, answer the questions.

1 **What is the purpose of the man's visit to Jeju Island?**
(a) To see a slide show of the island's features
(b) To take a tour of the island later during his trip
(c) To explore the geological features of the island
(d) To relax, rest, and perhaps take in a tour

2 **Choose the best summary.**
(a) A tour guide shows a foreign tourist a slide show of some volcanic features of Jeju Island before they start a tour of the island.
(b) A foreign tourist who is interested in volcanoes admires a tour guide's extensive knowledge of the volcanoes on Jeju Island.

Specific Questions Listen again. Mark T for true statements and F for false statements.

(1) There is only going to be one tourist on the tour of the island. ____
(2) The man and woman have some knowledge of volcanoes. ____
(3) Parasite cones are volcanoes independent of Halla Mountain. ____
(4) Pillar-shaped formations were created when lava cooled and cracked. ____

■ Listen to the lecture and complete the organizer.

9-4

Soil Composition

Soil Facts

• vital for human and animal life on Earth

<Formation>
1. (1)__________ of rock by wind and water
2. actions of (2)__________, animals, and (3)__________

Soil Layers

• called "horizons"
1. Horizon A - rich (4)__________ where (5)__________ grows
   - most useful part
2. Horizon B - has some (6)__________ washed down from the upper layer
   - less (7)__________, more (8)__________ and lighter
3. Horizon C - mostly (9)__________ and infertile
4. Horizon D - the more (10)__________ (11)__________

Soil Fertility

• depends on (12)__________ composition of soil → depends on the (13)__________ and the (14)__________ that grow in the soil
1. a lot of past (15)__________ activity → soil is rich - (16)__________ ash is very fertile
2. the actions of (17)__________ and fungi - help (18)__________ dead plant and animal matter, which creates <u>humus</u>
   ↓
   a dark, rich soil that is ideal for (19)__________

---

1 What is the lecture mainly about?

(a) Some characteristics of soil and how it is made
(b) Different layers of soil and how they are formed
(c) How soil—especially life-giving topsoil—is created
(d) The life forms which live in the layers of the soil

2 Choose the best summary.

(a) Soil is created through erosion and can be divided into several layers, with the top layer being the most important for mankind.
(b) Soil is created through several different methods and is organized in different layers, with the top layer being the most vital for the continuing existence of life.

3 Mark T for true statements and F for false statements.

(1) The chemical composition of soil is similar around the world.   _____

(2) Humus is very fertile due to decomposed plant and animal matter.   _____

(3) Horizon B of soil is composed of rocky material and is infertile.   _____

(4) Topsoil composed mainly of volcanic ash tends to be very fertile.   _____

4 What role do bacteria and fungi play in creating fertile topsoil?

(a) They are present in volcanic ash and turn it into humus.

(b) They are in the top layer of the soil and help erode rocks.

(c) They attack dead organisms and help them decompose.

(d) They shift through the layers of soil and feed soil creatures.

Dictation

■ Listen again and fill in the blanks.

w Soil is one of the _____________ of the geology of the Earth. ________,
most __________________, including crops, ______________, so it is
________________ and animal life. Soil is ______ mainly ________
________ of rock into ____________, with ______________ doing the work
over a long period of time. ____________ are also created through the
________, animals, and humans. ____________, or pedologists, __________
________ four main ________, which they call "________." At the top is horizon A, the most
________________, which is the ____________ where ____________. This can
be anywhere from a few centimeters to almost a ____________. Below that is horizon
B, which ____________ that water ____________ from the ____________.
However, horizon B is ____________ than horizon A and is more ______ and ______.
Under horizon B is the ______ horizon C, which is ______. Finally, the ______
bedrock is horizon D. Soil fertility ____________ its ____________, which
________ depends on the ______ and the plants that grow in the soil. If there was
____________ in the past, the soil will be rich as ____________ is very
fertile. Soil can also ____________ through the actions of bacteria and fungi. When plants
and animals die, the actions of bacteria and fungi ____________. Then, with the help of
________ and other ____________, this ____________ becomes humus, a dark, rich
soil that is ____________.

■ Listen and answer the questions.

9-5

1 What is the main idea of the talk?

(a) To discuss the benefits of different types of coal

(b) To examine the differences between coal and peat

(c) To discuss a geological process of the prehistoric Earth

(d) To prove that older coal is of the highest quality

(e) To describe how coal was created over time

2 Complete the table with the missing information on Lake Baikal.

Category	Information
Percent of World's Unfrozen Fresh Water	________ percent
Surface Area	31,722 square kilometers
Length	________ kilometers
Width	________ kilometers
Depth	________ meters
Age	________ years

3-4

3 What mainly accounts for the differences in the shape of river deltas?

(a) The building of dams across rivers that have a large river delta

(b) The amount of silt that the river drops off on the way to the mouth

(c) The average tidal speed in the body of water the river enters

(d) The power of the tides and waves where the river mouth is located

(e) The number of large storms with great wave power that occur yearly

4 What may happen to the Nile River delta in the future?

(a) It may be washed away if the dam blocking the Nile is destroyed.

(b) It will expand further into the Mediterranean due to the weak tides.

(c) It may disappear entirely because little new silt is being deposited.

(d) It will not be habitable as water levels rise due to Nile floodwaters.

(e) It could turn into a bird's foot delta like the Mississippi River delta.

5-6

Level up

5 Why are oil and gas likely to be found on a continental shelf?

(a) It was once exposed land where plants, and later fish, died.

(b) Shallow water has better conditions for making oil and gas.

(c) More fish die in shallow water than in deep water.

(d) The continental slope allows oil and gas to pool underground.

(e) Sea vegetation, such as seaweed, dies and becomes oil over time.

6 **Choose the statement that best summarizes the dialog.**

(a) Under coastal water lies shallow land called the continental shelf that suddenly gets deeper at the continental slope.

(b) Continental shelves have deposits of oil and gas as well as extensive fishing grounds and may have once served as continental land bridges.

(c) Fishing and petroleum exploration along continental shelves may be disrupted if water levels drop like they did in the past.

 7 **Listen to the question and answer choices and choose the correct answer.**

(a)　　(b)　　(c)　　(d)　　(e)

 8 **Listen to the question and answer choices and choose the correct answer.**

(a)　　(b)　　(c)　　(d)　　(e)

9 **What is NOT true according to the talk?**

(a) The urban heat island effect is made worse by taller buildings.

(b) Concrete and asphalt tend to absorb more heat than vegetation.

(c) Dark-colored buildings contribute to the urban heat island problem.

(d) The urban heat island effect has little influence outside of urban areas.

(e) Deaths during heat waves increase due to the urban heat island effect.

10 **Complete the table with the number of earthquakes that occurs per year at each intensity level.**

Intensity on Richter Scale	Number of Earthquakes per Year
Less than 2	
2 to 4	
4 to 6	
6 and higher	

 11 **Why is limestone an ideal rock for cave formation?**

(a) As limestone wears away, it leaves behind stalactites and stalagmites.

(b) Caves made from limestone are deeper and longer than other caves.

(c) Limestone is widespread worldwide, so many caves are made from it.

(d) Limestone is a soft rock that wears away more easily than other rocks.

(e) Limestone creates more stable and permanent caves than other rocks.

12 **Choose the statement that best summarizes the lecture.**

(a) Caves differ widely in how they are created, their composition, and their size, and they may range up to dozens of kilometers in length.

(b) Caves are mostly created through the action of water, which erodes rock and ice over time to form permanent underground sculptures.

(c) Caves are created in a variety of ways, but they all should be treated with caution when people explore them.

PRACTICE TEST

■ Listen and answer the questions.

9-6

1 What is NOT true according to the talk?

(a) Small islands covered with trees dot the Everglades swamp.

(b) Alligators and crocodiles coexist in the Everglades swamp.

(c) The Everglades swamp gets water from rain and river systems.

(d) The draining of the Everglades swamp is a fairly recent activity.

(e) Human use of Everglades swamp water is increasing yearly.

2-3

2 What is NOT true according to the dialog?

(a) The man's daughter did not understand what a peninsula is.

(b) The man has extensive knowledge of Korea and its people.

(c) The man had a very tiring day working in his office.

(d) The man will attend a conference while he is in Korea.

(e) One of the man's co-workers told him about the issue of the East Sea.

3 What will the father probably say next following his daughter's last comment?

(a) I don't know. Maybe I'll decide when I get there.

(b) I think I'll just go to the Sea of Japan in the west.

(c) Nowhere, as I won't have any free time in Korea.

(d) I love to swim, so the west coast sounds great.

(e) I'll fly to Jeju Island and stay there the whole trip.

4-5

4 Why is agriculture a precarious livelihood in a grassland area?

(a) Too much grazing of livestock can destroy the topsoil.

(b) The supply of water from year to year is very uncertain.

(c) Winds from storms blow away much of the vital topsoil.

(d) Mountains can prevent orchards from growing large trees.

(e) The land is too flat to protect the crops from erosion.

5 What can be inferred from the talk?

(a) There must be nearby mountains to create flat grasslands.

(b) Australians were raising rabbits just like herds of livestock.

(c) It would be difficult to find firewood in an area of grassland.

(d) The Dust Bowl resulted from too much land being farmed.

(e) Grasslands typically have the most productive farmland.

Level up

6 Listen to the question and answer choices and choose the correct answer.

(a)   (b)   (c)   (d)   (e)

Level up

7 Listen to the question and answer choices and choose the correct answer.

(a)   (b)   (c)   (d)   (e)

8 **Complete the chart with information on the layers of the Earth's atmosphere.**

Layer	Beginning	End
Troposphere		7-20 km
Stratosphere		50 km
Mesosphere		
Thermosphere	85 km	
Exosphere	685 km	

【Integrated Questions】

■ Read the following passage and listen to the lecture.

Cartography is the art of making maps—usually on a flat surface—that represent the features of the Earth. There are many kinds of maps, but the most common types show the layout of a town or city, the geography of a region or country, or the position of the continents and islands of the world. A common type of world map is called the Mercator projection. Dutch cartographer Gerardus Mercator created this map in 1569. The problem with Mercator's map, and many other maps, is that it tries to show the Earth in two dimensions on square or rectangular paper. However, the Earth is not flat, as it curves and narrows at the poles. To try to overcome this problem, Mercator used mathematical formulas to make his map fit rectangular paper and, at the same time, give his map straight lines of latitude and longitude while keeping the familiar shapes of small land formations. Unfortunately, since this map is laid flat and shows the whole world as if it were an unrolled cylinder and not a sphere, there are some distortions. In particular, the Northern Hemisphere appears larger than it really is, and continents such as South America, Africa, and Australia look correspondingly smaller than they are in reality.

■ Now answer the following questions based on what you read and heard.

9 **What is NOT true according to the reading and listening?**

(a) Mercator projection maps were once popular for sea navigation.

(b) The Mercator projection map was first created in the 17th century.

(c) There are maps that are more realistic than the Mercator projection.

(d) Not everyone agrees with the use of Mercator projection maps.

(e) Mercator projection maps make the far north and south seem larger.

10 **What can be inferred from the reading and listening?**

(a) Mercator projection maps are not the only ones that show distortions.

(b) The Dutch were famous for navigation during Mercator's lifetime.

(c) People in South America complained that Greenland was a smaller landmass.

(d) Navigators no longer use Mercator projection maps for sailing.

(e) Mercator projection maps have all been replaced with sinusoidal maps.

■ Listen and fill in the blanks. ● 9-7

1 M Coal is the ________ ________ ________ ________ that have undergone a ________ ________ over millions of years. After trees and plants died in ________ ________ ________ ________ ________ of inland seas and lakes, they quickly sank under the water and then were ________ ________ ________ of sand and mud. This process ________ ________ ________ ________ without ________ it to air or ________ ________ ________ ________. Over millions of years, this process was repeated many times and formed more and more layers of plant matter with ________ ________ ________ ________ ________. The plant matter ________ ________ ________ ________ tremendous amounts of heat and pressure. The ________ ________ in wood became ________ ________, then bitumen, and finally carbon. It was this ________ ________ when the plant matter was transformed into coal. A high carbon content indicates that a piece of coal is very old and is also of good quality. Most ________ ________ ________ was formed during the Carboniferous Period on the ________ ________ ________. This was a period about 360 to 290 million years ago. Coal from more ________ ________ ________ is usually not of as good a quality. The most ________ ________—from about 10,000 years ago—were transformed into peat. This is an early stage of coal transformation. Peat has a lot of ________ ________ ________, so it is useful for burning to heat homes. However, because it has no carbon content, it is not ________ ________ ________ ________.

2 W Did you find the information about lakes that we need for the project?

M Yes, and I think we ________ ________ ________ Lake Baikal in Russia.

W ________ ________ ________ about it?

M It has about 20 percent of the world's ________ ________ ________ that is not frozen, like in the ________ ________. Pretty amazing, huh?

W 20 percent? Are you sure? That sounds like someone is ________.

M No, it's true. In fact, Lake Baikal has more fresh water than the five Great Lakes in the U.S. combined.

W Then it must be huge. Do you have a picture?

M Yes, here it is, but it's ________ ________ ________. It's ________, and it's 636 kilometers long and 79 kilometers wide ________ ________ ________ ________. It has a surface area of ________ square kilometers.

W I think that's less than Lake Superior.

M You're right, but Baikal is the deepest lake in the world. It's ________ meters deep. That's why it has so much fresh water. Also, the bottom of the lake is ________ ________ ________, so the ________ ________ ________ is even deeper, at about 8 kilometers.

W What other interesting facts can we include in our report?

M Let's see. Oh, there are 72 islands in the lake. And it's also ________ to be about 25 million years old. Some geologists say it's ________ ________ ________ in the world.

W I think that's ________ ________ ________ ________ ________ our project.

3-4 M When a river ________ ________ the ocean, or sometimes into a lake, it can ________ ________ ________. This is an area of ________ ________ that forms over a long period of time. The term "delta" comes from the shape of the Nile River's delta. The ancient Greeks felt the shape was ________ ________ ________

________ "Δ" (delta) in the Greek alphabet. There are ________ ________ ________ ________ river deltas. The Nile River delta is a ________ ________ ________, which has slowly built up over a long period of time. The Mediterranean Sea has mostly ________ ________ but ________ ________ ________, which has allowed the Nile delta to expand, but not ________ ________ ________ ________. Since the construction of the Aswan High Dam on the Nile in the 1960s, the flow of silt to the delta ________ ________ ________, and, in recent decades, the Nile delta has shown a ________ ________. The other most common delta shape is the bird's foot delta, with the Mississippi River delta ________ ________ ________ ________ of this type. The great river ________ ________ the Gulf of Mexico, which has little tidal or wave power, allowing the Mississippi delta to expand very far. As it deposits silt, the river ________ ________ ________ and ________ ________ from the coastline. The different ________ ________ ________ fingers or toes and give the delta its ________ ________ ________ ________.

5-6

G It's such a nice day to ________ ________ ________, and this is a great beach. The water is great for swimming because it's really shallow here. There are also lots of ________ ________ ________.

B It's a great place for fishing because of the ________ ________ ________.

G What's the continental shelf?

B It's shallow, gently ________ ________ ________ that can extend into the ocean for a few or hundreds of kilometers. The shallow water provides ________ ________ ________ and other food for fish. The ________ ________ when the water suddenly gets deeper at a ________ ________ ________ ________ ________.

G So if I walk far enough in the water, I will suddenly fall?

B You'd have to ________ ________ ________, and the water isn't shallow enough to ________ ________ ________ ________.

G No, I don't think I'll try that. Wait. Is that an ________ ________ ________ ________ on the ________?

B Sure. Oil explorers have also found extensive oil and gas fields ________ ________ ________ ________.

G I thought oil only existed in the desert or places where ________ ________ ________ and animals died a long time ago.

B Fish die, too. The continental shelf was also ________ ________ in the ________ ________. The levels of the oceans ________ ________ over the years. During the ________ ________ ________, the world's oceans were around 100 meters lower than they are today due to ________ ________ ________ in the ________ ________.

G Oh, right. There was a land bridge between Asia and Alaska. I learned that was how the Native Americans probably went from Asia to North and South America.

7

G You've always got your ________ ________ ________ a book. What are you reading now?

B It's about a ________ ________, William Smith.

G I've never heard of him. Why's he so famous?

B He's often called the father of English geology. In the early 19th century, he made a ________ ________ ________ ________ of England that showed the ________ ________ ________ ________ all over the British Isles.

G Do you mean he showed the different types of land, ________ ________, and ________? That sort of thing?

B Yes, it's mostly what he is famous for. He also created what is called a ________ ________.
G That's ________ ________ ________ ________. What's a ________ ________?
B Smith was helping ________ a ________, and he noticed that different fossils were found in ________ ________ of rock, but the same fossils always appeared in the same layers.
G Wait. Let me ________ ________ ________. So because each layer had the same fossils in different areas, this was an ________ ________ ________ ________ of the rock layers and the fossils.
B You hit the nail right on the head. I guess it didn't all ________ ________ ________ ________ after all.

8 W The Northern Hemisphere has a great many more lakes than the Southern Hemisphere, ________ ________ ________ ________ ________. As the great ________ ________ ________ during the last ice age, they cut away the land and ________ ________ ________ by the tens of thousands. As the ice sheets ________ and ________, these depressions were filled with the ________ ________ ________ ________. Examples of glacial lakes include the five Great Lakes in North America, the largest examples of glacial lakes in the world. A lake can be ________ ________ a ________ ________ by certain ________ ________ that are located nearby. For example, small ________ ________ ________ ________ are often associated with glacial activity. The ________ ________ ________ the glacier stopped its movement usually has a ________ moraine, a long low hill that was created by the ________ ________ ________ and rock in front of it. These are both signs that a glacier was nearby and that the lake was most likely created by the ________ ________.

9 W An ________ heat island is a city area that is hotter than the surrounding countryside. Often, this ________ ________ may be ________ ________ ________ five ________ ________. With plenty of concrete and asphalt, plus tall buildings which have a larger surface area than houses and smaller buildings, ________ ________ ________ more sunlight and heat during the day. This ________ ________ is ________ very slowly at night, making city areas hotter than ________ ________ in the ________. Another problem is that tall buildings ________ ________ which could ________ ________ ________ more quickly. Heat from cars, factories, air conditioning systems, and other sources contributes to the higher temperatures in cities. The biggest ________ the ________ ________ ________ ________ has is to contribute to the ________ ________ during heat waves. In addition, there are some experts who believe the urban heat island effect is contributing to ________ ________ ________ and possibly to global warming. However, not all cities and not all city areas have these problems. Cities with a great many parks and ________ ________ ________ ________ have less of an urban heat island problem because ________ has a ________ ________. Some cities even have plans to build ________ ________ to reduce the urban heat island effect. Also, by using light-colored materials and ________ ________ to cover new buildings, the amount of heat absorbed during the daytime is ________ ________.

10 W Welcome to *Science Project*. Our guest today is Dr. Peter Beckman, an ________ ________ ________. What is ________, Dr. Beckman?
M It's the study of earthquakes.
W Great. We have an e-mail question here about earthquakes. Becky Johansson of Smith Falls wants to know how earthquakes are ________.

M Well, Becky, and all of you other kids out there watching, we measure earthquakes using a scale of measurement called the Richter scale.

W I think most of us have heard of the Richter scale. How does it work?

M It's kind of complex, but basically, we take measurements of the earthquake using instruments and then _________ _________ to get an _________ _________. We use a scale from 1 to 10.

W So 1 is good, and 10 is bad?

M _________ _________, yes. Earthquakes measuring less than 2 on the Richter scale are _________ _________ _________ by people, and they're the _________ _________. There are about 8,000 of them _________ _________ around the world.

W Eight thousand a day! I'm glad they aren't felt. At what intensity do people feel the earth shake?

M Between _________ and _________ _________ _________ _________, but this occurs less frequently—around _________ times per year.

W That seems like more... Oh, you said per year, not day.

M Yes. Next, an earthquake between 4 and 6 on the scale causes _________ _________ and usually minor—but sometimes a great deal of—damage. We have around 800 of these per year. After that, above 6 on the scale, the _________ can be very _________, and there will be many _________. Thankfully, these _________ _________ are _________, with only about _________ _________ per year, and sometimes they are not _________ _________ _________.

11-12 M A cave is a hole in the ground, in a cliff, or in a mountain, but that is a rather simple explanation. There are a _________ _________ _________, and they are _________ _________ by how they were created and their _________ _________. There are four main types of caves: _________, _________, _________, and _________. Solutional caves form where there are _________ _________ _________ _________ or other soft rocks which are _________ _________ by the _________ _________ of water over a long period of time. These caves can be very extensive, with some _________ _________ _________ _________, and they offer some of the most _________ _________ _________ in the _________ of large stalactites and stalagmites. The second type of cave is called a sea cave. Sea caves form _________ _________ _________ and are created by _________ _________ that wears away softer rock. These caves are usually not very large compared to other types of caves, _________ _________ _________ _________ _________ _________ _________ being the largest yet found. The third type of cave I mentioned is _________. These caves can form almost anywhere and are created by the actions of water or wind _________ _________ the rock over many years. In deserts, the wind _________ _________ _________ which act as a sandblaster and wear away rock to _________ _________ _________. The final type of cave I want to talk about is glacial caves. These are created in large ice formations—typically glaciers—and are made by _________, _________ _________. Glacial caves are not very stable and can move and _________ as the glacier moves or melts. _________ _________ any type of cave is dangerous and should only be done in a group that _________ _________ _________.

International Relations

PREPARATION

A **Read the definitions and write the correct word in each blank.**

deterrence	exacerbate	brinkmanship	petition	isolationism

1 ___________ the art of threatening one's opponent to gain an advantage
2 ___________ prevention of something by threatening, often with weapons or punishment
3 ___________ to make a formal request to someone in authority
4 ___________ to make something worse than it already is
5 ___________ a policy of nonparticipation in foreign affairs that do not directly affect a nation

■ Now listen to the words and definitions and check your answers.

B **Fill in the blanks with suitable words or phrases on the list. Change the forms if needed.**

treaty	negotiation	in hindsight	conflict	neutral	occupation	retaliation

1 The _____________ of a peace treaty was difficult as both sides were very stubborn.
2 In most cases, one nation will not attack another for fear of _____________.
3 _____________, it is clear to see that Britain and France could have stopped Hitler before World War II began.
4 The greatest _____________ in history was World War II, during which over 60 million people died.
5 The _____________ of Korea by Japan is still a sore point in the relations of the two nations.
6 Several European nations, including Switzerland and Sweden, remained _____________ during World Wars I and II and did not take part on either side.
7 The _____________ was negotiated in a few weeks and then signed by the combatants.

■ Now listen to the sentences and check your answers.

■ **Match each expression with its proper meaning.**

1 That about sums it up.
2 I don't know why there is such a fuss.
3 It makes my blood boil.
4 Could you fill in the blanks?
5 No one had the guts to stop him.
6 There's no use flogging a dead horse.
7 There is a lot of pride at stake.

ⓐ It makes me really mad.
ⓑ Nobody was brave enough to do anything to stop him.
ⓒ It's just a waste of time.
ⓓ That's correct.
ⓔ It is important for my sense of worth.
ⓕ Tell me more about it.
ⓖ Why is it a problem?

■ Now listen to the sentences and check your answers.

■ Listen to the monolog and complete the organizer.

🔵 10-2

Start of World War I (1914-___(1)___)

Immediate Cause

- ___(2)___ of Franz Ferdinand, ___(3)___ to the Austro-Hungarian ___(4)___, on June 28, 1914, in Sarajevo
  - → Austro-Hungarians demanded to send their ___(5)___ to Serbia
  - → Serbia refused this

Underlying Causes

- system of ___(6)___ between nations offered military support in case of war
  - Serbia had a treaty with ___(7)___; Russia with ___(8)___; ___(9)___ had an understanding with France; and ___(10)___ / Austro-Hungarian with ___(11)___
  - German military plan: must attack France & Russia first by marching through ___(12)___ Belgium
  - ___(13)___ declared war on Germany

General Questions Based on the organizer, answer the questions.

1 **What is the main purpose of the talk?**

(a) To describe the beginning battles of World War I

(b) To examine the factors behind World War I

(c) To discuss the assassination of Franz Ferdinand

(d) To look at the German strategy for war

2 **Choose the best summary.**

(a) The great powers of Europe went to war in 1914 when an assassination triggered a series of events that led to war.

(b) The assassination of Franz Ferdinand was the sole reason many nations went to war in 1914.

Specific Questions Listen again. Mark T for true statements and F for false statements.

(1) Franz Ferdinand was next in line for the Austro-Hungarian throne. _____

(2) Germany refused to support Austria-Hungary against Russia. _____

(3) The Russians and the British had a solid treaty of mutual protection. _____

(4) The violation of Belgium's neutrality brought Britain into the war. _____

■ **Listen to the dialog and complete the notes.**

10-3

> **Dokdo Island :** two small ___(1)___ located in East Sea between Korea and Japan
>
> **Value :** - may have ___(2)___ and ___(3)___ reserves underneath them
>
>   - has plenty of ___(4)___ nearby
>
> **Ownership:** currently owned by ___(5)___ - a fisherman and his wife; mostly occupied
>
>   by ___(6)___, military, and ___(7)___ groups
>
> **Issue :** ownership of the island is disputed by ___(8)___
>
>   → ___(9)___ have strong feelings over the issue

General Questions   **Based on the notes, answer the questions.**

1 What is the main topic of the dialog?

(a) The natural resources of Dokdo Island

(b) Some reasons why Dokdo Island belongs to Korea

(c) A territorial dispute between Korea and Japan

(d) The inhabitants of Dokdo and their jobs

2 Choose the best summary.

(a) Despite Korea's effectual ownership of Dokdo Island, the Japanese are still making claims on it, which is angering the Korean people.

(b) The issue of who owns Dokdo is mainly about national pride due to Japan's past occupation of Korea.

Specific Questions   **Listen again. Mark T for true statements and F for false statements.**

(1) There are potential gas and oil resources near Dokdo Island.   ____

(2) Only government officials live on Dokdo Island.   ____

(3) The Japanese have stubbornly refused to dismiss their claim.   ____

(4) At first, the boy believes Dokdo Island has no value.   ____

■ Listen to the lecture and complete the organizer.　10-4

The Cold War

a long struggle between the United States on the side of ⁽¹⁾__________ and the Soviet Union on the side of ⁽²⁾__________ from 1946 to ⁽³⁾__________

Causes

- a ⁽⁴⁾__________ left at the end of World War II
  - the United States & the Soviet Union- the ⁽⁵⁾__________ nations
  - France & Britain - ⁽⁶⁾__________ by the war
  - Germany & Italy - defeated in the war
- the Soviets set up a ⁽⁷⁾__________ of communist nations in ⁽⁸⁾__________ Europe
- the division of Europe: the democratic ⁽⁹⁾__________ states ← America
  - the communist ⁽¹⁰⁾__________ states ← the Soviet Union

Highlights

- ⁽¹¹⁾__________ in many places such as Berlin, China, and Korea
- each side had massive ⁽¹²⁾__________ and huge military forces
- the Soviets could not compete ⁽¹³⁾__________ → the communist system came to an end

1 What is the purpose of the lecture?

(a) To describe a period of international tension

(b) To examine the causes of the Cold War

(c) To show why communism lost the Cold War to democracy

(d) To explain the differences in two ideologies

2 Choose the best summary.

(a) The Cold War, which ended with the collapse of communism in 1991, was a long period of tension around the world between America and the Soviet Union.

(b) The Cold War was a series of conflicts between communism and democracy whose outcome was determined away from the battlefield.

3   Mark T for true statements and F for false statements.

(1) The Cold War was partially caused by the outcome of World War II.   _____

(2) The Soviets decided to build a buffer zone in Western Europe.   _____

(3) The Cold War was decided by the economic power of each side.   _____

(4) Both sides competed to attain large armies and nuclear weapons.   _____

4   Why was there a power vacuum in Europe after World War II?

(a) The Soviets and Americans took the place of the European powers.

(b) The former great powers has been defeated or weakened by the war.

(c) The war had devastated the whole continent and left it weakened.

(d) European countries had no resources left to restore their homelands.

Dictation

Listen again and fill in the blanks.

w The Cold War was a long __________ between the __________ __________ __________ and the __________ __________ __________ that lasted from 1946 to 1991. At the __________ __________ the Cold War was the ever-present __________ between the United States on the side of democracy and the Soviet Union on the side of communism. The Cold War began as World War II __________ . Following the war, a __________ __________ __________ in Europe, and the __________ were the United States and the Soviet Union. France and Britain __________ __________ by the war, and Germany and Italy __________ __________ and __________ . Germany __________ __________ the __________ Allies at the end of the war, and the __________ __________ —America, Britain, France, and the Soviet Union—each occupied a section of the country. During the war, the Soviets had __________ __________ __________ and __________ __________ . To prevent this from happening again in the future, they __________ a __________ __________ of __________ in Eastern Europe. In addition, in their zone of Germany, the Soviets __________ __________ a __________ __________ . Soon, Europe was divided into the __________ __________ __________ supported by America and the communist eastern states supported by the Soviet Union. From this beginning, the Cold War __________ __________ __________ around the world. __________ __________ were the city of Berlin, China, Korea, Vietnam, Afghanistan, and many smaller places. Each side built __________ __________ __________ and __________ __________ that had the potential to go to war in a very short time. In the end, the Soviets could not __________ __________ , and the whole communist system came to an end by 1991.

■ Listen and answer the questions.   ● 10-5

1 What is the main topic of the talk?

(a) The relationship between Kennedy and Khrushchev

(b) The events surrounding the missile crisis in Cuba in 1962

(c) The reason that Cuba allowed Soviet missiles on its land

(d) John F. Kennedy's skill in international negotiations

(e) The deal that ended the Cuban Missile Crisis in 1962

2 Complete the table with the missing information.

Nation	Year Acquired	Number of Weapons
United States	1945	
Russia		
	1952	200
France		350
	1964	200
Israel		possibly 80
India	1970	
Pakistan		60

3-4

3 How did deterrence helped prevent a nuclear war between Russia and America?

(a) Each side knew the other could destroy it even if the other were destroyed first.

(b) Each side knew the other would not retaliate unless it was in a desperate position.

(c) Each side wanted an advantage over the other but could not get it because of nuclear weapons.

(d) Each side was reluctant to start a war because neither could surprise the other.

(e) Each side wanted to occupy the other side's land, so using nuclear weapons was not an option.

4 What can be inferred from the talk?

(a) Deterrence is the main strategy of the United States.

(b) Deterrence has been a failure most of the time.

(c) Deterrence applies to many human activities, not just war.

(d) Deterrence only works with nuclear weapons.

(e) Deterrence is an effective way to attack a country.

5-6

Level up

5 What was the main purpose of the League of Nations?

(a) It was a place to discuss the problems left after World War I.

(b) It was an organization used to stop wars by using military force.

(c) It was used as a trial run for the creation of the United Nations.

(d) It was a body where nations could talk about disagreements.

(e) It was a system of nations that were dedicated to peace.

6 **Choose the statement that best summarizes the dialog.**

(a) The League of Nations was an attempt to make a world military force, but it failed when no one offered troops.

(b) The League of Nations was a forerunner of the United Nations, but it ultimately failed due to its inherent weaknesses.

(c) The League of Nations was a failure from the beginning because the United States refused to join it.

7 **Listen to the question and answer choices and choose the correct answer.**

(a)   (b)   (c)   (d)   (e)

8 **Listen to the question and answer choices and choose the correct answer.**

(a)   (b)   (c)   (d)   (e)

9 **What is NOT true according to the talk?**

(a) Four leaders met at the Munich conference.

(b) The Sudetenland was a German territory.

(c) Hitler had a desire for all of Czechoslovakia.

(d) The Munich Agreement seemed effective at first.

(e) Britain and France supported Poland in 1939.

10 **Complete the table with the missing information.**

Number of current missions	
Longest ongoing mission	
Number of military and police in current missions	
Civilian support personnel	
Fatalities on missions	

11 **Why did the American public want a return to isolationism after World War I?**

(a) They felt they had been duped into joining the war.

(b) They supported the actions of Italy, Germany, and Japan.

(c) They were reluctant to enter a new, bloody war.

(d) They believed that America would be defeated in war.

(e) They did not support Britain's and France's policies.

12 **Choose the statement that best summarizes the talk.**

(a) Isolationism served America well as a foreign policy, but the country was dragged into war twice when it was attacked.

(b) America's had an isolationist policy before World War II because it felt it could not win a conflict with Japan, Italy, and Germany.

(c) America's isolationism, while initially keeping America out of wars, ultimately failed to prevent America from getting involved in them.

■ Listen and answer the questions.

1 Why did some Arab states make peace with Israel?
(a) They were defeated every time they attacked Israel.
(b) They worried about Israel attacking their oil fields.
(c) The Palestinian Arabs now have their own state.
(d) The British and UN negotiated peace treaties.
(e) They no longer have any problems with Israel.

2-3

2 What can be inferred from the dialog?
(a) The woman has a relative fighting in Iraq.　　(b) The man has been to Iraq in the military.
(c) The rally is being opposed by a peace group.　　(d) The man and woman are both Americans.
(e) The man knows someone who is in Iraq.

3 What will the woman probably say after the man's last comment?
(a) You are just a war lover and think that all war is just fun and games.
(b) I don't understand why you are doing this. All war is wrong!
(c) I understand why you are doing it, but I can't get behind this war.
(d) The government should bring the soldiers back home and end the war.
(e) Rallies to support the troops are a nice idea, but I'm too busy.

4-5

4 Why did the United States begin bombing North Vietnam?
(a) It was done to support the French military forces.
(b) It was used as a preliminary to an invasion of North Vietnam.
(c) It was meant to scare the North Vietnamese into surrendering.
(d) It was done on the advice of special forces military advisors.
(e) It was a reaction to a naval battle in the Gulf of Tonkin.

5 What can be inferred from the talk?
(a) The French won a lot of battles but ultimately lost the war against the Vietnamese.
(b) Without American intervention, South Vietnam easily defended its land from the North Vietnamese.
(c) The North Vietnamese did not approve of the division of their country in 1954.
(d) The Americans left the warzone after they were confident North Vietnam was defeated.
(e) The Americans approved of the North Vietnamese attempts to unite the country.

Level up

6 Listen to the question and answer choices and choose the correct answer.
(a)　　(b)　　(c)　　(d)　　(e)

Level up

7 Listen to the question and answer choices and choose the correct answer.
(a)　　(b)　　(c)　　(d)　　(e)

8 **Fill in names of the countries and the missing information on the chart.**

Country	Active Troops (Million)	Reserve Troops (Million)	Aircraft	Aircraft Carriers
China		0.8		0
United States	1.5	1	over 3,000	
			1,500	1
		4.7	over _____	0

【Integrated Questions】

■ Read the following passage and listen to the lecture.

After World War I ended on November 11, 1918, the leaders of the victorious Allies gathered in Paris to make peace. After several months, they presented five treaties to the defeated Central Powers and forced them to sign them. The most controversial of these treaties was the Treaty of Versailles that the Germans signed on June 28, 1919. The treaty has often been blamed for being a cause of World War II. It was a humiliation for the German people and led many to seek revenge for their loss. Four things stood out more than any others. First, the Germans were blamed for causing the war in the first place. This so-called "War Guilt Clause" infuriated the Germans and was simply not true. Second, the Germans were forced to pay money for the destruction of property that resulted from German attacks. Third, Germany's military was reduced to only 100,000 men, and they were not allowed to have any tanks, airplanes, or submarines. Finally, Germany lost large parts of its territory in the east and west. The German politicians had no choice but to sign the treaty. Adolf Hitler later claimed the nation had been stabbed in the back and used these facts to help build support for his Nazi party in the interwar years.

■ Now answer the following questions based on what you read and heard.

9 **What factor concerning the Treaty of Versailles is NOT true according to the information presented in the reading and listening?**

(a) It was humiliating for the German people.

(b) It has been blamed for starting World War II.

(c) It completely eliminated the German military.

(d) It was used by Hitler to rally people to his cause.

(e) It was signed by the Germans under threat.

10 **How did Hitler become leader of Germany in 1933?**

(a) He was elected directly by the German people.

(b) He was appointed because he had a large following.

(c) His Nazi party won the most seats in the legislature.

(d) He tore up the Treaty of Versailles to win support.

(e) He was feared by France, Britain, and America.

DICTATION [Exercise]

■ Listen and fill in the blanks.　　　　　　　　　　　　　　　🔵 10-7

1　W　In 1962, the world almost ________ ________ ________ ________ in a nuclear holocaust. In October of that year, American spy planes ________ ________ ________ on the island of Cuba, only 145 kilometers from ________ ________. The Soviets had placed the missiles there ________ ________ ________ ________ Cuba's communist leader, Fidel Castro. For thirteen days, a ________ ________ ________ the world as the Americans and Soviets ________ ________ ________ ________ over the missiles. The Soviets said the missiles were ________ ________ ________ and were a response to American nuclear missiles in Turkey, which were ________ close to the Soviet homeland. The Americans wanted the missiles removed and threatened to invade Cuba unless they were ________ ________. At the center of this crisis were American President John F. Kennedy and Soviet leader Nikita Khrushchev. Kennedy was younger and ________ ________, but ________ ________ ________ at this game of ________. Khrushchev realized too late that he had made a mistake and that to remove the missiles would be a ________ ________ ________ Soviet ________. Fortunately, ________ ________ ________, and the two sides ________ ________ ________ for the Americans to remove the missiles from Turkey and the Soviets to do the same in Cuba. Publicly, however, it was great ________ ________ for Kennedy, as the Soviets appeared to have given up and ________ ________ ________ American pressure. For Khrushchev, it was a ________ ________, as the Cuban Missile Crisis failure was key to his ________ ________ ________ two years later.

2　M　North Korea just ________ ________ another ________ ________. That's two tests since 2006.

　　W　Should we be worried about North Korea attacking someone?

　　M　I'm not worried. They don't have that many ________ ________. Some experts think they only have enough ________ to ________ ________ ________ ________.

　　W　One would be ________ ________ ________. Which countries have ________ ________? I know America and Russia have them.

　　M　Russia has the most. It has around 15,000, and America has around 10,000. The United States was the first country to get nuclear weapons in 1945, and it was ________ ________ Russia in 1949.

　　W　What about China? The Chinese ________ ________ ________ nuclear weapons a long time ago, too.

　　M　Actually, China was the ________ ________. The British were the third in 1952 and they were followed by the French in 1960 and the Chinese in 1964. All have ________ ________. France has about 350 weapons, and the British and Chinese have around 200 each.

　　W　So, that's everyone? I mean, it's still too many, but at least there is ________ ________ now that the ________ ________ ________ ________.

　　M　Hold on. We forgot about India and Pakistan, and those two are ________. India ________ its first ________ ________ in 1970, and Pakistan did the same in 1998. Each country has about 60 ________. And then there is Israel, which many people ________ ________ ________ ________ in 1967 and has about 80 weapons, but the Israelis have never ________ this.

　　W　I wish they would just ________ ________ ________ all of them to make the world safe.

3-4　M　In any kind of strategy, whether it is in ________ ________, ________, business, or even a common everyday situation, ________ may ________ ________ ________. ________ is based on the idea that

someone can be stopped from doing something because he or she does not want to ________ ________
________ ________. For example, a nation wants another nation's oil. It can ________ and buy the oil,
or it could ________ and take the oil. However, the first nation knows that the nation with the oil has a
________ ________, so it decides to negotiate for the oil. The ________ ________ ________ of the nation
with the oil acts as a ________ ________ the first nation. The first nation ________ that the ________
________ ________ are too great, and, therefore, the first nation is ________ from attacking. Unfortunately,
________ has not always worked, and nations ________ ________ ________ ________ even when they
know the other side is strong. This is mainly because they believe they can ________ and ________ the
other nation quickly. However, since the ________ ________ ________ ________, a new kind of deterrence
has ________ ________ ________. Surprise and speed in an attack ________ ________ ________ when
the enemy nation can ________ nuclear missiles in a matter of seconds and ________ ________ ________.
During the Cold War, the Russians and the Americans knew they would just ________ ________ ________
each other and the world, so their nuclear weapons acted as a ________.

5-6

M So, Janice, what would you like to write your ________ ________ ________?

G I was thinking about doing it on the United Nations.

M Well, another student is already doing that. How about doing yours on the League of Nations?

G I don't know much about it. What is it?

M The League of Nations came about after World War I. It was ________ ________ ________ ________
________ where nations could take their problems and try to ________ ________ ________ rather than
________ ________ ________.

G ________ ________ ________ like the United Nations now, isn't it?

M Yes, they ________ ________ ________ ________ the same idea of having a place where nations could
________ ________ ________. Unfortunately, the League of Nations was a ________.

G Really? Why was it a ________? Could you ________ ________ ________ ________ for me?

M Sure. First, the United States never ________ ________ ________.

G Really? Why not?

M Well, US President Woodrow Wilson wanted to join, but the American Congress and many Americans
did not want to ________ ________ ________ the League of Nations. They wanted ________ ________
________ Europe after the war ended.

G So what happened to the League of Nations?

M It proved to be ________. The Japanese ________ ________ ________ the league after it condemned Japan's
invasion of China in 1931. In 1935, Italy invaded Ethiopia, but the league could do nothing because it had
no ________ ________. After that, no one ________ ________ ________ ________ it.

G And no one had the ________ to stop Hitler when he ________ ________ in the late 1930s, right?

M Exactly. The Second World War started, but the League of Nations could do nothing to prevent it. It was
finally ________ in 1945 when the UN was created.

7

B It's been over 60 years since the Americans used the A-bomb on Japan.

G Why did they have to do that? I mean, in our history class, the teacher said that Japan was already ________
and was ________ ________ ________.

B Not everyone wanted to ________. There was ________ in the Japanese government and military. Japan still had millions of men in the army in Japan and China in 1945.

G But its ________ ________ ________, and its ________ ________ was destroyed.

B True, yet the Americans believed the Japanese would ________ ________ if they invaded Japan. Using the ________ ________ was a way to get them to surrender with ________ ________ ________ ________ ________.

G But almost 200,000 people died at Hiroshima and Nagasaki.

B Yes, but if there had been an invasion, millions of people would have died. It seems ________, but those were the ________ ________ ________ ________ ________ in those days. ________ ________, many think the atomic bomb helped save lives.

G I understand, but I still think the Americans ________ ________ ________ ________ ________ harder to negotiate for Japan's surrender.

8 M ________ is the art of negotiating with other countries to ________ ________ ________ ________. These aims are often related to getting what you want by giving up ________ ________ ________ ________. In some cases, ________ can result as one side ________ ________ ________ of the other, and this can lead to ________ ________ ________ ________. In a ________ ________, Saddam Hussein, the leader of Iraq for many years, misunderstood the intentions of the United States prior to his invasion of Kuwait in August 1990. He ________ ________ ________ with the American ________ to Iraq a short time before the invasion, and Hussein believed that the Americans ________ ________ ________ ________ Kuwait and would not ________ an Iraqi invasion. However, he couldn't have been more wrong. When his forces invaded and occupied Kuwait, the Americans were ________ ________ ________ to condemn the actions, and they later ________ ________ ________ that defeated the Iraqi army and ________ Kuwait.

9 W Appeasement is a ________ ________ used to give one side what it wants in order to avoid a more ________ ________ from that side. As a ________ ________, it has proven useful ________ ________ ________, but it also has a lot of ________ attached to it since ________ ________ often ________ ________ the Munich Agreement of 1938. At that time, Adolf Hitler was ________ ________ ________ toward Czechoslovakia by claiming that parts of that nation, called the Sudetenland, really ________ ________ Germany. A ________ ________ ________ in Munich between Hitler, Benito Mussolini of Italy, British Prime Minister Neville Chamberlain, and French Premier Edourad Daladier. ________ ________ ________ ________ discussions, it was agreed that the Germans would be given the Sudetenland. The Czechs ________ ________ ________ ________ ________, but they gave up after Britain and France failed to support them. This act of ________ of Hitler was ________ at the time for avoiding war, but, ________ ________, it is now seen as a ________ ________. Hitler could not be ________, and, in early 1939, Germany ________ the rest of Czechoslovakia and then ________ ________ ________ toward Poland. When Germany attacked Poland in September 1939, it was clear to all that Hitler could not be stopped ________ ________ ________. Britain and France ________ ________ ________ Germany in support of Poland, and World War II began. Ever since, the word ________ has been associated with ________ ________ ________.

10   B   I just got our assignment from the teacher. We have to do a presentation on UN ________.

G   That sounds like it's going to be tough.

B   I've already found a few websites. Let's have a look. First, what's the ________ of ________?

G   It says here that ________ is the use of ________ ________ ________ to separate warring parties and to act as ________ to ensure that the ________ of a ________ ________ are ________ ________.

B   Sounds good. How many ________ ________ are there currently?

G   Right now, there are 19 peacekeeping missions worldwide. The longest ________ one is in the Middle East. It started in 1948 during the first Arab-Israeli war.

B   Okay, let me ________ that ________. Oh, and here it shows the number of ________ involved and where they're from. There are 83,326 ________ and ________ ________ involved in UN peacekeeping missions. They come from 117 different countries. There are also around 15,000 ________ used for ________.

G   Have any of them been hurt while on peacekeeping missions?

B   Since 1948, 2,386 people have been killed while doing peacekeeping missions.

G   Wow, that's a lot. I didn't expect the number to be so high. How did they get killed? I mean they ________ ________ ________ ________ ________ ________.

B   They are supposed to be, but sometimes they're not. Some were killed by ________ and bombs, and others were killed by ________. Still others were ________ and ________ ________.

G   That's awful. Why should countries send troops if that is what is going to happen to them?

B   I guess if the UN and its member countries did nothing, these ________ ________ could be a lot worse.

11-12   W   Isolationism was an American ________ ________ during the period between World War I and World War II. During this time, America tried to ________ ________ from ________ ________. Prior to the 20th century, the United States had a long history of ________ ________ ________ ________ ________. When World War I started in 1914, America stayed out of the war until forced to ________ ________ ________ Germany in 1917 after German ________ began sinking American ships that were carrying cargo to Britain and France. After the war, many Americans felt they had been ________ ________ ________ war by the British, the French, and the ________ who made money by ________ ________ ________. There were calls for a return to ________. During the 1930s, ________ ________ ________ aggressive actions on the world stage by Japan, Italy, and Germany ________ ________, ________ ________ due to American ________. Britain and France were the world's ________ ________ at that time, but they were ________ to ________ ________ any enemy without American help. They knew they ________ ________ ________ World War I with American help, and they were afraid of defeat and of millions more dead in a new war. When the Japanese attacked China, Italy attacked Ethiopia, and Germany ________ ________ Austria and Czechoslovakia, ________ ________ ________ ________ to stop them. American President Franklin Roosevelt wanted to break America's ________, but ________ ________ ________ prevented him from doing so. When World War II ________ ________ in 1939 in Europe, America was once again a ________ and did not join the war until December 7, 1941, when the Japanese attacked Pearl Harbor in Hawaii and ________ America ________ ________ but to enter the war.

Astronomy and Space Flight

PREPARATION

11-1

A **Read the definition and write the correct word in each blank.**

consortium	propaganda	disintegrate	extraterrestrial	hoax

1 ___________ to fall apart
2 ___________ a plan to fool people into believing that something fake is true
3 ___________ methods or information used to discredit an opponent or to enhance one's own position
4 ___________ a combination of organizations set up for a common purpose
5 ___________ originating or occurring outside the Earth

■ Now listen to the words and definitions and check your answers.

B **Fill in the blanks with suitable words or phrases on the list. Change the forms if needed.**

gullible	one step ahead	from that point on	cosmonaut
fill in the blanks	dock	out of control	

1 The US-Soviet Space Race ended in 1975. _____________, the two countries began limited cooperation in space exploration.
2 The history of space flight has some missing details, so historians are still trying to _____________.
3 The common term used for a space traveler in the Russian space program is _____________.
4 In the Space Race, the Americans were always _____________ of the Soviets.
5 The rocket was unstable and went _____________ a few seconds after blasting off.
6 Many people have proven they are _____________ by believing the moon landings were faked by the American government.
7 The Space Shuttle is now _____________ with the International Space Station.

■ Now listen to the sentences and check your answers.

■ **Match each expression with its proper meaning.**

1 Sorry I took the wind out of your sails.   ⓐ It's a desire that seems impossible to achieve.
2 It's kind of a touchy topic.   ⓑ I don't know how to proceed.
3 Sign me up for that.   ⓒ I don't have all of the information.
4 It's a pie-in-the-sky dream.   ⓓ I want to do that.
5 I'm at a bit of a loss.   ⓔ I don't want to talk about it.
6 The details are sketchy.   ⓕ Do what you want to do.
7 Suit yourself.   ⓖ I didn't mean to discourage you.

■ Now listen to the sentences and check your answers.

■ Listen to the monolog and complete the organizer. 11-2

Telescopes

- used to view distant objects
- first designed by three (1) ________ inventors in (2) ________ - improved by Galileo

Refracting Telescope

- sees the image (4) ________ through a (5) ________
- has size limits due to (7) ________ - largest possible is a (8) ________ lens

(3) ________ Telescope

- sees the image with a (6) ________ by gathering light and bouncing it
- no (9) ________ - largest is (10) ________ meters located in Hawaii
- the best telescope images come from the Hubble Space Telescope ←

no distortion by the Earth's (11) ________

General Questions   Based on the organizer, answer the questions.

1 What is the purpose of the talk?

(a) To discuss the types of design and size limits of telescopes

(b) To describe the invention of and two main types of telescope

(c) To examine the reasons why mirror telescopes are better

(d) To prove that Galileo did not invent the first telescope

2 Choose the best summary.

(a) The two main types of telescope differ greatly in function and size, and this difference has had an influence on the ability of humans to explore the universe.

(b) The creation of the two main types of telescope, while having limits such as their size and their ability to see distant objects, has greatly enhanced human knowledge of the universe.

Specific Questions   Listen again. Mark T for true statements and F for false statements.

(1) The telescope was invented in Europe in the early 17th century.   _____

(2) Refracting telescopes have size limits due to people's inability to make larger lenses.   _____

(3) Telescopes in space produce better images because there is no atmosphere.   _____

(4) The largest reflecting telescope is located in the United States.   _____

■ **Listen to the dialog and complete the notes.**　　　● 11-3

Woman: needs to pick a (1)______________ class - (2)__________ has to take at least one
　　　　- thinks (3)__________ is boring
　　　　→ (☐ she decides to take it / ☐ she decides to sign up for physics class)

Man: suggests the woman take (4)__________ - took the class last year

　　　　↓ Advantages
　　　- interesting class, learned a lot of cool things
　　　- the (5)__________ and tests are (6)_______
　　　- used (7)__________ and saw the Space Shuttle
　　　- there is some tricky (8)__________ but do assignments (9)______________
　　　- the professor (☐ expects a lot / ☐ doesn't expect much) from non-astronomy majors

General Questions　Based on the notes, answer the questions.

1 What is the main reason the woman talks to the man?

(a) She wants him to convince her to do something.

(b) She needs his advice in order to make a class selection.

(c) She wants to know what her professor is like.

(d) She hopes he can help her in a certain class.

2 Choose the best summary.

(a) A woman decides to register for a university class after talking about it with someone who has taken the class before.

(b) A woman cannot make up her mind about which class to take, so she asks around to see which class is the best.

Specific Questions　Listen again. Mark T for true statements and F for false statements.

(1) The woman has already attended at least one year of university.　　_____

(2) Freshmen at the university can decide not to take a science elective.　　_____

(3) Students in the astronomy class work in groups to do their class assignments.　　_____

(4) The man used a telescope in astronomy, but it was a rather boring experience.　　_____

LISTENING DRILL ②

Pluto's Status

Situation

- discovered in 1930 and considered one of the nine planets till 2006
- now downgraded to (1) ____________ status
- decision made at the IAU conference in 2006

- made a new classification system for the solar system
  - classical planets: eight remaining planets
  - (2) ____________: Pluto and two others
  - small solar system bodies: (3) ________, (4) ________, and other small objects
  ▸ (5) ________: objects that orbit the classical planets
      - considered (6) ________

- have an independent, (7) ________ orbit around the sun
- have only (8) ________

Reasons for Change

- Pluto's orbit - (9) ____________
- at times (10) ____________ to sun than Neptune
- Pluto's (11) ____________ Charon - very large; may be a (12) ____________ itself

---

1 What is the main purpose of the lecture?

(a) To discuss a new planet classification system

(b) To examine the orbits of the different planets

(c) To show why some planets are called dwarf planets

(d) To explain why one planet's status has changed

2 Choose the best summary.

(a) An international conference decided on a new classification system for planets, which effectively reduced the nine well-known planets to eight.

(b) Because of a decision at an international conference, Pluto has been downgraded to the dwarf planet class for a variety of reasons.

3 Mark T for true statements and F for false statements.

(1) Classical planets must have regular orbits and have cleared the area of their orbit of objects other than satellites.   _____

(2) Pluto's moon Charon may someday no longer be classed as a moon.   _____

(3) Pluto's orbit around the sun is similar to that of the eight classical planets.   _____

(4) A new class of object was created for space objects that do not qualify as classical planets, dwarf planets, or satellites.   _____

4 Why are satellites NOT considered classical planets?

(a) They are not large enough to qualify as planets.

(b) They do not have moons orbiting around them.

(c) They have elliptical orbits, not regular orbits.

(d) They do not have their own solar orbits.

Dictation

Listen again and fill in the blanks.

M Today, I'd like to ____________________ , which is no longer a ______ . Well, actually, this is old news since it hasn't been considered a planet ____________ . From 1930, when it was ____________ , until 2006, Pluto was ____________ one of the nine planets. Now there are only eight of what are now called "____________ ." Pluto has been ______ to ____________ . All of this was decided at a ______ of the International Astronomical Union, or IAU, in 2006. The members ____________ a new ____________ for the ____________ and made three groups: classical planets, ____________ the eight ______ planets, dwarf planets, consisting of Pluto and two others, and small solar system bodies, consisting of ______ , ______ , and other ____________ . Objects that ______ the classical planets are considered separate and are called satellites despite some being larger than classical planets and dwarf planets. For example, Titan, which orbits Saturn, is ____________ . The IAU ______ that a classical planet must have an ______ , ______ orbit around the sun. It also must not have any bodies—such as asteroids— ______ it other than satellites. Pluto ____________ since its orbit is rather elliptical, and, at times, Pluto is even closer to the sun than ______ . In addition, Pluto's moon Charon is so large it may ____________ as a dwarf planet. There were some ______ about this ______ for Pluto, but, for the most part, the ______ at the conference agreed that the change was ______ . Now we just have to ____________ saying there are eight planets, rather than nine.

EXERCISE

■ Listen and answer the questions.

1 What is the main purpose of the talk?

(a) To discuss the age of the universe

(b) To give some basic facts about galaxies

(c) To explain how galaxies are formed

(d) To describe the composition of galaxies

(e) To show why galaxies have size limits

2 Complete the table with the information about the Earth.

Average Distance from Sun	___________ kilometers
Period of Solar Rotation	________ Earth days
Period of Rotation on its Axis	___ h ___ m ___ s
Diameter at the Equator	___________ kilometers
Average Surface Temperature	___________________

3 What was the main reason the Russians lost four cosmonauts?

(a) Inexperience in operating complex spacecraft

(b) Inability to rescue cosmonauts in trouble

(c) Rushing to get untested spacecraft into flight

(d) Failure to set up the space station properly

(e) Mechanical failures of key spacecraft parts

4 What can be inferred from the talk about the *Columbia* shuttle disaster?

(a) The astronauts knew there was a hole in the wing but decided to land anyway.

(b) The crew had to try to land because *Columbia* was running out of fuel and oxygen.

(c) Ground control noticed the wing damage, but this information was withheld from the crew.

(d) There was no method set up to observe external damage to the shuttle during flight.

(e) Experts on the ground had done tests and did not believe that foam could damage the shuttle's wings.

5 What is a key factor in the size of a star and its longevity?

(a) The ability to convert helium into hydrogen and the masses involved

(b) The composition and mass of the initial material that forms the protostar

(c) The transition from a red giant to a planetary nebula to a white dwarf

(d) The size of the giant molecular cloud that the protostar comes from

(e) The size of the star's inner core before becoming a white dwarf

6 Choose the statement that best summarizes the dialog.

(a) Stars have life cycles like other living organisms and ultimately die out when their supply of hydrogen and helium is exhausted.

(b) Stars evolve through several stages of life as they burn brightly for a short time before transforming into the black inner core of the star.

(c) Stars go through many stages of life, with some differences depending on their mass and their ability to convert hydrogen into helium.

7 **Listen to the question and answer choices and choose the correct answer.**

(a)　　　(b)　　　(c)　　　(d)　　　(e)

8 **Listen to the question and answer choices and choose the correct answer.**

(a)　　　(b)　　　(c)　　　(d)　　　(e)

9 **What is NOT true according to the talk?**

(a) Solar eclipses do not have very long life spans.

(b) The sun covers the moon during a lunar eclipse.

(c) Earth blocks the moon's sunlight during a lunar eclipse.

(d) Eye protection is not needed during a lunar eclipse.

(e) The moon covers the sun during a solar eclipse.

10 **How long would it take a spaceship traveling at light speed to reach the sun from the Earth?**

(a) 51.6 minutes

(b) 310 seconds

(c) 9.3 minutes

(d) 8.6 minutes

(e) 1 second

11 **What is the main reason the lecture suggests the Northern Hemisphere would receive more people if the Earth were closer to the sun?**

(a) It would receive continuous sunlight for part of the year.

(b) It is very mountainous, so it would not flood from melting icecaps.

(c) Its polar ice cap would melt, thereby providing more water.

(d) It has more space than the Southern Hemisphere.

(e) It has more snow and ice so it would stay cooler.

12 **Choose the statement that best summarizes the lecture.**

(a) Earth's position in space supports life on Earth, and any slight change in this position would result in mass migrations.

(b) Earth is the only place that has life in the solar system because of its location, which makes it not too hot or cold.

(c) Earth is located in a position in space where life can exist, but any change in this position would end all life on Earth.

PRACTICE TEST

■ Listen and answer the questions.

11-6

1 **Which statement about sunspots is correct?**
(a) The umbra is the outer part of a sunspot.
(b) The maximum sunspot cycle is every 11.3 years.
(c) Sunspots have been recently discovered.
(d) Sunspots may affect weather on our planet.
(e) Less radiation is produced by sunspot activity.

2-3

2 **How do the boy's feelings at the beginning of the dialog compare with his feelings at the end?**
(a) Wishful thinking – Extreme sadness
(b) Hopeful desire – Reluctant acceptance
(c) Dark despair – Sudden hope
(d) Total indifference – Tragic depression
(e) Endless optimism – Complete apathy

3 **What will the girl probably say to the boy next?**
(a) you could start a campaign to raise money for it.
(b) you might just try to become wealthy and then build it yourself.
(c) it will happen in just a few years from now if we wish hard enough.
(d) perhaps your grandchildren will see your dream come true someday.
(e) we could write a letter to the government asking them to do it.

4-5

4 **What is NOT true according to the lecture?**
(a) Both the Soviets and Americans used captured German scientists in their space programs.
(b) The Americans launched the first satellite into orbit around the Earth.
(c) The Soviets launched a man into space only a short time before the Americans did.
(d) Reaching the moon before the Soviets became one of the priorities of the Kennedy administration.
(e) The Space Race ended in the 1970s after the Soviet Union and the U.S. had a change in relations.

5 **According to the lecture, why was the Space Race so important to the Soviet Union and the United States?**
(a) It was a sign of their economic and technical power.
(b) It was symbolic of the worth of their competing ways of life.
(c) It showed that even space was under their control.
(d) It proved that they were the best countries in the world.
(e) It was an alternative to going to war over their differences.

Level up

6 **Listen to the question and answer choices and choose the correct answer.**
(a)　　(b)　　(c)　　(d)　　(e)

Level up

7 **Listen to the question and answer choices and choose the correct answer.**
(a)　　(b)　　(c)　　(d)　　(e)

8 Complete the table with the missing star classification information.

Star Type (Largest to Smallest)	Color	Approximate Temperature (Kelvin)	Brightness (1 Equals the Sun)
O	blue		30,000 and higher
	blue-white	10,000–30,000	
A		7,000–10,000	5–25
	yellowish-white	6,000–7,000	1.5–5
G	yellow	5,000–6,000	
K	orange		0.08–0.6
M		2,000–4,000	Less than 0.08

9-10 〔Integrated Questions〕

■ Read the following passage and listen to the lecture.

A question that many people often raise is whether there is life outside the Earth. So far, the answer is, "No, there isn't." Scientific probe landings on Mars and flyby observations of other planets have not found any signs of life. This does not mean life doesn't exist somewhere else in the universe. Logically, with millions of galaxies, trillions of stars, and endless possibilities for solar systems and Earth-like planets, the conditions for life must be present somewhere. The main reason we haven't discovered this life is the great distances involved. Even sending scientific probes to the distant parts of the solar system took decades to achieve. In addition, the most powerful telescopes have spotted nothing to prove life exists elsewhere. Now, what about all of those UFO sightings and claims by people to have been abducted by aliens? Isn't this proof of life in the universe outside of Earth? Most of the claims for UFO sightings have had logical explanations when they were closely examined. Some were military aircraft, some were weather balloons, some were birds, and some were well-executed hoaxes. Have people been abducted by aliens? As the evidence is based entirely on the abductees' tales and without any independent proof, it is hard to agree whether these claims are true or not.

■ Now answer the following questions based on what you read and heard.

9 Why is it logically possible that there is life in the universe outside the Earth?

(a) There are people who say they have been captured by aliens.

(b) Telescopes have spotted what looks like life on other planets.

(c) The vast number of stars means that other Earth-like planets probably exist.

(d) The sheer number of UFO reports means that some must be true.

(e) Probes sent throughout the solar system have found evidence of life.

10 What can be inferred from the reading and listening about the claims of UFO sightings and alien abduction?

(a) There is a government plan to cover up all such incidents.

(b) There is evidence that extraterrestrial beings visited the earth in the past.

(c) No spaceships have ever visited or crashed on Earth.

(d) We may never know if some of the stories are true or not.

(e) It is all an elaborate hoax to fool the people of the world.

■ Listen and fill in the blanks. ● 11-7

1 W Galaxies are large ________ ________ ________ that form the basic units of the universe. It is estimated that there are millions upon millions of galaxies in the universe. They ________ ________ ________ and ________, but all formed in the ________ ________. Astronomers generally agree that the ________ ________ ________ the Big Bang about ________ ________ years ago. At this time, there were only ________ ________, helium, and hydrogen in the universe. Gradually, over the course of some ________ ________ ________, clumps of dark matter ________ and gathered together to ________ ________ ________. Eventually, they had enough mass to ________ ________, which ________ more dark matter, helium, and hydrogen. This early form of a galaxy is called a ________. The shape of the galaxy now ________ ________ another billion years. The helium and hydrogen moved toward the ________ ________ of the galaxy, called the ________, while the dark matter ________ ________ the ________ ________, which is called the halo. In the core, the helium and hydrogen ________ and began to create the first stars. Also, in the center of the core an ________ ________ ________ formed, which ________ the galaxy ________ ________ too large by ________ ________ ________ its center during the early period of the galaxy's formation. Without this black hole, astronomers believe there would be ________ ________ ________ how large a ________ ________ ________.

2 W The Earth is our home, yet a lot of people know very little about it. Today, I am ________ ________ Bruce Campbell, who is going to ________ ________ some of the ________ for us.

M Thanks, Wendy. Well, I'm at a bit of a loss. Where should I start?

W How about with a few basic facts about the Earth?

M Certainly. In ________ ________ ________, Earth is the third planet from the sun. It is, ________ ________, ________ ________ kilometers away from the sun, but it's sometimes a bit closer and sometimes a bit ________ ________.

W But not too close, I hope!

M No, no, just a few million extra kilometers. The Earth's ________ ________ ________ around the sun is ________ ________ ________.

W I've always thought it was 365 exactly. Is that why we ________ ________ ________?

M Yes, because the ________ is not exactly 365 days, ever four years we must add a day to our calendars to make up for the difference. Now you should also know that the day itself is not exactly 24 hours. It is 23 hours, 56 minutes, and 4.2 seconds long. This is the time it takes the Earth to ________ ________ ________ ________.

W Okay, what about some of the ________ ________ of the Earth?

M The Earth is about ________ kilometers in ________ at the ________, but, again, this is not the same in every direction as the Earth isn't a ________ ________. Finally, I guess I should mention the ________ ________ of the Earth's surface is ________ ________ ________, which is what makes life possible here.

3-4 W The exploration of space has ________ ________ ________ ________, not just ________ ________ ________ money but also in human lives. Since the Space Age began in 1957, many people have died in accidents on the ground, and 18 people have lost their lives in ________ ________. Four of the dead were Russian ________, who died in ________ ________ ________ during their return to Earth. In one accident in 1967, the spacecraft's ________ ________ ________ ________ properly, and the lone cosmonaut ________ ________ ________ ________ the Earth. In the second incident in 1971, three cosmonauts died from depressurization. A ________ had ________ ________ ________ properly when they were preparing to return to Earth after ________ ________ a ________ ________. The ________ 14 people died in the two American Space Shuttle disasters. The first ________ ________ January 28, 1986, when the shuttle *Challenger* ________ ________ ________, killing its seven occupants. A ________ ________ revealed that ________ ________ from one of the ________ ________ ________ had ________ the main fuel tank. The second Space Shuttle disaster involved the ________ ________ the *Columbia* on reentry on February 16, 2003. It was later determined that, ________ ________, a piece of ________ ________ the fuel tank had ________ ________, struck the ________ ________ of the left wing, and made a hole in the left wing. This was unknown to all, and, ________ ________, the wing began to disintegrate, causing the shuttle to ________ ________ ________ ________ and also to disintegrate, killing all seven astronauts ________ ________.

5-6

G So, what did you ________ ________ ________ for our project?

B One of the more ________ ________ ________ stars is that they have ________ ________ like ________ ________.

G But they aren't living things, are they? Stars are just ________ ________ ________ that come from ________ ________ ________ ________.

B Right. And these ________ ________ ________ ________ were mostly composed of helium and hydrogen. They collapsed, and ________ ________ into ________ ________, which formed the beginnings of stars, called ________.

G So, a ________ is the ________ ________ ________ a star?

B Yes. Eventually, most ________ ________ ________ stars by the fusion of hydrogen into helium.

G Just like in a ________ ________.

B Yes, but on a much more ________ ________. The size and life of the star ________ ________ the masses involved and the ability of the star to ________ hydrogen into helium.

G What did you find out about our sun?

B It's a medium-sized star that ________ ________, but, thankfully, it'll never ________ great mass. Our sun is currently about ________ ________ ________ ________ ________ years old.

G When will it die?

B One website said that by the time it is nine to ten billion years old, its ________ ________ will be ________. Then, the sun will ________ ________ a massive ________ ________ and will eventually explode and become a ________ ________.

G Right. That is a glowing cloud of ________ ________ ________ that eventually disappears. Is that the final stage of a star's life?

B No. What will remain is the collapsed ________ ________ of the sun, which will be about the size of the Earth. This is called a ________ ________. This remnant will continue to ________ ________ ________ for many millions of years and will finally just become a black rock, which is the final stage of star death.

7

W I heard that a Korean woman has ________ ________ ________ ________ astronauts. You must be proud of her and of your country.

M Yes, we are all very proud. Yi So-Yeon went into space in 2008 aboard a Russian spaceship. The ship ________ ________ the International ________ ________, and she spent around ten days there.

W That's amazing. What did she do while she was ________ ________ the space station?

M I'm not sure. I recall that she was ________ some ________ ________, something to do with ________ ________, and, maybe, I think, she observed Chinese ________ ________ ________ into Korea. But don't ________ me on that.

W Wasn't a man ________ ________ the first Korean to ________ ________ ________, but his flight was cancelled?

M Ah, not exactly. He was replaced. This is a little embarrassing and is ________ ________ a ________ ________.

W Oh, I'm sorry.

M It's okay. The reason they ________ ________ ________ was that the Russians think he ________ ________ ________ while he was training in Russia. The details are ________, so it's best not to say much about it.

W I understand.

8

W Approximately 50 ________ ________ from the sun, or fifty times the distance from the Earth to the sun, lies the Kuiper Belt. Astronomers believe this donut-shaped region is where all of the ________ ________ ________ the sun ________ ________ ________ come from. ________ are not the only objects in the Kuiper Belt. Astronomers estimate there are ________ ________ ________ in this region. Some are ________, some are ________, others are ________ ________ ________ ________, and many others have yet to be examined. Most of the objects examined are over 96 kilometers ________ ________, and six of them are larger than 800 kilometers ________ ________. Pluto is considered to be in the Kuiper Belt due to its distance from the sun. Astronomers are ________ ________ ________ ________ this region and are ________ many of the ________ ________ because some objects that could ________ ________ ________ the Earth in the future may come from the Kuiper Belt.

9

M There are two main types of eclipses—solar and lunar. Both types ________ ________ and only when there is a ________ ________ ________ the Earth, sun, and moon. During a solar eclipse, the moon covers the sun, but during a lunar eclipse, the Earth is between the moon and the sun and ________ ________ ________. Lunar eclipses can be seen over a large part of the world and can last for ________ ________ ________ ________, but solar eclipses can only be ________ ________ ________ ________ ________ several hundred kilometers wide and do not last for a long time—often ________ ________ ________ minutes. Solar eclipses can be either partial or total. During a ________ ________, only part of the sun may be covered by the moon's alignment with it. During a ________ ________, the entire sun is covered by the moon. The ________ ________ ________ is that, because of the distance the Earth is from the sun and the moon, both the sun and the moon appear to be the same size to an observer on Earth. ________ ________ a total solar eclipse need to ________ ________ ________ ________ ________. During a solar eclipse, people can ________ ________ ________ by the ________ ________ the sun's light when the eclipse ________ ________ ________. Using a viewer designed to observe solar eclipses is the best way to avoid this danger. With lunar eclipses, there is no such danger.

10

G Dad, what's a light year?

M Where did you hear that term?

G From this science fiction show. It said a planet was only a few hundred light years away, and then the spaceship was there _________ _________ _________ _________. That's not possible, right?

M _________ _________, that's for sure. It's not possible without a faster-than-light-speed ship. A light year? _________ _________ _________ _________ _________ I can, imagine the light from a flashlight. Now, if you took that light and _________ _________ _________ the sky, the distance that the light _________ in _________ _________ _________ is a light year.

G What's the speed of light?

M I don't know exactly. I guess we can _________ _________ _________.

G I'll do it. Hmm... This astronomy book says the speed of light is approximately _________ _________ per second, which is about _________ _________ per second.

M Let's do an experiment. How long would it _________ _________ _________ _________, say, the sun, from Earth, at the speed of light?

G You want me to _________ _________ _________?

M Sure, why not? How far is the sun from the Earth?

G That's an easy one because we did that in science class this term. I think it was _________ _________ miles.

M Right. Now, if your spaceship had a _________ _________, how long would it take to reach the sun?

G I need a calculator first. Let's see. Just one second... Ah, I've got it.

11-12

W Why is there life on Earth but not on Mars or Venus? It is because of _________ _________. Earth is in a unique position among the planets in that it is not too close to the sun so that _________ _________ _________, nor is it so far away that we're in a _________ _________ _________ winter. With an _________ _________ of _________ _________ _________, Earth is ideal for life. If the temperature were just a few degrees colder or hotter, our ecosystems on Earth would be _________ _________ that life might not survive. Imagine if _________ _________ somehow changed to make us closer to or _________ _________ _________ the sun, yet the change was so slight that life was still _________ _________. There would be _________ _________ in where people live. If the Earth moved closer to the sun, then the _________ _________ would become _________ _________, and people, animals, and plants could not survive there. There would be _________ _________ north and south, with most people going north due to its _________ _________. _________ _________ of the Northern Hemisphere, such as Canada, Alaska, and Russia would become _________ _________ _________ on an Earth that moved closer to the sun. Of course, things might get too unbearable if one moved too far north or south, since the _________ _________ get almost _________ _________ for part of the year. Also, the _________ _________ would most likely _________ _________ _________, _________ _________ a rise in the world's ocean levels, which would cause even more people to migrate. The opposite would occur _________ _________ _________ away from the sun. The _________ and _________ regions of the planet would be too cold to support life while the _________ _________ would be _________ by those escaping the cold.

Human Health

PREPARATION

12-1

A **Read the definitions and write the correct word in each blank.**

temptation	circadian	incubation	quarantine	inconclusive

1 ___________ to isolate people who have infectious diseases

2 ___________ the period when a disease is developing inside a host and when there are no symptoms

3 ___________ a desire or craving for something

4 ___________ uncertain; not decisive; not convincing

5 ___________ related to the daily cycles of living things

■ Now listen to the words and definitions and check your answers.

B **Fill in the blanks with suitable words or phrases on the list. Change the forms if needed.**

on edge	overwhelm	worse comes to worst	relapse	nausea	alleviate	waste away

1 I'm _____________ with work. I have too much to do and no time to do it.

2 Medication can _____________ the symptoms of many common illnesses.

3 Many people who quit smoking have a _____________ and begin again.

4 Some diseases cause the body to _____________, making a person weaker and more helpless until death.

5 Sorry, but I'm just a little _____________ because I am worried about my exam results.

6 I'd avoid that medication because it can cause _____________ and diarrhea.

7 If _____________, they will have to operate on me to fix the problem.

■ Now listen to the sentences and check your answers.

Expressions and Meanings

■ **Match each expression with its proper meaning.**

1 I'll give it my best shot.

2 They spoil him rotten.

3 Deal with these projects ASAP.

4 This constitutes a barrier.

5 Sure, fire away.

6 Maybe you could drop something.

7 It once more reared its ugly head.

ⓐ They give him whatever he wants.

ⓑ This is an obstacle.

ⓒ Give up something that you are involved in.

ⓓ Something bad occurred again.

ⓔ I'll try my hardest.

ⓕ Okay, go ahead.

ⓖ Take care of these things as soon as possible.

■ Now listen to the sentences and check your answers.

■ Listen to the monolog and complete the organizer.

12-2

Ginseng

Basic Facts of Ginseng

- a plant common to [1] _____________
- has a fork-shaped [2] _____________ which is taken

Healthy Benefits

- increased [3] _____________
- improved [4] _____________
- reduced [5] _____________
- reduced risk of [6] _____________
- used in treatment of diabetes
- may have an [7] _____________ effect on [8] _____________

Problems with Ginseng

- [9] _____________
- [10] _____________
- nausea
- diarrhea

studies on medicinal properties have been [11] _____________

General Questions Based on the organizer, answer the questions.

1 What is the main purpose of the talk?

(a) To examine the health properties of ginseng

(b) To describe the ways that ginseng is eaten

(c) To prove that ginseng has some health benefits

(d) To show that medical studies can be inconclusive

2 Choose the best summary.

(a) Despite years of study, the medicinal qualities of ginseng have not yet been proven true.

(b) While some healthy benefits of ginseng have been proven true, there is still more research needed.

Specific Questions Listen again. Mark T for true statements and F for false statements.

(1) People who take ginseng have shown no noticeable side effects. _____

(2) Ginseng helps prevent some types of cancer from coming back. _____

(3) Not all studies have proven that ginseng has medicinal benefits. _____

(4) Ginseng seems to be beneficial at curing infections. _____

■ **Listen to the dialog and complete the notes.**

12-3

Topic of the dialog: the girl's little brother's weight - (1) __________ than the girl

Boy's opinion: being overweight is not (2) __________ → her parents need to do something

▸ **What his mother does:** • never buys (3) __________

　　　　　　　　　　• only let him get ice cream on (4) __________ , like his (5) __________

　　　　　　　　　　• don't let him watch too much TV

Girl's opinion: blames her parents for her brother's problem

▸ **What her parents do:** • let her brother eat (6) __________

　　　　　　　　　　• let her brother watch cartoons and play (7) __________

　　　　　　　　　　• her mother works so she has no time to (8) __________

　　　　　　　　　　- eats a lot of (9) __________ → the girl (☐ likes / ☐ dislikes) it

---

General Questions — Based on the notes, answer the questions.

1 What is the main point of the dialog?

(a) Eating and living healthy should begin in childhood.

(b) The parents are to blame for a child's weight problems.

(c) Snack foods are a temptation that should be avoided.

(d) Weight gain is usually the result of an unhealthy lifestyle.

2 Choose the best summary.

(a) A girl laments that her parents do not show enough concern for her brother's health problems, which are related to his weight issues.

(b) A girl explains how her brother's weight issues are related to the way her parents treat him as well as the family's lifestyle.

Specific Questions — Listen again. Mark T for true statements and F for false statements.

(1) The boy noticed that the girls' brother has gained weight. _____

(2) The boy's family has a similar lifestyle to that of the girl's family. _____

(3) The girl's parents do not have enough time to prepare meals. _____

(4) The girl and her brother have the same tastes in food. _____

■ Listen to the lecture and complete the organizer.　　12-4

Genetically Modified Food

Basic Facts

- Definition: plants that have their [^(1)]________ altered
- Purpose: ① to make plants more [^(2)]__________ to insects or [^(3)]__________
  ② to make them less [^(4)]________ to herbivores
  ③ to [^(5)]________ slowly to have a longer [^(6)]__________
- Examples: soybeans, corn, rice, canola, potatoes, sugarcane, cotton /
  some attempts to modify [^(7)]________ and [^(8)]________

Benefits

- crops have greater chance of [^(9)]________
- crops can be [^(10)]________ in more places

➡ alleviate the world's hunger problems

Drawbacks

- concerns about possible health [^(11)]______________
  - [^(12)]________ and Japan: genetically modified food has to be labeled
  - [^(13)]______________: do not have to label genetically modified food
- are [^(14)]________ by the designers, and farmers in poor countries can't afford the seeds

---

1 Which is NOT a purpose of genetically modifying crops according to the lecture?

(a) To grow them almost anywhere　　(b) To solve global hunger problems

(c) To harvest them more easily　　(d) To make them stay fresh longer

2 Choose the best summary.

(a) While genetically modified food enables crops to be grown in more areas and ensures greater survivability, issues about possible health problems and availability make them controversial.

(b) Although genetically modified food can survive almost anywhere, many poor farmers cannot afford the seeds, a fact that prevents genetically modified food from spreading to poorer countries.

3 Mark T for true statements and F for false statements.

(1) Genetically modified plants have a greater chance of being harvested.   _____

(2) In Europe, food labels must give information on genetically modified food.   _____

(3) Genetically modified food is quite common in economically challenged areas.   _____

(4) It has been proven that there are health issues with genetically modified food.   _____

4 What is the main obstacle to genetically modified plants spreading to poor areas?

(a) Health concerns over the possible side effects of these plants

(b) Economic issues concerning the purchase of these plants

(c) Problems related to these plants adapting to different areas

(d) Difficulties related to the patent rights for these new plants

Dictation

■ Listen again and fill in the blanks.

M _____________________ is any food that has had its _____________ in some way. _____________ is almost always _____________ _____________ although there have been some _____________ to some _________. The main reasons for doing genetic alterations are to make the plants more _____________ or _________, to make them _____________ to herbivores, and to allow them to _____________ and thus have _____________. By making _____________ to the things that would have _____________, they have a greater _____________ and can be grown in more areas than possible _____________ genetic modifications. Currently, the most common genetically modified plants are _______, corn, rice, _______, potatoes, _________, and _______. There are also some _____________ to genetically _____________ and _______. Genetically modified food has _______ a _____________ whether it is _____________. There are fears that people _____________ as-yet-unknown side effects from eating genetically modified food. To _____________, in Europe, Japan, and several other countries, food _____________ to tell _______ if it is _____________. In North America, however, _____________ do not have to _____________ as such. There are some _____________ that genetically modified food _______ the world's _____________ because it can be grown in more areas and the _____________ more dangers. However, genetically modified plants are _____________ the designers, and farmers have to _____________ the right to _____________. For many poor farmers in the _______, this _____________ to them _______ and possibly enjoying any _____________ genetically modified crops.

EXERCISE

■ Listen and answer the questions. 

1 What is the main purpose of the lecture?

(a) To describe the way a disease is transmitted from animals to people

(b) To discuss how people changed their eating habits because of a disease

(c) To describe the negative effects of a disease on a certain industry

(d) To examine the media's role in causing a panic about a disease

(e) To prove that a certain disease is not as deadly as many people think

2 Complete the chart with information on blood pressure from the dialog.

Type of Blood Pressure	Systolic	Diastolic
Normal		
High	over 120	over 80
Low	under __________	under __________
Mr. Davis, 1st Reading		
Mr. Davis, 2nd Reading		

3 According to the talk, what is the major weakness of pathogens?

(a) They cannot survive after making someone ill.

(b) They depend on a host for long-term survival.

(c) They cannot be transmitted from humans to animals.

(d) They can only survive in water and food sources.

(e) They are destroyed by high doses of radiation.

4 What can be inferred from the talk?

(a) Viruses are the deadliest form of pathogen mentioned.

(b) Many cancer patients get infections after radiation treatment.

(c) Bats have a very strong immunity to many diseases.

(d) The smallpox virus needs a living host in order to live a long time.

(e) Prions cause more diseases than other types of pathogens.

5 Why won't the girl give up any of the things she is doing?

(a) She loves all of the things she does and does not want to stop.

(b) She hates everything she does but cannot find a way to quit.

(c) She needs to do some things, and others are just hobbies she likes.

(d) She has trouble saying no to people, so it is easier not to quit.

(e) She feels that she is too deeply committed to quit anything now.

6 Choose the statement that best summarizes the dialog.

(a) A boy tells a girl that the best way to reduce her stress is by doing school projects first every day.

(b) A boy advises a girl to work faster in order to reduce the amount of stress she has at present.

(c) A boy gives a girl some tips on reducing her stress and advises her to do less and to say no to people more often.

7 Listen to the question and answer choices and choose the correct answer.

(a)   (b)   (c)   (d)   (e)

8 Listen to the question and answer choices and choose the correct answer.

(a)   (b)   (c)   (d)   (e)

9 **What is NOT true according to the talk?**

(a) Korean women have longer life expectancies than men.

(b) A stroke can result from a very stressful lifestyle.

(c) Heart disease is currently the leading cause of death in Korea.

(d) It is uncertain whether kimchi causes stomach cancer or not.

(e) Liver illness is directly connected with the drinking of alcohol.

10 **Complete the information on the sleeping habits for the various age groups.**

Age Group	Average Hours of Sleep Per Day	Common Time for Falling Asleep
Babies		anytime
Children		
Teens	8-10 hours	
Adults		

11 **What can be inferred from the lecture?**

(a) The Odone family spent a fortune discovering the oils that make up Lorenzo's Oil.

(b) Although ALD is most common in boys, there have been some cases of girls getting the disease.

(c) A lack of certain food oils plays a role in the destruction of the myelin nerve coverings in ALD.

(d) There is as yet no method to detect if a boy has the genetic mutation which can cause ALD.

(e) The Odone family holds the patent rights to Lorenzo's Oil and has reaped substantial rewards from it.

12 **Choose the statement that best summarizes the lecture.**

(a) The deadly disease ALD has been cured largely through the efforts of Lorenzo Odone's parents, who created the oil named after him.

(b) Lorenzo's Oil is not a cure for ALD, but it is a treatment whose actual value is uncertain because not all boys who take the oil have signs of the disease.

(c) The hereditary disease ALD was a death sentence for Lorenzo Odone and other boys until his parents discovered a treatment for it in the 1980s.

■ Listen and answer the questions. 

1 Why is third-hand smoke considered a health problem?
(a) It can linger on people's clothes and cause skin trouble.
(b) Infants and children live in homes where people smoke.
(c) It harms the health of nonsmokers who breathe in the smoke.
(d) Residue from tobacco products can be taken in through the skin.
(e) It has negative effects on the health of those who smoke indoors.

2-3

2 What can be inferred from the dialog?
(a) Flossing is not really necessary for children and teens.
(b) The girl's school does not enforce the brushing of teeth after lunch.
(c) The girl's parents do not care about her dental health.
(d) Brushing one's teeth four times a day ensures good dental hygiene.
(e) Most people get nervous when they visit the dentist.

3 What will the dentist probably say to the girl next?
(a) Certainly. Just spit in this cup, and you can go.   (b) No, now I have to pull those decaying teeth.
(c) Not yet. You haven't been completely honest.   (d) After I tell your parents about your bad habits.
(e) Oh, no, now I need to look inside. Open wide.

4-5

4 Which health issue has green tea NOT been associated with?
(a) Fewer negative effects of Parkinson's and Alzheimer's disease
(b) A decrease in the incidence of breast cancer in women
(c) Reduced levels of lung cancer in Chinese and Japanese people
(d) Lower blood pressure and a smaller chance of heart disease
(e) Less incidence of cancer of the stomach and intestines

5 What can be inferred from the talk?
(a) Green tea is only beneficial if it is consumed every day.
(b) Other types of tea have similar health benefits as green tea.
(c) Green tea is beneficial at curing various types of cancer.
(d) The consumption of green tea is common outside of Asia.
(e) Research into green tea's health benefits is ongoing.

Level up

6 Listen to the question and answer choices and choose the correct answer.
(a)   (b)   (c)   (d)   (e)

Level up

7 Listen to the question and answer choices and choose the correct answer.
(a)   (b)   (c)   (d)   (e)

8 **Complete the graph showing the numbers of people who survived out of those who contracted Ebola in the years mentioned.**

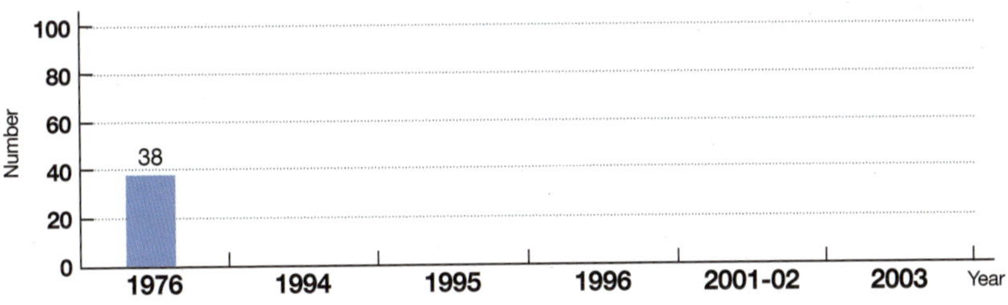

 【Integrated Questions】

■ Read the following passage and listen to the lecture.

A pandemic is an outbreak of a deadly disease that spreads widely and kills a great many people. In history, there have been several major pandemics, but none was as catastrophic as the Black Death. Now recognized as the bubonic plague, the Black Death may have originated somewhere in Asia or the Middle East. The plague first appeared in Europe in 1347, and, after six years, 30 million people had died in Europe while a further 45 million died in other lands. More recently, a form of influenza struck down approximately 50 million people worldwide between 1918 and 1920. This illness may have begun at army camps in America or Europe. It is also believed to have been passed from animals, possibly pigs or sheep, to humans. It killed mostly young people and spread at such a rapid rate that quarantine measures had little effect. Concerns over outbreaks of such a pandemic in modern times are well justified. In this modern age of air travel, a disease can spread around the world in a short time. Some pandemics may not be visible as a pandemic until after many years. The example of AIDS, which has spread from Africa around the world and has killed an estimated 22 million people since 1980, is but one example. The current H1N1 swine flu outbreak has not yet reached the same level as the 1918 outbreak, but it very easily could unless it is stopped in its tracks.

■ Now answer the following questions based on what you read and heard.

9 **Which is NOT correct about pandemics according to the reading and listening?**
(a) They occur quickly or take a long time to become a pandemic.
(b) They can be controlled through strict quarantine measures.
(c) They can spread through the use of international transportation.
(d) They occur once and do not appear in the same place again.
(e) They have been better controlled in modern times than in the past.

10 **What can be inferred from the reading and listening?**
(a) The Black Death has been eradicated worldwide.
(b) Some pandemics have a long incubation period.
(c) The current H1N1 flu is similar to the 1918 flu strain.
(d) All airports have temperature-sensing cameras.
(e) One third of the world died in the 1918 flu pandemic.

DICTATION (Exercise)

■ **Listen and fill in the blanks.** 12-7

1

M Okay, everyone, I'm sure you've heard about ________ ________ ________, or Creutzfeldt-Jakob disease. It is a disease that ________ ________ the ________ ________ and eventually ________ ________ ________. There is ________ ________ ________. It is ________ ________ ________ from animals, usually ________, which are ________. Humans ________ ________ the disease ________ ________ ________ of beef. People who are ________ ________ mad cow disease gradually ________ ________ ________ all of their ________ ________ until death occurs. The ________ of many cases in Britain in the 1980s ________ ________ ________ that ________ ________ over four million British ________ ________ ________, and many people ________ ________ ________ ________. In America and Canada, a few cases of the ________ ________ of the disease in beef cattle ________ ________ ________ of the beef industry in both nations. ________ ________ ________ over mad cow disease, only ________ ________, most of them in Britain, ________ ________ of it so far. However, many more people ________ ________ ________ because the disease has a ________ ________ ________—from many months to a few ________. In response to ________ ________ ________ of the disease, many people have ________ ________ ________ beef because of ________ ________ ________ mad cow disease. The ________ of beef has long been ________ ________ causing heart and ________ ________, which kill millions of people worldwide every year. ________, it took a disease that has killed very few to ________ ________ ________ that beef is an ________ food choice.

2

W So, Mr. Davis, it seems your ________ ________ is a ________ ________ ________.

M Oh, how high was it?

W Normal blood pressure is ________ ________ ________ over 60 to 80. ________ ________ ________ than this, we have a problem. Yours was a little high at ________ ________ ________.

M Ah, I really ________ ________ what you just said.

W We ________ ________ ________ with millimeters of mercury ________ ________ the old ________ ________ ________ that we used to use.

M Okay, I think I understand so far.

W Good. There are ________ ________ ________ blood pressure: systolic, which is the ________ ________ ________ ________ in the arteries, and diastolic, which is the lowest amount of pressure. ________ ________ ________ is 90 to ________ ________ of mercury. Normal diastolic pressure is 60 to 80.

M So my systolic was 130, and ________ ________ ________ ________?

W Yes. Let's ________ ________ ________. Some people ________ ________ when visiting a doctor. Try to ________ ________. Think of a ________ ________.

M Ah, okay, I'm thinking... Okay, I'm there.

W Just a moment... and there. Now it's ________ ________ ________. It's still a bit high on the systolic.

M What should I do?

W Lose a bit of weight, ________ ________, eat ________ ________, and ________ ________ ________.

M What happens if I can't get my ________ ________ ________?

W You could have a ________ ________ or a ________. If ________ ________ ________ ________, we can always ________ ________ ________ ________.

M I'll certainly ________ ________ ________ to ________ my blood pressure.

3-4   W   I would now like to _______ _______, which _______ _______, _______, viruses, and prions. _______ _______, a pathogen is any kind of _______ _______ that can introduce a disease into a host. Pathogens are _______ _______ the _______ _______ _______ in humans and animals. This transmission is usually the _______ _______ the _______ of water or food that is _______ _______ the pathogen. Once one animal or human is _______, then the pathogen can _______ _______ _______. Some pathogens _______ _______ _______ for a long time and _______ _______ _______ the animals but can still be _______ _______ _______. An example of this is the many types of _______ _______ _______ _______. These infections are _______ _______ to the bats but can _______ _______ or other animals if they _______ _______ by the bat. Sometimes, the pathogen is _______ _______ in animals and humans, such as with _______ _______ _______, which is _______ _______ prions. Humans and animals have _______ _______ that can _______ the body _______ _______ by pathogens, but sometimes this immune system is _______. For example, a person _______ _______ _______ for cancer may have a _______ _______ _______ that can allow a pathogen to _______ _______ _______ the person. Fortunately, many pathogens cannot survive _______ _______ a host body for long, so _______ _______. However, some, such as _______, can survive for a few years outside of a host body.

5-6   B   What's the matter? You _______ _______ and _______ _______ _______.

     G   There just never seems to be _______ _______ _______ _______ all of the things I have to do. I _______ _______.

     B   I think you _______ _______ _______ _______ in your life. You _______ _______ _______ more.

     G   I wish I knew how. I've _______ _______ _______ for the _______ _______ _______, I have two projects and two papers due in the next month, I'm _______ _______ _______ team, and I'm involved in student government.

     B   Maybe you could _______ _______ to _______ _______ _______ on yourself.

     G   No, I am _______ _______ _______ in everything. I can't _______ _______ _______. Not now.

     B   Then you need to _______ _______ _______ _______ _______ your stress. Are you getting enough sleep?

     G   About six hours a night.

     B   That's not enough. You need _______ _______ _______ _______ of good sleep.

     G   I'll try. What else can I do?

     B   _______ _______ _______ _______ in the evening. _______ _______ would be a bath. Don't drink coffee or _______ _______ _______ in it. And _______ _______ these projects ASAP. Get one of them _______ _______ _______. And do a little bit on the others each day. By _______ _______ _______ these problems, then you will _______ _______ _______.

     G   Got it.

     B   And there's one more thing. Don't try to do so much at the same time. _______ _______ _______ _______.

     G   I _______ _______ _______ to say no to people when they ask me to do stuff.

     B   _______ _______ _______ how to say no, or all of this stress is going to make your head _______ some day.

7   W   _______ _______ the Silver Sun Health Club, Mr. Watson.

     M   Hi. It's _______ _______ _______ in a health club, and I really _______ _______ _______ where to start. What kind of _______ _______ _______ _______ I do?

W You should do a ________ of ________, ________, and anaerobic exercises.
M Sorry, but could you ________ ________?
W There are two ________ ________ of exercise: aerobic and anaerobic. Aerobic exercise ________ your ________ ________ ________ and increases your ________. It's a lower-intensity exercise that is done for a long time.
M Ah, like when you ________ or ________ ________? That kind of thing?
W Yes, running is ________ ________ ________ ________ ________ exercises. Now, anaerobic exercise is for ________ ________ ________. It's an ________ ________ that is done for shorter periods. ________ ________ is the ________ ________ of anaerobic exercise. You ________ and ________ ________ ________ by doing different exercises. ________ ________ the weights helps ________ ________ ________ ________.
M What is the ________ ________ of muscle mass?
W First, it makes your body ________ ________. But, most importantly, increased muscle mass ________ your body's ________ ________ ________ fat and to maintain a healthy body.

8 W Since ________ ________, it has been known that ________ ________ have the ________ ________ ________ the health of the human body while a ________ ________ ________ ________ can cause problems. It ________ ________ the ________ ________ ________ that ________ ________ that certain elements in food, which we ________ ________ ________, were the reason for this. There are two main types of vitamins: ________ and ________ ________. Water-soluble vitamins are ________ by the body ________ ________ and therefore ________ ________ of the body ________ ________ ________ ________. These types of vitamins ________ vitamin B and C and ________ ________ ________ daily through food or ________. The second type is fat-soluble vitamins. They are absorbed by ________ ________ in the ________. As such, they can ________ ________ in the body for a long time and do not need to ________ ________ on a ________ ________. This group includes vitamin A, D, E, and K. Unfortunately, people sometimes ________ ________ ________ of these vitamins, so their bodies may have ________ ________, such as ________ ________.

9 M The ________ ________ of Koreans is ________ ________ ________ ________ and 80 years for females. ________ 275,000 people die in Korea each year. In 2008, the ________ ________ of death were ________, followed by cerebrovascular disease and ________ ________. The leading ________ ________ ________ in Korea are those that ________ ________ ________ ________, the stomach, and the ________. Cerebrovascular diseases are those ________ ________ the ________ ________ that ________ ________ to the brain. Sometimes, there is ________ of these blood vessels. This is called a ________, and it can lead to death or ________. Deaths for heart diseases can be ________ ________ into two types: ________ ________ and ischaemic heart problems. Cardiovascular problems are related to the ________ ________ ________ ________ while ischaemic heart problems ________ ________ ________ ________ ________ in and out of the heart. ________, some of these health problems are ________ ________ ________ the lifestyles of Koreans. In particular, high stress ________ ________ and ________ ________ ________ ________ cerebrovascular and heart disease. Cancer of the lungs and other parts of the ________ ________ is a result of the ________ ________ ________ ________ while liver problems are ________ ________ the ________ of alcohol. Finally, the high incidence of stomach cancer may or may not be the ________ ________ the ________ ________ Koreans enjoy. While some studies ________ that the overconsumption of ________ ________, in particular spicy kimchi, is the ________ ________ ________ ________, other studies suggest kimchi has ________ ________.

10

W James, that's the __________ __________ this month you have __________ __________ in my class. I want to know __________ __________ __________ in your life that is __________ __________ __________ __________.

B I'm sorry, Ms. Roberts, but your class __________ __________ 8:30 AM. It's just __________ __________ for me.

W What time do you go to sleep?

B About 1 or 2 AM. I know I should __________ __________ __________ __________. I tried that, but I __________ __________ __________ before then.

W Well, it's not really __________ __________. It's the __________ __________ of teenagers.

B The what?

W Circadian rhythms. They are what __________ your body's __________ __________. For example, __________ __________ seven or eight hours a night. They usually go to bed __________ 10 PM and midnight __________ __________ will sleep from __________ __________ __________ hours a day at any time of the day or night. __________ __________ __________ __________, the need for sleep __________, and the time we sleep changes. Children over five can sleep eight to ten hours and usually go to bed between 8 and 10 PM.

B What about __________?

W Teenagers sleep __________ __________ __________ __________ a day also, but many sleep __________ __________ __________ __________. Their circadian rhythms make them __________ __________ in the late evening than in the morning. Teens __________ __________ go to sleep between 10 PM and __________. However, many teens __________ __________ __________ because of __________ or __________ __________, or they watch TV or movies.

B That's about right. Then we __________ __________ __________ __________ and take these early classes.

W You are just __________. Your body __________ __________ __________ than you are getting. At least try to go to bed before midnight.

B I'll __________ __________ __________ __________ __________.

11-12

W There is a __________ __________ __________ genetically __________ __________, called ALD, which __________ __________ __________. ALD __________ usually __________ when the boy is __________ __________ and __________ __________ __________, and the __________ __________ about one to two years later. The __________ __________ myelin, which is the __________ __________ __________ __________, and this destruction __________ the nerves __________ __________ __________ to parts of the body. The body __________ __________ __________, and the child loses the __________ __________ __________, speak, see, and talk __________ __________ __________. There was no __________ __________ until an American couple found one __________ __________ __________ __________ in the 1980s. In 1984, five-year-old Lorenzo Odone __________ __________ __________ ALD, and his parents __________ __________ a cure. Eventually, they __________ __________ __________ a __________ of different oils __________ __________ __________ __________, which __________ __________ Lorenzo's Oil. The __________ __________ Lorenzo Odone's disease __________ __________ __________ in 2008 at the __________ __________ __________. Other __________ of ALD have had __________ __________, with some slowing and stopping the __________ of the __________ of the myelin nerve coverings. However, the oil is __________ __________ __________ but __________ __________ __________ that prevents the myelin covers __________ __________ __________. It is unknown if the oil prevents the __________ of ALD. Currently, boys who test for the __________ __________ causing ALD __________ __________ __________ before there are signs of the disease. However, not all boys with the genetic problem develop ALD. Therefore, if boys who are __________ __________ Lorenzo's Oil don't __________ __________ __________, it is not certain if it was the oil that prevented the disease __________ __________. In spite of that, for those parents whose sons have the __________ __________ and have not been __________ __________, Lorenzo's Oil is a __________ __________.

Listening AVIATOR

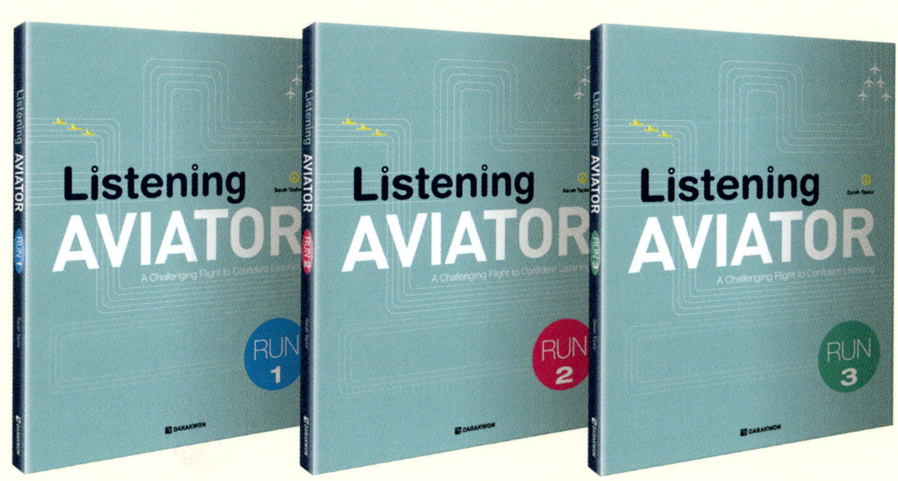

전반적인 리스닝 실력을 향상시키고 고난도 리스닝 연습에 대비하려는 중학생을 위한 교재

초급 이상의 리스닝 실력을 갖춘 중학생이 단계적 훈련을 통해 전반적인 리스닝 실력을 월등히 향상시킬 수 있도록 구성된 교재. 다양한 일상주제별 지문과 각종 리스닝 시험에 등장하는 주요 유형의 문제들을 단계적으로 익히고 훈련할 수 있다. 같은 초급 단계라도 1권에서 3권으로 갈수록 시문의 길이가 조금씩 길어지며, 문제 난이도도 점차 높아진다.

교재	구성	페이지	가격
Listening AVIATOR ⟨RUN⟩ 1	교재 + 해설집 + MP3 CD 1개	본책 152 pages + 해설집 72 pages	14,000원
Listening AVIATOR ⟨RUN⟩ 2	교재 + 해설집 + MP3 CD 1개	본책 152 pages + 해설집 72 pages	14,000원
Listening AVIATOR ⟨RUN⟩ 3	교재 + 해설집 + MP3 CD 1개	본책 152 pages + 해설집 80 pages	14,000원

Listening TOP

Answer Book

Reach for Excellence!

Listening TOP

Answer Book 3

DARAKWON

 UNIT 01 Psychology

Vocabulary Preview

A

1 **pigeon-hole**: 어떤 것을 특정 범주에 놓다
2 **credence**: 어떤 것이 사실이라는 믿음
3 **sadistic**: 잔인한 방식으로 행동하는 것과 관련이 있는
4 **relish**: 어떤 것을 굉장히 즐기다
5 **docile**: 온순하고 통제하기 쉬운

B

1 **compulsive** / 중독은 사람이 자신의 행동을 통제할 수 없는 충동적인 행동의 한 형태이다.
2 **got out of hand** / 경기가 제지할 수 없는 정도가 되어 심판들이 두 팀의 난폭한 플레이를 더 이상 통제할 수 없었다.
3 **foul mood** / 사장님이 하루 종일 기분이 안 좋아 별 이유 없이 사람들에게 소리를 지르고 있다.
4 **ticked off** / 나는 오늘 버스에서 한 남자가 핸드폰으로 큰 소리로 통화를 계속해서 정말 화가 났다.
5 **a pain in the neck** / 하루 종일 문제를 처리하는 것은 골치 아픈 일이어서 많은 스트레스를 야기할 수 있다.
6 **source of contention** / 어떤 정신 질환의 원인은 종종 심한 의견 차가 있는 전문가들 사이에 논쟁을 일으킨다.
7 **trauma** / 심한 심리적 스트레스를 받는 사람들은 정신적인 충격을 겪을 수 있다.

Expressions and Meanings

1 모든 이들이 하루 종일 성가시게 굴었어.
2 그는 젊음을 놓치기를 원치 않는다.
3 사람들이 어쩜 저렇게 뻔뻔스러울 수 있어!
4 그것은 전문가들 사이에서 논쟁의 여지가 있다.
5 난 모두를 실망시킬 거야.
6 난 고민을 털어 놓고 싶을 뿐이야.
7 그것은 사실에 근접해.

f 오늘 사람들이 나를 굉장히 귀찮게 했어.
a 그는 영원히 젊음을 유지하기를 원한다.
b 어떤 사람들은 하지 말아야 할 말을 해.
g 모든 사람이 그 해답에 동의하는 것은 아니다.
c 난 많은 사람들을 실망시킬 거야.
e 난 내 문제를 상의하고 싶을 뿐이야.
d 그것은 정답에 매우 가까워.

Monolog

O (1) immature (2) men (3) Peter Pan (4) responsibility (5) others (6) mistakes (7) wishes (8) younger (9) children (10) fact (11) burden (12) responsibilities

G 1 (c)   2 (b)

S (1) T (2) F (3) F (4) T

W Not many people want to get old, but most of us eventually outgrow our childish ways when we become adults. However, some people never want to let go of their youth. Some feel this way to the extent that it becomes a psychological problem. An American, Dr. Dan Kiley, created the term Peter Pan syndrome to describe this behavior, especially as it applies to a very immature adult male. The idea is based on British author J. M. Barrie's play about Peter Pan, a fictional boy who lives on an island where children never grow old. Kiley coined the term in 1983 in his book *The Peter Pan Syndrome: Men Who Have Never Grown Up.* Common characteristics associated with Peter Pan syndrome are the inability to accept responsibility, a desire to blame others for one's mistakes, failure to acknowledge others' wishes, and doing things usually associated with much younger people. Kiley's theory caused some controversy when it first came out. Women thought they had finally discovered the reason why men sometimes act like little children. Men felt that the idea of Peter Pan syndrome had no basis in fact or was a simplification of a more complex issue, the problem of society placing too many burdens on men, such as the burden to be a protector and provider for the family. Men claimed they only act like children at times to escape from the crushing burdens of responsibility society places on them.

▶ **outgrow** (성장하여 습관, 취미 등을) 벗어나다, 벗어버리다 **childish ways** 유치한 습관이나 버릇 **psychological problem** 정신적(심리적) 문제 **immature** 미숙한; 미발달의 **play** 연극; 희곡, 각본 **fictional** 꾸며낸, 허구의; 소설의, 소설적인 **coin the term** 용어를 만들다 **fail to acknowledge** 몰라주다 **controversy** 논쟁, 논의 **simplification** 편이화, 간이화; 단일화 **complex issue** 복잡한 문제 **burden** 부담 **protector** 보호자, 옹호자; 원조자 **provider** 가족 부양자; 공급자 **crushing** 압도적인, 결정적인

여 나이 들기를 원하는 사람은 많지 않지만 우리 대부분은 성인이 되면 유치한 습관에서 벗어나게 됩니다. 하지만 어떤 사람들은 젊음을 절대 놓으려고 하지 않습니다. 어떤 이들은 그것이 정신병이 될 정도로 집착하게 됩니다. 미국인 댄 카일리 박사는 특히 매우 미성숙한 성인 남자에게 적용되는 이 행동을 묘사하기 위해 피터팬 증후군이라는 용어를 만들었습니다. 이 개념은 아이들이 결코 나이가 들지 않는 섬에 사는 가상의 소년 피터 팬에 관한 영국 저자 J. M. 베리의 희곡에 기초하고 있습니다. 카일리는 1983년 그의 책『피터팬 증후군: 어른이 되지 않은 사람들』에서 그 용어를 만들었습니다. 피터 팬 증후군과 관련된 보편적인 특징은 책임을 지지 못하고, 자신의 잘못에 대해 남 탓을 하고, 다른 사람들이 원하는 것을 몰라주고, 대개 훨씬 어린 사람들이 하는 행동을 한다는 것입니다. 카일리의 이론은 처음 나왔을 때 논란을 일으켰습니다. 여자들은 마침내 남자들이 왜 어린 아이들처럼 행동할 때가 있는지를 알아냈다고 생각했습니다. 남자들은 피터팬 증후군이라는 개념에 근거가 없다고 생각하거나, 보다 복잡한 문제, 즉 남자들에게 가족의 보호자 및 부양자가 되어야 한다는 부담처럼 너무 많은 짐을 지우는 사회의 문제를 단순화한 것이라고 느꼈습니다. 남자들은 사회가 주는 엄청난 책임의 부담에서 벗어나기 위해 때때로 아이들처럼 행동하는 것일 뿐이라고 주장했습니다.

General Questions

1 담화의 주제는 무엇인가?
(a) 미성숙한 남자들과 여자들 사이의 관계
(b) 심각한 문제에 대한 문학적 은유 사용
(c) 심리학적 이론을 둘러싼 논란
(d) 남자들이 어른이 되지 않으려 할 때의 행동 방식

2 다음 중 가장 잘 요약된 것을 고르시오.
(a) 피터팬 증후군은 사람들이 늙어가면서 젊음을 유지하려는 방법과 관

련된 증명되지 않은 이론이다.
　(b) 피터팬 증후군이 철없이 행동하는 성인 남자들과 관련이 있기 때문에 남자들과 여자들은 피터팬 증후군의 타당성에 대해 이견이 많다.

Specific Questions

다시 듣고 옳은 문장에는 T, 틀린 문장에는 F를 쓰시오.
(1) 카일리 박사의 피터팬 증후군 이론은 J. M. 베리의 작품과 연관이 있다.
(2) 책임을 받아들이는 것은 남자들의 피터팬 증후군의 징후이다.
(3) 많은 여자들은 피터팬 증후군 이론의 진실성에 회의적이었다.
(4) 남자들은 자신들이 종종 아이 같은 행동을 하는 것을 사회가 너무 많은 책임을 지운 탓으로 돌린다.

Dialog

N (1) nervous / stage　(2) sick　(3) let　(4) down / becomes ready for the show / cheers up the boy　(5) nervous　(6) actors　(7) audience　(8) underwear

G 1 (a)　2 (a)

S (1) F　(2) T　(3) T　(4) F

G　Tomorrow's the night of the big play. Are you ready?

B　I've memorized all of my lines but... I think I'm going to quit.

G　What? That's crazy! You can't quit now. What's the matter?

B　I just can't do it. I'm scared to be in front of all of those people.

G　Oh, you just have a little stage fright, that's all.

B　No, really, I think I'll throw up if I have to stand on that stage for an hour and do the play. Just thinking about it is making me sick.

G　Relax. It's natural to get nervous before a performance. Even some of the biggest stars get nervous.

B　I can't help it.

G　Don't worry. Most people have some anxiety before they have to perform in front of so many people. But you realize it is too late to quit now.

B　Yeah, I guess I'd be letting everyone down. What can I do?

G　Before you go on stage, take some deep breaths and calm yourself. Then, look at the other actors. Don't look at the audience. Try to think of it like practice when no one is watching. If that doesn't work, imagine the audience in their underwear.

B　Ha ha. In their underwear? That'd be too funny.

G　See? You already feel better. And just remember that it's just a middle school play. It's not the most important thing in the world.

B　Thanks for all your advice. I think I'm ready for the show to go on.

▶ lines 대사　stage fright 무대 공포증　anxiety 걱정, 근심, 불안

여　내일밤이 대(大) 공연일이네. 준비됐어?
남　내 대사는 다 외웠지만… 난 그만둬야 할 것 같아.
여　뭐라고? 미쳤구나! 지금 그만둘 순 없어. 무슨 일이야?
남　그냥 못하겠어. 그 많은 사람들 앞에 서는 것이 두려워.

여　오, 넌 가벼운 무대공포증이 있는 것뿐이야, 그뿐이라고.
남　아니, 정말로 난 한 시간 동안 무대에 서서 연극을 해야 한다면 토할 것 같아. 생각하는 것만으로도 속이 울렁거려.
여　진정해. 공연 전에 긴장하는 건 당연해. 몇몇 대스타들조차도 긴장하니까.
남　난 어쩔 줄을 모르겠어.
여　걱정 마. 사람들은 대부분 많은 사람들 앞에서 연기를 하기 전엔 긴장을 해. 하지만 지금 그만두기에는 너무 늦었다는 걸 알잖아.
남　아는데, 모든 사람을 실망시키게 될 것 같아. 어떻게 해야 하지?
여　무대에 나가기 전에 심호흡을 하고 마음을 가라앉혀. 그러고 나서 다른 배우들을 봐. 관객을 보지 말고. 아무도 보지 않을 때 하는 연습이라고 생각하도록 해. 만약 그게 잘 되지 않으면 관객들이 속옷 바람이라고 상상해봐.
남　하하. 속옷 바람? 그럼 정말 웃기겠다.
여　봐. 벌써 기분이 나아졌잖아. 그리고 이건 그냥 중학교 연극이라는 것을 기억해. 세상에서 가장 중요한 일이 아니라고.
남　충고 고마워. 난 연극을 할 준비가 된 것 같아.

General Questions

1　소녀가 소년에게 이야기를 하는 주된 이유는 무엇인가?
　(a) 그가 긴장감을 이겨내도록 도와주기 위해
　(b) 그가 자기 대사를 알고 있는지 확인하기 위해
　(c) 더 나은 배우가 되기 위한 방법을 논의하기 위해
　(d) 그가 연기를 못할 정도로 아프지 않다는 것을 확인하기 위해

2　다음 중 가장 잘 요약된 것을 고르시오.
　(a) 소년은 연극 전에 심각한 무대 공포증을 겪고 있지만 그의 두려움은 친구의 좋은 조언으로 가라앉는다.
　(b) 소녀는 소년이 연극을 그만두고 싶을 정도로 심각한 무대 공포증을 겪게 되면 소년의 역할을 떠맡아야 한다.

Specific Questions

다시 듣고 옳은 문장에는 T, 틀린 문장에는 F를 쓰시오.
(1) 소녀는 연극에서 소년을 대신하고 싶어한다.
(2) 소년은 다른 배우들이나 관객을 실망시키고 싶지 않다.
(3) 소녀는 소년에게 마음을 가라앉히는 데 유머를 사용하라고 제안한다.
(4) 소년은 아파서 연극에서 연기를 안하고 싶어 한다.

Listening Drill 2　　　　　　　p. 12~p. 13

Long Lecture

O (1) inaccurate　(2) did nothing　(3) nothing　(4) someone else　(5) responsibility　(6) in danger　(7) help　(8) all theirs　(9) shared

1 (b)　　**2** (b)　　**3** (1) F　(2) T　(3) T　(4) F　　**4** (d)

Dictation 정답: 스크립트 밑줄 참조

M　There is a famous case in American criminal history that helped start an area of psychological research related to why people help or don't help people in distress. On the night of March 13, 1964, Kitty Genovese was murdered outside her apartment building in New York. A sensational newspaper article claimed that 38 people had witnessed the crime but did nothing to help the woman. This report was later proven inaccurate, but it caused an outrage and led to a deeper study of the way people behave when they are bystanders in a large crowd and witness an event where people are in distress. First, people in crowds often do not <u>call</u> <u>the</u> <u>police</u> when they witness a life-threatening event. When <u>asked</u> <u>why</u>, many thought someone else had already called the police. This <u>behavior</u> <u>suggests</u> they did not want to <u>accept</u> responsibility for calling the police, so <u>they</u> <u>assumed</u> someone else had already done so. Therefore, there was no <u>burden</u> <u>placed</u> <u>on</u> them. Second, when asked why they did not <u>help</u> <u>the</u> <u>victims</u> in these life-threatening situations, many people said that no one else was helping, so they <u>saw</u> <u>no</u> <u>reason</u> to get involved themselves. <u>Getting</u> <u>involved</u> would only <u>place</u> <u>them</u> <u>in</u> <u>danger</u> also. The <u>conclusion</u> <u>reached</u> by the researchers was that when in a group, people are <u>less</u> <u>likely</u> <u>to</u> <u>help</u> someone <u>in</u> <u>trouble</u> even if that trouble is life-threatening. However, studies done on <u>similar</u> <u>situations</u> where only one or a few people were <u>witnesses</u> showed that they almost always help the victims. <u>When</u> <u>alone</u> or in a small group, the <u>responsibility</u> is all theirs to do something, and it is <u>not</u> <u>shared</u> <u>among</u> so many, so they act.

▶ distress 고통, 비통, 비탄; 곤란   sensational 선정적인, 인기 끌기 위주의
witness 목격하다, 보다   report 보도, 기사   bystander 방관자, 구경꾼
life-threatening 생명을 위협하는   get involved 말려들다

남 곤경에 빠진 사람들을 왜 돕거나 돕지 않느냐에 관련된 심리학적 연구 분야가 시작되는 데 일조한, 미국 범죄 사상 유명한 사건이 있습니다. 1964년 3월 13일 밤에 키티 제노비스는 뉴욕에 있는 자신의 아파트 밖에서 살해되었습니다. 선정적인 뉴스 기사에서는 38명의 사람들이 그 범죄를 목격했지만 그 여자를 돕기 위해 아무것도 하지 않았다고 주장했습니다. 이 기사는 후에 부정확하다는 것이 증명되었지만 이는 분노를 일으켰고, 군중 속의 구경꾼으로서 사람들이 고통받는 사건을 목격했을 때 행동하는 방식에 대한 심층적인 연구를 하게 되는 원인이 되었습니다. 첫 번째로, 군중 속의 사람들은 종종 생명을 위협하는 사건을 목격하더라도 경찰에 신고하지 않습니다. 왜냐는 물음에, 많은 사람들은 다른 누군가가 이미 경찰에 신고를 했을 거라고 생각했다고 합니다. 이 행동은 경찰에 신고하는 책임을 지고 싶지 않은 나머지 다른 누군가가 이미 신고했을 거라고 생각한다는 것을 시사합니다. 그러니 그들에겐 어떠한 부담도 남지 않는 것이죠. 두 번째로 그들에게 왜 이 생명을 위협하는 상황에서 피해자들을 돕지 않았냐고 물었을 때 많은 사람들이 말하기를, 아무도 돕지 않고 있었기 때문에 자신도 말려들 이유가 없었다고 말했습니다. 거기 연루돼 봤자 자신들도 위험에 처하게 될 뿐이라는 거죠. 연구원들이 내린 결론은 사람들은 집단 속에 있을 때는 곤경에 빠진 사람들을 잘 안 도와주는 경향이 있다는 것입니다. 그 곤경이 생명을 위협하는 것이라도 말이죠. 하지만 단 한 명 또는 소수의 목격자가 있는 비슷한 상황에서 이루어진 연구에서는 목격자들이 거의 그 피해자를 돕는 것으로 나타났습니다. 혼자 또는 작은 무리에 있는 사람들은 어떤 일을 할 책임이 모두 자신에게 있고, 그 책임감을 많은 사람들과 공유할 수 없기에 행동을 취합니다.

1 강의의 주제는 무엇인가?
(a) 새로운 영역의 심리학이 처음 시작된 이유들
(b) 생명을 위협하는 상황을 목격하는 사람들의 반응
(c) 군중과 혼자인 사람들과의 차이점
(d) 군중의 본성과 어떻게 그들이 여러 가지 상황에 반응하는가

2 다음 중 가장 잘 요약된 것을 고르시오.
(a) 1964년에 일어난 살인 사건은 사람들이 생명을 위협하는 상황에 처하게 됐을 때의 반응에 대한 새로운 연구를 시작하는 촉매가 되었다.
(b) 1964년의 살인 사건은 위험한 상황에 처해 있는 사람을 보았을 때 군중과 개인들이 어떻게 반응하는가에 대해 조사하는 새로운 연구를 하게 되는 원인이 되었다.

3 옳은 문장에는 T, 틀린 문장에는 F를 쓰시오.
(1) 키티 제노비스 사건을 실었던 신문은 사실을 제대로 보도했다.
(2) 군중 속에 있는 개인들은 행동을 취해야 하는 의무를 많은 사람들과 공유한다고 느낀다.
(3) 개인이 경찰에 신고해 도움을 청하는 것보다 군중 속의 개인이 경찰에 신고해 도움을 청할 확률이 낮다.
(4) 군중은 생명을 위협하는 상황에서 사람이 생존할 수 있는 보다 나은 기회를 제공한다.

4 군중과 개인이 생명을 위협하는 상황을 보았을 때 반응하는 방식에는 왜 차이가 있는가?
(a) 혼자 있을 때보다 무리 속에 있을 때 위험을 공유하기 쉽다.
(b) 경찰을 부르는 것은 개인들에게 더 많은 문제를 일으킨다.
(c) 군중은 개인들보다 더 많이 책임감을 느끼는 경향이 있다.
(d) 개인들은 책임을 공유할 사람이 없다.

1 (d)   **2** 해설 참조   **3** (d)   **4** (b)   **5** (a)   **6** (b)   **7** (b)
8 (b)   **9** (d)   **10** 해설 참조   **11** (c)   **12** (c)

1

W An addiction is <u>any</u> <u>form</u> of <u>compulsive</u> <u>behavior</u> that has negative <u>side</u> <u>effects</u>. Examples of addiction include the use of drugs, whether legal or illegal, <u>alcohol</u> <u>consumption</u>, gambling, <u>overeating</u>, <u>compulsive</u> shopping, using the Internet for hours on end, watching too much TV, and a <u>multitude of</u> other <u>minor</u> <u>addictions</u>, such as a <u>fixation on</u> a certain food like chocolate. What causes an addiction is a source of much <u>contention</u> among medical doctors and psychologists. There is one school of thought that believes that addiction is caused by physical problems in the brain, which <u>results</u> <u>in</u> <u>behavioral</u> <u>problems</u> in the person. There is also a theory that there is a reward system associated with addiction. The brain <u>releases</u> <u>hormones</u>, like dopamine, which give pleasure to a person when a certain action, such as <u>taking</u> <u>a</u> <u>drug</u> or eating the food they enjoy, is <u>performed</u>. However, in a person who is addicted, the levels of dopamine need to be stronger and stronger to <u>produce</u> <u>the</u> <u>same</u> <u>effect</u> as before. Therefore, the person takes more drugs, or <u>gambles</u> or shops more often, to reach the same level of pleasure. A third theory is that addiction is related to a <u>genetic</u> <u>problem</u>. Studies of families with a history of alcoholism <u>tend</u> <u>to</u> <u>lend</u> <u>credence</u> to this theory. Finally, there is a moral theory of addiction; according to it, the person does not have a physical or psychological problem but <u>lacks</u> the moral character needed to <u>resist</u> <u>addiction</u>.

▶ compulsive behavior 충동적인 행동   on end 계속하여   a multitude of 다수의, 무수한   minor 중요치 않은   fixation 고착; 병적인 집착   contention 말다툼, 논쟁; 주장   school 학파, 주의, 학풍   reward 보수, 보상   dopamine 도파민(뇌 속의 신경 전달 물질)   genetic problem 유전적 문제   alcoholism 알코올 중독(증)
lend credence to 신뢰감을 실어주다   moral character 덕성, 품성

여 중독은 부정적인 부작용을 일으키는 충동적인 행동 유형입니다. 합법적이든 불법적이든, 중독의 예로는 약물복용, 알코올 섭취, 도박, 과식, 충동구매, 몇 시간

씹이고 인터넷을 계속하는 것, 과도한 텔레비전 시청, 초콜릿과 같은 특정 음식에 대한 병적인 집착처럼 심각하지 않은 무수한 중독들이 있습니다. 중독을 일으키는 원인에 대해서는 의사들과 심리학자들 사이에 많은 논쟁이 있습니다. 중독은 뇌 속의 물리적인 문제 때문에 생기며, 이것이 사람에게 행동상 문제를 일으킨다고 믿는 학파가 있습니다. 중독에 관련된 보상 체계가 있다는 이론도 있습니다. 뇌는 약물을 복용하거나 즐기는 음식을 먹는 것과 같은 특정한 행동을 했을 때 사람에게 즐거움을 주는 도파민과 같은 호르몬을 배출합니다. 하지만 중독자가 전과 같은 효과를 보기 위해서는 도파민의 정도가 점점 더 강해져야 합니다. 그래서 그 사람은 같은 수준의 즐거움에 다다르기 위해서 더 많은 약물을 복용하거나 더 자주 도박을 하거나 쇼핑을 해야 합니다. 세 번째 이론은 중독이 유전적 문제와 관련이 있다는 겁니다. 알코올 중독증 병력이 있는 가족에 대한 연구는 이 이론에 신빙성을 더해주기도 합니다. 마지막으로 중독에 대한 도덕적 이론이 있습니다. 이에 따르면, 중독자에게는 육체적, 심리적 문제는 없지만 중독에 저항하는 데 필요한 품성이 부족하다고 합니다.

1 담화의 목적은 무엇인가?
(a) 여러 가지 종류의 중독을 조사하려고
(b) 약물 중독은 심리적이라는 것임을 증명하려고
(c) 중독은 증상에 따라 다양하다는 것을 보여주려고
(d) 중독을 일으킬 수 있는 원인을 논하려고
(e) 약이 잘 맞지 않는 요인을 설명하려고

2

B This magazine article <u>seems</u> <u>all</u> <u>wrong</u> to me.

G What's it about?

B It says that when someone we love dies, there are <u>five</u> <u>stages</u> <u>to grief</u>: denial, anger, <u>bargaining</u>, depression, and acceptance.

G That sounds about right to me. I <u>went</u> <u>through</u> all of that when my mother died two years ago.

B Really? I didn't know you then. Do you want to talk about it?

G She had cancer, and the doctors only gave her a <u>few</u> <u>months</u> <u>to live</u>. At first, I couldn't believe it because she was so young. She was only 41.

B That is a young age to <u>die of</u> cancer.

G Then, I realized that the cancer wasn't <u>going</u> <u>away</u>, so I got angry, <u>bitter</u>, and mad at the world. I was mad at my father, the doctors, and everyone.

B It seems like you all had a hard time.

G It was so hard. And then I <u>started</u> <u>praying</u> to God, going to church, and asking him to save her. I said I would do anything if she could just live.

B But she didn't.

G No, it <u>got</u> <u>worse</u> each day. And then I <u>fell</u> <u>into</u> a deep, <u>black</u> <u>despair</u>. I didn't go to school. I <u>barely</u> <u>ate</u> or talked to anyone. And then she died.

B Have you finally accepted it?

G Yes. Just last week, I went to her grave, laid some flowers on <u>her</u> <u>headstone</u>, and had a long talk with her.

B It sounds just like what the writer of this article describes. I guess the magazine article was not <u>too</u> <u>far</u> <u>off</u> <u>base</u>.

▶ **denial** 부정, 부인 **bargaining** 거래, 교섭, 협상 **depression** 의기소침, 우울 **acceptance** 수락, 인정 **bitter** 쓴; 증오에 찬, 원통한 **despair** 절망; 자포자기

barely 거의 ~하지 않다: 간신히   headstone 묘석

남 이 잡지기사는 완전 잘못된 것 같아.

여 뭐에 관한 건데?

남 잡지기사에 의하면, 사랑하는 누군가가 죽으면 슬픔의 5단계를 겪게 된대. 즉 부정, 분노, 협상, 우울, 인정이지.

여 난 맞는 것 같은데. 난 어머니가 2년 전에 돌아가셨을 때 그 모든 걸 거쳤거든.

남 정말? 난 그 당시엔 널 몰랐잖아. 얘기 좀 해볼래?

여 어머니는 암이 있으셨어. 의사는 어머니가 몇 달밖에 못 사실 거라고 했지. 처음엔 어머니가 너무 젊으셔서 믿어지지가 않았어. 41세밖에 안 되셨거든.

남 암으로 돌아가시기엔 젊은 나이다.

여 그리고 나서 난 암이 치유가 되지 않을 거라는 것을 깨달았고, 세상에 화가 나고, 원통하고 노여웠지. 난 아버지, 의사, 모든 사람에게 화가 났어.

남 너희 가족 모두가 힘든 시간을 보냈겠구나.

여 너무 힘들었어. 그러고 나서 난 신에게 기도하고, 교회에 다니면서 어머니를 살려 달라고 빌기 시작했지. 만약 어머니가 살 수만 있다면 무슨 일이든 하겠다고 했어.

남 하지만 어머니는 돌아가셨구나.

여 맞아, 매일 점점 악화되었어. 그러고 나서 난 깊고 어두운 절망에 빠졌지. 난 학교에 가지 않았어. 먹지도 않고 얘기도 하지 않았지. 그러고 나서 어머니가 돌아가셨어.

남 결국은 받아들이게 됐니?

여 응. 지난주에 어머니 무덤에 가서 비석에 꽃을 놓고 어머니와 오랫동안 이야기를 나눴어.

남 이 기사를 쓴 저자가 묘사한 것과 똑같아. 그 잡지기사는 사실과 거의 같은가 봐.

2 다음 각 글이 어느 단계의 슬픔에 해당하는지 쓰시오.
(1) 난 어머니가 살 수만 있다면 뭐든 하겠다고 말했어. bargaining (협상)
(2) 난 어머니 무덤에 가서 비석에 꽃을 놓았어. acceptance (인정)
(3) 난 정말 원통했어. anger (분노)
(4) 난 깊고 어두운 절망에 빠졌어. depression (우울)
(5) 난 어머니가 너무 젊었기 때문에 믿을 수가 없었어. 부정

3-4

M For most people, one of the <u>hardest</u> <u>things</u> to do is talk to a <u>complete</u> stranger. People may be shy and <u>feel</u> <u>awkward</u> when <u>confronted</u> with someone they don't know. Sometimes, it is necessary to <u>talk</u> <u>to strangers</u>, such as when you need some important information. For example, I need to know the time a bus arrives, so I ask someone who is waiting at the bus stop. The person answers, and, from this <u>small</u> <u>beginning</u>, we could possibly have a longer conversation. By asking for <u>help</u> <u>from</u> someone, you can <u>overcome</u> <u>the</u> <u>initial</u> <u>awkwardness</u> that many people feel when talking to strangers. Who a person approaches to ask for help or information is <u>based on</u> some <u>unconscious</u> <u>perceptions</u>. We typically ask people of <u>our</u> <u>own</u> <u>race</u> due to the unconscious belief that they will speak the same language and be more willing to talk to a stranger who <u>looks</u> <u>similar</u> <u>to</u> them. We also <u>tend</u> <u>to</u> <u>ask</u> women more than men since women are <u>perceived</u> <u>to</u> <u>be</u> <u>gentler</u> and more <u>tolerant</u> of strangers' questions. Finally, we tend to ask <u>elderly</u> <u>people</u> more than younger ones since we unconsciously <u>associate</u> older people <u>with</u> <u>wisdom</u> and perhaps patience and kindness. Fortunately, most of our fears of strangers are <u>unfounded</u>. While some people may ignore you and some may be rude, most of the time, strangers will help and respond with kindness.

▶ a complete stranger 전혀 모르는 사람 awkward 어색한, 거북한
be confronted with 직면하다 initial 처음의, 최초의 unconscious 무의식의
perception 지각; 인식; 인지; 직관 be perceived to ~라고 인식되다
be tolerant of ~을 견뎌내다, ~을 관용하다 unfounded 근거 없는, 사실 무근의

남 대부분의 사람들에게 가장 어려운 일 중 하나는 낯선 사람에게 말을 하는 것입니다. 낯선 사람을 대면할 때는 수줍고 어색할 수 있습니다. 중요한 정보가 필요할 때처럼 낯선 사람에게 이야기를 해야 하는 경우가 있죠. 예를 들면 버스가 도착하는 시간을 알아야 해서, 버스 정거장에서 버스를 기다리는 어떤 사람에게 묻습니다. 그 사람은 버스 시간을 알려주고, 이 작은 시작으로부터 더 긴 대화를 할 수도 있죠. 어떤 사람에게 도움을 청함으로써, 낯선 이들에게 이야기할 때 많은 사람들이 느끼는 처음의 어색함을 극복할 수 있습니다. 도움을 청하거나 정보를 얻고자 누구에게 접근하는가는 무의식적인 직관을 기반으로 합니다. 우리는 대개 자신과 같은 인종의 사람들에게 묻습니다. 같은 언어를 사용할 거라는 믿음과, 비슷하게 생긴 이와는 더 기꺼이 얘기를 나누려고 할 것이라는 무의식적인 믿음 때문입니다. 우리는 또한 여성이 더 친절하고 낯선 사람의 질문을 잘 받아줄 거라고 인식하기 때문에 남자보다는 여자에게 물어보는 경향이 있습니다. 마지막으로, 우리는 무의식적으로 노인이라고 하면 지혜, 그리고 아마도 인내심과 친절을 연상하기 때문에 젊은이들보다는 노인들에게 물어보는 경향이 있습니다. 다행히 낯선 사람에 대한 우리의 두려움 대부분은 근거가 없는 것입니다. 일부는 여러분을 무시하고 어떤 사람들은 무례할 수도 있겠지만 대개의 낯선 사람들은 친절하게 도와주고 대답해 줄 것입니다.

3 왜 사람들이 낯선 사람들에게 말하는 것을 어려워하는가?

   (a) 대부분의 낯선 사람들이 도와줄 것처럼 보이지 않아서
   (b) 때때로 낯선 사람들은 도움을 요청하는 것을 묵살하기 때문에
   (c) 낯선 사람들은 사람들이 질문을 하면 어색해하기 때문에
   (d) 대부분의 사람들에게는 수줍음이 있기 때문에
   (e) 낯선 사람들은 모르는 이들에게 매우 무례할 수 있기 때문에

4 담화에 의하면 젊은 백인 남성은 어떤 사람에게 길을 물어보겠는가?

   (a) 젊은 백인 여성   (b) 나이가 든 백인 여성
   (c) 나이가 든 흑인 남성   (d) 젊은 흑인 여성
   (e) 나이가 든 백인 남성

5-6 Level up

M What a terrible day!

W I'm sorry to hear that. What happened?

M Everybody was in my face all day. I had no personal space whatsoever.

W I know what you mean. It's so hard getting any privacy these days. So what exactly ticked you off?

M First, on the subway, the guy sitting next to me just had to read his newspaper, and it was half in my face the whole time.

W I hate when people do that. Why couldn't he just fold the paper so it was smaller?

M I know! I said that to him, but he just glared at me and told me to mind my own business.

W The nerve of some people! I bet that put you in a foul mood all day.

M It sure did. And then on the elevator, it was so crowded I could smell what people had for breakfast on their breath.

W That's disgusting!

M It gets worse. They put a new person in my section at work today, and I have to share my desk and computer with him until they find him a spot. I just need more

personal space, you know? I don't want anyone around me and I don't need anyone bothering me.

W It's hard to have any personal space these days. The world is so crowded, and technology makes it worse. Cellphones, as useful as they are, can be a real pain in the neck when you want to avoid people or just relax for a little while.

M It's getting too hard just to be alone anymore.

▶ personal space 개인 공간(남과의 사이에서 불쾌감을 느끼지 않을 만큼의 공간)
whatsoever 〈문어〉 whatever(대대절, 도대체 무엇이, 도대체 무엇을)의 강조형
privacy 사생활; 사적 자유, 프라이버시 tick off 화나게 하다 glare at ~을 노려보다 mind one's own business ~의 일이나 제대로 하다 the nerve of ~! ~가 어쩜 그렇게[저렇게] 뻔뻔할 수 있어! be in a foul mood 심기가 불편하다; 기분이 나쁘다 a pain in the neck 불쾌감, 안달; 불쾌하게 하는 사람[것]

남 정말 끔찍한 날이었어.

여 안됐구나. 무슨 일이 있었니?

남 온종일 모두가 나를 귀찮게 했어. 도대체 혼자만의 공간이 없었다고.

여 무슨 말인지 알겠어. 요즘에는 사생활을 갖기가 정말 어려워. 그래서 넌 뭣 때문에 화가 났니?

남 먼저 지하철에서 옆에 앉은 남자가 신문을 읽는데 계속 내 얼굴의 반을 가리잖아.

여 사람들이 그럴 때 정말 싫더라. 왜 신문을 접어서 작게 만들지 못할까?

남 그러게 말이야! 그 사람한테 얘기했지만 나를 노려보면서 내 일에나 신경 쓰라는 거야.

여 어쩜 그렇게 뻔뻔할 수 있니! 그 일로 온종일 기분 나빴겠구나.

남 물론이야. 그리고 엘리베이터는 너무 붐벼서 사람들이 아침에 뭘 먹었는지 입냄새로 알 수 있을 정도였다니까.

여 구역질 나!

남 상황은 더 안 좋아졌어. 오늘 우리 부서에 새 직원이 왔는데 그 사람 자리가 만들어질 때까지 내 책상이랑 컴퓨터를 그와 함께 써야 해. 난 혼자만의 공간이 필요해. 알잖아? 난 누가 내 주위에 있는 걸 원치 않고, 날 귀찮게 하는 사람은 필요 없어.

여 요즘엔 혼자만의 공간을 갖기가 어려워. 세상이 너무 혼잡하고 기술이 그걸 더 악화시키지. 휴대폰은 유용하긴 하지만 사람을 피하거나 좀 쉬고 싶을 때는 정말 짜증난다니까.

남 혼자 있기가 너무 어려워지고 있어.

5 남자가 화난 이유가 아닌 것은 무엇인가?

   (a) 사람들이 계속 그의 휴대폰으로 전화를 해서
   (b) 직장의 엘리베이터가 너무 붐벼서
   (c) 지하철에서 한 남자가 그에게 매우 무례했기 때문에
   (d) 직장에 있는 누군가와 책상을 함께 써야 해서
   (e) 그의 생활에서 더 많은 사생활을 갖고 싶어서

6 대화를 가장 잘 요약한 문장을 고르시오.

   (a) 남자는 매일 만나는 사람들이 얼마나 무례하게 구는지에 대해 불평한다.
   (b) 남자와 여자는 혼자 있으면서 다른 사람들에게 방해 받지 않을 수 있는 곳을 찾기가 얼마나 힘든지에 대해 말한다.
   (c) 남자는 직장에서 그의 개인 공간이 잘 알지도 못하는 직장 동료에 의해 침해 받고 있기 때문에 화가 나 있다.

---

7 Level up

G I have a problem at school, Dad.

M What's the matter?

G I don't know. I think the teacher doesn't like me. I did well on all of my work and usually answered questions in class, but she still only gave me a B in the class.

M I'll have a talk with her.

G No, no. Don't do that.

M What? I <u>thought</u> <u>you</u> <u>had</u> a problem you wanted me to take care of.

G Why do men always want to take care of problems?

M Ah... because they are problems. That's what we <u>do</u> <u>with</u> <u>them</u>: We take care of them.

G I just wanted to talk about this. I don't expect you do anything about it.

M Now I'm <u>confused</u>.

G It's not your fault. You're a man. <u>You're</u> <u>programmed</u> <u>to</u> think with your head and to <u>solve</u> <u>difficult</u> <u>tasks</u>. I'm a woman, and we sometimes just want to talk about things to <u>get</u> <u>them</u> <u>off</u> our <u>chest</u>.

M That sounds <u>logical</u>. There I go again, thinking like a man. You know, you're <u>pretty</u> <u>smart</u> <u>for</u> a high school student.

G I know. That still won't change a B into an A. I guess I'll just have to <u>try</u> <u>harder</u>.

▶ confused 혼란스러운, 헷갈리는 be programmed to ~하도록 되어있다, ~하도록 프로그램 되어있다 get something off one's chest 고민을 털어놓다 There I go again. 또 시작이군.

여 아빠, 나 학교에서 문제가 있어요.

남 무슨 일이니?

여 모르겠어요. 선생님이 날 안 좋아하는 것 같아요. 난 과제를 전부 다 잘했고 수업 때는 질문에 대답도 했는데 선생님은 내게 B밖에 안 주셨어요.

남 선생님과 얘기해 볼게.

여 아니에요, 아니에요. 그러지 마세요.

남 뭐? 네 문제를 아빠가 해결해 주길 원하는 줄 알았는데.

여 왜 남자들은 항상 문제를 해결하길 원하는 거죠?

남 아… 그건 문제거리니까. 그게 남자들이 하는 일이지. 문제를 해결하는 것 말이야.

여 난 그냥 그 문제에 대해 얘기해 보고 싶었을 뿐이에요. 아빠가 그 문제에 대해 뭔가 해주시길 기대하진 않아요.

남 무슨 말인지 모르겠는걸.

여 아빠 잘못이 아니에요. 아빠는 남자기 때문에, 머리로 생각해서 어려운 일을 해결하도록 되어 있는 거예요. 난 여자예요. 우리는 고민을 털어 놓기 위해 그냥 말하고 싶을 때가 있죠.

남 그거 논리적인데. 내가 또 시작이군. 남자같이 생각하는 거 말이야. 있잖니, 넌 고등학생치곤 꽤 똑똑하구나.

여 알아요. 그렇지만 그게 B를 A로 바꾸진 못히잖아요. 더 열심히 해야겠어요.

7 What is the main difference in the ways men and women think according to the dialog? 대화에 따르면 남자들과 여자들의 사고방식의 주요 차이점은 무엇인가?

  (a) Men focus on feelings while women focus on situations.
      남자들은 감정에 치중하는 반면 여자들은 상황에 치중한다.
  (b) Men are task-oriented while women are emotion-oriented.
      남자들은 과제 위주인 반면 여자들은 감정 위주이다.
  (c) Men are more judgmental while women are more emotional. 남자들은 더 비판적인 반면 여자들은 더 감정적이다.
  (d) Men like to talk about problems, but women want to solve them. 남자들은 문제에 대해 이야기하는 것을 좋아하지만 여자들은 문제를 해결하길 원한다.
  (e) Men like to fix situations while women like them to stay the same. 남자들은 상황을 해결하길 좋아하는 반면 여자들은 그대로 머물러 있기를 좋아한다.

W In psychology, there are many <u>schools</u> <u>of</u> <u>thought</u> in how people <u>interpret</u> <u>their</u> <u>surroundings</u>. One such school is the Gestalt school, which originated in Berlin, Germany, in the early 20th century. This school believes the <u>brain</u> <u>organizes</u> our surroundings based on the ability of the <u>senses</u> <u>to</u> <u>recognize</u> <u>forms</u>. The <u>guiding</u> <u>principle</u> of Gestalt psychology is that something must be seen as a whole and not just in its individual parts. An <u>often-quoted</u> <u>phrase</u> used to describe Gestalt is "the whole is greater than the <u>sum</u> <u>of</u> its parts." Gestalt psychology often uses <u>diagrams</u> and <u>optical illusions</u> to allow people to use their brain in different ways to see the <u>whole</u> <u>object</u> rather than its smaller parts. Gestalt psychology also <u>has</u> insights <u>for</u> problem solving. With problem solving, Gestalt psychology divides it into two types: productive and reproductive thinking. Productive thinking uses an insight to solve a problem while reproductive thinking uses <u>previous</u> <u>experiences</u> to solve a problem.

▶ school of thought 생각(의견)을 같이하는 사람들, 학파 surroundings 주변(의 상황), 처지, 환경, 주위 Gestalt school 게슈탈트 학파 originate 시작되다, 비롯하다, 유래하다 organize 조직하다; 정리하다 guiding principle 지침, 원리, 신조 quote 인용하다; 예를 들다 sum 총계, 합계 diagram 도형; 도식; 도해; 도표 optical illusion 착시, 착각 insight 통찰력, 식견 productive thinking 생산적 사고 reproductive thinking 재생적 사고

여 심리학에는 사람들이 주변 상황을 어떻게 해석하느냐에 관한 많은 학파가 있습니다. 그런 학파의 하나가 게슈탈트 학파입니다. 게슈탈트 학파는 20세기 초 독일 베를린에서 시작되었습니다. 이 학파는 뇌가 형태를 인지하는 감각 능력을 기반으로 주변 상황을 조직한다고 믿습니다. 게슈탈트 심리학의 지침은 어떤 일은 반드시 전체로 보아야 하며 개별적인 부분으로 보아서는 안 된다는 것입니다. 게슈탈트를 묘사하기 위해 종종 인용되는 문구는 '전체는 그 부분들을 합한 것보다 더 크다'라는 것입니다. 게슈탈트 심리학은 사람들이 작은 부분보다는 전체 대상을 보게 하기 위해 종종 도표와 착시를 이용해 여러 방식으로 뇌를 사용하도록 합니다. 게슈탈트 심리학은 또한 문제 해결에 대해 통찰합니다. 게슈탈트 심리학은 문제 해결 방법을 생산적 사고와 재생적 사고, 이렇게 두 가지로 나눕니다. 생산적 사고는 문제를 해결하는 데 통찰력을 사용하는 반면 재생적 사고는 이전의 경험을 활용합니다.

8 What is the main purpose of the talk?
  남화의 목적은 무엇인가?

  (a) To discuss how optical illusions apply to psychology
      어떻게 착시가 심리학에 적용되는지 논하려고
  (b) To examine aspects of a branch of psychology
      심리학의 한 분파의 관점을 조사하려고
  (c) To describe the origins of a famous saying
      유명한 격언의 유래를 기술하려고
  (d) To show some ways that problems can be solved
      문제를 해결할 수 있는 몇 가지 방법을 보여주려고
  (e) To explain the origin of a school of psychology
      한 심리학 학파의 유래를 설명하려고

M You may have heard the saying "Laughter is the <u>best</u> <u>medicine</u>." What it means is that <u>laughing</u> <u>alone</u> <u>can</u> <u>cure</u> an illness. This may not be <u>as</u> <u>crazy</u> <u>as</u> it seems at first glance. Laughter causes the body to <u>release</u> endorphins, a type of hormone that helps to <u>relieve</u> <u>pain</u>. In addition, laughter can <u>widen</u> the <u>blood vessels</u>, allowing blood to flow more freely and <u>lowering</u> blood pressure. Laughter is also known to reduce stress, and some studies even show it <u>boosts the immune system</u>. But can laughter actually cure an illness? There are some <u>anecdotes</u> in medical history, and none is as famous as the story of Norman Cousins. He was an American journalist who <u>suffered from</u> a <u>variety</u> of illnesses <u>throughout</u> his life. At one point, he was <u>diagnosed with</u> a form of very painful arthritis that not many people survive. Cousins decided to try laughter as a therapy for his <u>chronic pain</u>. He watched hours of comedy movies and TV shows every day while he lay in bed and was <u>barely able to</u> move. After a few weeks, he found his pain <u>had lessened</u>, and he was able to move more. After many months of this therapy, Cousins was able to walk around and <u>could function</u> like he had before. He lived many years longer than others who had the <u>same form of</u> arthritis. Cousins finally died of a <u>heart attack at age</u> 75 in 1990.

▶ alone (명사·대명사 바로 뒤에서 그것을 수식하여) 다만 ~만, ~뿐　endorphin 엔도르핀　blood vessel 혈관　immune system 면역 체계　boost 증가하다; 돋우다　anecdotes (역사·전기 등의) 비사(秘史), 비화　journalist 저널리스트, 보도기자; 언론인　be diagnosed with ~을 진단받다　a form of 일종의　arthritis 관절염　therapy 요법, 치료　chronic pain 만성 통증　function 활동하다, 작용하다

남 여러분은 '웃음은 가장 좋은 약이다'라는 속담을 들어 본 적이 있을 것입니다. 무슨 의미인가 하면 웃음만으로 병을 치료할 수 있다는 것입니다. 이것은 알고 보면 말도 안 되는 소리는 아닙니다. 웃음은 고통을 줄이는 데 일조하는 호르몬의 일종인 엔도르핀이 몸에서 분비되게 해주죠. 더불어 웃음은 혈관을 넓혀주어 혈액이 좀 더 자유롭게 흐를 수 있게 해주고 혈압도 낮춰줍니다. 웃음은 또한 스트레스를 줄여주는 것으로 알려져 있고, 몇몇 연구에서는 웃음이 면역 체계를 촉진하는 것으로 나타나 있습니다. 하지만 웃음이 실제로 질병을 치료할 수 있을까요? 의학사에 몇몇 비화가 있지만 노먼 커즌스 이야기가 가장 유명하죠. 그는 일생 동안 여러 질병에 시달렸던 미국의 저널리스트였습니다. 한때 그는 소수만이 살아남는 매우 고통스러운 종류의 관절염을 진단받았습니다. 커즌스는 자신의 만성적인 통증을 치료하는 데 웃음을 사용해 보기로 결심했습니다. 그는 침대에 누운 채 거의 움직이지 못하는 동안 매일 수 시간씩 코미디 영화와 텔레비전 쇼를 보았습니다. 몇 주 후에 그는 고통이 줄어든 것을 깨달았고, 좀 더 움직일 수 있게 되었습니다. 이 웃음요법을 쓴 지 수 개월 후에 커즌스는 걸을 수 있었고 예전처럼 기능할 수 있었습니다. 그는 같은 종류의 관절염을 앓고 있었던 다른 사람들보다 오래 살았습니다. 커즌스는 결국 1990년에 75세의 나이에 심장마비로 사망했죠.

9 담화에 의하면 다음 중 사실이 아닌 것은?
　(a) 웃음은 몸의 정맥과 동맥을 확장하는 데 도움을 준다.
　(b) 노먼 커즌스의 웃음요법에는 텔레비전 시청이 포함되었다.
　(c) 웃음이 호르몬을 배출하면 고통이 감소될 수 있다.
　(d) 노먼 커즌스는 치료 불가능한 관절염 때문에 사망하였다.
　(e) 노먼 커즌스는 일생 동안 많은 고통을 겪었다.

10

M　Tonight on *Cross Talk*, we will examine a <u>report on depression</u> from the American Psychological Association. Here is Sue Delaney <u>with some details</u> from the report.

W　Thanks, Harry. First, what is depression? The <u>clinical definition</u> is that it is feelings and thoughts which <u>negatively affect</u> one's ability to function in everyday life. The most <u>startling statistic</u> from the report is that about <u>20 million</u> Americans currently suffer from depression.

M　That's around 7 percent of the population, isn't it?

W　Yes, Harry. And about <u>16 percent</u> of all Americans will suffer depression <u>at some point</u> in their lives.

M　What age groups suffer depression the most?

W　The report <u>indicates</u> that the age group from <u>18 to 29</u> suffers from depression more than any other age group.

M　Who suffers from depression more, men or women?

W　Nearly <u>twice as</u> many women have depression as men. So of those <u>20 million</u> people who have depression, about <u>two-thirds</u> are women.

M　What are the <u>signs of depression</u> according to the report?

W　The report states that <u>persistent sadness</u> and a lack of interest in activities a person used to enjoy are <u>classic early signs</u> of depression.

M　What are the best ways to treat depression?

W　There are two common ways: using <u>medications and psychoanalysis</u>. In fact, more anti-depressants are prescribed each year than any other kind of medicine in America. Around <u>107 million</u> prescriptions for anti-depressant drugs were given by doctors to patients in America last year.

M　Those are some <u>shocking statistics</u>. When we come back from a commercial break, we'll discuss the report with our <u>panel of experts</u>.

▶ clinical definition 임상적인 정의　startling 깜짝 놀라게 하는, 놀라운　statistic 통계치(량)　age group (특정한) 연령 집단　indicate 나타내다, 표시하다　persistent 계속적인, 끊임없는　classic 전형적인; 고전적인　psychoanalysis 정신 분석(학, 법)　anti-depressant 항우울증 치료제　prescribe 처방하다, 처방을 쓰다　statistics 통계 자료, 통계(표)　panel 패널, 토론자단

남 오늘 밤 〈크로스 토크〉에서는 미국 심리학 협회의 우울증에 대한 보고서를 살펴보도록 하겠습니다. 여기 그 보고서에 대한 상세한 설명을 해주실 수 딜레이니 씨께서 나오셨습니다.

여 고맙습니다, 해리. 우선, 우울증이란 무엇일까요? 임상적인 정의는 일상생활에서 활동하는 사람의 능력에 부정적으로 영향을 미치는 감정과 생각입니다. 보고서에서 가장 놀라운 통계치는 약 2천만 명의 미국인이 우울증을 앓고 있다는 것이죠.

남 그건 인구의 약 7%죠, 그렇지 않나요?

여 맞습니다, 해리. 그리고 미국인 중의 약 16%는 그들의 일생 중 어느 시점에 우울증을 앓게 되죠.

남 어떤 연령 집단이 가장 많이 우울증을 앓고 있나요?

여 보고서에는 18세에서 29세까지의 연령 집단이 다른 연령 집단보다 더 많이 우울증을 앓고 있다고 나타나 있습니다.

남 남성과 여성 중에 누가 더 우울증에 많이 걸리나요?

여 남성보다 여성이 거의 2배 더 우울증을 앓고 있습니다. 그래서 우울증을 앓는 2천만 명 중에 약 3분의 2가 여성이죠.

남 보고서에 따르면 우울증 증세에는 어떤 것이 있나요?

여 보고서에는 지속적인 슬픔과 평소에 즐겼던 활동에 흥미가 없어지는 것이 전형적인 우울증 초기 증세라고 되어 있습니다.

남 우울증을 치료하는 가장 좋은 방법은 무엇입니까?

여 두 가지 보편적인 방법이 있습니다. 약물 치료와 정신 분석이죠. 사실, 매년 미국에서는 다른 어떤 약보다도 더 많은 항우울증 치료제가 처방됩니다. 작년에 미국에서는 의사들이 약 1억 7백만 건의 항우울증 약 처방전을 환자에게 발급했습니다.

남 충격적인 통계 자료네요. 광고 후에 전문가 패널들과 보고서에 대해 이야기를 나눠 보겠습니다.

10 대화에 나온 정보로 표를 완성하시오.

구분	총계
현재 우울증을 앓고 있는 사람들	2천만
– 여성의 수	13.4 million (1천 3백 4십만 명)
– 남성의 수	6.6 million (660만 명)
일생 동안 우울증을 앓을 미국인 비율	16%
우울증에 가장 많이 영향을 받는 연령 집단	18–29
작년 우울증 처방전 건 수	107 million (1억 7백만)

11-12　**Level up**

W There is a <u>condition</u> <u>called</u> synesthesia in which people see color when they hear music or when they smell something, or they <u>associate</u> <u>certain</u> <u>letters</u> or numbers with a certain color. For example, "C" has to be red, and the number five has to be green. This <u>phenomenon</u> <u>occurs</u> more often in women than men, and there is a growing belief that it can be <u>hereditary</u>. The majority of people with synesthesia <u>associate</u> <u>colors</u> <u>with</u> <u>numbers</u> and letters. Many others see sounds, including music and voices, producing colors. A few people see colors when they <u>feel</u> pain or <u>smell</u> certain <u>odors</u>. Much of the research done on synesthesia is recent. Some experts believe that perhaps one in 2,000 people experience <u>heightened</u> <u>sensory</u> <u>awareness</u> of some type, but many of these people do not know what to call their condition, and others <u>were</u> <u>ridiculed</u> <u>as</u> <u>children</u> <u>for</u> <u>saying</u> that music had color or the number five was green. Perhaps in some cases, people feared they were <u>mentally</u> <u>unbalanced</u> and did not <u>seek</u> <u>any</u> <u>aid</u> because they believed that they would be <u>institutionalized</u>. However, there is <u>no</u> <u>correlation</u> <u>between</u> synesthesia and mental illness. Perhaps all people <u>exhibit</u> some <u>signs</u> of synesthesia as babies. Babies respond very <u>readily</u> <u>to</u> music, bright colors, and lights. There is a theory that a baby's <u>brain</u> <u>is</u> <u>wired</u> differently from an adult's, and, as we grow older, most of us <u>lose</u> <u>the</u> <u>connections</u> between the parts of the brain that <u>enable</u> <u>us</u> to see music as color. But not all do, and they are the ones who <u>grow</u> <u>up</u> to have synesthesia as adults.

▶ synesthesia 공감각(하나의 감각이 다른 감각을 작용케 하는 일) phenomenon 현상 hereditary 유전성의, 유전하는, 유전적인 heightened 강화된, 증가된 sensory awareness 감각지각 be ridiculed 놀림을 받다 unbalanced 불안정한; 착란한 be institutionalized 특수 병원에 수용되다 correlation 상호 관련, 상관 (관계) readily 쉽사리, 손쉽게

여 음악을 듣거나 냄새를 맡을 때 색깔이 보이는, 공감각이라고 불리는 상태가 있습니다. 아니면 특정한 글자나 숫자들에 대해 특정한 색깔을 연상하기도 합니다. 예를 들면 C는 빨간색이어야 하고 숫자 5는 녹색이어야 하는 것이죠. 이러한 현상은 남성보다는 여성에게 더 자주 발생하며, 유전적일 것이라는 믿음이 커지고 있습니다. 공감각을 가지고 있는 대부분의 사람들은 색깔을 숫자와 글자에 연관 지어 생각합니다. 또 다른 많은 사람들은 음악과 목소리를 포함한 소리가 색깔을 띠는 것을 봅니다. 몇몇 사람들은 고통을 느끼거나 냄새를 맡을 때 색깔을 보기도 하고요. 공감각에 대한 많은 연구는 최근에 이루어졌습니다. 일부 전문가들은 아마도 2천 명 중 한 명은 어떠한 유형의 강화된 감각지각을 경험하는 것으로 믿고 있습니다. 하지만 이 중 많은 사람들은 자신의 상태를 어떻게 불러야 할지 모릅니다. 그리고 어렸을 때 음악에 색깔이 있다고 하거나 숫자 5가 녹색이라고 했다가 놀림을 당한 사람들도 있습니다. 자신들이 정신적으로 불안정하다고 불안

해하며 정신병원에 수용될 것이라 생각해 어떠한 도움도 구하지 못했던 경우도 있었을 수 있습니다. 하지만 공감각과 정신병 사이에는 상호 관련이 없습니다. 모든 사람들은 아기 때 공감각 증후를 보일지도 모릅니다. 아기들은 쉽사리 음악, 밝은 색, 빛에 반응합니다. 아기의 뇌는 성인과 다르게 연결되어 있다가 나이가 들면서 대부분의 사람들은 음악을 색깔로 볼 수 있게 하는 뇌 부분들의 연결을 잃게 된다는 이론이 있습니다. 하지만 모든 사람이 그 연결 부분을 잃는 것은 아닙니다. 그래서 그 사람들이 어른으로 성장해도 공감각을 가지게 되는 것이죠.

11 강의에서 유추할 수 있는 것은?
(a) 공감각은 정신적인 문제가 있는 사람들에게만 영향을 미친다.
(b) 글자를 색깔로 보는 사람들은 숫자를 다른 색깔로 보지 않는다.
(c) 공감각으로 진단받지 않은 많은 사람들이 있다.
(d) 이상한 소리를 하는 아이들은 모두 공감각을 지니고 있다.
(e) 가족 중 한 사람 이상이 공감각을 가지고 있는 경우는 드물다.

12 다음 중 내용을 가장 잘 요약한 것을 고르시오.
(a) 공감각은 희귀하고 치료할 수 없는 정신병으로, 공감각 환자들의 감각이 어떻게 세상을 인지하느냐에 영향을 미친다.
(b) 공감각은 색깔이 대부분의 감각기능을 대신하는 정신 상태이다.
(c) 공감각은 감각들이 자극받았을 때 색깔을 인지하는 희귀한 상태이다.

Practice Test　　　　p. 16~p. 17

1 (a)	2 (e)	3 (d)	4 (d)	5 (d)	6 (b)	7 (d)
8 해설 참조		9 (c)	10 (d)			

1

W Racism is an active dislike—even hatred—of people who are of a different race. Whether racism is an instinctive thing that people have no control over or whether it is learned from a person's surrounding environment is a matter of debate among psychologists. Some studies suggest that racism has its roots in the human desire to belong to groups, whether they are racial groups or not. For example, people of all races support a certain sports team. They do not see themselves as members of individual races but as fans of this sports team. The fans of other sports teams would be considered outsiders to this group. Is this instinctive or learned? The answer is unclear, but studies show that children can perceive race at an early age. Studies done with young children show that as early as age three, children can identify races based on skin color and other distinguishing features and can identify themselves as belonging to a certain race. But why do some children grow up to hate other races? This seems more likely to be a product of their environment. If a child grows up with racist parents, then the child may believe that racism is normal. Sometimes, even entire societies can become racist by the use of propaganda against a certain group, such as the Nazi's propaganda against the Jews in Europe, which led to the Holocaust.

▶ racism 인종적 차별 have root in 기원하다, 뿌리를 두다 outsider 이단자, 외부인 distinguishing feature 구별되는 특징 racist 인종 차별주의자(의) propaganda 선전하는 주의[주장] Jew 유대인 the Holocaust (나치에 의한) 유대인 대학살

여 인종차별은 다른 인종 사람들을 아주 싫어하는, 심지어 증오하는 것입니다. 인종 차별이 통제할 수 없는 본능적인 것인가 아니면 주변 환경에서 학습되는가는 심리학자들 사이에 논란거리가 되고 있습니다. 어떤 연구는 인종차별이 집단에 속하고 싶은 인간의 욕망에 뿌리를 두고 있다고 합니다. 그 집단이 인종적인 집단이든 아니든 말이죠. 예를 들면 모든 인종의 사람들은 특정 스포츠 팀을 지지합니다. 그들은 자신들을 각 인종의 일원들로 보지 않고 이 스포츠 팀의 팬으로 봅니다. 다른 스포츠 팀 팬들은 이 집단에서 이단자로 여겨질 것입니다. 이것은 본능적인 것일까요, 아니면 학습되는 걸까요? 답은 명확하지 않지만, 어린이들이 어릴 때부터 인종을 인지할 수 있다는 것을 보여주는 연구들이 있습니다. 어린 아이들을 대상으로 한 연구에 의하면, 어린이들은 이르면 3세부터 피부색과 다른 특징을 기반으로 인종을 식별할 수 있다는 것과 자신들이 특정 인종에 속해 있다는 것을 알 수 있다고 합니다. 하지만 왜 일부 어린이들이 자라면서 다른 인종들을 증오하게 될까요? 이것은 환경의 산물인 것으로 보입니다. 만약 아이가 인종 차별주의자 부모 밑에서 자라게 되면 그 아이는 인종 차별이 정상적인 것이라고 믿게 될 수 있습니다. 때때로 특정 무리에 반대하는 선동으로 사회 전체가 인종 차별주의자가 될 수도 있습니다. 유럽에 있는 유대인에 대한 나치의 흑색 선전 같이 말이죠. 그리고 그 것은 대학살을 일으켰습니다.

1 담화에 의하면 다음 중 옳지 <u>않은</u> 것은?

(a) 인종 차별은 종종 스포츠 팬 집단에서도 볼 수 있다.
(b) 어린 아이들은 인종 간의 차이점을 구별할 수 있다.
(c) 사람들은 무리의 일원들이 되는 것을 좋아한다.
(d) 인종 차별은 본능적인 것인지 학습되는 것인지 확실하지 않다.
(e) 선동은 사람들을 인종 차별주의자로 만들 수 있다.

M Good morning, Darlene.

W Good morning, Dr. Silverman.

M How have you been since I last saw you?

W I'm feeling much better. I don't want to take those pills anymore.

M Let's have a chat, and then we'll talk about your medication later, okay?

W Okay.

M Good. Now, are you still experiencing stress and anxiety?

W No, I feel calm all day now. I don't even worry about work or my family anymore.

M And what about your relationships with your co-workers and your family? Have there been anymore outbursts of anger?

W No, we get along fine. I still hate my boss, but everyone at work hates him. My husband has been super nice, and my children are not as bratty as they used to be.

M And why do you think these changes have occurred?

W I don't know. I guess people are just being nice to me because they think I am sick.

M I'm sure that is partially true. But do you think the medication has made you a better person also? Maybe the medicine has reduced your stress levels and made you less angry and prone to outbursts of shouting.

W Maybe, but I think I am fine now and don't need to take the pills anymore.

M You seem to have your mind set on this. I'll tell you what. Let's try to go a few weeks without medication.

W That sounds great.

M ____

▶ outburst 폭발, 분출; 분격   bratty 개구쟁이의   prone to ~하기 쉬운
have one's mind set on ~하기로 마음을 굳히다, 작심하다

남 안녕하세요, 달린.
여 안녕하세요, 실버맨 선생님.
남 지난 번에 뵌 이후로 어떻게 지내셨어요?
여 훨씬 좋아졌어요. 더 이상은 약을 복용하고 싶지 않은데요.
남 대화를 좀 나눠 보죠. 그리고 나서 약에 대해서 얘기합시다, 괜찮죠?
여 예.
남 좋습니다. 자, 아직도 스트레스와 불안에 시달리고 있나요?
여 아니요, 지금은 하루 종일 편안해요. 일이나 가족에 대해서도 더 이상 걱정하지 않아요.
남 그럼 직장 동료들, 가족과의 관계는 어때요? 분노가 폭발한 적이 있었나요?
여 아니요, 우린 잘 지내요. 여전히 사장님은 몹시 싫지만 직장 사람들 모두가 그를 미워하니까요. 남편이 매우 잘 해 주고 아이들도 예전처럼 장난이 심하지 않아요.
남 왜 이러한 변화가 일어났다고 생각하나요?
여 모르겠어요. 내가 아프니까 사람들이 나에게 잘 하는 것 같아요.
남 어느 정도는 그렇겠죠. 하지만 약 또한 당신을 좀 더 나은 사람으로 만들었다고 생각하시나요? 약이 스트레스를 낮춰주고 덜 화나게 하고 소리를 덜 지르게 한 것일 수도 있어요.
여 그럴지도 모르죠. 하지만 난 지금 괜찮고 더 이상 약을 복용하고 싶지 않아요.
남 마음을 굳히신 것 같네요. 그럼 이렇게 하죠. 약 없이 몇 주 동안 지내 보도록 합시다.
여 좋아요.
남 ____

2 애초에 의사는 왜 여자에게 약을 처방해 주었나?

(a) 그녀는 회사 동료와 잘 지내는 데 어려움을 겪고 있었다.
(b) 그녀는 남편과 부부 문제가 있었다.
(c) 그녀는 일과 가족 문제로 우울해하고 있었다.
(d) 그녀는 신경과민 증세를 줄이기 위해 약을 복용하기를 원했다.
(e) 그녀는 스트레스를 받았고 주위 사람들에게 화를 내고 있었다.

3 의사는 다음에 뭐라고 말하겠는가?

(a) 그렇다면 난 당신이 약을 더 이상 복용할 필요가 없다고 생각해요.
(b) 당신 남편과 아이들을 다음 주에 보고 싶군요.
(c) 하지만 오늘은 새로운 약을 좀 처방해 드리고 싶네요.
(d) 그럼 몇 주 후에 기분이 어떠신지 보도록 하죠.
(e) 가시기 전에 처방전대로 조제하는 걸 잊지 마세요.

M Perhaps you may have heard about Sigmund Freud, the famous psychologist. He is credited with creating the field of psychoanalysis, in which the psychologist tries to understand the patients' issues by discussing their lives and thoughts. Freud established that the human psyche has three basic structures. He named them the id, ego, and superego. Freud discussed them in his writings in the early 1920s. These are not physical structures but parts of the mind. The id is present from birth and enables a baby to survive. It is an unconscious aspect of the mind and encompasses everything instinctual. The force behind the id is the "pleasure principle," which calls for instant satisfaction of all wants and needs. The ego is the part of the human psyche that deals with the reality of life. It helps to suppress the urges of the id and also satisfies the id in reasonable ways that do not clash with what society considers acceptable behavior. The ego is therefore part of the psyche that we are aware of since we use it to struggle with the id. The last part of the psyche, the superego, is composed of all that we learn as we grow up that is related to our sense of right and wrong. This is very similar to our morals. The superego strives to make a person conform to accepted standards of society.

▶ be credited with ~로 인정받고 있다, ~로 여겨지고 있다 psyche 정신, 영혼 establish 수립[확립]하다; 정하다 id (정신분석) 이드, 원아(原我), 자아(ego)의 기저(基底)를 이루는 본능적 충동 ego 자아(自我) superego 초자아(超自我), 상위(上位) 자아, 자아를 감시하는 무의식적 양심 encompass ~을 포함하다, 싸다 pleasure principle 쾌감 원칙 suppress 억제하다, 억누르다 urge (강한) 충동 clash (의견, 이해 등이) 충돌하다, (규칙 등에) 저촉되다 struggle with 싸우다; 격투하다 be aware of ~을 알아차리다, ~을 알다 morals 윤리(학); 도덕 strive to ~하도록 애쓰다[노력하다]

남 아마도 여러분은 유명한 심리학자 지그문트 프로이트에 대해 들어 보았을 것입니다. 그는 심리학자가 환자의 삶과 사고를 검토하여 환자의 문제를 이해하려고 하는 정신분석학 분야의 창시자로 인정받고 있습니다. 프로이트는 인간 정신에는 세 가지의 기본 구조가 있다는 개념을 확립했습니다. 그는 그 3대 기본 구조를 이드, 자아, 초자아라고 이름 지었습니다. 프로이트는 1920년대 초 그의 저술에서 3대 기본 구조에 대해 논했습니다. 이것들은 신체 구조가 아닌 마음의 일부입니다. 이드는 태어날 때부터 존재하며 아기가 생존할 수 있게 해줍니다. 이드는 마음의 무의식적인 면인데, 본능적인 모든 것을 포함합니다. 이드 배후에 있는 힘은 원하고 필요로 하는 모든 것에 대한 즉각적인 만족을 요구하는 '쾌감 원칙'입니다. 자아는 현실에 대처하는 인간 정신의 일부입니다. 자아는 이드의 충동을 억제하고 또한 사회에서 받아들일 수 있는 행동이라고 여겨지는 것과 상충하지 않는 합리적인 방법으로 이드를 만족시킵니다. 자아를 이용하여 이드와 싸우기 때문에, 자아는 우리가 알고 있는 정신의 일부입니다. 정신의 마지막 부분인 초자아는 우리가 성장하면서 배우는 옳고 그름에 대한 의식과 관련된 모든 것으로 이루어져 있습니다. 이것은 도덕과 매우 비슷합니다. 초자아는 용인된 사회 기준에 사람이 맞춰질 수 있도록 애쓰지요.

4 이드가 태어날 때부터 존재해야 하는 이유는?
  (a) 자아와 싸울 수 있게 발달할 시간을 주기 위해
  (b) 현실에 대처하는 방식을 가르쳐주기 위해
  (c) 아기 부모의 도덕을 전달하기 위해
  (d) 생존하기 위해 필요한 본능을 아기에게 주기 위해
  (e) 고통과 기쁨을 느끼는 방식을 알려주기 위해

5 담화에서 유추할 수 있는 것은?
  (a) 이드는 자아나 초자아의 통제를 극복할 수 없다.
  (b) 프로이트는 정신이 뇌의 신체적인 일부라고 믿었다.
  (c) 이드는 인간 뇌의 일부분으로 대표된다.
  (d) 초자아는 마지막으로 발달되는 정신의 부분이다.
  (e) 프로이트는 아기들이 정신을 갖고 태어나는 이유를 증명했다.

---

6 Level up

M Jenny, I'm home.

W Hi, Mr. Riggs. Where's Mrs. Riggs?

M She's going to stay at her mother's for the night. Her mother is not feeling well.

W I'm sorry to hear that.

M Thanks. Hey, how was Tommy?

W He's sleeping now, but he cried a lot when you and your wife left. He was really upset.

M I guess he's at that age when separation anxiety kicks in.

W Yeah, I've been babysitting a few years now, and I've seen it in other children. Usually around age one, they start to realize that their parents are someone special and that being away from them is upsetting.

M My wife and I already talked about one of us staying home from work.

W I don't know if that will help. I've been reading some books on the subject in my college psychology class. They say that sometimes it's better if the parents continue to work so that they can avoid having the children become too dependent on them.

M Maybe. But I think my wife has her heart set on spending more time with Tommy.

▶ separation anxiety 분리 불안(유아가 어머니로부터 분리될 때의 심리 상태) kick in (구어) 작동하다, 움직이다; 효력을 나타내다 have one's heart set on ~하기로 마음을 정하다; ~을 열망(갈망)하다

남 제니, 나 집에 왔어.
여 안녕하세요, 리그스 씨. 리그스 부인은 어디에 계세요?
남 장모님 댁에서 하룻밤 지낼 거야. 장모님이 몸이 편찮으셔.
여 안됐군요.
남 걱정해 줘서 고마워. 토미는 어땠어?
여 지금 자고 있어요. 하지만 두 분이 나가신 다음에 많이 울었어요. 아이가 난리였어요.
남 그 나이에는 분리 불안이 있을 때일 거야.
여 맞아요, 전 지금 아이를 봐준 지 몇 년 되었는데 다른 아이들에게도 분리 불안이 있는 걸 봤어요. 아이들은 대개 약 한 살에 부모님이 특별한 존재이고 부모님과 떨어지는 건 충격적인 일이라는 걸 깨닫기 시작하죠.
남 아내와 나는 우리 중 한 명이 일을 그만두고 집에 있을 것에 대해서도 이미 이야기를 나누었어.
여 그게 도움이 될지는 모르겠네요. 대학 심리학 수업에서 그 주제에 관한 책들을 읽고 있거든요. 부모님이 계속 일을 해서 아이들이 부모님한테 너무 의존하지 않게 하는 것이 더 나은 경우도 있다고 해요.
남 그럴지도 모르지. 하지만 아내는 토미와 더 많은 시간을 보내기로 마음먹은 것 같아.

6 What is NOT correct according to the dialog?
  대화에 따르면 다음 중 옳지 않은 것은?
  (a) The woman is babysitting for the Riggs family.
      여자는 리그스 가족의 아이를 봐주고 있다.
  (b) The baby boy was born very recently.
      남자아기는 바로 최근에 태어났다.
  (c) The mother of the baby boy did not come home.
      남자아기의 엄마는 집에 오지 않았다.
  (d) The woman has a lot of babysitting experience.
      여자는 아이를 봐준 경험이 많다.
  (e) The baby boy's grandmother is feeling sick.
      남자아기의 할머니는 아프다.

---

7 Level up

M Persuasion is the art of trying to get someone to do something for you or to give you something. There are a few methods that will help someone persuade someone else. First, ask for a lot more than you really want. The person is very likely to say no. Then you should ask for a lesser thing—the thing you really wanted all along. The person is now more likely to say yes to this request since he or she is mentally comparing it to the larger thing you just asked for. The person may also feel guilty for saying no to the first request, so the person will try to make himself or herself feel better by agreeing to the second, lesser request. For example, perhaps a teen asks his or her parents for 100 dollars. The parents immediately say no, after which the teen asks for 50 dollars, which the teen is now more likely to get for the reason I just explained.

▶ persuasion 설득, 납득; 설득력 method 방법, 방식 all along 줄곧, 처음부터; 끝에서 끝까지 mentally 정신적으로, 마음속으로 feel guilty (마음이) 꺼림칙하다; 잘못했다고[미안하다고] 생각하다

남 설득은 어떤 사람이 여러분을 위해 무엇을 하게 하거나 여러분에게 무엇을 주게 하는 기술입니다. 다른 사람을 설득하는 데 도움이 되는 몇 가지 방법이 있는데요. 먼저, 여러분이 정말로 원하는 것보다 훨씬 많은 것을 요구하십시오. 그 사람은 아마 거절할 것입니다. 그러고 나서 여러분은 더 적은 것을 요구해야 합니다. 애초에 여러분이 진정으로 원했던 것을 말이죠. 이제 그 사람은 마음속으로 그것과 여러분이 요구했던 더 큰 것을 비교하기 때문에 이 요청에 응할 가능성이 큽니다. 그 사람은 첫 번째 요청에 거절했던 것이 마음에 걸리기 때문에 두 번째의 더 적은 요청을 들어줌으로써 좀 더 편한 마음을 가지려고 할 것입니다. 예를 들면 한 십대 청소년이 부모님에게 100달러를 달라고 합니다. 부모님은 즉시 안 된다고 하겠죠. 그 후에 그 십대가 50달러를 달라고 하면 내가 방금 설명했던 이유로 아마 그 돈을 받게 될 것입니다.

7 What is the main topic of the talk? 담화의 주제는 무엇인가?
(a) The feeling of guilt that is associated with refusal
거절과 관련된 죄책감
(b) A way that enables teens to get higher allowances
10대들이 더 많은 용돈을 받을 수 있는 방법
(c) The reasons why people ask for more than they want
사람들이 원하는 것보다 더 많이 요구하는 이유
(d) A method to convince people to agree with a request
요구를 들어주도록 사람들을 설득하는 방법
(e) The ways people compare larger and smaller things
사람들이 더 큰 것과 더 작은 것을 비교하는 방식

8

W In ancient Greece, the doctor Hippocrates devised a system for categorizing people's character types based on their bodily fluids. While this connection of human character with bodily fluids is no longer made, there is still a belief that people have certain characters, or temperaments, that show their true personality. The four temperaments commonly referred to nowadays are sanguine, choleric, melancholic, and phlegmatic. A sanguine person is very carefree and lighthearted, is full of confidence, and has the ability to be a leader. However, a sanguine person can also be arrogant and impulsive and may be unable to finish things that he or she has started. Meanwhile, a choleric person has a lot of ambition and energy and has great charisma. On the negative side, choleric people can easily dominate other people, tend to be short-tempered, and want to have things their way. Next, melancholic people are very artistic and considerate. They are deep thinkers, perhaps too much so since melancholic people tend to

dwell on the bad things in the world, which can lead to depression. In addition, melancholic people strive for perfection to the point that they are very self-critical. The final temperament, phlegmatic, is associated with rationalism, consistency, and resistance to change. While some people may see themselves as fitting one of these four temperaments, it is hard to pigeon-hole each individual in just one temperament since most people exhibit characteristics of more than one of them.

▶ Hippocrates 히포크라테스(그리스의 의학자: 의학의 아버지라고 불림) devise 발명하다: 고안하다 categorize 분류하다: 특징짓다, 특징을 기술하다 bodily fluids 체액 temperament 기질, 성질, 성미 sanguine 다혈질의: 명랑한, 낙천적인 choleric 화를 잘 내는, 성마른 melancholic 우울질의, 우울한 phlegmatic 점액질의, 냉담한 carefree 근심[걱정]이 없는, 태평스러운: 무책임한 lighthearted 마음 편한: 쾌활한, 명랑한 arrogant 거만한, 오만한 impulsive 충동적인, 감정에 끌린 meanwhile 한편: 동시에 charisma 카리스마, 재능, 권능 dominate 좌우하다, 지배[위압]하다 short-tempered 성마른 considerate 사려깊은: 이해심이 있는 thinker 사색가, 생각하는 사람 dwell on (마음, 기억 따위가) ~에서 떠나지 않다, ~에 남다 self-critical 자기 비판적인 strive for perfection 완벽을 기하다 rationalism 합리주의: 이성주의 consistency 일관성, 언행일치 resistance 저항력, 반감 pigeon-hole 분류 정리하다

어 고대 그리스에서 히포크라테스 의사는 체액을 기반으로 해서 사람의 성격을 분류하는 시스템을 고안하였습니다. 인간의 성격과 체액을 연관짓는 것은 더 이상 행해지지 않지만 사람에게는 진정한 성격을 보여주는 특정한 성격이나 기질이 있다는 믿음은 여전히 있습니다. 오늘날 언급되는 네 가지 기질은 일반적으로 '다혈질', '담즙질', '우울질', '점액질'입니다. 다혈질인 사람은 매우 태평스럽고 쾌활하고 자신감이 넘치고 지도자가 될 능력을 갖추고 있습니다. 하지만 또한 오만하고 충동적이며 시작한 일을 끝맺지 못할 수 있습니다. 한편, 담즙질인 사람들은 큰 야망과 에너지 그리고 대단한 카리스마가 있습니다. 부정적인 면으로는 다른 사람들을 쉽게 좌우지할 수 있으며 화를 잘 내는 경향이 있고 자기 방식대로 일을 처리하려고 합니다. 다음으로 우울질인 사람들은 매우 예술적이고 사려가 깊습니다. 깊은 사색가인데, 그것이 너무 지나쳐서 세상의 나쁜 일에 대한 생각이 떠나지 않아 우울증이 올 수가 있습니다. 더불어 우울질인 사람들은 매우 자기 비판적이 될 정도로 완벽을 추구하려 애를 씁니다. 마지막으로 '점액질'은 이성주의, 일관성, 변화에 대한 반감과 관련이 있습니다. 어떤 사람들은 자신들이 이 네 가지 기질 중 하나와 맞는다고 보는 반면 대부분의 사람들은 한 가지 이상의 특성을 보이기 때문에 개인을 하나의 기질로만 분류하기는 어렵습니다.

8 성격과 네 가지 기질을 연결하시오. 각 기질에는 두 가지 특징이 있습니다.

성격
a. 충동적인
b. 우울한
c. 이성적인
d. 야심찬
e. 완벽주의자
f. 일관된
g. 쾌활한
h. 화를 잘 내는

(1) 다혈질 <u>a, g</u>
(2) 담즙질 <u>d, h</u>
(3) 우울질 <u>b, e</u>
(4) 점액질 <u>c, f</u>

9-10 Integrated Questions

Reading

▶ a position of authority 힘있는 자리: 권위가 있는 자리 subject 지배하다: 복종[종속]시키다 mock prison 모의 감옥 guard 교도관 get out of hand 과도해지다: 감당할 수 없게 되다 sadistic 가학적인, 사디스트적인 humiliateing 굴욕적인 rebellious 반항하는, 반역하는 docile 온순한, 유순한 compliant 유순한, 시키는 대로 하는, 고분고분한 emotional trauma 정신적 충격 emotional distress

정신적 고통, 심적 고통 relish 즐기다; 기쁘게 생각하다
be beyond one's control 제지할 수 없다; 마음대로 되지 않다

1971년 4월에 미국 스탠포드 대학에서 심리학 교수인 필립 짐바르도가 일부 사람들에게 힘 있는 자리를 주고 그 밖의 사람들에게는 그 힘에 복종하게 했을 때 어떤 일이 일어나는지를 가늠하기 위해 실험을 고안했다. 짐바르도는 대학 건물 지하에 지어진 모의 감옥 아이디어를 이용했는데, 어떤 학생들은 교도관으로, 그 밖의 학생들은 죄수로 지정했다. 그 실험은 2주간 지속될 예정이었지만 상황이 감당 못할 정도가 되어 6일 후에 끝내야만 했다. 교도관 역할을 한 학생들은 빠른 시간 안에 매우 잔인해졌고 심지어는 가학성을 띠기까지 했으며 굴욕적인 정신적, 육체적 학대로 학생 죄수들을 지배했다. 한편 처음에는 다소 반항적이었던 죄수들은 매우 온순해졌고 결국 시키는 대로 하게 되었다. 학생 죄수들 중 2명은 심한 정신적인 충격에 시달렸고 나머지 죄수들은 심적 고통의 징후를 보였다. 학생 교도관들은 자신들의 역할을 즐기는 것 같았고 실험이 일찍 끝났을 때는 실망감을 보이기까지 했다. 짐바르도는 모든 것을 관찰했고 자신이 제어할 수 없는 상황임이 명백해지자 속히 실험을 끝내야 했다.

M Okay, now that we have some background information on the Stanford Prison Experiment, I want to discuss it in terms of what can be learned from it. The experiment shows just how quickly normal people can become sadistic and how others can become subservient. The students involved in this famous case were all males and all of university age. They were mostly white and middle-class and were what would be considered normal from a psychological viewpoint. The professor designed the experiment to take away the human identity of the guards and prisoners. The guards all wore the same uniforms and sunglasses so that the prisoners could not see them as individuals. The prisoners wore a prison-type uniform with numbers and could not use their names. This enabled the guards to see them not as people but as objects. By the second day, the guards had started to abuse the prisoners. The prisoners eventually became traumatized by the abuse and became obedient despite earlier simmerings of rebellion. Because there were no signs of sadistic tendencies in any of the guards beforehand, the experiment showed that the sadistic behavior of the guards was a result of the situation they were in and not the result of the personalities of the people involved. Similarly, the student prisoners had no history of emotional problems, and their trauma was the result of the situation they were in. Similar results have been seen in other such experiments and, even tragically, in real life in the infamous case where American soldiers abused Iraqi prisoners of war.

▶ subservient 비굴한, 아첨하는 take away 제거하다 abuse 학대, 혹사
traumatize 충격을 주다, 정신적 충격(쇼크)을 주다 simmer 당장이라도 폭발하려 하다
rebellion 모반, 반란, 폭동 obedient 순종하는, 고분고분한 beforehand 사전에
Iraqi 이라크 사람(의), 이라크 말(의) infamous 악명 높은, 악독한, 악랄한

남 자, 스탠포드 대학 감옥 실험에 대한 배경 정보를 알았으니 거기서 무엇을 배울 수 있는가 하는 견지에서 이에 대해 논의해 보도록 하겠습니다. 실험은 정상인들이 얼마나 빨리 사디스트적이 될 수 있고 어떻게 비굴해질 수 있는지를 보여줍니다. 이 유명한 사례에 연관된 학생들은 모두 남성들이었고 대학생 나이였습니다. 대부분이 백인이었고 중산 계층이었으며 심리학적 관점에서 볼 때 정상적이었습니다. 교수는 교도관들과 죄수들의 인간적인 정체성을 제거하도록 실험을 설계했습니다. 교도관들은 모두 같은 유니폼과 선글라스를 썼기 때문에 죄수들이 그들을 개인으로 볼 수 없었습니다. 죄수들은 번호가 있는 죄수복을 입고 자기 이름을 사용할 수 없었습니다. 이로 인해 교도관들은 그들을 사람이 아닌 사물로

보았습니다. 두 번째 날부터 교도관들은 죄수들을 학대하기 시작했습니다. 초반에는 금방 폭동이 일어날 것 같았음에도 죄수들은 결국 학대에 의해 정신적 충격을 받게 되었고 고분고분해졌습니다. 이전에는 교도관들에게 그 어떤 사디스트적인 경향의 징후도 없었기 때문에, 실험은 교도관의 사디스트적인 행동이 그들이 처해 있는 상황의 결과이고, 관련된 사람들의 성격에서 나온 것이 아님을 보여주었습니다. 마찬가지로, 학생 죄수들에게도 감정적인 문제가 있었던 전력은 없었으므로 그들이 받은 정신적 충격은 그들이 처한 상황으로 인한 것이었습니다. 이와 같은 다른 실험에서도 유사한 결과가 나왔으며, 더욱 비극적이게도, 실생활에서는 미군 병사들이 이라크 전쟁 포로를 학대한 악명 높은 사례가 발생한 적이 있습니다.

9 읽기와 듣기 지문에 따르면 다음 중 사실이 <u>아닌</u> 것은?
(a) 교도관은 죄수를 처벌하기 위해 물리적인 수단을 사용하도록 허용되었다.
(b) 각 죄수는 번호를 할당받았고 그들의 이름은 전혀 사용되지 않았다.
(c) 죄수들에 대한 학대는 실험 첫날부터 시작되었다.
(d) 각 교도관은 사디스트적인 행동을 한 전력이 없었다.
(e) 죄수들은 반항할 계획이 있었으나 실행하지는 않았다.

10 읽기와 듣기 지문에서 유추할 수 있는 것은?
(a) 교수는 일부 실험에는 참석하지 않았다.
(b) 학생들은 심리학과 학생들이었다.
(c) 일부 교도관들은 실험이 끝났을 때 화를 냈다.
(d) 학생들은 실험을 위해 신중하게 선정되었다.
(e) 일부 죄수들은 실험이 계속되기를 원했다.

***Dictation 정답:** Exercise 스크립트 밑줄 참조

UNIT 02 Art and Culture

Preparation p. 23

Vocabulary Preview

A

1 commission: 예술가에게 예술 작품을 만들라고 주는 자금
2 perspective: 그림에 거리감을 창출해내기 위한 기법
3 vilify: 누군가에 대해 악의적인 말을 하거나 독설을 내뱉다
4 conventional: 일반적인 기준으로 여겨지는 것을 따라가는 경향이 있는
5 innovative: 특히 뭔가를 하는 방법이 새롭고 독창적인

B

1 acceptance rate / 일부 미술 학교와 음악 학교는 그들이 요구하는 높은 기준 때문에 경쟁률이 아주 낮다.
2 obscure / 어떤 미술 형식과 음악 형식은 너무 난해해서 아는 사람이 거의 없다.
3 referring to / 난 지금 숲 속에서 말을 타고 있는 남자 그림을 말하는 거야.
4 astounding / 미켈란젤로가 시스티나 성당에 그린 그림은 매우 경이롭다.
5 pay dividends / 미술 투자는 미래에 보상받을 수 있다.
6 conductor / 지휘자가 지휘봉을 들자 오케스트라는 연주를 하기 시작했다.
7 lauded / 모차르트는 겨우 여섯 살 때 신동이라고 칭송받았다.

Expressions and Meanings

1 그녀를 한 번만이라도 봤으면 좋겠어. 　⊙ 그녀를 만나 보고 싶어.

2 너에게 딱 맞는 일을 찾았구나. 　⊙ 넌 어떤 직업을 갖고 싶어하는지 알고 있구나.

3 내 그림은 조금 손질해야 해. 　⊙ 몇 가지 사소한 문제들을 수정해야 해.

4 넌 성적을 잘 유지해야 한다. 　⊙ 넌 학교 성적이 좋아야 해.

5 기적이 일어나야 가능할 거야. 　⊙ 성공 가능성이 낮아.

6 그는 전도유망한 화가야. 　⊙ 그는 나중에 유명해질 거야.

7 그 투자는 막대한 이익을 낳았다. 　⊙ 많은 수익이 생겼다.

Listening Drill 1　　　　　　　p. 24~p. 25

Monolog

O (1) prehistoric　(2) 2,000　(3) 16,000　(4) intricate detail　(5) in motion　(6) perspective　(7) bright　(8) natural minerals　(9) animal bones　(10) decoration　(11) hidden　(12) ceremonial　(13) religious　(14) hunters

G 1 (c)　2 (a)

S (1) F　(2) T　(3) F　(4) T

M Some of the best examples of prehistoric art are in the Lascaux Cave in southwestern France. The cave was discovered by four teenage boys out exploring on September 12, 1940. There are around 2,000 figures, mostly animals such as horses, bison, deer, and bulls, depicted on the walls of the cave. Experts believe that the paintings in the cave are over 16,000 years old. The skills of the artists were marvelous; they used intricate detail, showed the animals in motion, and had the ability to use perspective by crossing the animal's legs. The painters painted in very bright colors like red and yellow as well as using black charcoal. They created their paints by using natural minerals that were mixed with animal fat, spit, or blood to create a paste. The artists used many methods to apply the paint. These included feathers, sticks, and moss as well as their own hands and fingers. They also used hollow tubes from animal bones to blow the paint on the walls to create an airbrushed effect. Experts believe the paintings were not decorations because they are in hidden locations, are not easy to see, and are far from where the people lived. Perhaps the paintings had ceremonial or religious purposes, and some have suggested that they were instructions for hunters.

▶ bison 들소　depict 그리다, 묘사하다　intricate 복잡한　perspective 원근법　charcoal 숯, 목탄　spit 침, 타액　apply 바르다: 발라지다

남 선사시대 미술의 가장 훌륭한 예 중 일부는 프랑스 남서부의 라스코 동굴에 있습니다. 라스코 동굴은 1940년 9월 12일 야외 탐사를 하던 네 명의 십대 소년들에 의해 발견되었습니다. 동굴 벽에는 약 2,000여 개의 형상이 그려져 있는데요, 대부분 말, 들소, 사슴, 황소 같은 동물입니다. 전문가들은 동굴에 있는 벽화가 1만 6천년 이상 된 것이라고 생각하고 있죠. 벽화를 그린 화가들의 기술은 놀라울 정도입니다. 그들은 복잡한 세부 묘사를 활용했고, 움직이는 동물들을 보여주며, 동물의 다리를 교차시킴으로써 원근법을 사용할 줄 아는 능력이 있었습니다. 검은 목탄을 사용했을 뿐만 아니라 빨강과 노랑 같은 아주 밝은 색으로 채색했습니다.

그들은 천연 광물을 이용해 물감을 만들었는데요, 페이스트를 만들기 위해 동물의 지방이나 침, 피를 섞었죠. 그 동굴 벽화를 그린 화가들은 많은 방법을 이용해 물감을 칠했습니다. 자신들의 손과 손가락만이 아니라 깃털이나 막대기, 이끼도 사용했죠. 그들은 또한 동물의 뼈로 만든 속이 빈 관을 이용해 동굴 벽에 물감을 뿜어 에어브러시 효과를 냈습니다. 전문가들은 그 벽화가 쉽게 눈에 띄지 않는 숨겨진 곳에 있고, 사람들이 살던 곳에서 멀리 떨어져 있는 것으로 보아 장식품은 아니었을 것이라고 생각하고 있습니다. 아마도 그 벽화에는 어떤 의식이나 종교적인 목적이 있었을 겁니다. 몇몇 사람들은 그 벽화가 사냥꾼을 위한 지침서였을 거라고 생각하죠.

General Questions

1 담화에 가장 알맞은 제목은 무엇인가?
(a) 라스코 벽화의 의의
(b) 라스코 벽화의 발견
(c) 라스코 동굴 미술의 기법과 목적
(d) 고대 동굴 벽화의 몇가지 기법

2 다음 중 가장 잘 요약된 것을 고르시오.
(a) 프랑스의 라스코 동굴 미술의 궁극적인 목적은 알 수 없지만 그림을 그린 화가들이 사용한 재료와 기법은 규명되었다.
(b) 프랑스의 라스코 동굴 미술은 선사시대의 것으로 사람들에게 사냥법을 가르쳐주기 위해 제작되었을 것이다.

Specific Questions

다시 듣고 옳은 문장에는 T, 틀린 문장에는 F를 쓰시오.
(1) 라스코 동굴 벽화를 그린 화가의 솜씨는 매우 서툴렀다.
(2) 동굴 벽화를 그린 화가들이 사용한 물감은 재료가 다양했다.
(3) 라스코 동굴 벽화는 장식품이었을 것이다.
(4) 프랑스의 라스코 동굴 벽화는 1만년 이상 된 것이다.

Dialog

N (1) merchant's wife　(2) German　(3) Paris　(4) 1913　(5) two

G 1 (c)　2 (b)

S (1) T　(2) F　(3) F　(4) F

W Finally we're here in Paris at the Louvre, and today I'm going to see Leonardo da Vinci's *Mona Lisa*!

M I know it's supposed to be a great painting, but I don't really understand why.

W Actually, for a long time, it wasn't considered to be as great as many other artists' work, and it's only in the 20th century that it has achieved that status.

M Why do you think it's so special?

W It's hard to say, really, but, like everyone else, I think it's her smile which captures my attention. Also, the mystery of the woman in the painting makes it fascinating.

M Ah, she's not a mystery woman anymore. I heard that she was Lisa Del Giocondo, a rich merchant's wife. Some German researchers recently uncovered this fact.

W Yes, I heard that, too, but I meant she has a mysterious quality about her. It's like she has a secret. Also, it's the quality of the work that I find most impressive since it shows the great skill of Leonardo. The *Mona Lisa* was admired by French kings for centuries, and even

Napoleon had it hung in his bedroom when he was emperor.

M I think part of its fame also comes from it having been stolen in 1913 and having disappeared for two years.

W Yeah, that created a lot of interest at the time. Oh, wow! Look at the line. We're going to have to wait a while before we can finally see it.

M At least we know her smile will still be there when it's our turn to catch a glimpse.

▶ status 지위 catch a glimpse 힐끗 보다, 슬쩍 보다

여 드디어 파리의 루브르 박물관에 왔구나. 난 오늘 레오나르도 다 빈치의 〈모나리자〉를 보고야 말 거야!
남 그게 명화라는 건 아는데 그 이유는 진짜 모르겠어.
여 사실 그 그림은 오랫동안 다른 많은 화가들의 작품만큼 훌륭한 그림으로 여겨지진 않았어. 20세기 들어서야 지금의 지위를 얻었지.
남 넌 그 그림이 왜 그렇게 특별하다고 생각해?
여 말로 설명하기 정말 힘들어. 하지만 나도 다른 사람들처럼 시선을 사로잡는 그녀의 미소 때문이라고 생각해. 그림 속의 여자에 얽힌 수수께끼 덕에 더 매혹적이기도 하고.
남 아, 그녀는 더 이상 수수께끼의 여자가 아니야. 그녀는 부유한 상인의 아내였던 리자 델 지오콘도라는군. 몇몇 독일 연구자들이 최근에 그 사실을 밝혀냈어.
여 응, 나도 그 얘긴 들었어. 그런데 내 말은 그녀에게는 신비로운 면이 있다는 거야. 마치 뭔가 비밀을 갖고 있는 것 같잖아. 그리고 내가 제일 인상적으로 느낀 건 바로 그 작품의 우수성이야. 그 그림은 레오나르도의 뛰어난 솜씨를 보여주거든. 〈모나리자〉는 수세기 동안 프랑스 국왕들의 칭송을 받았고, 나폴레옹도 황제였을 때 그 그림을 침실에 걸어놓았대.
남 1913년에 도난 당해 2년 동안 사라졌었다는 사실도 그 그림의 명성에 한몫 하는 것 같아.
여 맞아. 그 당시에 대단한 관심을 불러일으켰지. 이런, 와! 저 줄 좀 봐. 그림 보려면 좀 기다려야겠다.
남 우리 차례가 되어 그림을 볼 수 있을 때까지 모나리자의 미소는 여전히 거기 있을 테니까 됐지 뭐.

General Questions

1 대화의 주제는 무엇인가?
(a) 한 화가의 가장 유명한 미술 작품
(b) 어떤 그림에 대한 프랑스 국왕들의 애정
(c) 어떤 그림이 그토록 유명한 이유
(d) 어떤 유명한 그림이 있는 장소

2 다음 중 가장 잘 요약된 것을 고르시오.
(a) 〈모나리자〉의 모델에 대한 수수께끼가 최근 풀리면서 그 그림에 대한 새로운 관심과 명성으로 이어졌다.
(b) 〈모나리자〉의 명성은 몇 가지 요인에 기인하는데, 그 요인에는 모델이 누구였는지에 관한 수수께끼와 도난 사건과 관련된 음모가 포함되어 있다.

Specific Questions

다시 듣고 옳은 문장에는 T, 틀린 문장에는 F를 쓰시오.
(1) 루브르는 파리의 주요 관광 명소로 보인다.
(2) 프랑스 연구자들은 〈모나리자〉의 모델 이름을 밝혀냈다.
(3) 〈모나리자〉는 1902년에 도난 당해 13년간 사라졌다.
(4) 두 사람은 곧바로 〈모나리자〉를 보러 들어간다.

Long Lecture

◉ (1) 1616 (2) 18 (3) unknown (4) 38 (5) 154 (6) acting (7) part owner (8) successful (9) plays (10) his death

1 (a) **2** (a) **3** (1) F (2) T (3) F (4) F **4** (c)

Dictation 정답: 스크립트 밑줄 참조

W In this term's English literature class, we will be examining the works of William Shakespeare. Today, we'll start with a brief introduction of his life before looking at his work. Shakespeare is considered the greatest writer in English literature. His fame rests on his lifetime work of 38 plays and 154 sonnets as well as some other poems. Shakespeare's plays have been performed more often than any other playwright's and have been translated into almost every major language. He was born in Stratford-upon-Avon, England, in 1564 and died 52 years later in 1616. Little is known about his childhood, but he most likely attended the local school in Stratford and studied the classics. He married a local woman, Anne Hathaway, at the age of 18, and she bore him three children—two daughters and a son. His son died at age 11, but the reason for his death is unknown. Not much else is known of Shakespeare's life after his marriage and prior to his start in the London theater world. Even when or why he started to write is veiled. He was in London acting by 1592, and some of his plays were being performed on London stages. In 1594, Shakespeare was a part owner in a playing company called the *Lord Chamberlain's Men*, which soon became the top performing company in London. Shakespeare became very successful over the next 20 years, and he invested in theaters and property and bought a large home in Stratford. It was only after Shakespeare's death that two of his company partners compiled his plays into a book. Of course, these plays have been staged nonstop ever since, and Shakespeare's legacy has only grown in the centuries since his death.

▶ playwright 극작가 the classics (고대 그리스, 로마의) 고전 문학
veil 감추다, 숨기다 part owner 공동 소유자 property 부동산, 토지
compile (자료를 모아 책을) 편찬(편집)하다 legacy 유산, 가치

여 이번 학기 영문학 수업에서는 윌리엄 셰익스피어의 작품을 공부할 겁니다. 오늘은 작품을 살펴보기 전에 그의 생애에 관해 간략하게 소개하면서 수업을 시작하도록 하죠. 셰익스피어는 영문학사에서 가장 위대한 작가로 간주됩니다. 그의 명성은 평생에 걸쳐 쓴 38편의 희곡과 154편의 소네트뿐만 아니라 몇 편의 시에 기인하죠. 셰익스피어의 희곡은 다른 어느 극작가의 작품보다 더 많이 공연되었으며 거의 모든 주요 언어로 번역되었습니다. 셰익스피어는 1564년에 영국의 스트래트포드 어폰 에이번에서 태어나 52년 뒤인 1616년에 죽었습니다. 그의 어린 시절에 관해서는 알려진 바가 거의 없지만 스트래트포드 지역에 있는 학교를 다니면서 고전 문학을 공부했을 가능성이 매우 큽니다. 셰익스피어는 18세 때 그 지역의 앤 해서웨이라는 여자와 결혼했습니다. 그녀는 딸 둘과 아들 하나, 이렇게 세 명의 아이를 낳았습니다. 아들은 열한 살 때 죽었는데 사인은 밝혀지지 않았죠. 그 외 결혼 후부터 런던 극장계에서 활동을 시작하기 전까지의 삶에 관해서는 알려진 게 별로 없습니다. 심지어는 그가 언제부터 왜 글을 쓰기 시작했는지조차 베일에 가려져 있죠. 셰익스피어는 1592년까지 배우 생활을 하면서 런던에 있었고, 그의 희곡 몇 편은 런던의 무대에서 공연되고 있었습니다. 1594년 셰익스피어는 궁내부장관극단이라는 극단의 공동 소유자가 되었고, 그곳은

곧 런던 최고의 극단으로 발돋움했습니다. 셰익스피어는 이후 20년 넘게 아주 큰 성공을 거두었고, 극장과 부동산에 투자했으며, 스트래트포드에 대저택을 구입했습니다. 그가 죽고 난 뒤에야 극단 공동 소유자 중 두 명이 셰익스피어의 희곡을 책으로 묶어 냈습니다. 물론 이 희곡들은 그 후 끊임없이 무대에 올려졌으며 셰익스피어의 유산은 그의 사후 수세기 동안 발전에 발전을 거듭했습니다.

1 강의의 목적은 무엇인가?
  (a) 셰익스피어의 전기를 설명하려고
  (b) 셰익스피어가 왜 그렇게 유명해졌는지 설명하려고
  (c) 셰익스피어가 사후에 거둔 성공을 보여주려고
  (d) 셰익스피어의 영감이 어디에서 비롯되었는지 논의하려고

2 다음 중 가장 잘 요약된 것을 고르시오.
  (a) 윌리엄 셰익스피어는 그의 성공적인 일생 동안 희곡과 소네트를 썼으며 그의 희곡은 오늘날에도 공연되고 있다.
  (b) 윌리엄 셰익스피어의 생애는 두 곳에 집중되어 있었다. 그가 초년 시절을 보냈던 스트래트포드 어폰 에이번과 여생을 보냈던 런던이 바로 그곳이다.

3 옳은 문장에는 T, 틀린 문장에는 F를 쓰시오.
  (1) 셰익스피어의 작품은 생전에 책으로 출판되었다.
  (2) 셰익스피어는 살아 있는 동안 명성과 부를 쌓았다.
  (3) 셰익스피어의 아들은 치명적인 전염병이 돌 때 죽었다.
  (4) 셰익스피어는 궁내부장관극단의 단독 소유자였다.

4 셰익스피어는 언제부터 희곡을 쓰기 시작했는가?
  (a) 런던에 이주해서 쓰기 시작했다.
  (b) 결혼 직후에 쓰기 시작했다.
  (c) 언제부터 쓰기 시작했는지 여전히 확실치 않다.
  (d) 아들을 잃고 나서 희곡을 쓰기 시작했다.

1 (a)	2 (b)	3 (b)	4 (e)	5 (e)	6 (b)	7 (d)
8 (d)	9 (c)	10 해설 참조	11 (c)	12 (a)		

1

M We can learn a lot about the history and daily lives of ancient civilizations through their art. For example, frescos can be found in the ruins of many ancient civilizations. A fresco is a type of wall painting or mural usually done in wet plaster. The paint is applied to the wet plaster, and, when it dries, it creates a permanent bond. Under the right conditions, a fresco can last thousands of years. One of the earliest examples of this type of fresco is found on the island of Crete in Greece and comes from the Minoan civilization. It dates from 1,500 B.C. and shows a youth jumping over a charging bull. Frescos have also been found in ancient Egyptian tombs and in caves in India. The Indian frescos show the life of Buddha and have been of great importance to scholars. The greatest collection of Roman frescos was found at Pompeii. The city was buried under volcanic ash in 79 A.D., which helped preserve the frescos for over fifteen hundred years. These frescos have given archaeologists and historians great insight into the daily lives of Romans. Frescos became a very common art form during the Renaissance. Michelangelo's *The Creation of Adam*, in which God gives life to the first man, Adam, is found on the ceiling of the Sistine Chapel and is considered the most famous fresco in history.

▶ mural 벽화, 천장화 plaster 회반죽 bond 접착 charge 돌진하다 A.D. 서기 archaeologist 고고학자 insight 식견; 통찰

남 우리는 고대 미술을 통해 고대 문명의 역사와 일상 생활에 관해 많은 것을 알 수 있습니다. 예를 들어 프레스코화는 많은 고대 문명의 유적에서 볼 수 있죠. 프레스코화는 보통 젖은 석회에 그리는 벽화나 천장화의 일종입니다. 젖은 석회에 물감을 칠한 뒤 그것이 마르면 영구적으로 착색되는데요. 조건만 맞으면 프레스코화는 수천 년도 견딜 수 있습니다. 이런 형태의 프레스코화의 가장 초기 사례 가운데 하나는 그리스의 크레테 섬에서 발견되었는데 이것은 미노스 문명의 것입니다. 기원전 1,500년 전의 것으로 한 젊은이가 돌진해오는 소를 뛰어넘는 그림이죠. 프레스코화는 고대 이집트의 고분과 인도의 동굴에서도 발견되었습니다. 인도의 프레스코화는 부처의 일생을 보여주고 있어 학자들에게는 대단히 중요하죠. 로마 프레스코화의 가장 훌륭한 작품들은 폼페이에서 발견되었습니다. 폼페이는 서기 79년에 화산재 아래 묻힘으로써 프레스코화들이 1,500년 넘게 보존될 수 있었습니다. 이 프레스코화들 덕분에 고고학자와 역사학자들은 로마의 일상 생활에 대해 많은 것을 알게 되었죠. 프레스코화는 르네상스 기간 동안 매우 일반적인 미술 양식이 되었습니다. 시스티나 성당 천장에 있는 미켈란젤로의 〈아담의 탄생〉은 신이 최초의 인간인 아담에게 생명을 불어넣어주는 그림인데 역사상 가장 유명한 프레스코화로 간주됩니다.

1 담화의 요지는 무엇인가?
  (a) 프레스코화로 과거의 삶을 알 수 있다.
  (b) 프레스코화의 역사적인 사례는 많다.
  (c) 고대 로마는 많은 훌륭한 프레스코화의 산실이었다.
  (d) 프레스코화는 역사상 가장 오래된 미술 양식 가운데 하나이다.
  (e) 많은 문명에서 그 문명만의 고유한 프레스코화 기법이 개발되었다.

2

W Welcome to my art gallery. If anything catches your eye, maybe we can talk about purchasing it.
M Sure thing. Say, these look nice. What do you call them?
W These are examples of still life. It's a very old form of painting in which the artist takes some common objects, such as fruit, arranges them, and then does the painting. It is a usual beginning work for amateur artists. In fact, these were done by some students at a local art school.
M I like that one there. It seems to be calling to me.
W Ah, excuse me, sir. Which one?
M The one with the apples and oranges.
W Sir, some of them have green apples, and some have red apples. Which is it?
M Three red apples and two oranges. I think there is a banana hidden behind... are those grapes?
W Yes, sir. Some of the works have purple grapes, and some have green grapes. Which are you referring to?
M I want to take a closer look at the painting with the red apples, oranges, one banana, and the bunch of green grapes.
W There are two very similar ones. One has the fruit on a table in the kitchen, and the other has the fruit on a

M The one in the kitchen. That's the one. How much is it?

W It was done by an <u>amateur</u> <u>artist</u> <u>after</u> <u>all</u>, so it's just 50 dollars.

M Okay, I'll <u>take</u> it. Oh, I'm hungry. Maybe <u>that's</u> <u>why</u> I like this painting so much.

▶ catch 끌다, 사로잡다 Sure thing. 그럴게요. 알았습니다. say 어머나, 저어
still life 정물화 arrange 배치하다, 배열하다 refer to 지시하다, 언급하다
take a close look at ~을 주의 깊게[세심히] 보다 bunch 송이, 다발

여 저희 화랑에 오신 것을 환영합니다. 마음에 드는 게 있으시다면 구입에 대해서도 의논하실 수 있답니다.

남 그럴게요. 어, 이거 괜찮네요. 뭐라고 하는 거죠?

여 그건 정물화예요. 아주 오래된 미술 양식으로, 화가가 과일 같은 일상적인 물건을 골라 배치해놓고 그리는 거죠. 아마추어 화가들이 보통 처음 시작할 때 그리는 그림이에요. 사실 이것들은 이 지역의 미술 학교 학생들이 그린 거랍니다.

남 저기 있는 저 그림이 마음에 드는군요. 마치 날 부르고 있는 것 같아요.

여 아, 죄송합니다만 어떤 것 말씀이신가요?

남 사과하고 오렌지가 있는 거요.

여 어떤 그림엔 파란 사과가 있고 어떤 그림엔 빨간 사과가 있는데요. 그 중에서 어떤 건가요?

남 빨간 사과 세 개와 오렌지 두 개가 있는 거요. 내 생각에는 뒤에 바나나가 한 개 숨어 있는 것 같은데… 저건 포도인가요?

여 네, 선생님. 어떤 건 자주색 포도가 있고 어떤 건 청포도가 있는데요. 그 중에서 어떤 걸 말씀하시는 거죠?

남 빨간 사과와 오렌지, 바나나 한 개, 청포도송이가 있는 저 그림을 좀 더 자세히 보고 싶어요.

여 무척 비슷한 게 두 점 있는데요. 하나는 주방 식탁 위에 과일이 있고 다른 하나는 야외 피크닉 테이블 위에 과일이 있네요.

남 주방에 있는 겁니다. 바로 그거요. 얼마죠?

여 아마추어 화가가 그린 것이라서 50달러밖에 안 합니다.

남 좋습니다. 그걸 사죠. 아, 배가 고프네요. 그래서 이 그림이 그렇게 좋은지도 모르겠네요.

2 다음 중 남자가 고른 그림은 어떤 것인가?

(a)  (b)  (c)  (d)  (e) 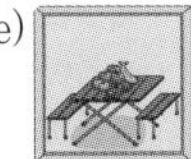

3-4

W Luciano Pavarotti <u>was</u> <u>renowned</u> <u>as</u> a world-class <u>opera</u> <u>singer</u>, but he didn't always <u>plan</u> <u>on</u> <u>pursuing</u> <u>this</u> <u>career</u>. Pavarotti was <u>born</u> <u>into</u> a poor Italian family in 1935 in Modena. His father was a <u>baker</u> and amateur singer and <u>struggled</u> <u>to</u> <u>provide</u> for his family. Pavarotti <u>enjoyed</u> <u>listening</u> to his father's <u>records</u> and <u>started</u> <u>singing</u> with his father in the <u>church</u> <u>choir</u> when he was 9 years old. When Pavarotti was young, his <u>real</u> <u>interest</u> was <u>soccer</u>, and he <u>wanted</u> <u>to</u> <u>be</u> a soccer player, but his mother <u>convinced</u> <u>him</u> that teaching was a <u>safer</u> <u>career</u> <u>choice</u>. He wasn't happy as a teacher, so at the age of 19, he <u>started</u> <u>to</u> <u>take</u> some <u>formal</u> <u>singing</u> <u>lessons</u> with a local singing teacher. Pavarotti became <u>a</u> <u>member</u> <u>of</u> his father's singing <u>chorus</u> from his hometown. In 1955, the group <u>traveled</u> <u>to</u> Wales and <u>won</u> <u>first</u> <u>place</u> in an <u>international</u> <u>singing</u> <u>contest</u>. After this, Pavarotti <u>quit</u> <u>teaching</u> and <u>devoted</u> <u>himself</u> full time to becoming a professional opera singer. He <u>made</u> <u>his</u> <u>début</u> in 1961

---

in Italy in the opera *La Boheme*, where he played the <u>part</u> <u>of</u> Rodolfo, and he made his <u>international</u> <u>début</u> playing the same part in London. Over the years, he was <u>lauded</u> <u>as</u> one of the greatest voices ever to <u>grace</u> <u>the</u> <u>stage</u>. His death at age 71 in 2007 <u>from</u> <u>cancer</u> was a <u>blow</u> for music lovers everywhere.

▶ pursue 종사하다 provide for 부양하다 laud 칭송하다, 찬미하다 grace 빛내다
blow 정신적 타격, 충격

여 루치아노 파바로티는 세계적인 오페라 가수로 유명하지만 그가 언제나 이 직업을 가지려고 했던 것은 아니었습니다. 파바로티는 1935년 모데나의 가난한 이탈리아 집안에서 태어났습니다. 아버지는 제빵업자이자 아마추어 가수로 어렵게 가족을 부양했는데요. 파바로티는 아버지가 갖고 있는 음반을 즐겨 들었고 9세 때 아버지와 함께 교회 성가대에서 노래하기 시작했죠. 파바로티가 어렸을 때 진짜 관심을 가졌던 것은 축구로, 그는 축구 선수가 되고 싶었지만 어머니는 교직이 더 안전한 직업 선택이라고 그를 설득했습니다. 교사로서 행복하지 않았던 그는 19세 때 그 지역의 노래 교사에게 정규 노래 수업을 받기 시작했습니다. 파바로티는 고향에서 아버지의 합창단 단원이 되었지요. 1955년 합창단은 웨일즈로 가 국제적인 노래 대회에서 1등을 했습니다. 이후 파바로티는 교직을 그만두고 전문적인 오페라 가수가 되는 데 전력을 다했습니다. 그는 1961년 이탈리아에서 오페라 〈라 보엠〉의 로돌포 역을 맡으며 데뷔했습니다. 그리고 같은 배역으로 런던에서 국제적인 데뷔를 했죠. 수십 년 동안 그는 무대를 빛낸 역사상 최고의 가수 가운데 한 명으로 칭송받았습니다. 2007년 71세에 암으로 인한 그의 죽음은 전 세계 음악 애호가들에게 큰 충격이었습니다.

3 파바로티가 전업 오페라 가수가 되는 데 가장 큰 영향을 미친 것은 무엇인가?
(a) 아버지에게서 받은 격려 (b) 국제 대회에서의 성공
(c) 축구 선수가 되지 못한 것 (d) 무대 경력을 쌓기 시작한 것
(e) 팬들로부터 받은 칭찬

4 담화에서 유추할 수 있는 것은 무엇인가?
(a) 파바로티의 아버지는 그 지역의 교회에서 노래를 배웠다.
(b) 파바로티의 어머니는 그다지 열렬한 축구 팬이 아니었다.
(c) 파바로티는 합창단의 리더였다.
(d) 파바로티의 재능은 어머니에게서 물려받은 것이었다.
(e) 파바로티의 어머니는 그에게 많은 영향을 미쳤다.

5-6 Level up

B You're really an <u>incredible</u> <u>dancer</u>, Katherine. <u>How</u> <u>long</u> have you been <u>taking</u> <u>lessons</u>?

G I started <u>studying</u> <u>ballet</u> when I was five. Since then, I've taken lessons in <u>tap</u>, <u>jazz</u>, and <u>modern</u> <u>dance</u>. I really love dancing.

B Are you planning to be a <u>professional</u> <u>dancer</u>?

G I hope so. When I <u>graduate</u>, I plan to <u>apply</u> <u>to</u> Julliard.

B I've <u>heard</u> <u>of</u> <u>it</u>. It's in New York City, right? I thought it was <u>mostly</u> a <u>music</u> <u>school</u>.

G It <u>started</u> <u>as</u> just a music school when it <u>was</u> <u>founded</u>, but it has since <u>expanded</u> <u>into</u> dance and acting.

B I guess it'll be tough to <u>get</u> <u>accepted</u> <u>there</u>.

G Yeah. The <u>acceptance</u> <u>rate</u> is around 6 percent. Some people say it's <u>more</u> <u>difficult</u> to <u>get</u> <u>into</u> than Harvard. It'll <u>take</u> <u>a</u> <u>miracle</u> to get accepted.

B You're really <u>amazing</u> though, so I'm sure <u>you'll</u> <u>get</u> <u>in</u>.

G Thanks. But it's also very expensive, so I might not

B even be <u>able to afford it</u>. So, what are you <u>planning to do after graduation</u>?

B I'm also planning to go to New York City.

G Oh, which university? Columbia?

B Nope. I'm going to the New York <u>Film Academy</u>. I'm going to be a <u>great movie director</u> like Steven Spielberg and Martin Scorsese.

G I didn't know you <u>were into making movies</u>.

B I really <u>got into it</u> over the summer after my dad bought a new video camera. I've been making some <u>short videos ever since</u>. I got some <u>editing software</u> and <u>do it all</u> on my computer at home. It's really great.

G It sounds like you've <u>found your calling</u>.

B I think so. If <u>you're interested</u>, I could <u>make a video</u> of you dancing. Maybe it will help you get into Julliard.

G That would be great!

▶ acceptance rate 경쟁률, 합격률   take a miracle 매우 어렵다, 하늘의 별따기이다
calling 직업, 천직

남 캐서린, 넌 정말 춤을 잘 추는구나. 강습을 얼마나 받았니?
여 난 다섯살 때 발레를 배우기 시작했어. 그때부터 탭 댄스와 재즈 댄스, 모던 댄스 강습을 받아왔지. 난 춤추는 게 정말 좋아.
남 프로 무용수가 될 생각이니?
여 그러고 싶어. 졸업하면 줄리어드에 지원할 계획이야.
남 나도 들어봤어. 뉴욕에 있는 거 맞지? 난 거기가 주로 음악 학교인 줄로만 알았는데.
여 처음 세워졌을 때는 그냥 음악 학교로 시작했지만 그 뒤로는 무용과 연기도 가르쳐.
남 입학하기가 꽤 힘들 것 같은데.
여 응. 합격률이 약 6%니까. 하버드 들어가는 것보다 더 어렵다는 말도 있어. 들어가기가 하늘의 별따기만큼 힘들지.
남 그래도 넌 진짜 잘하니까 꼭 합격할 거야.
여 고마워. 하지만 학비가 너무 비싸서 어쩌면 감당할 수 없을지도 모르겠어. 그건 그렇고 넌 졸업하면 뭐 할 거니?
남 나도 뉴욕에 갈 생각이야.
여 와, 어느 대학? 컬럼비아?
남 아니. 뉴욕 영화 학교에 갈 거야. 스티븐 스필버그와 마틴 스콜세지 같은 훌륭한 영화 감독이 되려고.
여 네가 영화 만드는 데 관심 있는지는 몰랐는걸.
남 아버지가 새 비디오 카메라를 사신 뒤로 여름 내내 거기에 푹 빠져 살았어. 그 뒤로 짧은 비디오를 몇 편 만들고 있어. 편집 소프트웨어도 구해서 전부 다 집에서 컴퓨터로 해. 정말 재미있어.
여 너에게 맞는 일을 찾은 것 같구나.
남 그런 것 같아. 관심 있다면 네가 춤추는 비디오도 찍어줄 수 있어. 아마 줄리어드에 들어가는 데 도움이 될 거야.
여 그거 괜찮겠다!

5 여학생은 왜 줄리어드에 합격하기가 힘들 것이라고 생각하는가?
   (a) 자신이 그 학교에 입학할 자격이 안 된다고 생각한다.
   (b) 지원자는 춤과 연기를 할 줄 알아야 한다.
   (c) 수업료를 낼 수 없을지도 모른다.
   (d) 지원하기 위해서는 비디오를 찍어야 한다.
   (e) 입학 정원은 적은데 경쟁이 치열하다.

6 다음 중 내용을 가장 잘 요약한 것을 고르시오.
   (a) 남학생은 여학생이 춤추는 것을 비디오로 찍어 그녀가 어느 유명한 학교에 들어가는 것을 도와주겠다고 제안한다.

   (b) 두 학생은 졸업한 뒤 예술 분야에서 더 공부하기 위해 뉴욕으로 갈 계획에 대해 이야기하고 있다.

   (c) 두 학생은 뉴욕에 있는 어느 유명한 학교에 입학할 수 있는 가능성에 관해 이야기하고 있다.

7 Level up

G Dad, where does the money <u>come from</u> to <u>pay</u> for museums and <u>orchestras</u>?

M Most of the money comes from the <u>government</u> or <u>private donations</u>. They also make some money from <u>ticket sales</u> and <u>admission fees</u>.

G How much money does the government give?

M Money for the arts comes from city, <u>provincial</u>, and <u>federal governments</u>, so it is hard to <u>say for sure</u>. In Canada, we have the Canada Council for the Arts, which had a <u>budget</u> of over 300 million dollars in 2008.

G That's a lot of money. What do they <u>spend it on</u>?

M The money is given as <u>prizes</u> in <u>national competitions</u>, and it <u>goes toward</u> young <u>filmmakers</u>, dancers, and artists as <u>grants</u> to <u>support their work</u>. It also goes toward paying all of the people who work in national museums and for <u>security</u>, <u>marketing</u>, <u>promotions</u>, and <u>maintenance</u>.

G I think they could use that money to <u>help poor people</u> or people who are sick.

M Maybe, but others feel that <u>art makes</u> the world a <u>better place</u> and can help to <u>inspire people</u> to help others.

▶ provincial 지방의   grant 보조금, 지원금   go toward ~에 충당되다

여 아빠, 미술관과 오케스트라에 들어가는 비용은 어디에서 나오나요?
남 대부분 정부에서 나오는 돈이나 개인적인 기부금이지. 표를 팔거나 입장료로 비용을 마련하기도 하고.
여 정부에서 얼마나 주는데요?
남 예술에 지원되는 돈은 시와 지방 자치단체, 그리고 연방 정부에서 나오기 때문에 확실히 말하기는 힘들단다. 캐나다에는 캐나다 예술 위원회가 있는데 2008년에는 3억 달러가 넘는 예산이 책정되었지.
여 큰돈이네요. 어디에 쓰는 거죠?
남 국가적인 대회에 상금으로 쓰이기도 하고 젊은 영화 제작자와 무용가, 예술가들의 작품 활동을 후원하기 위해 지원금으로 나가기도 해. 또 국립 미술관에서 일하는 직원들의 급료와 보안, 마케팅, 홍보, 유지비로도 나간단다.
여 제 생각에는 그 돈을 가난하거나 아픈 사람들을 돕는 데 쓸 수도 있을 것 같은데요.
남 그럴 수도 있겠지. 하지만 예술이 세상을 더 나은 곳으로 만들고, 또 사람들로 하여금 다른 이들을 돕고 싶은 마음이 들게 할 수 있다고 생각하는 사람들도 있거든.

7 What is the girl's opinion on giving money for the arts?
   예술에 돈을 지원하는 것에 대한 소녀의 생각은 무엇인가?
   (a) She believes the money is used for a good cause.
       타당한 명분에 돈이 쓰인다고 생각한다.
   (b) She feels it is useful for helping poor artists.
       가난한 예술가들을 돕는 데 도움이 된다고 생각한다.
   (c) She wants to stop all donations for the arts.
       예술 기부금을 모두 중단시키고 싶어 한다.
   (d) She thinks the money could be better used.
       그 돈이 더 나은 곳에 쓰일 수 있지 않을까 생각한다.
   (e) She feels the money is wisely spent.
       그 돈이 현명하게 쓰인다고 느낀다.

M Art as an <u>investment</u> is a <u>risky</u> <u>undertaking</u>. Paintings go <u>up</u> <u>and</u> <u>down</u> in <u>value</u> and are also <u>vulnerable</u> <u>to</u> <u>theft</u> and <u>damage</u>. It is not something that everyone can do since the most <u>valuable</u> <u>paintings</u> <u>sell</u> <u>for</u> millions of dollars. Although it is <u>not</u> <u>known</u> for certain what the <u>exact</u> <u>amount</u> <u>was</u>, it is believed that the <u>highest</u> <u>price</u> <u>ever</u> <u>paid</u> for a painting was an <u>astounding</u> 140 million dollars in a <u>private</u> <u>sale</u> made by media mogul David Geffen to an <u>unknown</u> <u>buyer</u>. The painting was by American artist Jackson Pollack, and it is <u>simply</u> <u>entitled</u> *No. 5, 1948*. It is an <u>abstract</u> <u>expressionist</u> <u>piece</u> which <u>depicts</u> <u>swirls</u> of yellow and brown paint on a large piece of <u>fiberboard</u>. While not everyone can <u>afford</u> <u>such</u> <u>rates</u>, a small <u>investment</u> in an up-and-coming artist may <u>pay</u> <u>dividends</u> in the future. The early works of artists who later <u>become</u> <u>famous</u> often <u>fetch</u> <u>great</u> <u>returns</u> on the investments.

▶ undertaking 사업, 시도 vulnerable 취약한, 피해를 입기 쉬운 mogul 거물 astounding 놀라운 swirl 소용돌이 fiberboard 섬유판 up-and-coming 유망한, 장래성이 있는 pay dividends 이익을 배당하다 fetch (값에) 팔리다, (값을) 부르다 returns 수익, 이익

남 투자 대상으로서의 예술은 위험한 사업입니다. 그림은 가치가 오르락내리락하고 도난과 파손을 당하기도 쉽죠. 가장 값비싼 그림들은 수백만 달러에 팔리기 때문에 이런 투자는 누구나 할 수 있는 게 아닙니다. 정확한 액수는 확실히 알려져 있지 않지만, 지금까지 그림에 지불된 가장 높은 가격은 미디어 황제 데이비드 게펜이 익명의 구매자에게 개인적으로 판매한 무려 1억 4천만 달러입니다. 그 그림은 미국 화가인 잭슨 폴록의 작품으로 〈5번, 1948년〉이라는 단순한 제목이 붙어 있습니다. 커다란 섬유판 위에 노란색과 갈색 물감이 소용돌이치는 것을 묘사한 추상표현주의 작품입니다. 모든 사람이 그 정도의 가격을 감당할 수는 없지만 유망한 화가에게 소액을 투자한다면 미래에 보상을 받을 수 있을지도 모릅니다. 나중에 유명해지는 화가들의 초기 작품은 투자해 놓으면 많은 수익을 안겨주기도 합니다.

8 What is the main topic of the talk? 담화의 주제는 무엇인가?
  (a) The vulnerability of paintings 그림의 취약성
  (b) The most expensive painting ever sold
      지금까지 가장 비싸게 팔린 그림
  (c) The best work by Jackson Pollack 잭슨 폴록의 대표작
  (d) The wisdom of buying works of art
      미술 작품을 구입하는 지혜
  (e) The early works of some famous artists
      몇몇 유명 화가들의 초기 작품

W Photography has many <u>purposes</u> and can be used in <u>both</u> <u>artistic</u> and <u>professional</u> <u>ways</u>. Photography <u>generally</u> <u>falls</u> <u>into</u> three categories: fine art photography, <u>photojournalism</u>, and <u>commercial</u> <u>photography</u>. The purpose of <u>fine</u> <u>art</u> photography is to <u>create</u> <u>an</u> <u>image</u> which <u>satisfies</u> the <u>artist's</u> <u>creative</u> <u>vision</u>. Photojournalism is used to <u>support</u> a <u>news</u> <u>story</u> and to <u>inform</u> <u>viewers</u> while commercial photography is used to <u>sell</u> <u>a</u> <u>product</u> or a service. Fine art photography is <u>further</u> <u>classified</u> by black-and-white or color photography. In addition, <u>subjects</u> <u>can</u> <u>be</u> <u>posed</u> or can be <u>spontaneous</u> and <u>get</u> <u>taken</u> as they happen. Photojournalism, on the other hand, almost always <u>consists</u> <u>of</u> <u>live</u> <u>action</u> photographs <u>except</u> <u>for</u> those <u>occasions</u> when someone such as a <u>government</u> <u>leader</u> or an <u>award</u> <u>winner</u> poses for a <u>shot</u>. Photojournalism has many <u>subcategories</u> such as sports photography and <u>entertainment</u> <u>photography</u>. A further subcategory of entertainment photography is the <u>paparazzi</u>, those <u>vilified</u> <u>photographers</u> that <u>chase</u> <u>celebrities</u> and wait outside their homes <u>while</u> hoping for a <u>chance</u> <u>to</u> <u>take</u> an embarrassing photo. In the world of commercial photography, most work is done with <u>models</u> in <u>fashion</u> <u>shoots</u>, and the <u>photographs</u> <u>are</u> <u>produced</u> for <u>magazines</u> or Internet sites. The <u>ultimate</u> <u>goal</u> of commercial photography is to <u>sell</u> <u>products</u>, so therefore most commercial photography is <u>manipulated</u> and <u>touched</u> <u>up</u> by using <u>airbrush</u> <u>techniques</u> or computer software.

▶ fine art 미술, 예술 spontaneous 자연 발생적인, 의식적이 아닌 live-action 생중계의, 실황의 vilify 헐뜯다, 비방하다 manipulate 조작하다 touch up 손질하다, 수정하다

여 사진 촬영에는 여러 가지 목적이 있으며, 예술적으로도 전문적으로도 사용될 수 있습니다. 사진은 일반적으로 예술 사진, 보도 사진, 상업 사진의 세 범주로 나뉘죠. 예술 사진의 목적은 작가의 창조적인 시선을 만족시키는 이미지를 창출하는 것입니다. 보도 사진은 기사를 뒷받침하고 보는 사람에게 정보를 전달하는 데 사용되는 반면 상업 사진은 상품이나 서비스를 판매하는 데 사용됩니다. 예술 사진은 좀 더 세부적으로 흑백 사진과 칼라 사진으로 분류됩니다. 뿐만 아니라 피사체가 포즈를 취한 것일 수도 있고 자연 발생적인 순간에 찍힌 것일 수도 있죠. 이에 반해 보도 사진은 정부 지도자나 수상자 같은 인물이 촬영을 위해 포즈를 취하는 경우 외에는 실제의 움직임을 담은 사진인 경우가 대부분입니다. 보도 사진에는 스포츠 사진과 연예 사진 같이 많은 하위 범주가 있는데요. 연예 사진의 좀 더 하위 범주는 연예인을 쫓아다니면서 당혹스러운 사진을 찍을 기회를 노리며 그들의 집 밖에서 기다리는 악의적인 사진가인 파파라치입니다. 상업 사진의 세계에서 대부분의 작업은 패션 사진으로, 모델과 함께 이루어지며 잡지나 인터넷 사이트에 쓰입니다. 상업 사진의 궁극적인 목적은 상품을 판매하는 것이죠. 따라서 대부분의 상업 사진은 에어브러시 기법이나 컴퓨터 소프트웨어를 이용해 조작되고 수정됩니다.

9 사진의 측면으로서 언급되지 <u>않은</u> 것은?
  (a) 스포츠 사진은 보도 사진에 속한다.
  (b) 어떤 보도 사진은 사진가를 위해 연출된다.
  (c) 예술 사진가의 목적은 사진 판매이다.
  (d) 사진은 예술의 한 형태로 볼 수 있다.
  (e) 상업 사진은 종종 원본과 다르다.

10

W Our topic for tonight's show is Broadway, and <u>our</u> <u>guest</u> is Charles Cabbage, who <u>has</u> <u>followed</u> Broadway over the years. His <u>recent</u> <u>book</u>, *Broadway's Rising Fortunes*, is <u>on</u> <u>sale</u> <u>now</u>. Welcome, Mr. Cabbage.

M Thank you.

W What is the <u>biggest</u> <u>difference</u> <u>between</u> Broadway in the past and today?

M Today it is a <u>grand</u> <u>moneymaking</u> <u>place</u>, which was not <u>always</u> <u>the</u> <u>case</u> in the past.

W Yes, your book gives a lot of <u>statistics</u> <u>on</u> how much money was <u>earned</u> <u>from</u> <u>ticket</u> <u>sales</u>. In 1960, sales were just <u>46</u> <u>million</u> dollars, and <u>attendance</u> at the <u>performances</u> was 7.9 million people.

M Yes. Now <u>look</u> <u>at</u> 2008. 12.3 million tickets <u>were</u> <u>sold</u>, which earned 939 million dollars. Clearly, the <u>big</u> <u>change</u> is the <u>higher</u> <u>ticket</u> <u>prices</u> today. Of course, in 1960, 46 million dollars was a lot of money.

W When did Broadway <u>turn</u> <u>into</u> this <u>super</u> <u>moneymaker</u>?

M The change was <u>gradual</u>. In 1970, there were 7.4 million tickets sold and 55 million dollars in <u>revenue</u> <u>collected</u>. Things <u>really</u> <u>dipped</u> for a while in the mid-1970s, but Broadway <u>rebounded</u> in the 1980s. In 1980, there were 11 million tickets sold and 197 million dollars <u>in profits earned</u>.

W That is a big change. <u>What</u> <u>happened</u> in the 1990s?

M By 1990, <u>attendance</u> <u>went</u> <u>down</u> a bit to 8 million people, but <u>revenue</u> <u>rose</u> <u>to</u> 282 million dollars. In 2000, attendance <u>went</u> <u>up</u> <u>even</u> <u>more</u> as 12 million tickets were sold, and there were 660 million dollars in <u>revenue</u> <u>collected</u>.

W I guess there is <u>no</u> <u>chance</u> that the bright lights of Broadway will be <u>dimming</u> <u>anytime</u> <u>soon</u>.

▶ follow 흥미를 가지고 연구하다(지켜보다): 주시하다 attendance 청중, 관중 moneymaker 돈벌이가 되는 일; 축재가 revenue 수익 dip 기울다, 감소하다 rebound 다시 일어서다

여 오늘 밤 저희 프로그램에서 다룰 주제는 브로드웨이이고요, 오늘 모신 손님은 몇 년 동안 브로드웨이에 대해 연구해오신 찰스 캐비지 씨입니다. 최신 저서 『브로드웨이의 떠오르는 부』가 현재 판매되고 있는데요. 어서 오십시오, 캐비지 씨.

남 감사합니다.

여 브로드웨이의 과거와 현재 가운데 가장 큰 차이점은 무엇인가요?

남 과거에는 꼭 그렇진 않았지만, 오늘날 브로드웨이는 엄청난 돈벌이가 되는 곳입니다.

여 네, 선생님 책에 입장권 판매로 벌어들인 돈의 액수에 관한 통계가 많이 나와 있더군요. 1960년에는 판매가 4천 6백만 달러에 불과하고 공연 관객 수도 7백 9십만 명이었죠.

남 네. 이제 2008년을 보시면요, 입장권이 1천 2백 3십만 장 팔려 9억 3천 9백만 달러를 벌어들였습니다. 오늘날 인상된 입장권 가격이 큰 변화인 것은 분명합니다. 물론 1960년에는 4천 6백만 달러가 큰돈이었죠.

여 언제 브로드웨이가 이렇게 어마어마한 돈벌이가 되었나요?

남 변화는 서서히 일어났습니다. 1970년에 7백 4십만 장의 입장권이 팔려 5천 5백만 달러의 수익을 올렸습니다. 1970년대 중반에는 잠깐 상황이 정말 안 좋았지만 브로드웨이는 1980년대에 다시 일어섰습니다. 1980년에 1천 1백만 장의 입장권이 팔리고 수익으로 1억 9천 7백만 달러를 벌어들였습니다.

여 굉장한 변화네요. 1990년대에는 어떤가요?

남 1990년까지는 관객이 8백만 명까지 조금 감소했지만 수익은 2억 8천 2백만 달러로 올랐습니다. 2000년에 관객 수는 훨씬 더 늘어서 1천 2백만 장의 입장권이 팔리고 6억 6천만 달러의 수익을 거뒀습니다.

여 브로드웨이의 불야성이 어두워질 가능성은 당분간은 없을 듯하군요.

10 1960, 1970, 1980, 1990, 2000, 2008년의 브로드웨이 입장권 판매 수익을 나타내는 그래프를 완성하시오.

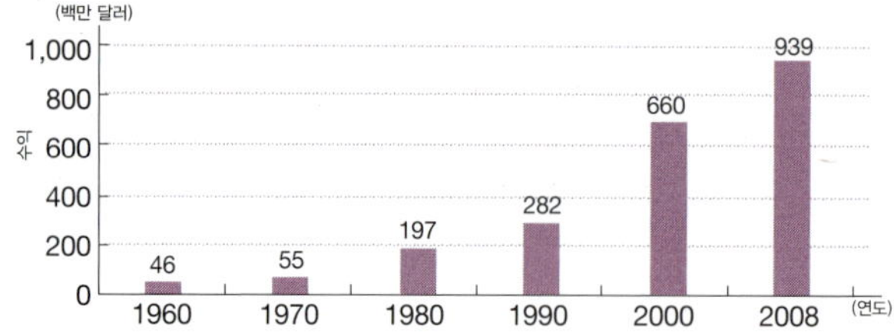

W Students, when we visit France next week, we will be <u>looking</u> around the <u>world's</u> <u>most</u> <u>visited</u> <u>museum</u>, the Louvre. Today, I <u>would</u> <u>like</u> <u>to</u> <u>tell</u> you a little more about this <u>celebrated</u> and <u>historic</u> museum. The Louvre was <u>originally</u> <u>built</u> as a <u>fortress</u> in Paris in the 12th century. Only a <u>small</u> <u>part</u> of the <u>original</u> <u>fortress</u> still <u>exists</u> because the French <u>enlarged</u> <u>the</u> <u>building</u> to become the Louvre Palace, which became the home of the <u>French</u> <u>royal</u> <u>family</u>. In 1674, however, King Louis XIV <u>decided</u> <u>to</u> <u>make</u> the Palace of Versailles his <u>permanent</u> <u>household</u>, so the Louvre Palace was then <u>used</u> <u>to</u> <u>display</u> <u>royal</u> collections of art and <u>antiques</u>. During the next hundred years, the palace was used as a <u>school</u> <u>for</u> <u>the</u> <u>arts</u>. When King Louis XV <u>reigned</u>, he <u>took</u> <u>an</u> <u>interest</u> in the Louvre Palace and <u>expanded</u> <u>it</u>. During the <u>French</u> <u>Revolution</u>, the government made the <u>palace</u> <u>into</u> <u>a</u> <u>museum</u> for the arts and sciences. It <u>officially</u> <u>opened</u> on August 10, 1793. The museum's collection has <u>grown</u> <u>steadily</u> over the years and now <u>holds</u> <u>over</u> <u>35,000</u> objects. The collection is <u>divided</u> <u>into</u> eight categories: Egyptian <u>artifacts</u>, Near Eastern artifacts, <u>Greek</u>, Etruscan, and Roman artifacts, Islamic art, <u>sculptures</u>, <u>decorative</u> <u>arts</u>, paintings, and prints and <u>drawings</u>. Throughout the year, the museum also <u>holds</u> <u>several</u> <u>temporary</u> <u>exhibitions</u> resulting from <u>expert</u> <u>research</u>. The museum also holds <u>concerts</u> <u>and</u> <u>lectures</u>, shows films, and holds <u>readings</u> <u>and</u> <u>performances</u> in its <u>large</u> <u>auditorium</u>. Last year, 8.5 million people visited the museum. They came to see <u>such</u> <u>famous</u> <u>works</u> of art as the *Mona Lisa* by Leonardo da Vinci and the *Venus de Milo*.

▶ celebrated 유명한, 이름 높은 fortress 요새 reign 군림하다, 지배하다 artifact 공예품

여 여러분, 다음 주에 프랑스에 가면 우리는 세계에서 가장 많은 관람객이 찾는 박물관인 루브르를 둘러볼 거예요. 오늘은 이 유명하고 역사적인 박물관에 대해 조금 이야기해보겠습니다. 루브르는 원래 12세기 파리에 요새로 지어졌어요. 원래 요새였던 부분은 아주 조금밖에 남아있지 않은데, 그 건물을 확장해서 루브르 궁을 만들었고, 프랑스 왕실이 사용하게 되었기 때문이죠. 그러나 1674년에 루이 14세가 베르사이유 궁을 거처로 결정하면서 루브르 궁은 왕실이 수집해온 미술품과 골동품 전시에 사용됩니다. 그 후 몇 백 년 동안 루브르 궁은 미술을 공부하는 학교로 이용되었습니다. 루이 15세가 즉위하면서 그는 루브르 궁에 관심을 갖고 궁을 확장했죠. 프랑스 대혁명 때 정부는 루브르 궁을 미술 및 과학 박물관으로 만들었습니다. 루브르 박물관은 1793년 8월 10일 공식적으로 개관했습니다. 루브르 박물관의 수집품은 오랜 세월 동안 꾸준히 증가해 현재 3만 5천 점이 넘게 소장되어 있습니다. 루브르의 소장품은 8개의 범주로 나뉩니다. 이집트 공예품과 근동 공예품, 그리고 그리스·에트루리아·로마의 공예품, 이슬람 예술, 조각, 장식 미술, 회화, 판화와 소묘지요. 루브르 박물관은 또한 연중 내내 전문가의 연구 결과로 임시 전시회도 개최합니다. 연주회와 강연을 개최하고 영화를 상영하며 대강당에서 낭독회와 공연도 엽니다. 작년에는 850만 명의 사람들이 루브르를 방문했습니다. 방문객들은 레오나르도 다 빈치의 모나리자와 밀로의 비너스 같이 유명한 작품을 보기 위해 루브르를 찾습니다.

11 프랑스 왕실은 1674년에 왜 루브르 궁을 떠났는가?
(a) 루브르 궁이 박물관이 되어서
(b) 프랑스 대혁명이 발발해서
(c) 그들이 다른 곳으로 이사 가서
(d) 루브르 궁을 미술 학교로 바꿔서
(e) 루브르 궁이 요새로 바뀌어서

12 다음 중 내용을 가장 잘 요약한 것을 고르시오.

(a) 유명한 루브르는 훌륭한 수집품을 소장하고 있는 박물관이지만 요새, 궁전, 미술 학교로서의 오랜 역사도 지니고 있다.

(b) 루브르 박물관의 엄청난 수집품은 프랑스 왕실 생활 중심지로서의 수백 년 동안의 유산이다.

(c) 프랑스 루브르 박물관에 있는 엄청난 수집품은 그리스, 로마, 이집트 같은 곳에서 온 것이다.

Practice Test

p. 30~p. 31

1 (b) **2** (d) **3** (c) **4** (e) **5** (d) **6** (c) **7** (b)
8 해설 참조 **9** (d) **10** (b)

1

M The Renaissance was an era of profound change in the way people viewed the world, and it had a great influence on the arts and sciences. It started around the beginning of the 14th century and lasted until the 17th century. Centered in the small Italian city-states and kingdoms of northern Italy, it eventually spread to other parts of Western Europe. The Renaissance had its roots in the revival of classical Greece and Rome. Around this time in Italy rose the Humanists, scholars who looked for inspiration in the past and attempted to interpret it in a new way. They studied the classics from the Greeks and Romans to try to understand the living world better. This was quite different from the previous religious views and people's attempts to try to understand the afterlife. During the Renaissance, art underwent a profound change. Previously, artists had worked for commissions from nobles or the Church, and most paintings had religious themes. Paintings were often two dimensional, flat, and without any nuance of shadow or lighting. Under the influence of Greek and Roman artistic methods, Renaissance art became highly realistic. Artists used perspective to add depth, and they studied light and shadow to add realism. They also studied human anatomy to create more detailed images. The height of Italian Renaissance art was the beginning of the 16th century, which saw such grandmasters as Michelangelo, Leonardo da Vinci, and Raphael.

▶ profound 깊은 commission 수수료; 의뢰, 주문 dimensional ~차원의
flat 단조로운; (타이어 등이) 펑크난 nuance 뉘앙스, 미묘한 차이; 음영
perspective 원근법 anatomy 해부학

남 르네상스는 사람들이 세계를 바라보는 방식에 근본적인 변화가 일어난 시기로, 미술과 과학에 지대한 영향을 미쳤습니다. 르네상스는 14세기 초쯤 시작되어 17세기까지 지속되었죠. 르네상스는 이탈리아의 작은 도시 국가들과 이탈리아 북부의 왕국들을 중심으로 서유럽의 다른 지역으로까지 확산되었습니다. 르네상스는 고전적인 그리스와 로마의 부흥에 뿌리를 두고 있었죠. 이 무렵 이탈리아에는 과거에서 영감을 찾아 그 영감을 새로운 방식으로 해석하고자 하는 학자들인 인문주의자들이 나타났는데요. 그들은 현실 세계를 더 잘 이해하기 위한 노력으로 그리스와 로마의 고전을 연구했습니다. 이것은 이전의 종교적 관점 및 사후를 이해하려고 노력하는 사람들의 시도와는 상당히 달랐죠. 르네상스 동안 미술은 큰 변화를 겪었습니다. 예전에 예술가들은 귀족이나 교회의 수수료를 받기 위해 작업했고, 그래서 대부분의 회화가 종교적인 주제였죠. 2차원적이고 단조로우며 명암의 미묘한 차이가 없는 회화가 흔했습니다. 그리스와 로마의 미술 기법의 영향으로 르네상스 미술은 매우 사실적이게 되었는데요. 화가들은 깊이를 더하기

위해 원근법을 이용했으며 사실성을 가미하기 위해 명암을 연구했습니다. 또한 좀 더 세밀한 이미지를 만들기 위해 해부학도 연구했죠. 이탈리아 르네상스 미술의 정점은 미켈란젤로, 레오나르도 다 빈치, 라파엘 같은 대가들이 활동했던 16세기 초였습니다.

1 담화에 따르면 다음 중 옳은 것은 무엇인가?

(a) 르네상스 예술가들은 인문주의자들의 작품을 연구했다.

(b) 르네상스 이전 회화는 주로 종교를 주제로 다뤘다.

(c) 그림자와 세부 묘사는 르네상스 이전의 미술에 흔했다.

(d) 르네상스 예술가들은 그리스 미술에서 원근법을 배웠다.

(e) 르네상스는 이탈리아 남부 도시들에 집중되었다.

2-3

W Hey, Sergio, do you want to come to my Oscar party next month?

M What is an Oscar party?

W You know, we dress up, watch the Oscars, talk about our favorite stars and movies, and try to guess who will win.

M I'm sorry, but I don't understand. Who is Oscar?

W You're serious? You really don't know?

M I've only been in America a few months, so I guess I haven't met him.

W Oscar isn't a "him." It's a "what." Oscar is the name of the gold statue given at the Academy Awards for awards such as best actor and best picture.

M Oh, yes, I know about that. That's when they give awards to all those Hollywood celebrities. They walk on a red carpet and have big parties afterward, right?

W Yes, that's right. My friends and I like to watch it on television, eat popcorn, check out all the latest fashions, and talk about the movies.

M That sounds interesting. I'd be happy to come. I've always wondered who votes for the winners and how it all works.

W It's all organized by the Academy of Motion Picture Arts and Sciences. Membership is only given to those people with close ties to the movie industry. They are the ones that vote for the awards.

M So once you make a movie, you can become a member, yes?

W Actually, no. You have to be recommended by two members, and you have to be selected by a special committee. You can also become a member if you are nominated for an award and the committee selects you.

M _______________________________________

▶ statue 조각상 vote for ~에게 찬성 투표하다; 제안하다
nominate 후보로 지명되다

여 세르지오, 다음 달에 내가 여는 오스카 파티에 올래?

남 오스카 파티가 뭐야?

여 그게, 정장을 입고 오스카를 보면서 좋아하는 스타와 영화에 대해 이야기하고 누가 상을 받겠는지 맞춰보는 거지.

남 미안한데 무슨 말인지 모르겠어. 오스카가 누구야?

여 진담이니? 정말 몰라?

남 내가 미국에 온 지 몇 달밖에 안 돼서 아직 그 사람을 못 만나 본 것 같은데.

여 오스카는 '누구'가 아니야. '무엇'이지. 오스카는 아카데미 시상식에서 최우수 배우나 최우수 작품에 주는 상의 황금 조각상 이름이야.

남 아, 그래, 뭔지 알겠어. 할리우드 스타들에게 상 주는 거 말하는 거지. 레드 카펫 위를 걸어가고, 끝나고 나서는 성대한 파티가 열리잖아, 맞지?

여 그래, 맞았어. 난 친구들하고 텔레비전으로 시상식 보면서 팝콘도 먹고 최신 패션도 확인하면서 영화에 대해 얘기하는 걸 좋아해.

남 재미있겠는걸. 갈게. 누가 수상자를 뽑고 그게 어떻게 돌아가는 건지 항상 궁금했거든.

여 모든 걸 영화 예술 과학 아카데미에서 주관해. 영화 산업에 밀접한 관련이 있는 사람들만 회원이 될 수 있지. 그들이 수상자를 뽑아.

남 그럼 일단 영화만 한 편 만들면 회원이 될 수 있는 거네, 그렇지?

여 사실, 그렇지 않아. 회원 2명의 추천을 받아야 하고 특별 위원회에 의해 선출돼야 해. 수상 후보가 되고 위원회가 선출하면 회원이 될 수도 있어.

남 ______________________________

2 오스카 파티가 무엇인지에 대해 남자가 어리둥절해 했던 주된 이유는?
(a) 남자는 영화 산업이나 시상식에 아무 관심이 없다.
(b) 남자는 미국에 산 지 오래되지 않았다.
(c) 남자는 지금까지 아카데미 시상식에 대해 들어본 적이 없다.
(d) 남자는 오스카가 상의 이름이라는 것을 몰랐다.
(e) 남자는 미국에서 파티에 별로 초대받지 못하고 있다.

3 남자는 다음에 뭐라고 말하겠는가?
(a) 회원이 되는 게 그렇게 어려운 것 같지는 않네.
(b) 너희 오스카 파티에 뭘 가져가면 되지?
(c) 회원이 되기가 힘든 것 같구나.
(d) 진짜 오스카 행사에 가고 싶어.
(e) 회원들이 올해 누구를 뽑을지 궁금해.

4-5

M In the United States, the Grammy Awards are given to the best groups and individuals in the music industry once a year. The National Academy of Recording Arts and Sciences started giving the awards in 1958. The awards have generated some controversy over the years mainly because of the nomination and voting process. Only members of the academy and selected members of the recording industry get to make nominations and then vote for the awards. Some musicians have suggested that the voters are easily swayed by personal prejudices and that the awards are not always given to the most deserving musicians. A further criticism of the awards is that too many are given out. There are now over a dozen categories of music and numerous technical, producing, writing, and arranging awards presented. Critics believe that with so many awards, the value of a Grammy is lessened. However, many musicians welcome the broadening of music categories that are up for awards. They state that only at the Grammy Awards ceremonies are all of the major forces of the music industry gathered at one time in one place. The public, on the other hand, feels that the Grammy Awards do not represent popular tastes and that the awards often go to obscure musicians. Different awards ceremonies, such as the People's Choice Awards, allow public voting, but the Grammy Awards, despite pressure to make changes, still has limited voting.

▶ **sway** 흔들다, 영향을 주다 **arrange** 편곡하다; 각색하다
obscure 세상에 알려지지 않은; 이해하기 어려운

남 미국에서 그래미 상은 일 년에 한 번 음악업계의 최고 그룹과 개인에게 주어집니다. 미국 음반 예술 과학 아카데미는 1958년에 상을 수여하기 시작했는데요. 그래미 상은 후보 지명과 투표 과정 때문에 오랫동안 약간의 논란을 일으켜왔습니다. 아카데미의 회원과 음반업계에서 선정된 회원만이 후보를 지명하고 상에 대해 투표하게 되죠. 일부 음악가들은 투표자가 개인적인 편견에 쉽게 움직이고, 가장 상을 받을 만한 음악인에게 항상 그 상이 수여되는 것도 아니라고 말합니다. 상을 너무 많이 나눠준다는 비판은 한층 거센데요. 현재 12개가 넘는 음악 부문이 있는 데다 수많은 기술 및 프로듀싱, 작곡 및 편곡 상이 수여됩니다. 비평가들은 상을 너무 많이 주는 바람에 그래미의 가치가 떨어진다고 생각하죠. 그러나 많은 음악인들은 상에 따라 음악 부문이 확대되는 것을 환영합니다. 음악 산업의 핵심 인물들이 한 번에 한 장소에 모이는 것은 그래미 상 시상식뿐이라는 것이 그들의 말이죠. 반면 대중들은 그래미 상이 대중의 기호를 반영하지 않으며 잘 알려지지 않은 음악가에게 상이 돌아가는 경우가 잦다고 생각합니다. 피플스 초이스 상과 같은 다른 시상식에서는 일반인 투표를 인정하지만, 변화를 요구하는 압력에도 불구하고 그래미 상은 여전히 제한된 투표를 실시합니다.

4 음악가의 관점에서 그래미 상에 대한 주된 비판은 무엇인가?
(a) 수상 음악 부문이 너무 많다.
(b) 음악가의 투표권이 없다.
(c) 투표자 규모가 너무 작아서 회원이 좀 더 필요하다.
(d) 투표가 좀 더 공개적이어야 하는데 비밀리에 실시된다.
(e) 투표자들이 개인적으로 선호하는 음악인을 선정한다.

5 만일 그래미 상이 일반인 투표로 선정된다면 무슨 일이 일어나겠는가?
(a) 피플스 초이스 상 같은 다른 시상식들이 폐지될 것이다.
(b) 그래미 상의 수가 인기있는 부문만으로 축소될 것이다.
(c) 미국 음반 예술 과학 아카데미가 필요 없어질 것이다.
(d) 당대 가장 인기 있는 음악인이 많은 상을 받을 것이다.
(e) 그래미 상의 투표 과정에 대한 비판이 더 많아질 것이다.

6   Level up

G Dad, I'd really like to take part in the school play, so I need you to sign a permission slip. Can I?

M I think it's great that you want to be in the school play. What play are you putting on?

G It's William Shakespeare's *Macbeth*.

M Wow, that's pretty serious. Does this mean you'll spend a lot of time after school practicing?

G Yes, and during lunchtime and study breaks, too.

M I'm a little worried about your grades. Are you going to be able to keep up your grades with all of this extra work?

G Of course I will. That's why I need permission.

M I'm not so sure about this.

G You know I study really hard. Also, it's good to do extracurricular activities. It can really help when applying to universities in a few years. It'll be a great experience.

M Yes, that's true, but I think we'll have to talk with your mother about this. She's the one who is going to have to pick you up after school.

G So if Mom agrees, it's okay?

M Yes.

G Great! I've already asked her, and she said, "Yes."

▶ **permission slip** 부모님 동의서 **put on** 상연하다 **keep up** 유지하다
extracurricular 정식 학과 이외의, 과외의

여 아빠, 학교 연극에 꼭 참가하고 싶은데 부모님 동의서에 서명이 필요해요. 저 해
도 돼죠?

남 학교 연극에 참여하고 싶다니 기특하구나. 공연하는 게 어떤 연극이니?

여 윌리엄 셰익스피어의 〈맥베스〉예요.

남 우와, 꽤 진지한 극이로구나. 연습하느라고 방과 후에 시간이 많이 들겠는걸?

여 네, 점심 시간이랑 쉬는 시간에도요.

남 네 성적에 대해 조금 걱정이 되는구나. 이런 과외 활동을 하면서 성적이 안 떨어
지게 할 수 있겠니?

여 그럼요. 그래서 부모님 동의가 필요한 거예요.

남 잘 모르겠구나.

여 제가 공부 열심히 한다는 거 아시잖아요. 게다가 과외 활동을 하면 좋다고요. 몇
년 후에 대학에 지원할 때 큰 도움이 될 수 있어요. 아주 좋은 경험이 될 거예요.

남 그래, 그 말은 맞다. 하지만 이 문제에 대해서 엄마와 이야기해봐야 할 것 같구나.
방과 후에 너를 데리러 가는 사람은 엄마니까 말이다.

여 그럼 엄마가 허락하시면 해도 되는 거죠?

남 그래.

여 아싸! 엄마한테 벌써 여쭤봤는데 엄마는 괜찮다고 하셨거든요.

6 Why is the father reluctant to let his daughter take part in
the play? 아빠는 딸의 연극 참여 허락을 왜 주저하는가?

  (a) He thinks that her mother will disapprove.
     엄마가 허락해주지 않을 거라고 생각해서

  (b) He feels that plays are a waste of time.
     연극은 시간 낭비라고 생각하므로

  (c) He is worried that her grades may suffer.
     딸의 성적이 나빠질까봐 걱정돼서

  (d) He thinks no one can pick her up after school.
     방과 후에 딸을 데리러 갈 사람이 없어서

  (e) He wants her to work on some other extra activities.
     딸이 다른 과외 활동을 좀 했으면 싶어서

---

7 Level up

W Today, we will examine one of the world's greatest
sculptors and his greatest work of art. I'm talking
about Michelangelo and his sculpture *David*. The
statue stands 5.17 meters and is of the biblical King
David just before his fight with Goliath. Two other
artists had worked on the statue before Michelangelo
had, but they had only started the beginnings of the
legs. A group of wealthy government officials had
commissioned the statue, and they were worried
that the huge block of expensive marble was being
damaged by the rain as it was left outside. The officials
contacted several artists to finish the work, and it was
young Michelangelo who got the job. Michelangelo
began to work on the statue of King David in 1501,
when he was just 26 years old, and he completed it
in 1504. Michelangelo believed that a statue's form is
already inside the marble and that it is the artist's job to
reveal it by cutting away the stone. With his great skill,
he created a true masterpiece for the ages.

▶ sculptor 조각가 work of art 예술품, 미술품 stand 높이가 ~이다
biblical 성경의, 성경에 있는 commission 의뢰하다, 주문하다

여 오늘은 세계에서 가장 위대한 조각가 중 한 사람과, 그의 최고 걸작에 대해 살펴
보겠습니다. 바로 미켈란젤로와 다비드상이죠. 다비드상은 높이 5.17미터로, 성
경에 나오는 다윗 왕이 골리앗과 싸우기 직전의 모습입니다. 미켈란젤로 이전에
두 명의 다른 조각가가 다비드 상 작업을 했지만 그들은 다리 부분의 초기 작업
만 했죠. 그 조각상을 의뢰한 부유한 정부 관료들은 그 거대한 고가의 대리석 덩
어리가 밖에 있어서 비에 훼손되는 것이 걱정이었습니다. 관료들은 그 작업을 완

성해달라고 여러 조각가에게 연락했고, 그 일을 맡게 된 것은 젊은 미켈란젤로
였습니다. 미켈란젤로는 겨우 26세였던 1501년에 다윗 왕 조각상 작업에 착수해
서 1504년에 완성했습니다. 미켈란젤로는 조각상의 형태가 이미 대리석 안에 존
재하고, 돌을 깎아내어 그 형태를 드러내는 것이 바로 조각가의 일이라고 생각했
습니다. 그는 놀라운 솜씨로 후세에 길이 남을 진정한 걸작을 창조했습니다.

7 What is the main topic of the talk? 담화의 주제는 무엇인가?

  (a) The number of artists that worked on the statue *David*
     다비드상을 작업한 조각가의 수

  (b) The history surrounding the making of the statue *David*
     다비드상의 제작을 둘러싼 역사

  (c) The people who commissioned the statue *David*
     다비드상을 의뢰한 사람들

  (d) The speaker's thoughts on how to make a statue like *David*
     다비드상 같은 조각상을 만드는 방법에 대한 화자의 생각

  (e) The physical characteristics of the statue *David*
     다비드상의 물리적 특징

8

M The modern orchestra has a layout that is relatively
common to most orchestras. Let's just look at this
diagram to help us understand the position of the
instruments. The orchestra is typically in a half-moon
setup, with the conductor at the base of the flat side and
in the center. The instruments are usually arranged with
the higher-pitched ones on the left and the deeper bass-
sounding ones on the right. Immediately in front of the
conductor in a semicircle are the string instruments, with
the first and second violins to the left and the violas and
cellos to the right. The violins occupy a large section of
the orchestra and fill the entire left side while there are
fewer violas and cellos, and they only fill a portion of
the right side. Behind the cellos are the double basses
while behind the violas are the oboes. Next to the oboes
are the flutes while immediately behind the flutes are
the clarinets. Beside the clarinets and behind the oboes
are the bassoons. Behind these woodwinds is the brass
section which includes, from left to the right from the
conductor's point of view, the French horns, trumpets,
trombones, and tubas. Finally, in the rear are the
remaining instruments, with the harp and the piano on
the left, an organ, if there is one, on the far right, and
all of the drums, cymbals, and remaining percussion
instruments in between.

▶ layout 배치 setup 배치 conductor 지휘자 at the base of ~의 근저[밑바닥]에
higher-pitched 고음의, 음조가 높은 deep (목소리 등이) 굵고도 낮은, 장중한
bass 저음의 semicircle 반원(형) rear 뒤, 후방

남 현대의 관현악단은 대부분 비교적 공통된 배치를 갖습니다. 악기의 위치에 대해
이해할 수 있도록 이 도표를 한번 봅시다. 관현악단은 일반적으로 반달형 배치로,
평평한 면 가장 아래쪽 중앙에 지휘자가 있습니다. 악기는 보통 왼쪽에 고음부
악기가, 오른쪽에 저음부 악기가 배치됩니다. 지휘자 바로 앞에는 현악기가 반원
으로 배치되는데 왼쪽이 제1 바이올린과 제2 바이올린, 오른쪽이 비올라와 첼로
입니다. 바이올린은 관현악단에서 상당한 비중을 차지하며 왼쪽을 거의 꽉 채우
는 반면 비올라와 첼로는 바이올린보다는 적은 수로 오른쪽의 일부분만 채웁니다.
첼로 뒤는 더블베이스, 비올라 뒤는 오보에입니다. 오보에 옆은 플룻이고, 플룻
바로 뒤는 클라리넷이죠. 클라리넷 옆이자 오보에 뒤는 바순입니다. 이 목관악기
뒤는 금관악기부로, 지휘자가 봤을 때 왼쪽에서 오른쪽으로 프렌치 호른, 트럼펫,
트롬본, 튜바 순입니다. 마지막으로 나머지 악기들이 맨 뒤에 놓이는데요, 하프
와 피아노가 왼쪽, 오르간이 있다면 제일 오른쪽, 그리고 그 사이에 드럼부와 심
벌즈, 나머지 타악기가 놓입니다.

8 오케스트라 그림에 있는 빈칸을 알맞은 악기로 채우시오.

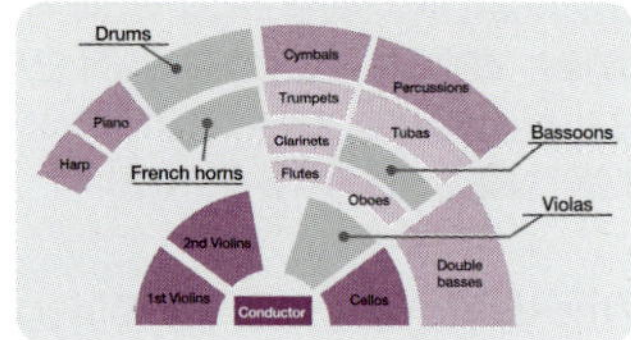

9-10   **Integrated Questions**

Reading

▶ **school** 학파, 유파   **innovative** 혁신적인   **shatter** 산산이 부수다, 분쇄하다
conventional 상투적인, 틀에 박힌   **accepted** 일반적으로 인정된, 용인된
disturbing 어지럽히는, 불안하게 하는   **mold** 성질, 성격; 틀, 주형
make room 장소를 내주다, 자리를 양보하다

예술이란 무엇일까? 이 질문은 다다이즘과 초현실주의 같은 미술 유파가 파블로 피카소 같은 혁신적인 예술가들과 함께 예술이 무엇인지에 대한 틀에 박힌 생각을 무너뜨렸던 20세기 초부터 수없이 제기되어왔다. 20세기 이전에는 대부분의 예술이 종교적인 주제나 일상 생활을 다루었고, 사람과 자연이 주된 주제였다. 이제는 거의 무엇이든 예술의 주제가 될 수 있다. 기술 또한 예술에 상당한 영향을 미쳤다. 처음에는 사진이, 다음에는 영화가 예술이라고 할 수 있는 것의 상식적인 경계에 도전했다. 사진은 예술인가? 영화는 예술에 속하는가? 그렇다는 사람도 있고, 아니라는 사람도 있다. 누구든 약간의 간단한 소프트웨어 도구로 수준 높은 작품을 만들어낼 수 있는 비디오와 컴퓨터 시대는 전통주의자들에게 더 큰 혼란을 안겨준다. 이들을 레오나르도 다 빈치나 피카소, 잭슨 폴록과 같은 성격의 예술가라고 부를 수 있을까? 아마도 아닐 것이다. 그러나 기술 혁명으로 가능해진 엄청나게 늘어난 예술 형태를 수용할 공간은 있어야 한다. 아마도 언젠가는 캔버스와 이젤과 붓이 컴퓨터 화면과 마우스 패드와 마우스로 영원히 대체될 것이며, 버튼을 한 번 클릭하는 것만으로 벽에 걸린 디지털 화면은 수많은 디지털화된 그림을 보여줄 것이다.

W   Technology has brought about many changes in art. Today, we'll look at a few of these changes. One of the biggest changes brought to the arts by technology was the rise of video art. Nam June Paik of South Korea is considered to be the father of video art. In the early 1960s, Paik began combining music, video, and performance to create a unique art form. The invention of the portable video camera by Sony in 1965 gave Paik much more freedom to record both video and audio. Paik used magnets to distort video images, created large towers made from television monitors, and used also live video feeds in his work. Meanwhile, the rise of computers led to another new type of art simply called computer art. Computer art is any art which uses computers either in its production or display. In the early days of computer art, this would have just been images, sounds, and animation. Now, we also have to consider CDs, DVDs, video games, websites, graphic design, and many other types of art. Even traditional arts now frequently use computers. This makes it difficult to define computer art. A purer form of computer art is digital art, which is art created at the digital level on a computer. It may also use a scanned image or an image created by other means such as a mouse or graphics tablet. This mixing of technology and art has led to a new field of study which combines science, art, and technology. Some university courses are now designed to help teachers find new and interesting ways to teach art and science through technology.

▶ **distort** 일그러뜨리다, 왜곡하다   **feed** 공급; 급송 (장치)   **graphics tablet** (도해 자료를 입력하는) 그래픽 태블릿, 도형 처리 평판

여   기술은 예술에 많은 많은 변화를 가져왔습니다. 오늘은 이러한 변화 몇 가지를 살펴보겠습니다. 기술이 예술에 가져온 가장 큰 변화 가운데 하나는 비디오 아트의 출현입니다. 한국의 백남준은 비디오 아트의 아버지로 간주됩니다. 1960년대 초, 백남준은 음악과 비디오, 퍼포먼스를 결합해 독특한 예술 형태를 창조했습니다. 1965년 소니에서 휴대용 비디오 카메라를 만들어내면서 백남준은 영상과 음향 모두를 훨씬 더 자유롭게 기록할 수 있었습니다. 백남준은 자석을 이용해 비디오 영상을 일그러뜨리고, 텔레비전 모니터로 이루어진 거대한 탑을 만들었으며, 작품에 실황 비디오 영상을 사용했습니다. 한편, 컴퓨터의 등장으로 간단히 컴퓨터 아트라고 불리는 새로운 형태의 또다른 예술이 나타났습니다. 컴퓨터 아트는 컴퓨터를 이용해 만들어지거나 전시되는 모든 예술을 가리킵니다. 초기 컴퓨터 아트는 영상, 소리, 동영상뿐이었죠. 지금은 CD, DVD, 비디오 게임, 웹사이트, 그래픽 디자인, 그리고 다른 여러 형태의 예술까지 염두에 두어야 합니다. 이제 전통적인 예술조차 컴퓨터를 사용하는 경우가 많습니다. 그래서 컴퓨터 아트는 정의하기 어렵습니다. 컴퓨터 아트의 좀 더 순수한 형태인 디지털 아트는 컴퓨터의 디지털 레벨에서 만들어지는 예술입니다. 디지털 아트는 스캔한 이미지를 사용할 수도 있고 마우스나 그래픽 태블릿 같은 다른 도구를 이용해 만든 이미지를 쓸 수도 있습니다. 기술과 예술의 이러한 혼합은 과학, 예술, 기술을 결합하는 새로운 연구 분야로 이어지고 있죠. 현재 어떤 대학 과정은 교수들이 기술을 통해 예술과 과학을 가르치는 새롭고 재미있는 방법을 찾는 데 도움이 되게끔 설계되어 있습니다.

9   읽기와 듣기 두 지문에 제시된 정보의 요지는 무엇인가?
(a) 전통적인 예술이 기술에 의해 대체되고 있다.
(b) 학교에서 기술을 이용해 미술을 가르치고 있다.
(c) 컴퓨터가 전통적인 미술 도구를 대신하고 있다.
(d) 기술로 인해 예술이 여러 모로 바뀌고 있다.
(e) 기술과 예술은 함께 갈 수 없다.

10   제시된 정보로부터 유추할 수 있는 것은 무엇인가?
(a) 한국은 비디오 예술의 가장 큰 고객이다.
(b) 예술의 본질은 끊임없이 변한다.
(c) 미술 학교에서는 더 이상 손으로 그림 그리는 것을 가르치지 않을 것이다.
(d) 많은 전통적인 예술가들이 컴퓨터를 사용하지 않는다.
(e) 컴퓨터는 전통적인 미술 도구를 쓸모 없게 만들었다.

*Dictation 정답: Exercise 스크립트 밑줄 참조

Preparation   p. 37

Vocabulary Preview

A

1   **monetary** : 돈, 특히 국가의 총 통화량과 관련된
2   **eye-catching** : 관심을 끌 수 있는
3   **fluctuation** : 예측 불가능한 방식으로 일어나는 변화
4   **investment** : 더 많은 돈을 벌기 위해 쓰여지는 돈
5   **gravitate** : 어떤 것을 향해 꾸준히 움직이다

B

1   **boom** / 1941년부터 1970년까지 미국은 경기 호황을 타서 모두가 풍

족함을 누렸다.

2 Currency / 통화 시장이란 하나의 통화를 다른 통화로 교환할 수 있는 곳이다.

3 government bonds / 정부가 손실을 막아주기 때문에 국채는 현명한 투자 대상이다.

4 rip-off / 그 식당에서 먹지 마. 완전 바가지야. 가격은 비싼 주제에 맛은 형편없어.

5 mint / 조폐국은 동전과 지폐를 제작하는 곳이다.

6 Low-yield / 수익률이 낮은 투자에는 저금리의 저축예금이 포함된다.

7 recession / 경제는 가끔 경제 성장이 더딘 시기인 불경기로 접어들기도 한다.

Expressions and Meanings

1 난 준비가 다 돼서 빨리 하고 싶어.　　**e** 시작하려니 막 들뜬다.

2 그건 돈이 너무 많이 들어.　　**a** 그건 너무 비싸.

3 간단히 말하자면 그런 얘기지.　　**d** 요약을 참 잘했구나.

4 한번 살펴보자.　　**g** 한번 살펴보자.

5 그것이 작용하게 될 것이다.　　**b** 그것은 중요한 요인이 될 것이다.

6 대개는 그런 법이다.　　**c** 대개는 그런 식이다.

7 판매량이 치솟았다.　　**f** 그들은 상품을 많이 팔았다.

Listening Drill 1　　p. 38~p. 39

Monolog

O (1) adults　(2) teens　(3) eye-catching　(4) slogans　(5) characters　(6) nag factor　(7) Teens　(8) income　(9) clothing　(10) entertainment　(11) designs　(12) brands

G 1 (c)　2 (b)

S (1) T　(2) T　(3) T　(4) F

M In the past, marketing focused on those people who had the money. They were most often adults. Now, however, there has been a shift in marketing strategies, which now focus more on children and teenagers. Children and teenagers have a large influence on how their parents spend money. Marketers have geared products to be eye-catching to children. They may have bright colors and funny slogans or characters so that children will desire this product. Then the nag factor comes into play. Children will pester their parents until the parents give in and buy the product the children desire. For teens, marketers are more direct. Teens often have their own income, either through a part-time job or an allowance that their parents give them. Marketers target the things teens favor the most: clothing, entertainment, and food. Most teens want to look fashionable and will spend their money on the latest fashions or will get their parents to buy them. Teens also want to have the latest cell phones, MP3 players, and computer games, so marketers come up with designs and brands targeted toward teens. With food, teens and children both tend to eat more unhealthy diets of snack and junk food. By advertising these food products during popular television shows that children and teens enjoy, the companies know that their sales will go through the roof.

▶ gear 맞추다, 조정하다　eye-catching 눈길을 끄는　nag factor (사 달라고) 조르기 요소　come into play 작동하기 시작하다　pester 괴롭히다, 조르다　give in 항복하다　come up with 제안하다, 마련하다　go through the roof 치솟다, 폭등하다

남　과거에 마케팅은 돈이 있는 사람들을 주 대상으로 삼았고, 그들은 대개 성인이었습니다. 하지만 지금은 마케팅 전략이 변해 아이들과 십대에게 더 초점을 맞춥니다. 아이들과 십대는 부모의 소비 방식에 큰 영향을 미치죠. 마케터는 상품이 아이들의 눈길을 끌 수 있게 만듭니다. 아이들이 그 상품을 원하게끔 밝은 색깔을 입히고 재미있는 선전 문구나 캐릭터를 넣기도 하죠. 그 다음에는 조르기가 시작됩니다. 아이들은 부모가 항복하여 자신들이 원하는 상품을 사줄 때까지 부모를 괴롭힐 것입니다. 십대의 경우, 마케터들은 좀 더 직접적이죠. 십대는 아르바이트를 해서 벌든 부모가 주는 용돈을 받든 보통 자신의 수입을 갖고 있습니다. 마케터는 십대가 가장 좋아하는 것들을 겨냥합니다. 바로 의류와 오락거리, 음식이죠. 대부분의 십대는 패셔너블하게 보이고 싶어서 최신 패션에 자기 돈을 쓰거나 부모가 사주게끔 만들 것입니다. 또한 십대들은 최신 휴대폰과 MP3 플레이어, 컴퓨터 게임기를 갖고 싶어하기 때문에 마케터들은 십대를 겨냥한 디자인과 브랜드를 선보이죠. 음식에 있어서는 십대와 아이들 모두 건강에 나쁜 간식거리와 인스턴트 식품을 더 많이 섭취하는 경향이 있습니다. 기업은 아이들과 십대가 즐겨 보는 인기 텔레비전 프로그램 중간에 이런 식품을 광고하면 판매량이 치솟을 것이라는 사실을 알고 있죠.

General Questions

1 담화에 가장 알맞은 제목은 무엇인가?
(a) 아이들과 십대의 구매력
(b) 효과적인 마케팅 전략: 조르기 요소
(c) 아이들과 십대를 겨냥한 마케팅 전략
(d) 아이들과 십대가 좋아하는 상품

2 다음 중 가장 잘 요약된 것을 고르시오.
(a) 아이들과 십대는 마케터가 현재 중점을 두고 있는 특정 상품을 즐겨 소비한다.
(b) 아이들과 십대는 그들의 부모에게 큰 영향을 미치기 때문에 마케터의 새로운 목표 대상이다.

Specific Questions

다시 듣고 옳은 문장에는 T, 틀린 문장에는 F를 쓰시오.
(1) 과거에는 돈을 버는 성인이 마케팅의 주요 대상이었다.
(2) 마케터는 상품에 재미있는 캐릭터를 써서 아이들의 흥미를 끈다.
(3) 십대들은 보통 부모 외에도 돈이 들어오는 수입원이 있다.
(4) 마케터는 모든 연령층에게 비슷한 디자인과 브랜드를 사용한다.

Dialog

N (1) 18th　(2) Scotland　(3) prosperous　(4) self-interest　(5) society　(6) value　(7) value　(8) division of labor　(9) separate　(10) assembly line

G 1 (b)　2 (b)

S (1) T　(2) T　(3) F　(4) T

B So, let's talk about our project on Adam Smith, the founding father of economics. What did you find out about Adam Smith?

G He was born in the 18th century in England, and he wrote a famous book called *The Wealth of Nations*.

B Right, except that he was born in Scotland. I found out he wrote *The Wealth of Nations* to explain why and how nations became prosperous.

G The main point of the book is that when people act in

their own self-interest, they are also helping society as a whole.

B That makes sense. One self-interest is to make money. We work to earn money, but to earn money we must be doing something of value to someone. If we didn't, they wouldn't pay us, right?

G Sure. Why should you get paid for doing nothing? This also explains why some types of work have more value than others and why people get paid different wages. A doctor should get paid more than a laborer.

B The teacher also said we should examine Smith's ideas on the division of labor.

G He thought the division of labor was one of the main causes of prosperity. Many workers working together doing separate tasks can produce more than if one worker tried to do all the tasks by himself. This is the main principle behind the modern assembly line.

B I think we have enough material to get started. Let's begin with a short biography.

G I'm ready and raring to go. Ah, where was he born again?

▶ founding father 창립자, 창시자 prosperous 번영하는, 번성하는 self-interest 이기심, 사리사욕 laborer (육체) 노동자 division of labor 분업 분할 prosperity 번영, 성공 assembly line 조립 라인 ready and raring to go 시작할 만반의 준비가 되어 빨리 시작하고 싶은

남 그럼 경제학의 창시자 애덤 스미스에 관한 우리 과제에 대해 이야기해보자. 넌 애덤 스미스에 대해 뭘 알아왔니?

여 그는 18세기에 영국에서 태어났고 『국부론』이라는 유명한 책을 썼어.

남 맞아, 그가 스코틀랜드에서 태어났다는 것만 빼고. 난 『국부론』이 국가가 번영하는 이유와 방법을 설명하기 위해 쓴 책이라는 걸 알았어.

여 책의 요점은 사람들이 자신의 이익에 따라 행동할 때, 그들은 또한 총체적으로는 사회에 기여하기도 한다는 거야.

남 일리가 있는 말이야. 개인의 이익 한 가지는 돈을 버는 거지. 우린 돈을 벌기 위해 일하지만 돈을 벌기 위해서는 누군가에게 가치 있는 어떤 일을 해야만 해. 그렇지 않으면 그들은 우리에게 돈을 지불하지 않을 테니까, 맞지?

여 물론이야. 아무것도 안 하는데 왜 돈을 받아? 이 책은 또 왜 어떤 종류의 일이 다른 일보다 더 가치 있고, 사람들이 왜 서로 다른 임금을 받는지도 설명해주고 있어. 의사가 육체 노동자보다는 더 많은 돈을 받아야 하지.

남 선생님께서 스미스의 분업 이론에 대해서도 조사하라고 하셨잖아.

여 스미스는 분업이 번영을 이루는 주요인 중 하나라고 생각했어. 많은 노동자들이 독립된 업무를 하면서 함께 일하면 한 사람이 혼자 모든 일을 하는 것보다 더 많이 생산해낼 수 있지. 이게 현대의 조립 라인 기저에 깔린 주된 원칙이야.

남 이만하면 시작하기에 충분한 것 같아. 간단한 일대기부터 시작해보자.

여 난 준비 됐으니 빨리 시작하자. 아, 그런데 그가 어디에서 태어났다고 했지?

General Questions

1 대화의 목적은 무엇인가?
  (a) 한 유명한 경제학자의 생애에 관해 이야기하려고
  (b) 한 유명한 경제학자의 사상에 대해 살펴보려고
  (c) 한 유명한 경제학자가 미친 영향을 살펴보려고
  (d) 한 유명한 경제학자의 이론을 반박하려고

2 다음 중 가장 잘 요약된 것을 고르시오.
  (a) 애덤 스미스의 경제학 사상은 그의 이론을 따른 많은 국가가 부강해지는 데 도움이 되었다.
  (b) 애덤 스미스의 이론은 사람들의 이익과 경제학 간의 관계 및 분업의 가치에 대해 다루고 있다.

Specific Questions

다시 듣고 옳은 문장에는 T, 틀린 문장에는 F를 쓰시오.
(1) 『국부론』은 국가가 부유해지는 이유와 방법을 설명하려고 했다.
(2) 애덤 스미스의 주요 경제 이론은 사람들이 자신의 이익에 따라 행동할 때 총체적으로 사회에 이득이 된다는 것이다.
(3) 애덤 스미스는 사람들이 서로 다른 일을 해도 똑같은 돈을 받아야 한다고 생각했다.
(4) 조립 라인은 애덤 스미스의 분업 이론에 따른 것이다.

Listening Drill 2
p. 40~p. 41

Long Lecture

◎ (1) supply (2) demand (3) greater (4) less (5) harvest
   (6) oil (7) hurricanes (8) 2008 (9) lifestyles
   (10) demand (11) down

1 (c) **2** (b) **3** (1) T (2) T (3) T (4) F **4** (b)

Dictation 정답: 스크립트 밑줄 참조

W You may often wonder about the price you pay for goods and services. How is the price determined? You've probably heard people complaining about rising prices for food and gas. You've also probably noticed that computer products tend to get cheaper over time. Why does this happen? A lot of it has to do with supply and demand. When the supply of something is greater than the demand by the public for this product—like computers, for example—then the price of that product will go down. If suppliers have too much of a product, they want to sell it, and they will drop their prices to get consumers to buy it. For instance, at harvest time, markets and shops are filled with fresh fruits and vegetables, so the prices go down. On the other hand, when there is not enough of a product and the demand is high, prices rise. In the summer of 2005, severe hurricanes in the Gulf of Mexico disrupted oil production there. As a consequence, oil prices in North America rose almost 50 percent in a few short weeks. The demand for oil hadn't changed, yet the supply did. This caused prices to rise. Still speaking of oil, in the summer of 2008, prices again skyrocketed for a variety of reasons. This time, the prices were so high that people decided to change their lifestyles to use fewer oil products. As a consequence, demand dropped. Soon, prices also began to drop. These changes and differences in price were the result of changes in supply and demand.

▶ gas 휘발유 disrupt 혼란시키다, 중단시키다 skyrocket (물가가) 급등하다

여 여러분은 종종 여러분이 지불하는 상품 및 서비스 가격에 대해 궁금해했을 거예요. 가격은 어떻게 결정되는 걸까요? 사람들이 식품이나 휘발유 가격 인상에 대해 불평하는 걸 들어봤을 겁니다. 또 컴퓨터 제품은 시간이 지나면서 싸지는 경향이 있다는 것도 알아챘을 거예요. 이런 일은 왜 일어나는 것일까요? 그 대부분은 공급 및 수요와 관련되어 있습니다. 예를 들어 컴퓨터 같은 어떤 상품의 공급이 그 상품에 대한 대중의 수요보다 많으면 그 상품의 가격은 떨어지겠죠. 공급업체가 어떤 상품을 지나치게 많이 갖고 있다면 그들은 그것을 팔고 싶어하고 따라서 소비자가 그 상품을 구입하게끔 가격을 낮출 것입니다. 예를 들어 수확철에는 시장과 상점에 신선한 과일과 채소가 가득하기 때문에 가격이 떨어집니다. 반

면에 상품은 충분하지 않은데 수요가 높을 때는 가격이 올라갑니다. 2005년 여름 멕시코 만에 심한 허리케인이 발생해 그 지역의 석유 생산이 중단되었습니다. 그 결과 북미 유가가 단 몇 주 만에 거의 50% 가까이 올랐습니다. 석유 수요는 변하지 않았는데 공급이 변했던 겁니다. 이 때문에 가격이 올랐죠. 역시 석유에 대한 건데요, 2008년 여름에는 여러 가지 이유로 가격이 또 한 차례 급등했습니다. 이번에는 가격이 워낙 비싸서 사람들이 석유 제품을 덜 쓰는 쪽으로 생활방식을 바꿨죠. 그 결과 수요가 줄어들었고 곧 가격도 떨어지기 시작했습니다. 가격의 이 같은 변화와 차이는 공급과 수요의 변화로 인한 결과였습니다.

1 강의의 주제는 무엇인가?
  (a) 상품 가격에 미치는 자연 재해의 영향
  (b) 어떤 상품에 대한 공급과 수요의 관계
  (c) 가격과 공급 및 수요의 관계
  (d) 소비자의 습관 변화로 인한 가격 변화

2 다음 중 가장 잘 요약된 것을 고르시오.
  (a) 상품의 가격 책정은 계절적인 변화 및 재해, 상품의 품질을 포함한 많은 요인과 관련되어 있다.
  (b) 상품의 가격은 그 상품의 구입 가능성과 해당 상품에 대한 소비자 욕구에 영향을 받는다.

3 옳은 문장에는 T, 틀린 문장에는 F를 쓰시오.
  (1) 연중 특정 시기에 식품이 더 싸진다.
  (2) 상품의 희소성은 흔히 상품 가격에 영향을 미친다.
  (3) 자연 재해는 일부 상품의 가격에 큰 영향을 줄 수 있다.
  (4) 소비자가 상품 가격에 미치는 영향은 미미하다.

4 강의에 따르면 2008년 여름에 석유 가격이 아주 많이 올랐다가 떨어진 이유는?
  (a) 정유 회사가 석유 공급을 늘렸다.
  (b) 소비자가 석유 제품의 사용을 줄였다.
  (c) 2008년 여름 이후에 자연 재해가 없었다.
  (d) 석유의 대체 상품이 개발되었다.

Exercise p. 42~p. 43

| 1 (a) | 2 해설 참조 | 3 (c) | 4 (d) | 5 (a) | 6 (c) | 7 (c) |
| 8 (d) | 9 (d) | 10 해설 참조 | 11 (e) | 12 (c) | | |

1

M A luxury item refers to any high-priced, high-quality good that people want. Such items can include almost any product or service, such as clothing, food, hotels, and transportation. Why do people spend so much money for these products and services? Common sense tells us that people will buy the best product they can for the lowest price possible. But with luxury items, there are two other factors at work. The first factor is the notion that high price means high quality. Of course, this is not always the case, and there are plenty of rip-offs out there, but when a brand name becomes associated with a reputation for quality, people know that they are getting good value for their money. This reduces the risk factor that is involved in almost any transaction. Second, there is the matter of prestige. People want to be associated with high-quality products. If they have worked hard and have made a good living, they want to show the world that they are

successful. By having the best car, watch, and clothes, by staying in the best hotels, by taking a limousine instead of a taxi, and by flying first class instead of economy, they show the world that they are among the elite. As long as there are people with money willing to buy these products and services, luxury items will continue to exist.

▶ refer to 가리키다, 적용되다 at work 작용하는 notion 관념, 생각 rip-off 바가지, 사기 transaction 거래, 매매 prestige 위신, 명망

남 사치품이란 사람들이 원하는 고가의 고급 상품을 말합니다. 여기에는 의류, 식품, 호텔, 교통수단 같은 거의 모든 상품이나 서비스가 포함될 수 있는데요. 사람들은 왜 이런 상품과 서비스에 그렇게 많은 돈을 쓰는 것일까요? 상식적으로 사람들은 가능한 한 가장 싼 가격에 가장 좋은 상품을 삽니다. 하지만 사치품에 관한 한 두 가지 다른 요인이 작용하죠. 첫 번째 요인은 높은 가격이 높은 품질을 의미한다는 생각입니다. 물론 언제나 그런 것은 아니며 세상에는 비싸기만 하고 형편없는 것들도 많죠. 그러나 어떤 브랜드명이 품질에 대한 명성과 관련될 때는 사람들은 값을 치른 만큼 훌륭한 가치를 얻는다는 것을 알고 있습니다. 이것은 어떤 거래에든 수반되기 마련인 위험 요소를 줄여주죠. 두 번째로는 위신의 문제가 있습니다. 사람들은 좋은 품질의 상품과 연관되고 싶어 합니다. 열심히 일해서 남부럽지 않게 살게 되면 자신이 성공했다는 것을 세상 사람들에게 보여주고 싶어지죠. 최고급 자동차와 시계, 옷을 소유하고 최고급 호텔에 묵으며 택시 대신 리무진을 타고 일반석 대신 일등석에 탐으로써 그들은 자신이 상류층에 속해 있다는 것을 세상에 과시합니다. 이런 상품과 서비스를 구매할 의사가 있는 부유한 사람들이 있는 한 사치품은 계속 존재할 것입니다.

1 담화의 주제는 무엇인가?
  (a) 사람들은 좋은 품질의 상품을 갖고 싶고 자신의 사회적 지위를 보여주고 싶어서 사치품을 산다.
  (b) 사치품은 상류층 사람들에게는 중요한 신분적 상징으로 인식된다.
  (c) 부유한 사람들은 미래를 위해 돈을 투자하는 하나의 방법으로써 사치품을 산다.
  (d) 사치품은 높은 가격에도 불구하고 믿을 수 있는 품질로 사람의 마음을 끈다.
  (e) 돈을 벌기 위해 열심히 일한 뒤 사람들은 그 노력의 대가로 사치품을 원한다.

2

M Welcome to *Business Week*. Our guest today is Susan Radcliff, a noted economist, and our topic is consumer demand. Susan, what are some factors that influence how much or how many of a product a person will buy?

W One of the biggest influences is the price of the product.

M Can you give some examples of this?

W Certainly. If a can of soda cost five dollars, you wouldn't buy it since you would think it costs an arm and a leg. If the price were three dollars, you might buy one as a special treat. If the price dropped to one dollar and 50 cents, you'd buy a few, and if it were fifty cents, you might buy a lot.

M It sounds very logical. How do economists express these concepts?

W We can put this information on a graph to show the demand curve.

M Can you explain that further?

W First, we put the price on the <u>vertical</u> <u>axis</u> and the amount bought on the <u>horizontal</u> <u>axis</u>. Let's use the soda example.

M Okay, so at five dollars, a person <u>would</u> <u>buy</u> <u>no</u> <u>sodas</u>, and at 3 dollars, the person would buy one, right?

W Yes, and when the price <u>drops</u> to one dollar and 50 cents, we'll say the person would buy three, and then <u>at</u> <u>fifty</u> <u>cents</u>, the person would buy eight. When we <u>connect</u> <u>the</u> <u>dots</u>, you can see that we have a <u>demand</u> <u>curve</u> which <u>slopes</u> <u>down</u> from the left to the right.

M So, <u>the</u> <u>cheaper</u> the price of a good, the more people will buy, and the <u>more</u> <u>expensive</u> <u>the</u> <u>good</u> <u>is</u>, the less of it you buy.

W Correct. Generally, demand goes down as prices rise and vice versa.

▶ cost an arm and a leg 많은 돈이 들다   treat 큰 기쁨, 특별한 즐거움을 주는 것
curve 곡선, 곡선 도표   vertical 수직의, 세로의   axis 축   horizontal 수평의, 가로의
slope 경사지다   vice versa 역(逆)도 또한 같음

남 〈비즈니스 위크〉를 시청해 주셔서 감사합니다. 오늘은 초대 손님으로 저명한 경제학자이신 수잔 래드클리프 씨를 모셨는데요, 오늘의 주제는 소비자 수요입니다. 수잔, 한 사람이 어떤 물건을 얼마어치, 그러니까 얼마나 많이 사는가에 영향을 미치는 요인에는 무엇이 있습니까?

여 가장 크게 영향을 미치는 것 중 하나는 상품의 가격이죠.

남 예를 좀 들어주시겠습니까?

여 물론이죠. 만약 사이다 한 캔이 5달러 한다면 너무 비싸다고 생각해서 안 살 겁니다. 가격이 3달러라면 특별히 하나 살지도 모르죠. 가격이 1달러 50센트로 떨어지면 조금 살 거고 50센트라면 많이 사겠죠.

남 굉장히 논리적인 것 같은데요. 경제학자들은 이런 개념을 어떻게 표현하나요?

여 이 정보를 그래프에 대입해 수요 곡선을 나타낼 수 있습니다.

남 좀 더 설명해주시겠습니까?

여 먼저 세로축에 가격을, 가로축에 구입한 양을 놓습니다. 사이다를 예로 들어보죠.

남 네, 5달러일 때는 사이다를 하나도 사지 않고 3달러일 때는 1개 살 거예요. 맞나요?

여 그렇습니다. 그리고 가격이 1달러 50센트로 떨어지면 3개를 살 거고 50센트일 때는 8개를 사겠죠. 이 점들을 연결하면 왼쪽에서 오른쪽으로 흘러내리는 수요 곡선이 만들어진 걸 보실 수 있을 거예요.

남 그러니까 상품의 가격이 쌀수록 사람들은 더 많이 사게 되고 상품이 비싸질수록 더 적게 사는군요.

여 맞습니다. 일반적으로 가격이 오르면 수요는 감소하고 그 반대도 마찬가지죠.

2 예로 든 사이다의 가격과 수요를 이용해 수요 곡선 그래프를 그리시오.

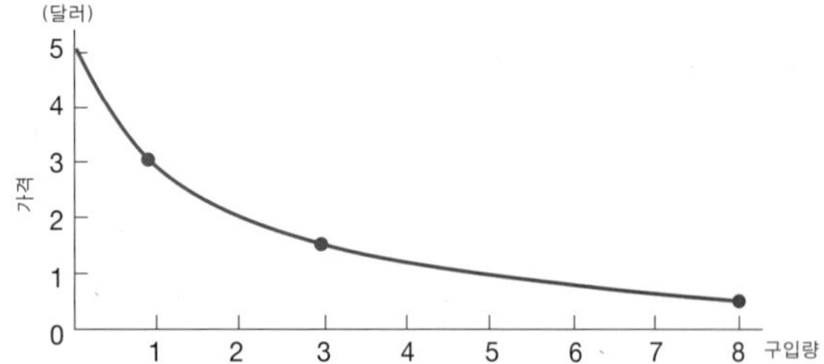

3-4

W One of the <u>major</u> <u>concerns</u> of <u>economists</u> is money. In fact, money is something that <u>concerns</u> <u>us</u> <u>all</u>, but economists look at money <u>in</u> <u>a</u> <u>different</u> <u>way</u> than most people. Economists think of money <u>based</u> <u>on</u> <u>its</u> <u>functions</u>—what it does—and to an <u>economist</u>, money has three functions. First, money is used as a <u>unit of</u>

<u>account</u>. This means that with money, we can <u>measure</u> <u>the</u> <u>values</u> of different goods and services and <u>compare</u> <u>them</u>. This also means that businesses have a <u>way of</u> <u>knowing</u> if their <u>business</u> <u>transactions</u> are <u>successful</u> <u>or</u> <u>not</u>. The second function of money is as a <u>medium</u> <u>of</u> <u>exchange</u>. This is perhaps its <u>most</u> <u>important</u> <u>function</u>. Money <u>allows</u> <u>for</u> <u>trading</u> or the exchange of <u>goods</u> <u>and</u> <u>services</u>. When we trade for goods or services without using money, it is <u>called</u> <u>barter</u>. This <u>requires</u> that <u>both</u> <u>parties</u> need what the <u>other</u> <u>party</u> <u>has</u>, which is not always the case. Money is <u>more</u> <u>useful</u> than <u>bartering</u> because it is <u>accepted</u> <u>as</u> <u>payment</u> for goods and services. This <u>leads</u> to the third function of money, which is the <u>store</u> <u>of</u> <u>value</u> function. People believe money is <u>worth</u> <u>something</u> and that it has value. People will <u>not</u> <u>trust</u> money as a <u>medium</u> of exchange if it does not <u>hold</u> <u>its</u> <u>value</u>. As a <u>definition</u>, money is anything which is accepted as a unit of account, a medium of exchange, and a store of value.

▶ account 계산, 셈   transaction 상거래, 매매   medium 수단, 매개물
barter 물물교환

여 경제학자의 가장 큰 관심사 중 하나는 돈입니다. 사실 돈은 우리 모두와 관련된 것이지만 경제학자는 보통 사람들과는 다른 관점에서 돈을 보는데요. 경제학자는 돈을 그 기능, 즉 돈이 무엇을 하는가에 근거해서 생각하는데, 경제학자에게 돈은 세 가지 기능을 갖고 있습니다. 첫째, 돈은 하나의 계산 단위로 사용되죠. 이것은 우리가 돈으로 서로 다른 상품과 서비스의 가치를 평가하고 비교할 수 있다는 뜻입니다. 이는 또한 기업이 자신들의 사업상 거래가 성공적인지 아닌지 알 수 있는 방법을 갖고 있다는 뜻이기도 하죠. 돈의 두 번째 기능은 교환 수단으로서의 역할인데요. 이것은 아마 돈의 가장 중요한 기능일 것입니다. 돈으로 상품과 서비스를 거래하거나 교환할 수 있죠. 돈을 사용하지 않고 상품이나 서비스를 거래할 때는 물물교환이라고 합니다. 이를 위해서는 양쪽 모두 상대편이 갖고 있는 것을 필요로 해야 하는데, 언제나 그런 것은 아니죠. 돈은 상품과 서비스에 대한 지불로 받아들여지기 때문에 물물교환보다 훨씬 유용하죠. 이로 인해 돈의 세 번째 기능이 생기는데 바로 가치 저장의 기능입니다. 사람들은 돈이 귀중한 것이고 가치가 있다고 믿습니다. 만약 돈에 가치가 없다면 사람들은 돈을 교환 수단으로 신뢰하지 않을 것입니다. 정의하자면, 돈은 계산 단위이자 교환 수단이며 가치의 저장으로 받아들여지는 어떤 것입니다.

3 화자가 돈을 '계산 단위'라고 말한 의미는 무엇인가?
   (a) 돈은 가치를 갖고 있어서 물건을 사는 데 쓰일 수 있다.
   (b) 돈을 저축하려면 은행에 보관한다.
   (c) 돈은 물건의 가치를 평가하는 데 쓰인다.
   (d) 돈은 어떤 것의 가치를 저장하는 수단으로서의 역할을 한다.
   (e) 돈은 사람들이 신뢰하는 정도에 따라 가치를 갖는다.

4 돈의 저장 가치가 현저하게 줄어든다면 어떤 일이 일어나겠는가?
   (a) 사람들은 교환 수단으로서 돈을 계속 신뢰할 것이다.
   (b) 사람들이 은행으로 몰려가 돈을 모두 인출할 수 있다.
   (c) 사람들은 돈을 더 많이 찍으라고 요구할 것이다.
   (d) 사람들은 옛날의 물물교환 체계로 돌아갈지 모른다.
   (e) 사람들은 돈을 모두 집에 모아놓기 시작할지도 모른다.

5-6   Level up

W When economists talk about <u>supply</u> <u>and</u> <u>demand</u>, they must also <u>consider</u> the concepts of <u>substitutes</u> and <u>complements</u>. Does anyone know what a <u>substitute</u> is?

B It's when you <u>replace</u> <u>one</u> <u>good</u> with another, such as when the good is in <u>short</u> <u>supply</u> or there is a <u>distribution</u> problem.

W <u>That's</u> <u>it</u> <u>in</u> <u>a</u> <u>nutshell</u>. For example, every morning you drink orange juice because it's healthy and <u>good</u> <u>for</u> <u>you</u>. Then there is a <u>big</u> <u>frost</u> in the great orange-growing <u>regions</u> of Florida, and many orange trees are <u>damaged</u> or <u>even</u> <u>destroyed</u> by the <u>cold</u> <u>weather</u>. What happens to the price of orange juice?

B The price of orange juice will <u>go</u> <u>up</u> because there is <u>less</u> <u>supply</u>.

W Right. So will your family <u>continue</u> <u>to</u> <u>buy</u> orange juice <u>even</u> <u>though</u> it's now very expensive?

B It <u>depends</u> <u>on</u> <u>how</u> <u>expensive</u> it is. If it gets really expensive, we probably <u>wouldn't</u> <u>keep</u> <u>buying</u> orange juice.

W So that's when <u>substitutes</u> <u>come</u> <u>into</u> <u>play</u>. What do you think is a <u>good</u> <u>substitute</u> <u>for</u> orange juice?

B Apple juice?

W Good choice. Apple juice is a substitute for orange juice. It <u>satisfies</u> <u>the</u> <u>same</u> <u>needs</u> as orange juice. When the price of one good <u>rises</u>, people <u>will</u> <u>switch</u> to a substitute if it's <u>available</u>.

B I understand. You also <u>mentioned</u> <u>complements</u>. What are they?

W A complement is when <u>two</u> <u>goods</u> <u>go</u> <u>together</u>. This means that they complement <u>each</u> <u>other</u>. A good example is <u>gas</u> <u>and</u> <u>cars</u>. When gas is cheap, people will buy large <u>sports</u> <u>utility</u> <u>vehicles</u> which use a lot of gas. When gas prices go up, people want to buy <u>smaller</u> <u>cars</u> which use less gas.

B So, <u>goods</u> <u>are</u> <u>complements</u> of each other when a change in the price of one good <u>affects</u> <u>the</u> <u>demand</u> for another good.

W Exactly.

▶ substitute 대체재 complement 보완재; 보완하다
in a nutshell 한 마디로, 아주 간단하게 come into play 작동하기 시작하다

여 경제학자들이 공급과 수요에 관해 이야기할 때 반드시 같이 고려해야 하는 게 대체재와 보완재 개념입니다. 대체재가 뭔지 아는 사람 있나요?

남 어떤 상품의 공급이 부족하거나 분배가 원활하지 않을 때 그 상품을 다른 것으로 대체하는 것을 말합니다.

여 바로 그거예요. 예를 들어 여러분은 건강에 좋기 때문에 매일 아침 오렌지 주스를 마시죠. 그런데 플로리다의 대규모 오렌지 재배 지역에 큰 서리가 내려 많은 오렌지 나무가 피해를 입거나 추운 날씨 때문에 죽습니다. 그럼 오렌지 주스의 가격은 어떻게 될까요?

남 공급이 줄어 오렌지 주스의 가격은 올라갈 겁니다.

여 맞아요. 그렇다면 여러분의 가족은 이제 오렌지 주스 가격이 아주 비싼데도 불구하고 계속 살까요?

남 얼마나 비싼가에 따라 다른데요. 만약 아주 비싸진다면 계속 오렌지 주스를 사지는 않을 거예요.

여 그때가 바로 대체재가 움직이게 되는 시점입니다. 오렌지 주스의 좋은 대체재로는 뭐가 있을까요?

남 사과 주스요?

여 훌륭한 선택입니다. 사과 주스는 오렌지 주스의 대체재입니다. 오렌지 주스와 동일한 필요를 충족시켜 주죠. 한 상품의 가격이 오르면 사람들은 가능하다면 대체재로 바꿀 거예요.

남 무슨 말씀인지 알겠어요. 보완재에 대해서도 언급하셨는데요. 그건 뭔가요?

여 보완재란 두 가지 상품이 같이 움직이는 것을 말합니다. 그 두 가지가 서로 보완한다는 뜻이죠. 휘발유와 자동차가 좋은 예입니다. 휘발유가 싸면 사람들은 휘발유를 많이 쓰는 커다란 스포츠 유틸리티 차량을 살 겁니다. 휘발유 가격이 오르면 휘발유를 적게 쓰는 소형차를 사고 싶어 하죠.

남 그러니까 한 상품의 가격 변동이 다른 상품의 수요에 영향을 줄 때 그 두 상품을 서로의 보완재라고 한다는 말씀이죠.

여 맞아요.

5 소비자가 대체재로 바꾸는 주된 이유로 담화에서 언급된 것은 무엇인가?
  (a) 일용품의 가격 차이   (b) 일용품을 바꾸려는 욕구
  (c) 일용품의 늘어난 효용성   (d) 일용품의 수요 감소
  (e) 일용품에 영향을 주는 보완재의 변화

6 다음 중 내용을 가장 잘 요약한 것을 고르시오.
  (a) 대체재와 보완재는 공급과 수요의 비율을 조절한다.
  (b) 보완재는 가격이 폭등했을 때 대체재를 대신한다.
  (c) 대체재와 보완재 사용은 가격 변화에 영향을 받는다.

7 **Level up**

G Dad, how do <u>banks</u> <u>work</u>?

M Banks use other people's money to <u>make</u> <u>money</u>. That's about <u>as</u> <u>simple</u> <u>as</u> I can make it.

G Do you mean they <u>use</u> <u>the</u> <u>money</u> people <u>deposit</u> in the bank?

M Right. Banks <u>offer</u> <u>people</u> a <u>safe</u> <u>place</u> <u>to</u> <u>keep</u> their money. They pay you to keep your money with them <u>through</u> <u>interest</u> <u>payments</u>, which are usually two or three percent per year.

G So then how do they make money?

M Banks <u>lend</u> <u>depositors'</u> <u>money</u> to people <u>who</u> <u>need</u> money to buy a house or a car or to <u>pay</u> <u>for</u> <u>university</u>. Banks <u>charge</u> these people a <u>higher</u> <u>interest</u> <u>rate</u>, which is usually between five and ten percent. This is the banks' <u>fee</u>, and it's how they make money.

G Can they lend all of their money? <u>What</u> <u>if</u> I want to <u>get</u> <u>my</u> <u>money</u> <u>back</u> and it's not there because they lent it?

M The <u>government</u> has <u>made</u> <u>rules</u> that banks must <u>keep</u> <u>a</u> <u>certain</u> <u>percentage</u> of their money <u>on</u> <u>hand</u> in the banks at all <u>times</u>. This is usually about 10 percent of <u>their</u> <u>total</u> <u>deposits</u>.

▶ deposit 예금하다; 예금(액) depositor 예금자 on hand 바로 곁에; 마침 가지고 있어

여 아빠, 은행은 어떻게 돌아가나요?

남 은행은 다른 사람들의 돈을 이용해 돈을 벌지. 이게 내가 할 수 있는 한 제일 간단하게 설명한 거야.

여 아빠 말씀은 사람들이 예금한 돈을 은행이 이용한다는 뜻인가요?

남 그래. 은행은 사람들에게 돈을 안전하게 보관할 수 있는 곳을 제공하지. 돈을 은행에 맡기는 대가로 이자를 주는데 보통은 일 년에 2, 3%란다.

여 그럼 은행은 어떻게 돈을 벌죠?

남 은행은 예금자들의 돈을 집이나 자동차를 사거나 대학 등록금을 내기 위해 돈이 필요한 사람들에게 빌려준다. 은행은 이런 사람들에게 높은 이율을 적용하는데 보통 5에서 10% 사이지. 이게 은행이 받는 수수료란다. 그렇게 해서 돈을 버는 거지.

여 은행은 갖고 있는 돈을 모두 빌려줄 수 있나요? 만약 제가 돈을 찾고 싶은데 은행이 그 돈을 빌려줘버려서 돈이 없으면 어떡해요?

남 은행은 언제나 일정한 비율의 돈을 갖고 있어야 한다고 정부가 규정을 만들었어. 그 돈은 보통 전체 예치금의 10% 정도지.

7 According to the dialog, what is the main way banks make money?   대화에 따르면 은행이 돈을 버는 주된 방법은 무엇인가?

(a) Banks collect interest directly from the money people deposit.   은행은 사람들이 예금한 돈에서 직접 이자를 받는다.

(b) Banks make money by spending all of their customers' deposits.   은행은 고객들의 예금을 모두 써서 돈을 번다.

(c) Banks earn interest by lending depositors' money.
은행은 예금자들의 돈을 빌려줌으로써 이자를 번다.

(d) Banks collect fees for the right to keep people's money safe.
은행은 돈을 안전하게 보관하는 권리에 대해 수수료를 받는다.

(e) Banks receive 10 percent interest from the government.
은행은 정부로부터 10%의 이자를 받는다.

---

8   Level up

W I'd like to speak a little about one of the <u>20th century's</u> <u>best-known</u> and most <u>influential economists</u>, Milton Friedman. He <u>was born in</u> New York in 1912. He is <u>best known for</u> his work at the University of Chicago, where <u>he taught</u> for 30 years. While there, he <u>helped to create</u> a group of <u>intellectuals</u> who would <u>become known as</u> the Chicago School of Economics. Many of the <u>school's principles</u> would be <u>adopted by governments</u> in the United States, Britain, and Canada in the 1980s. Freidman's <u>main theory</u> was that a government should not become <u>too involved in guiding</u> a nation's economy. He <u>authored</u> and <u>coauthored numerous books</u> on <u>monetary</u> history and theory. In 1976, he won the <u>Nobel Prize</u> for Economics. In addition, he won <u>several other awards</u> for economics in the United States <u>during his lifetime</u>. After his <u>retirement</u> in 1977, he traveled to many countries, <u>including</u> Eastern Europe and China, where he <u>gave lectures</u> and advice on economics. He was also an <u>economic advisor</u> to President Ronald Reagan from 1980 to 1988. Milton Friedman died in 2006 at the age of 94 in San Francisco.

▶ intellectual 지식인   school 학파, 유파   author 집필하다; 저자   coauthor 공동 집필하다   monetary 통화의

여 20세기의 가장 유명하고 영향력 있는 경제학자 가운데 한 사람인 밀턴 프리드먼에 관해 이야기해 볼까 합니다. 그는 1912년 뉴욕에서 태어났습니다. 프리드먼은 30년간 가르쳤던 시카고 대학에 재직했을 때의 성과로 가장 잘 알려져 있죠. 거기서 그는 후에 시카고 경제학파로 알려지게 될 지식인 그룹을 만드는 데 기여했습니다. 그 학파의 많은 원리들은 1980년대에 미국과 영국, 캐나다 정부에 의해 채택되었습니다. 프리드먼의 핵심 이론은 정부가 국가 경제를 이끄는 데 지나치게 개입해서는 안 된다는 것이었죠. 그는 통화의 역사와 이론에 관한 수많은 책을 집필하고 공저했습니다. 1976년 프리드먼은 노벨 경제학상을 수상했습니다. 뿐만 아니라 생전에 미국에서 몇 개의 다른 경제학상도 받았습니다. 1977년에 은퇴한 뒤에는 동유럽과 중국을 비롯한 많은 나라를 여행하면서 경제학에 관해 강의하고 조언을 해주었습니다. 그는 또한 1980년부터 1988년까지 로널드 레이건 대통령의 경제 고문이기도 했습니다. 밀턴 프리드먼은 2006년 94세의 나이로 샌프란시스코에서 사망했습니다.

---

8 What is NOT true about Milton Freidman?
밀턴 프리드먼에 관한 내용 중 사실이 <u>아닌</u> 것은?

(a) He was a presidential advisor in the 1980s.
그는 1980년대에 대통령의 고문이었다.

(b) His theories were used by several countries.
그의 이론은 몇몇 국가에서 이용되었다.

(c) He coauthored several books about money.

그는 통화에 관한 몇 권의 책을 공동 집필했다.

(d) He studied at the University of Chicago.
그는 시카고 대학에서 공부했다.

(e) He received the Nobel Prize in Economics.
그는 노벨 경제학상을 수상했다.

9

M Economics is very <u>concerned with measuring</u> how economies perform, and one of the most <u>important measurements</u> is <u>gross domestic product</u>, or GDP. This is a topic of <u>great concern</u> for newspapers, <u>corporations</u>, and <u>government</u>, and these <u>statistics</u> are usually <u>released on</u> a <u>yearly basis</u>. Simply put, GDP is a measurement of the <u>total output</u> of the <u>economy</u>. With this <u>figure</u>, economists can <u>determine</u> whether the economy is <u>getting stronger</u> and people's lives are <u>getting better</u> or whether there is a problem and people may need to <u>be helped</u>. The <u>simplest way</u> to do this is to <u>calculate</u> the <u>dollar value</u> of all final goods and services a <u>nation produces within</u> a period of time, <u>usually one year</u>. This is then <u>compared with</u> the <u>previous year</u>, and then economists can see if the economy has <u>improved or gotten worse</u>. The value of the dollar <u>changes over time</u>, and prices <u>tend to rise</u>, so it is important to <u>make adjustments</u> for these factors. The adjusted GDP is called the real GDP. When it is <u>not adjusted</u>, it is called the <u>nominal</u> GDP. One <u>other method</u> for calculating GDP is the <u>final goods approach</u>. In this method, GDP <u>equals consumption plus</u> investment plus government purchases plus <u>exports minus imports</u>. In the end, <u>no matter</u> which method is used, a strong GDP means a strong economy and <u>vice versa</u>.

▶ gross domestic product 국내총생산(=GDP)   release 발표하다; 출시하다   simply put 간단히 말해   nominal 이름뿐인, 명목상의   investment 투자, 투자금   vice versa 역 또한 같음; 거꾸로

남 경제학은 경제가 어떻게 돌아가는지를 측정하는 것과 밀접한 연관이 있습니다. 가장 중요한 측정치 가운데 하나는 국내총생산, 즉 GDP입니다. 국내총생산은 신문과 기업, 정부의 큰 관심사로, 이런 통계 자료는 보통 매년 발표됩니다. 간단히 말하면 GDP는 경제의 총산출량을 측정한 것인데요. 경제학자는 이 수치로 경제가 튼튼해지고 사람들의 생활이 나아지고 있는지, 아니면 문제가 있어서 사람들에게 도움이 필요한지 결정할 수 있습니다. 이를 결정하는 가장 간단한 방법은 보통 1년을 기준으로 하는 일정 기간 내에 국가가 생산한 모든 최종 상품과 서비스의 달러 가치를 계산하는 것입니다. 그런 다음 이것을 전년도와 비교해 보고 경제학자는 경제가 좋아졌는지 나빠졌는지 알 수 있죠. 달러 가치는 시간이 지나면서 변하고 가격은 오르는 경향이 있기 때문에 이 같은 요인들을 조정하는 것이 중요합니다. 그렇게 조정된 GDP를 실질 GDP라고 하며 조정되지 않았을 때는 명목 GDP라고 합니다. GDP를 계산하는 또 한 가지 방법은 최종재 접근 방식인데요. 이 방법에 의하면 GDP는 소비와 투자, 정부 구매, 수출을 더한 것에서 수입을 뺀 것과 같습니다. 결국 어떤 방법을 쓰든 튼튼한 GDP는 튼튼한 경제를 의미하며 그 반대 경우 역시 마찬가지입니다.

---

9 담화에 따르면 GDP에 관한 내용 중 사실이 <u>아닌</u> 것은?

(a) 정부의 큰 관심사이다.

(b) 과거의 GDP 측정치와 비교된다.

(c) 경제 발전 또는 퇴보의 신호이다.

(d) 상품과 서비스의 월간 측정치이다.

(e) 통화 가치의 변화에 따라 조정된다.

W The <u>government</u> <u>reports</u> are in on the 2008 <u>jobless</u> <u>rate</u> in America. I guess we need to do an <u>article</u> <u>on</u> <u>unemployment</u> for next month's magazine.

M You're right. Let's go to the <u>statistics</u> and see how we are doing <u>compared</u> to the past.

W Compared to the <u>Great</u> <u>Depression</u>, I am sure the unemployment rate is <u>much</u> <u>lower</u>.

M Let's have a <u>gander</u>. Ah, yes. In 1930, just as the <u>Great</u> <u>Depression</u> <u>started</u>, the <u>unemployment</u> <u>rate</u> was 8.9 percent, and 4.3 million people in a <u>workforce</u> of 44 million people were <u>out</u> <u>of</u> <u>work</u>.

W Let's just <u>stick</u> <u>with</u> the percentage and <u>make</u> <u>a</u> <u>graph</u> for the article <u>based</u> <u>on</u> <u>that</u>.

M Sounds like a plan. So we have 1930. Then, in 1940, it <u>got</u> <u>worse</u> as 14.9 percent were <u>unemployed</u>.

W That was just before World War II started. I'm sure the <u>1950</u> <u>figures</u> <u>were</u> <u>lower</u>.

M Yes, there was only 5 percent <u>unemployment</u> <u>in</u> <u>1950</u>. Then, in 1960, it was 5.5 percent, and, in 1970, it was even lower at <u>4.9</u> <u>percent</u>.

W Those were some <u>boom</u> <u>decades</u> in America. Now look at 1980. Unemployment <u>climbed</u> <u>to</u> 7.1 percent.

M Yes, but, by 1990, it was down to 5.6 percent, and, in 2000, it was the <u>lowest</u> <u>ever</u> <u>since</u> <u>1930</u> at 4 percent.

W Those were the <u>good</u> <u>old</u> <u>days</u> in 2000. And the <u>latest</u> <u>figures</u> for 2008 show it climbed to 6.1 percent.

M That's the result of the <u>latest</u> <u>economic</u> <u>recession</u>. I'm sure the figures for the <u>first</u> <u>half</u> of 2009 are also going to be high.

▶ in (기사 등이 책·잡지 등에) 실려, 게재되어 have a gander 한번 보다 out of work 실직한 workforce 노동 인구; 전 직원 stick with ~에 충실하다 boom 벼락 경기, 호황 the good old days 좋았던 옛날 recession (일시적) 경기 후퇴, 불경기

여 2008년 미국 실업률에 관한 정부 보고서가 나왔어요. 다음 달 잡지에는 실업률에 관한 기사를 실어야 할 것 같은데요.

남 맞아요. 통계를 보고 과거와 비교해 어떤지 살펴보죠.

여 대공황 때와 비교해보면 실업률이 아주 낮은 건 확실해요.

남 한빈 보자고요. 음, 그렇군요. 대공황이 막 시작되었던 1930년에는 실업률이 8.9%로 4,400만 명의 노동 인구 가운데 430만 명이 실직 상태였네요.

여 실업률에만 초점을 맞춰서 그걸 근거로 기사에 쓸 그래프를 만들어보죠.

남 좋은 계획이에요. 그럼 1930년 건 있고. 그 뒤 1940년에는 14.9%가 실직해서 상황이 더 나빠졌어요.

여 그때는 제2차 세계 대전 직전이었으니까. 1950년의 수치는 틀림없이 더 낮았겠죠.

남 맞아요. 1950년에는 실업률이 겨우 5%에 불과했네요. 그러다 1960년에는 5.5%, 1970년에는 4.9%까지 낮아졌어요.

여 그때는 미국의 호황기였죠. 이제 1980년을 봐요. 실업률이 7.1%까지 올라갔어요.

남 그렇네요. 하지만 1990년에는 5.6%로 내려갔고 2000년에는 1930년 이래 가장 낮은 4%였어요.

여 2000년은 좋은 시절이었죠. 그리고 2008년의 최근 수치를 보면 6.1%로 증가했어요.

남 그건 최근의 불경기 때문이에요. 난 2009년 상반기에도 역시 수치가 높을 거라고 봐요.

---

10 1930년에서 2008년까지의 미국 실업률 그래프를 완성하시오.

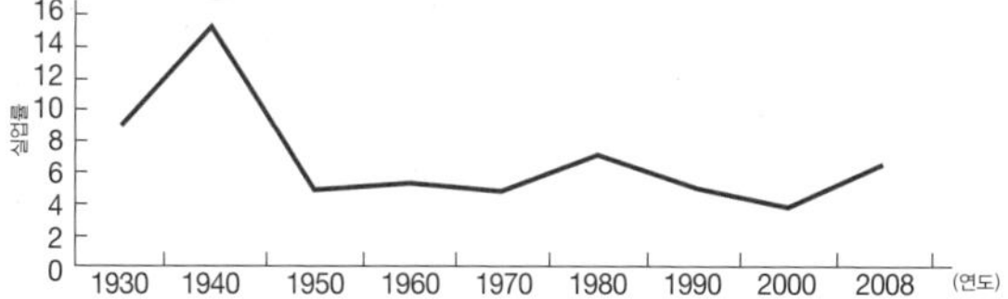

11-12 **Level up**

W Today, we are <u>going</u> <u>to</u> <u>discuss</u> the <u>money</u> <u>supply</u>. Quite simply, the money supply <u>refers</u> <u>to</u> the <u>amount</u> <u>of</u> <u>money</u> <u>available</u> in the economy at any point in time. It is <u>important</u> <u>to</u> <u>understand</u> the money supply because it can have a <u>wide</u> <u>number</u> <u>of</u> <u>effects</u> on an economy. <u>Most</u> <u>importantly</u>, it can <u>determine</u> <u>the</u> <u>prices</u> people pay for goods and services and the <u>interest</u> <u>rates</u> which banks <u>charge</u> <u>for</u> <u>loans</u>. The money supply is <u>regulated</u> <u>by</u> <u>governments</u>, usually through their central bank or other <u>institutions</u> like the Federal Reserve in the United States. The money supply <u>can</u> <u>be</u> <u>calculated</u> in three different ways. The <u>first</u> <u>definition</u> of the money supply is called M1. This is the <u>narrowest</u> of definitions and <u>includes</u> <u>all</u> <u>currency</u>, which is paper money and coins, plus <u>checkable</u> <u>deposits</u> and <u>traveler's</u> <u>checks</u>. Checkable deposits are money held in <u>bank</u> <u>accounts</u> which are easy for people to <u>access</u> by <u>writing</u> <u>checks</u>. The second definition of the money supply is M2. This includes all of the money in M1 plus money in savings accounts and time deposits of less than 100,000 dollars. <u>Time</u> <u>deposits</u> are savings which <u>cannot</u> <u>be</u> <u>accessed</u> for a certain period of time. The <u>final</u> <u>type</u> is called M3, which includes M1 and M2 plus time deposits <u>over</u> <u>100,000</u> dollars. When there is a <u>decrease</u> in the money supply, it means that there is <u>less</u> <u>money</u> <u>available</u> for <u>loans</u> and <u>investments</u>. In this case, banks can charge <u>higher</u> <u>interest</u> <u>rates</u>. When there is an <u>increase</u> in the money supply, it means that there is more money available, so banks <u>will</u> <u>lower</u> their interest rates to <u>encourage</u> <u>loans</u>.

▶ loan 융자금, 대여금 M1 협의통화 currency 통화 checkable deposit 요구불 예금 traveler's check 여행자 수표 write a check 수표를 끊다 M2 총통화 savings account 보통 예금 (계좌) time deposit 정기 예금 M3 총유동성

여 오늘은 통화 공급량에 관해 이야기해 보겠습니다. 간단히 말해, 통화 공급량이란 경제에서 언제라도 쓸 수 있는 돈의 총액을 가리킵니다. 통화 공급량은 경제에 폭넓게 많은 영향을 미칠 수 있기 때문에 이를 이해하는 것은 중요합니다. 가장 중요한 것은, 통화 공급량은 사람들이 상품 및 서비스에 지불하는 가격과 은행이 대출에 부과하는 이율을 결정할 수 있다는 것입니다. 통화 공급량은 정부에 의해 규제되는데, 보통 중앙은행이나 미국의 연방 준비 은행 같은 기타 기관을 통해 이루어집니다. 통화 공급량은 세 가지 방식으로 계산될 수 있습니다. 통화 공급량의 첫 번째 정의는 M1이라고 합니다. M1은 가장 좁은 의미의 정의로 지폐, 동전에 요구불 예금과 여행자 수표까지 모든 통화를 포함합니다. 요구불 예금이란 수표를 끊어서 쉽게 이용할 수 있는 은행 계좌에 있는 돈을 말합니다. 통화 공급량의 두 번째 정의는 M2입니다. M2는 M1의 모든 돈에 보통 예금과 10만 달러 이하의 정기 예금에 있는 돈을 더한 것입니다. 정기 예금은 일정 기간 동안 이용할 수 없는 예금입니다. 마지막 형태는 M3라고 하는데, M1과 M2에 10만 달러 이상의 정기 예금을 더한 것입니다. 통화 공급량이 감소한다는 것은 대출과 투자에 쓸 수 있는 돈이 줄었다는 것을 의미합니다. 이 경우 은행은 더 높은 이율을 적용할 수 있습니다. 통화 공급량이 증가했다는 것은 쓸 수 있는 돈이 많다는 것을 의미하므로 은행은 이율을 낮춰 대출을 장려할 것입니다.

11 강의의 주목적은 무엇인가?

(a) 통화 공급량이 증가하면 어떤 일이 일어나는지 설명하려고

(b) 은행이 정기 예금의 돈을 어떻게 계산하는지 설명하려고

(c) 통화를 규제하는 데 있어 정부의 역할을 논의하려고

(d) 통화 공급량이 증가하거나 감소하는 방법을 살펴보려고

(e) 정부가 어떻게 국가의 통화 공급량을 계산하는지 알아보려고

12 한 나라의 M3 통화 공급량이 증가하면 어떤 결과가 일어나겠는가?

(a) 은행은 대출 이율을 올릴 것이다.

(b) 예금자들은 돈을 더 많이 쓸 것이다.

(c) 사람들은 돈을 더 빌리려고 할 것이다.

(d) 정기 예금의 인기가 줄어들 것이다.

(e) 사람들은 돈을 집에 보관할 것이다.

Practice Test
p. 44~p. 45

1 (b) 2 (e) 3 (b) 4 (c) 5 (d) 6 (d) 7 (b)
8 해설 참조 9 (a), (e) 10 (c)

1

W Almost every country in the world has some form of a central bank. A central bank is a government's bank. The structures of central banks are different from country to country, but they all have very similar functions and purposes. The main purpose of any central bank is to be responsible for a country's monetary policy. It also oversees and monitors the banking system and acts as a bank for banks. The central bank's main duties are to keep a country's national currency strong and stable and to maintain control of the country's money supply. Some other functions a central bank may have are to regulate interest rates, to lend money to banks in times of financial crisis, and to print paper money and to mint coins. When governments in different countries do business with each other, it is usually conducted through their central banks. The central bank also holds a country's national reserve of gold and foreign currencies and manages a country's foreign exchange rates. Central banks also issue and sell government bonds. Central banks can be either public or private institutions, or, like the Federal Reserve of the United States, it can be semi-public. Central banks in most developed countries act independently from the government so as to avoid any political interference.

▶ mint (화폐를) 주조하다 conduct (업무 등을) 수행하다 reserve 준비금, 예비금 government bond 국채 semi-public 반공공(半公共)의, 반관반민(半官半民)의 interference 간섭, 방해

여 세계의 거의 모든 국가에는 어떤 형태의 중앙은행이 있습니다. 중앙은행은 정부 은행인데요. 중앙은행의 구조는 국가마다 다르지만 기능과 목적은 모두 아주 비슷합니다. 어떤 중앙은행이든 주목적은 국가의 통화 정책을 책임지는 것이죠. 중앙은행은 또한 은행 체계를 감독하고 관리하며 은행들의 은행 역할을 합니다. 중앙은행의 주업무는 국내 통화를 건실하고 안정적으로 유지하며 국가의 통화 공급량을 지속적으로 관리하는 것입니다. 중앙은행이 가질 수 있는 또 다른 기능은 이율을 규제하고, 재정 위기가 발생하면 은행에 돈을 빌려주며, 지폐와 주화를 찍어내는 것이죠. 서로 다른 국가의 정부들이 함께 거래를 할 때는 보통 자신들

의 중앙은행을 통해 업무를 처리합니다. 중앙은행은 또한 국가의 금과 외환 보유고를 맡고 환율을 관리합니다. 중앙은행은 국채를 발행하고 판매하기도 하죠. 중앙은행은 공공 기관이나 민간 기관일 수 있으며, 또는 미국의 연방 준비 은행처럼 반관반민의 형태일 수도 있습니다. 대부분의 선진국에서 중앙은행은 어떠한 정치적 간섭도 배제하기 위해 정부와는 독립적으로 운영됩니다.

1 한 국가의 중앙은행의 주목적은 무엇인가?

(a) 국가의 금 보유고를 유지하는 것

(b) 국내 통화를 안정시키는 것

(c) 국채를 발행하고 판매하는 것

(d) 어려움에 빠진 은행에 돈을 빌려주는 것

(e) 다른 국가들과 거래하는 것

2-3

W The interest rate on my car loan was really low. It's going to take me no time at all to pay off my loan. You work at a bank. Why is my interest rate so low?

M It has to do with the current economic crisis. A lot of people are not spending or borrowing money, which is hurting businesses and banks.

W So, people borrow more money in good economic times, and the interest rates are higher, right?

M Yes. A lot of people have no confidence in the future now, so they are saving their money and are putting off buying a new car or house. To encourage more borrowing, the banks lower the interest rate. What was your car loan rate?

W It was only four percent over five years. How do they set that rate anyway?

M Banks use many factors to determine their interest rates. The prime rate is usually set by the central bank from which other banks can borrow money. Banks also consider the risk involved in lending the money. Banks can't always be sure they will get all of their money back, which is the risk they take. So, a higher risk will mean a higher interest rate.

W That's how this whole crisis happened in the first place. Banks gave money to people who couldn't pay it back.

M True enough. But now they are worried that no one will borrow from them. Hence, the low interest rates. It's also a great time to borrow money to buy a house.

W ________________________

▶ no time 매우 짧은 시간, 곧 pay off (빚 등을) 모두 갚다 have to do with ~와 관계가 있다 put off 연기하다, 미루다 prime rate (우량 고객에 대한) 최저 대출 금리 in the first place 애당초, 처음부터; 첫째로 hence 따라서, 그러므로

여 내 자동차 대출금 이율은 굉장히 낮았어. 대출금을 금방 다 갚을 것 같다니까. 넌 은행에서 일하잖아. 내 이율이 왜 그렇게 낮은 거니?

남 그건 현재의 경제 위기와 관련 있어. 많은 사람들이 돈을 쓰지 않거나 빌려가지 않아서 기업과 은행이 손해를 보고 있거든.

여 그러니까 경기가 좋을 때는 사람들이 돈을 더 빌려가서 이율도 더 높은 거구나, 그렇지?

남 응. 지금은 많은 사람들이 미래에 대한 확신이 없기 때문에 돈을 저금하면서 새 차나 집을 사는 걸 미루고 있어. 대출을 늘리기 위해 은행은 이율을 더 낮추는 거지. 네 자동차 대출금 이율은 얼마였니?

여 5년에 겨우 4%였어. 그건 그렇고 은행은 어떻게 이율을 정하는 거니?

남 은행은 많은 요소를 이용해서 이율을 결정해. 최저 대출 이율은 보통 은행들이 돈을 빌릴 수 있는 중앙은행에 의해 결정되지. 은행은 돈을 빌려줄 때 있을 수 있

는 위험도도 고려해. 은행이 언제나 자기들 돈을 모두 돌려받을 거라고는 장담할
수 없거든. 그게 바로 은행이 떠안는 위험도라는 거지. 그래서 위험도가 높을수
록 이율도 더 높아지지.

여 애초에 이 위기가 모두 그렇게 해서 일어난 거구나. 갚을 능력이 없는 사람들에
게 은행이 돈을 빌려줬던 거네.

남 맞는 말이야. 하지만 지금은 아무도 은행에서 돈을 안 빌리려고 해서 걱정하고
있지. 그래서 이율이 낮은 거고. 집을 살 돈을 빌리기는 지금이 적기이기도 해.

여 ______________________________________

2 경제가 다시 좋아진다면 어떤 일이 일어나겠는가?

　(a) 돈을 빌리는 사람들이 더 적어질 것이다.

　(b) 사람들은 미래를 위해 더 많은 돈을 저축할 것이다.

　(c) 자동차 대출금 이율이 내릴 것이다.

　(d) 은행은 더 좋은 조건으로 주택 대출금을 제공할 것이다.

　(e) 이율이 다시 올라갈 가능성이 높다.

3 여자는 다음에 뭐라고 말하겠는가?

　(a) 난 경제가 좋아질 때까지 기다릴까봐.

　(b) 난 지금은 갚아야 할 대출 하나로 충분해.

　(c) 지금은 집을 사기 위해 모아놓은 현금이 충분치 않아.

　(d) 그럴 수도 있지. 난 갚지 못한 대출이 하나도 없으니까.

　(e) 난 신용이 낮아서 아무도 돈을 빌려주지 않을 거야.

4-5

M Competition is at the heart of economics. Economists believe that through competition, limited amounts of resources and workers end up where they are most highly valued. Competition takes place in what are called markets. Markets are where buyers and sellers meet to exchange goods and services. Usually, there are a few sellers and many more buyers. The sellers compete with each other to get the customers, and the consumers try to find the best deals possible to get the most for their money. Because of competition, sellers have to create more products in more varieties to get a customer's business. This is good for customers because they have more choices. Most experts identify three types of competition in economics. There is direct competition. This is the competition among almost the same products which satisfy the same need or want, such as the many types of chocolate bars that are on the market. Another form of competition is called substitute, or indirect, competition. This is when two products are different but could be considered substitutes for each other. This includes coffee and tea or butter and margarine. The final type of competition is called budget competition. This is a very broad form of competition and considers the buyer's budget or how much money a consumer has and is willing to spend. For example, if a consumer has ten dollars, that person could spend it on a movie, buy dinner, or get some flowers for his or her mother. How he or she spends the money is an individual choice, but the person may be influenced by the marketing tactics of sellers.

▶ **at the heart of** ~의 핵심에 있는, 밑바탕에 있는　**end up** 마침내 ~으로 되다
value (금전으로) 평가하다, 값을 매기다　**take place** 일어나다

남 경제학의 핵심에는 경쟁이 있습니다. 경제학자들은 한정된 자원과 노동자들이

경쟁을 통해 가장 높은 값을 받게 된다고 생각하죠. 경쟁은 시장이라고 불리는
곳에서 일어나는데요. 시장은 구매자와 판매자가 상품과 서비스를 교환하기 위
해 만나는 곳입니다. 대개는 소수의 판매자와 훨씬 더 많은 다수의 구매자가 존
재합니다. 판매자는 소비자를 잡기 위해 서로 경쟁하며 소비자는 자신이 갖고 있
는 돈으로 가장 큰 이득을 얻을 수 있는 최선의 거래를 하기 위해 노력합니다. 경
쟁 때문에 판매자는 소비자와 거래하기 위해 좀 더 다양한 제품을 더 많이 만들
어야 합니다. 선택의 폭이 넓어지므로 이것은 소비자에게 유리하죠. 대부분의 전
문가들은 경제학에는 세 가지 유형의 경쟁이 있다고 합니다. 직접 경쟁이 있는데,
이것은 시장에 있는 많은 종류의 초콜릿 바처럼 똑같은 필요나 욕구를 충족시키
는 거의 동일한 제품 간에 일어나는 경쟁입니다. 또 다른 형태의 경쟁은 간접 경
쟁인데 대체 경쟁이라고도 하죠. 대체 경쟁은 두 상품이 다르지만 서로 대체될
수 있다고 생각될 때 일어납니다. 여기에는 커피와 차 또는 버터와 마가린이 포
함됩니다. 마지막 유형의 경쟁은 예산 경쟁이라고 합니다. 예산 경쟁은 가장 폭
넓은 형태의 경쟁으로, 구매자의 예산 또는 소비자가 얼마나 갖고 있고 얼마를
쓸 의사가 있는지를 고려합니다. 예를 들어 어떤 소비자가 10달러를 갖고 있다
면 그 사람은 그 돈으로 영화를 볼 수도 있고 저녁을 사 먹거나 어머니를 위해 꽃
을 살 수도 있죠. 그 사람이 그 돈을 어떻게 쓸 것인지는 개인적인 선택이지만 판
매자의 마케팅 전술에 영향을 받을 수도 있습니다.

4 강의의 목적은 무엇인가?

　(a) 경쟁이 왜 일어나는지 설명하려고

　(b) 경쟁의 중요성을 논의하려고

　(c) 경쟁이 어떻게 이루어지는지 설명하려고

　(d) 유리한 거래를 하는 방법을 알려주려고

　(e) 시장에 대한 개념을 설명하려고

5 다음 중 강의에서 언급된 세 가지 형태의 경쟁에 관해 맞는 것은 무엇인
가?

　(a) 대체 경쟁은 한정된 액수의 돈을 갖고 있는 소비자와 관련이 있다.

　(b) 직접 경쟁은 하나의 제품을 다른 것으로 대체하는 것과 관계 있다.

　(c) 예산 경쟁은 비슷한 욕구를 충족시키는 비슷한 제품들과 관련 있다.

　(d) 직접 경쟁은 같은 종류의 제품과 관계 있다.

　(e) 대체 경쟁에는 많은 광고전이 필요하다.

6　**Level up**

M Professor, I heard some people on the news talking about the business cycle. What is that?

W The term business cycle is usually used to describe how the economy goes through periods of growth and expansion followed by periods of decline.

M A decline is a recession, right?

W Yes. During a recession, many people lose their jobs, and production goes way down in factories and industries. If a recession lasts a long time, it's called a depression.

M And a boom is when everybody has a job and there is an increase in production.

W Yes. Also, during a boom period, we may have an increase in prices because of inflation. In such a case, we say the economy is overheating.

M What causes this cycle to happen, and how often does it happen?

W Actually, it's not really known why or how business cycles occur. Many economists disagree as to the causes. Business cycles are very hard to predict, and they could last a few months, one or two years, or even several years. It's not actually a cycle at all but more of an economic fluctuation.

▶ **business cycle** 경기 순환 **go through** 통과하다, 겪다 **recession** 경기 후퇴, (일시적인) 불경기 **depression** 불황 **as to** ~에 관해 **fluctuation** 변동

남 교수님, 뉴스에서 사람들이 경기 순환에 대해 이야기하는 걸 들었는데요. 그게 뭔가요?

여 경기 순환이라는 말은 보통 경제가 어떻게 성장과 팽창기를 겪고, 쇠퇴기가 이어지는지 설명하는 데 쓰이죠.

남 쇠퇴라는 건 불경기를 말하는 거죠, 맞나요?

여 네. 불경기에는 많은 사람들이 직장을 잃고 공장과 기업의 생산이 하향세로 들어서죠. 불경기가 오래 계속되면 불황이라고 합니다.

남 그럼 호황은 모든 사람들이 일자리가 있고 생산이 증가할 때군요.

여 그래요. 또한 호황기에는 인플레이션 때문에 가격이 오를 수도 있습니다. 그런 경우에는 경제가 과열되었다고 하죠.

남 이런 순환을 일으키는 요인은 무엇인가요? 그리고 얼마나 자주 일어나죠?

여 사실 경기 순환이 왜, 어떤 식으로 일어나는지는 잘 알려져 있지 않아요. 그 원인에 관해서는 많은 경제학자들의 의견이 다르죠. 경기 순환은 예측하기가 매우 힘들며 몇 달 동안 지속되기도 하고 일이 년, 심지어는 몇 년 동안 지속될 수도 있습니다. 실제로는 순환이 아니라 경기 변동에 가까운 거죠.

6 Which statement about a recession and a depression is true according to the dialog?

대화에 따르면 다음 중 불경기와 불황에 관한 내용 중 사실인 것은?

(a) A recession occurs after a depression begins.
불경기는 불황이 시작된 뒤 일어난다.

(b) They are both almost exactly the same thing.
그 둘은 거의 똑같은 것이다.

(c) Recessions are economic booms, but depressions are not.
불경기는 호황이지만 불황은 그렇지 않다.

(d) A depression is a long-lasting recession.
불황이란 장기간에 걸친 불경기이다.

(e) A depression signals an upswing in an economy.
불황은 경기 회복의 신호이다.

---

7 Level up

W Let's talk about John Maynard Keynes today. He is one of the most famous and influential economists ever. He was born in 1883 in Britain. He had a strong and lasting influence on economic thought throughout the 20th century. He is best known for his work in laying the basis for the study of macroeconomics and for his books, which called for a large degree of government intervention in the economy. This was in direct opposition with classical theory, which stated that the economy would grow and reach its greatest potential if it were left alone to take care of itself. In the years of the Great Depression of the 1930s and following World War II, many Keynesian theories were put to use by the United States, Britain, and other governments. The prosperity of the 1950s and 1960s is believed to have been a result of these policies. The oil crisis of 1973, which was followed by a recession, changed many people's opinions, however, and Keynes's ideas fell out of favor and were replaced by those of Milton Friedman and the classical economists.

▶ **macroeconomics** 거시 경제학 **call for** 요구하다 **intervention** 개입, 간섭 **direct opposition** 정반대 **take care of itself** 자연히 해결되다 **fall out of favor** 인기를 잃다

여 오늘은 존 메이나드 케인스에 대해 이야기해봅시다. 그는 역사상 가장 유명하고 영향력 있는 경제학자 중 한 사람입니다. 1883년 영국에서 태어났죠. 케인스

는 20세기 내내 경제학 사상에 강력하고 지속적인 영향을 미쳤습니다. 그는 거시 경제학 연구의 토대를 마련한 업적으로 가장 잘 알려져 있으며 정부의 광범위한 경제 개입을 촉구하는 저서들로도 유명합니다. 이는 경제는 자연히 해결되도록 내버려두면 성장하면서 최대의 잠재력에 도달할 것이라는 전통적인 이론과는 정반대였습니다. 1930년대의 대공황과 뒤이은 제 2차 세계대전 동안 많은 케인스 학파 이론이 미국과 영국 그리고 다른 정부들에 의해 사용되었습니다. 1950년대와 1960년대의 번영은 이러한 정책들이 낳은 결과였다고 여겨지고 있지요. 그러나 경기 침체 뒤에 이어진 1973년의 석유 파동은 많은 사람들의 견해를 바꾸어 놓았고, 케인스의 사상은 인기를 잃고 밀턴 프리드먼과 고전 경제학자들의 사상으로 대체되었습니다.

7 What is the main topic of the talk?
담화의 주제는 무엇인가?

(a) The end of the influence of Keynes's economic theories
케인스의 경제학 이론의 영향력이 없어진 것

(b) The overall influence of the economic theories of Keynes
케인스의 경제학 이론이 미친 전반적인 영향

(c) The use of Keynes's school of economic thought in practice
실제로 이용된 케인스 학파의 경제학 사상

(d) The contrast between Keynesian theories and classical theories 케인즈 학파의 이론과 전통적인 이론의 대조점

(e) The use of Keynes's economic theories in various countries
여러 국가에서 이용된 케인스의 경제학 이론

8

M For the longest time, there was little equality between men and women in the workplace. In the last half of the 20th century, this situation began to change as women took many jobs that were traditionally men's jobs. However, there are still some differences in the numbers of working men and women in different occupations. Let's examine five key sectors of employment in the United States from 2006: management and professional jobs; the service industry; sales and office work; natural resources, construction, and maintenance; and finally, factory production and transportation. In the first category, management and professional work, the numbers are pretty equal at 24.9 million men and 25.5 million women. Next, in the service industry, there is a wider gap with 10.2 million men and 13.6 million women employed. In sales and office work, there is an even greater gap, with 22.8 million women employed compared to 13.3 million men. The opposite occurs in the last two categories as there were more men than women employed. In the natural resources, construction, and maintenance industries, there were 15 million men and only 700,000 women. Finally, in the factory production and transportation industries, there were 14 million men compared to 4.1 million women. What accounts for this difference? One key point is that fewer men than women go to university, which means that many men don't qualify for professional and management jobs. Another key point is that in the last two categories, a lot of physical labor is involved. These are jobs which women traditionally do not gravitate towards.

▶ **occupation** 직업 **sector** 부문, 분야 **natural resources** 천연자원 **maintenance** 정비 **account for** 원인이 되다, 설명하다 **gravitate** 끌리다

남　아주 오랫동안 일터에서는 남녀평등이 거의 이루어지지 않았습니다. 20세기 후반에 전통적으로 남성의 직업이었던 많은 일들을 여성이 하게 되면서 이런 상황은 변하기 시작했죠. 그러나 많은 직업에서는 아직도 일하는 남성과 여성의 수에 약간 차이가 있습니다. 2006년부터 미국의 5개 주요 고용 분야를 살펴보면 경영 및 전문직, 서비스업종, 영업 및 사무직, 1차 산업과 건설 및 정비, 그리고 마지막으로 공장 생산 및 운송 등이 있습니다. 첫 번째 분야인 경영 및 전문직에서는 남성 2천 4백 9십만 명, 여성 2천 5백 5십만 명으로 그 수가 꽤 비슷합니다. 그 다음 서비스업종에는 남성 1천 2십만 명, 여성 1천 3백 6십만 명이 종사하고 있어 격차가 좀 더 넓습니다. 영업 및 사무직에는 남성이 1천 3백 3십만 명인 데 비해 여성은 2천 2백 8십만 명이 종사하고 있어 격차가 더 크게 벌어지죠. 마지막 두 분야에서는 여성보다 남성이 더 많이 종사하고 있는 반대 현상이 일어나는데요. 1차 산업과 건설 및 정비업에는 남성은 1천 5백만 명, 여성은 7십만 명만이 종사합니다. 끝으로 공장 생산과 운송에는 남성은 1천 4백만 명이 종사하는 데 비해 여성은 4백 십만 명입니다. 이 같은 차이가 나는 원인은 무엇일까요? 한 가지 중요한 점은 여성보다 남성이 대학에 더 적게 진학한다는 것입니다. 그것은 많은 남성들이 전문직과 관리직에 요구되는 자격을 갖추지 못하고 있다는 것을 뜻하죠. 또 다른 중요한 점은 마지막 두 분야에는 많은 육체 노동이 필요하다는 점입니다. 이는 여성이 전통적으로 좋아하지 않는 직업들이죠.

8 언급된 5가지 직업 분야에 종사하는 남성과 여성의 수를 비교하는 막대 그래프를 완성하시오.

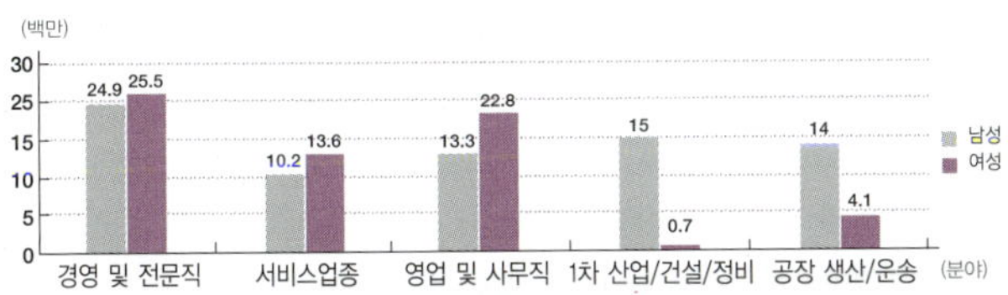

9-10　**Integrated Questions**

Reading

▶ keen 민감한　share 지분, 몫　regulator 단속자, 조정자　manipulate 조작하다

모든 국가의 경제에 매우 중요한 측면이자 경제학자들의 첨예한 관심사 가운데 하나는 바로 자본 시장이다. 자본이란 물론 돈의 다른 이름이다. 이 경우에는 기존의 기업에 투자하거나 새로 기업을 시작하는 데 사용되는 돈을 말한다. 자본 시장 내에는 주식시장과 채권시장이 있다. 기업과 정부는 주식과 채권을 팔아 사업을 확장하거나 도로, 다리, 고속도로 건설 같은 공공사업을 추진하는 데 필요한 돈을 마련할 수 있다. 주식은 한 기업에 대한 지분으로, 구매자에게 기업의 소유권을 부분적으로 나눠주는 것이다. 채권은 전혀 다른데, 누군가 채권을 산다는 것은 기업이나 정부에게 돈을 빌려주는 것과 같다. 정부나 기업은 그 돈에 5년 또는 10년처럼 확정된 시점에 이자를 덧붙여 그 사람에게 돈을 갚는다는 데 동의한다. 자본 시장에는 또한 누구도 불법적으로 시장을 기만하거나 조작하지 못하도록 하는 일종의 조정자도 있다. 대부분의 국가에는 투자자와 기업이 함께 모여 주식과 채권을 사고 팔고 거래할 수 있는 자본 시장이 있다. 가장 유명한 자본 시장은 뉴욕 증권 거래소이다.

W　Investing money is one of the most difficult things a person can do. There are many choices available, and all of them have benefits and risks. The typical rule of thumb is that for low risks, there are low returns, and for high risks, there are high returns. There are four main ways a person can make his or her money grow. First, a bank deposit with a low interest rate—usually 2 or 3 percent—is attractive because it is secure. In most developed nations, the government guarantees bank deposits up to a certain amount, so the depositors cannot lose all of their money. The second method is to buy bonds from banks or governments. These have slightly higher interest rates—about 3 or 4 percent and usually over a longer term, such as five or ten years. They are also guaranteed by governments. Next

are mutual funds, which offer higher interest rates—usually between 5 and 12 percent. Mutual funds are pools of money people invest in. A fund manager takes this money and invests in a portfolio of many different stocks. Each individual investor does not make the decisions regarding the investment; the fund manger does. In some nations, such as Canada, mutual funds are guaranteed by the government up to 75 percent of the original investment. Finally, there is the stock market, which anyone can invest in. A stock's value may climb a great deal, and a great profit can be made, or the investor can lose all of his or her money. There are no guarantees.

▶ rule of thumb 경험칙(경험상 대개는 틀림없는 법칙), 경험에 바탕을 둔 방법
returns 수익　pool 공동 출자, 공동 기금　portfolio 포트폴리오, 투자 자산

여　돈을 투자하는 것은 사람이 할 수 있는 가장 어려운 일 가운데 하나입니다. 많은 선택이 가능하며 그 모두가 수익성과 위험도를 안고 있죠. 일반적인 경험칙은 위험도가 낮으면 수익도 낮고 위험도가 높으면 수익도 높다는 것입니다. 개인이 돈을 불릴 수 있는 방법에는 크게 네 가지가 있는데요. 첫째로 은행 예금은 보통 2, 3%로 이율은 낮지만 안전하기 때문에 매력이 있습니다. 대부분의 선진국에서는 정부가 일정 금액까지 은행 예금을 보장해주므로 예금자가 돈을 모두 잃을 염려는 없죠. 두 번째 방법은 은행이나 정부의 채권을 사는 것입니다. 채권은 보통 5년이나 10년처럼 장기간에 걸쳐 이율이 3, 4% 정도로, 은행 예금보다 약간 더 높습니다. 채권 역시 정부에 의해 보장됩니다. 다음으로 뮤추얼 펀드가 있는데 보통 5에서 12% 사이의 좀 더 높은 이율을 제공하죠. 뮤추얼 펀드는 사람들이 투자하는 공동 기금입니다. 펀드매니저는 이 돈을 다양한 주식으로 구성된 포트폴리오에 투자합니다. 각각의 개인 투자자가 투자에 대한 결정을 내리지 않고 펀드매니저가 합니다. 캐나다 같은 일부 국가에서는 정부가 뮤추얼 펀드의 원금을 75%까지 보장해주죠. 마지막으로는 누구나 투자할 수 있는 주식시장이 있습니다. 주가가 크게 올라 상당한 수익을 낼 수도 있지만 가진 돈을 모두 잃을 수도 있죠. 주식에는 어떤 보장도 없습니다.

9 읽기와 듣기 지문에서 제시된 정보에 따르면 주식과 채권의 주된 차이점은 무엇인가? 해당하는 정답을 모두 고르시오.
(a) 주식은 높은 위험도에 높은 수익을 제공하는 반면 채권은 위험도는 낮지만 낮은 투자 수익률을 제공한다.
(b) 채권을 사는 것은 투자금이 완벽하게 안전하다는 것을 보장하는 방법인 반면 주식은 안전이 보장되지 않는다.
(c) 주식 투자는 안전한 금융 시장 거래소를 통해서만 가능한 반면 채권은 어디서나 투자할 수 있다.
(d) 채권은 투자자에게 직접적으로 금융 시장과 거래하는 방법을 제공하지만 주식은 펀드매니저 같은 다른 사람에 의해 처리된다.
(e) 주식에 투자하면 기업에 대한 부분적인 소유권을 주지만 채권에 투자하는 것은 단지 기업에게 돈을 빌려주는 것과 같다.

10 제시된 정보에 따르면 캐나다의 뮤추얼 펀드 투자자는 8천 달러를 투자해서 실패하면 얼마를 돌려받겠는가?
(a) $8,000
(b) $7,500
(c) $6,000
(d) $3,500
(e) $0

***Dictation 정답**: Exercise 스크립트 밑줄 참조

Vocabulary Preview

A

1 foliage: 나뭇잎
2 buoyancy: 액체 위에 뜨는 능력
3 metabolic: 생물이 음식을 태워 에너지로 전환하는 것과 관련된
4 vertebrate: 골조직과 척추가 있는 생물
5 nocturnal: 야행성의

B

1 Coniferous / 침엽수는 바늘 같은 잎과 원뿔 모양의 큰 씨앗으로 알아볼 수 있다.

2 Diurnal / 주행성 동물은 낮에 활동하고 밤에 쉰다.

3 predators / 대부분의 포식 동물은 노리는 먹잇감에 집중할 수 있도록 눈이 앞을 향하고 있다.

4 creep up on / 포식 동물들은 먹이 쪽으로 몰래 다가가서 먹잇감을 깜짝 놀라게 하곤 한다.

5 slimy / 지렁이들은 흙을 소화하고 나서 흙이 서로 엉기게 하는 점액성의 물질을 분비한다.

6 feline / 고양잇과 동물은 집고양이와 들고양이 둘 다 포함한다.

7 pesky / 벌이 쏠 수 있을 정도로 가깝게 접근하면 심하게 성가실 수 있다.

Expressions and Meanings

1 난 원예에 재능이 있어.
2 그건 우리 집안 내력이야.
3 이 업계에서는 늘상 있는 일이야.
4 날 들볶을 필요는 없잖아.
5 나중에 후회하기보다는 안전한 게 나아.
6 마음에 드는 것 있어?
7 적은 양도 큰 도움이 돼.

d 난 원예에 대해 많이 알아.
a 우리 가족에게는 공통적인 거야.
f 이 활동을 하다 보면 흔하게 일어나는 일이야.
b 그 일로 날 그만 괴롭혀.
g 최악의 상황에 대비해야 해.
c 네 마음에 드는 게 있니?
e 많이는 필요하지 않아.

Monolog

O (1) antennae (2) smell (3) touch (4) sucking (5) middle (6) three (7) wings (8) rear (9) reproductive (10) digestion (11) stinger

G 1 (b) 2 (a)

S (1) F (2) T (3) F (4) T

W Insects have three body segments: the head, the thorax, and the abdomen. Each part has a function which is common in most insects, but there are some variations. The head contains the antennae, which come in various shapes and sizes, the eyes, the mouth, and, of course, the brain. The antennae are sensory organs, and some insects use them for smell while the majority uses them for touch. The mouths of insects are either constructed for chewing, like in a grasshopper, or are constructed for sucking, like in a mosquito. The thorax is the middle section of the insect's body and consists of three segments. Each segment has a pair of legs, giving it six in total. The thorax is also where an insect's wings are located. That is, if it has wings because not all insects do. There are either one or two pairs of wings. The rear portion of an insect's body is the abdomen. This is where its reproductive organs are. The final stages of digestion also take place here. On some insects, like bees, there is also a stinger. The digestive tract of insects is a long alimentary tube going from the mouth through the thorax and then through the abdomen.

▶ segment 체절, 환절; 부분, 조각   thorax 흉부, 흉곽, 흉강   abdomen 복부, 배   variation 변화, 변동   antennae 촉각, 더듬이, antenna의 복수형   sensory organ 감각 기관   that is 즉, 다르게 말하면   rear portion 뒷부분, 맨 뒷부분   reproductive organs 생식기   digestion (음식의) 소화   stinger 침   digestive tract 소화관   alimentary tube 소화관

여 곤충의 몸은 머리, 흉부, 복부 세 부분으로 나뉩니다. 각 부위의 기능은 대부분의 곤충에게 공통적이지만 몇 가지 차이도 있습니다. 머리에는 여러 가지 모양 및 크기의 더듬이, 눈, 주둥이, 그리고 물론 뇌도 있습니다. 더듬이는 감각 기관으로, 일부 곤충은 냄새를 맡기 위해 사용하는 한편, 대부분의 곤충은 접촉을 위해 씁니다. 곤충의 입은 메뚜기처럼 씹기 위한 구조이거나 모기처럼 빨기 위한 구조입니다. 흉부는 곤충 몸의 중간 부위로 세 부분으로 구성되어 있습니다. 각 부분에 다리가 한 쌍씩 있으니 모두 6개의 다리가 있는 것입니다. 흉부는 또한 곤충의 날개가 있는 곳이죠. 모든 곤충이 날개가 있는 것은 아니니, 날개가 있는 곤충이라면 그렇다는 말이죠. 날개는 한 쌍 또는 두 쌍이 있습니다. 곤충 몸의 맨 아랫부분은 복부입니다. 복부는 생식기가 있는 곳입니다. 소화의 마지막 단계 또한 이곳에서 이루어집니다. 벌과 같은 몇몇 곤충은 이곳에 침도 있죠. 곤충의 소화관은 입에서 흉부를 지나 복부로 통하는 긴 소화기관이랍니다.

General Questions

1 담화의 목적은 무엇인가?
  (a) 곤충의 복부 기능을 논하려고
  (b) 곤충의 몸을 구성하는 부분을 설명하려고
  (c) 곤충의 주둥이의 다양한 유형을 묘사하려고
  (d) 곤충의 신체 기능을 조사하려고

2 다음 중 가장 잘 요약된 것을 고르시오.
  (a) 곤충의 몸은 뚜렷하게 세 부분으로 나뉘며 거기에는 더듬이, 날개, 다리, 소화기와 같은 여러 신체 부위가 있다.
  (b) 곤충은 세 부분으로 이루어진 몸, 6개의 다리, 2쌍의 날개가 있어 다른 작은 생물과 구별된다.

Specific Questions

다시 듣고 옳은 문장에는 T, 틀린 문장에는 F를 쓰시오.
(1) 곤충의 더듬이는 접촉과 청각에 이용된다.
(2) 날개가 없다는 것은 그 생물이 곤충이 아니라는 의미는 아니다.
(3) 곤충의 다리는 세 쌍으로 복부에 붙어 있다.
(4) 곤충의 주둥이는 각 종의 곤충이 먹는 먹이의 유형에 맞게 달라졌다.

N (1) earthworms / doesn't know (2) Earthworms
(3) soil (4) soil (5) open spaces (6) air (7) water
(8) lower (9) roots (9) soil particles (10) eroded
(11) wind (12) water

G 1 (b) 2 (b)

S (1) F (2) F (3) T (4) T

B Grandma, do you need some help in your garden?

W Yes, dear. Just carry that bucket of dirt and follow me.

B Okay... Hey, something is moving in the dirt... Oh, that's disgusting. It's full of earthworms. Are you going fishing?

W No, silly. I need them to make a healthy garden.

B How can earthworms make your garden healthy?

W They are a vital part of soil health. You should be thanking the earthworms. Much of life as we know it could not exist without them. Now, just put the bucket there and start scooping the dirt and worms around the garden.

B Sure thing, Grandma. So, just how do earthworms help the soil?

W It's rather simple. When earthworms eat food, they also eat soil because the gritty soil helps them break down food matter in their stomachs. Also, as they tunnel through the soil, they act like an underground plow. This leaves open spaces where air and water can reach the lower levels of soil.

B So, if the earthworms didn't plow the soil, then it would become very compacted.

W Exactly. Plant roots could not grow because air and water could not penetrate the lower layers of soil.

B Oh, these earthworms are just so slimy!

W That slime also helps. When soil passes through earthworms, it comes out the other end with this sticky slime. This helps the particles of soil stick together and prevents them from being eroded away by wind and water.

B You sure know a lot about earthworms and gardening, Grandma.

W Oh, I've always had a green thumb. It runs in the family.

▶ **vital part** 절대적으로 필요한 요소 **scoop** 퍼올리다; 퍼내다 **gritty** 모래가 든, 모래투성이의 **plow** 쟁기; 갈다 **compacted** 꽉 찬; 탄탄한 **penetrate** 스며들다; 침투하다 **slimy** 끈적끈적한, 점액성의 **slime** 끈적끈적한 것; 끈적끈적한 지렁이 **particle** 입자, 미립자 **erode** 침식하다, 부식시키다

남 할머니, 정원일 도와드릴 것 있어요?

여 그래, 얘야. 그 흙 양동이를 들고 나를 따라오렴.

남 알겠어요… 어, 뭔가가 흙 속에서 움직이고 있어요… 으악, 징그러. 지렁이가 한 가득이에요. 낚시하실 거예요?

여 아니다. 실없기는. 건강한 정원을 만들려면 지렁이가 필요하단다.

남 어떻게 지렁이가 정원을 건강하게 만들 수 있어요?

여 지렁이는 토양 건강에 절대적으로 필요한 요소란다. 지렁이에게 고마워해야 해. 우리가 아는 많은 생물들은 지렁이가 없다면 살아갈 수 없을 테니 말이다. 자, 거기에 양동이를 놓고 흙과 지렁이를 정원 여기저기에 퍼넣으렴.

남 그럴게요, 할머니. 그런데, 지렁이가 토양에 어떻게 도움을 주나요?

여 간단해. 지렁이는 먹이를 먹을 때 흙도 같이 먹는단다. 모래가 든 흙이 지렁이 뱃속에서 음식을 잘게 부수는 작용을 하기 때문이지. 또한 지렁이는 흙에 터널을 파서 땅속에서 쟁기 역할을 하기도 해. 이렇게 해서 공기와 물이 흙의 깊은 곳까지 도달할 수 있는 공간이 생기게 되는 거지.

남 그럼, 만약 지렁이가 흙을 갈지 않는다면 흙이 매우 단단해지겠네요.

여 바로 그거야. 식물 뿌리는 공기와 물이 토양의 밑부분까지 스며들지 못하면 자랄 수 없게 돼.

남 아, 이 지렁이들은 꽤 끈적끈적하네요!

여 그 끈적끈적한 점액 또한 도움을 준단다. 지렁이의 몸속을 통과한 흙은 이 끈적끈적한 점액과 같이 배출되는데, 이게 토양 입자들을 서로 들러붙게 해서 바람이나 물에 토양이 침식되는 것을 막아 주지.

남 할머니는 정말 지렁이와 원예에 대해 많이 아시네요.

여 아, 난 원예에 재능이 있단다. 집안 내력이지.

1 대화의 주제는 무엇인가?
(a) 소년이 지렁이를 좋아하지 않는 이유
(b) 토양 건강에 있어서 지렁이의 역할
(c) 지렁이의 소화 방법
(d) 원예에 지렁이를 이용하는 최적의 방법

2 다음 중 가장 잘 요약된 것을 고르시오.
(a) 지렁이는 흙을 더 영양분이 풍부하게 만들어 식물을 더 잘 지라게 하기 때문에 정원에 꼭 필요하다.
(b) 지렁이는 흙에 공기와 물이 통할 수 있는 공간을 터주고 토양 침식을 막아주기 때문에 원예에 큰 도움이 된다.

다시 듣고 옳은 문장에는 T, 틀린 문장에는 F를 쓰시오.
(1) 소년은 왜 지렁이가 정원에 좋은지에 대해 많이 알고 있다.
(2) 지렁이는 흙을 먹고 끈적끈적한 점액을 배출해서 식물이 토양에 더 잘 달라붙도록 도와준다.
(3) 지렁이 굴이 물이 토양의 깊은 곳까지 닿을 수 있도록 흙을 푸석푸석하게 만들어준다.
(4) 지렁이가 섭취하는 흙은 지렁이가 먹이를 소화하는 데 도움을 준다.

Listening Drill 2 p. 54~p. 55

Long Lecture

O (1) winter (2) cold (3) warm-blooded (4) body temperature (5) consuming food (6) food (7) winter (8) reduced (9) a lot of (10) inactivity (11) hot (12) cold-blooded (13) air temperature (14) snail (15) shady (16) underground (17) mud (18) heat

1 (a) **2** (b) **3** (1) F (2) T (3) F (4) T **4** (c)

Dictation 정답: 스크립트 밑줄 참조

M Now I'm sure everyone knows that <u>bears</u> <u>hibernate</u> during the winter. Many other <u>species</u>, such as <u>squirrels</u>, also do the same. However, it may surprise you that some <u>creatures</u> in <u>warmer</u> <u>climates</u> also become <u>inactive</u> <u>when</u> <u>it</u> <u>gets</u> <u>too</u> <u>hot</u>. The <u>term</u> for this action, I mean, when creatures in hot climates "<u>hibernate</u>," is called aestivation. Okay then. Why do creatures <u>hibernate</u> or <u>aestivate</u> when it gets too cold or too hot? Most animals are <u>either</u> <u>warm-blooded</u> or <u>cold-blooded</u>. Mammals are warm-blooded and regulate their body temperature by consuming food and burning energy. In cold weather, however, there is sometimes not enough food, so some species, like the squirrel, hibernate. During hibernation, the metabolic rate of the animals is reduced, allowing them to consume energy more slowly. Hibernating animals consume a lot of food before winter arrives, so they get fatter and can survive the long period of inactivity. Meanwhile, other creatures are cold-blooded, meaning their body temperature depends on the external air temperature. Cold-blooded animals living in a desert, for example, usually try to find a shady spot when it gets hot. When the temperature is too extreme, they aestivate. In many types of terrain, species such as frogs, snakes, crocodiles, and turtles find cool places—typically underground or under mud—where they can escape extreme heat and remain mostly inactive. Some species of snails aestivate by climbing up fence posts, trees, and buildings. They do this to find shade in order to escape the extreme heat of the ground during high temperatures. How long a creature hibernates or aestivates depends on the species. Some sleep or stay inactive for many months while others do that for shorter periods of time.

▶ hibernate 동면하다, 겨울잠자다 aestivation 여름잠; 피서 mammal 포유동물
regulate 조절(조정)하다 metabolic rate 대사율 meanwhile 한편; 동시에
shady spot 그늘진 곳, 응달진 곳 terrain 지역, 지대 fence post 말뚝

남 자, 곰이 겨울 동안 동면한다는 건 다들 알겠지요. 다람쥐 같은 다른 많은 종도 동면을 합니다. 하지만 더운 기후에서 사는 몇몇 동물도 날씨가 너무 더워지면 활동하지 않게 된다는 사실을 알면 놀랄 거예요. 이러한 행위를 지칭하는 용어, 즉 더운 기후의 동물들이 '동면하는 것'을 여름잠이라고 부릅니다. 자, 그럼 왜 동물들은 날씨가 너무 추워지거나 너무 더워지면 동면에 들어가거나 여름잠을 자는 걸까요? 대부분의 동물은 온혈동물 아니면 냉혈동물입니다. 포유류는 온혈동물이며 먹이를 먹고 에너지를 태움으로써 체온을 조절합니다. 하지만 날씨가 추워지면 먹이가 충분하지 않은 경우가 있기 때문에 다람쥐와 같은 몇몇 종은 동면을 합니다. 동면을 하는 동안 동물의 대사율이 감소되어 에너지를 더 천천히 소비할 수 있게 됩니다. 동면하는 동물은 겨울이 오기 전에 먹이를 많이 먹습니다. 그렇게 살을 찌워 장기간 활동하지 않아도 생존할 수 있게 되는 거죠. 한편, 나머지는 냉혈동물인데요. 냉혈동물이란 체온이 외부의 공기 온도에 좌우된다는 의미죠. 예를 들면, 사막에 사는 냉혈동물들은 대개 날씨가 더워지면 그늘진 곳을 찾으려고 하죠. 기온이 너무 뜨거워지면 냉혈동물은 여름잠을 잡니다. 여러 지역에 사는 개구리, 뱀, 악어, 거북이 같은 종들은 무더위를 피하고 거의 활동을 하지 않은 채 있을 수 있는 서늘한 곳, 대체로 지하 또는 진흙 밑 같은 곳을 찾습니다. 어떤 달팽이 종은 말뚝이나 나무, 빌딩에 기어올라가 여름잠을 잡니다. 고온이 계속되는 동안 땅에서 발산되는 엄청난 열기에서 벗어날 수 있는 그늘을 찾기 위해 이렇게 하는 거죠. 얼마나 오래 동면을 하거나 여름잠을 자는가는 동물의 종에 따라 다릅니다. 어떤 종들은 몇 달 동안 자거나 활동을 안 하는 반면, 다른 종들은 더 짧은 기간 동안 그렇게 하지요.

1 강의의 주제는 무엇인가?
(a) 동물은 일정 기간 활동을 하지 않음으로써 온도 변화에 대응한다.
(b) 동면과 여름잠은 같은 것이지만 다른 동물에게 영향을 미친다.
(c) 온혈동물과 냉혈동물은 온도에 다르게 반응한다.
(d) 한 해의 특정한 시간에 식량 부족 때문에 동물은 동면을 하거나 여름잠을 잔다.

2 다음 중 가장 잘 요약된 것을 고르시오.
(a) 뜨거운 사막 기후에 서식하는 파충류의 여름잠을 유발하는 이유가

온도 변화와 먹이 부족인 반면, 겨울에 포유동물이 동면을 하는 주원인은 식량 공급 문제 때문이다.
(b) 동면과 여름잠은 일부 동물들이 극한의 온도와 식량 공급 부족과 같은 통제 불가능한 외부 요인으로부터 자신을 보호하는 방법이다.

3 옳은 문장에는 T, 틀린 문장에는 F를 쓰시오.
(1) 먹이 부족은 일부 동물이 여름잠을 자는 주요 원인이다.
(2) 자신의 체온을 조절할 수 없는 동물은 여름잠을 잘 가능성이 크다.
(3) 몇몇 달팽이는 온도가 너무 높아지면 땅 밑으로 들어간다.
(4) 동면기간 동안에는 소량의 음식도 큰 도움이 된다.

4 동면과 여름잠은 어떤 점에서 비슷한가?
(a) 동면과 여름잠이 일어나는 계절
(b) 동면과 여름잠의 지속기간
(c) 동물의 활동 수준
(d) 동면과 여름잠이 발생하는 지역

1 (b) **2** 해설 참조 **3** (b) **4** (c) **5** (b) **6** (a) **7** (b)
8 (a) **9** (b) **10** 해설 참조 **11** (c) **12** (e)

1

W Okay, today I want to discuss the class of animals called marsupials. The most well-known of these animals is the kangaroo, and other well-known species include the koala bear and the opossum. There are over 300 species of marsupials on Earth, and two-thirds of them are native to Australia. What distinguishes marsupials from most other animals is the way their offspring are born. In most mammals, the female has a placenta in its womb, which allows the offspring to use the mother's blood supply to get nourishment. However, in marsupials, the womb is more like the yolk of a bird's egg and only supplies nutrition for a short time. Therefore, the mother carries the offspring inside her for only a short period of time—about a month—and then the offspring is born. The offspring climbs into a pouch on the front of the female marsupial's abdomen. Here it may remain for several more months as it develops and grows stronger. Inside the pouch are the female marsupial's nipples, which the offspring latches onto and suckles to receive milk and nutrition. Fossilized remains of marsupials have been found on all continents, but the vast majority of marsupials today live in South America and Australia. It is believed marsupials died off outside of these two continents because placenta-born mammals out-competed them. The hot climates of South America and Australia seem to have made the marsupial form of birth an advantage, and therefore marsupials have flourished in these lands.

▶ class (동식물 분류상의) 강(綱) marsupial 유대류(有袋類)의 포유동물(캥거루 등)
opossum 주머니쥐 offspring 자식, 새끼 placenta 태반 more like 오히려
~에 가까운 yolk (알의) 노른자위, 난황 carry (아이·새끼를) 배고 있다 pouch
작은 주머니; 주머니 모양의 것 nipple 젖꼭지; 고무젖꼭지 latch onto ~을 꽉
쥐다, 쥐고 놓지 않다 fossilize 화석으로 만들다(되다) remains 유골, 유해; 잔해
die off (종족 등이) 차차 멸망하다; 차례로 죽다(말라죽다) flourish 번성하다

여 좋아요, 오늘은 유대류 포유동물이라고 불리는 동물 강에 대해 이야기하려고 해요. 이 가운데 가장 잘 알려진 동물은 캥거루입니다. 그리고 잘 알려진 다른 종으로는 코알라와 주머니쥐가 있죠. 지구상에는 300종이 넘는 유대류 포유동물이 있고 그 중 3분의 2는 호주가 원산지입니다. 다른 동물과 유대류 포유동물을 구별짓는 것은 새끼가 태어나는 방식입니다. 대부분의 포유동물은 암컷이 자궁에 태반을 가지고 있어 새끼가 어미의 혈액을 통해 영양분을 취할 수 있습니다. 하지만 유대류 포유동물의 경우에는 자궁이 새알의 노른자에 가까워 짧은 시간 동안만 영양을 공급할 뿐입니다. 그래서 어미가 한 달 정도의 짧은 기간 동안만 새끼를 배고나면 새끼가 태어나게 됩니다. 새끼는 유대류 포유동물 복부 앞에 있는 작은 주머니 속으로 기어 올라갑니다. 여기서 새끼는 몇 달 더 살면서 발육하고 힘이 세지지요. 암컷 유대류 포유동물의 주머니 안에는 새끼가 젖과 영양분을 얻을 수 있도록 꼭 쥐고 빨 수 있는 젖꼭지가 있습니다. 유대류 포유동물의 화석 유골은 모든 대륙에서 발견되지만 오늘날 대부분의 유대류 포유동물은 남아메리카와 호주에서 삽니다. 태반 태생인 포유동물들이 경쟁에서 이겼기 때문에 이 두 대륙 외의 지역에 살던 유대류 포유동물들은 자연소멸된 것으로 여겨지고 있습니다. 더운 기후의 남아메리카와 호주는 유대류 포유동물의 출산에 유리했으며, 따라서 유대류 포유동물은 이 땅들에서 번성하였습니다.

1 담화의 목적은 무엇인가?
(a) 현대와 고대의 유대류 포유동물이 있는 곳에 대해 논하려고
(b) 유대류 포유동물의 특이한 출산 방법에 대해 설명하려고
(c) 호주에서 유대류 포유동물이 번성하는 이유에 대해 조사하려고
(d) 유대류 포유동물이 한때 모든 대륙에서 살았다는 것을 증명하려고
(e) 유대류 포유동물이 다른 포유동물과 어떻게 같은지를 보여주려고

2

W Thanks for inviting me to your bee farm, David. I'm really looking forward to seeing how you make honey.

M First, we have to put on these protective suits so the bees can't sting us.

W I've been stung before, and it's no picnic. That's for sure.

M I think I've been stung by every kind of bee, wasp, and hornet. I guess that goes with the territory when you collect honey for a living.

W Which stings hurt the most: bees, wasps, or hornets?

M It's hard to say since everyone feels pain a little differently. An American professor made a pain index which shows how painful a sting can get. It just has numbers from one to four, with one being mild pain and four being extreme pain. It's in this magazine. Ah, here it is.

W It looks like wasps cause the worst pain. The paper wasp rates a three, and the pepsis wasp rates a four on the pain index.

M Yeah, those can be pesky devils if you get stung. In comparison, hornets and bees usually rate only a two. But even ants can have painful stings.

W Oh, this is the harvester ant! It looks like the ants I had in my ant farm when I was in school.

M Most likely. It's usually docile, but it has a sting as powerful as paper wasps.

W Do all ants cause such pain?

M Oh, no. The fire ant rates even below the hornets and bees on the chart. But they attack in swarms, so they can be dangerous.

▶ protective suits 보호복 sting 쏘다, 찌르다; 쏨; 침 It's no picnic. (구어) 장난[쉬운 일]이 아니다. wasp 말벌 hornet 호박벌 That goes with the territory.

<hr>

이런 일을 하다 보면 으레 있는 일이다. pain index 고통지수 paper wasp 크기가 1.9 cm~2.5 cm 정도로 죽은 나무와 식물의 줄기를 모아 타액을 섞어 집을 짓는 말벌의 종류 pepsis wasp 타란툴라 애벌레를 먹이로 사냥하기 때문에 tarantula hawk라고도 하며, 크기가 5cm로 가장 큰 말벌 중의 하나임 pesky 귀찮은, 성가신 harvester ant 수확개미(풀을 먹고 그 씨를 비축함. 미 남서부산) most likely 아마, 필시 docile 온순한, 유순한 in swarm 떼 지어

여 벌 농장에 초대해 줘서 고마워, 데이비드. 난 어떻게 꿀을 만드는지 정말 보고 싶어.

남 우선, 우리는 벌들이 쏘지 못하도록 보호복을 입어야 해.

여 전에 벌에 쏘인 적이 있는데, 장난 아니더라고. 정말이야.

남 난 온갖 종류의 벌, 말벌, 호박벌에게 쏘여 본 것 같아. 벌꿀 채집이 직업이면 감수해야 하는 일이겠지.

여 어떤 벌에 쏘이면 가장 아프니? 벌, 말벌, 아니면 호박벌?

남 사람마다 고통을 조금씩 다르게 느끼기 때문에 한마디로 설명하긴 어려워. 한 미국인 교수는 쏘였을 때 얼마나 아픈지를 보여주는 고통지수를 만들었어. 고통지수는 가벼운 통증 1에서 극심한 통증 4로 1에서 4까지의 수치로 되어 있어. 이 잡지에 나와 있어. 아, 여기 있다.

여 말벌이 가장 심한 고통을 일으키는 것 같구나. 고통지수가 종이말벌은 3이고 펩시스말벌은 4야.

남 그래, 그 벌들에 쏘이면 정말 괴롭지. 비교해 보자면, 호박벌과 벌은 보통 고통지수가 2정도밖에 안 돼. 하지만 개미도 물면 아파.

여 오, 이건 수확개미야! 내가 학교에 다닐 때 우리 개미농장에 있던 개미같이 생겼어.

남 아마 그럴 거야. 그건 대개 온순하지만 종이말벌만큼이나 강한 침을 가지고 있지.

여 모든 개미가 쏘면 그렇게 아프니?

남 아, 아니야. 불개미는 고통지수 차트에서 호박벌과 벌보다도 낮은 순위야. 하지만 불개미는 떼 지어 공격하기 때문에 위험할 수 있어.

2 고통지수에 따라 각 곤충의 올바른 통증 수준으로 표를 완성하시오.

곤충	고통지수 척도에 따른 통증 수준
종이말벌	3
펩시스말벌	4
벌	2
호박벌	2
수확개미	3
불개미	1

3-4

W The albatross is one of the great travelers among birds. The southern islands of the Indian, Pacific, and Atlantic oceans, and the northwest Pacific, are home to these large birds. Albatrosses can fly across vast expanses of water for hundreds of kilometers at a time. They have a unique body structure that enhances this long-range flight and also have several techniques that they use to prolong flight. First off, the albatross has an almost hollow bone structure, which makes it lighter than its size would suggest. There is also a tendon in its wings that locks them in place so the wings are immobile and do not tire easily from being held still with just the bird's muscles. The wings are large and have a great surface area for catching more lift while the bird glides. For flight, the albatross relies on its special gliding ability and the use of the winds and the waves. The albatross dives toward the ocean, builds up speed, and then pulls up and converts this speed to height and distance. For every 30 centimeters it drops toward the ocean, it can move six meters forward and then do this repeatedly for hundreds of kilometers without touching the ocean. A second technique of flight relies on the <u>ocean</u> <u>waves</u>. The albatross will <u>fly</u> <u>low</u>—just above wave height—and will <u>gain</u> <u>lift</u> from the wind that is <u>rising</u> <u>above</u> the waves. As each <u>wave</u> <u>passes</u>, the albatross gains more lift and <u>continues</u> <u>on</u> its long journey.

▶ vast expanses of water 드넓은 바다 enhance 높이다, 강화하다
long-range 장거리에 달하는; 장기간의 prolong 늘이다, 길게 하다; 연장하다
first off 우선, 첫째로; 곧 hollow 속이 빈; 텅 빈 tendon 힘줄 immobile 움직일
수 없는, 고정된 lift 상승력; 들어올림 glide 활공하다 dive 급강하하다; 잠수하다
surface area 면적 pull up 서다; 차를 세우다 convert 전환하다

여 앨버트로스는 새들 가운데 가장 훌륭한 여행자 중 하나에 속합니다. 인도양의 남쪽 섬, 태평양, 대서양, 북서태평양은 이 큰 새들의 보금자리이죠. 앨버트로스는 한 번에 수 백 킬로미터의 드넓은 바다를 날 수 있습니다. 앨버트로스는 이 장거리 비행 능력을 향상시켜주는 독특한 신체 구조를 가지고 있고, 또한 비행을 오래하기 위해 사용하는 몇 가지의 기술이 있습니다. 우선, 앨버트로스는 골격의 속이 거의 비어 있어 크기에 비해 더 가볍답니다. 또한 날개가 움직이지 않도록 제자리에 고정시키는 힘줄이 있어서 그냥 근육만으로 움직이지 않고 가만히 떠 있어도 피로를 쉽게 느끼지 않습니다. 날개가 크고 표면적이 넓어 새가 활공하는 동안 상승력이 더 좋지요. 앨버트로스는 비행하기 위해 특별한 활공능력과 바람과 파도를 이용합니다. 앨버트로스는 바다를 향해 급강하하여 속력을 올리고 난 후 멈춰서 이 속도를 높이와 거리로 전환합니다. 앨버트로스는 바다를 향해 30 센티미터를 급강하할 때마다 6미터를 앞으로 이동할 수 있는데, 이 행동을 반복하여 바닷물을 건드리는 일 없이 수백 킬로미터를 비행합니다. 비행의 두 번째 기술은 바다의 파도에 의지하는 것입니다. 앨버트로스는 파도 바로 위로 낮게 비행하여 파도 위에 생기는 바람으로부터 상승력을 얻게 됩니다. 파도가 지나갈 때마다 앨버트로스는 더 큰 상승력을 얻어 장기간의 여행을 계속합니다.

3 앨버트로스가 활공할 때 도움이 되는 신체적인 특징은 무엇인가?
(a) 속이 빈 뼈 구조 (b) 날개의 넓은 면적
(c) 큰 날개의 부동성 (d) 날개에 있는 특별한 힘줄
(e) 전반적으로 가벼운 체중

4 담화를 통해 앨버트로스에 대해 유추할 수 있는 것은?
(a) 앨버트로스는 바닷물 위에 떠다닐 수 없다.
(b) 앨버트로스는 장기간 비행 후에 집으로 돌아간다.
(c) 앨버트로스는 비행하는 동안 거의 날갯짓을 하지 않는다.
(d) 앨버트로스는 주로 육지에서 먹이를 먹는다.
(e) 앨버트로스는 나는 데 도움이 되는 특별한 깃털을 가지고 있다.

5-6   Level up

M It's a nice day for a <u>walk</u> <u>in</u> the <u>forest</u>.

W Thanks for helping me <u>go</u> <u>mushroom</u> <u>hunting</u>. There should be lots of them <u>around</u> <u>here</u>. This was the <u>best</u> <u>spot</u> last year.

M I think I see some now.

W No, <u>don't</u> <u>pick</u> those. They are not very <u>edible</u>, and some are very <u>poisonous</u>.

M That's some information I <u>could</u> <u>have</u> <u>used</u> a bit earlier. How can I tell a <u>poisonous</u> mushroom <u>from</u> <u>a</u> <u>safe</u> mushroom?

W It's hard. That's why I have <u>brought</u> <u>along</u> this mushroom <u>identification</u> <u>guidebook</u>. The ones to <u>avoid</u> are the little brown ones because they are the <u>hardest</u> <u>to</u> <u>classify</u>. Even a small <u>difference</u> <u>can</u> <u>indicate</u> a different species, and some are <u>poisonous</u>.

M Do you mean I could die <u>from</u> <u>eating</u> a mushroom?

W Yes, it has happened. A <u>whole</u> <u>family</u> in Canada died after eating a type of mushroom <u>they</u> <u>thought</u> was safe, but it was <u>another</u> <u>type</u>.

M Now you've <u>made</u> <u>me</u> <u>paranoid</u>. Is that type of mushroom around here?

W No, and the mushrooms that <u>grow</u> <u>here</u> are not very poisonous. Some types will <u>make</u> <u>you</u> <u>sick</u> <u>though</u>.

M What about <u>toadstools</u>? Are they around here?

W There is no such thing as a toadstool. That's just a <u>name</u> <u>given</u> <u>to</u> dangerous mushrooms a long time ago in Europe.

M So, <u>many</u> <u>types</u> <u>of</u> bad mushrooms could be what people call toadstools?

W <u>Exactly</u>. Oh, stop! You just about <u>tramped</u> <u>on</u> those mushrooms. Now those are <u>good</u> <u>for</u> <u>eating</u>.

M Are you sure?

W Yes. Why? Don't you <u>trust</u> <u>me</u>?

M Maybe I'll just have a sandwich for lunch.

▶ edible 먹을 수 있는, 식용에 알맞은 poisonous 유독〔유해〕한 identification 식별 classify 분류하다 indicate 나타내다 paranoid 피해망상의; 지나치게 의심이 많은 toadstool 독버섯 tramp 짓밟다, 밟아 뭉개다

남 숲 속을 걷기에 좋은 날씨야.
여 버섯 따러 가는 걸 도와줘서 고마워. 이 근처에 많이 있을 거야. 작년에 가장 많이 있었던 곳이거든.
남 이제 좀 보이는 것 같아.
여 아니야, 그것들은 따지 마. 먹을 수 있는 게 아니고, 어떤 것들은 강한 독성이 있어.
남 좋은 정보네. 좀 더 일찍 알았으면 좋았을 텐데. 독버섯과 안전한 버섯을 어떻게 구분할 수 있지?
여 어려워. 그래서 내가 이 버섯 식별 가이드북을 가져온 거야. 피해야 할 버섯은 작은 갈색 버섯이야. 가장 분류하기 힘들기 때문이지. 작은 차이로도 다른 종류일 수 있고 어떤 것들은 독이 있어.
남 네 말은 버섯을 먹고 죽을 수도 있다는 거야?
여 그래, 그런 일이 실제로 있었어. 캐나다에서 한 가족이 안전하다고 생각하고 먹었다가 죽었어. 다른 종류의 버섯이었던 거지.
남 이제 넌 날 피해망상으로 만들고 있구나. 그런 종류의 버섯이 이 근처에 있어?
여 아니. 여기에서 자라는 버섯은 독성이 그리 강하진 않아. 하지만 어떤 종류는 구토를 일으키지.
남 토드스툴은 어때? 이 근처에 있어?
여 토드스툴이라는 것은 없어. 그건 그냥 유럽에서 오래 전에 위험한 버섯에 붙인 이름일 뿐이야.
남 그럼, 여러 종류의 나쁜 버섯이 사람들이 말하는 토드스툴이라는 거야?
여 바로 그거야. 아, 멈춰! 이 버섯들을 밟아 뭉갤 뻔 했잖아. 이건 먹어도 좋은 것들이야.
남 확실해?
여 응. 왜? 너 나 못 믿어?
남 난 그냥 점심으로 샌드위치나 먹어야겠다.

5 대화에 따르면 다음 중 사실이 <u>아닌</u> 것은?
(a) 어떤 종류의 버섯은 먹으면 치명적일 수 있다.
(b) 여러 가지 버섯을 구분하는 것은 꽤 쉽다.
(c) '토드스툴'은 일부 버섯에 붙여진 이름일 뿐이다.
(d) 버섯과 관련된 비극적인 사고가 일어난 적이 있다.
(e) 다른 종류의 버섯들이 비슷해 보일 수 있다.

6 다음 중 내용을 가장 잘 요약한 것을 고르시오.

(a) 많은 버섯이 먹어도 좋은 반면 토드스툴은 그렇지 않다. 그렇기 때문에 전문가의 안내 없이 야생 버섯을 채집해서는 안 된다.

(b) 안전한 버섯과 위험한 버섯을 구분하는 특별한 버섯 가이드북이 있는 한 야생 버섯을 채집해도 안전하다.

(c) '토드스툴'은 먹을 수 없는 많은 종류의 버섯에 붙여진 이름일 뿐이기 때문에 버섯과 토드스툴은 똑같은 것이다.

---

7 **Level up**

W That's a cute cat. What's its name?

M Bubbles. She's a <u>female</u> <u>feline</u>.

W Oh, I think she <u>sees something</u> <u>she wants</u>. It looks like she's <u>about to hunt</u>.

M Yeah, she does that when she sees a bird. Cats are <u>better hunters</u> at night though. They have <u>great night vision</u>.

W I <u>get spooked</u> when I see a <u>cat's eyes shining</u> in the dark.

M Yeah, it is <u>kind of creepy</u>. Have you ever <u>noticed</u> that some animals have eyes <u>on the sides</u> of their heads <u>while others</u> have them in the <u>front</u>?

W Yeah, I <u>have noticed that</u>. I imagine it <u>has something</u> to <u>do with</u> the type of animal. For instance, I think most <u>predators</u> have forward-facing eyes. Look at your cat, other cats, like lions and tigers, and even dogs.

M That's all the <u>better to hunt with</u>. Forward-facing eyes <u>enable</u> them to <u>keep the target</u> in sight.

W And <u>prey animal</u> have eyes on the sides of their heads.

M Now that <u>makes sense</u>. So the prey animals can see if a predator is coming from the <u>flank</u> to <u>attack</u> them.

W That sounds <u>logical</u>.

▶ feline 고양잇과의 동물　night vision 야간 시력, 암시(暗視) 시력　spooked 겁먹은　creepy 소름이 끼치는; 으스스한　predator 포식 동물, 육식 동물　target (공격) 목표; 표적　keep ... in sight 놓치지 않도록 지켜보다　flank 측면　logical 논리적인

여 귀여운 고양이네. 이름이 뭐야?

남 버블스. 암컷이야.

여 오, 원하는 걸 본 모양인데. 곧 사냥을 할 태세야.

남 응, 새를 보면 그래. 하지만 고양이는 밤에 사냥을 더 잘해. 야간 시력이 무척 좋거든.

여 난 밤에 빛나는 고양이 눈을 보면 겁이 나.

남 그래, 좀 으스스하지. 너 어떤 동물들은 머리 양 옆에 눈이 있는 반면에 그 외의 다른 동물들은 앞에 눈이 있는 거 알고 있었니?

여 응, 알고 있었어. 그건 동물 종류와 관련이 있는 것 같아. 예를 들면 대부분의 포식 동물들은 앞쪽을 향하는 눈을 가지고 있는 것 같아. 네 고양이와 사자, 호랑이 같은 다른 고양잇과의 동물들, 심지어 개들을 보라고.

남 사냥을 하기에 더 낫기 때문이지. 앞쪽을 보는 눈은 표적을 놓치지 않고 볼 수 있게 해주지.

여 그리고 먹잇감은 머리 양옆에 눈이 있지.

남 말 된다. 그러면 먹잇감은 포식 동물이 측면에서 공격을 하러 오는지 볼 수 있잖아.

여 그거 논리적인데.

---

7 Why do some animals have eyes on the sides of their heads?　왜 어떤 동물들은 머리 양 옆에 눈이 있는가?

(a) To allow them to see better during the night
밤에 더 잘 볼 수 있도록

(b) To prevent surprise attacks by predators
포식 동물에 의한 기습 공격을 막을 수 있도록

(c) To focus on prey as they are attacking it
공격하는 동안 먹잇감에 집중할 수 있도록

─(d) To allow them to see for long distances
먼 거리를 볼 수 있도록

(e) To see their flanks while they are hunting
사냥하는 동안 측면을 볼 수 있도록

---

8 **Level up**

M Most plants <u>get their nutrition</u> from soil and <u>through active photosynthesis</u>. However, there are a few plants that <u>get nutrition</u> from eating other <u>life forms</u>—usually <u>insects</u> and sometimes small animals, <u>like rats</u>. These are <u>carnivorous plants</u>. They are usually found in <u>regions</u> with <u>poor soil</u>, such as <u>swampy areas</u> or <u>bogs</u>, which may <u>explain why</u> these plants have <u>evolved to eat</u> other life forms. Carnivorous plants <u>trap insects</u> in several ways. The Venus flytrap, for example, <u>snaps its leaves</u> on an insect very quickly—just <u>like a trap</u>—and then uses <u>digestive enzymes</u> to consume it. The <u>pitcher plant</u> has a long, <u>rolled, enclosed leaf</u> that has digestive enzymes <u>at the bottom</u>. Insects <u>fall in</u> and can't <u>get out</u>, so they are <u>consumed by</u> the plant. Other carnivorous plants have <u>sticky substances</u> that trap insects, they have traps like <u>lobster pots</u> where the insects <u>can get in</u> but can't get out, or they have a <u>bladder</u> that <u>sucks insects</u> in like a <u>vacuum sucks in dirt</u>.

▶ photosynthesis 광합성　life form 생물, 생명체　carnivorous plant 식충 식물　swampy area 늪, 습지　bog 소택지, 습지; 수렁　evolve 진화하다; 점진적으로 변화하다　trap 덫으로 잡다; 함정에 빠뜨리다　Venus flytrap 끈끈이주걱　snap 잡아채다, 홱 집다　digestive enzymes 소화효소　pitcher plant 낭상엽 식물 (벌레잡이통풀 등)　enclose 에워싸다, 둘러싸다　fall in ～에 빠지다, 떨어지다　substance 물질; 재질, 재료　lobster pot 왕새우잡이 통발　bladder 바람 주머니

남 대부분의 식물은 토양과 활발한 광합성을 통해 양분을 얻습니다. 하지만, 몇몇 식물들은 대개 곤충, 그리고 때로는 쥐 등의 작은 동물과 같은 다른 생물들을 먹어서 영양분을 취하죠. 이런 식물들을 식충식물이라고 합니다. 식충식물은 대개 늪이나 습지와 같은 척박한 토양이 있는 지역에서 발견되는데, 바로 그 점이 왜 이 식물들이 다른 생물들을 먹도록 진화되었는지 설명해 줍니다. 식충 식물은 여러 가지 방법으로 곤충을 잡습니다. 예를 들어 끈끈이주걱은 자신의 잎으로 곤충을 마치 덫처럼 재빨리 잡아채서 소화효소를 사용하여 먹이 버립니다. 낭상엽 식물은 바닥에 소화효소가 있는 길고 돌돌 말려 둘러싸인 잎을 가지고 있습니다. 곤충들은 그 안에 빠져 헤어나올 수 없기 때문에 그 식물에게 잡아 먹히고 말죠. 다른 식충식물에는 곤충을 잡는 끈적끈적한 물질이 있습니다. 그 식물들은 곤충들이 들어갈 수는 있지만 나올 수는 없는 왕새우잡이 통발 같은 덫을 가지고 있거나 먼지를 빨아들이는 진공청소기처럼 곤충들을 빨아들이는 바람 주머니가 있습니다.

---

8 Which is NOT a method carnivorous plants use to trap prey?　식충식물이 먹이를 잡을 때 쓰는 방법이 <u>아닌</u> 것은?

(a) Barbs that prey gets impaled on　먹잇감을 찌르는 가시

(b) Leaves that snap quickly over prey
먹잇감을 재빨리 잡아채는 잎

(c) Liquid-filled tubes into which prey fall
먹잇감이 빠지는, 액체가 들어있는 관

(d) Substances to which prey sticks　먹잇감이 들러붙는 물질

(e) Traps that prey can enter but not exit
먹잇감이 들어갈 수는 있지만 나올 수는 없는 덫

9

W In the animal kingdom, competition for food is one of the prime aspects of daily life. Many species, such as lions and wolves, choose a territory and defend it against all outsiders. The food resources within this territory can support a certain number of predators but no more than that number, so it is vital for the predators to claim and defend their territory. They warn away other members of the same species by marking the boundaries of their territory with urine or other secretions from the body. These secretions give off distinctive smells that signal to intruders that this territory has been claimed. However, this does not prevent all intrusions. Members of different species may not recognize the stay-away warnings or may be intent on taking over the territory. Hyenas, for example, frequently stray through lion territories. There is even some evidence that the lions allow this so that the hyenas can make a kill. Then the lions chase the hyenas away so they can consume the dead animal. But when other lions enter a lion pride's territory, the occupying lions are not so forgiving. A prime reason for male lions to enter a territory is to fight those male lions that have claimed it. This action is done to obtain a food supply as well as to take over the lion pride and to make a claim on the female lions. In this way, these intruders may kill or drive away the males and take their place.

▶ prime 주요한, 가장 중요한 territory 세력권, 텃세권 a certain number of 일정 수의 vital 극히 중대한, 절대 필요한 claim 권리를 주장하다 secretion 분비물 warn away 접근하지 않도록 경고하다 distinctive 특유의, 특이한 signal 신호를 보내다 intruder 침입자 recognize 알아보다, 인정하다 intent 의도: 목적 stray 헤매다, 방황하다 chase away 쫓아버리다 pride (사자의) 떼, 집단 forgiving 관대한, (쾌히) 용서하는 drive away 쫓아내다, 몰아내다

여 동물 세계에서 먹이를 차지하기 위한 경쟁은 일상생활의 가장 중요한 요소 중 하나입니다. 사자나 늑대와 같은 많은 종들은 세력권을 고르고 외부 동물들에 대항해 이를 지키죠. 이 세력권 내에 있는 먹이로 일정수의 포식 동물들을 먹여 살릴 수 있지만 그 이상은 감당할 수 없기 때문에, 포식 동물들에게는 자신의 세력권을 주장하고 지키는 것이 매우 중요합니다. 이 포식 동물들은 오줌이나 몸에서 나오는 다른 분비물로 자신의 세력권 경계를 표시함으로써 같은 종의 다른 포식 동물들이 접근하지 않도록 경고한답니다. 이 분비물은 특이한 냄새를 냄으로써 침입자들에게 이 지역에 임자가 있다는 신호를 보내죠. 하지만, 이것이 침입을 다 막지는 못합니다. 다른 종들의 동물들이 가까이 오지 말라는 경고를 인지하지 못하거나, 그 세력권을 장악하려는 의도를 품을 수 있거든요. 예를 들면 하이에나는 사자의 세력권에서 자주 어슬렁거립니다. 심지어 사자가 이것을 묵인하여 하이에나들이 동물을 죽이도록 한다는 증거도 있습니다. 그러고 나서 사자들은 죽은 동물을 먹으려고 하이에나를 쫓아버립니다. 하지만 다른 사자들이 한 사자 집단의 세력권으로 들어오면 그 영역을 차지하고 있던 사자들은 그다지 관대하지 않죠. 수컷 사자들이 세력권에 들어가는 가장 큰 이유는 그 지역의 소유권을 주장하는 수컷 사자들과 싸우기 위함입니다. 이러한 행동은 그 사자 집단을 차지하고 암컷 사자들에 대한 권리를 주장할 뿐만 아니라 먹이를 얻기 위해 이루어지는 것이죠. 이러한 방법으로 이 침입자들은 수컷 사자들을 죽이거나 쫓아내어 그들의 자리를 차지하게 됩니다.

9 담화에 따르면 다음 중 사실이 아닌 것은?
(a) 하이에나는 먹잇감을 죽이지만 때로는 사자에게 뺏기기도 한다.
(b) 세력권 다툼은 대개 암컷을 차지하기 위해 이루어진다.
(c) 수컷 사자는 다른 수컷 사자들의 집단을 차지하기 위해 싸운다.
(d) 동물들은 냄새나는 분비물로 자기 영역을 표시한다.
(e) 세력권 안에 있는 먹이는 많은 포식 동물들을 먹여 살리지 못한다.

G Hello, Dr. Hibbert.

M Hello, Sally. Hello, Pookie. What can I do for you?

G Pookie is sick.

M Why do you think your dog is sick, Sally?

G She is very lazy lately. She doesn't want to run around as much. And she's eating too much and is getting very fat. Look at her.

M Well, let me do a quick examination, and we'll see what the trouble is. Okay... oh, I see what's going on now.

G What's wrong with Pookie, Dr. Hibbert?

M Sally, Pookie is going to be a mommy dog soon.

G Oh, wow. Puppies! How many puppies?

M It's hard to say. We'll know more in a few weeks.

G How long do I have to wait?

M The normal gestation period for dogs is about 63 days. I'd say Pookie has about 45 more days to go.

G Gestation? What does that mean?

M The time it takes an animal to give birth. Cats are about the same as dogs. Their gestation period is around 61 days.

G Which animal takes the longest time to have babies?

M I'd say the elephant. Its gestation period is about 2 years, which is around 660 days.

G Wow, that's a long time. Which animal takes the shortest time to have babies then?

M I'm not exactly sure, but mice usually have babies within 21 days of becoming pregnant.

G What about rabbits? I had a pet rabbit once.

M I remember. A rabbit's gestation is very short; it's only 31 days.

▶ gestation period 잉태 기간 about the same 비슷비슷하다

여 안녕하세요, 히버트 선생님.
남 안녕, 샐리. 안녕, 푸키. 뭘 도와줄까?
여 푸키가 아파요.
남 왜 네 개가 아프다고 생각하지, 샐리?
여 푸키가 요새 아주 굼떠요. 별로 뛰어다니려고 하지도 않고요. 그리고 너무 많이 먹고 살이 많이 찌고 있어요. 보세요.
남 음, 잠깐 진찰 좀 해보자. 그럼 뭐가 문제인지 알게 될 거야. 그래… 아, 무슨 일인지 알겠다.
여 푸키에게 무슨 일이 있는 거죠, 히버트 선생님?
남 샐리야, 푸키는 곧 엄마가 될 거야.
여 와. 강아지라고요! 강아지가 몇 마리나 있나요?
남 말하기 힘들단다. 몇 주 후에는 더 알 수 있을 거야.
여 얼마나 오래 기다려야 하죠?
남 개의 정상 잉태 기간은 약 63일이야. 푸키는 약 45일이 더 남은 것 같구나.
여 잉태? 그게 무슨 뜻이죠?
남 동물이 새끼를 낳을 때까지 걸리는 시간을 의미하지. 고양이는 개와 비슷해. 고양이의 잉태 기간은 약 61일이야.
여 어느 동물이 새끼를 낳는 데 시간이 가장 오래 걸리죠?
남 코끼리겠지. 코끼리의 잉태 기간은 약 2년이야. 약 660일 정도지.
여 와, 정말 기네요. 그럼 어떤 동물이 새끼를 낳는 데 시간이 가장 짧게 걸리나요?
남 확실하지는 않지만 쥐는 새끼를 가지고 대개 21일 안에 낳지.
여 토끼는 어때요? 전에 애완용 토끼가 있었거든요.
남 나도 기억나. 토끼의 잉태 기간은 매우 짧아서, 31일밖에 안 되지.

10 개, 고양이, 코끼리, 토끼, 쥐의 잉태 기간을 나타내는 그래프를 만드시오.

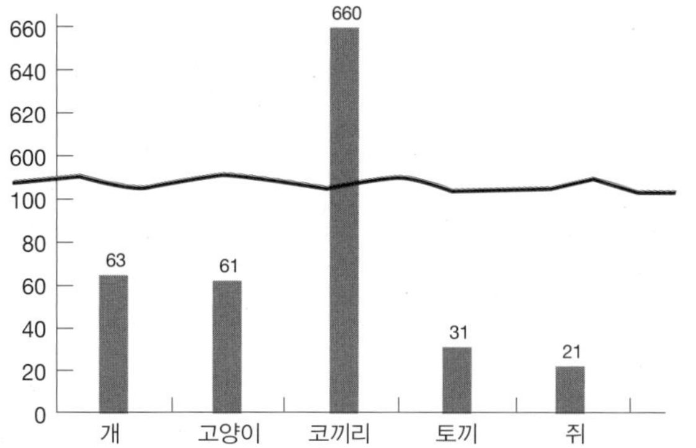

11-12 Level up

M There are almost 300,000 different types of plants already identified by botanists, and there may be many more. So, how can we classify plants? The simplest way—without getting into all of the scientific name stuff—is by examining the plant's tissue structure, its seed structure, and its height. There are two types of tissue structures: vascular and nonvascular. Most plants are vascular plants. They have leaves, stems, and root systems. Nonvascular plants don't have leaves, stems, or root systems. Mosses are a good example of nonvascular plants. Next, plants are divided by their types of seeds. There are three types of seeds: spores, naked seeds, and covered seeds. Mosses and several types of ferns produce spores. They are blown around by the wind and grow wherever they land. Plants with naked seeds usually have cones and they are called gymnosperms. Spruce, pine, and fir trees are some examples of this type. Covered-seed plants are called angiosperms. They have their seeds covered inside fruits or nutshells. Almost all plants with flowers are angiosperms. Angiosperms are further divided into two types, depending on their internal veins and the number of seeds they bear. Some have parallel internal veins for the movement of nutrients and also have one-seed leaves. Grasses and palms are in this group. The second type has internal veins like a net and two-seed leaves. Cherry trees and coffee plants fall into this group. Finally, plants are characterized by their height. At the bottom are the mosses and the lower growing grasses, flowers, and bushes, and, finally, there are the trees at various heights.

▶ botanist 식물학자 classify 분류하다 scientific name 학명 tissue 조직
vascular plant 관다발 식물 moss 이끼 spore 아포, 포자, 홀씨 naked seed
나출종자(과피나 과육으로 덮어 있지 않은 식물의 종자) fern 양치류 cone 방울 열
매, 솔방울 gymnosperm 겉씨[나자]식물 spruce 가문비나무, 전나무 fir (서양)
전나무 angiosperm 속씨식물, 피자식물 nutshell 견과(堅果)의 껍질 vein (식물)
엽맥(葉脈) parallel 평형의, 나란한 nutrients 영양분; 영양소 palm 야자나무
fall into ~으로 나뉘다, 분류되다 characterize ~에 특성을 부여하다

남 거의 30만 종의 식물이 이미 식물학자들에 의해 식별되었고 더 많은 종이 있을
것으로 보고 있습니다. 그럼, 어떻게 식물을 분류할 수 있을까요? 학명 같은 것
을 따질 필요 없이 가장 간단한 방법은 식물의 조직 구조, 씨앗의 구조, 키를 조
사하는 것입니다. 조직 구조에는 두 가지 종류, 즉 관다발, 무관다발이 있습니다.
대부분의 식물은 관다발 식물입니다. 관다발 식물은 잎, 줄기, 뿌리가 있습니다.
무관다발 식물은 잎, 줄기 뿌리가 없습니다. 이끼가 무관다발 식물의 좋은 예입

니다. 다음으로 식물은 씨앗의 종류로 나누어집니다. 씨앗의 종류에는 포자, 나
출종자, 피자종자, 이렇게 세 종류가 있습니다. 이끼와 몇몇의 양치류는 포자를
만듭니다. 그것들은 바람에 흩날려 어디든 닿는 땅에서 자라게 됩니다. 나출종자
식물에는 대개 겉씨식물이라 불리는 방울 열매가 있죠. 가문비나무, 소나무, 전
나무가 그 예입니다. 피자종자는 속씨식물이라고 불립니다. 피자종자는 씨앗이
과일이나 견과의 껍질 안에 싸여 있습니다. 꽃이 있는 거의 모든 식물들은 속씨
식물입니다. 속씨식물은 내부 엽맥과 맺는 씨앗 수에 따라 두 가지 종류로 나눕
니다. 어떤 속씨식물들은 영양소의 이동을 위한 평행으로 된 내부 엽맥을 가지고
있고, 또한 외떡잎이 있습니다. 풀과 야자나무가 이 그룹에 속합니다. 두 번째 종
류로는 그물 같은 내부 엽맥과 쌍떡잎이 있죠. 체리나무와 커피나무가 이 그룹에
속합니다. 마지막으로 식물은 키에 따라 특징 지어집니다. 아래쪽에는 이끼와 낮
게 자라는 풀, 꽃, 덤불이 있고 마지막으로 여러 높이의 나무들이 있습니다.

11 강의의 주요 목적은 무엇인가?
  (a) 여러 가지 종류의 식물과 그 기능에 대해 논하려고
  (b) 식물이 어떻게 학명으로 분류되는지 보여주려고
  (c) 식물이 분류되는 여러 가지 방법을 조사하려고
  (d) 식물 분류를 위한 더 나은 과학적 체계를 개발하려고
  (e) 어떻게 식물이 새로운 곳으로 퍼질 수 있는지 설명하려고

12 속씨식물과 겉씨식물의 가장 큰 차이점은 무엇인가?
  (a) 내부 엽맥 조직의 특성 (b) 최대한 자랄 수 있는 키
  (c) 안에 있는 씨앗의 수 (d) 씨앗을 퍼뜨리기 위해 사용하는 방법
  (e) 씨앗 외피의 특성

Practice Test
p. 58~p. 59

1 (c)	2 (c)	3 (d)	4 (c)	5 (d)	6 (a)	7 (d)
8 해설 참조	9 (d)	10 (a)				

1

W All living creatures go through cycles that are influenced by the rising and setting of the sun and by the change of the seasons. These patterns are related to the animals' daily needs, such as eating and sleeping, or to more long-term aspects, such as breeding, hibernating, and migrating. The feeding and sleeping patterns animals follow daily are called circadian cycles. Animals are either nocturnal or diurnal. Nocturnal animals are awake during the night and hunt and feed during this time. Diurnal animals are the opposite; they maintain their feeding activities in daylight and fall asleep at night. In contrast, circannian cycles are patterns that animals follow on a yearly basis. Mating is one type of circannian cycle. Some animals have a scheduled reproductive cycle since they have the ability to reproduce only at certain times of the year. Experts call this a mating season. For example, mammals in northern lands reproduce in the spring to allow their offspring time to grow before the winter cold arrives. Other circannian patterns are related to hibernation and migration. When cold weather arrives, some animals, such as bears and squirrels, hibernate in order to use less energy. The annual migrations of birds are common sights in northern lands. How animals know when to follow these circadian and circannian patterns is still not totally understood. Some experts believe hormones are involved while others think it is an instinctive urge that has been in them for generation after generation.

▶ daily needs 일용품 breeding 번식 migrating 이주하는, 이동하는 circadian cycle 24시간 주기 nocturnal 야행성의 diurnal 주행성의 in contrast 그에 반해서, 그와 대조적으로 circannian cycle 1년 주기 mating 교미, 짝짓기 reproduce 생식하다, 번식하다 mating season 발정기 offspring 새끼; 자손 generation after generation 자손 대대로 instinctive urge 본능적인 충동

여 모든 살아있는 생물체는 일출과 일몰, 그리고 계절의 변화에 영향을 받는 주기를 따릅니다. 이 패턴은 먹는 것과 수면같이 일상에 필요한 것 또는 번식, 겨울잠, 이동과 같은 좀 더 장기적인 면과 관련이 있습니다. 동물들이 날마다 따르는 섭취와 수면 패턴을 24시간 주기라고 부릅니다. 동물들은 야행성 아니면 주행성이죠. 야행성 동물은 밤 동안 깨어 있어 이때 사냥을 하고 먹이를 먹습니다. 주행성 동물은 그 반대죠. 낮 동안 먹이 활동을 하고 밤에는 잠을 잡니다. 그에 반해서 1년 주기는 동물이 1년 단위로 따르는 유형입니다. 짝짓기는 1년 주기의 한 종류죠. 일부 동물들은 1년의 특정한 기간에만 번식 능력을 가지기 때문에 정해진 번식 주기가 있습니다. 전문가들은 이것을 발정기라고 부릅니다. 예를 들면 북부지방의 포유동물들은 겨울 추위가 오기 전에 새끼가 자랄 수 있도록 봄에 번식을 합니다. 다른 1년 주기의 형태는 겨울잠 및 이동과 관련이 있죠. 날씨가 추워지면 곰, 다람쥐 같은 일부 동물들은 에너지를 적게 쓰기 위해서 겨울잠을 잡니다. 새가 매년 이동하는 것은 북부지방에서 흔히 볼 수 있는 광경입니다. 동물들이 이 24시간 주기와 1년 주기 패턴을 언제 따라야 하는지를 어떻게 아는가에 대해서는 아직 그다지 알려져 있지 않습니다. 일부 전문가들은 호르몬과 관련이 있다고 믿는 한편, 다른 전문가들은 대대로 그들에게 남아있는 본능적인 충동이라고 생각합니다.

1 담화에 따르면 다음 중 옳은 것은?
    (a) 호르몬이 동물의 24시간 주기와 1년 주기를 결정한다.
    (b) 24시간 주기는 겨울잠, 이주, 짝짓기와 관련이 있다.
    (c) 봄에 새끼가 출생하는 것은 1년 주기의 한 예이다.
    (d) 야행성 동물은 밤에 자고 낮에 사냥을 한다.
    (e) 태양의 움직임은 1년 주기를 촉발하는 열쇠이다.

2-3

G Min-woo, let's review for our biology test.

B Do you think we have to? My head is about ready to explode from all of this studying.

G Come on. You need a good grade. You barely squeaked by on the last test.

B Okay, okay. There's no need to nag me. So, I guess we should start with trees.

G Great. First question. What's the difference between a deciduous and a coniferous tree?

B Coniferous trees have needle-like leaves, stay green all year around, and have cones instead of seeds.

G So they are gymnosperms.

B Right. I forgot about that one. And deciduous trees are... What is it...? Ah... No, don't tell me... Angiosperms. They have covered seeds.

G Correct. And they have broad leaves which change color and fall off every year. Now, what's another name for coniferous trees?

B Evergreens because they stay green all year.

G What are some typical coniferous trees?

B Spruce, pine, fir, some types of oaks, and holly.

G Good so far. Now, what is the tallest species of tree in the world?

B That's not going to be on the test.

G You never know. It might be a bonus question on the test. It's better to be safe than sorry.

B You always worry too much.

G Just answer the question.

B The tallest tree in the world is the Redwood tree in California.

G Good. Now, how tall is the tallest Redwood ever found and measured?

B Aaargghh! I don't know! ___________________________

▶ squeak by 간신히 성공하다 deciduous 낙엽성의 coniferous 침엽수의 gymnosperm 겉씨식물 angiosperm 속씨식물 evergreen 상록수 spruce 전나무, 가문비나무 fir 전나무 oak 상수리나무 holly 서양호랑가시나무

여 민우야, 우리 생물 시험에 대비해 복습하자.
남 그래야 할까? 이 모든 공부 때문에 내 머리는 터지기 일보 직전이라고.
여 자, 어서. 넌 좋은 성적을 받아야 하잖아. 저번 시험에서도 간신히 통과했으면서.
남 알았어, 알았어. 잔소리할 필요는 없잖아. 그럼, 나무에서부터 시작해야겠네.
여 좋아. 첫 번째 문제. 낙엽수와 침엽수의 차이점은 무엇인가?
남 침엽수는 바늘과 같은 나뭇잎이 있고 일 년 내내 푸르지. 그리고 씨앗 대신 방울 열매를 가지고 있어.
여 그리고 침엽수는 겉씨식물이지.
남 맞아. 그건 잊어버렸다. 그리고 낙엽수는… 뭐였지? … 아니야, 말하지 마… 속씨식물. 그것들은 피자종자를 가지고 있어.
여 맞아. 그리고 낙엽수는 해마다 색깔이 바뀌고 낙엽으로 떨어지는 넓은 잎이 있어. 그럼 침엽수의 다른 이름은 뭐지?
남 상록수야. 왜냐하면 침엽수는 1년 내내 푸르거든.
여 대표적인 침엽수로는 어떤 게 있어?
남 가문비나무, 소나무, 전나무, 상수리나무 몇 종, 서양호랑가시나무가 있지.
여 지금까지는 잘하고 있어. 자, 세계에서 가장 키가 큰 나무는?
남 그건 시험에 안 나올 거야.
여 알 수 없지. 시험에 보너스 문제로 나올 수도 있잖아. 나중에 후회하는 것보단 확실하게 해두는 편이 낫지.
남 넌 항상 걱정이 너무 많아 탈이야.
여 묻는 말에 대답이나 하시지.
남 세계에서 가장 큰 나무는 캘리포니아에 있는 레드우드 나무야.
여 좋아. 자, 지금까지 발견된 레드우드 중 가장 큰 것의 높이는 어떻게 되니?
남 으악! 몰라! ___________________________

2 대화를 통해 유추할 수 있는 것은?
    (a) 두 화자는 남매 간이다.
    (b) 침엽수는 낙엽수보다 크다.
    (c) 소녀는 소년보다 학교 성적이 더 좋다.
    (d) 소년은 지난 번 생물 시험을 잘 봤다.
    (e) 시험에 보너스 문제가 있을 것이다.

3 소년은 다음에 뭐라고 말하겠는가?
    (a) 이 시험 준비하는 거 도와줘서 고마워.
    (b) 그냥 내 대신 시험 보는 게 어때?
    (c) 그건 379피트, 즉 115미터 높이야.
    (d) 그만 됐어! 이제 내가 물어볼 차례야.
    (e) 너 완전히 정신이 나갔구나.

M In nature, sometimes two organisms help each other to achieve some benefits. This is called mutualism. For example, ants protect aphids from attacking beetles. In return, the ants get to suck the sweet nectar that aphids produce. This form of mutualism is called facultative mutualism since both species can survive without the other but maintain a relationship for the benefits it gives. While the aphids might suffer losses if beetles attack and no ants are around to protect the aphids, a severing of the ant-aphid relationship in no way means that the aphids will die. Other relationships are more complex and are called obligatory mutualism. If the relationship between the two species involved is severed, then one or both species may die. In the oceans, coral reefs are an example of organisms in an obligatory relationship. Small organisms called zooxanthellae live within the coral. The coral protects the zooxanthellae and provides them with nutrients they need to accomplish photosynthesis. In return, the products of the zooxanthellae photosynthesis give the coral most of its energy. Zooxanthellae will leave the coral if the temperature of the water changes, if there is too much pollution, or if there is too much radiation from the sun at lower water levels. Because zooxanthellae provide the pigments which color the coral, a loss of this organism will cause the coral to turn white. This is called coral bleaching. If the zooxanthellae do not return soon, the coral then dies.

▶ organism 유기체: 생물 mutualism 상리 공생 aphid 진디, 진딧물
in return 답례로: 그 대신에 nectar 과즙, 넥타: 화밀(花蜜) facultative 선택적인,
임의의 sever 끊다, ~의 사이를 가르다 obligatory 필수의, 의무적인
coral reef 산호초 radiation 복사 (에너지): 발광(發光) water level 수위(水位)
pigment 색소 bleaching 표백

남 자연계에서는 때때로 두 종류의 생물이 이득을 얻기 위해 서로 돕습니다. 이것을 상리 공생이라고 부르죠. 예를 들면, 개미는 딱정벌레의 공격으로부터 진딧물을 보호합니다. 그 보답으로 개미는 진딧물이 만들어 내는 달콤한 즙을 빨아먹을 수 있게 되지요. 이러한 형태의 상리 공생은 두 종 모두 다른 한 종이 없어도 살 수는 있지만 그 종이 주는 혜택 때문에 관계를 유지하기 때문에 선택적인 상리 공생이라고 부릅니다. 딱정벌레가 공격할 때 진딧물을 보호할 개미가 주위에 없어서 피해를 입게 될지라도, 개미-신딧물의 관계가 끊어진다는 것이 진딧물이 죽는다는 의미는 아닙니다. 다른 관계는 더 복잡한데요. 이것은 의무적인 상리 공생이라고 부릅니다. 만약 두 종의 관계가 끊어진다면 한 종 또는 두 종 모두 다 죽게 되는 것이죠. 바다에 사는 산호초는 의무적인 관계에 있는 생물들의 한 예입니다. 공생조(共生藻)라고 불리는 작은 생물은 산호 안에서 살죠. 산호는 공생조를 보호하고 광합성에 필요한 영양소를 제공합니다. 그 보답으로 산호는 필요한 대부분의 에너지를 공생조가 광합성으로 만든 산물에서 얻게 됩니다. 만약 수온이 바뀌거나 너무 오염이 되었거나 낮은 수위에 태양 복사열이 너무 많을 경우 공생조는 산호를 떠나게 됩니다. 공생조는 산호를 물들이는 색소를 제공하기 때문에 이 생물이 없으면 산호의 색깔이 하얘집니다. 이것을 산호 표백이라고 부르죠. 공생조가 곧 돌아오지 않으면 산호는 죽게 됩니다.

4 왜 개미와 진딧물의 관계를 선택적인 상리 공생이라고 부르는가?
(a) 만약 개미와 진딧물 사이의 관계가 끊어지게 되면 둘 다 살아남을 수 없기 때문에
(b) 개미가 딱정벌레의 공격으로부터 진딧물을 보호하는 것은 선택적인 상리 공생의 전형적인 징조이기 때문에
(c) 두 종 모두 그 관계에서 이득을 취하는 한편, 다른 한 종이 없다 해도 둘 다 살아남을 수 있기 때문에
(d) 개미와 진딧물은 공동의 적이 있으므로 힘을 합쳐야 하기 때문에
(e) 그들의 관계는 너무 오랫동안 계속되어 관계를 끝내는 것이 거의 불가능하기 때문에

5 담화를 통해 유추할 수 있는 것은?
(a) 개미는 딱정벌레와 성공적인 전투를 치른 후에야 진딧물의 즙을 보상으로 받는다.
(b) 산호가 하얗게 변하면 짧은 시간 내에 반드시 죽을 것이다.
(c) 상리 공생은 동물 사이의 관계에서만 존재하고 식물 사이에서는 존재하지 않는다.
(d) 공생조는 산호가 죽기 전에 산호 숙주에게 돌아가기도 한다.
(e) 진딧물은 공격하는 딱정벌레에 대항해 싸울 그 어떤 방어체계도 가지고 있지 않다.

6 Level up

M You certainly have a lovely garden. There are so many different flowers and bushes.

W Thank you very much. Is there anything that strikes your fancy?

M I think those are some pretty flowers. What are they called?

W That's the Miss Kim lilac.

M Who's Miss Kim, and why does she have a flower named after her?

W The flower originates from Korea. It was named after the typist of an American official. He brought the seeds to America in 1947.

M I'm glad he did. Wow, they smell great.

W Yes, the Miss Kim lilac is one of the most fragrant of all flowers. Some people say it smells even better than roses.

M It also has a wonderful lavender and burgundy red color.

W Yes, it is usually green and lavender, but its green leaves change color in the fall.

M How big does it get?

W It can grow to about two meters in height and spread out about two meters.

M Is it hard to take care of?

W No, not really. The only problem is water. If it goes without water for some time, it will shed its foliage.

▶ fancy 기호, 선호 official 관리, 공무원 lavender 라벤더 색(엷은 자주색)
burgundy 암홍색 spread out (가지 등이) 활짝 퍼지다 shed (잎, 씨 등이) 떨어지다 foliage 잎

남 정말 정원이 예쁘군요. 여러 가지 꽃과 관목이 정말 많네요.
여 고마워요. 마음에 드는 게 있나요?
남 저 꽃들이 참 예쁘네요. 이름이 뭐죠?
여 미스 김 라일락이라고 해요.
남 미스 김이 누군데요? 왜 꽃에다 그 이름을 붙인 거죠?
여 그 꽃의 원산지는 한국이에요. 그 꽃은 한 미국 관리의 타이피스트 이름을 따서 붙였죠. 그 관리는 1947년에 미국으로 씨앗을 가져왔어요.
남 그 사람이 씨앗을 가져와서 다행이네요. 와, 정말 향이 좋군요.
여 네, 미스 김 라일락은 가장 향기로운 꽃 중 하나죠. 어떤 사람들은 장미보다 향이 더 좋다고도 해요.
남 멋진 라벤더 색과 암홍색도 있네요.
여 네, 대개 녹색과 라벤더 색이지만 가을에는 녹색이었던 잎의 색깔이 변하죠.

남 얼마나 커지나요?

여 키는 2미터 정도까지 자랄 수 있고 가지는 약 2미터 정도 퍼져나가죠.

남 돌보기가 힘든가요?

여 아니, 별로요. 유일한 문제는 물이에요. 물을 안 주면 잎이 떨어지거든요.

6 **What aspects of the Miss Kim lilac does the man find special?**
남자가 특별하다고 느낀 미스 김 라일락의 특징은 무엇인가?

  (a) The fragrance and the colors of the plant
   식물의 향기와 색깔

  (b) The size and the name of the plant   식물의 크기와 이름

  (c) The colors and the height of the plant   식물의 색깔과 키

  (d) The fragrance and the origin of the plant
   식물의 향기와 원산지

  (e) The size and the colors of the plant   식물의 크기와 색깔

7 **Level up**

W Alligators are very good swimmers, and what makes them so is the structure of their lungs. An alligator's lungs are not just for breathing; they also play an important role in the creature's ability to dive, surface, and roll over to the left and right while in the water. A special set of muscles attached to the lungs and liver pulls these organs back when the alligator wants to dive. The buoyancy of the alligator shifts, and this helps tilt the alligator's head downward, making diving easier. When the alligator wants to surface, it relaxes these muscles to shift its buoyancy forward, which allows the alligator to raise its head more easily. When the alligator wants to roll to the right, its breathing muscles on the right side contract, which squeezes the lungs smaller, so there is more air in the left lung. Because of this greater amount of air, the left side has more buoyancy and rises upward, and then the alligator can roll to the right more easily.

▶ alligator 악어 lung 폐 surface (고래 등이) 떠오르다, 부상하다 roll 구르다, 뒹굴다 liver 간 organ 장기: 기관(器官) buoyancy 부력: 부양성(浮揚性) shift 바뀌다: 위치가 변경되다 tilt 기울다: 기울이다 relax 늦추다: ~의 힘을 빼다 contract 수축하다: 수축시키다 squeeze 압착하다, 죄다

여 악어는 수영을 매우 잘하는데요, 이것은 악어의 폐 구조 때문이죠. 악어의 폐는 숨을 쉬기 위한 것만은 아닙니다. 악어의 폐는 악어가 잠수하고 물에 떠오르고 물속에서 몸을 왼쪽, 오른쪽으로 굴리는 데에도 중요한 역할을 합니다. 폐와 간에 붙어 있는 특수한 근육이 악어가 잠수하려고 할 때 폐와 간을 뒤로 잡아당깁니다. 악어의 부력이 바뀌면서 악어의 머리가 밑으로 기울도록 도와줘 잠수가 쉬워지죠. 악어가 물에 떠오르려고 할 때는 이 근육들의 힘을 빼서 부력을 앞으로 이동해 머리를 더 쉽게 들어올릴 수 있습니다. 악어가 오른쪽으로 구르려 할 때는 오른쪽에 있는 호흡 근육이 수축하게 되고 이로써 폐를 더 작게 압착해 왼쪽 폐에 더 많은 공기가 들어가게 됩니다. 그만큼 더 많은 양의 공기로 왼쪽 부분이 더 큰 부력을 갖게 돼서 위로 올라가게 되고 악어는 오른쪽으로 더 쉽게 구를 수 있게 되는 것이죠.

7 **What is NOT true according to the talk?**
담화에 따르면 다음 중 사실이 <u>아닌</u> 것은?

  (a) The lungs have more than one function in alligators.
   악어의 폐는 한 가지 이상의 기능을 한다.

  (b) Forward buoyancy helps an alligator to surface.
   전방 부력은 악어가 수면에 떠오르는 데 도움이 된다.

  (c) Increased left lung air causes a roll to the right.

늘어난 왼쪽 폐는 오른쪽으로 구를 수 있게 해준다.

  (d) Muscles pull the lungs forwards when alligators dive.
   악어가 잠수할 때 근육은 폐를 앞으로 잡아당긴다.

  (e) Muscles pull the lungs and liver forward and back.
   근육은 폐와 간을 앞과 뒤로 잡아당긴다.

8

M Humans and animals hear in a variety of ways. Most vertebrates have ears which direct sound to a membrane or bones which then vibrate. The brain then interprets these sounds. Sounds are measured by the frequency of the sound waves per second in units called hertz. The normal range of audible sound for humans is from 16 to a little over 16,000 hertz. Sounds above 20,000 hertz are called ultrasound. In the animal kingdom, many animals can hear in the ultrasound range, and hearing ability varies from species to species. The mouse can hear as high as 91,000 hertz but has trouble with lower frequency sounds and cannot hear sounds below 1,000 hertz. Dogs are well known for their hearing ability, which covers a range from 67 to 45,000 hertz. Cats have even more sensitive hearing, which goes from 45 to 64,000 hertz. Bats have the greatest range of hearing among land mammals. It goes from 2,000 to 110,000 hertz, and they use their hearing to "see" in the dark by echolocation. Bats send out high-pitched screeches and then judge the distance to objects by the time the echo takes to return to their ears. Some marine mammals can hear at a greater range than the bat. The porpoise has the greatest range; it starts at 75 hertz and goes to at least 40,000 hertz above the bat's range.

▶ vertebrate 척추동물: 척추의 direct 돌리다, 향하게 하다 membrane 세포막 vibrate 진동하다: 진동시키다 frequency 주파수 audible 들리는, 들을 수 있는 ultrasound 초음파 echolocation 반향 정위(박쥐 등이 발사한 초음파의 반향으로 물체의 존재를 측정하는 능력) high-pitched (감도 등이) 높은: 음조가 높은 screech 날카로운 외침, 쇳소리 marine 바다의, 해양의 porpoise 돌고래 (무리)

남 인간과 동물은 여러 가지 방법으로 소리를 듣습니다. 대부분의 척추동물은 소리를 세포막이나 뼈로 향하게 한 다음 진동시키는 귀를 가지고 있습니다. 그러면 뇌는 이 소리를 해석합니다. 소리는 헤르츠라고 하는 초당 음파의 주파수로 측정됩니다. 인간이 들을 수 있는 소리의 정상 범위는 16에서 1만 6,000헤르츠를 약간 넘습니다. 2만 헤르츠 이상의 소리는 초음파라고 부릅니다. 동물계에서는 많은 동물이 초음파를 들을 수 있고 청력은 종에 따라 다양합니다. 쥐는 9만 1천 헤르츠까지 들을 수 있지만 낮은 주파수를 듣기는 어려워서 1,000헤르츠 미만의 소리는 들을 수 없습니다. 개는 청력이 좋은 것으로 유명한데 67에서 4만 5,000헤르츠까지의 영역을 들을 수 있습니다. 고양이는 더 예민한 청력을 가지고 있어서 45에서 6만 4,000헤르츠까지 들을 수 있습니다. 박쥐는 육지 포유동물 중에서 가장 넓은 범위를 들을 수 있는 청력을 가지고 있습니다. 박쥐는 2,000에서 11만 헤르츠까지 들을 수 있고, 청력을 이용해 반향 정위로 어둠 속에서 '볼 수' 있습니다. 박쥐는 음조가 높은 날카로운 소리를 내어 메아리가 박쥐의 귀에 들리는 시간으로 물체와의 거리를 판단합니다. 일부 바다 포유동물은 박쥐보다 더 넓은 범위를 들을 수 있습니다. 돌고래는 가장 넓은 범위를 들을 수 있습니다. 75헤르츠에서 시작하여 박쥐가 들을 수 있는 영역보다 적어도 4만 헤르츠 높은 영역까지 들을 수 있습니다.

8 언급된 동물들이 들을 수 있는 가청 범위를 넣어 표를 완성하시오.

동물	가청 범위 (헤르츠)
쥐	1,000 – 91,000
개	67 – 45,000
고양이	45 – 64,000
박쥐	2,000 – 110,000
돌고래	75 – 150,000

9-10 Integrated Questions

Reading

▶ primates 영장류 herbivore 초식동물 carnivore 육식동물; 식충동물
colobus 콜로부스 속(屬) 원숭이(꼬리가 발달한 아프리카 원숭이) colony 집단, 군생
game 사냥감; 표적, 목적물 sharpen 깎다, 뾰족하게 하다 bush baby 갈라고
원숭이 make headlines 신문에 크게 취급되다 controversy 논쟁, 논의

영장류는 인간을 동물 세계와 연결시키는 가장 밀접한 연결 고리이다. 이러한 이유로 영장류는 널리 연구되어 왔다. 대부분의 영장류는 초식동물인데, 이는 그 동물들이 식물을 먹는다는 의미이다. 몇몇 종, 특히 침팬지는 육식 동물로, 서아프리카의 침팬지들은 빨간 콜로부스 속 원숭이를 열심히 사냥해 죽이고 먹었다. 보다 최근에 전문가들은 서아프리카 세네갈에 있는 침팬지 집단이 몸집이 작은 사냥감을 사냥할 때 창 같이 생긴 막대기를 무기로 사용하는 것을 관찰했다. 영장류가 도구를 사용한다는 것은 알려져 있었지만 도구를 만드는 이유는 알려져 있지 않다. 침팬지를 상당 기간 관찰한 후에 연구원들은 그 해답을 알게 되었다. 침팬지는 작은 나뭇가지의 잎은 떼어 버리고 이빨로 한쪽 끝을 뾰족하게 한 다음 이 창처럼 생긴 무기를 갈라고 원숭이라는 작은 동물들이 흔히 낮잠을 청하는 나무줄기 구멍 속에 찔러 넣는 데 사용했다. 학자들은 적어도 40건의 사례에서 이러한 활동을 관찰했다. 침팬지가 다른 동물들을 죽이기 위해 적극적으로 도구를 만든다는 소식이 전 세계에 알려지자 이는 대서특필되었고 침팬지의 이러한 도구 사용의 의미와 이유에 관한 논쟁도 일어났다.

W Primates are very similar to humans in many ways, including their use of tools. Primates use twigs to dig termites out of logs as well as rocks to open nuts and hard-shelled fruits. Rocks have even been used as weapons. Chimps are the main primates observed using tools. Tool use among chimps received a lot of attention in 2007 when reports came out that chimps were deliberately making spears and hunting small game with them in West Africa. These reports caused a media frenzy as reporters and editors attempted to sensationalize the story. Images of chimps wielding and throwing spears at running game came to the readers' minds. But this was far from the truth. In reality, the chimps used the spears to stab sleeping bush babies, a small species of animal, in holes in tree trunks. Some primate experts stated that the activity wasn't really hunting because the bush babies were sleeping when killed. An ever greater controversy arose from the fact that the observers noted that it was the females and young chimps that did the hunting while no adult males were involved. This went against most current views on chimpanzee behavior, which saw adult males as dominant player since they are more aggressive and violent than females and young. In addition, there is some difficulty with primate experts recognizing chimps of both sexes and all ages exhibiting humanlike behavior. Most experts in primate studies are warned in their early days of study to avoid seeing primates as humanlike. Placing human values and characteristics on animals is called anthropomorphizing. However, with chimps, it is hard not to do this since they are perhaps our closest relatives in the animal kingdom.

▶ twig 잔가지, 작은 가지 termite 흰개미 frenzy 열광; 격분; 광포 deliberately 의식적으로, 고의로 sensationalize 선정적으로 보도하다 wield (칼, 도구 등을) 휘두르다, 사용하다 stab 찌르다, 찔러 죽이다 go against 반대하다, ~에 반하다 dominant 지배적인; 우세한 anthropomorphize (신, 동물을) 인격화하다, 의인화하다

여 영장류는 도구 사용을 포함한 많은 면에서 인간과 매우 흡사합니다. 영장류는 견과류와 딱딱한 껍질이 있는 과일을 깔 때뿐만 아니라 통나무에서 흰개미를 파내는 데에도 잔가지를 사용합니다. 바위는 무기로도 사용되어 왔습니다. 침팬지는 도구를 사용한다고 알려진 주요 영장류입니다. 2007년에 침팬지가 서아프리카에서 의도적으로 창을 만들어 작은 사냥감을 사냥한다는 보고가 나오자 침팬지의 도구 사용이 큰 주목을 받았습니다. 리포터들과 편집자들이 그 이야기를 선정적으로 보도하려고 하면서, 이 보고는 대중 매체에 광풍을 일으켰죠. 독자의 머리엔 도망가는 사냥감에게 창을 휘두르고 던지는 침팬지의 모습이 떠올랐죠. 하지만 이것은 진실과는 거리가 멀었습니다. 실제로 침팬지는 나무줄기의 구멍에서 잠자는 작은 종의 동물인 갈라고 원숭이를 찌르려고 창을 사용했습니다. 어떤 영장류 전문가들은 갈라고 원숭이들이 자고 있었기 때문에 이것은 진정한 의미의 사냥이 아니라고 말했습니다. 또한 그 관찰자들이 암컷과 어린 침팬지가 사냥을 하는 반면 어른 수컷은 사냥에 참여하지 않는 것을 발견하자, 이는 더 큰 논쟁을 불러일으켰습니다. 이것은 장성한 수컷이 암컷과 어린 침팬지보다 더 공격적이고 폭력적이기 때문에 어른 수컷을 주도자로 보는 침팬지 행동에 대한 대부분의 최근 관점에 반하는 것이었으니까요. 게다가 영장류 전문가는 인간처럼 행동하는 암수 및 온갖 연령의 침팬지를 식별하는 데 어려움을 겪습니다. 영장류를 연구하는 대부분의 학자들은 연구 초기에 영장류를 인간과 같이 보지 말라고 주의를 받습니다. 인간의 가치와 특성을 동물에게 두는 것을 의인화라고 합니다. 하지만 침팬지는 동물계에서 우리의 가장 가까운 동족이기 때문에 이렇게 안 하기가 힘듭니다.

9 읽기와 듣기 지문에 따르면 다음 중 사실이 <u>아닌</u> 것은?

(a) 서아프리카의 침팬지가 무기로 작은 동물들을 죽이는 것이 관찰되었다.
(b) 대개 장성한 수컷이 사냥을 하고 공격적인 행동을 보인다.
(c) 때때로 침팬지는 다른 종의 원숭이를 잡아먹기 위해 공격해 죽인다.
(d) 침팬지가 창과 같은 도구를 사용한다는 보고서는 폭넓은 학술적 지지를 받았다.
(e) 유인원 학자들은 침팬지가 인간과 매우 비슷하다고 생각해서는 안 된다. 그러한 태도는 연구를 왜곡할 수 있기 때문이다.

10 읽기와 듣기 지문에서 유추할 수 있는 것은?

(a) 2007년 전에는 침팬지가 창을 사용하는 것이 관찰된 적이 없다.
(b) 서아프리카는 살아 있는 침팬지가 많이 사는 서식지이다.
(c) 갈라고 원숭이는 대개 공격을 당할 때 자신을 방어한다.
(d) 침팬지는 때때로 자신보다 더 큰 동물을 적극적으로 사냥하고 공격한다.
(e) 암컷 침팬지는 관찰자 앞에서 공격적인 성향을 숨긴다.

*Dictation 정답: Exercise 스크립트 밑줄 참조

Preparation
p. 65

Vocabulary Preview

A

1 hypocrite: 자신이 믿는 것과 반대되는 행동을 하는 사람
2 self-esteem: 사람이 자신에 대해 어떻게 생각하는지
3 conscience: 옳고 그름에 대한 판단력
4 counterfeiting: 속이기 위해 어떤 것을 베끼는 행위
5 purging: 어떤 것을 쫓아내는 것

B

1 lethal force / 때때로 경찰은 위험한 범죄자들을 잡기 위해 치명적 위력[총기]을 써야 한다.
2 defamation / 블로거들은 자기 블로그에 다른 사람들에 대한 거짓말을 쓸 경우 명예 훼손죄로 기소될 수 있다.
3 copycat / 유명한 사람이 자살을 하는 경우 스타의 죽음을 함께하고 싶은 광팬들의 모방 자살이 속출하곤 한다.
4 terminally ill / 사람은 죽을 병에 걸리면 의사에게 자살을 도와달라고 부탁할지도 모른다.
5 Knockoff / 모조품은 제조업자들에게 매년 수십억의 이윤손실을 안기고 있다.
6 gave in / 나쁘다는 것을 알았지만 존은 친구들의 압력에 못 이겨 담배를 피웠다.
7 alimony / 그녀는 이혼 후에 전남편이 위자료를 제때 지불하지 않아 고생했다.

Expressions and Meanings

1 난 매우 건강해.	**f** 난 매우 건강해.
2 너 기운 없어 보인다.	**a** 너 슬퍼 보여.
3 우린 같은 처지야.	**g** 우리는 비슷한 처지에 처했어.
4 정부를 상대로 싸우는 것은 무모한 짓이야.	**b** 정부에 대항하는 것은 어려워.
5 현실을 인정해야 해.	**c** 상황을 있는 그대로 받아들여.
6 그것의 중요성은 너무 과장되어 있어.	**e** 그것은 실제보다 더 중요한 것처럼 보여.
7 정부가 감시하고 있어.	**d** 정부가 국민들을 감시하고 있어.

Listening Drill 1
p. 66~p. 67

Monolog

O (1) obese (2) body image (3) dieting (4) underweight (5) exercise (6) chews gum (7) eat (8) large (9) guilt (10) overeating (11) get rid of (12) vomiting (13) emotional (14) self-esteem (15) in control of

G 1 (b) 2 (a)

S (1) F (2) T (3) T (4) F

W Eating disorders are very serious problems that affect many young people. Eating disorders are caused by eating too much or not eating enough food and are usually a symptom of a deeper, more serious emotional problem. The two most common forms of eating disorders are anorexia nervosa and bulimia nervosa. People suffering from anorexia nervosa think they are obese and are sensitive about how others may think of them. Since they are obsessed with their body image, they are constantly dieting and counting calories and are almost always underweight. Many of them may even stop eating and starve themselves. Anorexics also engage in strenuous exercise in an effort to burn more calories. They may also take diet pills, smoke cigarettes, and chew gum to control their eating. On the other hand, people suffering from bulimia nervosa have a different problem. They eat large amounts of food in a short time, which is called binging. Afterwards, they feel extreme guilt about this overeating and try to get rid of the food by either self-inducing vomiting or taking laxatives. This process is called purging. Both bulimics and anorexics usually have low self-esteem and feel the need to be in more control of their lives. Bulimia and anorexia are more common with teenage girls and younger women, but there has been a recent increase in the number of males affected with these disorders.

▶ eating disorder 섭식장애 symptom 증후, 증상 anorexia nervosa 신경성 무식욕증, 거식증 bulimia nervosa 신경성 과식증 obese 비만의 be obsessed with ~에 집착하다 body image 신체상(身體像), 자신의 신체에 대해 가지는 심상(心像) starve 굶주리다: 단식하다 anorexic 신경성 무식욕증 환자; 식욕 부진의 strenuous 격렬한 binge 진탕 먹고 마시다, 말처럼 대식하다 afterwards 그 후에: 후에, 나중에 laxative 설사하게 하는: 완하제(緩下劑), 하제 purge 하제를 써서 제거하다: 깨끗이 하다 self-esteem 자존심, 자부심

여 섭식장애는 많은 젊은이들에게 악영향을 미치는 매우 심각한 문제입니다. 섭식장애는 너무 많이 먹거나 음식을 충분히 먹지 않아 초래되며, 대개는 더 뿌리 깊고 심각한 정서적 문제의 증후입니다. 가장 보편적인 형태의 두 가지 섭식장애는 거식증과 폭식증입니다. 거식증을 앓고 있는 사람은 자기가 비만이라고 생각하면서 남들이 자신에 대해 어떻게 생각할지에 민감합니다. 거식증 환자는 자신의 신체 이미지에 집착하기 때문에 계속 다이어트를 하고 칼로리를 계산하며 거의 늘 저체중입니다. 많은 거식증 환자들이 심지어 먹지도 않고 굶습니다. 또한 칼로리를 더 많이 연소시키기 위한 노력의 일환으로 격렬한 운동을 하죠. 그들은 또한 먹는 것을 조절하기 위해 다이어트 약을 복용하고 담배를 피우며 껌을 씹기도 합니다. 반면 폭식증을 앓는 사람들에게는 다른 문제가 있습니다. 폭식증 환자들은 단시간에 많은 양의 음식을 먹는데요, 그것을 '대식'이라고 합니다. 그 후에 그들은 과식한 것에 대해 굉장한 죄책감을 느껴 스스로 구토를 유도하거나 설사약을 복용해서 먹은 음식을 빼내고자 하죠. 이러한 과정을 '축출'이라고 합니다. 폭식증 환자나 거식증 환자는 둘 다 자존감이 낮으며 자신의 삶을 더 관리할 필요가 있습니다. 폭식증과 거식증은 십대 소녀와 젊은 여성에게 더 흔하지만 최근에는 이 병을 앓는 남성의 수도 증가하고 있습니다.

General Questions

1 담화의 주된 목적은 무엇인가?
 (a) 십대 소녀들이 다이어트하는 이유를 설명하려고
 (b) 젊은이들 사이의 섭식문제를 기술하려고
 (c) 폭식을 유발하는 심리에 대해 조사하려고
 (d) 몇 가지 위험한 살빼는 방법에 대해 경고하려고

2 다음 중 가장 잘 요약된 것을 고르시오.
 (a) 섭식장애는 음식문제가 중심에 놓여 있지만, 실제 원인은 치료되지 않은 심리적 상태에 있을지도 모른다.
 (b) 많은 젊은이들, 특히 여성들은 자신의 신체 이미지에 너무 집착하여 섭식장애를 겪게 된다.

다시 듣고 옳은 문장에는 T, 틀린 문장에는 F를 쓰시오.
(1) 거식증을 앓는 사람들은 과체중이다.
(2) 낮은 자존감은 섭식장애와 관련 있는 한 가지 문제이다.
(3) 폭식증을 앓는 사람들은 너무 많이 먹은 것에 대해 죄책감을 느낀다.
(4) 먹은 음식을 억지로 빼내는 행위는 거식증 환자에게 흔하다.

Dialog

N (1) month (2) depressed (3) school nurse (4) last year (5) girl's mother / avoid (6) depressed / agrees / convinced by girl's persuasion

G 1 (b) 2 (b)

S (1) F (2) T (3) T (4) T

G Hey, Tim. How's it going? I haven't seen you in a while.

B Oh, hey, Jenny. I'm fine.

G You don't seem fine. I haven't seen you in like a month. Have you been sick?

B No, I'm right as rain.

G Really? Well, a bunch of us are going to the park after school. You want to come?

B Sorry. I've got things to do.

G Oh? Such as?

B Just stuff.

G You seem a little bummed out, Tim. You look like you haven't washed your hair in weeks. What's going on?

B It's nothing. It's just...

G What? Tell me. Come on!

B Ah, forget about it.

G Tim, I think maybe you should talk with someone. Are you having trouble at home? I think maybe you're feeling depressed.

B Only old people get depressed.

G No, that's not true. A lot of young people feel depressed. It's not so uncommon. We're under a lot of pressure from school and our parents. And sometimes things happen at home which we can't control, so we don't know what to do. You really should talk with someone who can help you. You know, I was feeling pretty bad last year after my mom got sick and I didn't know what to do. Then, one day, I just went to see the school nurse, and we talked. It really helped.

B The school nurse can help?

G Yeah. She's really nice. Why don't you go talk to her? We can go together if you want.

B Okay, maybe that's a good idea.

▶ depressed 우울한; 의기소침한 pressure 압박, 중압 school nurse 양호선생님

여 안녕, 팀. 어떻게 지내? 정말 오랜만이야.
남 오, 안녕, 제니. 난 잘 지내.
여 잘 지내는 것처럼 보이지 않는데. 근 한 달 정도 못 봤었네. 너 어디 아프니?
남 아니야, 나 무척 건강해.
여 정말? 아무튼, 방과 후에 몇 명 모여서 공원에 갈 건데, 너도 같이 갈래?
남 미안. 할 일이 있어.

여 그래? 무슨 일?
남 그냥 할 일.
여 너 좀 기운 없어 보여. 머리도 몇 주 안 감은 것 같고. 무슨 일이야?
남 아무 것도 아니야. 그냥…
여 뭐야? 말해봐. 어서!
남 야, 관두자.
여 팀, 난 네가 누군가에게 털어놓아야 한다고 생각해. 집에 무슨 문제 있니? 우울한 것 같은데.
남 나이 든 사람들이나 우울해하지.
여 아냐, 그렇지 않아. 젊은 사람들 중에도 우울해하는 사람은 많아. 그렇게 드문 일이 아니라고. 우리는 학교와 부모님으로부터 많은 압박을 받고 있잖아. 게다가 집에 우리가 통제할 수 없는 일이 생겨서 어떻게 해야 할지 모를 때도 있고. 널 진짜로 도와줄 수 있는 사람과 얘기를 해야 해. 너도 알다시피 작년에 난 엄마가 아프시고 나서 어떻게 해야 할지 몰라 마음이 무척 힘들었잖아. 그러던 어느 날, 양호선생님을 찾아가서 이야기를 나눴어. 정말 도움이 되더라고.
남 양호선생님이 도움이 될까?
여 응. 굉장히 좋은 분이셔. 양호선생님께 가서 이야기를 해 보는 게 어떨까? 원한다면 같이 갈 수도 있어.
남 좋아, 좋은 생각인 것 같아.

1 대화의 요지는 무엇인가??
   (a) 소년은 자신이 앓고 있는 병의 증상에 대해 묘사한다.
   (b) 소녀는 정서적 문제를 가지고 있는 친구를 도우려 한다.
   (c) 소년은 몸이 좋지 않아 양호선생님을 찾아간다.
   (d) 소녀는 자신의 우울증에 대해 친구와 이야기하는 것을 이상하게 생각한다.

2 다음 중 가장 잘 요약된 것을 고르시오.
   (a) 소년은 문제가 심각하지 않다고 생각하기 때문에 그 문제를 극복할 수 있게 도움을 주려는 친구의 제안을 거절한다.
   (b) 소년의 친구는 최근 소년이 평소와 다르다고 느껴서 그에게 도움을 받도록 권한다.

다시 듣고 옳은 문장에는 T, 틀린 문장에는 F를 쓰시오.
(1) 소년은 소녀랑 그 친구들과 함께 공원에 몹시 가고 싶어했다.
(2) 소녀는 도움이 필요하다는 것을 소년이 인정할 때까지 그와 계속 이야기했다.
(3) 소녀는 양호선생님이 소녀을 도울 자격이 있다고 생각한다.
(4) 과거에 소녀는 소년이 지금 느끼는 것과 비슷하게 우울해했다.

Listening Drill 2   p. 68~p. 69

Long Lecture

O (1) manmade (2) male (3) pill (4) skin gels (5) creams (6) muscle mass (7) aggressive (8) acne (9) sterility (10) increase (11) baldness (12) growth (13) deepening (14) masculine (15) shrinkage (16) baldness

1 (b)   **2** (b)   **3** (1) T (2) F (3) F (4) T   **4** (d)

Dictation 정답: 스크립트 밑줄 참조

M Some recent studies <u>have</u> <u>shown</u> that there has been an increase in the use of <u>anabolic</u> <u>steroids</u> by teenagers in America. Many teenage <u>athletes</u> are <u>under</u> a lot of pressure to <u>make</u> <u>sports</u> <u>teams</u> and to perform well. Instead of taking the time to <u>train</u> <u>properly</u>, eat well, and <u>get</u> <u>healthy</u>, a lot of these amateur athletes <u>end</u> <u>up</u> <u>using</u> <u>steroids</u>. Steroids are <u>manmade</u> <u>hormones</u> that have the <u>same</u> <u>effects</u> <u>as</u> the natural male hormone testosterone. Users take steroids in <u>pill</u> <u>form</u>, <u>inject</u> <u>them</u> with a needle, or use skin gels and creams that <u>contain</u> <u>steroids</u>. Steroids aid in the development of <u>muscle</u> <u>mass</u> and <u>strength</u>, but they also have a lot of <u>dangerous</u> <u>side</u> <u>effects</u>, which many young people <u>are</u> <u>unaware</u> <u>of</u> or just <u>ignore</u>. The most common side effects in teenage boys are an increase in <u>aggressive</u> <u>behavior</u>, the development of <u>more</u> <u>acne</u>, <u>liver</u> <u>damage</u>, possible <u>sterility</u>, an increase in breast size, and early <u>baldness</u>. There is also the <u>risk</u> that the <u>user</u> <u>will</u> <u>stop</u> <u>growing</u>. The increased amount of testosterone may <u>fool</u> <u>the</u> <u>body</u> <u>into</u> <u>thinking</u> the user is an adult, so it will stop <u>producing</u> <u>growth</u> <u>hormones</u>. It's not just teenage boys using steroids though. Some teenage girls use them because they want the <u>lean</u>, <u>muscular</u> <u>bodies</u> common with the <u>celebrities</u> they see in magazines. For teenage girls, the side effects of <u>taking</u> <u>male</u> <u>hormones</u> are a <u>deepening</u> of the voice, a more <u>masculine</u> <u>appearance</u>, <u>baldness</u>, and <u>shrinkage</u> of the breasts. <u>Bad</u> <u>breath</u> and <u>body</u> <u>odor</u> are also possible side effects for both men and women.

▶ anabolic steroid 단백 동화 스테로이드(근육 증강제) under pressure 압력을 받아, 강요되어 end up 마침내 ~으로 되다; 끝나다 manmade 인조의, 인공의; 합성의 testosterone (화학) 테스토스테론 (남성 호르몬의 일종) inject 주사(주입)하다 side effect 부작용 acne 여드름 sterility 불임(증) baldness 대머리 lean 마른, 야윈 celebrity (유명) 연예인 masculine 남성적인 shrinkage 수축; 축소 body odor 체취; 암내

남 최근의 몇몇 연구에서 미국 십대들의 스테로이드 사용이 증가하고 있는 것으로 나타났습니다. 많은 십대 운동선수들은 스포츠 팀에 들어가서 실력을 발휘하는 것에 대해 많은 스트레스를 받습니다. 적절히 훈련하고, 잘 먹고, 건강해지는 데 시간을 들이는 대신 많은 아마추어 선수들이 스테로이드를 사용하고 맙니다. 스테로이드는 천연 남성 호르몬인 테스토스테론과 동일한 효과를 가지는 인공 호르몬입니다. 스테로이드 사용자들은 알약 형태로 스테로이드를 섭취하거나, 주사를 맞거나, 스테로이드가 함유된 스킨 젤과 크림을 사용합니다. 스테로이드는 근육량과 힘을 늘리는 데 도움을 주지만 위험한 부작용도 많습니다. 그러나 많은 젊은이들이 그것에 대해 모르거나 그냥 무시해 버리죠. 십대 소년들 사이에서 가장 보편적인 부작용으로는 공격적인 성향의 증가, 여드름 증가, 간 손상, 불임 가능성, 가슴이 커지는 것, 탈모의 조기 발생이 있습니다. 스테로이드 사용자의 성장이 멈출 위험도 있습니다. 증가한 테스토스테론은 스테로이드 사용자를 성인이라고 인식하게끔 사용자의 몸을 속여 성장 호르몬의 생산을 멈추게 할 수도 있습니다. 하지만 십대 소년만 스테로이드를 사용하는 것은 아닙니다. 일부 십대 소녀들도 잡지에 나오는 유명 연예인들에게 공통적인 날씬한 근육질의 몸매를 갖고 싶어 스테로이드를 사용합니다. 십대 소녀들이 남성 호르몬을 섭취하면서 생기는 부작용은 굵은 목소리, 남성적 외모, 탈모, 가슴 축소입니다. 입 냄새와 암내도 남성과 여성 둘 다에게 나타날 수 있는 부작용입니다.

1 강의 주제는 무엇인가?
(a) 스테로이드의 올바른 사용법
(b) 십대에게 나타나는 스테로이드 부작용
(c) 젊은이들이 스테로이드를 사용하는 이유
(d) 어린 운동선수들 사이의 스테로이드 남용

2 다음 중 가장 잘 요약된 것을 고르시오.
(a) 스테로이드는 사람의 운동능력을 향상시켜 주지만 신중하게 소량으로 섭취해야 한다.
(b) 비록 스테로이드에 몇 가지 긍정적인 효과가 있지만 부작용이 있을 수 있어 사용하기에는 위험하다.

3 옳은 문장에는 T, 틀린 문장에는 F를 쓰시오.
(1) 일부 미국 십대들은 스테로이드 복용을 팀에서 좋은 성적을 내는 매우 효과적인 방법이라고 생각한다.
(2) 스테로이드는 남성 호르몬인 테스토스테론과 같은 작용을 하는 천연 호르몬이다.
(3) 스테로이드는 원래 자라기로 예정돼 있던 키보다 더 자라게 돕는다.
(4) 스테로이드를 섭취하는 젊은 여성은 더 남성적인 외모를 갖게 된다.

4 소년들 사이에서 나타날 수 있는 스테로이드 부작용으로 언급되지 <u>않은</u> 것은?
(a) 성격이 매우 공격적으로 변할 수 있다.
(b) 스테로이드로 일찍부터 탈모를 겪을 수 있다.
(c) 미래에 아이를 갖는 것이 어려울 수도 있다.
(d) 스테로이드 복용으로 가슴이 작아질 수 있다.

1 (d)	**2** 해설 참조	**3** (b), (e)	**4** (d)	**5** (c)	**6** (b)
7 (d)	**8** (b)	**9** (b)	**10** 해설 참조	**11** (d)	**12** (b)

1

W An important issue facing children and teens everywhere is <u>peer</u> <u>pressure</u>. It's <u>vital</u> for young people to understand what peer pressure is and <u>how</u> <u>to</u> <u>handle</u> <u>it</u>. Firstly, your peers are the people who are your friends, the people <u>in</u> <u>your</u> <u>class</u>, and the people who are <u>around</u> <u>the</u> <u>same</u> <u>age</u> as you. Peer pressure occurs when these people <u>encourage</u> <u>you</u> to do something that you <u>really</u> <u>don't</u> <u>want</u> to do. It could also be something you think you would like to do or are <u>curious</u> <u>about</u> but that your <u>conscience</u> <u>tells</u> you is wrong. It may also be some <u>form</u> <u>of</u> <u>behavior</u> which <u>breaks</u> <u>the</u> <u>rules</u> of the school or the rules <u>set</u> <u>by</u> <u>your</u> <u>parents</u>. There are many reasons why you may want to <u>give</u> <u>in</u> to peer pressure. Most young people want to <u>be</u> <u>accepted</u>, to <u>fit</u> <u>in</u>, to have friends, and to <u>be</u> <u>liked</u> by other people. These are very <u>normal</u> <u>feelings</u>. You may also worry that people will <u>tease</u> <u>you</u> or <u>bully</u> <u>you</u> if you don't <u>go</u> <u>along</u> <u>with</u> them. It's very difficult to say "no" in the <u>face</u> <u>of</u> <u>peer</u> <u>pressure</u>, but you need to be able to do it. You should <u>trust</u> <u>your</u> <u>conscience</u> and the opinions and rules of your parents. It also helps if you have a friend who <u>shares</u> <u>your</u> <u>opinions</u> and beliefs so that you can say "no" together.

▶ peer pressure 동료 집단으로부터 받는 사회적 압력 handle 다루다, 처리하다 conscience 양심 give in 항복하다, 굴복하다; 따르다 fit in 조화하다, 적합하다 tease 놀리다, 희롱하다, 괴롭히다 bully 곯리다, 겁주다 in the face of ~의 정면에서; ~에도 불구하고

여 어린이와 십대들이 어디에서나 직면하게 되는 중요한 문제는 또래 집단으로부터 받는 압력입니다. 청소년들이 또래 집단 압력이 무엇인지, 어떻게 처리해야 하는지에 대해 이해하는 것은 매우 중요합니다. 첫 번째로, 또래는 여러분의 친구들,

급우들, 여러분과 비슷한 나이의 사람들을 말합니다. 또래 집단 압력은 이 또래들이 여러분이 그다지 원하지 않는 일을 하도록 부추길 때 일어납니다. 아니면 그것은 여러분이 하고 싶어하거나 호기심을 갖는 일이지만 양심상 옳지 않다고 여겨지는 일일 수도 있죠. 교칙을 어기는 행동이거나 부모님이 정해 놓은 규칙을 어기는 행동일 수도 있고요. 여러분이 또래 집단 압력에 굴복하려 하는 이유는 여러 가지가 있습니다. 대부분의 청소년들은 인정받고, 사람들과 어울리며, 친구를 사귀고, 다른 사람들이 자신을 좋아하기를 원합니다. 이것들은 매우 정상적인 감정입니다. 만약 사람들과 잘 지내지 않으면 그들이 여러분을 놀리거나 겁줄 거라고 걱정할 수도 있겠죠. 또래 집단 압력에 직면하여 "안 돼"라고 말하는 것은 매우 어렵지만 그것을 할 수 있어야 합니다. 여러분은 자신의 양심과 부모님의 의견과 규칙을 믿어야 합니다. 또한 여러분의 의견과 신념을 공유하는 친구가 있다면 함께 "안 돼"라고 말할 수 있을 것입니다.

1 담화에 가장 알맞은 제목은 무엇인가?

    (a) 여러분의 진정한 친구는 누구인가
    (b) 동료들, 모든 규칙을 어기다
    (c) 학교에서의 또래 집단 압력
    (d) 또래 집단 압력의 모든 것
    (e) 언제 승낙하고 언제 반대할 것인가

2

W I read an <u>interesting</u> <u>article</u> about <u>obesity</u> and kids in the library this morning. There were some really <u>surprising</u> <u>statistics</u>.

M What was so surprising?

W It said that in today's America, <u>one in five</u>, or 20 percent, of kids are <u>obese</u>. That's four times higher than the number in the 1970s.

M That is a big change.

W I was also surprised that it wasn't just in America. The article said that <u>worldwide around</u> 22 million kids under the age of five were <u>considered to be overweight</u> and that it was a problem in <u>developing countries</u> also.

M With everything we know about <u>diets and exercise</u>, it's really surprising. I think parents <u>should be teaching</u> their kids better, especially kids so young.

W That's where the problem begins. It's up to parents to give kids <u>healthy food choices</u> and to <u>encourage</u> them to be <u>active</u>. Anyway, the article said that 80% of <u>obese children grow up</u> to be overweight adults. I checked the World Health Organization website, and it said that more than 1 <u>billion people worldwide</u> were overweight. About 300 million of them are children 12 and under.

M That's really <u>incredible</u>. There are so many <u>medical problems</u> that obese people can get, like heart disease and <u>diabetes</u>. What's the difference between <u>being overweight</u> and <u>obese</u> anyway?

W You're overweight if you <u>weigh more</u> than you should for your body type and <u>height</u>. You're <u>considered obese</u> if that amount is <u>at least</u> 10 percent higher than it should be.

▶ obesity 비만, 비대 statistics 통계 World Health Organization 세계 보건 기구 incredible 놀라운; 믿어지지 않은 diabetes 당뇨병 body type 체형

여 오늘 아침에 도서관에서 비만과 어린이들에 관한 재미있는 기사를 읽었어. 정말 놀라운 통계가 있었지.

남 뭐가 그렇게 놀라웠는데?

여 오늘날 미국에서 5명 중 1명, 즉 20%의 어린이들이 비만이라고 나와 있었어.

여 1970년대에 비해 4배나 높은 수치야.

남 엄청난 변화구나.

여 그게 미국만의 일이 아니라는 것에 또 한 번 놀랐지. 전 세계 약 2천 2백만 명의 5세 미만 아이들이 과체중이고, 그건 개발도상국의 문제이기도 하다는 군.

남 다이어트와 운동에 대해 그렇게 많이들 알고 있는데 그 기사는 정말 의외다. 부모님들이 아이들을 더 잘 가르쳐야 한다고 생각해. 특히 아주 어린 아이들의 경우에는 말이지.

여 그게 바로 문제의 시작이야. 아이들에게 건강식품을 선택하게 하고 활발하게 활동하도록 북돋우는 것은 부모에게 달려 있는 일이지. 어쨌든, 기사에는 80%의 비만 아동들이 자라 과체중 성인이 된다고 나와 있었어. 세계보건기구 웹사이트에 들어가 봤는데 전 세계적으로 10억 이상의 사람들이 과체중이라고 나와 있더라. 그 중 3억이 12세 이하의 아이들이야.

남 정말 놀랍다. 비만인 사람들이 걸릴 수 있는 질병이 정말 많잖아. 심장병과 당뇨병 같은 거. 그건 그렇고, 과체중과 비만의 차이점은 뭐니?

여 만약 체형과 키에 비해 몸무게가 더 나간다면 과체중인데, 만약 그 초과량이 표준보다 적어도 10% 더 높으면 비만인 거지.

2 빈칸을 채워 표를 완성하시오.

미국의 비만 아동 비율 – 현재	20%
미국의 비만 아동 비율 – 1970년대	5%
5세 미만의 비만 아동 수 – 전 세계	22 million (2천 2백만 명)
12세 이하의 비만 아동 총 수 – 전 세계	300 million (3억 명)
비만 성인이 되는 비만 아동의 비율	80%
전 세계 비만인의 총 수	1 billion (10억 명)

3-4

W AIDS is a very <u>serious disease</u> which has killed <u>millions of people</u> around the world every year. Since AIDS <u>first arose</u> in the 1980s, there have been <u>great medical advances</u> in the development of drugs to <u>treat</u> AIDS. This <u>has allowed</u> AIDS patients now to live 10 or 20 years <u>longer than</u> they had in the past. The problem is that these drugs are very expensive. The drug companies which <u>manufacture these drugs</u> can <u>charge high prices</u> because they <u>own the patents</u> for them. Africa has the largest numbers of AIDS cases but also some of the poorest countries in the world, <u>making it difficult</u> to <u>obtain</u> AIDS drugs for all of those who are ill. To <u>bypass</u> the drug companies, one African nation, South Africa, <u>decided to enact</u> a law which would <u>allow domestic</u> drug companies to <u>manufacture</u> the same AIDS drugs and to sell them <u>at reduced prices</u>. In addition, the law <u>permitted</u> South Africa to <u>import</u> AIDS drugs from other countries where they were <u>cheaper</u>. However, these actions were <u>against</u> international law due to <u>complex international trade relations</u>, and South Africa needed permission from the drug companies to do this. The South African government <u>argued</u> that millions of people <u>were dying</u> and that life was <u>more precious</u> than the drug companies' profits. The drug companies <u>sued</u> the South African government, <u>claiming</u> they needed the money to pay for the development of new drugs. Many Africans <u>protested against</u> the drug companies, and the companies eventually <u>dropped their lawsuit</u>.

▶ arise 발생하다, 생기다 patent 특허(권) case 환자; 사례 bypass 우회하다; 무시하다; 회피하다 enact a law 법을 제정하다 domestic 국내의; 국산의, 자국의 international trade relation 국제 무역 관계 argue 주장하다; 논쟁하다 protest against ~에 항의하다 drop the lawsuit 소송을 철회하다

여 에이즈는 매년 전 세계적으로 수백만 명의 생명을 앗아가는 매우 심각한 질병입니다. 에이즈가 1980년대에 처음 발생한 이래로 에이즈를 치료하는 약물 개발은 크게 발전해 왔습니다. 이로 인해 에이즈 환자가 과거보다 10년에서 20년 더 살 수 있게 되었죠. 문제는 이 약들이 매우 비싸다는 것입니다. 이 약들을 제조하는 제약회사들은 약에 대한 특허권을 가지고 있기 때문에 가격을 높게 책정할 수 있습니다. 아프리카에는 가장 많은 에이즈 환자가 있을뿐 아니라 그 중 몇몇 국가들은 세계에서 가장 가난한 나라들이어서 아픈 사람들 모두가 에이즈 약을 구하기는 어렵습니다. 기존의 제약회사들을 거치지 않기 위해, 한 아프리카 국가인 남아프리카공화국은 자국의 제약회사에서 같은 에이즈 약을 제조하는 것을 허용하고 할인된 가격으로 약을 판매하게 하는 법을 제정하기로 결정했습니다. 또한 그 법률에 따라 남아프리카공화국은 에이즈 약을 값이 더 저렴한 다른 나라들에서도 수입할 수 있었습니다. 하지만 이러한 조치는 복잡한 국제 무역 관계 때문에 국제법에 어긋나는 것이었고, 남아프리카공화국이 그렇게 하기 위해서는 제약회사들의 허가가 필요했습니다. 남아프리카공화국 정부는 수백만 명의 사람들이 죽어가고 있고, 생명이 제약회사의 이윤보다 더 소중하다고 주장했습니다. 제약회사들은 남아프리카공화국 정부를 고소하고 신약을 개발하기 위해 돈이 필요하다고 주장했습니다. 많은 아프리카인들이 제약회사에 항의했고, 제약회사들은 결국 소송을 철회했습니다.

3 담화에 따르면 남아프리카공화국 법률에서 시도한 것은 무엇인가? 해당되는 것을 모두 고르시오.

(a) 제약회사들에게 에이즈 약 가격을 낮추도록 강제
(b) 남아프리카공화국에서 주요 에이즈 약을 모방해 제조
(c) 남아프리카공화국에서 에이즈 신약을 개발하고 생산
(d) 에이즈 신약을 인간에게 직접 실험하는 것을 합법화
(e) 다른 나라에서 더 저렴한 에이즈 약을 구입

4 담화에서 유추할 수 있는 것은 무엇인가?

(a) 남아프리카공화국 이외의 아프리카 국가들은 남아프리카공화국만큼 에이즈 관련된 사망이 많지 않다.
(b) 에이즈 약을 만드는 주요 제약회사 중 몇 군데는 원래 남아프리카공화국에서 설립되었다.
(c) 남아프리카공화국에 더 저렴한 에이즈 약을 판매하고자 했던 나라들도 제약회사에 고소당했다.
(d) 남아프리카공화국의 국내 제약회사들은 더 저렴한 주요 에이즈 약을 제조하려고 준비하고 있다.
(e) 남아프리카공화국 제약회사들은 기존의 제약회사들로부터 에이즈 약을 만들어도 된다는 허가를 받았다.

5-6　　**Level up**

M That's a really nice bag. It must have been very expensive.

W Well, actually, it's not real. It's a <u>knockoff</u>. I only paid 75 dollars for it. I think a lot of companies <u>charge way too much</u> for their products just because of their <u>brand names</u>. Why shouldn't I be able to get a <u>quality bag</u> at a <u>reasonable price</u>?

M Lots of reasons. For instance, <u>counterfeiting robs</u> companies of millions of dollars every year. When the companies <u>lose money</u>, they have to <u>close factories</u> and move to <u>cheaper countries</u>. That means thousands of people here could lose their jobs.

W I hadn't <u>thought about that</u>. But I still think the prices they charge are just way too high, especially for things like <u>accessories</u> and <u>clothing</u>. A lot of the clothing is already made in countries with <u>cheap labor</u>.

M Maybe, but the clothing companies spend a lot of money on <u>marketing</u> and <u>advertising</u>. They also have

to <u>develop new styles</u> and ideas, which <u>takes time</u> and money.

W Okay. Maybe you're right about that, too. But you <u>download games</u> and music all the time, and you don't pay for them.

M Oh, ah, yeah, well, you <u>got me there</u>. I guess I look like a <u>real hypocrite</u>, right? But you know games and CDs are also really expensive. If the prices were cheaper, I <u>would buy them</u> from the store.

W It's the same thing with me and my bag. I guess we are both in the <u>same boat</u>.

M It looks like it. But it's not like we're alone. Everyone is doing it, so we'd be stupid to <u>pay the full price</u> for something, right?

W <u>Somehow</u>, what you just said <u>feels wrong</u>.

▶ brand 상표, 브랜드　knockoff 모조품, 가짜　counterfeit 위조의; 모조품; 위조하다　labor 노동력　you got me there. 네 말이 맞아.　hypocrite 위선자, 겉으로 착한 체하는 사람　somehow 어쩐지, 아무래도; 아무튼

남 정말 멋진 가방이네. 엄청 비싸겠는걸.

여 음, 사실, 진품이 아니야. 모조품이지. 75달러밖에 안 들었어. 많은 회사들이 브랜드 이름만으로 제품을 너무 비싸게 팔고 있는 것 같아. 왜 저렴한 가격에 질 좋은 가방을 살 수 없는 거지?

남 많은 이유가 있지. 예를 들면, 모조품 때문에 기업들이 매년 수백만 달러의 돈을 손해보고 있어. 회사가 돈을 잃으면 공장 문을 닫아야 하고 더 싼 비용으로 제품을 만들 수 있는 나라로 이전해야 해. 그건 여기 있는 수천 명의 사람들이 직장을 잃게 될 수도 있다는 것을 의미하지.

여 그건 생각 못했어. 하지만 그래도 가격이 너무 높잖아. 특히 액세서리와 옷 같은 것들 말이지. 이미 많은 옷이 값싼 노동력을 가진 나라에서 만들어지고 있잖아.

남 그럴지도 모르지. 하지만 의류업체들은 마케팅과 광고에 많은 돈을 써. 새로운 스타일과 아이디어도 개발해야 하고. 그것 역시 시간과 돈이 들지.

여 그래. 그 점에 있어서도 네 말이 맞아. 하지만 너도 항상 게임과 음악을 다운로드 하면서 돈은 내지 않잖아.

남 오, 아, 그래, 음, 네 말이 맞아. 내가 정말 위선자처럼 보이겠구나, 그렇지? 하지만 게임과 CD도 정말 비싸. 가격이 더 싸다면 상점에서 살 텐데 말이지.

여 그건 나랑 내 가방의 경우와 똑같은 거잖아. 우린 둘 다 같은 처지인 것 같은데.

남 그런 것 같다. 그런데 우리만 그런 것 같진 않아. 모두 다 그렇게 하는데, 제 값 다 주고 물건을 사는 건 어리석은 짓 아니냐?

여 아무래도, 네가 방금 말한 것은 잘못된 것 같다.

5 대화 중 한 시점에서 남자는 왜 자신을 '위선자'라고 불렀는가?

(a) 남자는 모조품을 구입했다고 여자를 꾸짖었지만 그도 역시 같은 방법으로 옷을 산다.
(b) 남자는 여자에게 음악과 비디오 게임을 다운로드 받는 것은 잘못된 것이니까 자신은 그것을 그만둘 것이라고 말했다.
(c) 남자는 모조품을 사는 것에 대해 여자를 훈계했지만 자신은 불법으로 음악과 비디오 게임을 다운로드한다.
(d) 남자는 모든 사람이 공짜로 비싼 게임과 음악을 얻기 때문에 같은 짓을 하지 않는 것은 어리석은 일이라고 느낀다.
(e) 남자는 무료로, 또는 싼 가격에 물건을 얻는 것은 잘못이라고 생각하지만 제 값을 다 주고 살 돈이 없다.

6 다음 중 내용을 가장 잘 요약한 것을 고르시오.

(a) 모조품을 사는 것과 다운로드를 하는 것은 다르다. 왜냐하면 전자는 원래의 제조업자들에게서 돈을 빼앗는 일이기 때문이다.
(b) 사람들은 비싼 가격 때문에 모조품을 사게 되지만, 원래 제조업자들이 돈을 받지 못하게 되기 때문에 잘못된 것이다.
(c) 사람들은 좋은 제품을 갖고 싶은 욕망 때문에 모조품을 산다. 하지만

모두들 그렇게 하기 때문에 용서될 수 있다.

7 Level up

M Hey, Sharon. Do you ever <u>worry about</u> the government in Washington <u>spying on you</u>?

W What are you talking about? Why would the government want to spy on me?

M Well, maybe not you but your parents or your older brother. I read in the paper that recently the government has been <u>spying on</u> a lot on <u>ordinary citizens</u> while <u>looking for</u> terrorists. They're listening to people's phone calls, <u>monitoring their Internet usage</u>, and even <u>checking</u> what library books they borrow.

W How can they <u>accomplish</u> all of that?

M It's really easy with <u>today's technology</u>. They use <u>supercomputers to check</u> for key words like "<u>bomb</u>" or "<u>blow-up</u>" that people might say on the phone or <u>search for</u> on the Internet. Also, if someone <u>checks out</u> books about <u>certain topics</u>, the government starts watching them <u>more closely</u>.

W It's like George Orwell's book *1984*. Big Brother is <u>watching you</u>. What about my <u>right to privacy</u>?

M They <u>figure</u> that <u>protecting people</u> from <u>terrorists</u> is more important than your privacy.

W We have to <u>make a stand</u> against this.

M <u>Count me out</u>. You know you can't fight city hall.

▶ spy on 감시하다: 염탐하다 monitor 감시하다, 관리하다 bomb 폭탄
blow-up 폭파 check something out 조회하다: (책을) 대출하다
make a stand 멈추다, 저항하다 count me out 난 빼줘.
fight city hall 관권을 상대로 무익한 싸움을 하다

남 이봐, 섀론. 워싱턴에 있는 중앙정부가 너를 감시하고 있다고 걱정한 적 있어?
여 무슨 소리야? 왜 정부가 날 감시해?
남 음, 너는 아니라도 너희 부모님이나 오빠를 감시할 수는 있지. 난 최근에 정부가 테러리스트를 색출하면서 많은 일반 국민들을 감시하고 있다고 신문에서 읽었어. 정부가 사람들의 전화를 엿듣고 인터넷 사용을 감시하고 도서관에서 무슨 책을 빌리는지도 조사하고 있다.
여 정부가 그런 걸 어떻게 다 할 수 있지?
남 요즘 기술을 사용하면 매우 쉽지. 정부는 슈퍼컴퓨터를 사용하여 사람들이 전화 상으로 말하거나 인터넷에서 검색할 수도 있는 '폭탄' 또는 '폭파'와 같은 키워드를 조사해. 그리고 어떤 사람들이 특정 주제에 관한 책들을 도서관에서 대출하면 정부는 그들을 자세히 감시하기 시작하는 거지.
여 조지 오웰의 책 『1984년』 같군. 정부가 국민들을 감시하고 있다. 내 사생활 보호권은 어떻게 되는 거야?
남 정부는 국민을 테러리스트로부터 보호하는 것이 사생활 보호보다 더 중요하다고 생각하는 거지.
여 우리는 이 일에 맞서야 돼.
남 난 빼줘. 정부를 상대로 무익한 싸움을 할 수는 없는 거잖아.

---

7 What is the government's main reason for spying on its citizens according to the dialog?
대화에 따르면 정부가 국민을 감시하는 주요 이유는 무엇인가?

(a) To research the book-reading habits of the citizens
국민의 독서 습관을 조사하려고

(b) To examine the frequency that certain words are used
특정한 단어가 사용되는 빈도를 조사하려고

(c) To attempt to discover cases of fraudulent Internet use
부당한 인터넷 사용의 사례를 발견해 내려고

(d) To try to find people who wish to do harm to the nation
국가에 해가 되는 일을 하고자 하는 사람들을 찾아내려고

(e) To test its supercomputers by studying the citizens
국민을 조사함으로써 정부의 슈퍼컴퓨터를 테스트하려고

8 Level up

W <u>Political corruption</u> is a serious problem which <u>all citizens</u> of a nation should <u>be aware of</u>. It is when a <u>government official</u> uses his or her <u>political power</u> for <u>illegal private gain</u>. The most <u>common form</u> of political corruption is <u>bribery</u>, which happens when an official <u>receives money</u> or gifts to do a <u>favor for someone</u>. Another type is called <u>patronage</u>, which is when government officials help someone who helped them in the past <u>by giving</u> that person a <u>government job</u>. Nepotism is another form of corruption and is when an official uses his or her power to help a <u>relative</u> get a job or <u>government contract</u>. Government officials may also be <u>involved in embezzlement</u>, which is the <u>stealing</u> of government money or <u>property</u>. Some officials <u>in charge of</u> government projects <u>employ people</u> who then <u>give back</u> some of their salary to the official <u>who hired them</u>. This is called a <u>kickback</u>. Finally, some government officials have worked closely with <u>organized crime</u> to help these groups <u>make huge profits</u> and to <u>hide their illegal activities</u>.

▶ political corruption 정치적 부패 gain 이득, 벌이; 수익 bribery 뇌물 수수
do someone a favor ~의 청을 들어주다, ~을 위하여 힘쓰다
patronage (자신의 정당이나 정치 운동의 지지자에 대한) 관직 제공
nepotism 친척 등용, 족벌주의 embezzlement (위탁금 등의) 도용, 횡령, 착복
government money 공금 in charge of ~담당인 kickback (임금의 일부를)
가로채기; 정치 헌금, 상납 organized crime 조직 범죄

여 정치적 부패는 모든 국민들이 알고 있어야 할 심각한 문제입니다. 정치적 부패는 정부 관료가 불법적인 사적 이익을 위해 정권을 이용하는 것입니다. 정치적 부패의 가장 보편적인 형태는 뇌물 수수인데, 이것은 관리가 어떤 사람의 편의를 봐주기 위해 돈이나 선물을 받을 때 일어납니다. 또 다른 형태로는 관직 제공이 있습니다. 이것은 정부 관료들이 과거에 자신들을 도왔던 사람에게 관직을 주어서 그를 돕는 것이죠. 족벌주의는 또 다른 형태의 부패입니다. 족벌주의는 정부 관료가 자신의 권력을 이용해 친척이 직업을 구하거나 정부와의 계약을 따도록 도와주는 것입니다. 또한 정부 관료들은 횡령에 연루될 수 있는데요, 이는 정부 돈이나 재산을 훔치는 행위입니다. 정부 프로젝트를 담당하는 일부 정부 관료들은 사람들을 고용하고, 고용된 사람들은 급여의 일부를 자신들을 고용한 그 관리에게 돌려줍니다. 이것을 상납이라 부르죠. 마지막으로, 일부 정부 관료들은 조직 범죄와 긴밀히 협력하여 이러한 무리들이 엄청난 이윤을 챙기도록 돕고 자신들의 불법행위를 숨겼습니다.

8 What is the main purpose of the talk?
담화의 주된 목적은 무엇인가?

(a) To explain how governments and criminals are connected
정부와 범죄자가 어떻게 결탁되어 있는지를 설명하려고

(b) To describe some illegal activities taking place in government
정부에서 일어나는 몇 가지 불법 행위들에 대해 묘사하려고

(c) To discuss how some people can get a government job
어떤 사람들이 어떻게 공직을 갖게 되는지를 논하려고

(d) To demonstrate how some government officials make extra money
일부 정부 관료가 어떤 식으로 가욋돈을 버는지 설명하려고

(e) To show that politicians are not very honest people
정치가들이 그다지 정직한 사람들이 아니라는 것을 보여주려고

9

M In today's <u>social</u> <u>studies</u> <u>class</u>, we're going to look at how families can change due to changes in <u>social</u> <u>values</u> and the <u>economy</u>. One of the biggest changes is an <u>increase</u> <u>in</u> <u>divorce</u> in different nations. A good example of this is South Korea. For a long time, South Korea had a very <u>low</u> <u>divorce</u> <u>rate</u>, and families were seen as very <u>stable</u> <u>and</u> <u>enduring</u>. This has changed <u>dramatically</u> in the last 10 years, and there are <u>several</u> <u>social</u> and <u>economic</u> <u>reasons</u> which <u>may</u> <u>explain</u> <u>why</u>. Socially, divorce laws have changed in South Korea. Many <u>female</u> <u>politicians</u> have helped to <u>change</u> <u>divorce</u> <u>laws</u>, which used to be <u>favorable</u> to men. The current laws are <u>more</u> <u>equal</u> and also make getting a divorce <u>easier</u> <u>than</u> it once was. Another change has been the <u>rising</u> <u>economic</u> <u>power</u> of women. Modern Korean women <u>tend</u> <u>to</u> be very <u>well</u> <u>educated</u> and make a good living, giving them an economic base even if they <u>get</u> <u>divorced</u>. This is very different from just a <u>generation</u> <u>ago</u>, when Korean women tended to be stay-at-home wives. In the past, women who wanted to get divorced were <u>reluctant</u> <u>to</u> <u>do</u> so since they had <u>no</u> <u>financial</u> <u>support</u> if their husband refused to <u>pay</u> <u>alimony</u>. With the <u>increasing</u> <u>ability</u> of women to make money, the <u>financial</u> <u>obstacle</u> to divorce is <u>removed</u>.

▶ social studies 사회학 enduring 영속하는, 영구적인 dramatically 극적으로; 급격하게 favorable 유리한; 호의적인 current law 현행법 equal (법, 영향력 등이) 평등한, 공평한 make a good living 수입이 꽤 좋다; 잘 살다 reluctant 마음이 내키지 않는; 마지못해 하는 alimony 위자료 obstacle 장애물, 방해물

남 오늘 사회학 수업에서는 사회적 가치 및 경제 변화에 따라 어떻게 가족이 변화할 수 있는지에 대해 살펴볼 것입니다. 가장 큰 변화 중 하나는 여러 나라에서의 이혼 증가입니다. 이것의 좋은 보기가 한국입니다. 오랫동안 한국은 이혼율이 매우 낮았고, 가정은 매우 안정적이며 지속적으로 보였습니다. 이 모습이 지난 10년 동안 급격하게 변했습니다. 이를 설명해 주는 몇몇 사회적·경제적 이유가 있는데요. 사회적으로는 한국의 이혼법이 바뀌었습니다. 많은 여성 정치인들이 남성에게 유리했던 이혼법을 바꾸는 데 일조하였습니다. 현행법 상에서는 더 평등해졌고, 또 예전보다 이혼이 쉬워졌습니다. 또 하나의 변화는 여성의 경제력이 향상되었다는 것입니다. 현대 한국 여성들은 매우 좋은 교육을 받고 수입이 좋은 편이어서 이혼을 하더라도 경제적 기반이 있습니다. 이것이 전업주부였던 바로 전 세대의 한국 여성들과 매우 다른 점입니다. 과거에 이혼을 원했던 여성들은 남편이 위자료 지불을 거부하면 아무런 재정적 지원을 받을 수 없었기 때문에 이혼을 꺼려했습니다. 여성의 경제 능력 향상으로 이혼하는 데 재정적 걸림돌이 제거된 것이죠.

9 한국에서 이혼이 증가한 이유로 언급된 것이 <u>아닌</u> 것은?
(a) 요즘 한국 여성들은 더 많은 재정적 안정을 누리고 있다.
(b) 이혼이 과거처럼 금기시되지 않는다.
(c) 남성에게 더 많은 권한을 주었던 이혼법이 바뀌었다.
(d) 한국 여성들이 예전보다 더 큰 정치적 영향력을 미치고 있다.
(e) 이혼을 하는 것이 과거처럼 어렵지 않다.

10

M What do you think about <u>capital</u> <u>punishment</u>, Lena?

W I really think it's wrong. I don't see why we have to <u>kill</u> <u>people</u> as a <u>way</u> of <u>punishment</u>. <u>Putting</u> <u>someone</u> in <u>jail</u> for life is punishment enough.

M Most people <u>argue</u> that the main reason for capital punishment is to <u>deter</u> criminals from <u>committing</u> <u>serious</u> <u>crimes</u>.

W I've heard that, too, but I don't think it's true. Most states in America have the <u>death</u> <u>penalty</u>, but they still have more serious crime than Canada, which <u>abolished</u> the death penalty years ago.

M That's interesting. I <u>wonder</u> how many countries <u>still</u> <u>have</u> the death penalty.

W It should be <u>easy</u> <u>to</u> <u>find</u> on the Internet. Just a sec... (pause) Right. These are the 2008 <u>figures</u>. There are 197 countries <u>listed</u> on this website. It says here that 92 countries have <u>completely</u> <u>abolished</u> the death penalty. The <u>remaining</u> 105 countries still have the death penalty as law, but 10 of those countries <u>only</u> <u>use</u> <u>it</u> in very <u>special</u> <u>circumstances</u>, such as in cases <u>involving</u> <u>terrorism</u>. The <u>rest</u> <u>practice</u> the death penalty <u>mostly</u> <u>for</u> <u>major</u> <u>crimes</u> such as <u>murder</u>.

M But of those countries, 36 of them still have it as a law but <u>haven't</u> <u>used</u> <u>it</u> in more than 10 years. In 2008, only 25 countries <u>actually</u> <u>executed</u> a criminal.

W I really wish that no country would use the death penalty. <u>What</u> <u>if</u> they <u>make</u> <u>a</u> <u>mistake</u> and they <u>sentence</u> someone to death who didn't commit a crime?

M Unfortunately, it has happened. Recent DNA <u>evidence</u> has proven that some <u>innocent</u> <u>people</u> have been executed.

▶ capital punishment 사형 punishment 형벌, 처벌 jail 감옥 for life 종신의, 무기의 deter (못하게) 막다, 단념시키다 death penalty 사형 abolish 폐지하다 circumstance 상황, 환경 terrorism 테러리즘, 테러행위(수단) execute 사형에 처하다, 처형하다 sentence someone to death ~에게 사형을 선고하다

남 리나, 사형에 대해 어떻게 생각하니?

여 난 사형이 정말 잘못된 거라고 생각해. 형벌의 수단으로 왜 사람을 죽여야 하는지 이해할 수 없어. 평생 감옥에서 살게 하는 것만으로도 충분한 형벌이잖아.

남 대부분의 사람들은 범죄자로 하여금 중범죄를 저지르지 못하도록 막는 것이 사형의 주요 이유라고 주장하지.

여 나도 들었어. 하지만 그게 사실이라고 생각하진 않아. 미국 대부분의 주에 사형 제도가 있는데도 수 년 전에 사형을 폐지한 캐나다보다 중범죄가 더 많이 발생하거든.

남 그거 흥미롭네. 아직도 사형 제도가 있는 나라들이 얼마나 되나 궁금해.

여 인터넷에서 찾는 게 쉬울 거야. 잠깐만… (사이) 좋아. 2008년 수치가 있네. 이 웹사이트에 197개국이 열거되어 있는데, 이 중 92개국이 사형 제도를 완전히 폐지했다고 나와 있어. 나머지 105개국은 아직도 법으로 사형 제도를 유지하고 있지만 그 중 10개국은 테러 행위와 관련된 경우와 같은 매우 특별한 상황에서만 사형을 집행하고 있어. 나머지 국가들은 주로 살인과 같은 중범죄일 때 사형을 집행하고.

남 하지만 그 나라들 중에서 36개국은 아직까지 사형을 법으로 정하고 있지만 10년이 넘도록 사형시킨 적이 없네. 2008년에 실제로 범죄자를 처형한 것은 25개국뿐이야.

여 난 정말 어떤 나라에서도 사형이 없기를 바라. 만약 실수로 범죄를 저지르지 않은 사람에게 사형을 선고하면 어떡해?

남 불행하게도, 그런 일이 있었어. 최근 DNA 증거로 몇몇 무고한 사람들이 사형당했다는 것이 증명됐지.

10 사형에 관한 정보로 빈칸을 채워 표를 완성하시오.

구 분	총 197개국
사형이 폐지된 나라	92
법적으로 사형이 허용되고 특별한 경우(테러 행위)에 사용되는 나라	10
법적으로 사형이 허용되지만 10년 이상 시행되지 않은 나라	36
2008년에 사형이 집행된 나라	25

W In the modern media-frenzied world, <u>celebrities</u> <u>have</u> <u>power</u> out of proportion to their importance. Businesses have <u>tapped</u> <u>into</u> this power of celebrity by <u>hiring</u> <u>famous</u> <u>faces</u> to <u>endorse</u> <u>their</u> <u>products</u> and services in order to <u>encourage</u> <u>people</u> <u>to</u> <u>use</u> them. Sometimes, however, the power of celebrities <u>goes</u> <u>too</u> <u>far</u>. Many young people like to <u>mimic</u> <u>the</u> <u>behavior</u> of their favorite star, even to the <u>point</u> <u>of</u> <u>death</u>. This is <u>known</u> <u>as</u> the Werther effect. It is <u>named</u> <u>after</u> a character in the novel *The Sorrows of Young Werther*, which <u>was</u> <u>written</u> <u>by</u> Goethe over 200 years ago in Germany. The story ends with the <u>main</u> <u>character</u> Werther <u>committing</u> <u>suicide</u> by <u>shooting</u> <u>himself</u> while dressed in boots, a yellow vest, and a blue jacket as he was sitting at a desk. Over the next few years, so many young men <u>killed</u> themselves in the <u>same</u> <u>manner</u> that the book <u>was</u> <u>banned</u> in parts of Europe. In a <u>more</u> <u>modern</u> case in the United States, the famous singer Kurt Cobain <u>shot</u> <u>himself</u> in 1994. During the following year, an <u>alarming</u> <u>number</u> <u>of</u> <u>teenagers</u> killed themselves while listening to his music. <u>Psychologists</u> have been aware of this <u>phenomenon</u> for some time, but it has only recently <u>gained</u> <u>public</u> <u>attention</u>. They <u>blame</u> <u>the</u> <u>media</u> for their role in <u>reporting</u> <u>the</u> <u>suicides</u> of famous people <u>in</u> <u>every</u> <u>detail</u>, with the stories lasting for days and weeks. Many experts believe this may give people the <u>courage</u> <u>to</u> <u>commit</u> <u>suicide</u> if they are already thinking about suicide. Young people are <u>especially</u> <u>vulnerable</u>, according to the experts, because of their strong <u>attachment</u> <u>to</u> <u>celebrities</u>.

▶ frenzied 열광적인: 광포한 power 영향력: 힘 out of proportion 과장된: 다른 것과 비교하여 비현실적인 비율로(받아야 할 이상의 주의를 받거나 필요 이상의 중요성을 두는 경우) tap into ~을 활용하다 endorse (상품을) 추천하다 go too far 도를 지나치다 mimic 흉내 내다 Werther effect 베르테르 효과 commit suicide 자살하다 ban 금지하다: 금지 alarming 놀라운, 심상치 않은 in every detail 모든 면에서: 세세하게 vulnerable (유혹 등에) 넘어가기 쉬운 attachment 애착, 애정

여 대중 매체에 열광하는 현대 사회에서 유명 연예인은 그 존재의 실질적인 중요성에 비해 지나치게 큰 영향력을 갖고 있습니다. 기업은 사람들이 자사의 상품과 서비스를 사용하도록 부추기기 위해 유명 스타를 고용하여 자기네 상품과 서비스를 추천하도록 함으로써 유명 인사의 영향력을 활용합니다. 하지만 유명 인사의 영향력이 도를 넘을 때도 있습니다. 많은 젊은이들이 좋아하는 스타의 행동을 흉내 내기를 좋아합니다. 심지에 죽음까지 말이죠. 이것은 베르테르 효과라고 알려져 있습니다. 200년도 더 전에 독일의 괴테가 쓴 『젊은 베르테르의 슬픔』이라는 소설의 등장인물 이름을 딴 것인데요. 이야기는 주인공인 베르테르가 부츠를 신고, 노란 조끼와 파란 재킷을 입은 채 책상에 앉아 권총 자살을 하는 것으로 끝납니다. 그 후 수년간 너무 많은 젊은이들이 같은 방식으로 자살을 해서 유럽의 몇몇 나라에서는 그 책이 출판 금지되었습니다. 미국에서 발생한 보다 최근 사례로는 유명 가수였던 커트 코베인이 1994년 권총 자살을 한 사건이 있는데요. 그 다음해에 엄청나게 많은 십대들이 그의 노래를 들으면서 자살을 했죠. 심리학자들은 한동안 이 현상을 인식하고 있었지만 최근에 와서야 대중의 주목을 받게 되었습니다. 심리학자들은 유명한 사람들의 자살 기사를 며칠에서 몇 주 동안 세세하게 보도하는 대중 매체의 역할을 비난합니다. 많은 전문가들은 이미 자살을 생각하고 있는 사람이라면 이를 통해 자살을 감행할 용기를 낼 수도 있다고 믿고 있습니다. 전문가들에 따르면 젊은이들은 유명 연예인들에게 강한 애착을 보이기 때문에 특히 자살의 유혹에 넘어가기 쉽다고 합니다.

11 대중 매체는 사람들이 결국 모방 자살을 하기로 결정하는 데 어떠한 역할을 하는가?

(a) 대중 매체는 종종 자살을 선정적으로 보도하여 사람들이 쉽게 그 방법을 따라할 수 있다.

(b) 사람들이 자살하고 싶어질 때까지 유명한 사람의 자살을 계속 보도한다.

(c) 모방 자살을 하는 사람들은 자신들도 동등한 수준으로 언론에 다뤄질 것이라 믿는다.

(d) 유명 연예인의 자살에 대한 과도한 보도는 일부 사람들이 자살을 하는 데 필요한 촉매제가 될 수 있다.

(e) 유명 연예인의 자살에 대한 계속적인 보도는 유명 연예인조차 자살할 정도라면 삶이 얼마나 각박한 것인지를 사람들에게 상기시킨다.

12 다음 중 내용을 가장 잘 요약한 것을 고르시오.

(a) 모방 자살은 수세기 동안 계속되었고, 유명 인사에 대한 숭배 때문에 앞으로도 계속될 것이다.

(b) 자신의 우상이 자살한 것처럼 자살하는 유명 연예인의 광팬들은 그 연예인이 세상을 떠나기 전부터 이미 죽기를 바랐을지도 모른다.

(c) 유명한 사람들은 젊은이들에게 강한 영향력을 미치지만 정신적인 문제가 있는 젊은이들만이 유명 인사들의 죽음을 따른다.

Practice Test

p. 72~p. 73

1 (e)	2 (b)	3 (a)	4 (e)	5 (d)	6 (d)	7 (b)
8 해설 참조	9 (c)	10 (e)				

1

M The right to own a gun in the United States is ingrained in the American Constitution's Second Amendment. In addition, many states have laws that make it legal for a property owner to defend his or her land and home with lethal force if necessary. The whole American gun issue became very controversial on an international level in 1992 when a Japanese university exchange student was shot to death in Louisiana by a homeowner who thought the student was a criminal on his property. Yoshiro Hattori and a friend were dressed in costumes for a Halloween party and mistakenly went to the wrong home, where owner Rodney Peairs shot and killed Yoshiro Hattori. Peairs later claimed that the student was acting in an aggressive manner and kept walking toward him in his driveway after he yelled freeze, so he shot him. The case caused an outrage in Japan, more so when a court found Peairs not guilty of manslaughter. While it took place many years ago, the case still generates anger and is a classic example of how different cultures interpret events. To the Japanese, Peairs committed murder and should have been punished. Yoshiro Hattori's family feels they never received the justice that they thought was their due because Peairs killed their son and walked away free. However, in the United States, the federal and state laws protected Peairs's right to own a gun and to use it to protect his property.

▶ ingrained 바탕부터의: 타고난 constitution 헌법 amendment 개정, 수정(안) property owner 지주, 집주인 lethal force 흉기 controversial 쟁점이 되는, 물의를 일으키는 driveway 사유 차도(도로에서 집·차고까지의) 진입로 freeze (명령형으로) 꼼짝 마: 얼어붙다 outrage 격분, 격노, 분개

manslaughter 살인; 과실 치사   generates anger 분노를 유발하다
classical example 전형적인 예   due 당연한 권리

남 미국의 총기 소유 권리는 미국 헌법 수정 조항 제 2조에 바탕을 둔 것입니다. 더불어 많은 주에서는 땅 주인이 자신의 땅이나 집을 보호하기 위해 필요한 경우 총기를 사용하는 것이 합법입니다. 미국의 총기 문제는 루이지애나에서 한 일본인 교환 대학생이 자신의 집에 침입한 범죄자라고 생각한 집주인의 총에 맞아 사망한 일을 계기로 1992년에 국제적인 수준으로 쟁점화되었습니다. 요시로 하토리와 그의 친구는 할로윈 파티 의상을 입은 채 실수로 집을 잘못 들어갔고, 그 집의 주인인 로드니 페어스는 총을 쏘아 요시로 하토리를 죽였습니다. 페어스는 후에, 그 학생이 공격적인 태도를 취하고 있었고, 멈추라고 소리쳤는데도 진입로에서 계속 그를 향해 걸어와서 그 학생에게 총을 쏘았다고 주장했습니다. 이 사건으로 일본인들은 격분했고, 법원이 페어스에게 무죄를 선고하자 그들의 분노는 더 커졌습니다. 수년 전의 일임에도 불구하고 그 사건은 아직도 분노를 유발하고 있고, 다른 문화권에서는 사건을 어떻게 해석하느냐에 대한 전형적인 사례가 되었습니다. 일본인들에게는 페어스가 살인을 저질렀으므로 벌을 받았어야 했습니다. 요시로 하토리의 가족은 그들의 당연한 권리라고 생각했던 정의가 실현되지 않았다고 여깁니다. 페어스가 아들을 죽이고도 무죄로 풀려났기 때문이죠. 하지만 미국의 연방 법과 주(州) 법은 페어스가 총기를 소지하고 자신의 재산을 보호하기 위해 총을 사용할 수 있는 권리를 보호했습니다.

1 담화에 따르면 요시로 하토리 사건에 대한 내용 중 사실이 <u>아닌</u> 것은?

(a) 로드니 페어스는 요시로 하토리에게 움직이지 말라고 경고했다.

(b) 요시로 하토리는 미국의 한 대학에서 공부하고 있었다.

(c) 루이지애나 법원은 그 사건과 관련해 로드니에게 무죄를 선고했다.

(d) 요시로 하토리가 총에 맞아 사망했을 때 그는 혼자가 아니었다.

(e) 로드니 페어스는 그 사건에서 살인죄로 기소되었다.

2-3

W In your paper on population, David, I asked you to look into the issue of aging. First of all, let's see what you have researched already. Can you tell me why many nations' populations are getting older?

B I think the reason is that older people live much longer than they used to.

W Yes, that's definitely one factor. Now we have medicines and medical procedures that can extend people's lives into the 80s and beyond. Can you tell me another reason?

B In some countries, like America, people are having fewer children, so there are more elderly people than younger people. My father had six brothers and sisters, but, these days, most families only have one or two kids.

W That's referred to as a declining birthrate. What problems do you think our society might have because of an aging population?

B I think one might be rising medical costs. In many countries, the government helps pay for older people's medical care, and that money comes from taxes. If there are fewer younger people working, there might not be enough taxes collected to help pay to take care of older people.

W Very good. Also, if people live longer and there is less support from the government, then maybe many older people won't have enough money to take care of themselves.

B In addition, because of rising costs, many older people won't have enough money saved after they retire and

can no longer work. How might these factors influence younger people who are planning for their future?

W ____

▶ look into ~을 조사(연구)하다   aging 노화, 나이 먹음   medical procedure 의료 시술   declining 기우는, 쇠퇴하는   aging population 노령화 인구, 인구 고령화

여 데이비드, 인구에 관한 리포트에서 내 노화문제에 대해 조사하라고 했지. 우선, 네가 무엇을 조사했는지 봐야겠구나. 많은 국가의 국민 연령이 왜 점점 높아지고 있는지 말해 볼래?

남 그 이유는 과거에 비해 노인들이 훨씬 오래 살기 때문이라고 생각해요.

여 맞아, 확실히 하나의 요인이지. 이젠 약과 의료 시술로 사람의 수명을 80세 이상까지 연장할 수 있으니 말이다. 다른 이유도 말해 볼까?

남 미국과 같은 일부 나라에서는 사람들이 아이들을 덜 낳기 때문에 젊은이보다 노인이 더 많아요. 저희 아버지에게는 6명의 형제자매가 있었지만 요즘 대부분의 가정은 아이를 한두 명만 갖죠.

여 그것을 출산율 저하라고 한다. 인구 고령화 때문에 우리 사회가 겪을 수 있는 문제에는 무엇이 있다고 생각하니?

남 하나는 의료비의 증가라고 생각해요. 많은 나라에서는 정부가 노인들의 의료 비용을 부담하는데, 그 돈은 세금에서 나오죠. 만약 일하는 젊은이들이 적다면 노인들을 돌볼 비용을 지불하기 위한 세금이 충분히 징수되지 않을 거예요.

여 잘했어. 또한, 만약 사람들이 더 오래 살고 정부의 지원이 적어지면 많은 노인들이 자신을 돌볼 돈이 부족하게 될 거야.

남 게다가 비용 상승으로 인해 많은 노인들이 은퇴하고 더 이상 일할 수 없게 된 후에는 저축해둔 돈이 충분치 않을 거예요. 이러한 요소들이 미래를 계획하는 젊은이들에게 어떻게 영향을 미칠까요?

여 ____

2 대화에서 유추할 수 있는 것은?

(a) 출산율 저하는 노인 인구 증가의 결과이다.

(b) 소득세는 노인들을 지원하기 위한 정부의 주요 수입원이다.

(c) 노인의 의료 비용은 젊은이들보다 더 비싸다.

(d) 노인들은 자신의 의료 비용을 지불하기 위해 저축을 하고 있다.

(e) 가족 구성원이 적어진다는 것은 조만간 노인들이 줄어들 것임을 의미한다.

3 소년의 마지막 질문 후에 여자가 뭐라고 말하겠는가?

(a) 젊은이들은 은퇴를 위해 저축하는 것에 대해 좀 더 고려해야 할 거야.

(b) 젊은이들은 퇴직 후에 충분한 돈이 있을지에 대해 그다지 신경 쓰지 않지.

(c) 젊은이들은 이 문제를 해결하기 위해 다음 세대가 세금을 충분히 내야 한다고 생각하지.

(d) 젊은이들은 자신들의 퇴직연금이 나중에 들 비용에 대한 부담을 없애줄 것으로 믿고 있어.

(e) 젊은이들은 부모와 조부모처럼 퇴직할 수 있을 거라 생각하지.

4-5

M The Internet is now considered to be a form of media similar to newspapers, television, and radio. There are laws and rules which these older, established types of media must obey. These include not spreading lies or false news and not insulting people. Some of the possible crimes are spreading racial hatred and making death threats. Others relate to defamation, which is the writing or saying of insulting comments directed at certain people or groups. If people break these rules, they can be fined or sentenced to prison. The rules are still being formed for the Internet because it is so new, but there is some agreement that the rules should be similar to other forms of media. However, many people still believe the Internet should be free from any such restrictions. The problem is not so much the rules as it is the actual policing of the Internet. With the Internet being a worldwide tool that anybody can access from many places at any time, tracking down and arresting those breaking the laws will be difficult. In addition, many people don't realize that such rules exist or that they relate to the Internet. Many others think they can hide their identity on the Internet, so they feel safe to write what they want. However, some cases have already been made against Internet users. For instance, in South Korea, a blogger was arrested for spreading false rumors relating to the recent economic crisis.

▶ established 확립된, 확정된 insult 모욕하다 racial hatred 인종적 증오심
death threat 살해 위협 defamation 중상, 비방 comment 비판, 비평: 논평
fine ~에게 벌금을 과하다 be sentenced to prison 형을 선고 받다 agreement
합의: 협정 restriction 제약, 규정 not so much … as …이라기보다는 오히려 ~
police 단속하다 track down 철저하게 조사하다 against ~에 불리하게

남 인터넷은 이제 신문, 텔레비전, 라디오와 유사한 대중 매체의 형태로 간주되고 있습니다. 오래되고 확립된 형태의 대중 매체에게는 따라야 할 법과 규정이 있죠. 여기에는 거짓말이나 잘못된 뉴스를 퍼뜨리고 사람을 모욕하지 않는다는 것이 포함되어 있습니다. 발생 가능한 범죄로는 인종적 증오심을 퍼뜨리는 것과 살해 위협이 있고, 다른 것은 명예 훼손과 관련이 있습니다. 명예 훼손이란 특정 사람들이나 집단을 겨냥해 모욕적인 내용을 글로 쓰거나 말하는 것입니다. 만약 사람들이 이러한 규정을 어기면 벌금을 물거나 형을 선고 받을 수 있습니다. 인터넷에서 지켜야 할 규정들은 여전히 만들어지고 있는 상태입니다. 왜냐하면 인터넷은 생긴 지 얼마 안 되었기 때문이죠. 하지만 그 규정이 다른 형태의 대중 매체와 비슷해야 한다는 합의는 있습니다. 그러나 아직도 인터넷이 그러한 제한으로부터 자유로워야 한다고 믿는 사람들이 많습니다. 문제는 규정에 있는 것이 아니라 인터넷에 대한 실제적인 단속에 있습니다. 인터넷이 누구나 여러 곳에서 아무 때나 접속 가능한 전 세계적인 도구가 됨에 따라, 법을 어긴 사람들을 철저하게 조사하고 체포하는 것은 어려울 것입니다. 게다가 많은 사람들은 그러한 규정이 존재한다는 것이나 그 규정들이 인터넷과 관련이 있다는 것을 알지 못합니다. 그 밖의 많은 사람들은 인터넷에서 자신의 신분을 숨길 수 있다고 생각해서 자신들이 원하는 바를 안전하게 쓸 수 있다고 느낍니다. 하지만 이미 인터넷 사용자들에게 불리하게 적용된 몇몇 사례가 있습니다. 예를 들어 한국에서는 최근의 경제 위기와 관련해 잘못된 루머를 퍼뜨린 죄로 한 블로거가 체포되었습니다.

4 왜 아직도 인터넷에서 허용되는 것과 그렇지 않은 것에 대해 혼란이 있는가?
(a) 전체 인터넷을 조사할 경찰이 충분치 않다.
(b) 나라마다 법이 달라 혼란을 일으킨다.
(c) 많은 사람들은 새로운 인터넷 규정에 무지하다.
(d) 꽤 많은 인터넷 사용자들이 규정이 없어야 한다고 믿고 있다.
(e) 인터넷을 규제하는 규정이 아직 확실히 결정되지 않았다.

5 담화에서 설명된 대중 매체 규정 위반이 인터넷에도 적용된 예는 다음 중 무엇이겠는가?
(a) 한 학생이 채팅방에서 특정 비디오 게임을 아주 싫어한다고 말한다.
(b) 한 교수가 수업에서 인터넷 규정이 위헌이라고 주장한다.
(c) 한 시민이 대통령에게 협박 편지를 쓰는 데 자신의 컴퓨터를 사용한다.
(d) 한 블로거가 싫어하는 연예인에 대한 악의적인 공격성 글을 쓴다.
(e) 웹 디자이너가 새로운 프로젝트에 유명 브랜드명을 사용한다.

B I didn't see you in class yesterday.

G I was at my grandmother's funeral.

B Oh, I'm sorry to hear that. Were you close to her?

G In a way. We both liked to do needlepoint, and she gave me some tips on how to do it better. Also, she often made me great tea. I'll miss her.

B My grandmother passed away when I was just six years old. I cried a lot. I didn't really understand it all, but I still cried, mostly because my mom was crying.

G I didn't cry that much. I guess we're getting older. It's a reality of life that people die. Someday, it will be our parents and then us.

B Don't say that.

G Face the facts. Everyone dies eventually. We just have to enjoy life while we can.

B I don't think I'll ever be ready for someone else to die in my family.

G No one ever is, but you have to be prepared because it is going to happen.

▶ in a way 한편으로는, 아마도 needlepoint 바늘로 뜬 레이스(자수)
reality of life 인생의 참모습

남 너 어제 수업시간에 안 보이더라.
여 할머니 장례식에 갔었어.
남 아, 유감이구나. 할머니랑 친했니?
여 그런 편이었지. 우리 둘 다 레이스 자수를 하는 걸 좋아했는데, 할머닌 내게 잘할 수 있는 요령을 몇 가지 알려주셨어. 종종 맛있는 차도 만들어 주셨지. 할머니가 그리울 거야.
남 우리 할머니는 내가 겨우 여섯 살 때 돌아가셨어. 많이 울었지. 그 모든 것을 제대로 이해하진 못했지만, 그래도 울었어. 거의 엄마가 우셔서 나도 운 거었어.
여 난 그다지 많이 울지 않았어. 우리도 늙어갈 거잖아. 사람들이 죽는 것은 인생의 참모습이야. 언젠가 우리 부모님 차례가 될 것이고 그 다음에는 우리가 되겠지.
남 그런 말 하지 마.
여 현실을 직시해. 모든 사람은 언젠가 죽기 마련이야. 우리는 할 수 있는 동안 인생을 즐겨야 해.
남 우리 가족 중 누군가가 죽는 것에 대해서는 결코 준비가 될 것 같지 않아.
여 누군들 준비가 되겠어. 하지만 일어날 일이니까 준비를 해두어야 해.

6 What is NOT mentioned in the dialog?
대화에서 언급되지 않은 것은?
(a) The age the boy was at the time his grandmother died
할머니가 돌아가셨을 때 소년의 나이
(b) The special memories the girl has of her grandmother
소녀가 할머니와 함께 한 특별한 추억들
(c) The reason that the girl missed class the day before
소녀가 그 전날 수업에 빠진 이유
(d) The things the boy and his grandmother did together
소년과 할머니가 함께 했던 일들
(e) The girl's way of thinking about living and dying
삶과 죽음에 관한 소녀의 사고방식

M One growing controversy around the world is the right to die when we are ready to die. The correct term is called euthanasia, or sometimes assisted suicide, but most advocates of the practice prefer to call it the right to die with dignity. Essentially, a person is assisted in dying, either with someone providing the person with the means to kill himself or herself—most often drugs—or with doctors removing medical aid that is keeping the person alive, such as a breathing apparatus. Several countries, including the Netherlands and Japan, allow the practice, but, in other nations, such as in America, the practice is considered murder. In the few nations that allow euthanasia, the person must be terminally ill and have no chance of recovery. In addition, the person has to be of sound mind, meaning that the person must be thinking clearly enough to make the choice to die by himself or herself.

▶ controversy 논쟁, 논의 term 말, 용어 euthanasia 안락사 advocate 옹호자, 지지자 with dignity 위엄 있게, 기품 있게 essentially 본질적으로, 원래 means 수단, 방법 breathing apparatus 산소 호흡기 be terminally ill 죽을 병에 걸리다 sound mind 건전한 정신, 제정신

남 전 세계적으로 논란이 커지고 있는 한 가지 쟁점은 준비가 되었을 때 죽을 수 있는 권리입니다. 정확한 용어로는 안락사 또는 자살 방조라고도 불립니다. 하지만 대부분의 안락사 옹호자들은 안락사를 품위있게 죽을 권리라고 부르기를 선호합니다. 본질적으로, 사람이 죽을 때는 약물과 같은 자살 수단을 제공하는 사람, 또는 생명을 유지시키는 산소 호흡기와 같은 의료 기구를 제거해주는 의사의 도움을 받게 됩니다. 네덜란드와 일본을 포함해 일부 국가에서는 안락사를 허용하지만, 미국 같은 다른 나라에서는 안락사가 살인으로 간주됩니다. 안락사를 허용하는 몇몇 나라에서는 죽을 병에 걸려서 회생 가능성이 없는 사람만이 안락사 대상자가 됩니다. 게다가 그 사람은 정신이 온전해야 하는데, 그 사람 스스로가 죽음을 선택할 수 있을 정도로 제대로 생각할 수 있어야 한다는 의미입니다.

7 What is the main topic of the talk? 담화의 주제는 무엇인가?

(a) Countries that do not allow euthanasia
   안락사를 허용하지 않는 나라들
(b) Methods and rules for euthanasia 안락사의 방법과 규칙
(c) Legal issues concerning euthanasia 안락사에 관한 법률 문제
(d) Reasons for practicing euthanasia 안락사를 하는 이유
(e) Alternate terms for euthanasia 안락사의 다른 용어

8

W A very serious social issue these days that everyone should be concerned with is child labor, which often means employing a person under the age of 16. While millions of young people are going to school, there are millions of other children working long hours for very little money. A recent study estimates that 246 million children are child laborers, and, of them, 73 million are less than 10 years old. Around 22,000 children die each year in work-related accidents. The largest number of working children can be found in some poor countries in the Asian-Pacific region, where there are 127 million working children 15 years of age and younger. However, child labor does not just happen in poor countries. About 2.5 million children are working in developed countries. About 70 percent of child labor occurs in the agriculture, forestry, and commercial hunting and fishing sectors. Child laborers also work in manufacturing, sales, restaurants, and hotels and do domestic work such as cleaning and cooking in people's homes. Many of these children work in terrible and dangerous conditions and earn only a couple of dollars a week. Some of these children are even trapped in slavery. There are some cases, however, where the children really want to work. They work to earn money to help their families or to pay for their education in the future.

▶ child labor 미성년 노동 estimate 추정하다, 어림하다 agriculture 농업 forestry 임업; 산림 관리 commercial 상업상의; 영리적인 manufacturing 제조 (공업) slavery 노예의 몸, 노예의 신세

여 요즈음 모든 사람들이 관심을 가져야 할 매우 심각한 사회 문제는 아동 노동입니다. 아동 노동은 16세 미만의 사람을 고용하는 것을 의미합니다. 수백만 명의 어린이들이 학교를 다니고 있는 동안, 다른 수백만 명의 아이들은 아주 적은 돈을 벌기 위해 장시간 일하고 있습니다. 최근의 한 연구에서는 2억 4천 6백만 명의 아이들이 아동 노동자이며 그 중 7천 3백만 명은 10세 미만이라고 추산하고 있습니다. 약 2만 2천명의 아이들이 일과 관련된 사고로 사망합니다. 일하는 아이들은 아시아-태평양 지역에 있는 일부 가난한 나라에서 가장 많이 찾을 수 있는데, 거기에서는 1억 2천 7백만 명의 15세 이하의 아이들이 일을 하고 있습니다. 하지만 아동 노동은 가난한 나라에만 있는 것이 아닙니다. 약 2백 5십만 명의 아이들이 선진국에서 일하고 있죠. 아동 노동의 약 70%는 농업, 임업, 상업적인 사냥과 어업에서 일어납니다. 아동 노동자들은 또한 제조업, 판매, 음식점, 호텔에서 일하고 있으며 남의 집에서 청소와 요리 같은 일을 하기도 합니다. 이 아이들 중 많은 수가 열악하고 위험한 조건에서 일하며 일주일에 2달러밖에 벌지 못합니다. 이런 아이들 중 일부는 노예로 붙잡혀 있기도 합니다. 하지만 아이들이 진정으로 일하고 싶어하는 경우도 있습니다. 그 아이들은 자기 가족을 돕거나 앞으로 자신들의 교육비에 쓸 돈을 벌기 위해 일합니다.

8 아동 노동에 관한 정보로 빈칸을 채워 표를 완성하시오.

구 분	수
아동 노동자: 전 세계	2억 4천 6백만 명
아동 노동자: 10세 미만	73 million (7천 3백만 명)
아동 노동자: 10~15세	173 million (1억 7천 3백만 명)
아동 노동자: 아시아 · 태평양 지역	127 million (1억 2천 7백만 명)
아동 노동자: 그 외 지역	119 million (1억 1천 9백만 명)

9-10   Integrated Questions

Reading

▶ adoption 입양 welfare 복지 orphan 고아 unintentional 고의가 아닌, 부지불식간의 case study 사례 연구 readily 손쉽게; 즉시 adapt 적응하다 custom 관습, 풍습 identify with ~와 자기를 동일시하다; 일체감을 가지다 abandon 버리다; 포기하다 in addition to ~에 더하여, ~일 뿐 아니라 communicate with ~와 의사소통하다 government agency 정부 기관 cultural barrier 문화적 장벽 awkward 어색한, 거북한

국제 입양이 전 세계적으로 늘고 있다. 고아의 복지가 큰 관심사인 한편, 몇몇 의도하지 않은 해악이 생기기도 한다. 같은 문화나 인종이 아닌 가족에게 입양된 것에 부정적인 반응을 보이는 아이들의 사례 연구가 많다. 이는 대개 아이들이 입양된 나이에 따라 달라진다. 아이가 매우 어리면 입양한 부모의 문화에 쉽게 동화되고 언어와 관습을 배우며 쉽사리 적응을 한다. 하지만 입양아가 나이가 있고 이미 친부모의 문화, 인종, 언어에 자기를 동일시한다면 적응은 더 어려워질 수 있다. 입양아들은 또한 누가 자신들의 친부모인지, 왜 친부모가 자신들을 버렸는지에 대해 의문을 품을 수도 있다. 친부모를 찾는 것은 국외 가정에 입양된 아이들에게는 훨씬 어렵다. 모국과 거리가 떨어져 있을 뿐만 아니라, 모국에 있는 정부기관과 의사소통하는 데 언어 문제가 있을 수 있다. 설령 이 입양아들이 누가 친부모인지 알아냈다고 하더라도, 슬픈 사실은 모든 친부모가 자기 아이들을 보고 싶어하지는 않는다는 것이다. 그리고 친부모가 자기 아이를 보고 싶어한다 할지라도 때로는 언어와 문화 장벽이 너무 커서 만남이 어색하고 고통스럽기 때문에 아예 친부모가 누구인지 모르는 편이 나을 것 같기도 하다.

M Recently in the news, there have been many stories, both positive and negative, relating to celebrities and international adoption. In particular, Madonna and Angelina Jolie have been at the center of this controversial issue. Many people feel that international adoption is a good thing for both the child and the adoptive parents. Quite a few of these children are from poor and underdeveloped countries where they would have little chance to be adopted locally, or they live in cultures where adoption is not an accepted practice. The adopting parents are usually from a more affluent, developed nation and have the financial resources to take good care of these children. They would be able to get a good education and might not have to worry about material needs. It also tends to be easier for the adoptive parents to adopt children from poorer countries as there are not as many legal restrictions as in developed countries. However, there are people opposed to international adoption for a number of reasons. The main concern is that the children will lose their cultural identity, language, and heritage by living in a different country, usually with people who are from a different culture and often a different race from themselves. This may cause confusion for the adopted children as they get older. Another issue is that because of the lack of rules and regulations in some poorer countries, there is no way to check if the adoptive parents are good people and will take good care of the child. Finally, in many cases, the children have relatives who can't afford to take care of them but are worried about losing contact with a family member.

▶ undeveloped 미발전의, 미발달의 affluent 부유한, 풍부한
financial resource 재원 identity 주체성, 독자성 heritage 전승, 전통

남 최근 뉴스에는 유명 연예인들과 국외 입양에 관련된 긍정적이고 부정적인 많은 이야기들이 있습니다. 특히 마돈나와 안젤리나 졸리가 이 논란의 중심에 있었죠. 많은 사람들은 국외 입양이 아이와 입양 부모 모두에게 좋은 것이라 생각합니다. 상당수의 아이들이 현지 입양의 기회가 거의 없는 가난한 후진국 출신이거나, 입양이 받아들여지지 않는 문화권에서 살고 있습니다. 입양 부모는 대개 좀 더 부유한 선진국 사람들이고 이 아이들을 잘 돌볼 수 있는 재원을 가지고 있습니다. 입양아들은 좋은 교육을 받을 수 있고 물질적인 부분에 대해 걱정할 필요가 없을 것입니다. 가난한 나라에는 선진국만큼 법적인 제한이 많지 않기 때문에 입양 부모도 그런 나라의 아이들을 입양하는 것이 더 쉬운 편입니다. 하지만 여러 가지 이유로 인해 국제 입양을 반대하는 사람들이 있습니다. 주된 우려사항은 다른 나라에서 대개 문화가 다르고 종종 인종도 다른 사람들과 살면서 아이들이 자신의 문화적 주체성, 언어, 전통을 잃어버릴 수 있다는 겁니다. 나이가 들수록 이것은 입양아들에게 혼란을 줄 수 있습니다. 또 다른 문제는, 가난한 나라에는 규칙과 규정이 부족하기 때문에 입양 부모가 좋은 사람인지, 아이를 잘 보살필 것인지를 확인할 방법이 없다는 것입니다. 마지막으로, 아이에게는 아이를 돌볼 여유는 없지만 가족들과 연락이 끊기는 것에 대해 걱정하는 친척들이 있는 경우가 많다는 것입니다.

9 읽기와 듣기 지문에 따르면 다음 중 국외 입양에 대해 사실이 <u>아닌</u> 것은?

  (a) 국외 입양에 대한 한 가지 우려는 일부 나라에서 입양 부모에 대한 신원 조회를 잘 하지 않는 것이다.

  (b) 입양된 사실에 적응하는 것은 아이마다 다르고 입양 당시 아이의 나이에 많이 좌우된다.

  (c) 언어와 문화적 장벽은 아주 어린 입양아들과 새로운 부모들 간의 유대에 방해가 될 수도 있다.

  (d) 국외 입양아들에게 누가 친부모인지 알아내는 것은 더 힘들다.

  (e) 국외 입양아들의 친척들은 아이가 입양되면 연락이 끊길까 봐 걱정한다.

10 국외 입양에 대한 주된 우려사항으로 읽기와 듣기 지문에서 모두 언급된 것은?

  (a) 많은 유명 연예인들이 국외 입양에 대해 너무 많은 관심을 보이고 있어 국외 입양에 나쁜 이미지를 주고 있다.

  (b) 국외 입양아는 원래 가족을 만나거나 그들의 소식을 다시는 들을 수 없게 될 수도 있어 입양아와 원래 가족 모두에게 해가 될 수 있다.

  (c) 친부모를 찾아다니는 것은 친부모를 찾든 아니든 간에 입양아에게 큰 실망을 줄 수 있다.

  (d) 일부 나라는 관련된 아이들에게 충분한 관심이 없기 때문에 입양법이 부실해 절차가 너무 쉽다.

  (e) 입양아는 인종과 문화가 다른 부모에게 입양되면 특히 자신의 정체성을 잃을 수 있다.

***Dictation 정답**: Exercise 스크립트 밑줄 참조

Vocabulary Preview

A

1 espouse: 어떤 신념이나 정책, 견해를 지지하다
2 revitalize: 어떤 것에 다시 새로운 힘을 불어넣다
3 disseminate: 특히 정보 같은 것을 유포하다
4 intermittent: 규칙적이거나 지속적으로 일어나지 않는
5 procrastinate: 어떤 일을 하는 것을 미루다

B

1 put forth / 고고학자들은 현대 인류의 기원이 아프리카라는 이론을 개진했다.

2 Etching / 뜨겁게 달군 청동 핀으로 뼈에 새기는 것이 중국인들이 글을 쓴 초기 방법이었다.

3 eking out / 그는 자신의 유명한 역사소설이 출판되기 전에는 교사로 간신히 생계를 이어가고 있었다.

4 fostered / 마케도니아 정복자들은 패전국인 페르시아 제국에 자신들의 문화를 심었다.

5 humanoids / 초기 원인(原人)의 두개골과 치아, 턱뼈가 동아프리카의 유적지에서 발견되었다.

6 sect / 한 종파의 이집트 사제들은 나일 강의 신에게 해마다 홍수가 나게 해달라고 기도했다.

7 incursion / 13세기 몽고의 유럽 침입은 1242년 헝가리에서 멈추었다.

Expressions and Meanings

1 그들은 그것을 합법적으로 구입했다.
2 난 역사광이야.
3 바로 시작합시다.
4 너무 무리하지 마.
5 터무니없어!
6 거기에 대해서는 나도 잘 모르겠어.
7 그것 때문에 그들의 일정이 혼란스러워졌다.

  ⓕ 불공정 행위는 전혀 없었다.
  ⓖ 난 역사 공부를 정말 좋아해.
  ⓗ 시작해 볼까요?
  ⓐ 감당할 수 없는 일은 하지 마.
  ⓒ 재미있는 이야기지만 사실은 아니야.
  ⓓ 그게 뭔지 확실히는 모르겠어.
  ⓔ 그것은 그들의 일정을 망쳐놓았다.

Monolog

(O) (1) Africa   (2) seven   (3) volcanic   (4) potassium-argon   (5) humanoid   (6) settlements   (7) different humanoid groups   (8) 17,000   (9) descended   (10) humanoids   (11) cradle   (12) mankind

(G) 1 (b)   2 (b)

(S) (1) T   (2) F   (3) T   (4) T

M In Tanzania in eastern Africa lies a long, narrow valley called the Olduvai Gorge. Early in the 20th century, the remains of early humanoids and their settlements were discovered in the gorge. Over the last century, researchers have discovered fossils of humanoids, tools, fire pits, animal butcher sites, and many other indicators of settlement. The discoveries were made in seven different layers of exposed rock and soil, which were mostly of volcanic origin. Due to the volcanic nature of the rocks and stone tools, the researchers were able to use the potassium-argon dating method to date some of the remains to as far back as two million years. Skeletal remains found in the seven different layers were from different humanoid groups, and most of the remains found were teeth, jawbones, and skulls. One complete skeleton of a modern man, dated to 17,000 years ago, was unearthed. Famed Kenyan researcher Louis Leakey and his wife Mary are the most prominent of those who have studied and written about the Olduvai Gorge. Through patient and tireless investigation of the sites in the gorge and nearby it, the Leakeys and other researchers have concluded that these humanoid remains represent the earliest examples of man's ancestors. They put forth the now well-accepted theory that all humans on Earth are descended from these early humanoids and that the Olduvai Gorge is the cradle of all mankind.

▶ gorge 골짜기, 협곡   remains 유물, 유적   humanoid 원인(原人)   pit 구멍, 구덩이   potassium-argon dating 칼륨아르곤 연대 측정   unearth 발굴하다, 파내다   prominent 저명한, 두드러진   put forth 발표하다; 개진하다   cradle 요람

남 동아프리카의 탄자니아에는 올두바이 협곡이라는 길고 좁은 계곡이 있습니다. 20세기 초, 초기 원인(原人)과 그들의 거주 유적이 이 협곡에서 발견되었습니다. 20세기 내내 연구자들은 원인(原人)의 화석, 도구, 화덕, 동물을 도살하던 곳을 비롯해 그 밖에도 인간이 거주했음을 보여주는 많은 지표를 발견했습니다. 유적은 노출된 암석과 토양으로 된 일곱 개의 서로 다른 층에서 발견되었는데 대부분 화산으로 인해 형성된 것이었습니다. 암석과 석기들의 화산성 성질 덕분에 연구자들은 칼륨아르곤 연대 측정법을 이용해 일부 유적의 연대가 200만 년 전까지 거슬러 올라간다고 추정할 수 있었습니다. 일곱 개의 다른 층에서 발견된 뼈 유적은 상이한 원인(原人) 집단의 것으로, 대부분이 치아와 턱뼈, 두개골이었습니다. 현대 인류의 완벽한 해골이 하나 발굴되었는데, 1만 7천 년 전의 것이었습니다. 케냐의 저명한 연구자인 루이스 리키와 그의 아내 메리는 올두바이 협곡에 관해 연구하고 저술한 사람들 가운데 가장 유명합니다. 끈기를 갖고 꾸준히 협곡과 인근 유적지를 조사한 리키 부부와 다른 연구자들은 이 원인(原人) 유적이 인류 조상의 초창기 표본이라는 결론을 내렸습니다. 그들은 지구상의 모든 인간은 이 초기 원인(原人)의 자손이며 올두바이 협곡은 모든 인류의 요람이라는 지금은 널리 받아들여진 이론을 발표했습니다.

<u>General Questions</u>

1 담화의 요지는 무엇인가?
 (a) 아주 오래된 물체의 연대를 매기려면 화산암이 필요하다.
 (b) 현대 인류의 기원은 올두바이 협곡이다.
 (c) 유명한 리키 가족은 올두바이 협곡에 관해 연구했다.
 (d) 올두바이 협곡은 많은 인류 유적지 가운데 하나이다.

2 다음 중 가장 잘 요약된 것을 고르시오.
 (a) 인류학자들은 아프리카의 올두바이 협곡에서 잘 보존된 인류의 유적을 발굴했는데, 그곳은 화산 활동으로 형성된 곳이었다.
 (b) 아프리카의 올두바이 협곡에서 초기 인류의 주거지 유적이 발견되었는데 그곳은 모든 인류의 요람일 가능성이 높다.

<u>Specific Questions</u>

다시 듣고 옳은 문장에는 T, 틀린 문장에는 F를 쓰시오.
(1) 올두바이 협곡의 고고학적 유적은 토양과 암석으로 이루어진 일곱 개의 서로 다른 층에 있다.
(2) 고고학자들은 탄소 14 연대측정법을 사용해 그 유적의 연대를 측정했다.
(3) 루이스 리키와 메리 리키는 올두바이 협곡이 초기 인류가 살았던 곳이라고 주장했다.
(4) 고고학자들은 올두바이 협곡에서 서로 다른 유형의 초기 인류 유적을 발견했다.

Dialog

(N) (1) 1626 / myth / fair and square / true story   (2) 60   (3) 24   (4) glass beads   (5) 60   (6) English   (7) 1664

(G) 1 (c)   2 (b)

(S) (1) T   (2) F   (3) T   (4) T

G What a howler our history teacher told in class today!

B Tell me what he said.

G He said that the Dutch bought Manhattan Island in New York City from the natives for only 24 dollars. Can you believe it?

B Why is that a howler? It's mostly a true story. I've heard my grandmother tell it.

G It certainly isn't a true story. It's just a myth.

B There's a bit of truth to that myth. And it wasn't exactly for 24 dollars. That's a figure that was added to the story later. Supposedly, on May 24, 1626, Peter Minuit, one of the directors of the Dutch We India Company, paid a band of natives 60 guilders for the rights to the land on the island of Manhattan.

G What's 60 guilders in dollars?

B I don't know exactly, but, later on, a New York historian said that the price was 24 dollars, and, even later, someone else came up with a story that the island was bought for some glass beads and other simple supplies.

G So how do we know which story is true?

B There is a letter in the Dutch We India Company records telling the story of buying the land for 60 guilders.

G Then the Dutch bought the land fair and square from the natives.

B Maybe, but some historians think the natives had no concept of land ownership like the Europeans did, so they didn't even realize what they had done.

G Was there any trouble over the deal?

B No, I don't think so. The Dutch called the area New Amsterdam and stayed until the English defeated them in 1664.

▶ howler 포복절도할 오답, 허풍 myth 지어낸 이야기; 근거 없는 통념
band 무리, 일당 guilder 길더(네덜란드의 화폐 단위) fair and square 공정하게

여 오늘 수업 시간에 역사 선생님이 어찌나 터무니없는 얘기를 하시던지!
남 뭐라고 하셨는지 말해봐.
여 네덜란드인이 뉴욕의 맨해튼 섬을 원주민한테서 겨우 24달러에 샀다지 뭐야. 믿어져?
남 그게 왜 터무니없는 말이야? 대부분 사실인데. 나도 할머니가 말씀하시는 걸 들은 적이 있어.
여 그건 절대 실화가 아니야. 그냥 근거 없는 이야기일 뿐이라고.
남 그 이야기에도 어느 정도 진실은 있어. 그리고 정확히 24달러에 산 건 아니었지. 그건 나중에 그 이야기에 덧붙여진 숫자일 뿐. 네덜란드 서인도 회사 총독 가운데 한 명이었던 피터 미누잇이 1626년 5월 24일에 맨해튼 섬의 땅에 대한 권리를 얻는 대가로 원주민 무리에게 60길더를 지불한 걸로 되어 있어.
여 60길더면 달러로 얼마야?
남 정확히는 모르지만 나중에 어떤 뉴욕 역사가가 그 가격이 24달러였다고 했어. 한참 뒤에 누군가 그 섬이 유리 구슬 몇 개와 다른 간단한 공급품에 팔렸다는 이야기를 지어냈지.
여 그럼 어느 이야기가 사실인지 어떻게 알지?
남 네덜란드 서인도 회사의 기록 중에 편지 한 통이 있는데 거기에 그 섬을 60길더에 샀다는 이야기가 나와.
여 그럼 네덜란드인은 그 섬을 원주민한테서 정당하게 산 거네.
남 그렇다고 할 수도 있지. 하지만 그 당시 원주민은 유럽인처럼 땅에 대한 소유권 개념이 없어서 자신들이 뭘 했는지도 몰랐을 거라는 게 일부 역사가들의 생각이야.
여 그 거래로 무슨 문제라도 있었어?
남 아니, 없었을 거야. 네덜란드인은 그 지역을 뉴암스테르담이라고 부르며 1664년 영국에게 패할 때까지 정착해 살았거든.

General Questions

1 대화에서 나타나는 소년의 의도는 무엇인가?
 (a) 초기 미국 역사에 관한 이야기를 반박하려고
 (b) 대부분은 사실이 아닌 역사 이야기를 하려고
 (c) 미국 역사에서 일어난 어떤 사건에 대해 진짜 설명을 해주려고
 (d) 어떤 이야기가 어느 정도는 진실이라는 것을 납득시키려고

2 다음 중 가장 잘 요약된 것을 고르시오.
 (a) 네덜란드인이 1626년에 맨해튼 섬을 원주민에게서 24달러에 구입한 거래는 정당했다.
 (b) 네덜란드인의 맨해튼 섬 구입에 관한 이야기는 실제로 일어난 사건에 근거하고 있지만 세부적인 내용은 세월이 지나면서 바뀌었다.

Specific Questions

다시 듣고 옳은 문장에는 T, 틀린 문장에는 F를 쓰시오.
(1) 소녀는 역사 선생님이 한 이야기가 사실이라기엔 너무 터무니없다고 생각했다.
(2) 네덜란드 서인도 회사는 피터 미누잇에게 맨해튼에 대한 권리의 대가를 지불했다.
(3) 맨해튼의 구입가는 세월이 흘러 이야기가 구전되면서 바뀌었다.
(4) 1664년 네덜란드인은 결국 영국인에게 맨해튼의 통치권을 내주었다.

Long Lecture

O (1) farmland (2) delta (3) farming (4) floods
(5) nutrient-rich (6) flooding (7) floods (8) August
(9) September (10) transportation (11) kingdom
(12) barrier (13) civilization

1 (a) 2 (a) 3 (1) F (2) F (3) T (4) F 4 (d)

Dictation 정답: 스크립트 밑줄 참조

W Without the Nile River, the <u>ancient</u> <u>civilization</u> in Egypt would most likely never have developed. The Nile <u>provided</u> several things for the people of ancient Egypt, including a <u>source</u> <u>of</u> <u>drinking</u> <u>water</u>, a <u>means</u> of <u>transportation</u>, and a method to <u>revitalize</u> the soil of <u>farmland</u> during the <u>annual</u> <u>Nile</u> <u>floods</u>. Some <u>evidence</u> <u>points</u> to the land around the Nile being <u>semi-arid</u> <u>farmland</u> in the past, but, by about 8,000 B.C., the land in Egypt <u>surrounding</u> the Nile was <u>desert</u>. The Egyptian people <u>lived</u> <u>along</u> <u>the</u> <u>banks</u> of the Nile and in the <u>wide</u> <u>delta</u> that forms at <u>its</u> <u>mouth,</u> where it <u>flows</u> into the Mediterranean Sea. Even today, almost all of Egypt's people live along or near the Nile River and its delta. In ancient Egypt, farming was the <u>main</u> <u>method</u> people used to <u>eke</u> <u>out</u> an <u>existence,</u> and the <u>floods</u> of the Nile helped farmers by <u>bringing</u> <u>nutrient-rich</u> <u>silt</u> to their farmland. Some years, the Nile floods were <u>too</u> <u>great</u> and <u>caused</u> a <u>great</u> <u>amount</u> <u>of</u> <u>destruction,</u> and other years they were <u>insufficient</u>. In order to get the <u>right</u> <u>amount</u> <u>of</u> flooding, the ancient Egyptians <u>prayed</u> <u>to</u> the Nile River god to <u>bring</u> <u>the</u> <u>floods</u> each year, which usually <u>occurred</u> in late August or early September by our <u>modern</u> <u>calendar</u>. The god was called Hapy, and a <u>whole</u> <u>sect</u> <u>of</u> Egyptian <u>priests</u> <u>was</u> <u>dedicated</u> <u>to</u> this god and the <u>controlling</u> <u>of the</u> <u>annual</u> Nile floods. Besides providing rich soil for farming, the Nile River provided an <u>easy</u> <u>means</u> of transportation and <u>allowed</u> <u>greater</u> <u>control</u> of the <u>kingdom</u>. Finally, the deserts surrounding the <u>fertile</u> Nile River provided a <u>barrier</u> to <u>enemy</u> <u>invaders</u>. The <u>longevity</u> of the Egyptian civilization, which <u>lasted</u> for thousands of years, is mostly due to these facts.

▶ revitalize 회복시키다 semi-arid 강우량이 적고 증발이 심한, 반건조성의
bank 강둑, 강기슭 delta 삼각주 mouth 강어귀 Mediterranean Sea 지중해
eke out ~을 겨우 이어 나가다 existence 생활, 생계 silt 모래보다 잘고 진흙보다
거친 침적토, 미사 insufficient 불충분한 sect 종파, 분파 fertile 비옥한
longevity 장수 barrier 방벽, 장벽 dedicate 헌납하다; 바치다; 전념하다
means 방법, 수단

여 나일 강이 없었다면 고대 이집트 문명은 결코 발달하지 못했을 것입니다. 나일 강은 고대 이집트인들에게 식수원과 운송 수단, 해마다 나일 강이 범람할 때 농지의 토양을 회복시키는 방법을 포함한 몇 가지를 제공해주었습니다. 과거에는 나일 강 유역의 땅이 반건조성 농지였음을 나타내는 증거가 몇 가지 있지만, 기원전 8,000년경 나일 강 주변의 이집트 땅은 사막이었죠. 이집트인은 나일 강기슭과 지중해로 흘러들어가는 강어귀에 형성된 넓은 삼각주에 살았습니다. 오늘날에도 거의 모든 이집트인들은 나일 강과 삼각주, 또는 그 근방에 살고 있습니다. 고대 이집트에서는 농업이 생계를 이어갈 수 있는 주된 방법이었고, 나일 강의 범람은 농지에 자양분이 풍부한 미사를 실어 와 줘서 농부들에게 도움이 되었습니다. 어떤 해에는 나일 강이 너무 많이 범람해서 엄청난 손실을 입히기도 했

고 또 어떤 해에는 범람이 불충분하기도 했습니다. 강의 적당한 범람을 위해 고대 이집트인들은 나일 강의 신에게 강이 매년 범람하게 해달라고 기도했는데, 범람은 대개 현대 달력으로 8월 말이나 9월 초에 일어났습니다. 그 신은 하피라고 불렸고, 모든 종파의 이집트 사제들은 이 신을 모시면서 해마다 나일 강의 범람을 조절하는 데 전념했습니다. 나일 강은 농사 지을 기름진 토양을 제공하는 것 외에 편한 운송 수단도 제공해주어 왕국의 통치가 더 강화될 수 있었습니다. 마지막으로, 비옥한 나일 강을 둘러싼 사막은 침입자들을 막아주는 방벽이 되었습니다. 이집트 문명이 수천 년 동안 지속될 수 있었던 것은 대부분 이 같은 요소들 덕분입니다.

1 강의의 주목적은 무엇인가?
(a) 나일 강이 이집트에게 주는 이점을 살펴보려고
(b) 나일 강에 대한 종교적인 숭배에 관해 이야기하려고
(c) 매년 일어나는 나일 강 범람의 특징을 설명하려고
(d) 나일 강이 어떻게 이집트 문명을 보호했는지 살펴보려고

2 다음 중 가장 잘 요약된 것을 고르시오.
(a) 나일 강은 고대 이집트인들에게 많은 혜택을 주었으며, 나일 강이 없었다면 이집트 문명은 결코 존재하지 않았을지도 모른다.
(b) 나일 강은 이집트인들이 농지를 경작할 수 있도록 물을 공급했으며, 그래서 그들의 문명이 발달했다.

3 옳은 문장에는 T, 틀린 문장에는 F를 쓰시오.
(1) 나일 강의 범람을 조절하는 책임은 이집트 파라오에게 있었다.
(2) 나일 강의 범람은 매년 똑같은 수위였다.
(3) 나일 강은 이집트의 파라오들이 더욱 쉽게 국민을 통치할 수 있게 해주었다.
(4) 이집트는 많은 침략에 시달렸으며 적에게 자주 점령당했다.

4 강의에서 언급된 바에 따르면 고대 이집트의 어떤 측면이 오늘날에도 여전히 사실인가?
(a) 이집트인들은 아직도 범람에 의존해 농사를 짓는다.
(b) 하피 같은 신들에 대한 숭배는 여전히 흔한 일이다.
(c) 이따금 일어나는 나일 강의 범람은 여전히 이집트에 엄청난 피해를 끼친다.
(d) 대부분의 이집트인들은 아직도 나일 강 주변과 삼각주에 살고 있다.

Exercise

p. 84~p. 85

1 (c) 2 해설 참조 3 (b) 4 (b) 5 (b) 6 (c) 7 (d) 8 (c) 9 (a)
10 해설 참조 11 (c) 12 (b)

1

M The <u>ancient civilization</u> known as Sumer was the first place where <u>humans settled</u> in great numbers, developed <u>intensive agriculture</u>, and created <u>institutions</u> of civilization similar to what we have today. Sumer was <u>located in</u> the region <u>known as</u> Mesopotamia, the land between the Tigris and Euphrates rivers in what is now southern Iraq. <u>Archaeologically</u>, the evidence shows that <u>early settlers</u> of Sumer <u>came from</u> the northern region of modern Iraq. The first cities, which were really more like small towns, <u>arose around</u> 5,300 B.C. The <u>fertile floodplains</u> of the Tigris and Euphrates rivers <u>enabled</u> the early Sumerians to grow a <u>surplus of food</u> through <u>intensive agriculture</u> and <u>extensive irrigation</u> based on the waters of the two rivers. This enabled the people to <u>remain</u> in one place and to <u>develop civilization</u>. By 4,000 B.C., many cities <u>had arisen</u>, and elements such as <u>religion</u>, military forces, <u>slavery</u>, government, and <u>bureaucracy</u> had been established. The <u>earliest kind of</u> human writing, called cuneiform, was <u>also developed</u> in the region around 3,500 B.C., which gives us the <u>oldest known records</u> from any civilization of the past. These records show <u>intermittent warfare</u> between the various Sumerian city-states. Different city-states on occasion <u>managed to establish</u> themselves as the <u>preeminent power</u>. The <u>decline</u> of Sumer <u>began around</u> 2,000 B.C., when a <u>greater salinity</u> of the soil led to <u>reduced crop yields</u>, which in turn <u>resulted in</u> many people leaving the area. Around 1,700 B.C., the Babylonians <u>conquered</u> the area, effectively ending the Sumer period of Mesopotamia's history.

▶ intensive 집약적인 institution 제도, 관습 floodplain 범람원(홍수 때 강물이 평상시의 물길에서 넘쳐 범람하는 범위의 평야) surplus 여분, 잉여 irrigation 관개, 물을 끌어들임 bureaucracy 관료 (제도) cuneiform 설형 문자 intermittent 간헐적인 preeminent 뛰어난, 걸출한 salinity 염분, 염도

남 수메르로 알려진 고대 문명지는 인류가 대규모로 정착해서 집약적인 농업을 발전시키고 현재 우리가 갖고 있는 것과 유사한 문명 제도를 만든 첫 번째 장소입니다. 수메르는 지금의 이라크 남부에 있는 티그리스 강과 유프라테스 강 사이의 메소포타미아로 알려진 지역에 위치해 있었습니다. 고고학적인 증거에 의하면 수메르의 초기 정착자들은 현대 이라크의 북부 지역에서 왔다는 것을 알 수 있습니다. 사실상 작은 읍에 더 가까운 최초의 도시는 기원전 5,300년 경에 생겨났습니다. 초기 수메르 인들은 티그리스 강과 유프라테스 강의 기름진 범람원 덕분에 집약적인 농업과 두 강물을 바탕으로 한 대규모 관개를 통해 잉여 식량을 수확할 수 있었습니다. 이로써 사람들이 한 곳에 머무르면서 문명을 발전시킬 수 있게 되었죠. 기원전 4,000년까지 많은 도시들이 생겨났으며 종교, 군대, 노예 제도, 정부, 관료 제도 같은 요소들이 확립되었습니다. 기원전 3,500년에는 설형 문자라고 불리는 가장 초기 형태의 글이 그 지역에서 나타나기도 했는데, 그것은 과거 어떤 문명에서보다도 오래된 기록으로 알려져 있습니다. 이 기록을 통해 수메르의 다양한 도시 국가들 사이에 간헐적으로 전쟁이 있었다는 것을 알 수 있습니다. 이런저런 도시 국가들이 이따금 막강한 강대국이 되기도 했습니다. 수메르 문명은 토양의 염도가 더욱 높아지면서 농작물 수확이 줄자 많은 사람들이 그 지역을 떠나면서 기원전 2,000년경에 쇠퇴하기 시작했습니다. 기원전 1,700년경 바빌로니아 인들이 그 지역을 정복하면서 메소포타미아 역사에서 수메르 시대는 사실상 막을 내리게 되었습니다.

1 담화에 가장 알맞은 제목은 무엇인가?
(a) 수메르 인의 기원
(b) 세계 최초의 문명: 수메르
(c) 고대 수메르의 흥망성쇠
(d) 수메르 도시의 발전
(e) 인류에 대한 수메르 인의 공헌

2

W Today on *History Speaks*, we are <u>discussing</u> the Battle of Thermopylae from <u>ancient Greek history</u> with Professor Higgins from the local university. First, Professor, <u>could you explain</u> the battle?

M Yes. To <u>put it simply</u>, the Persians <u>invaded</u> Greece in 480 B.C. A force of Greeks <u>led by</u> the Spartans <u>blocked</u> the Persian advance in a <u>narrow coastal area</u> called Thermopylae. After three days of <u>intense battle</u>, the Persians <u>managed to defeat</u> the Greek force.

W Now, this action by the Greeks is <u>considered</u> <u>heroic</u> because so few men <u>held off</u> tens of thousands of Persians. Is that correct?

M Yes, but there is some <u>dispute over</u> the <u>exact numbers</u> on both sides. <u>Traditionally</u>, it was said that only 300 Spartans <u>delayed over</u> 200,000 Persians.

W But there were some other Greeks <u>alongside</u> the Spartans.

M Correct. There were <u>at least</u> 7,000 Greeks at the battle. There were 4,000 from the Peloponnesian Peninsula, where Sparta was located. That <u>total includes</u> the 300 Spartans. And there were about 3,000 other Greeks, including 400 Thebans and 700 Thespians, <u>who also died</u> to the last man.

W And what about the <u>number of Persians</u>?

M This is <u>more difficult to ascertain</u>. Confusion <u>exists</u> because perhaps <u>half a million</u> Persians came to Greece, but only around 200,000 Persians <u>fought at</u> Thermopylae.

W What were the <u>total casualties</u> on each side?

M The best guess is that in <u>three days of battle</u>, the Persians lost about ten percent of their men while the <u>Greeks lost</u> all of the Spartans, Thebans, and Thespians. Most of the rest of the Greek force <u>retreated</u>.

▶ put it simply 간단히 말하자면 advance 전진, 진군 intense 격렬한
action 교전, 전투; 군사 행동 hold off 막다 alongside (~의) 쪽에
peninsula 반도 to the last man 최후의 한 사람까지
ascertain 확인하다, 확실히 하다 casualty 사상자 retreat 퇴각, 후퇴

여 오늘 〈역사는 말한다〉에서는 고대 그리스 역사에서 테르모필레 전투에 관해 이 지역 대학의 히긴스 교수님과 함께 얘기를 나눠보겠습니다. 교수님, 먼저 그 전투에 대해 설명해 주시겠습니까?

남 네. 간단히 말씀 드리자면 기원전 480년에 페르시아가 그리스를 침략했습니다. 스파르타가 이끄는 그리스 군대가 테르모필레라고 불리는 좁은 해안 지역에서 페르시아의 진군을 막아냈죠. 3일간의 치열한 전투 뒤에 페르시아는 간신히 그리스 군대를 물리쳤습니다.

여 너무나 적은 인원으로 수만 명의 페르시아 군을 막아냈기 때문에 그리스의 이 전투는 오늘날 영웅적인 것으로 간주되고 있죠. 맞습니까?

남 네, 하지만 양측의 정확한 숫자에 대해서는 약간의 논란이 있습니다. 예전부터 전해지기로는 겨우 300명의 스파르타 군이 20만 명이 넘는 페르시아 군을 지연시켰다고 했었죠.

여 하지만 스파르타 군 측에는 다른 그리스군도 조금 있었잖아요.

남 맞습니다. 최소한 7,000명의 그리스 군이 전투에 참가했죠. 스파르타가 위치해 있던 펠로폰네소스 반도에서 온 사람들이 4,000명이었습니다. 이 합계에는 300명의 스파르타 군이 포함되어 있죠. 그리고 테베 군 400명과 테스피아 군 700명을 포함해 약 3,000명의 다른 그리스 군이 있었는데 모두 전사했습니다.

여 그럼 페르시아 군의 숫자는 어떻게 되나요?

남 이건 확인하기가 더 어렵습니다. 왜냐하면 50만 명의 페르시아 군이 그리스에 왔을 텐데 테르모필레 전투에서는 20만 명 정도밖에 싸우지 않았기 때문에 애매한 점이 있거든요.

여 양측의 총 사상자 수는 어떻게 되죠?

남 가장 그럴듯한 추측은 3일간의 전투에서 페르시아는 병력의 약 10%를 잃은 반면 그리스는 스파르타 군과 테베 군, 테스피아 군을 모두 잃었다는 겁니다. 남은 그리스 군 대부분은 후퇴했죠.

---

2 테르모필레 전투에 관해 빠진 정보를 채워 표를 완성하시오.

병사	수
전체 그리스 군	7,000
– 스파르타 군	300
– 테베 군	400
– 테스피아 군	700
그리스 군 사망자	1,400
전체 페르시아 군	200,000
페르시아 군 사망자	20,000

3-4

W Many details about <u>early Chinese history</u> come from a form of writing called <u>oracle bone script</u>. This type of writing was done with a <u>heated bronze</u> pin <u>etching on</u> animal bones or sometimes on the <u>underside of turtle shells</u>. The <u>earliest examples</u> of oracle bone script <u>come from</u> the Shang Dynasty, in about 1,400 B.C. The <u>style of writing</u> on bones or turtle shells <u>lasted until</u> around 1,100 B.C., when the Shang Dynasty ended. At the time, oracle bone script <u>was used</u> for <u>purposes of divination</u>, which I guess we would call <u>fortune telling today</u>. The bones or turtle shells were <u>inscribed</u> with a question and then <u>heated over</u> a fire. An <u>expert interpreted</u> the <u>resulting cracks</u> in the bone or turtle shell as an answer to the question. <u>Topics for</u> the divination questions <u>included issues</u> like <u>war, trade</u>, the health of the royal family, and the weather as it <u>related to agriculture</u>. Oracle bone writing was also used to <u>record information</u> about the Shang Dynasty and its events. These are the earliest examples of historical records in China. However, where exactly the oracle bone script <u>originated is still unknown</u>. There are examples of <u>what appear</u> to be writing from early times, but there are <u>disputes among scholars</u> over these samples. There has as yet been <u>no connection made</u> between them and oracle bone script. Therefore, it is <u>entirely possible</u> that oracle bone script is the <u>origin of</u> all modern Chinese writing.

▶ oracle bone script 갑골문(甲骨文) etch (동판 등에) 식각하다, 에칭하다
underside 아래쪽, 밑면 divination 점(占) inooribo 새기다, 파다

여 갑골문(甲骨文)이라고 불리는 형태의 글에는 중국의 초기 역사에 관한 자세한 내용이 많이 나와 있습니다. 갑골문은 불에 달군 청동 바늘로 동물의 뼈나 때로는 거북이 껍질의 밑면에 새긴 것입니다. 갑골문의 가장 초기본은 기원전 1,400년경인 상(商) 왕조 시대의 것입니다. 뼈나 거북이 껍질에 글을 쓰는 방식은 기원전 1,100년경 상 왕조가 끝날 때까지 계속되었습니다. 당시 갑골문은 점복의 용도로 사용되었는데, 오늘날에는 이것을 점(占)이라고 부를 겁니다. 뼈나 거북이 껍질에 질문을 새겨 넣고 불 위에서 가열합니다. 전문가는 그렇게 해서 뼈나 거북이 껍질에 나타난 금을 질문에 대한 대답으로 해석했죠. 점을 쳐서 물어보는 질문의 내용은 전쟁, 무역, 왕족의 건강, 농업과 관련된 날씨 같은 것들이었습니다. 갑골문은 상 왕조에 관한 정보와 당시 일어난 일들을 기록하는 데에도 사용되었습니다. 이 기록들이 중국의 가장 오래된 역사 기록본입니다. 그러나 갑골문이 정확히 어디에서 유래했는지는 아직 알려지지 않았습니다. 고대부터 써온 것처럼 보이는 사례들이 있긴 하지만 이 표본들에 관해서는 학자들 사이에 논란이 있습니다. 현재로서는 그 표본들과 갑골문 사이에 아무런 연관이 없습니다. 따라서 갑골문이 모든 현대 중국 문자의 기원일 가능성은 충분합니다.

3 상 왕조의 갑골문의 주된 용도는 무엇이었는가?
  (a) 당대의 농업 기록을 남기기 위해
  (b) 점복을 치기 위한 질문을 적기 위해

(c) 후대의 중국 문자를 위한 토대를 마련하기 위해
(d) 왕실의 신성을 보여주기 위해
(e) 초기 문자 형태의 기록을 보존하기 위해

4 갑골문에 대해 담화로부터 유추할 수 있는 것은 무엇인가?
(a) 뼈보다 거북이 껍질에 쓰는 것이 더 쉬웠다.
(b) 깊이 새겨졌기 때문에 오래 보존되었다.
(c) 당시 사용되고 있었던 많은 글쓰기 방법 가운데 하나였다.
(d) 상 왕조 이후에도 계속 사용되었다.
(e) 목판 인쇄로 대체되었다.

M Hi, Joanna, I'm Eric. I'm going to be your <u>history tutor</u>.

G Hi. I have a <u>project</u> to <u>do</u>, so <u>let's jump</u> to it, okay? Do you know anything about Mongolia?

M Yes. <u>What</u> aspect of Mongolia are you doing <u>your project on</u>?

G Its empire. I know the Mongols <u>conquered parts of</u> Europe in the 13th century, but I'm a little <u>foggy on the</u> details.

M Let's do some <u>research</u> in the textbook.

G Okay. Let's see... page 342... the <u>Mongol</u> invasion of Europe. Mongol leader Genghis Khan died in 1227, and the first Mongol <u>raids into</u> European Russia began in the 1230s.

M What was the extent of the Mongol <u>incursion into</u> Europe?

G They <u>went into</u> modern-day Russia and then <u>as far as</u> Poland and Hungary. Then they <u>withdrew</u> in 1242.

M Right so far. Now, why didn't the Mongols conquer all of Europe, and why did they withdraw?

G Give me a minute. Ah. Here it is. The <u>successor</u> to Genghis Kahn was his son Ogedei, who died in 1241. Ogedei's wife <u>tried to take power</u> and was <u>opposed by</u> many nobles. As a result, there was a four-year period of <u>indecision</u>. This led to the <u>beginning of the decline</u> of the Mongol Empire.

M It <u>seems like</u> you know more than <u>you thought</u>. I think you have <u>enough information</u> without <u>dealing with</u> the <u>demise</u> of the later Mongol Empire. You don't want to <u>bite off</u> more than <u>you can chew</u>.

G That sounds like a good idea. Now I need to <u>write a paper</u> on it.

M <u>Let's get started</u>.

G Now? I mean, it's not due for another three days.

M It's better to get started now than to <u>procrastinate</u> and have to <u>cram everything into</u> the last day.

▶ jump to it 빨리빨리 착수하다, 서두르다 foggy 불확실한, 막연한 raid 습격, 기습
extent 면적, 범위 incursion 습격, 침입 indecision 결단력이 없음, 우유부단
demise 서거, 소멸 bite off more than one can chew 분에 넘치는 일을 하다
procrastinate 꾸물거리다, 질질 끌다 cram 벼락치기 하다

남 안녕, 조안나. 난 에릭이야. 이제부터 내가 네 역사 개인 교사가 될 거란다.
여 안녕하세요. 제가 해야 할 과제가 있거든요. 그러니까 바로 시작하죠, 괜찮죠?
    몽고에 관해 아세요?

남 응. 몽고의 어떤 면에 대한 과제를 하고 있니?
여 몽고 제국요. 몽고가 13세기에 유럽의 여러 지역을 정복했다는 건 알고 있는데
    자세한 건 잘 모르겠어요.
남 교과서를 한번 살펴보자.
여 네. 어디 보자… 342쪽. 몽고의 유럽 침략. 몽고의 지도자 칭기즈칸은 1227년
    에 죽었고 유럽계 러시아에 대한 몽고의 첫 침략은 1230년대에 시작되었어요.
남 몽고가 유럽을 침략한 범위는 얼마나 되지?
여 오늘날의 러시아를 침략한 다음 폴란드와 헝가리까지 진격했어요. 그러고 나서
    1242년에 철수했죠.
남 거기까지는 맞아. 그럼 왜 몽고는 유럽을 모두 정복하지 않고 철수했을까?
여 잠깐만요. 아, 여기 있다. 칭기즈칸의 후계자는 아들 오게데이였는데 1241년에
    죽었어요. 오게데이의 아내가 권력을 쥐기 위해 노력했는데 많은 귀족들의 반대
    에 부딪쳤죠. 그 결과 4년간의 공백 기간이 생겼어요. 이 때문에 몽고 제국은 쇠
    퇴하기 시작했고요.
남 넌 네가 생각하는 것보다 더 많은 걸 알고 있는 것 같구나. 그 정도면 이후의 몽
    고 제국의 몰락에 관해 다루지 않아도 될 만큼 충분한 정보인 것 같다. 감당할 수
    있을 만큼만 해야지.
여 좋은 생각인 것 같아요. 그럼 거기에 관해 과제를 써야겠네요.
남 그럼 시작해보자.
여 지금요? 제 말은, 기한이 아직 사흘이나 남았는걸요.
남 지금 시작하는 게 질질 끌다가 마지막 날 전부 벼락치기해야 하는 것보단 낫지.

5 소녀는 무엇이 어렵다고 생각하는가?
(a) 학교의 역사 과제에 쓸 주제를 결정하는 것
(b) 몽고 제국에 관한 세부적인 내용을 명확하게 정리하는 것
(c) 인터넷을 이용해 역사 조사를 하는 것
(d) 몽고의 정복 연대를 암기하는 것
(e) 본격적으로 리포트를 쓸 시간을 내는 것

6 다음 중 내용을 가장 잘 요약한 것을 고르시오.
(a) 학생과 그녀의 개인 교사는 13세기에 몽고의 유럽 침략이 실패한 이
    유를 바탕으로 과제 작성을 마친다.
(b) 개인 교사는 조사를 위해 교과서를 이용하는 방법을 학생에게 가르쳐
    주고, 몽고의 유럽 침략에 대한 과제에 대해 몇 가지 조언을 해준다.
(c) 학생은 몽고의 유럽 침략에 관한 몇몇 측면을 이해하는 데 어려움을 겪
    고 있어서 개인 교사의 도움으로 교과서에서 자세한 내용을 찾아본다.

M I'm doing a <u>crossword puzzle</u>. What's a five-letter word for an <u>ancient civilization</u>?

W I bet the answer is China.

M No, it <u>doesn't fit</u>. Wait. There was Egypt... No, it doesn't fit either.

W Then it has to be the <u>Indus civilization</u>.

M You mean India, right?

W No, Indus. I-N-D-U-S. <u>Does it fit</u>?

M Yeah, <u>perfectly</u>. What was the Indus civilization?

W One of the <u>world's original civilizations</u>. It was located <u>along</u> the <u>Indus River Valley</u> in the area of Pakistan and India today. It <u>lasted from</u> about 5,000 to 1,700 B.C.

M Oh, now I remember. I think we <u>learned about it</u> in school. Didn't it have a lot of cities?

W Yes, but there are no <u>great monuments</u> or <u>pyramids</u> like in Egypt and no Great Wall like in China. Maybe that's why the Indus is <u>not</u> as <u>famous as</u> other civilizations.

M <u>What happened to</u> the Indus civilization?

W No one knows for sure. By 1,700 B.C., most of its people had left or died. Some researchers think there was a change in the climate that reduced food supplies or that the river systems may have been diverted by earthquakes.

▶ monument 기념물, 유물; 기념비   divert 딴 데로 돌리다, 전환하다

남 지금 낱말 맞추기 퀴즈를 풀고 있는데 다섯 글자로 된 고대 문명이 뭐지?
여 정답은 분명히 중국일 거야.
남 아니야, 안 맞아. 잠깐만. 이집트가 있었지… 아니야, 이것도 안 맞네.
여 그럼 분명히 인더스 문명일 거야.
남 그러니까 인도 말하는 거지, 그렇지?
여 아니, 인더스. I-N-D-U-S. 맞아?
남 응. 딱 맞아. 인더스 문명은 어떤 거였어?
여 세계 최초의 문명 가운데 하나야. 오늘날의 파키스탄과 인도 지역에 있는 인더스 강 계곡을 따라 있었지. 기원전 5,000년부터 1,700년경까지 이어졌어.
남 아, 이제 기억난다. 학교에서 거기에 대해 배웠던 것 같아. 도시들이 많이 있지 않았어?
여 응, 하지만 이집트처럼 거대한 기념물이나 피라미드도 없고 중국 같은 만리장성도 없어. 아마 그래서 인더스가 다른 문명들만큼 유명하지 않은 걸 거야.
남 인더스 문명은 어떻게 되었어?
여 누구도 확실히는 몰라. 기원전 1,700년까지 그 문명의 사람들이 대부분 떠나거나 죽었거든. 일부 연구자들은 식량 공급을 감소시킨 기후 변화가 있었거나 지진으로 강의 흐름이 바뀌었을 수도 있다고 생각하지.

7 Why does the woman think the Indus civilization is not as famous as those of ancient China or Egypt?
여자는 왜 인더스 문명이 고대 중국이나 이집트 문명처럼 유명하지 않다고 생각하는가?

(a) It is no longer a country like China or Egypt.
더 이상 중국이나 이집트 같은 국가가 아니다.
(b) It is not commonly studied in school.
학교에서 일반적으로 배우지 않는다.
(c) Its people died a long time ago.
그곳 사람들이 오래 전에 죽었다.
(d) It did not leave any monumental structures.
어떠한 기념비적인 구조물도 남기지 않았다.
(e) It did not have great cities like the others.
다른 문명들처럼 큰 도시가 없었다.

8 Level up

M In ancient Korea for a time, there were three main kingdoms: the Silla, the Baekje, and the Goguryeo. The Silla kingdom developed an elite corps of male youths called the *Hwarang*, or "Flower Youths," who were dedicated to the kingdom. Information about the formation of this group is scanty, but all accounts seem to agree that sometime in the early 6th century A.D., after the Silla kingdom adopted Buddhism, the *Hwarang* were founded. The members were selected from the best young males of elite families. At first, it is believed it was more like a social club, but, gradually, the *Hwarang* took on a military aspect. Its members learned hand-to-hand combat skills, archery, horsemanship, and other necessary military skills. They espoused Buddhist principles and also followed a doctrine of loyalty to the state, to their families, and to each other. Stories of the *Hwarang* being at the forefront of fighting to unite the three kingdoms are legion, and they may have been instrumental in the final unification of ancient Korea in 688 A.D.

▶ corps 군단, 병단   scanty 빈약한, 불충분한   hand-to-hand combat 백병전   archery 궁술   horsemanship 승마술   espouse 신봉하다, 지지하다   doctrine 원칙; 주의; 교리   forefront 최전선, 선봉   legion 많은, 무수한   instrumental 도움이 되는, 수단이 되는

남 고대 한국에는 한동안 세 왕국이 있었는데 바로 신라, 백제, 고구려였습니다. 신라 왕국은 젊은 남성들로 이루어진 화랑(花郞), 즉 '꽃 같은 젊은이들'이라는 정예 부대를 양성했는데 그들은 신라 왕국에 헌신했습니다. 이 단체의 구성에 대한 정보는 충분치 않지만 신라 왕국이 불교를 받아들이고 난 다음인 서기 6세기 초의 어느 시점에 화랑 제도가 설립되었다는 점에 대해서는 모든 기록이 일치하는 것 같습니다. 낭도들은 상류 가문의 가장 훌륭한 젊은 남성들 가운데서 뽑혔습니다. 처음에는 사교 모임에 가까웠던 것으로 보이지만, '화랑'은 점차 군사적인 면모를 갖추게 되었습니다. 낭도들은 백병전 기술, 궁술, 승마술, 그리고 다른 요긴한 군사 기술들을 배웠습니다. 그들은 불교의 계율을 신봉했으며 또한 국가와 가족, 서로에 대해 충성한다는 원칙을 따랐습니다. 세 왕국을 통일하기 위한 싸움의 선봉에 있던 '화랑'의 이야기는 무수히 많으며, 그들은 서기 688년 고대 한국을 최종적으로 통일하는 데 도움이 되었을 것입니다.

8 Which is NOT mentioned in the talk?
다음 중 담화에서 언급되지 않은 것은?

(a) The political situation in ancient Korea
고대 한국의 정치적인 상황
(b) The skills of the ancient Flower Youths   고대 화랑의 기술
(c) The names of some famous Flower Youths
몇몇 유명한 화랑의 이름
(d) The special military force of the Silla kingdom
신라 왕국의 특수 부대
(e) The beliefs of the ancient Flower Youths   고대 화랑의 신념

9

W The term Hellenism is used to describe the influence of Greek culture in the Mediterranean world and the Middle East after the period of Alexander the Great's conquests in the late 4th century B.C. Alexander was a king of Macedonia, a land to the north of modern-day Greece. He conquered the Persian Empire and invaded India before his death in 323 B.C. As he marched, Alexander founded cities, and his heirs set up Greek kingdoms in the former lands of the Persian Empire. They spoke Greek dialects and fostered Greek ideas on their new subjects. This cultural exchange was not a totally one-way street as the Greeks adopted customs from the locals, and there was much intermarrying. However much the higher classes interacted with the Greeks, there was probably not much change in the lives and cultures of the lower classes of the conquered lands. One of the greatest contributors to the spread of Hellenism was the library in the city of Alexandria in Egypt. Alexander laid the foundation for the city, which became the main seat of scholarly learning in the known world and the center of Hellenism for hundreds of years. Scholars from all over the Mediterranean world made their way to Alexandria and its famous museum, which is more like what we would call a library today. Through its large collection of scrolls and manuscripts, the Library of Alexandria stored and disseminated knowledge from all corners of the known world.

▶ heir 후계자 dialect 방언, 지방 사투리 foster 마음에 품다; 육성하다, 촉진하다
subject 백성, 국민 one-way street 일방 통행로 scroll 두루마리
manuscript 필사본, 원고 disseminate 퍼뜨리다

여 헬레니즘이라는 용어는 기원전 4세기 말 알렉산더 대왕의 정복 시대 이후 지중해 연안 국가들과 중동에 미친 그리스 문화의 영향에 관해 이야기할 때 사용됩니다. 알렉산더는 오늘날의 그리스 북부 지역에 해당하는 마케도니아의 왕이었습니다. 그는 페르시아 제국을 정복했으며 죽기 전인 기원전 323년에 인도를 침략했습니다. 알렉산더는 진격해나가면서 여러 도시를 발견하게 되었고 그의 후계자들은 예전에 페르시아 제국이었던 땅에 그리스 왕국을 건설했습니다. 그들은 그리스어를 썼고 자신들의 새로운 백성들에게 그리스의 사상을 심어주었습니다. 그리스 역시 그 지역 사람들의 관습을 받아들였기 때문에 이러한 문화 교류가 완전히 일방적인 것만은 아니었으며, 서로 다른 종족 간의 결혼도 많았습니다. 점령지의 상류층이 그리스와 아무리 많은 영향을 주고받았다고 해도 하층민들의 삶과 문화에는 별다른 변화가 없었을 것입니다. 헬레니즘의 확산에 가장 크게 공헌한 것 중 하나는 이집트의 도시인 알렉산드리아에 있던 도서관이었습니다. 알렉산더가 토대를 마련한 알렉산드리아는 당시 세계의 학문 탐구의 요람이자 수백 년 동안 헬레니즘의 중심지가 되었습니다. 지중해 세계 전역의 학자들이 알렉산드리아와 그곳의 유명한 박물관을 찾았는데, 그 박물관은 말하자면 오늘날의 도서관에 더 가까웠습니다. 알렉산드리아 도서관은 방대한 양의 두루마리와 필사본 소장 도서를 통해 당시 세계 구석구석에서 온 지식을 보관하고 퍼뜨렸습니다.

9 담화에 따르면 다음 중 사실이 <u>아닌</u> 것은?
(a) 헬레니즘의 확산은 모든 계층의 사람들에게 영향을 미쳤다.
(b) 그리스인들 역시 그들이 정복한 땅에서 많은 것을 배웠다.
(c) 알렉산더는 이집트의 도시인 알렉산드리아의 설립자였다.
(d) 알렉산드리아의 도서관은 방대한 양의 정보를 소장하고 있었다.
(e) 그리스 정복자들은 때때로 비 그리스인과 결혼했다.

10

B All we <u>have left to do</u> for our project on ancient China is to <u>find out</u> what it has <u>contributed to</u> the world.

G I found an <u>article</u> about the four <u>great inventions</u> of ancient China. They were paper, <u>printing</u>, the <u>compass</u>, and <u>gunpowder</u>.

B I think you're wrong about printing. Some people say the Koreans <u>invented printing</u> before the Chinese.

G Well, then we can <u>mention</u> the Koreans in the paper, but we still have to <u>talk</u> about <u>printing</u> in China.

B Okay, so what's the date for the <u>first known use</u> of printing in China?

G Well, no one knows the <u>exact date</u>. Some <u>sources say</u> as early as 200 A.D., but the first book is from 868 A.D.

B We'll <u>use that</u> date. Now, what about paper? When was it invented?

G The article gives a date of 105 A.D., but there is a <u>possible example from</u> the 8th century B.C. No, wait... Sorry. That's 8 B.C.

B Let's go with the <u>most certain answer</u>, which is 105 A.D.

G Okay. Now, <u>for the compass</u>, there is also some <u>uncertainty</u>. There is a <u>reference</u> to it in a book from the 4th century A.D., but I'm not sure if that is <u>what we call</u> a compass today. A <u>better choice</u> would be a <u>reference</u> in a book from 1088.

B Then 1088 it is. Finally, <u>what about gunpowder</u>?

G Gunpowder was known in the 9th century A.D., but the <u>first written record</u> of it is from 1044. So I guess we should <u>go with that date</u>.

▶ gunpowder 화약 reference 언급

남 이제 고대 중국에 관한 과제 중에 남은 건 중국이 세계에 기여한 것을 조사하는 것뿐이야.
여 내가 고대 중국의 네 가지 위대한 발명품에 대한 기사를 찾았어. 종이, 인쇄술, 나침반, 화약이었지.
남 내 생각에 인쇄술은 아닌 것 같은데. 한국이 중국보다 먼저 인쇄술을 발명했다는 말도 있거든.
여 음, 그럼 과제에 한국을 언급하면 되겠네. 하지만 그래도 중국의 인쇄술에 대해서는 이야기해야 해.
남 좋아, 그럼 중국에서 처음으로 인쇄술이 사용된 건 언제지?
여 음. 누구도 정확한 연대는 몰라. 몇몇 기록에 의하면 서기 200년이라고 하는데 최초의 책은 서기 868년에 나왔거든.
남 그 연대를 써야겠네. 그럼 종이는? 그건 언제 발명된 거야?
여 기사에 따르면 서기 105년이라고 하는데 기원전 8세기로 추정되는 표본도 있어. 아니다, 잠깐만… 미안. 기원전 8년이네.
남 제일 확실한 답으로 하자. 서기 105년으로 말이야.
여 그래, 이제 나침반인데 약간 불확실해. 서기 4세기의 책에 나침반에 관한 언급이 나오긴 하지만 그게 요즘 말하는 나침반인지는 확실치 않아. 더 정확한 건 1088년의 책에 나와 있는 기록일 거야.
남 그럼 1088년이네. 마지막으로 화약은?
여 화약은 서기 9세기로 알려져 있지만 그것에 관한 문서 기록은 1044년에 처음 나와. 그러니까 그 연대로 해야 할 것 같아.

10 중국의 발명품에 관한 빠진 정보를 채워 표를 완성하시오.

발명품	최초의 증거(연대)	확실한 증거(연대)
인쇄술	서기 200년	868 A.D. (서기 868년)
종이	8 B.C. (기원전 8세기)	서기 105년
나침반	4th century A. D. (서기 4세기)	1088 (1088년)
화약	서기 9세기	1044 (1044년)

11-12 Level up

W All right, the Byzantine Empire is our <u>next topic</u>. It <u>stems directly from</u> the Roman Empire, and, in fact, the Byzantine Empire was <u>originally known as</u> the Eastern Roman Empire. In 285 A.D., the Roman Emperor Diocletian <u>decided to split</u> the <u>vast empire</u> into two parts for <u>purely administrative reasons</u>. He created a system where <u>two emperors</u> would <u>rule jointly</u>—one from the east and the other from the west. Then, in 330 A.D., the Emperor Constantine <u>moved the capital</u> of the Roman Empire to the city of Byzantium, which he renamed Constantinople. This is now the <u>modern city</u> of Istanbul in Turkey. In 395 A.D., the Emperor Theodosius the Great <u>died and bequeathed</u> the <u>two halves</u> of the empire to two different sons. <u>Thereafter,</u> the two halves <u>were never reunited</u>. The western empire <u>fell to</u> Germanic <u>tribal invasions</u> by 476 A.D. The Byzantine Empire, I mean the Eastern Roman Empire, <u>outlasted Rome</u> by almost a thousand years. Much of this was <u>due to its wealth</u>, which it used to <u>pay off barbarian leaders</u> like Attila the Hun as well as to <u>strengthen its military forces</u> and to <u>defend</u> its capital city. While the western empire fell to the <u>barbarian hordes</u>, the Byzantine Empire <u>flourished</u> and even for a time reconquered the <u>western empire</u>. However, a <u>new enemy arose</u> in the form of Islam. For many centuries, the Byzantines <u>clashed with</u> the Muslims. Gradually, the empire <u>declined</u>. It lost <u>territory</u> and even had its capital <u>sacked by</u> a band of <u>crusaders</u> in 1204. During the empire's last days, only the city of Constantinople

<u>remained</u>, and when it fell to the Muslims in 1453, the <u>last bastion</u> of the Roman Empire was gone.

▶ stem from ~에서 생기다, 유래하다   bequeath 유언으로 증여하다, 물려주다
pay off 매수하다   barbarian 야만인(의)   horde 유목민 무리, 약탈자 무리
clash with 충돌하다, 부딪치다   sack 약탈하다   crusader 십자군 전사
bastion 보루   fall to (적의 손에) 떨어지다, 함락되다, 굴복하다

여 자, 이제 우리가 다룰 다음 주제는 비잔틴 제국입니다. 비잔틴 제국은 로마 제국에서 직접적으로 유래했는데, 사실 원래는 동로마 제국으로 알려져 있었습니다. 서기 285년 로마 황제 디오클레티아누스는 순전히 행정적인 이유로 광대한 두 제국을 둘로 나누기로 결정했습니다. 그는 동쪽과 서쪽의 두 황제가 같이 통치하는 체제를 만들었죠. 그 뒤 서기 330년, 콘스탄티누스 황제가 로마 제국의 수도를 비잔틴으로 옮기고 도시의 이름을 콘스탄티노플로 바꾸었습니다. 이 도시가 현재 오늘날의 터키 이스탄불이죠. 서기 395년에 테오도시우스 대제가 죽으면서 두 제국을 두 아들에게 각각 물려주었습니다. 그 후 두 제국은 다시 통일되지 못했습니다. 서로마 제국이 게르만족의 침입으로 서기 476년 무너졌거든요. 비잔틴 제국, 즉 동로마 제국은 로마보다 거의 천 년이나 더 오래 지속되었습니다. 가장 큰 이유는 부유했기 때문인데요. 그 부유함은 군대를 강화하고 수도를 방어할 뿐만 아니라 훈족의 아틸라 같은 야만인 지도자들을 회유하는 데에도 사용되었습니다. 서로마 제국이 야만인 무리에게 멸망한 반면 비잔틴 제국은 번성해서 한동안 서로마 제국을 재정복하기도 했습니다. 그러나 이슬람이라는 형태의 새로운 적이 등장했습니다. 비잔틴은 수세기 동안 이슬람과 충돌했습니다. 제국은 점차 기울어갔죠. 비잔틴은 영토를 잃고 1204년에는 십자군에게 수도를 빼앗기기까지 했습니다. 제국 말기에는 콘스탄티노플만 남게 되었고 1453년 콘스탄티노플이 이슬람교도에게 함락되면서 로마 제국의 마지막 보루는 사라졌습니다.

11 왜 비잔틴 제국이 서로마 제국보다 오래갈 수 있었는가?
   (a) 공격을 계속하여 서로마 제국을 재정복했다.
   (b) 제국을 침략하려고 했던 적들을 성공적으로 물리쳤다.
   (c) 제국의 영토를 지키기 위해 돈과 군사 기술을 이용했다.
   (d) 서로마 제국만큼 많은 야만인들의 침략을 받지 않았다.
   (e) 침략자들에게 많은 땅을 내주며 타협했다.

12 다음 중 내용을 가장 잘 요약한 것을 고르시오.
   (a) 비잔틴 제국은 로마 제국의 마지막 유산이었으며 1453년 콘스탄티노플이 이슬람교도에게 점령되자 멸망했다.
   (b) 비잔틴 제국은 로마 제국의 일부이기는 했으나 독립하여 이슬람에 패할 때까지 로마보다 더 오래 지속되었다.
   (c) 비잔틴 제국은 로마 제국 내의 문제 때문에 생긴 산물이어서 1,000년 동안 독립적으로 지낼 수밖에 없었다.

Practice Test
p. 86~p. 87

1 (e)   2 (c)   3 (a)   4 (d)   5 (b)   6 (d)   7 (b)
8 해설 참조   9 (a)   10 (c)

1

W Marco Polo of Venice was the son of a merchant and later became famous for his journey to the Far East, in particular the years he spent in China. Polo was not the first European to make the long, difficult overland journey to China during the days before there were large oceangoing ships. However, he is perhaps the most famous, and through his writings he became the most influential. Polo left Venice with his father and uncle in 1271, when he was 17 years old, and did not return home for 24 years. During most of that time,

he and his father and uncle were guests of the Mongol leader of China, Kublai Khan. Upon his return to Venice, Polo was imprisoned for a time by the city-state of Genoa, which was at war with Venice. During his imprisonment, Polo dictated an account of his travels in the east to a fellow prisoner. The book became *The Travels of Marco Polo*. However, the original manuscript has been lost, and there are many versions of the book. This is due to changes and mistakes due to hand-copying in a time of no printing presses as well as the embellishments of translators. So there is no definitive way to know the accuracy of Polo's writing. But, as the first thorough account of the eastern lands, this book became highly influential and was read by Christopher Columbus and others seeking a shorter route to China.

▶ overland 육상의, 육로의   oceangoing 외양(원양) 항행의
embellishment 윤색, 꾸밈   definitive 명확한

여 베니스의 마르코 폴로는 상인의 아들로 나중에 극동 지역, 그 중에서도 특히 중국에서 보낸 몇 년 간의 여행으로 유명해졌습니다. 폴로가 대양을 항해하는 거대한 선박이 등장하기 전의 시대에 중국까지 멀고도 험한 육로 여행을 한 최초의 유럽인은 아니었습니다. 그러나 폴로가 가장 유명할 텐데요. 그는 자신이 쓴 글 덕분에 가장 영향력 있는 인물이 되었습니다. 폴로는 1271년 그의 나이 17세 때 아버지와 삼촌을 따라 베니스를 떠난 뒤 24년 동안 고향에 돌아오지 않았습니다. 그 대부분의 기간 동안 폴로와 그의 아버지, 삼촌은 중국의 몽고 지도자인 쿠빌라이 칸의 손님으로 있었습니다. 베니스로 돌아오자 마자 그는 베니스와 전쟁 중이었던 도시 국가 제노바에 의해 잠시 투옥되었습니다. 감옥에 갇혀 있는 동안 그는 동료 수감자에게 자신의 동방 여행에 관한 이야기를 받아 적게 했습니다. 그 책이 『마르코 폴로의 여행기』가 되었죠. 그러나 최초의 필사본은 유실되었고 그 책의 판본들이 많이 있습니다. 이는 번역자들의 윤색뿐만 아니라 인쇄기가 없던 시대에 손으로 베껴 써서 생긴 변화와 실수 때문입니다. 그래서 폴로가 쓴 글의 정확성을 알 수 있는 확실한 방법은 없습니다. 그러나 이 책은 동방에 관한 최초의 꼼꼼한 보고서로서 큰 영향력을 갖게 되어 크리스토퍼 콜럼버스와 중국으로 가는 더 빠른 길을 찾는 여러 사람들에게 읽혀졌습니다.

1 마르코 폴로의 동방 여행 이야기에 다소 불확실한 면이 있는 가장 큰 이유는?
   (a) 자신이 직접 그 책을 쓰지 않고 다른 사람에게 받아쓰게 했다.
   (b) 책을 베껴 쓸 때 많은 사람들이 자신의 여행담을 덧붙였다.
   (c) 인쇄기로 찍어낸 초판본에 실수가 있었다.
   (d) 최초의 필사본이 한동안 유실되었다가 최근에야 발견되었다.
   (e) 베껴 쓰고 번역하는 과정에서 실수가 생겨 현재 많은 판본들이 존재한다.

2-3

G What are you going to do for your summer vacation?

B My family is taking a trip to Southeast Asia. We're going to Vietnam first and then maybe to Cambodia.

G Wow. That's great. Make sure to tell your parents to visit Angkor Wat if you go to Cambodia.

B Is that the big temple that's buried in the jungle?

G Yes, it's a temple, but it's not buried in the jungle. I read something about it for a school project once. It's part of a complex of over a thousand temples and the ancient city of Angkor nearby. It's one of the largest temples in all of Southeast Asia.

B How old is it?

G The city was built during the Khmer time in Cambodia. Ah, I'm not sure of the exact date, but it was sometime around 900 A.D. So, the temple is more than a thousand years old.

B That's really old. So, what happened to the city and the people?

G It was attacked by people from Thailand in the 1400s, and eventually the whole area was abandoned except for the temple at Angkor Wat.

B I heard the temple is a big tourist attraction now, but the Cambodians really don't want people to go there.

G No, that's not exactly true. They want tourists to come so they can collect money to restore the temple and the city. But they just don't want people walking everywhere and damaging these historical places.

B That makes sense. I don't know if my parents are really interested in such a place, but I'll try to convince them to go there.

G You should try really hard. It's a trip they will never regret taking.

B ____

▶ abandon 버리고 떠나다　tourist attraction 관광 명소

여 여름 방학 동안 뭐 할 거니?

남 우린 가족은 동남아시아로 여행 갈 거야. 먼저 베트남에 갔다가 다음에 캄보디아로 갈 것 같아.

여 와. 정말 좋겠다. 캄보디아에 가면 부모님께 꼭 앙코르와트에 가보자고 해.

남 정글 속에 묻혀 있는 그 거대한 사원 말이니?

여 응, 사원은 맞는데 정글 속에 묻혀 있지는 않아. 전에 학교 숙제 때문에 앙코르와트에 관해 좀 읽어봤거든. 1,000개가 넘는 사원들로 이루어진 복합 건축물의 일부이자 인근의 고대 도시 앙코르에 속해 있기도 해. 동남아시아 전체에서 가장 큰 사원 중 하나지.

남 얼마나 오래된 거야?

여 그 도시는 캄보디아의 크메르 시대에 세워졌어. 어, 정확한 연대는 잘 모르겠지만 서기 900년쯤이었어. 그러니까 사원은 1,000년 이상 된 셈이지.

남 정말 오래됐네. 그 도시와 거기 살던 사람들은 어떻게 됐어?

여 1400년대에 타이 사람들의 공격을 받아서 결국 앙코르와트에 있는 그 사원만 빼고 그 지역 전체가 버려졌어.

남 지금은 그 사원이 굉장한 관광 명소라고 듣긴 했지만 캄보디아인들은 사람들이 그곳에 가는 걸 별로 원하지 않잖아.

여 아니, 꼭 그런 건 아니야. 캄보디아인들은 사원과 도시를 복원할 돈을 모을 수 있게 관광객들이 오기를 바라. 하지만 사람들이 여기저기 돌아다니면서 그 역사적인 장소를 훼손하는 걸 원하지 않을 뿐이지.

남 일리가 있어. 부모님이 그런 데 관심이 있으신지는 잘 모르겠지만 가보자고 설득해봐야겠다.

여 열심히 노력해봐. 부모님도 가보시면 절대 후회 안 하실 테니까.

남 ____

2 대화에서 유추할 수 있는 것은 무엇인가?
　(a) 관광 산업은 앙코르 지역의 가장 큰 수입원이다.
　(b) 타이 사람들은 앙코르를 정복하는 데 실패했다.
　(c) 관광객들이 앙코르와트를 조금 훼손했다.
　(d) 사원 건축에 쓰인 일반적인 재료는 사암이었다.
　(e) 크메르 사람들이 한때 앙코르에서 캄보디아를 지배했다.

3 소년은 소녀에게 다음에 뭐라고 말하겠는가?
　(a) 내가 뭘 할 수 있을지 생각해볼게.
　(b) 거기 갔다 온 것처럼 말하네.
　(c) 너한테 약속할 수 있어.
　(d) 너도 아마 우리와 같이 가야 될 거야.
　(e) 틀림없이 내가 너보다 더 좋은 여름을 보낼 거야.

4-5

M The Mayan civilization flourished for over a thousand years in what are now modern Guatemala and the Yucatan Peninsula of Mexico. The Mayan culture had declined a great deal prior to the arrival of the Europeans, and they were eventually conquered by the Spanish. The legacy of the Mayan civilization is the great cities they built. One of the most important of these cities was Quirigua, which was located in Guatemala. Although not large compared to other Mayan cities and ruins, Quirigua has a great number of well-preserved and tall structures. The complex was built between about 550 A.D. and 900 A.D. The main material used was sandstone. This particular sandstone was strong, which enabled the Mayans to build very tall monuments that have survived until today without cracking or much wearing. Most of the buildings and monuments were built in the latter half of the 700s. Quirigua was a city controlled by the nearby larger and more powerful city of Copan. In the 730s, Quirigua rebelled against Copan. In 737, the Quirigua king captured the king of Copan and had him beheaded in a ritual ceremony. Then, for almost forty years, Quirigua remained independent, and the king set out to build great plazas, temples, and monuments, many of which were copied from the style at Copan. Eventually, like the rest of the Mayan cities, Quirigua declined and was unknown to the world until it was rediscovered in 1840.

▶ flourish 번창하다, 번성하다　rebel against 반란을 일으키다　behead (사람의) 목을 베다, 참수하다　ritual 의식의, 제식의; 의식, 예식　set out 착수하다, 시작하다　plaza 대광장

남 마야 문명은 오늘날의 과테말라와 멕시코에 있는 유카탄 반도에서 천 년 넘게 번성했습니다. 마야 문명은 유럽인이 도착하기 전에 매우 쇠퇴해 있었으며 결국 스페인에게 정복당했습니다. 마야 문명의 유산은 그들이 세운 거대한 도시입니다. 이 가운데 가장 중요한 도시 중 하나가 과테말라에 있던 퀴리구아였습니다. 마야의 다른 도시와 유적에 비해 크지는 않지만 퀴리구아에는 잘 보존된 높은 건축물이 많이 있습니다. 그 건축물들은 약 서기 550년에서 900년 사이에 세워졌습니다. 주로 쓰인 재료는 사암이었죠. 이 특별한 사암은 단단했기 때문에 마야인은 오늘날까지도 금이 가거나 크게 닳지 않고 남아 있는 매우 높은 기념물을 세울 수 있었습니다. 대부분의 건물과 기념물은 700년대 후반에 지어졌습니다. 퀴리구아는 인근에 있는 더 크고 강력한 도시인 코판의 지배를 받는 도시였습니다. 730년대에 퀴리구아는 코판에 반기를 들었습니다. 737년, 퀴리구아의 왕은 코판의 왕을 붙잡아 제사 의식에서 참수시켰습니다. 그 뒤 거의 40년 동안 퀴리구아는 독립국으로 있었고 왕은 거대한 광장과 사원, 기념물을 짓기 시작했는데 대부분 코판의 양식을 모방했죠. 결국 나머지 마야 도시들처럼 퀴리구아는 몰락했고 1840년에 다시 발견될 때까지 세상에 알려지지 않았습니다.

4 퀴리구아는 왜 고대 마야 문명의 중요한 유적지인가?
　(a) 퀴리구아의 왕과 전쟁에 관한 역사적인 기록이 잘 알려져 있다.
　(b) 가장 거대하고 가장 잘 보존된 마야 유적이 있다.
　(c) 수십 년 동안 마야 문명의 중심지였다.

(d) 잘 보존된 높은 기념물이 많이 있다.
(e) 사암이 광범위하게 사용된 유일한 유적지이다.

5 담화에서 유추할 수 있는 것은 무엇인가?

(a) 마야인은 많은 도시에서 화강암을 사용했다.
(b) 마야 문명은 복잡한 정치 구조를 갖고 있었다.
(c) 마야의 도시 국가들 사이에는 전쟁이 흔했다.
(d) 마야인은 적들을 보통 참수형에 처했다.
(e) 퀴리구아는 유적지 때문에 유명한 관광지이다.

---

6 Level up

B What are you studying for?

G We have a history test on the American Revolutionary War next week.

B Oh, I'm a real history buff. Is there anything I can help you with?

G I'm reading about the Battle of Saratoga now.

B You mean the Battles of Saratoga. There were two battles in roughly the same place, near Saratoga, New York. The first was on September 19, 1777, and the second was on October 7, 1777.

G That was something I didn't know. Why were there two battles?

B The British kept attacking. That's why. They were trying to divide New England from the rest of the 13 colonies. They won a small victory in the first battle. Then they attacked again but were totally defeated in the second battle. Ten days later, that British army surrendered to the Americans.

G Okay, but what significance did this battle have?

B It was the first major American victory. Also, after Saratoga, the French decided to join America in the war against Britain. Without French help, perhaps the war would never have been won.

▶ Revolutionary War (미국사) 독립 전쟁 buff ~팬, ~광

남 뭐 공부하고 있니?
여 다음 주에 미국 독립 전쟁에 관한 역사 시험을 보거든.
남 아, 내가 진짜 역사 좋아하는데. 뭐 도와줄 거라도 있니?
여 지금 사라토가 전투에 대해 읽고 있어.
남 그 사라토가 전투들 말이구나. 뉴욕 사라토가 근처의 엇비슷한 장소에서 두 번의 전투가 있었어. 첫 번째는 1777년 9월 19일에 있었고 두 번째는 1777년 10월 7일에 있었지.
여 그건 몰랐네. 왜 전투가 두 번이나 있었어?
남 영국이 계속 공격했거든. 그게 이유지. 영국은 뉴잉글랜드를 나머지 13개의 식민지에서 분리하려고 했어. 첫 번째 전투에서는 영국이 작은 승리를 거두었지. 그리고 나서 영국이 다시 공격했는데 두 번째 전투에서는 완전히 참패했어. 10일 후에 영국군은 미국에 항복했지.
여 알겠어. 그런데 이 전투가 어떤 의미를 갖는 거야?
남 미국이 처음으로 거둔 큰 승리였어. 또 사라토가 전투 이후에 프랑스가 영국에 대항해 미국과 참전하기로 결정했고. 프랑스의 도움이 없었다면 아마 전쟁에서 결코 이기지 못했을 거야.

6 What is correct about the Battles of Saratoga?
사라토가 전투들에 관해 옳은 것은 무엇인가?

(a) The battles took place more than a month apart.
전투들은 한 달 이상의 간격으로 일어났다.

(b) The French helped the Americans win both battles.
프랑스는 미국이 두 전투에서 이기도록 도왔다.

(c) The Americans beat the British in the first battle.
미국은 첫 번째 전투에서 영국을 물리쳤다.

(d) The British were attacking the Americans.
영국이 미국을 공격하고 있었다.

(e) The Americans surrendered after both battles.
미국은 두 전투 후 항복했다.

---

7 Level up

W Much of modern medical practice owes a debt to a Persian scientist called Avicenna. That's his Western name. His real name was Ibn Sina, and he was born in Persia in 980 A.D. Avicenna was an expert in a wide variety of fields, and wrote on mathematics, philosophy, astronomy, physics, and chemistry. However, much of his fame rests on his medical knowledge and his writings on diseases, drugs, and medical experimentation. His most famous written works are *The Canon of Medicine* and *The Book of Healing*. The latter was a book of scientific thought and philosophy. The *Canon of Medicine* had 14 volumes and covered all of Avicenna's medical knowledge. It was used in universities throughout the Islamic world and Europe for hundreds of years as a standard medical textbook. Its influence was also felt on medical practice in India and China. The work covered a wide variety of medical areas, including drug use, psychology, and afflictions of the brain. It is also noted for establishing many of the experimentation methods used to diagnose illnesses.

▶ practice 업무, 행위 canon 규범, 근본 원리 affliction 고통 diagnose 진단하다

여 현대 의료 행위의 많은 부분이 아비세나라는 페르시아의 과학자 덕을 보고 있습니다. 아비세나는 그의 서양식 이름입니다. 진짜 이름은 이븐 시나인데, 서기 980년에 페르시아에서 태어났습니다. 아비세나는 다양하고 폭넓은 분야의 전문가로 수학, 철학, 천문학, 물리학, 화학에 관해 책을 썼습니다. 그러나 아비세나의 명성은 대부분 그의 의학 지식과 질병, 약품, 의학 실험에 관한 저술을 바탕으로 하고 있습니다. 그의 가장 유명한 저술은 『의학 전범』과 『치유의 서』입니다. 『치유의 서』는 과학적인 사고와 철학에 관한 책입니다. 『의학 전범』은 14권으로 나뉘어 있으며 아비세나의 모든 의학 지식을 포괄했습니다. 그 책은 수백 년 동안 이슬람 세계와 유럽 전역의 대학에서 표준 의학 교과서로 사용되었습니다. 그 책의 영향력은 인도와 중국의 의료 행위에서도 감지되었죠. 『의학 전범』은 약물 사용, 심리학, 뇌 질환을 포함해 아주 다양한 의학 영역을 다루었습니다. 그 책은 또한 질병을 진단하기 위해 이용되는 많은 실험 방법을 확립한 것으로도 유명합니다.

7 What is NOT true about Avicenna?
아비세나에 관해 사실이 아닌 것은?

(a) He was born in Persia over a thousand years ago.
1,000년도 더 전에 페르시아에서 태어났다.

(b) He was involved in teaching medicine at universities.
대학에서 의학을 가르치는 데 종사했다.

(c) He wrote books that universities used for centuries.
수세기 동안 대학에서 사용한 책들을 저술했다.

(d) He has had an influence on modern medical practices.
현대 의료 행위에 영향을 미쳤다.

(e) He wrote many works on many different subjects.
다양한 주제에 관해 많은 책을 저술했다.

M In 1588, a Spanish fleet, called the Armada, was utterly defeated by skillful English seamanship and the ravages of the sea. The battle occurred mainly because Protestant England supported the Protestant United Provinces, which are now the Netherlands, in a revolt against their Catholic Spanish masters. The Spanish planned to sail up the English Channel and destroy the English fleet in battle. Then they would go to the United Provinces, board an army, and invade England. The Armada had about 130 ships and was outnumbered by the 200 ships of the English, but the Spanish ships were bigger, and each had many more guns. However, the English ships were better handled and had better gunnery. The English sailed around the Spanish ships and sank two ships in a several-day running battle up the English Channel. On July 27, 1588, the Armada anchored at Calais, France, near where the army was to board. That night, the English sent in fire ships—old hulks that they had set on fire—which disrupted the Armanda's defensive position. Fearing destruction by fire, the Armada scattered. The English closed for battle and sank five Spanish ships. The Armada now sought to escape and, in a long voyage around the British Isles, lost a lot of its ships to bad weather and rocky shores. Only 67 ships returned to Spain. The English had lost none. This battle marked the beginning of English naval dominance, which was to last until the mid-20th century.

▶ the Armada (스페인의) 무적 함대 utterly 완전히 seamanship 선박 조종술
Protestant 신교도의 ravage 파괴의 맹위 revolt 반란, 폭동
English Channel 영국 해협 board ~에 승선(탑승)시키다 outnumber ~보다
수적으로 우세하다 gunnery 포격, 사격법 running battle 장기전, 끊임없는 싸움
hulk 폐선 close (대열을) 좁히다, (대열이) 밀집하다
naval dominance 바다에 대한 지배권, 제해권

남 1588년, 무적 함대로 불리던 스페인 함대는 영국의 노련한 선박 운용술과 맹위를 떨치는 바다에 의해 완전히 패했습니다. 전투가 일어난 주된 이유는 가톨릭계 스페인 총독들에 대항해 일어난 반란에서 개신교를 믿는 영국이 현재의 네덜란드에 해당하는 개신교 연합 주를 지원했기 때문입니다. 스페인은 영국 해협까지 항해해 가서 전투를 벌여 영국 함대를 파괴할 계획이었습니다. 그런 다음 연합 주로 가서 육군을 승선시켜 영국을 침공하려고 했죠. 무적 함대는 약 130척의 배를 갖고 있었기 때문에 200척을 갖고 있는 영국에 비해 수적으로 불리했으나 스페인 함선은 크기가 더 크고 각 함선에 더 많은 대포를 장착하고 있었습니다. 그러나 영국 함대의 조종과 포술이 더 나았습니다. 영국은 영국 해협 북단에서 며칠간 계속된 전투에서 스페인 함선들을 둘러싸 2척을 침몰시켰습니다. 1588년 7월 27일, 무적 함대는 육군을 태우기로 한 곳 근처에 있는 프랑스의 칼레에 정박했습니다. 그날 밤 영국은 낡은 폐선에 불을 붙인 화선(火船)들을 보내 무적 함대의 방어 대열을 교란시켰습니다. 불이 붙어 부서질까봐 겁을 먹은 무적 함대는 뿔뿔이 흩어졌습니다. 영국은 전투 대열로 좁혀 5척의 스페인 함선을 침몰시켰습니다. 이제 무적 함대는 후퇴를 시도했고, 영국 제도를 빙 돌아가는 긴 항해 도중 악천후와 암초투성이의 해안에 많은 함선을 잃었습니다. 67척의 함선만이 스페인에 돌아갔죠. 영국은 단 한 척도 잃지 않았습니다. 이 전투는 영국이 제해권을 쥐기 시작한 전기가 되었으며 이는 20세기 중반까지 계속되었습니다.

---

8 영국과 스페인의 함대에 관한 내용으로 표를 완성하시오.

구분	수
영국 함대의 총수	200척
스페인 함대의 총수	130척
영국이 잃은 함선	0척
스페인이 잃은 함선	63척
– 영국의 공격에 의해 격침된 함선	7척
– 날씨와 암초투성이 해안으로 침몰한 함선	56척

9-10　Integrated Questions

Reading

▶ wait out (위기 등이) 지나가기를 기다리다 intact 손대지 않은, 손상되지 않은
flee 달아나다, 피하다

폼페이는 로마 제국의 고대 마을로, 나폴리 인근에 위치해 있었다. 서기 79년 8월 24일, 인근의 베수비오 화산이 폭발했다. 폼페이 주민들은 처음에는 화산 분출이 대수롭지 않기를 바라며 폭발이 끝나기를 기다리려고 했다. 하지만 다음 날 재와 뜨거운 가스로 된 구름이 격렬하게 폭발하면서 폼페이 마을은 바위와 재 아래 묻혔고 대부분의 주민은 죽었다. 폼페이와 역시 화산 폭발로 묻혀버린 인근 도시 헤르쿨라네움은 거의 1,700년 동안 세상에 존재하지 않았다. 그러다 18세기 중반에 두 도시가 다시 발견되었다. 그 도시들은 화산재 덕분에 벽에 그려진 그림조차 손상되지 않은 채 그대로 남아 있을 정도로 잘 보존되어 있었다. 두 도시는 주요 관광 명소이자 고대 로마의 생활을 연구할 수 있는 자료가 되었다. 베수비오 화산으로 인한 멸망에 관한 중요한 이야기 가운데 하나는 로마의 행정관이었던 소(小) 플리니우스의 편지에 나온다. 그는 그 사건을 건너편 나폴리 만에서 지켜보았다. 그의 삼촌인 대(大) 플리니우스는 그 지역의 해군을 책임지고 있었는데, 그 재난으로부터 도망치려는 사람들을 구하기 위해 선박들을 이끌던 중 사망했다. 당시의 기록들과 고고학적 증거에 의하면 약 2만 명의 주민 가운데 1만 6천 명 정도가 죽은 것으로 추산된다.

W Pompeii's destruction by the volcanic eruption of Vesuvius is an important historical event because of the well-preserved ruins of the town. Pliny the Younger was an eyewitness to this event, and he later gave an account to the famous Roman historian Tacitus. Pliny was on the far side of the Bay of Naples, but, even from a distance, he felt the volcano's power as earthquakes accompanied the eruption and ash and rocks fell all around the Bay of Naples. Pliny and others give the date of August 24, 79 A.D., for the eruption of Vesuvius. This was accepted for a long time. However, after the ruins of Pompeii were uncovered, evidence indicates that the eruption took place later in the year, mostly likely in late October. Such evidence includes the clothing the victims were wearing, which was heavier for the fall season, and the finding of a coin minted in September 79 A.D. Despite these minor discrepancies, the uncovered ruins have provided a wealth of historical evidence about life in the early Roman Empire and are of great benefit to social historians. In addition, as engraved images from the ruins spread around Europe in the 18th century, it led to the birth of the Neoclassical Movement. This revival in the interest of Rome had a profound effect on the art and architecture of the late 18th and early 19th centuries. Even into the 20th century, the tragedy of Pompeii's destruction has captured the attention of many, and several theatrical performances and films have used the event to depict stories about the lives of Romans at the time of the eruption.

▶ eyewitness 목격자, 목격 증인 Pliny the Younger 소(小) 플리니우스, 그의 숙부인 (大) 플리니우스(Pliny the Elder)와 구분한 호칭 mint (화폐를) 주조하다 discrepancy 모순, 불일치 social history 사회사 engrave 새기다, 조각하다 depict 묘사하다

여 베수비오 화산 폭발로 인한 폼페이의 멸망은 중요한 역사적 사건입니다. 잘 보존된 그 마을의 유적 때문이죠. 소(小) 플리니우스는 이 사건의 목격자였는데 나중에 로마의 유명한 역사가인 타키투스에게 그 이야기를 해주었습니다. 플리니우스는 나폴리 만의 끝에 있었지만 멀리에서도 화산의 위력을 느꼈습니다. 폭발과 함께 지진이 일어났고 재와 바위가 온 나폴리 만에 떨어졌으니까요. 플리니우스를 비롯한 다른 사람들은 베수비오 화산이 폭발한 날짜가 서기 79년 8월 24일이라고 했습니다. 이는 오랫동안 받아들여졌습니다. 그러나 폼페이 유적이 발굴된 뒤 나타난 증거들은 화산 폭발이 그해 말, 아마 10월 하순에 일어났으리라는 것을 말해줍니다. 그런 증거에는 희생자들이 입고 있던, 가을철에 입기에는 너무 두꺼운 옷도 포함되며, 발견된 동전 하나는 서기 79년 9월에 주조된 것이었습니다. 이런 사소한 불일치에도 불구하고 발굴된 유적은 초기 로마 제국의 생활에 대한 풍부한 역사적 증거를 제공해주어 사회사를 연구하는 역사가에게 많은 도움이 됩니다. 게다가 유적에서 출토된 새김 이미지들은 18세기에 유럽 전역으로 퍼져나가 신고전주의 운동을 낳게 했습니다. 로마에 대한 이 같은 새로운 관심은 18세기 말과 19세기 초의 예술과 건축에 깊은 영향을 미쳤습니다. 심지어는 20세기 초까지도 폼페이의 멸망에 얽힌 비극은 많은 이들의 주목을 받았으며 몇몇 연극과 영화는 그 폭발이 있었던 시대의 로마인의 삶에 대한 이야기를 묘사하기 위해 그 사건을 이용하기도 했습니다.

9 읽기와 듣기 지문에 따르면 사실이 <u>아닌</u> 것은 무엇인가?
   (a) 베수비오 화산은 갑자기 폭발해서 폼페이 사람들이 눈치채지 못하는 사이에 덮쳤다.
   (b) 폼페이는 18세기에 재발견될 때까지 잊혀져 있었다.
   (c) 대(大) 플리니우스는 베수비오 화산 폭발로 죽었다.
   (d) 베수비오 화산 폭발때 폼페이 시민이 모두 죽은 건 아니었다.
   (e) 폼페이의 예술과 건축은 화산재 덕분에 보존되었다.

10 읽기와 듣기 지문은 어떤 점에 있어서 서로 일치하지 않는가?
   (a) 베수비오 화산으로 인해 멸망한 마을들의 사망자 수
   (b) 대(大) 플리니우스와 그의 생존자 해상 구조에 관한 이야기
   (c) 베수비오 화산이 폭발해서 폼페이를 멸망시킨 정확한 날짜
   (d) 유적의 특성과 그 유적의 역사적 연구 가치
   (e) 폼페이의 재발견이 예술과 건축에 미친 영향

*Dictation 정답: Exercise 스크립트 밑줄 참조

Preparation
p. 93

Vocabulary Preview

A

1 discredit : 누군가 혹은 무엇인가에 부정적인 감정을 갖다
2 equilibrium : 균형잡힌 상태, 균등
3 condescending : 다른 사람들에게 잘난 척 행동하는
4 synthetic : 천연적인 것이 아닌; 인공적인
5 spatial : 물리적인 공간과 관련된

B

1 bonding / 수십억 개 물분자의 분자결합은 눈송이를 만든다.

2 fortuitous / 많은 과학적 발견은 뜻밖의 일로 이루어졌다.
3 dissolve / 산은 접촉하는 것들을 대부분 녹인다.
4 optical illusion / 그 사진은 사람이 어떻게 보느냐에 따라 다른 이미지를 보여주는 착시이미지였다.
5 electrode / 학생이 전선을 전극봉에 연결하자 전구에 불이 들어왔다.
6 particle / 힉스 입자라고 불리는 소립자에 대한 조사가 그 대규모 실험의 주제이다.
7 circuit / 완성된 회로는 전기로 전자 장치를 작동하는 데 꼭 필요하다.

Expressions and Meanings

1 그만 투덜대.	ⓑ 그만 불평해.
2 나 배꼽 빠지겠다.	ⓓ 그거 정말 웃긴다.
3 멍청한 짓 좀 그만해.	ⓖ 어리석은 짓 그만해.
4 책을 펴자.	ⓒ 공부 시작하자.
5 정말 끝내줬어.	ⓐ 우린 멋진 시간을 보냈어.
6 잠깐 기다려봐.	ⓔ 잠깐만.
7 여기까지는 이해돼.	ⓕ 여기까지는 이해했어.

Monolog

Ⓞ (1) chemistry (2) tax collector (3) executed/died
    (4) conservation of mass (5) mass (6) enclosed
    (7) change (8) physical properties (9) air (10) oxygen
    (11) water (12) hydrogen (13) chemicals

Ⓖ 1 (c)   2 (b)

Ⓢ (1) T (2) T (3) F (4) T

M One of the fathers of modern chemistry is the Frenchman Antoine-Laurent de Lavoisier. He lived in the late 18th century and was well known as the foremost chemist of his day. Lavoisier's work includes the theory of the conservation of mass. This theory states that the mass of an object in an enclosed system will not change no matter how its physical properties are changed. For example, if a piece of paper is burned inside a closed area, then the mass of the remaining ashes should equal the mass of the original piece of paper. In theory, this principle is sound, but, practically, it is extremely difficult to create an enclosed system that is not affected in some way by external factors. Lavoisier is also credited with work that proved that air is made up of different gases, and he named the part of air that animals and people breathe "oxygen." In addition, Lavoisier is noted for his contributions to the discovery that water consists of hydrogen and oxygen and to the creation of a system for naming different chemicals. Unfortunately, this great man died during the French Revolution, when some revolutionaries executed him in 1794 for his former ties to the French nobility and for his work as a tax collector for the royal regime that the revolution was against.

▶ foremost 으뜸가는; 선두의 conservation of mass 질량 보존의 법칙 physical property 물리적 특성; 물리적인 성질 principle 법칙, 원리 sound 논리적으로 옳은, 바른 practically 실제로는; 사실상 be credited with ~에 인정을

71

받다 be noted for ~(으)로 유명하다 contribution 공헌, 기여 oxygen 산소 hydrogen 수소 French Revolution 프랑스 혁명 revolutionaries 혁명당원; 혁명론자 execute 처형하다, 사형에 처하다 nobility 귀족 (계급) ties 인연; 연줄, 유대 royal regime 왕정 tax collector 세금 징수원(공무원)

남 근대 화학의 아버지 가운데에는 프랑스인인 앙투안-로랑 드 라부아지에가 있습니다. 그는 18세기 후반에 살았으며 당대 일류 화학자로 잘 알려져 있었습니다. 라부아지에의 업적 중에는 질량 보존의 법칙이 있습니다. 이 이론은 밀폐된 공간에 있는 물체의 질량은 그 물체의 물리적 특성이 어떻게 변하든 바뀌지 않는다는 것입니다. 예를 들어 종이 한 장이 밀폐된 장소 안에서 타면 남아 있는 재의 질량은 원래 종이의 질량과 같다는 것이죠. 이 법칙은 이론상으로는 옳지만 실제로는 어떤 식으로든 외부 요소의 영향을 받지 않는 밀폐된 공간을 만드는 것은 극히 힘듭니다. 라부아지에는 또한 공기가 여러 가지 기체로 이루어져 있다는 것을 증명했다고 인정받고 있습니다. 그는 동물과 사람이 호흡하는 공기 중의 한 성분을 '산소'라고 이름지었습니다. 또한 물은 수소와 산소로 이루어져 있다는 것을 발견했고 여러 가지 화학물질을 명명하는 체계를 만드는 데 공헌한 것으로 유명합니다. 안타깝게도 이 위대한 인물은 프랑스 혁명 기간에 세상을 떠났습니다. 혁명주의자들이 그가 예전에 프랑스 귀족과 관계가 있었고 혁명이 반대하는 왕정의 세금 징수원으로 일했다는 이유로 1794년 그를 처형했던 것이죠.

General Questions

1 담화의 목적은 무엇인가?
  (a) 위대한 화학자의 삶과 죽음을 고찰하려고
  (b) 질량에 관련된 과학이론을 설명하려고
  (c) 위대한 화학자의 과학적 업적을 논하려고
  (d) 어떻게 화학명이 만들어졌는지 기술하려고

2 다음 중 가장 잘 요약된 것을 고르시오.
  (a) 앙투안-로랑 드 라부아지에의 질량 보존의 법칙과 물 구조 이론도 그가 프랑스 국민을 거스른 범죄로 처형되는 것을 막지 못했다.
  (b) 앙투안-로랑 드 라부아지에는 화학 분야에서 많은 새로운 발견을 이루었지만 그의 삶은 프랑스 혁명기에 갑자기 끝나고 말았다.

Specific Questions

다시 듣고 옳은 문장에는 T, 틀린 문장에는 F를 쓰시오.
(1) 라부아지에의 이론인 질량 보존의 법칙은 폐쇄된 공간에서만 적용된다.
(2) 라부아지에는 인간이 호흡하는 공기 성분을 명명한 것으로 인정받는다.
(3) 라부아지에는 다른 과학자들이 개발한 화학물질 명명 체계를 사용했다.
(4) 라부아지에는 혁명 전에 프랑스 왕정을 위해 일했다는 것 때문에 처형되었다.

Dialog

(N) (1) electricity (2) conducted (3) electric circuit / actively / prepared / set up the apparatus
(4) grade / not prepared / (5) football

(G) 1 (c) 2 (a)
(S) (1) F (2) F (3) T (4) T

B Sorry I'm late. What experiment are we doing in lab class today?

G We are proving that electricity can be conducted through a human being.

B What? That's a little shocking. Ha ha. Get it? Shocking?

G I'm in stitches. That's a real knee-slapper. Quit fooling around and help me set up the apparatus.

B Oh, oh, Mr. Patterson is already going around and checking the other teams' work.

G Just set up the circuit breaker while I screw in the light bulb.

B How is this supposed to work anyway?

G Didn't you prepare for class? It was in the lab instruction manual.

B No, I had football practice until late last night.

G Oh, brother. I don't need a lab partner who doesn't prepare for class.

B Quit whining. Tell me about the experiment before the teacher gets here.

G Fine. Electricity needs a completed circuit to light the light bulb.

B But the circuit isn't complete. There's a gap between these two electrodes.

G I know. When you and I touch these electrodes with one hand and then hold our other hands together, the circuit will be complete, and the bulb will light up.

B Hold hands? With you? Now, that is shocking.

G Don't be such a jerk. If I don't get a good grade in this class, I will haunt you forever.

B Okay, okay. Ready? Now, take my hand and... Wow! The bulb lit up!

G Don't be so dramatic. I knew it would work.

▶ electricity 전기 conduct (열, 전기, 소리 등을) 전도하다 shocking '충격적인'의 의미와 '감전(electric shock)'의 의미를 동시에 표현한 말장난 be in stitches 배꼽을 잡고 웃다 knee-slapper (무릎을 치고 웃을 만큼) 기막힌 농담 set up 설치하다 apparatus (한 벌의) 기구(器具), 기계, 장치 circuit breaker 회로 차단기 light bulb 전구 electrode 전극, 전극봉 haunt 괴롭히다, 늘 따라다니다 dramatic 극적인; 연극 같은

남 늦어서 미안. 오늘 실습시간에 무슨 실험을 하는 거니?

여 인간을 통해 전기가 전도될 수 있다는 것을 증명할거야.

남 뭐라고? 그건 좀 쇼킹하다. 하하. 농담 이해했어? 쇼킹?

여 배꼽 빠지겠다. 정말 기막힌 농담이야. 장난 그만하고 기구 설치나 도와줘.

남 아, 아, 패터슨 선생님이 벌써 돌아다니시면서 다른 조들이 어떻게 했는지 체크하고 계셔.

여 내가 전구를 돌려 끼우는 동안 넌 회로 차단기나 설치해.

남 그건 그렇고 이거 어떻게 작동하는 거야?

여 너 수업 준비 안했어? 실험 매뉴얼에 있었잖아.

남 안 했어. 어젯밤 늦게까지 풋볼 연습을 했거든.

여 오, 맙소사. 난 수업 준비하지 않는 실험 파트너는 필요 없어.

남 그만 좀 투덜대. 선생님이 여기 오시기 전에 실험에 대해 얘기해 보라고.

여 좋아. 전기가 전구를 밝히기 위해서는 완성된 회로가 필요해.

남 하지만 회로가 완성되지 않았어. 이 두 전극봉 사이에 틈이 있잖아.

여 알아. 너와 내가 한 손으로 이 전극봉들을 만지면서 다른 쪽 손을 마주잡으면, 회로가 완성되어서 전구에 불이 들어오는 거야.

남 손을 잡는다고? 너랑? 그거 쇼킹한데.

여 멍청한 소리 좀 그만해. 내가 이 수업에서 좋은 성적을 받지 못하면 널 영원히 괴롭힐 거야.

남 알았어, 알았어. 준비됐어? 자, 내 손을 잡아, 그리고… 우와! 전구에 불이 들어왔어!

여 그렇게 법석떨지 마. 난 작동될 줄 알았다고.

General Questions

1 대화문은 주로 무엇에 관한 것인가?
  (a) 학교 실험실에서 전자 회로 고치기

(b) 왜 소년이 실험에 늦었는지
(c) 인간 전도로 전구 불 밝히기
(d) 과학 실험이 어떻게 이루어지는지

2 다음 중 가장 잘 요약된 것을 고르시오.
(a) 두 명의 실험 파트너는 사이가 별로 좋지 않지만 수업 중에 과학 실험을 성공적으로 함께 해낸다.
(b) 전기에 관한 실습 중에 두 파트너는 이 실험 수업 이외에는 별로 공통점이 없다는 것을 알게 된다.

Specific Questions

다시 듣고 옳은 문장에는 T, 틀린 문장에는 F를 쓰시오.
(1) 소년은 소녀가 실험에 열심히 참여하지 않는다고 생각한다.
(2) 실험은 인체가 감전을 견뎌낼 수 있다는 것을 증명하기 위해 설계되었다.
(3) 학생들은 수업 전에 실험을 준비하도록 되어 있었다.
(4) 여자는 실험의 성공을 매우 확신하였다.

Listening Drill 2

p. 96~p. 97

Long Lecture

ⓞ (1) stable (2) spatial relationship (3) gas (4) dry ice
(5) liquid (6) Liquids (7) close (8) volume (9) shape
(10) vaporization (11) Gases (12) freely (13) expand
(14) plasma (15) deposition (16) condensation
(17) ionized gas (18) high temperatures (19) gases
(20) expand

1 (d)　　**2** (a)　　**3** (1) T (2) T (3) F (4) T　　**4** (c)

Dictation 정답: 스크립트 밑줄 참조

---

w Traditionally, there are three <u>states of matter</u>: solid, liquid, and gas. A fourth, plasma, may also <u>be added to</u> this list. A state of matter <u>indicates</u> the form that matter takes. The <u>solid form</u> of matter is <u>fixed</u> and <u>stable</u>. The <u>molecules</u> in a solid are in a <u>fixed spatial relationship</u>, meaning that the molecules do not <u>move or change</u> unless an <u>external force</u> like heat is <u>applied</u>. A liquid is a state of matter where the molecules of the matter are still in a <u>close relationship</u>, but the relationship is <u>no longer fixed</u>. The <u>volume</u> of the matter <u>remains the same</u>, but the shape changes. Thus, in the <u>liquid state</u>, the matter will <u>take the shape</u> of any <u>container</u> it is in. A gas is a state of matter where the <u>molecules freely move</u> and will <u>expand</u> as far as they can if they are not contained. Meanwhile, <u>plasma</u> is created from a <u>partially ionized gas</u>. Only gases can become plasma, and this happens only at <u>extremely high temperatures</u>. Plasma has <u>similar properties</u> as gases and can expand <u>unless contained</u>. The states of matter can change from one to another. Solids become liquids <u>through melting</u> when heat is used. A solid can also go directly to a <u>gaseous state</u> through a process called <u>sublimation</u>. For example, the solid form of carbon dioxide, often called dry ice, will <u>turn into</u> a gaseous form under <u>atmospheric pressure</u> without becoming a liquid first. Liquids become solids by <u>freezing</u> and become gases by <u>vaporization</u>. Gases become liquids by <u>condensation</u> and become solids by <u>deposition</u>. An example of deposition is when water vapor <u>changes</u> <u>directly</u> to ice if the temperature is low enough.

▶ plasma 플라즈마, 전리(電離) (원자핵과 전자가 분리된 가스 상태) fixed 고정된, 정착된 stable 안정된; 영구성이 있는 molecule 분자 spatial 공간의; 장소의; 우주의 volume 부피, 양 thus 예를 들면, (그) 한 예로서 container 그릇, 용기 ionize 이온화하다; 이온을 발생시키다 sublimation 승화 carbon dioxide 이산화탄소, 탄산가스 atmospheric pressure 기압 freezing 냉동, 결빙 vaporization 증발 (작용), 기화 condensation 액화; 응결, 냉축 deposition 퇴적, 침전

여 예로부터, 물질에는 고체, 액체, 기체의 세 가지 상태가 있습니다. 네 번째 상태, 플라즈마도 이 리스트에 추가돼야 할지 모르겠군요. 물질의 상태는 물질이 취하는 형태를 나타냅니다. 물질의 고체 형태는 고정되고 안정적입니다. 고체분자는 고정된 공간 관계에 있습니다. 열과 같은 외부적인 힘이 작용되지 않는 한 분자가 움직이거나 바뀌지 않는다는 의미죠. 액체는 물질의 분자가 여전히 가까운 관계에 있지만 그 관계가 더 이상 고정적이지 않은 물질 상태입니다. 물질의 부피는 같지만 모양은 변하죠. 예를 들면, 액체 상태의 물질은 그것이 담겨 있는 그릇 모양을 그대로 취합니다. 기체는 분자가 자유롭게 움직이고 용기에 담겨 있지 않는 한 끝없이 팽창할 수 있는 물질 상태입니다. 한편 플라즈마는 부분적으로 이온화된 기체에서 만들어집니다. 기체만이 플라즈마가 될 수 있는데, 이것은 극히 높은 온도에서만 발생합니다. 플라즈마도 기체와 비슷한 속성을 가지고 있어서 용기에 담겨 있지 않으면 팽창할 수 있습니다. 물질 상태는 한 상태에서 다른 상태로 변할 수 있습니다. 고체는 열을 사용하면 녹아서 액체가 됩니다. 고체는 또한 승화라고 하는 과정을 거쳐서 곧바로 기체 상태가 될 수 있습니다. 예를 들면, 드라이아이스라 불리는 이산화탄소의 고체 형태는 먼저 액체가 되지 않고 기압을 받아 기체 형태로 바뀝니다. 액체는 얼리면 고체가 되고 증발시키면 기체가 됩니다. 기체는 액화를 통해 액체가 되고 침전을 통해 고체가 됩니다. 침전의 예로는 온도가 충분히 낮아지면 수증기가 바로 얼음이 되는 것이 있죠.

1 강의의 주목적은 무엇인가?
(a) 물질 상태가 변하는 방법을 설명하려고
(b) 네 번째 물질 상태의 필요성에 대해 논하려고
(c) 가장 안정적인 물질 상태를 기술하려고
(d) 물질 상태의 특성을 대략적으로 살펴보려고

2 다음 중 가장 잘 요약된 것을 고르시오.
(a) 물체 분자의 안정성은 그 물질의 상태를 결정하며, 대부분의 상태는 다른 상태로 바뀔 수 있다.
(b) 물질의 네 가지 상태는 다른 속성을 갖고 있고 네 가지 상태는 모두 한 상태에서 다른 상태로 바뀔 수 있다.

3 옳은 문장에는 T, 틀린 문장에는 F를 쓰시오.
(1) 고체는 가장 고정된 공간적 관계에 있는 분자들을 가진다.
(2) 기체만이 다른 세 가지 물질 상태로 변할 수 있다.
(3) 물질은 액체와 기체 상태일 때 그 부피를 유지한다.
(4) 플라즈마는 팽창하지 않으려면 용기가 필요하다.

4 다음 중 승화란 무엇인가?
(a) 기체가 먼저 액체가 되지 않고 플라즈마가 되는 것
(b) 액체가 먼저 고체가 되지 않고 기체가 되는 것
(c) 고체가 먼저 액체가 되지 않고 기체가 되는 것
(d) 기체가 먼저 고체가 되지 않고 액체가 되는 것

1 (d)   2 해설 참조   3 (b)   4 (e)   5 (b)   6 (c)   7 (b)
8 (a)   9 (c)   10 (1) Barium (2) Copper (4) Calcium
(5) Iron   11 (d)   12 (b)

1

M Have you ever heard the story about no two snowflakes being exactly the same? Well, it turns out not to be a story but an actual fact. The reason lies behind how snowflakes are formed in the first place. Snowflakes form in clouds and start as water molecules which form around a nucleus. In very cold air—about minus 35 degrees Celsius—the nucleus is several frozen water droplets. In warmer air—about minus 18 degrees Celsius—the nucleus must be a piece of dust since the temperature is too warm for an ice nucleus to form on its own. After the nucleus forms, then it grows as water vapor in the cloud freezes around the nucleus. Billions of tiny water molecules make up each snowflake and bond with the nucleus. Exactly how this bonding takes place is still unclear. As the snowflake builds mass, it falls and passes through different layers of moisture and temperature in clouds before it reaches the ground. Variables such as the moisture content of the air and the temperature at different heights, plus the nature of the water molecule bonding, all play roles in producing a unique snowflake each and every time. Attempts to prove snowflakes can be the same shape have produced some positive results in labs, but, as yet, no two identical snowflakes have been found in nature.

▶ snowflake 눈송이   in the first place 애당초, 처음부터   lie behind ~의 이유이다   nucleus (기상) 핵   droplet 작은 물방울   water vapor 수증기   on its own 스스로, 제 힘으로   unclear 명백하지 않은, 막연한   moisture 습기, 수분, 물기   content 함유량, 산출량   variable 변수   play a role in 일조하다, ~의 역할을 하다   as yet 아직까지, 지금까지는   identical 똑같은, 꼭 같은

남 두 개의 눈송이가 완전히 똑같이 생길 수 없다는 이야기, 들어 본 적 있나요? 음, 그건 그냥 이야기가 아니라 실제 사실입니다. 그 이유는 처음에 눈송이가 어떻게 만들어지는가에 있습니다. 눈송이는 구름에서 형성되는데, 핵 주위에 형성되는 물 분자 형태로 시작합니다. 약 섭씨 영하 35도의 매우 차가운 공기에서 핵은 몇 개의 얼어있는 작은 물방울 상태입니다. 섭씨 영하 18도 정도의 좀 더 따뜻한 공기에서는 스스로 얼음 핵을 만들기에는 기온이 너무 따뜻하기 때문에 핵은 먼지 입자 형태여야만 합니다. 핵이 형성된 후에는 구름 안의 수증기가 주위에서 얼면서 핵이 커집니다. 수십억 개의 작은 물 분자들이 각각의 눈송이를 만들고 핵과 결합합니다. 이 결합이 정확히 어떻게 일어나는지는 아직 명확하지 않습니다. 눈송이가 덩어리가 되면 떨어지면서 땅에 닿기 전에 구름 속의 여러 수분 및 기온 층을 지나가게 됩니다. 공기의 수분 함량과 다양한 고도에서의 기온과 같은 변수, 거기에 물 분자 결합의 특성이 더해져 이 모든 것이 매번 각각 독특한 눈송이를 만드는 데 일익을 담당합니다. 실험실에서 눈송이가 똑같은 모양으로 만들어질 수 있다는 것을 증명하려는 시도가 긍정적인 결과를 낳은 바 있습니다. 하지만 아직까지 자연에서는 똑같은 눈송이가 발견되지 않았습니다.

1 왜 똑같은 눈송이는 없는가?
(a) 수분 함량이 정확히 맞아야 하기 때문에
(b) 눈은 일정한 온도에서만 만들어지기 때문에
(c) 각 눈송이에는 다른 핵들이 있기 때문에
(d) 눈송이 생성 과정에 너무 많은 변수가 작용하기 때문에
(e) 어떤 것들은 차가운 구름에서 만들어지는 반면 다른 것들은 따뜻한 구름에서 만들어지기 때문에

2

G Sorry I was absent from lab class. What did I miss?

B Oh, it was a blast today. We got to use the Bunsen burners to test the flame reaction of metals.

G Before you explain the experiment, give me the background.

B Metals react to flame by giving off certain colors. This way, we can determine if a metal is present in a sample of ore or another mixed sample of rocks and minerals.

G Okay. What are some examples of some flame tests you did in class? And speak slowly so I can take notes.

B Sure. First, we checked for copper, which gives off a blue-colored flame.

G Copper is blue. Got it. Okay, what was next?

B Then we looked at calcium, which is a really dull red. I guess you could say it is the color of a brick.

G Did the teacher say that, or are you making it up?

B The teacher said, "Brick red," so, no, I'm not making it up.

G Sorry. What was next?

B Magnesium, which was a yellowish green. We were lucky we had on our dark goggles because it burned very brightly.

G It's often used in flares. Any more?

B Barium, which was kind of like an apple green. And, yes, that's how the teacher described it, too.

G So there were only four tests.

B No, there was one more. The last one was iron, which had a kind of gold-colored flame.

▶ blast 매우 재미있거나 즐거운 경험·사건; 큰 파티   Bunsen burner (독일의 화학자 이름에서) 분젠 가스 버너(주로 화학 실험실용)   flame 불꽃, 화염   background (문제를 이해하는 데 필요한) 배경 정보, 예비지식   ore 광석   mineral 광물; 무기물   copper 구리, 동   dull (색, 빛, 음색 등이) 분명(뚜렷)치 않은; 우중충한   goggles 보호 안경; 먼지 막는 안경   flare 조명탄, (해상 등에서 쓰는) 발광 신호   iron 철

여 미안, 실습시간에 결석했어. 실습시간에 뭐 했니?
남 아, 오늘 굉장했어. 우리는 금속 불꽃 반응을 테스트하기 위해 분젠 가스 버너를 사용했지.
여 실험에 대해 설명하기 전에 배경지식 좀 줘.
남 금속은 특정한 색깔을 내면서 불꽃에 반응하지. 이렇게 해서 금속이 광석 샘플에 존재하는지 아니면 다른 암석과 광물의 혼합 샘플에 존재하는지 측정하는 거야.
여 알겠어. 수업에서 했던 불꽃 테스트는 어떤 것이었니? 천천히 얘기해. 메모 좀 하게.
남 물론이지. 먼저, 우리는 파란색 불꽃을 일으키는 구리를 실험했어.
여 구리는 파란색. 알겠어. 다음은 뭐였니?
남 그러고 나서 우리는 아주 어두운 빨간색인 칼슘을 실험했어. 벽돌색깔이라고 보면 될 것 같아.
여 선생님이 그렇게 말씀하신 거니, 아니면 네가 만들어낸 말이야?
남 선생님이 '붉은 벽돌색'이라고 하셨어. 그러니까 내가 지어 낸 게 아니라고.
여 미안해. 다음은 뭐였니?
남 노란색이 도는 녹색인 마그네슘이었어. 마그네슘이 굉장히 밝게 탔는데 짙은 보호 안경을 쓰고 있어 다행이었어.
여 마그네슘은 종종 조명탄으로 사용되지. 더 있어?
남 녹색 사과 색과 비슷한 바름이야. 그리고 맞아, 선생님도 그렇게 설명하셨어.
여 그럼 네 개만 실험한 거네.
남 아니야, 하나 더 있었어. 마지막으로는 철이었어. 약간 금빛 불꽃이었지.

2 각각의 불꽃 그림 옆의 올바른 원소를 쓰시오.

(1) 바륨　(2) 구리　(3) 마그네슘　(4) 칼슘　(5) 철

3-4

W　Now that you <u>understand</u> <u>gravity</u> and Sir Isaac Newton's role in <u>defining</u> it, I want to look at Newton's three <u>laws</u> <u>of</u> <u>motion</u>. They were first <u>defined</u> in his <u>famous</u> <u>work</u> *The Mathematical Principles of Natural Philosophy* in 1687. I will put the three laws <u>as</u> <u>simply</u> <u>as</u> I can and then <u>give</u> <u>some</u> examples. The first law of motion is that a body will <u>remain</u> <u>at</u> <u>rest</u> or will move in a <u>straight</u> <u>line</u> at a <u>constant</u> <u>rate</u> unless an <u>external</u> <u>force</u> is placed on that body. For example, a ball on a <u>pool</u> <u>table</u> is not moving. But <u>once</u> <u>you</u> <u>hit</u> the white cue ball and the cue ball hits another ball, that second ball is <u>no</u> <u>longer</u> <u>at</u> <u>rest</u> but is moving. The second of Newton's laws of motion tells us how much force <u>is</u> <u>applied</u> when an <u>object</u> <u>strikes</u> another object. The second law <u>states</u> that the force is <u>equal</u> to the mass of the object plus its <u>acceleration</u>. Now, what about the third law? The third law of motion states that for every action, there is an <u>equal</u> <u>and</u> <u>opposite</u> <u>reaction</u>. For example, you and a friend <u>push</u> <u>against</u> <u>each</u> <u>other</u> with the palms of your hands. You push one way while your friend pushes the other way, and <u>neither</u> <u>of</u> <u>you</u> <u>moves</u>. Of course, one person may be <u>stronger</u> and push the other person <u>backwards</u>. Newton's law doesn't <u>dispute</u> this result could happen but <u>merely</u> <u>states</u> that forces of motion work in both directions.

▶ **gravity** 중력　**define** 정의를 내리다　**put** 설명하다, 말하다; 두다　**at rest** 휴지[정지]하여; 잠들어, 휴식하여　**constant rate** 일정한 속도　**in a straight line** 일직선으로　**pool table** 당구대　**cue ball** 〈당구〉 큐볼, 칠 공　**mass** 크기, 양, 부피　**acceleration** 가속도　**opposite reaction** 반작용　**dispute** 이의를 제기하다; 논쟁하다

여　여러분이 중력과, 중력을 정의하는 데 있어 아이작 뉴튼 경의 역할에 대해 배웠으니, 뉴튼의 세 가지 운동법칙에 대해 살펴보기로 하겠습니다. 이 운동법칙들은 1687년 뉴튼의 유명한 저서 『자연철학의 수학적 법칙』에서 처음으로 정의되었죠. 되도록 간단하게 세 가지 법칙을 설명하고 나서 예를 들도록 하겠습니다. 첫 번째 운동법칙은 외부의 힘이 가해지지 않는 물체는 정지해 있거나 일정한 속도로 일직선으로 움직인다는 것입니다. 예를 들면 당구대에 있는 당구공은 움직이지 않습니다. 하지만 흰색 큐볼을 치고 그 공이 다른 공을 친다면 그 두 번째 공은 더 이상 정지해 있지 않고 움직이게 됩니다. 뉴튼의 두 번째 운동법칙은 한 물체가 다른 물체를 칠 때 얼마나 강한 힘이 적용되는지를 보여줍니다. 두 번째 법칙은 그 힘이 물체의 질량에 가속도를 더한 것과 같다는 것을 말해 줍니다. 자, 세 번째 법칙은 어떨까요? 세 번째 운동 법칙은 모든 행동에는 작용과 반작용이 있음을 나타냅니다. 예를 들어 여기 한 학생과 그 친구가 손바닥을 마주대고 서로를 민다고 합시다. 그 학생은 한 방향으로 밀고 친구는 반대 방향으로 밀겠죠. 그러면 둘 다 움직이지 않게 됩니다. 물론, 한 사람이 더 힘이 세서 다른 한 사람이 뒤로 밀릴 수도 있겠지요. 뉴튼의 법칙은 이런 결과에 이의를 제기하는 것이 아니라 단순히 운동의 힘이 양방향으로 작용한다는 것을 나타내는 겁니다.

3　뉴튼의 운동법칙에 따르면 같은 힘의 두 물체가 서로 일직선으로 맞선다면 어떤 일이 생기겠는가?

(a) 더 무거운 물체가 더 가벼운 물체를 매우 쉽게 내칠 것이다.

(b) 각 힘이 똑같게 유지되는 한 두 물체는 움직이지 않을 것이다.

(c) 두 물체의 힘이 오랜 시간 후에 소진될 것이다.

(d) 큰 물체는 작은 물체를 새로운 방향으로 밀 것이다.

(e) 두 물체의 가속도가 크게 증가할 것이다.

4　담화를 통해 유추할 수 있는 것은?

(a) 뉴튼의 운동법칙은 많은 실질적인 문제에 적용되지 않는다.

(b) 첫 번째 운동법칙은 움직이지 않는 물체에 적용되고 움직이는 물체에는 적용되지 않는다.

(c) 현재 경로에서 움직이는 물체를 밀려면 엄청난 힘이 필요하다.

(d) 운동법칙이 폭넓게 인정받는 데는 몇 세기가 걸렸다.

(e) 무거운 물체는 가벼운 물체보다 더 큰 힘으로 다른 물체를 친다.

5-6　Level up

M　Welcome to the Nikola Tesla Museum of Electrical History. Before we <u>begin</u> <u>the</u> <u>tour</u>, are there any questions?

G　Yes. Who was Nikola Tesla?

M　Nikola Tesla was one of the <u>great</u> <u>pioneers</u> of the <u>electrical</u> <u>age</u>. He is <u>best</u> <u>known</u> <u>for</u> the creation of the system of <u>alternating</u> <u>current</u>, or AC, that is used in most <u>power</u> <u>grid</u> <u>systems</u> today.

G　I thought Thomas Edison created the <u>systems</u> <u>of</u> <u>electricity</u> we use today.

M　Actually, Edison and Tesla had a long-running <u>disagreement</u> <u>over</u> which system of electricity was better, DC or AC.

G　DC is <u>direct</u> <u>current</u>, and AC is alternating current, right?

M　Yes. Direct current <u>flows</u> <u>in</u> one direction while alternating current moves <u>back</u> <u>and</u> <u>forth</u>, first going one way and then going another.

G　So, why do we use Tesla's alternating current <u>rather</u> <u>than</u> Edison's direct current system?

M　Direct current was used in the late 19th century when electrical systems <u>were</u> <u>first</u> <u>introduced</u>. But DC <u>had</u> <u>some</u> <u>problems</u>. First, it couldn't be sent <u>over</u> <u>long</u> <u>distances</u> since its <u>power</u> <u>diminished</u> due to <u>resistance</u> in <u>copper</u> <u>wires</u>. Second, it had a <u>low</u> <u>voltage</u>, which was fine for things such as <u>light</u> <u>bulbs</u> and small motors but was <u>impractical</u> <u>for</u> <u>machines</u> that needed a higher voltage. AC power used high voltage to <u>avoid</u> <u>these</u> <u>problems</u>, and it used <u>transformers</u> <u>to</u> <u>reduce</u> <u>voltage</u> for light bulbs and small motors.

G　It <u>seems</u> <u>strange</u> that a man as smart as Thomas Edison would not see that AC was the <u>better</u> <u>system</u>.

M　Edison had a lot of time and <u>money</u> <u>invested</u> in DC systems. So, he fought to have AC systems <u>discredited</u>. In the end, he lost, and AC systems <u>were</u> <u>adopted</u> almost everywhere in the world.

▶ **pioneer** 선구자, 개척자　**alternating current** 〈전기〉 교류　**grid** (가스, 전기, 수도 등의) 시설망　**long-running** 장기간에 걸친　**direct current** 직류　**back and forth** 앞뒤로; 이리저리　**voltage** 전압　**transformer** 변압기, 트랜스　**discredit** 평판을 나쁘게 하다, 불신하다　**adopt** 채용[채택]하다

남　니콜라 테슬라 전기 역사 박물관에 오신 것을 환영합니다. 투어를 시작하기 전에 질문 있나요?

여　예. 니콜라 테슬라가 누구예요?

남　니콜라 테슬라는 전기 시대의 위대한 개척자 중 한 명이었습니다. 그는 오늘날 대부분의 전력 시설망 시스템에서 쓰이는 교류, 즉 AC 시스템을 만든 것으로 잘 알려져 있죠.

여　전 토마스 에디슨이 오늘날 쓰이는 전기 시스템을 만들었다고 생각했는데요.

남　사실, 토마스 에디슨과 테슬라는 DC와 AC 중 어느 전기 시스템이 나은지를 놓고 오랫동안 이견을 보였어요.

여　DC는 직류고 AC는 교류죠?

남　맞습니다. 직류는 한 방향으로 흐르는 반면 교류는 처음에는 한 방향으로 갔다가 다음에는 다른 방향으로 가면서 왔다갔다 움직이죠.

여　그럼 왜 우리는 에디슨의 직류 시스템보다 테슬라의 교류 시스템을 더 많이 사용하는 건가요?

남　직류는 전기 시스템이 처음 소개되었던 19세기 후반에 사용되었습니다. 하지만 DC는 약간 문제가 있었습니다. 첫째는 구리선의 저항 때문에 전력이 소실되기 때문에 전기가 장거리를 갈 수 없죠. 둘째는 전압이 낮아서 전구와 작은 모터 같은 것은 괜찮지만 더 높은 전압이 필요한 기계에는 비실용적이었습니다. AC 전력은 이러한 문제를 막을 수 있도록 높은 전압을 사용했고 전구나 작은 모터를 사용하는 데는 전압을 줄이기 위해 변압기를 이용했죠.

여　토마스 에디슨 같이 똑똑한 사람이 AC가 더 낫다는 걸 알지 못했다는 게 이상하네요.

남　에디슨은 DC 시스템에 많은 시간과 돈을 투자했습니다. 그래서 그는 AC 시스템의 평판을 떨어뜨리기 위해 싸웠던 거죠. 결국, 그는 졌고 AC 시스템이 세계 거의 모든 곳에서 채택되었죠.

5　에디슨의 DC 시스템과 테슬라의 AC 시스템의 주요 차이점은 무엇인가?

(a) DC는 왔다갔다 흐르는 반면 AC는 한 방향으로만 흐른다.
(b) AC는 더 높은 전압을 가지고 있어 더 먼 거리까지 갈 수 있다.
(c) DC는 높은 전압을 가지고 있어 전구에 쓰일 수 있다.
(d) AC와 DC는 모두 왔다갔다 흐르지만 AC가 더 높은 전압을 가지고 있다.
(e) DC는 작은 모터에 사용할 때는 전력을 줄일 수 있는 변압기가 필요하다.

6　다음 중 내용을 가장 잘 요약한 것을 고르시오.

(a) 토마스 에디슨은 자신의 직류 시스템이 교류 시스템으로 대체되는 것을 막기 위해 오랜 싸움을 벌였다.
(b) 토마스 에디슨과 니콜라 테슬라는 실용적인 전기 시스템을 개발했지만 테슬라의 시스템이 설치하고 사용하기에 더 쉬웠다.
(c) 니콜라 테슬라의 교류 시스템이 더 실용적이었기 때문에 토마스 에디슨의 직류 시스템을 능가했다.

▶ laundry detergent 세탁세제　underestimate 과소평가하다: 낮게 어림하다
grease 기름　dirt 때, 먼지　surround 에워싸다, 둘러싸다　dissolve 용해하다, 녹이다　simplistic 극단적으로 단순화한　That will do. 그만하면 됐어, 그것으로 족하다

여　네 손이 너무 더럽구나. 옷도 마찬가지고. 너 뭐했니?

남　축구요, 엄마. 우리가 3대2로 이겼어요. 제가 한 골 넣었어요.

여　잘했구나. 자, 저녁식사가 거의 준비됐어. 가서 옷을 갈아입고 벗은 옷은 세탁기에 넣고 먹기 전에 손을 씻으렴.

남　그 어떤 세제도 이 옷을 다시 깨끗하게 만들 수는 없을 것 같아요.

여　좋은 비누나 세제의 힘을 과소평가하지 마.

남　전 비누가 어떻게 때를 빼는지 항상 궁금했어요.

여　그건 비누의 화학적 특성과 관련이 있단다. 비누 분자는 피부나 옷에 있는 기름기나 때 분자를 에워싸지. 그러면 비누 분자가 기름이나 때 분자를 물에 녹일 수 있게 된단다.

남　정말요? 단순하네요. 틀림없이 그것보다는 훨씬 더 복잡할텐데요.

여　물론이지. 하지만 지금은 그 설명으로 충분해. 엄마는 몇 년 전에 대학에서 화학 수업을 들었는데 많이 잊어버렸어.

남　나중에 인터넷에서 확인해 볼게요.

7　What was the son's reaction to the mother's explanation for how soap gets things clean? 어떻게 비누가 사물을 깨끗하게 만드는지에 관한 엄마의 설명에 아들의 반응은?

(a) He felt it was too complicated to understand.
이해하기 너무 복잡하다고 생각했다.
(b) He really wanted a more in-depth explanation.
더 자세한 설명을 원했다.
(c) He thought she knew a lot about the subject.
엄마가 그 문제에 대해 많이 안다고 생각했다.
(d) He understood her but did not really trust her.
엄마를 이해했지만 그다지 신뢰하지는 않았다.
(e) He decided to ask her more about it later.
나중에 엄마에게 그것에 대해 더 많이 물어보기로 마음먹었다.

▶ equilibrium 평형 상태, 균형　transfer 이동하다　conduction 전도

convection 전달 vibration 진동, 떨림 radiation 복사 free electron 자유전자
composition 구성, 합성 electromagnetic wave 전자파

남 열은 온도의 평형 상태에 도달하기 위해 뜨거운 물체에서 차가운 물체로 흐릅니
다. 열은 전도, 전달, 복사의 세 가지 주된 방법으로 이동합니다. 전도는 고체, 액
체, 기체 상태에서 일어납니다. 전도는 분자들의 진동과 자유전자에 의한 에너지
이동의 결과입니다. 전도는 다른 상태보다 고체 상태에서 더 빨리 일어납니다.
금속의 화학적 구성이 열 이동을 좀 더 빠르게 하기 때문에 열전도는 금속에서
가장 잘 됩니다. 전달은 기체나 액체의 실제 움직임에 의한 기체나 액체 상태에
서의 열 이동입니다. 예를 들면 따뜻한 물은 상승하고 시원한 물은 가라앉으면서
물이 담겨진 공간의 밑부분에서 윗부분으로 열이 이동하게 됩니다. 복사는 전자
파에 의해 열이 빈 공간을 통해 이동하는 것입니다. 태양열은 복사열 이동의 가
장 알기 쉬운 유형입니다.

8 What is NOT true according to the talk?

담화에 따르면 다음 중 사실이 **아닌** 것은?

(a) Convection in some solids is easier than in liquids.
일부 고체에서의 전달은 액체 상태에서의 전달보다 더 쉽다.

(b) Warm water rises, and cold water sinks in a container.
용기에 담긴 따뜻한 물은 상승하고 찬물은 가라앉는다.

(c) Conduction is quicker in solids, especially metals.
전도는 고체, 특히 금속에서 더 빠르다.

(d) The movement of liquids and gases causes convection.
액체와 기체의 움직임은 전달을 일으킨다.

(e) Heat transfer can take place without objects touching.
열 이동은 물체를 건드리지 않고 일어날 수 있다.

9

W Deep beneath the Franco-Swiss <u>border</u> <u>lays</u> a device that may change how the <u>universe is viewed</u>. This is the Large Hadron Collider, the <u>largest particle accelerator</u> ever built. A particle accelerator is a device <u>used to search for</u> the smallest elements in the universe. This search is done by <u>colliding atomic nuclei</u> and parts of atoms, like <u>positrons</u> and <u>electrons</u>, and then using <u>specialized systems</u> of computers to <u>read the results</u>. The atoms must be <u>speeded up</u> to collide head on, and thus the collider must be very large. The Large Hadron Collider is 27 kilometers long, <u>shaped in</u> a great circle, and is about 100 meters <u>deep underground</u>. Proton beams <u>shoot around</u> the circle and are <u>held in place</u> and turned by <u>hundreds of magnets</u>. By colliding protons, the scientists hope to <u>find proof</u> that a <u>small particle</u> called the Higgs boson <u>actually exists</u>. The Higgs boson may <u>hold the key</u> to many <u>unanswered questions</u> about the universe, such as how <u>mass is created</u> in the first place. The existence of the Higgs boson <u>was predicted</u> over 30 years ago, but, as yet, no one has seen <u>evidence</u> for such a particle. Some scientists call it the God particle since it may <u>hold the answers</u> to many <u>mysteries</u> of the universe. Unfortunately, the first <u>attempt to test</u> the Large Hadron Collider in 2008 failed. The device <u>was tested again</u> in late 2009, with more positive results, but, as yet, the Higgs boson remains elusive.

▶ Franco- (연결형) 프랑스(의) border 국경, 경계 particle accelerator 입자(분자)
가속기 element 원소; 요소 collide 충돌하다 atomic nuclei 원자핵
atom 원자 positron 양전자 electron 전자 collide head on 정면으로 충돌 하다
collider 입자 가속기 proton 양자, 프로톤 beam 광선; 광속
Higgs boson 힉스 입자(전기적으로 중성인 불안정한 가상의 입자)

elusive 찾기 힘든, 잡히지 않는, 정의하기 어려운

여 프랑스-스위스 국경 아래 깊숙이에는 우주를 보는 관점을 바꿀 수도 있는 장치
가 있습니다. 그것은 라지 하드론 콜라이더로, 지금까지 만들어진 것 중 가장 큰
입자 가속기입니다. 입자 가속기는 우주에 있는 가장 작은 원소를 찾기 위해 사
용되는 장치입니다. 이 조사는 원자핵과 양전자, 전자 같은 원자의 일부를 충돌
시키고 특화된 컴퓨터 시스템을 이용해 그 결과를 판독하는 방식으로 이루어졌
습니다. 원자들이 정면으로 충돌할 때까지 속도를 높여야 하기 때문에 입자 가속
기는 매우 커야 합니다. 라지 하드론 콜라이더는 길이가 27킬로미터이고 커다란
원형이며 지하 약 100미터 깊이에 있습니다. 양자 광선이 원형 주위에 방사되고
수백 개의 자석으로 고정되어 회전합니다. 과학자들은 양자 충돌로 힉스 입자라
고 하는 작은 입자가 실제로 존재한다는 증거를 찾고자 합니다. 힉스 입자는 처
음에 질량이 어떻게 생기는가와 같은, 해답을 찾지 못한 우주에 대한 많은 질문
의 열쇠를 쥐고 있을 수 있습니다. 힉스 입자의 존재는 30년도 더 전에 예측되었
지만 아직까지 아무도 이러한 입자에 대한 증거를 목격한 바 없습니다. 어떤 과
학자들은 그것이 우주의 많은 미스터리에 대한 해답을 쥐고 있을 수 있기 때문
에 신의 입자라고 부릅니다. 아쉽게도, 2008년에 라지 하드론 콜라이더를 시험
하려는 첫 시도는 실패했습니다. 2009년 후반에 그 장치를 다시 시험하여 좀 더
긍정적인 결과를 얻었지만, 힉스 입자는 아직까지 손에 잡히지 않은 채로 남아있
습니다.

9 담화에 따르면 다음 중 사실이 **아닌** 것은?

(a) 라지 하드론 콜라이더는 프랑스와 스위스 지하에 있다.

(b) 라지 하드론 콜라이더를 사용한 첫 번째 테스트는 실패했다.

(c) 힉스 입자는 30년 전에 처음 발견되었다.

(d) 우주에 질량이 존재하는 이유는 알려지지 않았다.

(e) 라지 하드론 콜라이더는 실험에 양자 광선을 사용한다.

10

B It's time to study chemistry. Mr. Wilkes is <u>known for giving pop quizzes</u> on Fridays.

G Let's <u>crack</u> the books then. What's first?

B Chapter 6, the noble gases. Why are they called "noble"?

G Wait. Here it is. The noble gases are called "noble" because they have <u>full outer</u> valences of electrons and therefore do not <u>bond well</u> with other <u>elements</u>. Okay, so what are the noble gases?

B There are helium, neon, argon, krypton, xenon, and radon.

G Krypton? As in Superman's <u>weakness</u>?

B That's just a <u>comic book</u>. Come on. This is serious.

G Okay. So now we need to know the <u>atomic numbers</u>. Helium is 2, neon 10, argon 18, krypton 36, xenon 54, and radon 86.

B I'll <u>never remember</u> all that by tomorrow.

G Wait a second. We can use a <u>simple method</u>. Start with helium, whose atomic number is 2. <u>Then add 8</u>, and you get 10 for the <u>atomic number of neon</u>. Then add 8 again and you have the atomic number of argon, 18. Then add 8... No, wait. <u>That doesn't work</u>.

B Close, but no cigar. Hey, <u>hold your horses</u>. If we then double 18, we get 36 the atomic number of krypton. Then <u>add 18 again</u> and we have 54, the atomic number of xenon.

G But the last one is radon, whose atomic number is 86. <u>Nothing so far adds</u> up to 86.

B We'll just have to remember it, like helium. So, helium

is 2, plus 8 <u>equals</u> <u>10</u> for neon, plus 8 equals 18 for argon, plus <u>18</u> equals 36 for krypton, plus 18 equals 54 for xenon, and the final one, radon, is... I can't remember!

G 86!

▶ pop quiz 예고 없는 시험 noble gas 희(稀)가스 valence electron 〈화학〉 원자가 전자 helium 헬륨(기호 He, 원자번호 2) neon 네온(기호 Ne, 원자번호10) argon 아르곤(기호 A 또는 Ar, 원자번호 18) krypton 크립톤(기호 Kr, 번호 36) xenon 크세논(기호 Xe, 원자번호 54) radon 라돈(기호 Rn, 번호 86) atomic number 원자번호 Close, but no cigar. 아슬아슬하다, 아주 가깝다 hold one's horses (보통 명령문으로) 조급해지는 마음을 억제하다 double 두 배로 하다 add up to 합계 ~이 되다

남 화학 공부할 시간이야. 윌키스 선생님은 금요일마다 쪽지시험을 내는 걸로 유명해.

여 그럼 책을 펴자. 뭐지?

남 6장, 희가스야. 왜 '희(稀)'라고 불리는 걸까?

여 잠깐. 여기 있다. 희가스에는 전자 외부의 원자가가 꽉 차 있어서 다른 원소들과 결합을 잘 안 해. 좋아, 그럼 희가스에는 뭐가 있지?

남 헬륨, 네온, 아르곤, 크립톤, 크세논, 라돈이 있어.

여 크립톤? 수퍼맨의 약점 말이야?

남 그건 만화책일 뿐이고. 야, 이건 장난이 아니라고.

여 알았어. 그럼 이제 원자번호를 알아야겠구나. 헬륨은 2, 네온은 10, 아르곤은 18, 크립톤은 36, 크세논은 54, 라돈은 86.

남 난 내일까지 이거 절대 다 못 외워.

여 잠깐만. 간단한 방법을 써보자. 원자번호 2번인 헬륨부터 시작해. 거기 8을 더하면 네온의 원자번호 10이 되잖아. 거기에 다시 8을 더하면 아르곤의 원자번호인 18이 되고 거기에 8을 더하면… 아니야, 잠깐만. 안 되네.

남 아주 근접했어. 이봐, 잠깐 기다려봐. 18을 두 배로 하면 크립톤의 원자번호인 36을 얻을 수 있어. 그러고 나서 다시 18을 더하면 크세논의 원자번호인 54가 된다.

여 하지만 마지막 라돈은 원자번호가 86이야. 더해서 합계가 86이 되는 게 없어.

남 그건 헬륨처럼 기억해야겠어. 그럼, 헬륨은 2, 더하기 8은 10 네온, 더하기 8은 18 아르곤, 더하기 18은 36 크립톤, 더하기 18은 54 크세논, 그리고 마지막으로 라돈은… 기억이 안 나!

여 86이잖아!

10 각 희가스의 원자번호로 표를 완성하시오.

희가스	원자번호
헬륨	2
네온	10
아르곤	18
크립톤	36
크세논	54
라돈	86

11-12 Level up

M The <u>three</u> <u>main</u> <u>parts</u> of an <u>atom</u> are <u>electrons</u>, protons, and neutrons. Protons are <u>positively</u> <u>charged</u>, and neutrons <u>have</u> <u>no</u> <u>charge</u>. They both <u>make</u> <u>up</u> the <u>center</u> <u>of</u> <u>an</u> <u>atom</u>, which is <u>called</u> <u>the</u> <u>nucleus</u>. Electrons are negatively charged, <u>spin</u> <u>around</u> the nucleus very <u>quickly</u>, and form what is called the <u>electron</u> <u>cloud</u>. Let's use a few <u>examples</u> <u>of</u> <u>elements</u> to explain this <u>in</u> <u>more</u> <u>depth</u>. Hydrogen is the <u>simplest</u> <u>element</u> because it has one electron, one proton, and no neutrons. The <u>opposite</u> <u>electrical</u> <u>charges</u> of the proton and the electron are what <u>keep</u> <u>them</u> <u>together</u>. The second simplest atom is the <u>helium</u> <u>atom</u>. It has two protons and two electrons. It also has two neutrons, which are <u>necessary</u> <u>to</u> <u>maintain</u> the <u>cohesion</u> of the atom. The two positively charged protons <u>would</u> <u>repel</u> <u>each</u> <u>other</u> if there were no neutrons, which <u>sort</u> <u>of</u> <u>act</u> like a <u>glue</u> that keeps the helium atom together. These types of atoms, which are <u>neither</u> <u>positively</u> <u>nor</u> <u>negatively</u> charged, are called neutral atoms. In each neutral atom, there are an <u>equal</u> <u>number</u> of protons and electrons. Atoms are <u>measured</u> <u>by</u> their atomic number or atomic mass. The atomic number <u>equals</u> the <u>number</u> <u>of</u> <u>protons</u> in an atom. The atomic mass equals the mass of the electrons, protons, and neutrons in an atom. Sometimes, an atom can have <u>more</u> <u>or</u> <u>fewer</u> <u>electrons</u> than protons. Positively charged atoms have fewer electrons than protons, and <u>negatively</u> <u>charged</u> <u>atoms</u> have more electrons than protons. These charged atoms <u>are</u> <u>called</u> <u>ions</u>. Sometimes, atoms can also have more neutrons than protons. These atoms are called isotopes of the atom.

▶ electron 전자 proton 양성자, 프로톤 neutron 중성자 positively 양전기로 charge 충전하다; 전하(電荷) atom 원자 in depth 깊이 있게, 철저히 hydrogen 수소 cohesion 응집력; 결합 repel 쫓아내다 neutral atom 중성원자 atomic mass 원자질량 ion 이온 isotope 동위원소, 동위체; 핵종

남 원자의 주요 세 부분은 전자, 양성자, 중성자입니다. 양성자는 양의 전하를 띠고 있고 중성자는 전하가 없습니다. 양성자와 중성자 둘 다 원자의 중심을 이루는데, 이를 핵이라고 부릅니다. 전자는 음전하를 띠며 핵 주위를 매우 빠르게 돌면서 전자구름이라고 하는 것을 형성합니다. 몇 가지 원소를 예로 들어 더 심도 있게 설명하도록 하겠습니다. 수소는 전자 한 개, 양성자 한 개, 중성자는 없는 가장 단순한 원소입니다. 양성자와 전자는 서로 전기적으로 반대되는 전하를 가지고 있기 때문에 함께 있게 되는 것이죠. 두 번째로 단순한 원자는 헬륨 원자입니다. 헬륨 원자는 양성자 두 개와 전자 두 개를 가지고 있습니다. 헬륨 원자 또한 이 원자의 응집력을 유지하는 데 필수적인 두 개의 중성자를 갖고 있습니다. 헬륨 원자를 서로 붙게 하는 접착제 역할을 하는 중성자가 없다면 양전하를 가진 양성자 두 개가 서로를 밀쳐내게 될 것입니다. 양전하 하나 음전하를 띠지 않는 이러한 종류의 원자를 중성원자라고 합니다. 각각의 중성원자에는 같은 수의 양성자와 전자가 있습니다. 원자는 원자번호와 원자질량으로 측정됩니다. 원자번호는 원자의 양성자 개수와 같습니다. 원자질량은 원자 한 개에 있는 전자, 양성자, 중성자의 질량과 같습니다. 원자는 양성자보다 더 많은 수 또는 적은 수의 전자를 가지고 있을 때도 있습니다. 양전하를 띠는 원자는 양성자보다 적은 전자를 가지고 있고, 음전하를 띠는 원자는 양성자보다 더 많은 전자를 가지고 있습니다. 이런 원자를 이온이라고 부릅니다. 때때로 원자는 양성자보다 많은 중성자를 가질 수도 있습니다. 이러한 원자를 원자 동위원소라고 부릅니다.

11 강의의 주목적은 무엇인가?
  (a) 이온과 동위 원소가 만들어지는 방법을 기술하려고
  (b) 원자 인력의 특성에 대한 세부적인 설명을 하려고
  (c) 원자의 요소와 그것들이 어떻게 측정되는지 보여주려고
  (d) 원자의 요소와 그것들이 움직이는 방식을 설명하려고
  (e) 원자 구조에서 전자적인 인력을 조사하려고

12 강의에서 유추할 수 있는 것은?
  (a) 전자보다 양성자가 더 많은 원자는 음전하를 띤다.
  (b) 수소는 양성자가 하나이기 때문에 중성자가 필요 없다.
  (c) 동위 원소는 헬륨과 같은 중성원자의 이온에서 형성된다.
  (d) 원자의 원자번호는 원자가 이온이 되면 변한다.
  (e) 원자질량은 중성원자와 동위 원소에서는 아무런 변화가 없다.

1 (c)　2 (b)　3 (b)　4 (b)　5 (d)　6 (a)　7 (b)
8 해설 참조　9 (d)　10 (e)

1

W Most of you probably know about magnetism from using a compass, which was the first practical use of magnetism. A compass always points to magnetic north. But why? And what causes magnetism in the first place? Originally, magnetism was thought to be found only in certain metals, such as iron, which were called ferromagnetic. Then, in the 19th century, a Danish researcher, Hans Christian Oersted, was doing an experiment with electricity when he saw a nearby compass needle pointing toward his experiment. By this fortuitous stroke of luck, the scientist accidentally realized that magnetism was created by electric currents. Further research showed that if two electric currents are parallel and facing the same way, they attract each other. If the electric currents are not parallel, then they repel each other. For example, when two magnets are placed together, one side repels or attracts the other. This research led to the theories of electromagnetism. The basic theory is related to the structure of the atom. In each atom of a material, there are electrons rotating around protons and neutrons. If all of the electrons of a material line up in a certain way, then a magnetic field is created. This does not happen in all matter though, and some things, such as copper, water, and gases, cannot produce a magnetic field.

▶ magnetism 자기, 자력　compass 나침반　magnetic north 자북극(자침이 가리키는 북쪽 끝)　originally 원래, 처음에는　ferromagnetic 강(强)자성의; 강자성체　fortuitous 뜻밖의; 우연한; 행운의　stroke of luck 행운, 운수대통　accidentally 우연히, 뜻하지 않게　electric current 전류　parallel 〈전기〉 병렬의　magnet 자석　electromagnetism 전자기(학)　line up 한 줄로 늘어서다　magnetic field 자기장

여 여러분 중 대부분은 자력을 최초로 실용적으로 사용한 경우인 나침반을 써보고 자력에 대해 알게 되었을 것입니다. 나침반은 항상 자북극을 가리킵니다. 왜 그럴까요? 그리고 맨처음 무엇이 지력을 일으키는 걸까요? 원래 지력은 강자성체라고 불리는 철과 같은 특정한 금속에서만 발견되는 것으로 여겨졌습니다. 그 후 19세기에 한스 크리스티안 외르스테드라는 덴마크 연구원이 전기 실험을 하고 있을 때 근처에 있던 나침반 바늘이 그의 실험 장치로 향해 있는 것을 보았습니다. 이 뜻밖의 행운으로 그 과학자는 자력이 전류에 의해 형성된다는 것을 우연히 깨닫게 됩니다. 추후의 연구는 두 개의 전류가 병렬이고 같은 방향을 향하고 있다면 서로 끌어당긴다는 것을 보여줍니다. 만약 그 전류들이 병렬이 아니라면 서로 밀쳐내게 됩니다. 예를 들어 두 개의 자석이 함께 놓여 있다면 한쪽은 다른 한쪽을 밀치지 않으면 끌어당긴다는 것입니다. 이 연구로 전자기학이 생겨나게 되었죠. 기본 이론은 원자의 구조와 관련되어 있습니다. 물질의 각 원자에는 양성자와 중성자 주위를 도는 전자가 있습니다. 만약 물질의 모든 전자가 일정한 방향으로 늘어서 있다면 자기장이 만들어집니다. 그러나 이것은 모든 물질에서 일어나는 것은 아닙니다. 구리, 물, 기체와 같은 물질은 자기장을 만들 수 없습니다.

1 담화에 의하면 사실이 <u>아닌</u> 것은?
 (a) 나침반은 자력을 처음으로 실용적으로 사용한 사례였다.
 (b) 덴마크 연구원은 우연히 전자기를 발견하였다.
 (c) 자력은 구리와 같은 금속에서 발견된다고 여겨졌다.
 (d) 자력은 원자 안에서 전자의 일렬 정렬에 의해 만들어진다.
 (e) 어떤 종류의 물질은 자기장을 만들 수 없다.

2-3

W It's a nice day for a walk.

M It sure is. Hey, what's that sound?

W I think it's an ambulance. Here it comes... And there it goes. Wow, that was so loud!

M It sure was. I think my eardrums are about to burst.

W Did you notice that it seemed louder as it was far away but not as loud when it just passed by us?

M Yeah. That's because of the Doppler effect.

W The what effect?

M The Doppler effect. It was named for an Austrian physicist, Christian Doppler.

W So, what does it have to do with an ambulance and the sound it makes?

M Let's see if I can make this simple without sounding condescending. When a sound source approaches an observer, such as us, here taking a walk on this road, the sound's pitch seems to be higher.

W Okay, I'm with you so far.

M Then the pitch appears to be lower when the sound source recedes from the person. The ambulance's siren sounded very loud first. Yet, as soon as the ambulance passed by, the pitch was much lower, and the sound was quieter.

W What causes the Doppler effect in the first place?

M Let me see if I can get this straight.

W Do your best.

M Okay. The effect is caused by a change in the frequency and length of the sound waves when they are approaching and receding from an observer. That's all I remember.

W Oh, I understand. ______________________

▶ eardrum 고막, 귀청　have to do with ~ ~와 관계(관련)가 있다　condescending (아랫사람에게) 짐짓 겸손한 체하는; 생색내는 듯한　pitch 음조, 음의 고저　recede 멀어지다; 물러가다　frequency 주파수　sound wave 음파

여 산책하기에 좋은 날이야.

남 정말 그래. 어, 무슨 소리지?

여 앰뷸런스 소리 같은데. 여기로 오네… 그리고 저기로 가버렸다. 와, 정말 시끄러웠어!

남 그래. 고막이 터지는 줄 알았어.

여 너 앰뷸런스가 멀리 있을 때는 소리가 시끄러운 것 같았지만 우리를 지나갈 때만 큼은 아니었다는 거 눈치 챘니?

남 응. 그건 도플러 효과 때문이야.

여 무슨 효과?

남 도플러 효과. 도플러 효과는 오스트리아 물리학자인 크리스티안 도플러의 이름을 딴 거야.

여 그런데 그게 앰뷸런스와 앰뷸런스가 내는 소리랑 무슨 상관이 있는데?

남 잘난 척하는 것 같지 않으면서도 간단하게 설명할 수 있는지 한번 볼까. 여기 도로에서 걷고 있는 우리와 같은 관찰자에게 음원이 도달하면 음조가 더 높은 것 같이 들리지.

여 좋아, 지금까지는 알겠어.

남 그러고 나서 음원이 그 사람으로부터 멀어지면 음조가 낮아진 것 같지. 그 앰뷸런스의 사이렌은 처음에는 매우 시끄러웠지만 앰뷸런스가 지나가자마자 음조가 훨씬 낮아졌고 더 조용해졌잖아.

여 애당초 무엇이 도플러 효과를 일으키는 거지?

남　내가 이걸 확실히 설명할 수 있을지 모르겠네.

여　최대한 해 봐.

남　알았어. 그 효과는 관찰자에게 접근했다가 멀어질 때 주파수와 음파 길이가 변화해서 일어나. 그게 내가 기억하고 있는 전부야.

여　아, 이해된다. ________________________________

2　대화에서 유추할 수 있는 것은?

  (a) 남자는 자신의 기억력에 매우 자신이 있다.

  (b) 남자는 과거에 물리학을 공부한 적이 있다.

  (c) 그들은 집 근처를 걷고 있다.

  (d) 도플러 효과는 증명되지 않은 이론이다.

  (e) 음조는 음량과 관련이 있다.

3　여자는 다음에 뭐라고 말하겠는가?

  (a) 하지만 그것을 왜 도플러 효과라고 부르지?

  (b) 설명하기가 그렇게 어려운건 아니었네, 그렇지?

  (c) 다른 방법으로 그 이론을 테스트해야 해.

  (d) 아무도 심하게 다치지 않았길 진심으로 바라.

  (e) 그건 앰뷸런스 사이렌에만 적용되는 거니?

4-5

M　A neutrino is a non-electrically charged particle that has a mass so small that it can't be measured. Neutrinos are perhaps the most numerous particles in the universe, and every second of every day, almost 50 trillion of them pass through our bodies. Most of the neutrinos we come in contact with are produced by the nuclear reactions of the sun, and many of the others come from nuclear reactions in other stars. There are three main types of neutrinos: electron, muon, and tau. They can "oscillate," or move in waves, and one type of neutrino can change into another type. They also move at close to the speed of light and move in the same direction, no matter what happens to them. It is believed that if all of the neutrinos in the universe were measured, they would weigh more than all of the stars and planets combined. The idea for neutrinos started out as just a theory in the 1930s. Many attempts have been made to detect neutrinos, and a few have been successful, but no one has found a way to weigh them. The greatest success so far in neutrino detection has been in Japan in the town of Kamioka. In 1998, in an old zinc mine 1,000 meters underground, researchers managed to stop and record evidence of several thousand neutrinos for a short time. The hope is that one day we can capture, control, and use neutrinos for various applications.

▶ neutrino 〈물리〉 중성미자(微子)　numerous 다수의, 수많은, 셀 수 없이 많은　trillion 1조　muon 〈물리〉 뮤온, 뮤입자(중간자)　tau 〈물리〉 타우입자　oscillate 진동하다　wave 파동, 전파　zinc mine 아연광산　capture 포착하다; 붙잡다

남　중성미자는 질량이 너무 작아 측정할 수 없고 전기를 띠지 않는 입자입니다. 중성미자는 아마도 우주에서 가장 많은 입자일 것입니다. 매순간 거의 50조의 중성미자가 우리 몸을 관통합니다. 우리가 접촉하는 대부분의 중성미자는 태양의 핵반응으로 생성되고, 그 밖의 많은 것들은 다른 별들의 핵반응에서 나오는 것입니다. 중성미자에는 전자, 뮤온, 타우, 이렇게 세 가지 종류가 있습니다. 중성미자는 '진동', 즉 파동 속에서 움직일 수 있고, 중성미자의 한 종류는 다른 종류로 바뀔 수 있습니다. 중성미자는 무슨 일이 있든 빛의 속도에 가깝게 움직이고 같은 방향으로 움직입니다. 만약 우주에 있는 모든 중성미자를 측정한다면 모든 별

과 행성을 합한 것보다 더 무거울 것이라고 여겨지고 있습니다. 중성미자에 대한 생각은 1930년대에 이론으로 시작되었습니다. 중성미자를 탐지하기 위한 많은 시도가 있었는데요. 일부는 성공적이었지만 그 누구도 중성미자의 무게를 잴 방법을 알아내지 못했습니다. 중성미자 탐색에서 지금까지 가장 크게 성공한 사례는 일본 가미오카의 마을에서 있었습니다. 1998년에 1,000미터 지하의 오래된 아연광산에서 학자들은 잠시 동안 간신히 수천 개의 중성미자를 멈추고 그 증거를 기록하였습니다. 언젠가는 중성미자를 포착·조절하고 다양하게 응용하여 사용할 수 있다는 희망이 생겼습니다.

4　중성미자에 대해서 다음 중 사실이 <u>아닌</u> 것은?

  (a) 중성미자는 한 종류에서 다른 종류로 변할 수 있다.

  (b) 중성미자는 전기적인 전하와 적은 질량을 가지고 있다.

  (c) 중성미자는 멈추지 않고 일직선으로 움직인다.

  (d) 중성미자는 우주에서 가장 많은 입자이다.

  (e) 중성미자는 믿을 수 없을 만큼 빠른 속도로 움직인다.

5　담화를 통해 중성미자에 대해 유추할 수 있는 것은?

  (a) 중성미자의 무게는 너무 가벼워 측정할 수 없다.

  (b) 중성미자는 다양하게 많이 응용된다.

  (c) 중성미자는 이동을 시작하면 방향을 바꿀 수 있다.

  (d) 어떤 중성미자는 원자력 발전소의 핵반응에서 나온다.

  (e) 중성미자가 몸에 들어가면 건강상 문제를 일으킬 수 있다.

6　**Level up**

G　Are you going to the library after lunch?

B　Yeah, why do you ask?

G　I just need you to Xerox some class notes I missed when I was sick last week. I don't have any time.

B　Ah, what does Xerox mean?

G　Make photocopies. Haven't you ever heard that term before?

B　No, I don't think so. Why did you use the word Xerox? Isn't that a photocopy machine company?

G　Yes, but it's also the name of the dry process for making copies invented in 1938. The inventor called it xerography, from the Greek words for dry, *xeros*, and writing, *graphos*. Now people just say *Xerox*. It's a noun for the company name and a verb for the process of making photocopies using xerography.

B　Why use the word "dry"? No one makes copies that are wet.

G　No, but they used to use liquid chemicals to make copies before the invention of xerography. Xerography uses no liquids but has dry toner that is attached to the paper during the process. So can you help me or not?

B　Sure, I can make some "Xeroxes" for you.

G　Thanks. You're a lifesaver.

▶ Xerox 제록스: 제록스로 복사하다　make photocopy 복사하다　dry process 건식　xerography 제로그라피(건식 전자 사진 복사의 한 방식)　chemicals 화학약품　be attached to ~에 연결되어 있다　toner (전자 복사의) 현상약　lifesaver 곤경에서 구해 주는 사람, 구원자

여　점심식사 후에 도서관 갈 거니?

남　응, 왜?

여　지난주에 내가 아파서 빠진 수업의 노트 좀 제록스 해주었으면 해서. 난 시간이 없거든.

남　어, 제록스가 무슨 말이야?

여 복사한다는 뜻이야. 그 용어 들어본 적 없어?

남 응, 없어. 왜 제록스라는 단어를 썼어? 그거 복사기 회사 이름 아니야?

여 맞아, 하지만 제록스는 1938년에 발명된 건식 복사 과정의 이름이기도 해. 그 발명가가 건식 복사를 제로그라피라고 불렀어. '물기 없는'이라는 뜻의 그리스어 '제로스'랑 '쓰기'라는 의미의 그리스어 '그라포스'에서 이름을 딴 거지. 이제 사람들은 그냥 제록스라고 해. 제록스는 회사 이름으로 명사이기도 하고 제로그라피를 이용한 복사 공정을 나타내는 동사이기도 해.

남 왜 '물기 없는' 이라는 단어를 사용하지? 아무도 물기 젖게 복사하지 않잖아.

여 그렇지, 하지만 제로그라피가 발명되기 전에는 액체 화학약품을 사용해서 복사하곤 했어. 제로그라피는 액체를 사용하지 않고 복사 과정 동안 종이에 연결되어 있는 물기 없는 토너를 사용하지. 그건 그렇고 너 나 도와줄 거야 말 거야?

남 도와주고말고. 내가 너를 위해 '제록스'해줄게.

여 고마워. 넌 내 구세주야.

6 What is correct according to the dialog?

대화에 따르면 다음 중 옳은 것은?

(a) Xerography is not the first form of copying.
제로그라피는 복사의 최초 형태가 아니다.

(b) The girl has to go to a class after lunch.
소녀는 점심시간 후에 수업에 가야 한다.

(c) Liquid chemical copying is still in use.
아직도 액체 화학약품을 사용한 복사를 하고 있다.

(d) The girl missed a whole week of classes.
소녀는 일주일 내내 수업에 빠졌다.

(e) The word "Xerox" is Greek for writing.
'제록스'라는 단어는 그리스어로 '쓰기'라는 뜻이다.

W Have you ever put a straw in a glass of water and then noticed that the straw seems to be bent or even broken, depending on the angle you look at the glass? This optical illusion is caused by the principle of refraction, which refers to the slowing down of light waves as they pass through a different medium. For example, when light passes through air, it has one speed. When light passes through water or glass, such as an eyeglass lens, it moves at a slower speed. This causes a distortion of the image that the human eye sees and the brain interprets. The principle of refraction has been known for a long time, and it was the basis by which refractive lenses for telescopes and eyeglasses were first developed. This principle also works with sound. Sound waves slow down in different mediums, such as water. In the ocean, sound wave speed can be altered by the temperature, salinity, and pressure of a layer of water. Underwater acoustics must take these factors into account.

▶ optical illusion 착시현상　refraction 굴절 (작용)　refer to 일컫다, 가리키다　light wave 광파(光波)　medium 도체(導體), 매체　one 같은, 동일한　refractive lens 굴절 렌즈　salinity 염분, 염도　alter 변경하다, 바꾸다　underwater 수중의　acoustics 음향 상태[효과]　take ~ into account ~을 고려하다

여 여러분은 유리컵에 빨대를 넣고 나서 컵을 보는 각도에 따라 빨대가 구부러지거나 부러진 것처럼 보인다는 것을 알게된 적이 있나요? 이 착시현상은 굴절법칙에 의해 일어나는데, 이것은 다른 매개물을 통과할 때 광파가 느려지는 것을 말합니다. 예를 들면 빛이 공기를 통과할 때는 일정한 속도를 유지합니다. 빛이 물이나 안경 렌즈와 같은 유리를 통과할 때는 속도가 느려집니다. 이것은 사람의 눈이 보고 뇌가 판단하는 이미지에 변형을 일으킵니다. 굴절법칙은 오랫동안 알려져 있었고, 이를 기초로 하여 망원경과 안경에 쓰는 굴절 렌즈가 처음 개발되

었습니다. 이 법칙은 소리에도 적용됩니다. 음파는 물과 같은 다른 매개체에서는 속도가 느려지죠. 바다에서는 음파 속도가 기온, 염도, 바다 층의 압력에 의해 변할 수 있습니다. 물속의 음향 상태는 이 요소들을 고려해야 합니다.

7 What is the main purpose of the talk?

담화의 주목적은 무엇인가?

(a) To describe a possible scientific theory related to light and sound
빛과 소리에 관련된 확립 가능한 과학적 이론을 기술하려고

(b) To explain why and how different mediums affect light and sound 다른 매개물들이 왜 그리고 어떻게 빛과 소리에 영향을 미치는지를 설명하려고

(c) To prove that light and sound waves do not have constant speeds
빛과 음파는 일정한 속도를 가지고 있지 않다는 것을 증명하려고

(d) To discuss how telescope and eyeglass lenses improve vision 어떻게 망원경과 안경 렌즈가 시력을 향상시키는지에 대해 논하려고

(e) To examine why people hear and see differently from each other
왜 사람들이 다른 사람들과 다르게 듣고 보는지를 조사하려고

8

M Diamonds are a girl's best friend, or so the saying goes. Society has placed a high value on these gemstones, which are little more than a form of carbon. Diamonds are an allotrope of carbon. This means the atoms of carbon are arranged and bonded differently in different carbon-based materials, such as diamonds and graphite. This unique bonding gives diamonds their strength and hardness. As you already know, diamonds are the hardest of all minerals. Approximately 26,000 kilograms of diamonds are mined each year around the world. Natural diamonds are usually found in two places: alluvial deposits at the mouths of rivers and in lava pipes from ancient volcanoes. Lava pipes are the most common places to find diamonds. In the lava pipes, there is a special rock called kimberlite, which is the most common hiding place of diamonds. Kimberlite is so rare that only a few countries have diamonds in sufficient enough quantities to mine. About 50 percent of natural diamonds come from Africa, with most of them coming from South Africa. Outside of Africa, Russia has about one-fifth of the world's diamonds while Canada, Australia, Brazil, and India have most of the rest. Most diamonds are intended to be gems in jewelry, which leaves little leftover for industrial uses, so researchers created the first synthetic diamonds in 1954. These artificial diamonds were created to meet the demand for industrial uses, such as for cutting tools and producing semiconductors. Approximately 100,000 kilograms of synthetic diamonds are made worldwide each year.

▶ gemstone 보석의 원석　carbon 탄소　allotrope 동소체(同素體)　graphite 그래파이트, 흑연, 석묵(石墨)　strength 강도(強度)　hardness 경도(硬度)　mine 채굴하다　alluvial deposit 퇴적층　at the mouths of a river 강어귀에　lava 용암　pipe 관상 광맥　gem 보석; 귀중품　industrial use 공업용　synthetic diamond 인조 다이아몬드　semiconductor 반도체

남 다이아몬드는 여자의 가장 친한 친구죠. 어쨌든 속담에 의하면 그렇다고 하네요. 세상은 탄소의 형태에 보다 가까운 이 원석에 높은 가치를 두었습니다. 다이아

몬드는 탄소 동소체입니다. 이것은 탄소 원자가 다이아몬드와 흑연 같은 탄소를 기반으로 하는 다른 물질에서는 다르게 배열되고 결합된다는 의미입니다. 이 독특한 결합은 다이아몬드에 강도와 경도를 부여합니다. 이미 알다시피 다이아몬드는 모든 광물 중에서 가장 단단하죠. 전 세계에서 매년 약 2만 6천 킬로그램의 다이아몬드가 채굴됩니다. 천연 다이아몬드는 대개 강어귀에 있는 퇴적층과 오래된 화산의 용암광맥 두 곳에서 발견됩니다. 용암광맥은 다이아몬드가 가장 흔하게 발견되는 장소입니다. 용암광맥에는 다이아몬드가 가장 많이 숨어 있는, 킴벌라이트라는 특수한 암석이 있습니다. 킴벌라이트는 매우 귀해서 채굴할 수 있을 만큼의 다이아몬드는 단 몇 개국에만 있죠. 약 50%의 천연 다이아몬드는 아프리카에서 나오는데, 그 대부분이 남아프리카에서 나옵니다. 아프리카 외에 러시아에서 전 세계의 5분의 1 정도의 다이아몬드가 생산되는 한편 캐나다, 호주, 브라질, 인도에서 그 나머지 대부분이 생산됩니다. 대부분의 다이아몬드는 보석으로 쓰여 공업용으로는 거의 남아 있지 않습니다. 그래서 학자들은 1954년에 처음으로 인조 다이아몬드를 만들었습니다. 이러한 인조 다이아몬드는 절단기를 만드는 데 쓰거나 반도체를 생산하는 것과 같은 공업용 수요를 위해 제조되었습니다. 매년 약 십만 킬로그램의 인조 다이아몬드가 전 세계에서 제조됩니다.

8 다이아몬드와 관련된 정보에서 빠진 부분을 채우시오.

범주	숫자/날짜
매년 채굴되는 천연 다이아몬드의 양	26,000 kg
아프리카에서 채굴되는 천연 다이아몬드의 양	13,000 kg
러시아에서 채굴되는 천연 다이아몬드의 양	5,200킬로그램
매년 만들어지는 인조 다이아몬드의 양	100,000 kg
인조 다이아몬드가 처음 만들어진 해	1954

9-10 **Integrated Questions**

Reading

▶ densely populated area 인구 밀집 지역   pesticide 구충제, 살충제   hazardous 위험한   manufacture 제조, 제작; 생산   investigation 조사, 수사, 연구   reveal 밝히다; 폭로하다   explosion 폭발, 파열   deadly 치명적인, 치사의   fume (유해하거나 불쾌한) 연기   release 내뿜다, 방출하다   blame 책임; 비난   urban area 도시 지역   safety standard 안전기준   to this day 오늘날까지   disgruntled 불만인; 심술 난   sabotage 사보타주(쟁의 중인 노동자가 공장 설비·기계 등을 파괴하고 생산을 방해하는 것)

화학제품은 인간에게 많은 혜택을 주지만 동시에 위험하고 치명적이기까지 할 수 있다. 이 사실이 가장 비극적으로 극명하게 드러난 사건은 1984년 12월 2일과 3일 밤에 인도 보팔에서 일어난 화학재해로, 결국 거의 2만 5천 명의 목숨을 앗아갔다. 보팔의 인구 밀집 지역 인근에 미국 회사인 유니온 카바이드 소유의 화학공장이 위치해 있었다. 공장은 제초제를 생산했는데, 제조 과정에서 위험한 화학제품을 사용했다. 후에 수사팀은 화학제품이 담겨 있는 큰 탱크에 물이 들어가 탱크 안 온도가 폭발 도달점까지 올라갔음을 밝혀냈다. 치명적인 가스가 누출되어 그 지역 전체로 퍼져나갔다. 사람들은 그 가스를 마셨고 그 중 일부는 즉사했으며 그 밖의 사람들은 며칠, 몇 달 심지어 몇 년 후에 사망했다. 다른 이들은 가스가 누출되었을 때 그 지역을 대피하면서 시작된 공황 속에서 목숨을 잃었다. 결국, 유니온 카바이드사와 인도 정부가 책임을 분담했다. 공장은 도시 지역과 너무 가깝게 있었고 안전 기준은 부실했다. 그 재해가 사고였는지 아니면 불만을 품은 노동자의 의도적인 사보타주였는지에 대해서는 오늘날까지 아직도 논란이 있다.

W In the world of chemistry, there is no more dreaded word than Bhopal. Say this, and people will get an immediate picture of dead children in the streets of this Indian city. The disaster that took place there in December 1984 was one of the greatest tragedies involving chemicals ever to happen. The blame for the disaster should lie squarely on the owners of the plant, Union Carbide, and the Indian government. In order to save money, the company did not replace faulty and worn-out equipment, did not have enough supervisors, and did not properly train the workers in disaster prevention. The company was using chemicals that were known to be hazardous and more unstable than others. The company also used large storage tanks when it was more normal and safer to store chemicals in smaller containers like steel drums. When the gas leaked, it was heavier and denser than the air and went low to the ground. Because the gas was so low to the ground, many victims were children and women, who are of shorter height than men. Also, a lot of people were asleep when the disaster happened, so many of the first victims died in bed. Bhopal had no disaster management plans for such an unexpected incident, and the local government and medical services were overwhelmed by the event. Eventually, Union Carbide paid a settlement of 470 million dollars to the victims. But with so many dead, and hundreds of thousands of others affected, compensation amounted to less than 1,000 dollars per person.

▶ dread 무서워하다, 두려워하다   squarely 공평하게   lie on ~의무[책임]이다: ~에 의하다   faulty 결점이 있는, 불완전한   worn-out 닳아 해진, 써서 낡은   supervisor 감독자; 관리인   steel 강철   leak 새다   dense 짙은; 농밀한   overwhelm 당황하게 하다, 압도하다   settlement 합의, 해결   hundreds of thousands of 수천수만의, 수많은   compensation 배상금, 보상금

여 화학업계에서는 보팔보다 무서운 단어는 없습니다. 이 얘기를 하면 사람들은 이 인도 도시 거리에서 죽어간 어린이들부터 떠올릴 것입니다. 1984년 12월 그곳에서 일어난 재해는 화학제품과 관련된 가장 큰 비극 중 하나였습니다. 그 재해에 대한 책임은 공장의 소유사인 유니온 카바이드와 인도 정부가 똑같이 져야 합니다. 경비를 절약하기 위해 회사는 결함이 있고 낡아빠진 설비를 교체하지 않았고, 감독관을 충분히 두지 않았으며, 직원들에게 재해 방지를 위한 훈련도 제대로 시키지 않았죠. 회사는 다른 것보다 위험하고 불안정하다고 알려진 화학약품도 사용하고 있었습니다. 또한 강철 드럼 같은 작은 용기에 화학제품을 보관하는 것이 보통이고 안전한 데도 불구하고 큰 저장 탱크를 사용했습니다. 가스가 샐 때는 공기보다 더 무겁고 짙기 때문에 바닥으로 깔렸죠. 가스가 바닥에 아주 낮게 깔렸기 때문에 남자들보다 키가 작은 아이들과 여자들이 많이 희생되었습니다. 또한 재해가 발생했을 때 많은 사람들이 자고 있어서 많은 1차 희생자들은 자다가 목숨을 잃었습니다. 보팔은 그런 예기치 않은 사건에 대한 재해 관리 계획이 없었고 지방 정부와 의료 기관은 당황했습니다. 결국 유니온 카바이드가 피해자들에게 4억 7천만 달러의 합의금을 지불했습니다. 하지만 너무나 많은 사람들이 죽었고 그 밖의 수많은 사람들도 영향을 받았기 때문에 보상금은 일인당 1천 달러 미만에 지나지 않았습니다.

9 읽기와 듣기 지문에 따르면 옳은 것은?
(a) 공장은 인구 밀집 지역에서 상당히 먼 거리에 있었다.
(b) 재해의 피해자들은 보살핌을 잘 받았다.
(c) 공장 노동자들은 광범위한 훈련을 거쳤다.
(d) 재해의 피해자들은 장기간에 걸쳐 사망하였다.
(e) 회사는 통상적인 화학제품 보관 방법을 사용했다.

10 읽기와 듣기 지문에서 유추할 수 있는 것은?
(a) 보팔지역에는 피해자들을 위한 병상이 충분하게 있었다.
(b) 회사 감독관들은 재해가 닥쳤을 때 공장에 있지 않았다.
(c) 인도 정부는 보상금 기금에 기부했다.
(d) 사고는 고의적인 사보타주 행위로 일어났다.
(e) 가스 누출을 사람들에게 알릴 경보 시스템이 구축되지 않았다.

***Dictation** 정답: Exercise 스크립트 밑줄 참조

Preparation

p. 107

Vocabulary Preview

A

1 platform: 정당이나 후보가 선거 바로 전에 공표하는 정책과 공약
2 legislature: 의회와 같이 법을 만들거나 바꿀 수 있는 힘을 가진 사람들 집단
3 abstain: 논점에 대해 투표를 하지 않다
4 entrenched: 굳게 확립된; 바꾸기 힘든
5 affiliated: 어떤 사람이나 사물과 관련된

B

1 referendum / 그 도시에서 도박을 허용할지 여부를 가리는 일반 투표는 큰 표 차로 부결되었다.
2 concede / 패배한 시장은 그의 적수에게 선거 패배를 인정할 것이다.
3 landslide / 로널드 레이건은 1984년 선거에서 50개 주 중 49개 주에서 승리했는데, 그것은 미국 역사상 가장 큰 압승 중 하나였다.
4 wait with bated breath / 후보들은 이 접전에서 최종 선거 결과를 숨죽이고 기다릴 것이다.
5 representative / 우리 지역 정부 대표는 지난 선거에서 패배해 이제 공직에서 물러난다.
6 turn of events / 기이한 사태의 반전은 유력한 후보자를 선거전에서 낙마시킨 추문으로 이어졌다.
7 follow the party line / 정치인들은 개인적인 견해가 있어도 종종 당의 노선을 따라야 한다. 그렇지 않으면 정당에서 쫓겨나게 된다.

Expressions and Meanings

1 무슨 일이 벌어지고 있어.	ⓔ 재미있는 일들이 일어나고 있어.
2 그들에게는 내부 사정에 정통한 사람이 있었어.	ⓓ 거기서 일하는 사람이 그 범죄자들을 도왔어.
3 그건 부질없는 기대일 뿐이었지.	ⓐ 난 뭔가를 정말 바랐지만 그 일은 일어나지 않았어.
4 그에겐 추문이 있었어.	ⓖ 그는 몇 가지 악행에 연루되어 있었어.
5 그건 그 문제의 본질이야.	ⓒ 관련된 그 쟁점은 중요해.
6 난 끝까지 싸울 거야.	ⓑ 난 포기하지 않을 거야.
7 그는 태연한 척하고 있어.	ⓕ 그는 자신감을 유지하려 노력하고 있어.

Listening Drill 1

p. 108~p. 109

Monolog

Ⓞ (1) country (2) political (3) power (4) citizens (5) provinces (6) provincial (7) reside (8) province (9) positions (10) cities (11) towns (12) city (13) town (14) different (15) dies (16) resigns (17) nonelection

Ⓖ 1 (c) 2 (a)

Ⓢ (1) T (2) F (3) F (4) T

W Depending on the country, there could be more than one type of election. In Canada, for instance, there are three main types of elections: federal, provincial, and local. Federal elections are for the whole country and decide which political party will be in power and who will represent the people from each district in the country. Provincial elections are for the provinces, such as Ontario, British Columbia, and Quebec, and they decide the same things as the federal election except at the provincial level. Local elections are for positions of power, such as the office of mayor, in cities and towns. All citizens can vote in federal elections while only those who reside in a province, city, or town can vote in the provincial and local elections. This three-level system is common in many democracies in the world though the names of the elections may differ. Occasionally, there are other elections called by-elections, which happen when a government representative dies or resigns while in office and the legislature seat is vacant during a nonelection period. Elections can be set for a certain year, like in the United States, which has presidential elections every four years, or they can be called at any time. For example, in Canada, the government must call a federal election every five years. Also, when the political party in power feels it is in a strong position, it can call an election anytime. This is done in the hope of retaining its number of seats in Parliament or even increasing its majority.

▶ federal 연방의 provincial 주(성)의, 도(道)의 the whole country 전국 positions of power 직권 office 직책, 직무 occasionally 때때로, 이따금 by-election 보궐선거 in office 재직 중에 legislature 주의회; 입법부 presidential election 대통령 선거 in a strong position 확고한 입지에 있는 retain 보유[유지]하다 majority 득표차; 과반수

여 나라에 따라 한 가지 형태 이상의 선거가 있을 수 있습니다. 예를 들면 캐나다에는 연방선거, 주 선거, 지방선거 이렇게 세 가지 주요 형태의 선거가 있습니다. 연방선거는 전국에서 시행되는 것인데, 어떤 정당이 권력을 잡을 것인지, 누가 국가의 각 지역 사람들을 대표할지를 결정합니다. 주 선거는 온타리오, 브리티시 콜롬비아, 퀘벡처럼 주에서 시행되는 것이고, 주 단위에서 시행된다는 것을 제외하면 연방선거와 똑같은 것을 결정합니다. 지방선거는 도시와 자치도시에서 시장직과 같은 지위를 뽑기 위한 것입니다. 모든 국민은 연방선거에서 투표할 수 있지만 주 선거와 지방선거는 특정 주나 도시 또는 자치도시에 사는 사람들만이 투표할 수 있습니다. 이 세 가지 형태의 선거 시스템은 세계의 많은 민주주의 국가에서 흔히 볼 수 있습니다. 비록 선거 명칭은 다를 수도 있지만요. 때때로 보궐선거라는 또 다른 선거도 있습니다. 보궐선거는 정부 대표가 임기 중에 죽거나 사임하여 비(非)선거 기간에 의석이 비었을 때 시행됩니다. 선거는 4년마다 대통령 선거가 있는 미국과 같이 특정 해에 치러지기도 하고 어느 때나 치러질 수도 있습니다. 캐나다를 예로 들면, 정부는 5년마다 연방선거를 치러야 합니다. 또한 집권당은 당의 입지가 확고하다고 생각되면 언제든지 선거를 치를 수 있습니다. 이것은 의회의 의석 수를 유지하거나 늘리기 위해 시행됩니다.

General Questions

1 담화의 주목적은 무엇인가?
(a) 캐나다의 여러 가지 선거 형태를 기술하려고
(b) 여러 단위의 선거를 논하려고
(c) 선거의 여러 가지 형태를 조사하려고
(d) 여러 국가의 선거를 보여주려고

2 다음 중 가장 잘 요약된 것을 고르시오.

(a) 몇 가지 보편적인 선거 유형이 있지만 선거 시스템이 어떻게 운영되느냐는 나라마다 다양하다.

(b) 선거 형태와 시기가 장소마다 다양한 것과 같은 점들로 인해 여러 국가에서 치르는 선거는 다르다.

Specific Questions

다시 듣고 옳은 문장에는 T, 틀린 문장에는 F를 쓰시오.

(1) 국민이면 누구나 캐나다 연방선거에서 투표할 수 있다.

(2) 보궐선거에서는 대개 누가 도시나 자치도시의 시장이 되는가를 결정한다.

(3) 미국 대통령 선거는 5년마다 치러진다.

(4) 캐나다의 주 선거나 지방선거에서 투표할 때는 행정 구획이 중요하다.

Dialog

N (1) voting (2) president (3) vending machines
(4) yearbook (5) dress code / Timmy Parsons
(6) real power (7) teachers (8) constructive
(9) dress code / can't (10) voting

G 1 (d) 2 (b)

S (1) F (2) F (3) T (4) T

G Did you vote yet in the student election?

B No, I'm going to do that at lunchtime.

G Who are you going to vote for president?

B My vote is secret, and you shouldn't be going around asking people who they voted for.

G Ah, come on. It's just for student government. No one really cares that much.

B You sound like you care. Besides, it's the principle of the matter. A person's vote is his or her business and no one else's.

G I voted for Timmy Parsons. There. Now you know my secret.

B Timmy Parsons? He's a terrible choice. His election platform was to have more junk food vending machines in the school.

G I know. Everyone thinks that's a cool idea. He's not like Tammy Miller. All she promised was to raise more money for the yearbook and to push the school to relax the dress code.

B But the dress code is the big issue. We can't wear the clothes we want to wear. No T-shirts, no ripped jeans, no baseball caps in class, and no makeup for girls.

G I guess that's important, but, anyway, the student president has no real power. The student election is just something the teachers allow so the students feel like they are taking part in something constructive.

B Maybe, but it's important because we get a chance to see how an election works, and we get a chance to use our voting power.

G You're going to vote for Tammy Miller, right?

B For the last time, it's a secret!

▶ **There.** (승리, 반항 등을 나타내어) 거봐, 자 **election platform** 선거 공약
yearbook 졸업 앨범; 연감 **dress code** 복장 규정 **ripped jeans** 찢어진 청바지

84

---

take part in ~에 참여하다 **constructive** 건설적인 **voting power** 투표권

여 학생선거 투표했니?

남 아니, 점심시간에 하려고.

여 넌 학생회장으로 누굴 뽑을 거니?

남 비밀이야. 그리고 넌 사람들에게 누굴 뽑을 건지 물어 보고 다니면 안 돼.

여 아, 왜 그래. 겨우 학생회 투표잖아. 아무도 그렇게 신경 쓰지 않아.

남 너는 신경 쓰는 것 같은데. 게다가, 이건 문제의 본질에 관한 얘기라고. 투표는 자기 일이지 다른 사람의 일이 아니잖아.

여 난 티미 파슨스에게 투표했어. 자, 이제 넌 내 비밀을 알게 되었어.

남 티미 파슨스? 끔찍한 선택이야. 걔의 선거 공약은 학교에 더 많은 인스턴트식품 자판기를 두겠다는 거잖아.

여 맞아. 모두가 멋진 생각이라고 여기고 있어. 그는 태미 밀러와 달라. 걔가 공약으로 내세운 것은 졸업 앨범을 위해 돈을 더 마련하고 복장 규정을 완화하도록 학교 측을 압박하겠다는 것뿐이잖아.

남 하지만 복장 규정은 중요한 문제지. 우리는 입고 싶은 옷을 입을 수 없잖아. 티셔츠와 찢어진 청바지도 안되고, 수업 시간에 야구모자도 못 쓰고 여자애들은 화장도 못 하고.

여 그건 중요하다고 생각하지만 어쨌든, 학생회장에게는 실질적인 힘이 없어. 학생선거는 학생들이 건설적인 일에 참여한다고 느끼게 해주려고 선생님들이 허용해 주는 일일 뿐이야.

남 그럴지도 모르지. 하지만 어떻게 선거가 치러지는지 알 수 있고 우리가 투표권을 행사할 수 있는 기회를 가질 수 있기 때문에 학생선거는 중요해.

여 너 태미 밀러에게 투표할 거구나, 그렇지?

남 마지막으로 말하는데, 비밀이야!

General Questions

1 소녀가 소년과 이야기하는 주된 이유는 무엇인가?

(a) 선거 후보에 대해 논하려고

(b) 선거 문제에 대해 이야기하려고

(c) 몇몇 교칙에 대해 살펴보려고

(d) 그가 누구에게 투표할 것인지 알아내려고

2 다음 중 가장 잘 요약된 것을 고르시오.

(a) 학생선거에 두 명의 학생회장 후보가 있는데, 그 둘 다 학생들이 직면하고 있는 중요한 문제에 대해 의견을 같이한다.

(b) 학생선거는 두 학생 간에 비밀 투표의 가치와 후보들의 장점에 대한 의견 차이를 불러일으킨다.

Specific Questions

다시 듣고 옳은 문장에는 T, 틀린 문장에는 F를 쓰시오.

(1) 학생선거 투표장은 점심시간 전에 문을 닫았다.

(2) 태미 밀러는 학교에 더 많은 자판기를 원한다.

(3) 학생들은 학교에서 특정한 옷을 입지 못하게 되어있다.

(4) 선생님들은 학생선거를 치르도록 허용하였다.

Listening Drill 2　　　p. 110~p. 111

Long Lecture

O (1) Term (2) highest (3) office (4) one (5) five (6) two
(7) four (8) amendment (9) 1951 (10) most seats
(11) head (12) abuse (13) entrenched (14) popular
(15) step down (16) suitable

1 (d) 　**2** (b) 　**3** (1) F (2) T (3) T (4) F 　**4** (c)

Dictation 정답: 스크립트 밑줄 참조

M　How long should a politician be allowed to hold office? In the case of a nation's legislature, many countries have no limits. However, when it comes to the highest office, which is usually president or prime minister, most nations have term limits. For instance, the president of Korea is limited to one term of five years, and no one can be elected to the office of president of the United States for more than two terms of four years each. This wasn't always the case in America. President Franklin Roosevelt held the office for 12 years from 1933 to his death in 1945, and he won the presidential election four times. However, the government made an amendment to the Constitution in 1951 limiting the American president to two full terms. In some nations, there is no limit to how long someone can hold the highest office. In the British parliamentary system, which is used in many countries, the prime minister is the leader of a political party. He or she can be the leader as long as his or her party maintains the most seats in the legislature and as long as that person is the head of his or her political party. The main benefit of having a limit on presidential terms is that it serves as a check on the abuse of power. The longer a politician remains in power, the more entrenched and powerful he or she can become. On the other hand, a drawback to presidential term limits is that a popular, respected, and energetic leader is forced to step down and may be replaced by someone not as suitable for the position.

▶ hold office 재직하다 when it comes to ~에 관한 한 prime minister 수상 the highest office 최고의 지위 amendment 개정, 수정 Constitution 헌법 British parliamentary system 영국 내각제 political party 정당 check 저지, (갑작스러운) 방해 abuse of power 권력 남용 entrench 자기 몸을 지키다, 자기 입장을 굳히다 drawback 약점, 결점 respected 훌륭한; 높이 평가되는 energetic 유력한, 강력한 step down 퇴진(사직)하다

남　정치인의 임기는 얼마 동안이어야 할까요? 국가 의회의 경우는 많은 나라에서 제한을 두지 않습니다. 하지만 대개 대통령이나 수상과 같은 최고의 지위에 관한 한 대부분의 국가에는 임기 제한이 있습니다. 예를 들면 한국 대통령의 임기는 5년 1회로 제한되어 있습니다. 미국에서는 각 4년씩, 2회 이상 대통령직에 선출될 수 없습니다. 미국이 항상 그런 것은 아니었는데요. 프랭클린 루즈벨트 대통령은 1933년부터 1945년 사망할 때까지 12년 동안 대통령으로 재직했습니다. 그는 대통령에 4번 당선되었죠. 하지만 1951년 정부가 미국 대통령의 임기를 2번으로 제한하는 헌법 개정을 했습니다. 일부 국가에서는 그 최고위직 임기에 제한을 두지 않습니다. 많은 국가들이 채택하고 있는 영국 내각제에서는 수상이 정당 지도자입니다. 그는 자신의 정당이 의회에서 가장 많은 의석수를 유지하고 자신이 정당의 우두머리인 한 지도자가 될 수 있습니다. 대통령 임기에 제한을 두는 주요 이점은 권력 남용을 막는 역할을 할 수 있다는 건데요. 정치가가 권좌에 오래 있으면 있을수록 점점 더 자기 입장을 고수하면서 강력해질 수 있습니다. 반면에 대통령 임기 제한의 단점은 인기 있고 훌륭하고 유력한 지도자가 어쩔 수 없이 물러나게 되어 그 지위에 적합하지 않은 사람이 그 자리를 대신할 수도 있다는 것입니다.

1　담화에 가장 알맞은 제목은 무엇인가?
(a) 정치 요직 임기 제한: 좋은가, 나쁜가?　(b) 미국 대통령 임기 제한
(c) 전 세계 지도자들의 임기 제한　(d) 정치 요직 재직 제한

2　다음 중 가장 잘 요약된 것을 고르시오.
(a) 정치 요직 임기 제한은 종종 특정 지도자들이 오랫동안 국정을 잘 운영할 수 있느냐의 여부를 증명하는 것에 기초한다.
(b) 정치 요직 임기 제한은 전 세계적으로 다르다. 하지만 임기 제한의

장점과 단점은 개개의 정치가에 의해 좌우된다.

3　옳은 문장에는 T, 틀린 문장에는 F를 쓰시오.
(1) 미국 대통령 임기는 나라의 역사가 시작될 때부터 2회로 제한되었다.
(2) 영국 수상 임기에는 법적인 제한이 없다.
(3) 정치 요직 임기 제한은 정치가의 힘이 너무 커지는 것을 막기 위한 것이다.
(4) 한국 대통령의 임기는 각 5년씩, 2회로 제한된다.

4　정치 요직 임기 제한의 한 가지 단점은 무엇인가?
(a) 한 정당이 오랫동안 권력을 잡을 수 있다.
(b) 일부 요직의 임기가 너무 짧다.
(c) 좋은 정치가들이 권좌에서 물러나야만 한다.
(d) 일부 지도자들이 권좌에서 결코 물러나지 않을 수도 있다.

| 1 (c) | 2 해설 참조 | 3 (c) | 4 (b) | 5 (b) | 6 (a) | 7 (a) |
| 8 (d) | 9 (d) | 10 해설 참조 | 11 (a) | 12 (c) | | |

1

W　During an election campaign, there are many polls taken to determine who is most likely to win the election. Polls are surveys done by major political parties or companies that specialize in such matters. The survey companies ask a random sampling of people, either in person or by telephone, or sometimes by the Internet these days, what they think of the major issues or who they would most likely vote for on election day. These polls have margins for error, but they are often a good source to predict who the winner will be on election day. Even on election day, polls are taken of people leaving the voting stations. Predictions on who the winner will be are done based on these polls even before the voting is finished or the votes counted. Candidates use the polls to plan strategy and to see where they are losing votes. A candidate might concentrate his or her campaigning in an area where he or she is down in the polls if that area is vital to the election result. The candidate may also find out that people do not like his or her position on an important issue. Therefore, the candidate may switch to the more popular opinion on the issue. For example, abortion is always a controversial issue in American elections, and candidates must be careful to know where the people stand on such an issue.

▶ poll 여론 조사 specialize in ~을 전문으로 하다 survey 표본 조사 random 임의의 sampling 표본 추출; 추출 견본 margin 여지; 차, 오차 error 〈통계〉 오차 source 근거, 출처 strategy 전략 popular opinion 여론 abortion 낙태 stand ~에 찬성(반대)의 태도를 취하다

여　선거운동 기간 동안 누가 당선될 것인가를 판단하기 위해 많은 여론 조사가 행해집니다. 여론 조사는 주요 정당이나 그러한 일을 전문으로 하는 회사에 의해 이루어지는 표본 조사입니다. 표본 조사 회사는 임의로 추출한 사람들에게 직접 또는 전화로, 요즘에는 인터넷으로, 주요 사안에 대한 의견이나 선거일에 누구를 뽑을 것인지를 묻습니다. 이러한 여론 조사는 오차의 여지가 있지만, 흔히 선거일에 누가 당선될 것인지를 예측할 수 있게 하는 좋은 근거가 됩니다. 선거일에도 투표소를 나서는 사람들에게 여론 조사가 이루어집니다. 당선자 예측은 투표

가 끝나기 전이나 개표 전에 이런 여론 조사를 토대로 이루어집니다. 후보들은 여론 조사를 활용하여 전략을 세우고 자신들이 어디에서 표를 잃고 있는지 봅니다. 여론 조사에서 밀리는 지역이 선거 결과에 매우 중요한 곳이라면 그곳의 유세에 집중하겠죠. 후보는 또한 중요한 사안에 대한 자신의 입장을 사람들이 좋아하지 않는다는 것을 알아낼 수도 있습니다. 따라서 후보는 그 사안에 대해 보다 대중적인 의견 쪽으로 선회할 수도 있죠. 예를 들면 낙태는 미국 선거 때마다 논란이 되는 쟁점인데요, 후보들은 사람들이 그러한 문제에 어떠한 태도를 취하는지를 신중히 알아내야 합니다.

1 담화의 목적은 무엇인가?

(a) 선거 여론 조사의 오차 여지를 조사하려고
(b) 선거 여론 조사가 어떻게 이루어지는지 조사하려고
(c) 선거 여론 조사와 그것의 용도를 논하려고
(d) 선거 예측이 어떻게 이루어지는지를 설명하려고
(e) 선거 여론 조사의 장점을 보여주려고

2

G　This is so <u>frustrating</u>!

M　What's the matter, dear?

G　I'm studying politics, Dad, and we have to <u>write a paper on</u> the 2000 election campaign. I can't understand why George Bush won when Al Gore had more votes than him.

M　It's the Electoral College system.

G　I found that out, but I really don't understand it.

M　Each state has <u>a number of</u> Electoral College voters called "electors," and they decide who the <u>president</u> will be. There are 538 electors, and <u>whichever</u> candidate wins the majority of them wins the <u>presidential election</u>.

G　How does the government determine <u>the number of electors</u>?

M　The number in each state <u>corresponds</u> to the number of members in the Senate and House of Representatives from that state. There are also three electors from the District of Columbia.

G　And these electors <u>pick the president</u>?

M　Yes. They <u>are affiliated with</u> the major political parties. The <u>ballots</u> have the name of the <u>presidential candidate</u>, but, in reality, people are voting for the electors that are from these parties.

G　So, what's the point of the <u>popular vote being counted</u>?

M　To know which party's electors <u>get to cast their</u> votes. In 2000, Bush won Florida by only a <u>slim margin of popular votes</u>, but that was enough to win the votes of the 25 electors who were Republicans and give him a majority of 271 Electoral College votes. Gore got the rest <u>except for</u> one elector who <u>abstained from voting</u>.

G　But Gore had more popular votes across the country! More people wanted him as president.

M　But he didn't have enough Electoral College electors and their votes.

▶ frustrate 좌절시키다, 꺾다　Electoral College system 선거인단제도　correspond to ~에 해당하다　the Senate and House of Representative 상하원　District of Columbia 컬럼비아 특별구(미국 연방 정부 소재지; 일반적으로 Washington, D.C.라고도 함)　be affiliated with ~와 관계가 있다; ~와 사귀다

---

ballot 〈투표용〉후보 명부, 〈무기명〉투표　popular vote 〈미〉일반 투표(대통령 후보의 선출처럼 일정 자격이 있는 선거인이 하는)　cast one's vote 투표권을 행사하다　a slim margin 근소한 차이　Republican 공화당원　a majority of 대다수의　abstain from voting 기권하다

여　정말 짜증난다!

남　무슨 일이니, 얘야?

여　정치학을 배우고 있는데요, 아빠. 2000년 선거운동에 대한 리포트를 써야 하는데, 어떻게 조지 부시가 득표수가 더 많았던 앨 고어를 이긴 건지 이해할 수 없어요.

남　그건 선거인단제도 때문에 그래.

여　그건 알아냈어요. 하지만 이해가 잘 안 돼요.

남　각 주에는 '선거인'이라고 불리는 선거인단 유권자들이 있어. 그들이 누가 대통령이 될 것인지를 결정하지. 538명의 유권자들이 있는데, 그들의 표를 가장 많이 받은 후보가 대통령에 당선되는 거야.

여　정부는 어떻게 선거인의 수를 결정하죠?

남　각 주의 선거인 수는 그 주의 상하원 의원의 수와 같아. 컬럼비아 특별구에는 3명의 선거인이 있지.

여　그리고 이 선거인들이 대통령을 뽑는 건가요?

남　그래. 선거인들은 주요 정당들과 관계가 있어. 후보 명부에는 대통령 후보의 이름이 있지만, 실제로는 사람들은 이 정당들 출신의 선거인들에게 투표하는 거지.

여　그럼 일반 투표를 개표할 이유가 없잖아요?

남　그건 어떤 정당의 선거인들이 투표권을 행사하는지를 알기 위해서란다. 2000년에 부시는 플로리다 주 일반 투표에서 근소한 차로 간신히 이겼어. 하지만 그것은 공화당원이었던 선거인단 25명의 표를 얻고 선거인단 271표 대부분을 그에게 안겨주기에 충분했지. 고어는 기권한 한 명의 표를 제외한 나머지 표를 얻었고.

여　하지만 전국적으로는 고어가 일반 투표에서 더 많이 득표했잖아요! 고어가 대통령이 되길 원한 사람들이 더 많았는데.

남　하지만 고어에겐 선거인단 선거인들이 충분치 않았고 그들의 표를 충분히 얻지 못했단다.

2 선거인단에 대한 정보로 표를 완성하시오.

구분	수
선거인단 선거인들	538
주 출신의 선거인들	535
컬럼비아 특별구 출신의 선거인들	3
2000년 부시의 선거인단 투표수	271
2000년 고어의 선거인단 투표수	266

3-4

M　In politics, there are several ways the people of a country can have their <u>views represented</u> in the government. Two common types are <u>direct representation</u> and <u>proportional representation</u>. In direct representation, the people <u>vote directly for</u> the political candidates in their <u>election district</u>. These candidates usually <u>represent major political parties</u>, but they can also be <u>independent</u>. They campaign in their district, and, on election day, the people vote for them. When the votes <u>are counted</u>, the candidate with the most votes wins the district and will <u>represent the people of the district</u>. Proportional representation is different. There are many forms, but very often in countries that use the system, the people <u>cast their votes</u> for political parties, not <u>individuals</u>. When all of the votes are counted, a certain percentage of votes <u>determines</u> each party's number of seats <u>in the legislature</u>. If a party gets 50% of the vote, for instance, it gets 50% of the seats. Even the smallest party with the fewest votes can <u>have a member sitting</u> if that party gained a large enough percentage to get a seat. The party with the most votes, and therefore the most seats, can <u>control</u> <u>the</u> <u>legislature</u> and <u>form</u> <u>a</u> <u>government</u>. This type of voting is common in <u>continental</u> Europe. However, it is often <u>blamed</u> <u>for</u> <u>causing</u> <u>weak</u> <u>governments</u> as too many parties <u>dilute</u> the voting pool, so no party can <u>gain</u> <u>a</u> <u>strong</u> <u>majority</u> and <u>run</u> the government successfully without help from other parties.

▶ represent (선거·선거민을) 대표하다 direct representation 직접대표제 proportional representation 비례대표제 form a government 내각을 구성하다, 정부를 구성하다 continental Europe 유럽 대륙 be blamed for ~에 대해 비난받다 dilute 강도〔효력〕을 약하게 하다

남 정치에는 국민이 정부에 자신들의 의견을 대표하도록 할 수 있는 여러 가지 방법들이 있습니다. 두 가지 보편적인 형태로는 직접대표제와 비례대표제가 있습니다. 복수대표제에서는 사람들이 자신의 선거구에서 후보들을 직접 투표합니다. 이 후보들은 대개 주요 정당을 대표하지만 무소속일 수도 있습니다. 그들은 자신들의 선거구에서 유세를 하고 선거일에 사람들은 그들에게 투표를 합니다. 개표가 되었을 때 가장 많은 표를 얻은 후보는 그 선거구에서 승리하여 그 선거구 사람들을 대표하게 됩니다. 비례대표제는 다릅니다. 많은 형태가 있지만 그 제도를 사용하는 나라에서는 사람들이 종종 개인이 아닌 정당을 보고 투표를 합니다. 표가 모두 개표되면 표의 일정 퍼센트는 각 정당의 의회 의석수를 결정합니다. 예를 들어 만약 정당이 투표수의 50%를 얻는다면 의석수의 50%를 갖습니다. 가장 적은 득표를 한 가장 작은 정당조차도 정당이 의석을 가질 만큼의 투표율을 얻는다면 의석을 가질 수 있죠. 가장 많은 득표를 하여 의석수를 가장 많이 가진 정당은 의회를 통제하고 내각을 구성할 수 있습니다. 이런 형태의 투표는 유럽 대륙에서는 흔합니다. 하지만 정당들이 너무 많아 표밭을 희석시켜 놓아서 그 어떤 정당도 대다수의 득표를 하지 못하게 되므로 다른 정당의 도움 없이는 성공적으로 국정을 운영할 수 없는 힘이 약한 정부를 만든다는 비난을 종종 받습니다.

3 비례대표제 투표에 비해 직접대표제 투표의 장점은 무엇인가?
(a) 투표에 더 많은 선택권이 있다.
(b) 몇몇 후보들만이 각 선거구에서 입후보한다.
(c) 사람들이 정확히 누구를 투표할 것인지를 알 수 있다.
(d) 같은 정당이 오랫동안 통치할 수 있다.
(e) 선거 결과를 더 쉽게 알 수 있다.

4 담화를 통해 유추할 수 있는 것은?
(a) 직접대표제 투표에 의해 선출된 사람들은 국가의 모든 투표권자들의 소망을 대표한다.
(b) 내각을 구성하는 정당들의 연합은 비례대표제 제도의 통상적인 결과이다.
(c) 비례대표제는 영국에서 의회 의원을 선출하는 일반적인 형태이다.
(d) 직접대표제 투표 방식의 후보들은 자신이 출마하는 선거구 출신일 필요는 없다.
(e) 비례대표제는 각 정당이 의석을 가질 수 있으므로 더 나은 투표 방식이다.

5-6 **Level up**

W What's in the newspaper today?

M It looks like <u>something</u> <u>is</u> <u>brewing</u> <u>over</u> in City Hall. The newspaper says there are <u>calls</u> <u>for</u> <u>an</u> <u>investigation</u> into the recent <u>mayoral</u> <u>election</u>.

W Did some people <u>get</u> <u>caught</u> <u>with</u> <u>their</u> <u>hands</u> in the ballot box?

M It seems so. The losing candidate is claming <u>fraud</u> <u>at</u> <u>the</u> <u>highest</u> <u>levels</u>. She says she wants a <u>recount</u> and an <u>examination</u> of certain voters who registered at the last minute.

W <u>That</u> <u>old</u> <u>trick</u>. My father said that in the old days, they <u>dragged</u> people <u>off</u> the street, gave them a bit of cash, and handed them a voter registration card with some <u>dead</u> <u>person's</u> <u>name</u> <u>on</u> <u>it</u>. Some guys voted ten times in one election.

M Things are a bit more <u>sophisticated</u> now. Everyone has to <u>resister</u> <u>with</u> <u>proper</u> <u>ID</u> and also show proper ID at the voting station.

W If the <u>fraud</u> really happened, I wonder how they did it.

M The paper says the only way was to have someone on the inside changing the <u>voter</u> <u>registration</u> <u>lists</u>. That's where the investigation will begin.

W It doesn't matter if it's true or not. The <u>mayor</u> will be <u>tarred</u> with the <u>scandal</u> <u>brush</u>, and he'll never win another election. It's probably best if he resigns now.

M He says it's all <u>unfounded</u> <u>lies</u> and that he will fight to the <u>bitter</u> <u>end</u>.

▶ brew (음모 등이) 꾸며지다 investigation 조사 mayoral election 시장 선거 get caught with one's hands 현장에서 발각되다 ballot box 투표함 fraud 사기 행위, 부정 수단 old trick 상투적인 수법 drag 잡아끌 듯 데려가다 sophisticated 매우 복잡한, 정교한 be tarred with the scandal brush 오명을 뒤집어쓰다 resign 사임하다, 사직하다 unfounded 근거 없는, 사실 무근의

여 오늘 신문에 뭐가 나왔니?
남 시청에서 무슨 일이 벌어지고 있는 것 같아. 최근에 있었던 시장 선거에 대해 조사 요구가 있다고 신문에 나오네.
여 사람들이 투표함에 부정행위를 한 게 걸렸나?
남 그런 것 같아. 낙선한 후보가 주장하기로는 고도의 부정행위가 있었다는군. 그녀는 재개표와 마지막 순간에 등록했던 특정 유권자들에 대한 조사를 원한대.
여 상투적인 수법이지. 아버지가 그러시는데 옛날에는 사람들을 끌고 가서 돈을 좀 주고 죽은 사람의 이름이 적힌 투표 등록 카드를 건네주었대. 어떤 사람들은 한 선거에서 10번이나 투표했다고 하더라고.
남 지금은 좀 더 정교해졌어. 모든 사람은 신분증을 가지고 등록해야 하고, 투표소에서도 신분증을 보여줘야 하지.
여 만약 정말 부정행위가 있었다면 어떻게 했을지 궁금해.
남 신문에 의하면 유일한 방법은 내부인사를 시켜 투표 등록 리스트를 바꿔치기 하는 거래. 바로 그 부분에서 조사가 시작될 거야.
여 사실인지 아닌지는 중요하지 않아. 그 시장은 오명을 뒤집어쓰게 될 것이고 다른 선거에서 절대 이길 수 없을 거야. 지금 사퇴하는 게 최선이겠어.
남 그는 모든 것이 사실 무근의 거짓말이고 끝까지 싸울 거라네.

5 신문기사에 의하면 어떻게 선거 사기가 일어났나?
(a) 죽은 사람들 이름이 가짜 등록 카드에 사용되었다.
(b) 선거 시스템에서 일하는 사람이 뭔가를 바꿨다.
(c) 가짜 등록 카드를 가진 사람들이 10번 투표를 했다.
(d) 시장은 투표함에 선거용지를 추가로 넣다가 적발됐다.
(e) 신분증을 확인하기 위해 설치된 시스템이 잘 작동되지 않았다.

6 다음 중 내용을 가장 잘 요약한 것을 고르시오.
(a) 낙선 후보가 사기행위를 주장하고 당선자는 일고의 가치가 없는 말이라고 하기 때문에 시장 선거가 논란에 휘말렸다.
(b) 시장 선거를 둘러싼 추문은 악행에 가담하지 않았다 하더라도 관련된 모든 사람들에게 해를 초래할 것이다.
(c) 시장은 최근 선거 결과를 조작했다는 비난 때문에 강제로 사직될 수도 있다.

B My father was really <u>mad</u> last night.

G What did you do wrong this time?

B Nothing! He <u>was</u> <u>mad</u> <u>at</u> some politician who <u>got</u> <u>arrested</u>.

G Oh, I heard about that. They say he stole some money. My mom said you can't <u>trust</u> <u>any</u> politicians these days.

B My dad said that, too. He even helped when that politician came to town, and he asked people to vote for him. Now my dad <u>feels</u> really <u>embarrassed</u>.

G I'd be too if I had supported someone who <u>turned</u> <u>out</u> <u>to be a</u> <u>crook</u>.

B He said he's never going to <u>take</u> <u>part</u> <u>in</u> an election or vote the rest of his life.

G I think that's a little silly. Just because of <u>one</u> <u>bad</u> <u>apple</u>, you can't say all politicians are bad.

B I don't know. You only hear about politicians when something bad happens.

G That's partly the <u>media's</u> <u>fault</u>, too. They are always looking for some <u>scandal</u>.

B Maybe the media should be <u>looking</u> <u>harder</u>. People trust politicians to do <u>a</u> <u>good</u> <u>job</u> <u>of</u> <u>representing</u> them. Instead, we have ones like this guy who was just trying to get rich.

▶ **embarrassed** 당혹한, 창피한, 난처한 **turn out** 결국은 ~임이 밝혀지다 **crook** 사기꾼, 도둑 **bad apple** 악당, 못 믿을 인간: 망나니

남 우리 아버지 어젯밤에 정말 화나셨어.

여 너 이번엔 뭘 잘못했니?

남 아무것도 안했어! 아버지는 체포된 정치가에게 화가 나신 거라고.

여 아, 그거 들었어. 그 사람이 돈을 훔쳤다고 하던데. 엄마가 요즘에는 믿을 정치인이 없다고 하셨어.

남 우리 아빠도 그러셨어. 아빠는 그 정치가가 왔을 때 도와주기도 했고 사람들에게 그를 뽑으라고 부탁하기도 했거든. 지금은 정말 창피해하셔.

여 내가 지지했던 사람이 사기꾼으로 밝혀지면 나라도 그렇겠다.

남 아빠는 남은 인생 동안 절대로 선거에 참여 안 하실 거고 투표도 안 하실 거래.

여 그건 좀 아닌 것 같다. 악당 한 명 때문에 모든 정치가가 나쁘다고 할 수는 없는 거잖아.

남 모르겠어. 정치가에 대한 얘기가 언급될 때는 뭔가 나쁜 일이 일어날 때뿐인지라.

여 그건 부분적으로는 대중매체의 잘못이기도 해. 항상 스캔들을 찾아다니잖아.

남 대중매체가 더 열심히 찾아야 할 거야. 사람들은 정치가들이 자신들을 대표해 좋은 일들을 한다고 믿고 있어. 하지만 그 사람처럼 단지 부자가 되기만을 바라는 정치가들도 있잖아.

7 What was the main reason the boy's father was angry?
소년의 아버지가 화가 난 주요 이유는 무엇이었나?

(a) The boy's father had supported a politician who got arrested. 소년의 아버지는 체포된 정치인을 지지했었다.

(b) The boy had done something wrong that angered his father. 소년은 아버지가 화를 낼 만한 나쁜 짓을 했다.

(c) The politician had been a friend of the boy's father.
그 정치가는 소년 아버지의 친구였다.

(d) The boy's father knew that a politician was a crook.
소년의 아버지는 정치가가 사기꾼이라는 것을 알았다.

(e) The media had told some lies about a politician.
대중 매체가 정치가에 대한 거짓말을 했다.

W During an election campaign, each <u>candidate</u> presents his or her <u>election</u> <u>platform</u> to the <u>voting</u> <u>public</u>. The voters then often use the <u>opinions</u> <u>of</u> <u>the</u> <u>candidates</u> on these issues to help them decide whom to vote for during the election. Issues can be national ones, which <u>affect</u> <u>the</u> <u>whole</u> <u>nation</u>, or they can be local ones, which affect one state or city. Some typical issues of a candidate's platform include <u>foreign</u> <u>policy</u>, <u>taxes</u>, education, <u>abortion</u>, the environment, and <u>employment</u>. Often, candidates follow the <u>party</u> <u>line</u>, which means they follow the opinions of their <u>political</u> <u>party</u>. A common part of any election campaign is a <u>debate</u> between the candidates. These <u>debates</u> are important as they show the public what the candidates' platforms are and how well they can <u>handle</u> <u>a</u> <u>pressure-filled</u> <u>situation</u>. These debates <u>are</u> <u>done</u> <u>live</u> in front of an audience and are typically <u>broadcast</u> on TV, radio, and the Internet. A <u>moderator</u> and / or audience members ask the candidates questions, and each candidate <u>is</u> <u>allotted</u> some time to answer.

▶ **platform** 연설, 강연 **foreign policy** 외교 정책 **debate** 토론, 토의, 논쟁 **party line** (정당의) 강령, 정책 노선 **typically** 대체로, 일반적으로 **moderator** (토론 등의) 사회자 **allot** 할당하다, 분배하다

여 선거운동 기간 동안 각 후보는 유권자들에게 자신의 공약을 내놓습니다. 그러면 유권자들은 선거기간 동안 이 현안들에 대한 후보들의 의견을 듣고 누구를 뽑을 것인가를 결정하곤 합니다. 현안은 국가 전체에 영향을 미치는 국가적인 것일 수도 있고 한 주나 도시에 영향을 미치는 지역적인 것일 수도 있습니다. 후보 공약에 들어가는 전형적인 현안에는 외교 정책, 세금, 교육, 낙태, 환경, 고용 등이 있습니다. 종종 후보들은 정당의 정책 노선을 따르는데, 이는 후보들이 소속 정당의 의견을 따른다는 것을 의미합니다. 선거운동에서 보편적인 부분은 후보들 간의 토론입니다. 이런 토론은 후보들의 공약이 무엇인지와 후보들이 압박감 가득한 상황에 얼마나 잘 대처할 수 있는지를 대중에게 보여주는 것이기 때문에 중요합니다. 이런 토론은 관중 앞에서 생방송으로 진행되며 대개 텔레비전, 라디오, 인터넷으로 방송됩니다. 토론 사회자와 관중들은 후보들에게 질문을 하고 각 후보에게는 대답할 시간이 할당됩니다.

8 Which statement is NOT correct according to the talk?
담화에 의하면 다음 중 옳지 않은 것은?

(a) Election issues can be both national and local issues.
선거 현안에는 국가적인 것과 지역적인 것 둘 다 있을 수 있다.

(b) Election debates are commonly shown as they happen.
선거 토론은 대개 공개된다.

(c) Candidates typically use the platform of their political party. 후보들은 대체로 자신들이 속한 정당의 강령을 사용한다.

(d) Voters often decide how to vote without regard to the issues.
유권자들은 종종 현안과 상관없이 어떻게 투표할지 결정한다.

(e) Audience members can ask candidates questions during debates. 관중들은 토론 중에 후보자에게 질문할 수 있다.

9

M In most <u>democratic</u> <u>nations</u>, and even in some not-so-democratic ones, political parties are a <u>central</u> <u>feature</u> of politics. Some <u>well-known</u> <u>political</u> <u>parties</u> are the Republican and Democratic parties in America, the Conservative and Labor parties in Britain, the Green Party in Germany, and the Communist Party in Russia and in many other nations. Political parties are often called left, right, or center depending on their platform. These terms come from the period of the French Revolution in the late 18th century. The assembly of the French representatives to government sat in a semi-circle, with those most radical on the far left, those most conservative on the right, and those neither very radical nor very conservative in the center. In modern terms, the Communist Party is very much a leftist party while the British Conservative and American Republican parties are more toward the right. Leftist parties are often popular with the poor and the working classes since leftist platforms center on more government assistance for the people, such as free education, medical care, and unemployment benefits. Parties on the right are attractive to the wealthy and businesspeople, who do not want the high taxes that come with more assistance to the common people. Many parties have more centralist platforms and try to attract both the wealthy and working classes with promises to help both sides with their issues.

▶ central feature 주요 특징 Republican Party 공화당 Democratic Party 민주당 Conservative Party 보수당 Labor Party 노동당 Green Party 녹색당 Communist Party 공산당 French Revolution 프랑스 혁명 assembly 〈입법〉 의회, 입법부 semi-circle 반원 radical 급진적인 conservative 보수적인 leftist 좌파, 좌익, 급진파 working class 노동계급 medical care 의료, 건강관리 unemployment benefit 실업 급여 businesspeople 사업가들

남 대부분의 민주주의국가, 또한 그다지 민주적이지 않은 국가에서도 정당은 정치의 주요 특징입니다. 미국에서 잘 알려진 정당에는 공화당과 민주당이 있고, 영국에는 보수당과 노동당, 독일에는 녹색당, 러시아와 또 다른 많은 나라에는 공산당이 있습니다. 정당은 정당 강령에 따라 종종 좌익, 우익, 중도파라고 불립니다. 이 용어는 18세기 후반 프랑스 혁명 기간 동안에 생겨났습니다. 프랑스 의회 의원들은 반원 형태로 앉아 있었는데 가장 급진적인 의원들은 맨 왼쪽, 가장 보수적인 의원들은 오른쪽, 그다지 급진적이지도 보수적이지도 않은 의원들은 중간에 앉았습니다. 현대적인 용어로 하자면, 공산당은 매우 아주 좌파 정당인 한편 영국 보수당과 미국의 공화당은 좀 더 우파 성향입니다. 좌파 정당들은 정당 강령이 무상 교육, 의료, 실업 급여와 같은 국민에 대한 좀 더 많은 정부 지원에 중점을 두기 때문에 빈민과 노동 계층 사이에서 인기가 있는 편입니다. 우파 정당은 보통 사람들에 대한 더 많은 원조에 수반되는 높은 세금을 원하지 않는 부자와 사업가들 입장에서 볼 때 매력적입니다. 많은 정당들은 중도피의 강령을 기지고 있고 부유한 사람들과 노동 계급의 문제 해결을 돕는다는 공약으로 이 두 계층 모두의 지지를 얻고자 합니다.

9 담화에 따르면 정당에 대해 사실이 <u>아닌</u> 것은?
(a) 노동 계급의 사람들은 좌파 정당에게 투표하는 경향이 있다.
(b) 중도파 정당은 모든 계층의 사람들에게 공약을 한다.
(c) 우파 정당은 부자들의 요구에 비위를 맞추는 경향이 있다.
(d) 정당은 18세기 프랑스 혁명 때 생겼다.
(e) 민주적이지 않은 국가에도 정당은 존재한다.

10

M Welcome back to *Election Night 2009* at RKO Radio. We'll have all of the results in the state elections in just a few moments. Now let's go over to our correspondent, Debbie Taylor, who is at the governor's campaign headquarters. Debbie?

W Jake, there is a lot of nervous tension over here as the vote for governor is too close to pick a winner yet. At present, Governor Walker is 250 votes behind the leading challenger, Joseph Mellon, who has 34,560 votes. In third place is Stella Hawking with 24,678 votes. There is just one more district to count, and we are waiting for this result.

M Governor Walker was expected to win in a landslide. How is he handling this turn of events?

W He is putting on a brave face and remaining upbeat, but word is that his advisors are scratching their heads and trying to figure out what went wrong. All the polls showed the governor ahead, but... wait. Yes, the final results are coming in now.

M All of our listeners are waiting with bated breath, Debbie.

W And it's official. The new governor of the state will be Joseph Mellon. He added another 2,342 votes in the last district while Governor Walker only managed 2,241, and Stella Hawking received 1,030 votes. That was not enough for either Hawking or Walker to overcome the lead of Joseph Mellon.

M I must say this is quite a shock. Can we get a word with Governor Walker?

W Perhaps soon, but right now I think we are about to hear Governor Walker concede the election to Joseph Mellon. Stand by for the governor's speech.

▶ correspondent 특파원, 통신원 governor 주지사; 통치자 headquarters 본부 win in a landslide 대승리를 거두다 turn of events 사태의 반전 put on a brave face 태연한 체하다; 허세를 부리다 upbeat 낙관적인; 즐거운 advisor 고문, 조언자; 보좌관 scratch one's head (어쩔 줄 몰라) 머리를 긁다; 곤혹스러워 하다 with bated breath 숨을 죽이고 concede 인정하다, 시인하다

남 RKO 라디오의 〈2009 선거의 밤〉을 다시 청취해주셔서 감사합니다. 잠시 후면 주 선거 결과가 모두 나올 것입니다. 이제, 주지사 선거운동 본부에 있는 저희 특파원 데비 타일러에게 가보도록 하죠. 데비?

여 제이크, 당선자를 가려내기에는 아직 주지사 후보 득표수 차이가 너무 근소해, 여기는 긴장감이 고조되고 있습니다. 현재 워커 주지사는 선두를 달리고 있는 도전자 조셉 멜론의 34,560표에 250표 차로 뒤지고 있습니다. 3위는 24,678표를 얻고 있는 스텔라 호킹입니다. 이제 선거구 한 곳의 개표만이 남아 있어 그 결과를 기다리고 있는 중입니다.

남 워커 주지사의 압승이 예상됐었는데요 그는 이 사태의 반전에 어떻게 대처하고 있나요?

여 그는 태연한 표정으로 낙관적인 태도를 유지하고 있습니다만 그의 보좌관들은 무엇이 잘못되었는지 알아내려고 곤혹스러워하고 있다는 전언입니다. 모든 여론 조사에서는 주지사가 앞서는 것으로 나왔지만… 잠시만요. 네. 최종 결과가 곧 나오겠습니다.

남 모든 청취자들이 숨을 죽이고 기다리고 있습니다, 데비.

여 공식 결과입니다. 새 주지사는 조셉 멜론이 될 것입니다. 그는 마지막 선거구에서 2,342표를 추가로 얻었지만 워커 주지사는 2,241표를 얻었을 뿐이네요. 그리고 스텔라 호킹은 1,030표를 받았습니다. 그 표로는 호킹이나 워커가 선두 조셉 멜론을 넘어서기엔 역부족이었습니다.

남 꽤 충격적인 일이네요. 워커 주지사와 이야기를 나눌 수 있을까요?

여 곧 가능할 것입니다. 하지만 지금은 워커 주지사가 조셉 멜론에게 패배를 인정하는 연설을 할 것 같습니다. 주지사 연설을 기다려주십시오.

10 주지사 선거 개표 결과에 대해 빠진 수치를 채워 표를 완성하시오.

후보자	마지막 선거구 개표 전의 결과	최종 결과
조셉 멜론	34,560	36,902
워커 주지사	34,310	36,551
스텔라 호킹	24,678	25,708

W While voting in an election is a right that many people have, sometimes they don't exercise this right. This is reflected in voting statistics, such as with the less than 50 percent of eligible voters coming to the polls in America in 1996 and barely more than 50 percent in 2000. There are many reasons why people don't vote. These include disinterest in the election process, problems associated with following the election rules, and the person's inability to vote on election day. Many people feel that their vote has no bearing on the outcome or simply believe that the choice of candidates is so bad that it is not worth voting. The second reason people don't vote is that they can't due to mistakes they make following election rules. Usually, a person must register to vote before the election. Failure to register means a person can't vote. In some cases, such as in Canada, if a person moves to a new election district less than six months before an election, that individual can't vote in any elections. Sometimes, people are overseas and fail to register or vote on time. The final issue with failing to vote is trouble actually voting on election day. Many elderly people have limited mobility and cannot easily get to and from the voting station. Other people have no car or easy access to public transportation. If the weather is bad, many people will decide to stay home and not vote. Other people have to work even if the election is on a declared holiday. Whatever the case, many people fail to vote, and this can have an impact on the outcome of an election.

▶ eligible 자격이 있는 the polls 투표소 bearing 의미; 관계 outcome 결과; 과정 mobility 이동성; 기동력 declared holiday 공표된 휴일 impact 영향

여 투표권은 많은 사람들이 가지고 있는 권리인데, 사람들은 이 권리를 행사하지 않을 때가 있습니다. 이것은 투표 통계에 반영되죠. 1996년 미국에서 50% 미만의 유권자가 투표를 했으며 2000년에는 간신히 50% 넘는 수가 투표를 했다는 것과 같이 말이죠. 사람들이 투표를 하지 않는 이유는 많습니다. 이 중에는 선거 과정에 대한 무관심, 선거 규정을 따르는 데 수반되는 문제, 선거일에 투표를 할 수 없는 사정 등이 포함됩니다. 많은 사람들은 자신의 표가 결과와 상관없다고 여기거나 단순히 후보자들이 너무 형편없어 투표를 할 가치가 없다고 믿습니다. 사람들이 투표를 안 하는 두 번째 이유는 사람들이 선거 규정을 따르다 저지르는 실수 때문에 투표를 못하기 때문입니다. 대개 선거 전에 투표 등록을 해야 합니다. 등록을 하지 않는다는 것은 투표를 할 수 없다는 의미죠. 캐나다의 경우에는 선거가 6개월이 안 남은 상태에서 새로운 선거구로 이사를 가면 그 사람은 어떤 선거에서도 투표를 할 수 없습니다. 해외에 있어 제때 투표 등록이나 투표를 하지 못할 때도 있죠. 투표를 못하게 되는 마지막 문제는 선거일에 실제로 투표하는 불편입니다. 많은 노인들은 움직임에 제한이 있어 투표소를 쉽게 오갈 수 없습니다. 차가 없거나 대중교통 수단을 이용하기 쉽지 않은 사람들도 있습니다. 날씨가 나쁘면 많은 사람들은 집에 머물면서 투표를 하지 않기로 마음먹겠죠. 그 밖의 사람들은 선거일이 공휴일일지라도 일을 해야 합니다. 경우야 어떻든 많은 사람들이 투표를 못합니다. 그리고 이것은 선거 결과에 영향을 줄 수 있습니다.

11 강의에 따르면 많은 노인들이 선거일에 부딪치는 문제는 무엇인가?
  (a) 투표소에 가는 데 애를 먹는다.
  (b) 선거에서 누구에게 투표할지 결정하지 못한다.
  (c) 대부분 대중교통을 이용할 수 없는 시골에 산다.
  (d) 투표를 하고 싶어하나 종종 다음 선거 등록을 잊어버린다.
  (e) 해외에 살아 선거 등록을 제때 하지 못한다.

12 다음 중 내용을 가장 잘 요약한 것을 고르시오.
  (a) 투표는 일부 사람들이 어떻게 투표를 하는지 모르거나 선거일에 너무 바빠 행사하지 않는 권리이다.
  (b) 비록 일부 사람들이 투표 문제에 무관심하거나 후보들을 신뢰하지 않아서 투표를 안하기는 하지만 대부분의 사람들은 선거일에 투표를 하려 한다.
  (c) 선거에 대한 무관심, 선거 과정의 성가스러움, 또는 선거일의 곤란한 사정을 포함해 선거일에 투표를 못하는 이유는 많다.

Practice Test   p. 114~p. 115

1 (b) **2** (c) **3** (b) **4** (b) **5** (b) **6** (b), (e) **7** (c)
8 해설 참조 **9** (c) **10** (c)

1

W The American system of government has three main branches and is based on a series of checks and balances. The three branches are the executive branch, the legislative branch, and the judicial branch. The executive branch consists of the president, the vice president, and the various offices under the president's authority, such as the National Security Council. The legislative branch is the Senate and the House of Representatives, which consists of the members of these bodies plus several other offices such as the Government Accountability Office. Finally, there is the judicial branch, which contains the Supreme Court of the United States and the many lesser courts across the land. Each branch has powers, but those powers are limited. For example, the authority to deal with foreign governments rests with the executive branch, but the president cannot declare war without the approval of the legislative branch. The legislative branch makes and passes laws, but the executive branch has the power to veto these laws. The judicial branch has legal authority over the nation, but its senior members are appointed by the executive branch and must be approved by the legislative branch. These checks and balances are a byproduct of the creation of the United States, which grew out of rebellion against an authoritative British king who had few checks on his authority. At times, the system does not work, such as when President Johnson authorized military forces to Vietnam in 1965 without declaring war, thus avoiding the need for approval of the legislative branch.

▶ branch 부문, 분과(分課); 지부 checks and balances (입법, 사법, 행정 간의) 견제와 균형 executive branch 행정부 legislative branch 입법부 judicial branch 사법부 National Security Council 국가 안전 보장 회의 the Senate and the House of Representatives 상하 양원 Government Accountability Office 회계 감사원 Supreme Court 최고 법원, 대법원; 연방 대법원 declare war 전쟁을 선포하다 pass (의안 등이) 통과하다, 가결되다 veto (제안, 의안 등을) 거부하다 legal authority 법적 권한 by-product 부차적 결과, 부산물 rebellion 저항, 도전; 폭동

여 미국 정부제도에는 세 개의 주요 부문이 있는데, 일련의 견제와 균형에 기초하고 있습니다. 그 세 개의 부문은 행정부, 입법부, 사법부입니다. 행정부에는 대통령, 부통령, 국가 안전 보장 회의와 같은 대통령 직속의 여러 관청이 있습니다. 입법부는 상하원 의원들과 더불어 회계 감사원과 같은 여러 다른 관청으로 구성되어 있는 상하 양원입니다. 마지막으로 사법부는 미국 대법원과 전국 각지의 많은 법

원들을 포함하고 있습니다. 각 부문은 힘이 있지만 그 힘은 제한되어 있습니다. 예를 들면 외국 정부를 담당하는 권한은 행정부에 있지만 대통령은 입법부의 승인 없이는 전쟁을 선포할 수 없습니다. 입법부는 법을 만들고 통과시키지만 행정부는 이 법을 거부할 수 있습니다. 사법부는 전국에 법적 권한이 있지만 사법부 선임들은 행정부에 의해 임명되고 반드시 입법부의 승인을 받아야 합니다. 이러한 견제와 균형은 권력에 견제를 거의 받지 않았던 위압적인 영국 왕에 저항하여 미국이 건국될 때 생겨난 부산물입니다. 이 제도는 제 역할을 못할 때도 있습니다. 1965년에 존슨 대통령이 입법부의 승인 절차를 피하기 위해 전쟁을 선포하지 않고 베트남에 병력 사용을 허가한 것과 같이 말이죠.

1 담화에 의하면 다음 중 옳은 것은?
   (a) 대법원은 입법부에 의해 통과된 법을 거부할 수 있다.
   (b) 대통령은 전쟁 선포 없이 군대에 참전을 명령할 수 있다.
   (c) 미국 정부 제도는 영국 제도에 기초한다.
   (d) 미국 정부의 세 부문은 대통령의 통제 하에 있다.
   (e) 대통령이 국정을 운영하는 권한에는 견제가 거의 없다.

2-3

B Our teacher is going to Africa next week.

G Really? Do we have class off?

B Sadly, no. We'll have a substitute for five or six days.

G Oh, well. That's just wishful thinking on my part. So, why is she going to Africa?

B To be a monitor in an election there. I forgot which country she's actually going to, but they are having an election, and she is a part of it.

G But she's an American. How can she take part in an election in Africa?

B I'm not sure. I think she is just part of a group that makes sure the election is conducted fairly.

G I don't get it. Do you mean they count the votes and stuff like that?

B Maybe. Or maybe it's just to make sure the votes are real and that no one tries to add fake votes to the ballot boxes.

G Someone would actually do that?

B I guess so. The way I figure it, if I were running for president and I didn't think I was going to win, maybe I'd do something to make sure I won. Like adding more votes that aren't real.

G I guess some people would do that if they wanted power badly enough. But isn't it dangerous for our teacher to be one of the people who makes sure that doesn't happen?

B I think my father said the UN also had soldiers there to watch the election process. The country wants them there—wants the monitors—because they want the election to look fair so the government has more standing.

G _______________________________________

▶ substitute 대리인, 보결   wishful thinking 부질없는 기대   conduct 처리하다, 수행하다   figure 생각하다, 판단하다   standing 명성, 명망

남 우리 선생님은 다음 주에 아프리카에 가신대.
여 정말? 우리 수업 없는 거야?
남 슬프게도, 있어. 임시교사가 5, 6일 동안 가르치실 거야.

여 아, 음. 내 부질없는 소망일 뿐이었네. 그런데 왜 선생님이 아프리카에 가시는 거니?
남 거기서 선거 감시원을 하신대. 정확히 어느 나라에 가시는지는 잊어버렸지만 그 나라 사람들이 선거를 하고, 선생님은 거기에 참여하시는 거야.
여 하지만 선생님은 미국인이잖아. 어떻게 선생님이 아프리카 선거에 참여를 할 수 있지?
남 잘 모르겠어. 선생님은 그냥 선거가 공정하게 치러지는지 확인하는 무리의 일원인 것 같아.
여 이해가 안 돼. 개표 같은 거 하는 걸 말하는 거야?
남 아마도. 아니면 표가 진짜이고 그 누구도 투표함에 가짜 표를 넣지 않았다는 것을 확인하기 위해서일지도 모르지.
여 그런 짓을 하는 사람이 정말로 있어?
남 그런 거 같아. 내 생각으로는 만약 내가 대통령에 출마하고 있는데 승산이 없다면 아마도 확실히 승리할 수 있게 뭔가를 할 거야. 진짜가 아닌 표들을 더한다든지 말이지.
여 권력을 몹시 원한다면 일부 사람들은 그렇게 할 거라고 생각해. 하지만 우리 선생님이 그런 일이 안 일어나도록 확인하는 사람들의 일원이 되는 것은 위험하지 않을까?
남 우리 아버지가 거기에는 선거 과정을 지켜보는 UN군도 있다고 하셨던 것 같아. 그 군인들이 거기에서 감시하기를 그 나라가 원한다는 거야. 왜냐하면 선거가 공정해 보이도록 하면 정부의 권위가 더 서기 때문이지.
여 _______________________________________

2 대화를 통해 유추할 수 있는 것은?
   (a) 선거 참관인들은 아프리카 UN에서 일한다.
   (b) 선생님은 과거에 아프리카의 선거 참관인이었다.
   (c) 한 아프리카 국가가 선거 참관인들에게 와달라고 요청했다.
   (d) 학생들은 임시교사로부터 아프리카 선거에 대해 배울 것이다.
   (e) 여분의 표를 추가하는 것은 아프리카 선거에서 흔히 일어나는 일이다.

3 소년의 마지막 말 후에 소녀는 뭐라고 말하겠는가?
   (a) UN은 이번 선거에서 곤란을 겪게 될 것 같아.
   (b) 그들은 합법적인 정부로 인식되고 싶은가 보다.
   (c) 선생님이 거기 계시는 동안 즐겁게 지내셨으면 좋겠어.
   (d) 난 우리나라에도 선거 참관인이 있어야 한다고 생각해.
   (e) 아프리카에서는 선거에 문제가 없을 거라고 생각했어.

4-5

M During elections in the United States, there are often questions added to the ballot with "yes" and "no" as answer choices. These are called referendums. For example, during the 1998 election in California, voters were asked to vote yes or no on allowing casinos to be built on Native American land. While this issue may not seem important, it was important enough that the Californian government decided to ask the citizens directly for their opinion. For a referendum to pass, it must receive more than 50 percent of the vote. The main point of a referendum is to let the people decide an issue instead of having government leaders do so. In this way, the people feel they have more power, and the leaders take less criticism if they choose to favor an unpopular issue. The drawback to referendums is that they require only a little more than 50 percent of the vote to be successful. If 49 percent of the people vote against an issue, it means that a lot of people are unhappy with the outcome. There is also the problem of voters being influenced. Those with a direct interest in referendums, such as the people who wanted to build the casinos on Native American land in California,

▶ ballot 투표용지, 투표   referendum 국민투표, 일반투표   drawback 약점, 결점
sum 금액

남 미국에서는 선거 때 대개 투표용지에 yes와 no를 선택하는 질문들이 추가됩니다. 이것을 일반투표라고 부릅니다. 예를 들면 1998년 캘리포니아에서 치러진 선거 때 유권자들은 아메리칸 원주민 땅에 카지노 설립을 허용할 것이냐는 질문에 yes 아니면 no로 투표하도록 요청 받았습니다. 이 쟁점이 중요하지 않은 것 같을 수도 있지만 캘리포니아 정부가 시민들의 의견을 직접 물어보기로 결정할 만큼 중요한 사안이었습니다. 일반투표가 통과되기 위해서는 과반수가 넘는 표를 받아야 합니다. 일반투표의 요지는 정부 지도자들이 결정하는 대신 국민들이 결정하도록 한다는 것입니다. 이렇게 하면 국민들은 자신들에게 좀 더 힘이 있다고 생각하게 되고, 지도자들은 별로 인기 없는 쟁점을 지지하기로 결정했을 때 비판을 덜 받게 되죠. 일반투표의 결정은 안건이 통과되는 데 50%를 약간 상회하는 표만 받으면 된다는 것입니다. 만약 49%의 사람들이 반대투표를 한다면 많은 사람들이 그 결과에 만족하지 않는다는 의미입니다. 유권자들이 영향을 받는다는 것도 문제입니다. 캘리포니아의 아메리칸 원주민 땅에 카지노를 짓고 싶은 사람들처럼 일반투표에 직접적인 이해관계가 얽힌 사람들은 선거운동에 막대한 돈을 써서 유권자들이 자신들에게 유리한 방향으로 투표하게끔 합니다. 유권자들이 어떻게 결정하든 일반투표는 특정 문제들에 대해서는 미약한 해결책인 듯합니다.

4 담화에 의하면 국민 투표의 가장 큰 약점은 무엇인가?
 (a) 사람들이 안건에 찬성하거나 반대하도록 설득하기 위해 많은 돈이 선거운동에 쓰인다.
 (b) 설령 일반투표가 과반수의 찬성으로 통과된다 할지라도 꽤 많은 사람들은 그 쟁점에 여전히 반대할 수도 있다.
 (c) 정치인들이 결정할 책임을 피하기 위해 일반투표를 사용하는 것뿐이다.
 (d) 대부분의 사람들은 일반투표의 안건이 중요하지 않다고 생각해서 투표하려고 애쓰지 않는다.
 (e) 유권자는 영향을 받기 때문에 설령 안건에 반대한다 할지라도 대부분의 사람들은 일반투표에서 yes라고 투표할 것이다.

5 담화에서 유추할 수 있는 것은?
 (a) 캘리포니아의 모든 아메리칸 원주민 종족들은 그들의 땅에 카지노가 들어서기를 원했다.
 (b) 일반투표 안건의 양측 지지자들은 돈을 들여서 유권자들에게 영향을 미치려 한다.
 (c) 일반투표에서 yes 또는 no를 선택하지 않은 유권자들이 투표를 망쳐 왔다.
 (d) 일반투표를 활용하는 정부 지도자들이 활용하지 않는 지도자들보다 권력을 더 오래 유지한다.
 (e) 어떤 쟁점들에는 대개 일반투표를 하는 것보다 더 나은 해결책이 있다.

6   Level up

▶ democracy 민주주의, 민주제, 민주 정치   obligation 의무   guarantee (일의 실현, 확실성 등을) 장담하다, 확언하다   make provision 준비하다, 대비책을 마련하다
community service 사회봉사

남 너 호주 같은 몇몇 국가에서는 선거일에 사람들이 강제로 투표한다는 거 아니?
여 강제로 투표를 한다고? 그건 민주주의가 아닌 것 같은데.
남 그러게 말야. 난 투표는 권리지 의무는 아니라고 항상 생각해 왔거든.
여 왜 사람들이 강제로 투표를 하니?
남 주요 이유는 선거가 선택일 경우 투표하는 사람들뿐만이 아닌, 모든 사람들에 의해 선택된 정부가 되어야 하기 때문인 거지. 모든 사람들이 투표를 할 수 있게 하려면 정부가 대비책을 마련해야만 한다는 주장도 있어. 정부는 주말을 선거일로 정해 모든 사람이 투표소에 갈 수 있도록 하고 있어.
여 하지만 비밀투표라면 투표를 강제로 하게 하는 데 반대하는 항의 표시로 투표용지에 표시를 하지 않거나 모든 후보를 다 찍을 수도 있잖아.
남 그렇지. 그게 문제야.
여 선거일에 투표소에 가지 않으면 어떻게 되니?
남 호주에서는 벌금을 물거나 사회봉사를 해야 해. 하지만 만약 지병이라든지 적절한 이유가 있다면 그렇게 안해도 되고.

6 What is a reason for forcing people to vote in elections in Australia? Choose ALL that apply.
호주에서 사람들에게 강제로 투표하게 하는 이유는 무엇인가? 해당하는 것을 모두 고르시오.
 (a) To collect money from those who do not vote on election day   선거일에 투표하지 않은 사람들에게서 돈을 걷으려고
 (b) To make sure all of the people pick the government representatives
반드시 모든 사람들이 정부 대표를 뽑도록 하려고
 (c) To ensure that ballots with none or all of the candidates picked are invalid   아무도 뽑지 않거나 모든 후보를 뽑은 표는 무효라는 것을 확실히 하려고
 (d) To prove that the nation is a democracy by having all of the citizens vote   모든 국민이 투표하게 함으로써 민주주의 국가임을 증명하려고
 (e) To get those who would normally not turn out to vote actually to vote
보통은 투표하러 오지 않는 사람들을 실제로 투표하게 만들려고

7   Level up

party in power may select the boundaries of the election district so that it encompasses groups of people more favorably toward their party. Gerrymandering was especially common in the United States, where, in the past, people often settled in groups based on their country of origin, race, or religion, and these groups are still present to this day. At times, they may favor one political party more than another. For example, African-Americans have a history of regularly voting for the Democratic Party. The term gerrymandering comes from Massachusetts in 1812. Governor Elbridge Gerry created a new election district that was so long and thin that it looked liked a salamander. Since then, the governor's name and the back half of the word salamander have been combined to create the word "gerrymander" to describe the creation of such election districts.

▶ much-maligned 비난을 많이 받는 gerrymandering 자기 당에 유리한 선거구 재편 encompass 포함하다, 싸다 salamander 도룡뇽

여 어떤 국가나 자치도시, 그리고 도시는 선거구로 나뉘어져 있습니다. 각 선거구에서는 의회에서 그 지역을 대표할 한 사람을 투표로 뽑습니다. 어떤 곳의 인구가 늘어나게 되면 새로운 선거구가 생기기도 합니다. 이것은 많은 비난을 불러 일으킨, 이른 바 게리맨더링으로 이어졌습니다. 정권을 잡고 있는 정당은 자신의 정당에 좀 더 우호적인 집단이 포함되도록 선거구의 경계를 선택할 수 있습니다. 게리맨더링은 과거에 출신 국가나 인종 또는 종교를 기반으로 집단을 이루어 정착한 미국에서 특히 흔했습니다. 그리고 이 집단들은 현재까지도 여전히 존재하고 있죠. 때때로 그들은 특정한 정당을 다른 정당보다 더 지지할 수도 있습니다. 예를 들어 아프리카계 미국인들은 민주당에 지속적으로 투표하는 역사를 가지고 있습니다. 게리맨더링이라는 용어는 1812년 매사추세츠에서 유래되었습니다. 엘브리지 게리 주지사는 너무 길고 가늘어서 도룡뇽처럼 보이는 새로운 선거구를 만들었죠. 그 이후 이러한 선거구를 만드는 것을 묘사하기 위해 주지사의 이름(Gerry)과 도룡뇽(salamander)의 단어 뒷부분을 결합한 gerrymander라는 단어가 생겨났습니다.

7 What is the purpose of the talk? 담화의 목적은 무엇인가?

(a) To discuss the history of election districts in Massachusetts 매사추세츠의 선거구 역사를 논하려고

(b) To examine where people settled in different election districts 사람들이 여러 다른 선거구의 어느 곳에 정착했는지 조사하려고

(c) To show a disreputable method of making new election districts 새로운 선거구를 만드는, 평판이 좋지 않은 방법을 보여주려고

(d) To prove that election districts are created based on many factors. 많은 요소를 기초로 해서 선거구가 만들어진다는 것을 증명하려고

(e) To demonstrate a word's meaning and how it was created 한 단어의 의미와 그 단어가 어떻게 만들어졌는지를 설명하려고

8

M In the United States, there are two main bodies in the legislative branch of the government: the Senate and the House of Representatives. Together, they form the United States Congress. The total number of senators is set at a fixed rate of two per state. Since the addition of Alaska and Hawaii as states in 1959, the number of states has been set at 50 and is unlikely to change in the future unless a territory like Puerto Rico gets state status. The two senators from each state are called the senior and junior senator based on their experience in government. Senators are elected for six-year terms, so only one-third of them are up for election every two years. The number of members of the House of Representatives, usually called congressmen or congresswomen, per state depends on the population of the state. The number is set at 435 members, so states with greater populations, such as California, have the most representatives. Congressmen and women are up for election every two years. Each congressman or woman represents about 690,000 American citizens, but the numbers vary slightly from district to district. Every state, regardless of population, has at least one member in the House of Representatives. The number of representatives per state is decided every ten years when the official national census is calculated.

▶ main body 주요부 United States Congress 미국 국회 senator 상원의원 fixed rate 고정요율, 고정금리 be up for election 입후보하다 regardless of ~에 상관 없이 census 인구 조사 calculate 산정하다, 추산하다

남 미국에는 상하 양원, 합쳐서 미국 의회라고 하는 정부 입법부의 두 개 주요 부문이 있습니다. 상원의원의 총수는 주(州)당 2명으로 고정되어 있습니다. 1959년에 알래스카와 하와이 주가 더해져서 이 수는 50개로 정해졌고, 푸에르토리코와 같은 지역이 주의 지위를 얻지 않는 한 앞으로 이 개수가 변할 것 같지는 않습니다. 각 주에서 나온 2명의 상원의원들은 정부에서 일한 경력을 바탕으로 하여 선임 상원의원과 후임 상원의원이라고 불립니다. 상원의원은 6년 임기로 선출되어 그 중 3분의 1만이 2년마다 입후보합니다. 대개 의회의원이라고 부르는 하원 의원들의 수는 각 주당 주의 인구에 따라 달라집니다. 의회의원의 수는 435명으로 설정되어 있어 캘리포니아와 같이 인구가 많은 주에 가장 많은 의회의원이 있습니다. 의회의원은 2년마다 입후보합니다. 각각의 의회의원은 약 69만 명의 미국 국민을 대표하지만 그 숫자는 선거구마다 약간 달라집니다. 인구 수에 상관 없이 각 주에는 적어도 한 명의 하원의원이 있습니다. 주당 의회의원의 수는 공식적인 국가 인구수가 산정되는 매 10년마다 결정됩니다.

8 미국 의회에 대한 정보로 표를 완성하시오.

구분	총수
상원의원의 수	100
하원의원의 수	435
매년 입후보하는 상원의원의 퍼센트	약 33%

9-10 **Integrated Questions**

Reading

▶ bloc 블록 (정치, 경제상의 특수 이익을 위하여 제휴한 몇몇 국민, 단체의 일단), 권(圈) in line (~와) 일치[조화]하여 filibuster 의사 진행 방해: 의사 진행 방해자 announce a vote 개표 결과를 공표하다 confrontation 대립, 직면 supposedly 아마도, 추측건대 dignified 생각건대, 위엄 있는; 기품 있는 brawl 싸움하다, 악다구니치다: 말다툼, 싸움

정치에서는 정부와 정당의 일원들이 자신들의 정치적 목적을 달성하기 위해 여러 가지 작전을 쓴다. 대부분의 정당은 당원 모두가 현안에 찬성하거나 반대함으로써 몰표로 투표를 한다. 각 당에는 당원들의 의견을 조율하여 정당이 원하는 방향으로 투표하도록 하는 일을 담당하는 당원들이 있다. 때때로 당원들은 정당의 강령을 따르지 않기도 하지만 대개는 따른다. 투표가 시작되었을 때, 투표가 정당이 원하는 방향으로 가기에는 부족한 수의 당원만이 출석할 때도 있다. 이런 경우에는 투표를 지체시키는 전술이 있다. 미국에는 그러한 전술의 하나로 시간을 끌기 위해 한 당원이 긴 연설을 하는 의사 진행 방해 행위가 있다. 다른 나라에서는 의회의원들이 개표 결과를 공표하려는 사람들을 물리적으로 막아서 표결을 막으려고 한다. 아니면 투표가 원하는 방향으로 가기 위해 반대당의 당원들이 의회 건물에 들어오는 것을 막는다. 이것은 대만과 한국과 같은 곳에서 기품 있어야 할 국회의원들이 국회 건물 앞

이나 때로는 안에서까지 싸움을 벌이는 물리적 충돌을 낳기도 했다.

W Politics is all about power. Political parties fight for power, and often the people of a country are the ones that suffer. It is sad to say, but the major weakness in most governments comes not from the inability of the election winners to do their jobs but from those legislature members who form the opposition to the government. In most nations, this opposition is made up of the political party which received the second-highest number of seats in the legislature. While they are supposed to be working for the people to ensure the leading political party is doing its job, the reality in most cases is that the opposition wants the government to appear weak in order to force it from power. In countries where there are scheduled elections, like the United States, there can usually be no change in power until a set date. In other nations, like Britain and Canada, the government leadership can change at any time if there is enough opposition to it. In the British parliamentary system, the legislature members can call for a vote of no confidence. This means that the people do not believe the government is doing a good enough job. If a majority of legislature members agree, then the government falls—it loses power—so there must be a new election. No matter what the system, the opposition can paralyze government action if it has a large enough number of seats in the legislature. The opposition does this by always voting against government-supported laws. In this political game, the real losers are the people, who suffer from ineffective government leadership.

▶ inability 무능, 무력 be made up of 구성되다, 이루어지다 leading party 다수당 a vote of no confidence 불신임 투표 a majority of 대다수의, 과반수의 paralyze 마비시키다; 쓸모없게 만들다 ineffective 효과가 없는; 무능한, 무력한

여 정치는 모두 권력에 관한 것입니다. 정당은 권력을 위해 싸우고, 고통 받는 이들은 국민들인 경우가 많죠. 그러나 슬프게도 대부분의 정부들의 가장 큰 약점은 당선자들이 본분을 다하지 못하는 무능함에서 나오는 것이 아니라, 정부에 대해 반대 세력을 형성하는 의회의원들에게서 비롯됩니다. 대부분의 국가에서 이러한 반대 세력은 의회에서 두 번째로 많은 의석수를 차지한 정당으로 이루어져 있습니다. 그들은 다수당이 자신의 일을 확실히 할 수 있도록 국민을 위해 일해야 하지만, 현실에서는 대부분의 경우 정부 내각을 권좌에서 강제로 끌어내리기 위해 정부 내각이 약해 보이기를 원합니다. 미국처럼 예정된 선거가 있는 국가에서는 정해진 날짜까지 권력의 변동은 대체로 있을 수 없습니다. 영국과 캐나다 같은 다른 국가에서는 반대 세력의 수가 충분하다면 언제든지 정부의 지도권이 바뀔 수 있습니다. 영국 의회제도에서는 의회의원들이 불신임 투표를 결의할 수 있습니다. 이것은 국민들이 정부 내각이 제대로 못하고 있다고 믿고 있다는 뜻입니다. 만약 과반수의 의회의원이 동의하면 정부 내각이 몰락하여, 즉 힘을 잃어, 선거를 새로 해야 합니다. 제도가 어떻든 간에 반대 세력이 의회에서 많은 의석수를 차지하고 있다면 정부 활동을 마비시킬 수 있습니다. 반대 세력은 항상 정부가 지지하는 법률에 반대하는 투표를 함으로서 정부 활동을 마비시킵니다. 이 정치게임에서 진정한 피해자는 무력한 정부 지도권에 시달리는 국민들입니다.

9 읽기와 듣기 지문 둘 다에서 언급된 정치적 전술의 하나는 무엇인가?
   (a) 의회의원들은 원하는 대로 투표할 수 있다.
   (b) 육체적인 싸움은 투표를 막는 보편적인 전술이다.
   (c) 정당 간의 싸움은 약한 정부를 만든다.
   (d) 어떤 정부는 언제든지 권좌에서 물러날 수 있다.
   (e) 정부는 중요한 투표가 이루어지는 동안 문을 잠근다.

10 읽기와 듣기 지문에서 유추할 수 있는 것은?
   (a) 정당이 원하는 방향으로 투표를 하지 않는 당원들은 정당에서 축출될 수 있다.
   (b) 영국 정부는 의회 불신임 투표로 자주 정권이 전복된다.
   (c) 국민들이 원하는 법이 의회의 정치적 내분 때문에 통과되지 못할 수 있다.
   (d) 의회에서 두 번째로 많은 의석수를 가진 정당은 무너진 정부를 대신한다.
   (e) 의회에서 물리적인 싸움마저 포함하는 지연 전술은 합법적인 것이다.

*Dictation 정답: Exercise 스크립트 밑줄 참조

UNIT
09 **Earth Sciences**

Preparation   p. 121

Vocabulary Preview

A

1 **depression**: 주위보다 더 낮은 땅
2 **encroachment**: 지역을 점점 더 장악하는 행동
3 **moraine**: 빙하에 의해 생긴 낮은 봉우리
4 **retrograde**: 초기의 더 나쁜 상황으로 돌아가는
5 **distortion**: 원래 형태에서 어떤 점에 변화가 생기는 것

B

1 **infertile** / 돌이 많고 메마른 토지는 대개 척박하여 농사에 적합하지 않다.
2 **decompose** / 죽은 식물과 동물은 부패하여 토양을 더 비옥하게 해준다.
3 **protrude** / 플로리다의 에버글레이즈 습지에는 습지 물 밖으로 튀어나와 있는, 나무에 덮인 작은 섬들이 많이 있다.
4 **take exception** / 과학자들은 자신들의 이론이 논쟁을 일으키는 것에 대해 화를 내고 이의를 제기할 때가 있다.
5 **dubbed** / 초대륙은 한 독일 과학자에 의해 판게아라 불러졌다.
6 **fossil index** / 표준 화석은 암석 지각의 다양한 층에 있는 고대 동식물의 화석에 관한 기록이다.
7 **humus** / 그 농지는 표토가 대부분 부식토이기 때문에 매우 비옥했다.

Expressions and Meanings

1 한번 얘기해 봐.   e 어서 말해봐. 난 준비됐어.
2 난 그것에 당장 착수하겠어.   d 난 당장 그 일을 하겠어.
3 그는 항상 책에 코를 박고 있어.   g 그는 항상 공부해.
4 네 설명은 항상 이해가 안 돼.   a 그건 이해하기에 너무 어려워.
5 바로 그거야.   f 네가 맞아.
6 넌 그 주제에 관해서는 꽤 잘 아는구나.   b 너 정말 그것에 대해 많이 알고 있구나.
7 내가 그 나머지를 추측해 볼게.   c 난 무슨 일이 일어났는지 추측할 수 있을 것 같아.

Monolog

- (1) continental drift (2) continents (3) shape
  (4) position (5) 1920 (6) supercontinent (7) 250
  (8) drifted apart (9) several (10) fossils
  (11) geological formations
- **G** 1 (a) 2 (a)
- **S** (1) T (2) F (3) T (4) F

M The prevailing theory of how the Earth's continents obtained their present shape and position is called continental drift. The theory proposes that the Earth's crust is made up of many plates—some small and some large—which drift apart and sometimes collide with each other. At some point in the past, all of these plates, and thus all of the continents, were joined together in a single landmass that has been dubbed Pangaea. German scientist Alfred Wegener created the term in 1920 when he presented his theories on continental drift. Pangaea is thought to have formed about 250 million years ago. Later, this supercontinent drifted apart, and eventually the Earth's surface took the shape we know today. According to the theory, Pangaea was not the first supercontinent, and there may have been several occasions when all of the Earth's land was joined together and then drifted apart during the Earth's 4-billion-year-plus history. Support for the existence of Pangaea includes fossils and geological evidence. Fossils of the same species have been found on different continents that are now a great distance from each other. For example, a certain ancient lizard's fossilized remains have only been found in Brazil and West Africa. This fact, along with the similar geological formations of the two areas, suggests that at one point in the past, West Africa and Brazil were joined as a single landmass.

▶ prevailing theory 널리 일러진 이론 continental drift 대륙 이동(설) crust 지각 plate 플레이트 (지각을 구성하고 있는 암판) drift 표류하다, 떠다니다 landmass 광대한 땅, (특히) 대륙 Pangaea 판게아(트라이아스기 이전에 존재했다는 가설적인 대륙; 그 후 북의 Laurasia와 남의 Gondwana로 분리되었음) dub (~을 …이라고) 부르다 supercontinent 초대륙 drift apart 표류하여 뿔뿔이 흩어지다; 따로따로 흩어지다 fossil 화석 geological evidence 지질학상의 증거 fossilized remain 화석으로 된 유골[시체]

남 어떻게 지구의 대륙들이 현재의 형태와 위치를 갖게 되었는지에 대한 유력한 이론을 대륙 이동설이라 부릅니다. 그 이론은 지구의 지각이 따로 흩어져 때때로 서로 충돌하는 크고 작은 많은 플레이트로 이루어져 있다고 주장합니다. 과거의 어느 시점에 이 모든 플레이트, 요컨대 모든 대륙은 판게아라고 불리는 하나의 광대한 땅으로 합쳐졌습니다. 독일 과학자 알프레드 베게너는 대륙 이동설에 대한 이론을 발표했던 1920년에 그 용어를 만들었습니다. 판게아는 약 2억 5천만 년 전에 형성되었다고 여겨집니다. 후에, 이 초대륙은 표류하여 뿔뿔이 흩어졌고 마침내 지구 표면은 우리가 오늘날 알고 있는 모양이 되었습니다. 이론에 따르면 판게아는 첫 번째 초대륙이 아니었고 지구의 40억년 역사 동안에 지구 전체의 육지가 붙었다가 따로따로 흩어진 경우가 몇 번 있었습니다. 판게아의 존재에 대한 증거에는 화석과 지질학적인 증거가 있습니다. 같은 종의 화석이 지금은 서로 매우 멀리 떨어진 서로 다른 대륙에서 발견되었습니다. 예를 들면 어떤 고대 도마뱀의 화석화된 유골은 브라질과 서아프리카에서만 발견되고 있습니다. 이 두

지역의 비슷한 지질학적 형태와 함께 이 사실은 과거의 어느 시점에 남아프리카와 브라질이 하나의 대륙으로 붙어 있었다는 것을 말해 줍니다.

General Questions

1 담화의 목적은 무엇인가?
  (a) 한 과학적 이론과 그것을 뒷받침하는 증거를 설명하려고
  (b) 한 이론의 과학적 근원을 논하여 그것이 맞다는 것을 증명하려고
  (c) 한 과학적 이론을 지지하고 반박하는 증거를 기술하려고
  (d) 한 과학적 이론이 아직 만족스럽게 증명되지 않았다는 것을 보여주려고

2 다음 중 가장 잘 요약된 것을 고르시오.
  (a) 화석과 지질학상의 증거는 지구 육지가 한때는 하나의 큰 땅덩어리였다는 것을 주장하는 대륙 이동설을 뒷받침한다.
  (b) 지구의 육지가 한때 하나의 큰 땅덩어리였다는 이론은 1920년에 처음 독일 과학자에 의해 주장되었으나 아직 증명되지는 않았다.

Specific Questions

다시 듣고 옳은 문장에는 T, 틀린 문장에는 F를 쓰시오.
(1) 지구는 육지가 합쳐졌다가 분리되는 주기를 몇 차례 겪었다고 여겨지고 있다.
(2) 판게아는 대륙이 움지임을 묘사하기 위해 만들어진 신조어이다.
(3) 대서양의 양쪽에서 발견된 화석은 서로 닮았다.
(4) 대륙 이동설의 지질학상의 증거는 좀 불충분하다.

Dialog

- (1) tour guide / geology (2) formations (3) Mt. Halla
  (4) blocked (5) lava (6) cooling / tourist (7) volcanoes
- **G** 1 (c) 2 (a)
- **S** (1) T (2) T (3) F (4) T

W Welcome to Jeju Island. I'm Park Jin-hee. I'll be your tour guide, Mr. Davis.

M I really appreciate you taking the time to give this tour just to me. I came here because I'm interested in volcanoes.

W The pleasure is all mine. First, I will give you a slide show showing the geology of Jeju Island, since you said you were interested in that. Then we'll take a trip around the island to see various formations. Are you ready?

M Yes, it sounds like a good plan.

W Okay. First, we have Halla Mountain, the main volcano of Jeju Island. Geologists estimate it erupted about 2 million years ago and created the island.

M What are the many small volcanoes in the pictures?

W These are called parasite cones. Sometimes, the lava tubes for Halla Mountain were blocked, so then the lava would burst forth from weak spots in the rock and create small volcanic cones.

M We'll have to visit one of them.

W Certainly. Now this here's a large tunnel which was created by a lava tube. We'll take a tour of this cave and walk deep underground.

M I'm looking forward to it. Wait. Stop the slides. What

are those strange formations?

W These are the pillar-shaped joints along the cliffs near the seashore. They appear to be like columns supporting a building.

M They are most likely made of basalt.

W Correct. They are the result of cracking that occurred when the lava was cooling.

M Well, this is all very interesting. You're no slouch when it comes to geology. I can't wait for the tour to begin. Let's go!

▶ **formation** 형성, 구성; 계층, 층, 물질의 퇴적작용 **geologist** 지질학자 **estimate** 추정하다, 어림하다 **erupt** 폭발하다, 분화하다 **parasite cone** 기생 화산 **lava tube** 용암굴 **volcanic cone** 화산 원뿔 **burst forth** 분출하다, 터지다 **pillar-shaped joint** 주상절리 **column** 기둥 **basalt** 현무암 **be no slouch** 꽤 잘하다[좋다] **geology** 지질학

여 제주도에 오신 것을 환영합니다. 저는 당신의 투어 가이드 박진희입니다, 데이비스 씨.

남 나만을 위해 이 투어에 시간을 내주셔서 정말 감사합니다. 난 화산에 관심이 있어서 여기에 오게 됐어요.

여 별 말씀을요. 우선, 화산에 관심 있다고 하셨으니 제주도의 지형을 보여주는 슬라이드 쇼를 보여드리겠습니다. 그 후 섬을 여행하면서 여러 가지 지형을 보도록 하죠. 준비되셨습니까?

남 네, 좋은 계획 같네요.

여 좋습니다. 우선 제주도의 주화산인 한라산이 있습니다. 지질학자들은 한라산이 약 2백만 년 전에 폭발하여 섬을 형성했다고 추정하고 있습니다.

남 사진에 있는 많은 작은 화산들은 뭐죠?

여 이것들은 기생 화산이라고 불립니다. 한라산 용암굴이 막혀있을 때도 있었기 때문에 용암이 암석의 약한 곳을 뚫고 터져서 작은 화산 원뿔을 만들었겠죠.

남 우리 그곳도 한번 가보기로 하죠.

여 물론이죠. 여기 이것은 용암굴에 의해 만들어진 큰 굴입니다. 우리는 이 동굴을 둘러보고 깊은 지하로 걸어가 볼 거예요.

남 기대되네요. 잠깐만요. 그 슬라이드 좀 멈춰보세요. 이 이상하게 생긴 것들은 뭔가요?

여 이것들은 해변 근처의 절벽을 따라 있는 주상절리입니다. 빌딩을 지지하는 기둥처럼 보이지요.

남 현무암으로 만들어진 것 같은데요.

여 맞아요. 용암이 식었을 때 생긴 틈 때문에 형성된 거지요.

남 음, 정말 흥미롭네요. 지질학에 대해 꽤 많이 아시는군요. 투어를 얼른 시작했으면 좋겠어요. 갑시다!

General Questions

1 남자가 제주도를 방문한 목적은 무엇인가?
   (a) 섬의 특징에 대한 슬라이드 쇼를 보려고
   (b) 여행기간 동안 나중에 섬을 여행하려고
   (c) 섬의 지질학적인 특징을 조사하려고
   (d) 편히 쉬고 어쩌면 관광도 하려고

2 다음 중 가장 잘 요약된 것을 고르시오.
   (a) 투어 가이드는 섬 여행을 시작하기 전에 외국 관광객에게 제주도 화산의 특징에 대한 슬라이드 쇼를 보여준다.
   (b) 화산에 관심이 있는 외국 관광객은 투어 가이드의 제주도 화산에 대한 폭넓은 지식에 감탄한다.

Specific Questions

다시 듣고 옳은 문장에는 T, 틀린 문장에는 F를 쓰시오.
(1) 섬 투어에 오직 한 명의 여행객만이 있을 것이다.

(2) 남자와 여자는 화산에 대한 지식이 좀 있다.
(3) 기생 화산은 한라산과는 독립적인 화산이다.
(4) 주상절리는 용암이 식어 갈라져서 생겼다.

Long Lecture

○ (1) erosion (2) plants (3) humans (4) topsoil
(5) vegetation (6) minerals (7) fertile (8) compact
(9) rocky (10) solid (11) bedrock (12) chemical
(13) climate (14) plants (15) volcanic (16) ash
(17) bacteria (18) decompose (19) growing crops

1 (a)　　**2** (b)　　**3** (1) F (2) T (3) F (4) T　　**4** (c)

Dictation 정답: 스크립트 밑줄 참조

W Soil is one of the <u>most important aspects</u> of the geology of the Earth. <u>Without</u> soil, most <u>types of vegetation</u>, including crops, <u>could not grow</u>, so it is <u>vital for human</u> and animal life. Soil is <u>formed</u> mainly <u>through the erosion</u> of rock into <u>smaller particles</u>, with <u>wind and water</u> doing the work over a long period of time. <u>Smaller amounts</u> are also created through the <u>actions of plants</u>, animals, and humans. <u>Soil scientists</u>, or pedologists, <u>divide soil into</u> four main <u>layers</u>, which they call "<u>horizons</u>." At the top is horizon A, the most <u>useful part</u>, which is the <u>rich topsoil</u> where <u>vegetation grows</u>. This can be anywhere from a few centimeters to almost a <u>meter thick</u>. Below that is horizon B, which <u>has minerals</u> that water <u>washes down</u> from the <u>upper layer</u>. However, horizon B is <u>less fertile</u> than horizon A and is more <u>compact</u> and <u>lighter</u>. Under horizon B is the <u>rockier</u> horizon C, which is <u>infertile</u>. Finally, the <u>more solid</u> bedrock is horizon D. Soil fertility <u>depends on</u> its <u>chemical composition</u>, which <u>in turn</u> depends on the <u>climate</u> and the plants that grow in the soil. If there was <u>plenty of volcanic activity</u> in the past, the soil will be rich as <u>volcanic ash</u> is very fertile. Soil can also <u>become fertile</u> through the actions of bacteria and fungi. When plants and animals die, the actions of bacteria and fungi <u>decompose them</u>. Then, with the help of <u>earthworms</u> and other <u>soil creatures</u>, this <u>decomposing matter</u> becomes humus, a dark, rich soil that is <u>ideal for growing crops</u>.

▶ **vegetation** 초목 **erosion** 부식; 침식 **particle** 아주 작은 조각, 극소량 **pedologist** 토양학자 **horizons** 지평층, 층위(層位) **topsoil** 표토(表土) **upper layer** 상층(上層) **wash down** 쓸어내리다 **mineral** 광물; 광석; 무기물 **compact** 조밀한; 빽빽한 **infertile** 불모의; 메마른 **bedrock** 기반암(基盤岩) **in turn** 차례로, 번갈아, 이번에는 **chemical composition** 화합물 **rich** (토지가) 기름진, 비옥한 **volcanic ash** 화산재 **fungi** fungus(진균류, 효모균; 버섯)의 복수형 **decompose** 부패시키다 **humus** 부식, 부식질, 부식토

여 토양은 지구 지질학의 가장 중요한 요소 중 하나입니다. 토양이 없다면 농작물을 포함한 대부분의 초목이 자랄 수 없기 때문에 인간과 동물의 삶에 극히 중요하지요. 토양은 주로 암석이 오랜 세월 동안 바람과 물의 작용으로 작은 조각으로 부식되어 형성됩니다. 또한 그보다 적은 양은 식물, 동물, 사람들의 작용으로도 만들어집니다. 토양 과학자, 즉 토양학자는 토양을 4개의 주요 층으로 나누는데, 그것을 '층위'라고 부릅니다. 가장 윗부분은 층위 A이고 초목이 자라는 비옥

한 표토라서 가장 유용한 부분입니다. 층위 A는 몇 센티미터에서 거의 1미터 두께로 다양합니다. 그 밑에는 층위 B가 있으며 여기에는 상층으로부터 물이 쓸어내린 광물이 있습니다. 하지만 층위 B는 층위 A보다 덜 비옥하고 더 조밀하고 가볍습니다. 층위 B 밑에는 더 바위가 많아 불모인 층위 C가 있습니다. 마지막으로 더 단단한 기반암인 층위 D가 있습니다. 토양의 비옥도는 화합물에 따라 달라지며 그 화합물은 기후와 토양에서 자라는 식물에 따라 달라집니다. 만약 과거에 활발한 화산활동이 있었다면 화산재가 매우 비옥하기 때문에 토양이 기름집니다. 토양은 또한 박테리아와 진균류의 활동을 통해 비옥해질 수 있습니다. 식물과 동물이 죽으면 박테리아와 진균류의 활동은 식물과 동물을 부패시킵니다. 그러고 나면 지렁이와 다른 토양 생물들의 도움으로 이 부패된 물질은 농작물이 자라기에 더할 나위 없는 검고 비옥한 토양인 부식토가 됩니다.

1　강의는 주로 무엇에 관한 것인가?
　(a) 토양의 몇 가지 특징과 토양이 만들어지는 방법
　(b) 토양의 여러 가지 층과 그것들이 형성되는 방법
　(c) 어떻게 토양, 특히 생명력을 주는 표토가 만들어지는가
　(d) 토양층에 서식하는 생명체

2　다음 중 가장 잘 요약된 것을 고르시오.
　(a) 토양은 부식을 통해 만들어지고 몇 개의 층으로 나누어질 수 있으며
　　　최상위층은 인류에게 가장 중요하다.
　(b) 토양은 여러 다른 방법을 통해 만들어지고 여러 층으로 구분되는데,
　　　최상위층은 생물체가 계속 생존하는 데 가장 중요하다.

3　옳은 문장에는 T, 틀린 문장에는 F를 쓰시오.
　(1) 토양 화합물은 전 세계적으로 비슷하다.
　(2) 부식토는 부패된 식물과 동물질 때문에 매우 비옥하다.
　(3) 층위 B 토양은 바위가 많은 물질로 이루어져 비옥하지 않다.
　(4) 주로 화산재로 이루어진 표토는 매우 비옥한 경향이 있다.

4　박테리아와 진균류는 비옥한 표토를 만드는 데 어떤 역할을 하는가?
　(a) 화산재에 존재하며 화산재를 부식토로 만든다.
　(b) 토양의 최상위층에 있으며 바위를 부식시키는 데 도움을 준다.
　(c) 죽은 유기체를 공격하여 부패시키는 데 도움을 준다.
　(d) 토양의 여러 층을 이동하며 토양 생물체의 먹이가 된다.

Exercise

p. 126~p. 127

1 (e)	**2** 해설 참조	**3** (d)	**4** (a)	**5** (a)	**6** (b)	**7** (c)
8 (c)	**9** (d)	**10** 해설 참조	**11** (d)	**12** (c)		

1

M　Coal is the <u>remains</u> of <u>dead</u> <u>vegetation</u> that have undergone a <u>chemical</u> <u>transformation</u> over millions of years. After trees and plants died in <u>swamps</u> <u>or</u> <u>along</u> <u>the</u> <u>shores</u> of inland seas and lakes, they quickly sank under the water and then were <u>buried</u> <u>by</u> <u>layers</u> of sand and mud. This process <u>trapped</u> <u>the</u> <u>plant</u> <u>matter</u> without <u>exposing</u> it to air or <u>causing</u> <u>it</u> <u>to</u> <u>decompose</u>. Over millions of years, this process was repeated many times and formed more and more layers of plant matter with <u>sand</u> <u>and</u> <u>mud</u> <u>on</u> <u>top</u>. The plant matter <u>was</u> <u>then</u> <u>subjected</u> <u>to</u> tremendous amounts of heat and pressure. The <u>cellulose</u> <u>matter</u> in wood became <u>humic</u> <u>acid</u>, then bitumen, and finally carbon. It was this <u>carbon</u> <u>stage</u> when the plant matter was transformed into coal. A high carbon content indicates that a piece of coal is very old and is also of good quality. Most <u>high</u> <u>quality</u> <u>coal</u> was formed during the Carboniferous Period on the <u>geological</u> <u>time</u> <u>scale</u>. This was a period about 360 to 290 million years ago. Coal from more <u>recent</u> <u>geological</u> <u>periods</u> is usually not of as good a quality. The most <u>recent</u> <u>deposits</u>—from about 10,000 years ago—were transformed into peat. This is an early stage of coal transformation. Peat has a lot of <u>fibrous</u> <u>plant</u> <u>matter</u>, so it is useful for burning to heat homes. However, because it has no carbon content, it is not <u>as</u> <u>prized</u> <u>as</u> <u>coal</u>.

▶ coal 석탄　transformation 변형, 변질　remains 잔해; 유골　inland 내륙의, 내륙으로　expose 노출시키다　trap 좁은 장소에 가두다　be subjected to ~을 받다 〔당하다〕　cellulose matter 셀룰로오스, 섬유질　humic acid 부식산(腐植酸)　bitumen 역청　carbon 탄소　be transformed into ~로 변형되다　Carboniferous Period 석탄기[계, 층]　geological time scale 지질연대표　geological time periods 지질시대　deposit 퇴적물, 침전물　peat 토탄(土炭)　fibrous 섬유의, 섬유질의　prized 중요한, 가치 있는

남　석탄은 수백만 년 세월에 걸쳐 화학적 변형을 일으킨 죽은 초목의 잔해입니다. 습지나 내륙의 바다와 호수를 따라 난 나무와 식물은 죽은 후에 빠르게 물 밑으로 가라앉아 모래와 진흙에 의해 묻히게 됩니다. 이 과정으로 인해 식물질은 공기에 노출되거나 부패되지 않게 가둬진 것이지요. 수백만 년 동안 이 과정은 여러 번 반복되어 점점 더 많은 모래와 진흙에 덮인 식물질층을 형성하게 되었습니다. 그후 식물질은 엄청난 양의 열과 압력을 받습니다. 나무의 섬유질은 부식산이 된 후 역청이 되고 마침내 탄소가 됩니다. 식물질층이 석탄으로 변형되는 때가 바로 이 탄소 단계입니다. 탄소 함량이 높다는 것은 매우 오래되고 품질 좋은 석탄이라는 것을 나타냅니다. 대부분의 고품질 석탄은 지질연대표에 따르면 석탄기에 형성되었습니다. 석탄기는 약 3억 6천만 년에서 2억 9천만 년 전에 있었습니다. 좀 더 최근의 지질시대의 석탄은 대개 그다지 좋은 품질이 아닙니다. 약 만 년 전에 형성된 가장 최근의 퇴적물은 토탄으로 변형되었습니다. 이것은 석탄 변형의 초기 단계입니다. 토탄은 섬유질의 식물질이 많아 난방용으로 유용합니다. 하지만 탄소 함량이 없기 때문에 석탄만큼 가치 있지는 않습니다.

1　담화의 목적은 무엇인가?
　(a) 여러 가지 종류의 석탄의 이점에 대해 논하려고
　(b) 석탄과 토탄의 차이점을 조사하려고
　(c) 선사시대 지구의 지질학적 과정을 논하려고
　(d) 더 오래된 석탄이 고품질이라는 것을 증명하려고
　(e) 어떻게 석탄이 오랜 세월에 걸쳐 만들어지는가를 기술하려고

2

W　Did you find the information about lakes that we need for the project?

M　Yes, and I think we <u>should</u> <u>concentrate</u> on Lake Baikal in Russia.

W　<u>What's</u> <u>so</u> <u>special</u> about it?

M　It has about 20 percent of the world's <u>fresh</u> <u>water</u> <u>supply</u> that is not frozen, like in the <u>polar</u> <u>icecaps</u>. Pretty amazing, huh?

W　20 percent? Are you sure? That sounds like someone is <u>exaggerating</u>.

M　No, it's true. In fact, Lake Baikal has more fresh water than the five Great Lakes in the U.S. combined.

W　Then it must be huge. Do you have a picture?

M　Yes, here it is, but it's <u>not</u> <u>that</u> big. It's <u>crescent-shaped</u>, and it's 636 kilometers long and 79 kilometers wide <u>at</u> <u>its</u> <u>widest</u> <u>point</u>. It has a surface area of <u>31,722</u> square kilometers.

97

W I think that's less than Lake Superior.

M You're right, but Baikal is the deepest lake in the world. It's 1,642 meters deep. That's why it has so much fresh water. Also the bottom of the lake is mostly soft sediment, so the hard rock layer is even deeper, at about 8 kilometers.

W What other interesting facts can we include in our report?

M Let's see. Oh, there are 72 islands in the lake. And it's also estimated to be about 25 million years old. Some geologists say it's the oldest lake in the world.

W I think that's more than enough to begin our project.

▶ Lake Baikal 바이칼 호(시베리아의 호수) polar icecaps 극지의 만년설 fresh water 담수, 민물 exaggerate 과장하다 crescent-shaped 초승달 모양의 square kilometer 평방미터 Lake Superior 슈피리어 호(북미에 있는 세계 최대의 담수호) soft sediment 부드러운 침전물

여 우리 연구 과제에 필요한 호수들에 대한 정보 찾았니?
남 응, 그리고 난 우리가 러시아에 있는 바이칼 호에 중점을 둬야 한다고 생각해.
여 그곳이 뭐가 그렇게 특별한데?
남 그 호수는 극지의 만년설 같이 얼어 있지 않은 담수 공급원으로서 세계의 약 20%를 차지하고 있어. 놀랍지 않아?
여 20%? 정말이야? 조금 과장한 것 같은데.
남 아니, 맞아. 사실 바이칼 호는 미국의 5대호를 합친 것보다 더 많은 담수를 가지고 있어.
여 그럼 정말 거대하겠구나. 사진 있니?
남 응, 여기 있어. 하지만 그렇게 크진 않아. 초승달 모양이고 길이가 636킬로미터에 가장 넓은 부분의 너비가 79킬로미터야. 그리고 표면적이 31,722평방미터야.
여 슈피리어 호보다 작은 것 같은데?
남 맞아. 하지만 바이칼 호는 세계에서 가장 깊은 호수야. 깊이가 1,642미터지. 그래서 그렇게 담수가 많은 거야. 게다가 호수 바닥 대부분이 부드러운 침전물로 되어 있어서 단단한 암석층은 더 깊어. 약 8킬로미터가 되지.
여 우리 리포트에 넣을 다른 재미있는 사실들이 있니?
남 보자. 오, 호수에 72개의 섬이 있어. 또 바이칼 호는 약 2천 5백만 년이 된 것으로 추정되고 있어. 일부 지질학자들은 바이칼 호가 세계에서 가장 오래된 호수라고 하지.
여 우리 연구 과제를 시작하기에 충분하고도 남을 것 같다.

2 바이칼 호에 대한 정보로 표를 완성하시오.

구분	정보
세계의 얼지 않은 담수 중 비율	20%
표면적	31,722평방미터
길이	636킬로미터
넓이	79킬로미터
깊이	1,642미터
나이	25 million years (2천 5백만 년)

3-4

M When a river emerges into the ocean, or sometimes into a lake, it can form a delta. This is an area of silt deposits that forms over a long period of time. The term "delta" comes from the shape of the Nile River's delta. The ancient Greeks felt the shape was similar to the letter "Δ" (delta) in the Greek alphabet. There are two major types of river deltas. The Nile River delta is a classic fan-shaped delta, which has slowly built up over a long period of time. The Mediterranean Sea has mostly weak tides but strong wave power, which has allowed the Nile delta to expand, but not to a great extent. Since the construction of the Aswan High Dam on the Nile in the 1960s, the flow of silt to the delta has been negligible, and, in recent decades, the Nile delta has shown a retrograde movement. The other most common delta shape is the bird's foot delta, with the Mississippi River delta being the most famous of this type. The great river flows into the Gulf of Mexico, which has little tidal or wave power, allowing the Mississippi delta to expand very far. As it deposits silt, the river divides into channels and spreads away from the coastline. The different channels look like fingers or toes and give the delta its classic bird's foot appearance.

▶ delta 삼각주 silt 미사(微砂), 침니(沈泥) (모래보다 잘지만 진흙보다 굵은 침적토) deposit 침전물, 퇴적물; 침적[퇴적]시키다 Mediterranean Sea 지중해 tide 조수, 조류; 간만 to a great extent 크게 Aswan High Dam 아스완하이댐(이집트 아스완 댐 상류 7km 지점에 있는 댐) negligible 무시해도 좋은; 대수롭지 않은, 하찮은 retrograde movement 퇴행적인 움직임 channel 수로, 운하

남 강물이 바다 또는 때때로 호수에 들어가면 삼각주를 형성합니다. 삼각주는 오랜 시간 형성된 침니 침전물 지역입니다. '삼각주'라는 용어는 나일 강의 삼각주 모양에서 유래되었습니다. 고대 그리스 사람들은 그 모양이 그리스 알파벳 Δ(델타)와 비슷하다고 생각했습니다. 강 삼각주에는 두 가지 주요 형태가 있습니다. 나일 강 삼각주는 전형적인 부채 모양의 삼각주로 오랜 시간 동안 천천히 형성된 것입니다. 지중해는 대부분 조수가 약하지만 파도의 힘이 강합니다. 이 강한 파도의 힘은 나일 강의 삼각주를 확장시키지만 그렇게 크게 확장시키지 못합니다. 1960년대 나일 강 아스완하이댐의 축조 이래로 삼각주로의 침니의 흐름이 그다지 크지 않았고, 최근 몇 십년간 나일 강 삼각주는 퇴행적인 움직임을 보이고 있습니다. 또 다른 가장 보편적인 삼각주 형태는 새 발 모양의 삼각주인데, 미시시피 강 삼각주가 이 형태로 가장 유명합니다. 큰 강이 조수와 파도의 힘이 미약한 멕시코 만으로 흘러 들어가므로 미시시피 삼각주는 매우 멀리까지 확장할 수 있습니다. 그것이 침니를 침전시킴으로써 강은 수로들로 나뉘게 되고 해안선으로부터 펼쳐집니다. 여러 수로들은 손가락들이나 발가락들 같이 생겨 삼각주가 전형적인 새 발 모습을 띠게 되었습니다.

3 주로 무슨 이유로 강 삼각주 모양에 차이가 있나?
(a) 큰 삼각주가 있는 강을 가로지르는 댐의 축조
(b) 강물이 강어귀로 흘러가는 동안 떨어뜨린 침니의 양
(c) 강이 흘러 들어갈 때 물줄기의 평균 조수 속력
(d) 강어귀가 있는 곳의 조수와 파도의 힘
(e) 해마다 강한 파도를 일으키는 큰 폭풍의 횟수

4 장차 나일 강 삼각주에는 무슨 일이 일어나겠는가?
(a) 나일 강을 막고 있는 댐이 부서지면 휩쓸려 없어질 것이다.
(b) 약한 조수로 인해 지중해까지 더 확장될 것이다.
(c) 새로운 침니가 거의 퇴적되지 않으므로 완전히 사라질 것이다.
(d) 나일 강의 홍수로 인해 수면이 높아져 거주하기 적당하지 않을 것이다.
(e) 미시시피 강 삼각주와 같이 새 발 모양의 삼각주로 변하게 될 것이다.

5-6　Level up

G It's such a nice day to take a break, and this is a great beach. The water is great for swimming because it's really shallow here. There are also lots of colorful fishing boats.

B It's a great place for fishing because of the extensive continental shelf.

G What's the continental shelf?

B It's shallow, gently <u>sloping</u> <u>underwater</u> <u>land</u> that can extend into the ocean for a few or hundreds of kilometers. The shallow water provides <u>plenty</u> <u>of</u> <u>plankton</u> and other food for fish. The <u>shelf</u> <u>ends</u> when the water suddenly gets deeper at a <u>boundary</u> <u>called</u> <u>the</u> <u>continental</u> <u>slope</u>.

G So if I walk far enough in the water, I will suddenly fall?

B You'd have to <u>walk</u> <u>pretty</u> <u>far</u>, and the water isn't shallow enough to <u>walk</u> <u>the</u> <u>whole</u> <u>way</u>.

G No, I don't think I'll try that. Wait. Is that an <u>oil</u> <u>rig</u> <u>out</u> <u>there</u> on the <u>horizon</u>?

B Sure. Oil explorers have also found extensive oil and gas fields <u>under</u> <u>the</u> <u>continental</u> <u>shelves</u>.

G I thought oil only existed in the desert or places where <u>lots</u> <u>of</u> <u>vegetation</u> and animals died a long time ago.

B Fish die, too. The continental shelf was also <u>exposed</u> <u>land</u> in the <u>distant</u> <u>past</u>. The levels of the oceans <u>have</u> <u>fluctuated</u> over the years. During the <u>last</u> <u>ice</u> <u>age</u>, the world's oceans were around 100 meters lower than they are today due to <u>water</u> <u>being</u> <u>frozen</u> in the <u>ice</u> <u>sheets</u>.

G Oh, right. There was a land bridge between Asia and Alaska. I learned that was how the Native Americans probably went from Asia to North and South America.

▶ shallow 얕은　extensive continental shelf 대규모의 대륙붕　gently sloping 완만하게 경사진　plenty of 많은, 충분한　plankton 플랑크톤, 부유 생물　continental slope 대륙 사면(斜面)　the whole way 내내, 끝까지　oil rig 석유 굴착 장치　field 매장 지대　exposed 노출된, 드러난　fluctuate 오르내리다, 변동하다　ice sheet 대륙 빙하, 대빙원; 빙상　land bridge 육지 다리; 해륙 수송(해상 운송과 육상 운송을 결합시킨 운송 방식)

여 쉬기에 딱 좋은 날씨인 데다 정말 멋진 해변이야. 여기는 물이 정말 얕아서 수영하기에 좋네. 여러 색깔의 고깃배도 많고.

남 대규모 대륙붕 때문에 고기잡이 하기에 좋은 곳이야.

여 대륙붕이 뭐야?

남 바닷속 몇 킬로미터 또는 수백 킬로미터까지 뻗은 얕고 완만하게 경사진 수중 육지야. 얕은 물에는 물고기가 먹을 플랑크톤과 다른 먹이가 풍부하지. 대륙붕은 대륙 사면이라고 불리는, 물이 갑자기 깊어지는 경계에서 끝나게 돼.

여 그럼 내가 물속 멀리까지 걸어 나가면 갑자기 빠지게 되는 거야?

남 꽤 멀리까지 걸어 나가야 할 걸. 그리고 끝까지 걸어갈 수 있을 정도로 물이 얕진 않아.

여 아니, 그렇게 해보겠다는 건 아니야. 잠깐. 저기 수평선에 있는 건 석유 굴착 장치 아니야?

남 맞아. 석유 탐사자들이 대륙붕 밑에서 대규모의 석유와 가스 매장지대도 발견했거든.

여 난 석유가 사막이나 많은 초목과 동물들이 오래 전에 죽은 곳에만 있는 줄 알았어.

남 물고기도 죽잖아. 그리고 대륙붕도 먼 옛날에는 노출된 땅이었어. 해수면이 세월이 흐르는 동안 오르내렸지. 마지막 빙하기에는 물이 얼어 빙하가 돼서 세계의 바다가 지금보다 약 100미터 낮았어.

여 오, 맞다. 아시아와 알래스카 사이에 육지 다리가 있었잖아. 아마 그것 덕분에 미국 원주민들이 아시아에서 북아메리카와 남아메리카로 건너갔을 거라고 배웠어.

5 왜 석유와 가스가 대륙붕에서 발견되겠는가?

(a) 한때는 식물들이 죽었고 후에는 물고기들이 죽었던 노출된 땅이었기 때문에

(b) 얕은 물이 석유와 가스를 만드는 데 더 나은 조건이기 때문에

(c) 깊은 물 보다는 얕은 물에서 물고기들이 더 많이 죽기 때문에

(d) 대륙 사면으로 인해 석유와 가스가 지하에 고여서

(e) 해초와 같은 바다 초목이 죽어 오랜 시간에 걸쳐 석유가 되기 때문에

6 다음 중 내용을 가장 잘 요약한 것을 고르시오.

(a) 연안 바다 밑에는 대류 사면에서 갑자기 깊어지는 대륙붕이라고 부르는 얕은 육지가 있다.

(b) 대륙붕에는 대규모 어장이 있을 뿐 아니라 석유와 가스의 퇴적물이 있고 한때는 육지 다리로 이용되었을 수도 있다.

(c) 만약 해수면이 과거에 그랬던 것처럼 낮아지면 대륙붕을 따라 행해지는 어업과 석유 개발은 중단될 수도 있다.

G You've always got your <u>nose</u> <u>stuck</u> <u>in</u> a book. What are you reading now?

B It's about a <u>famous</u> <u>geologist</u>, William Smith.

G I've never heard of him. Why's he so famous?

B He's often called the father of English geology. In the early 19th century, he made a <u>map</u> <u>of</u> <u>the</u> <u>geology</u> of England that showed the <u>composition</u> <u>of</u> <u>the</u> <u>land</u> all over the British Isles.

G Do you mean he showed the different types of land, <u>rock</u> <u>formations</u>, and <u>minerals</u>? That sort of thing?

B Yes, it's mostly what he is famous for. He also created what is called a <u>fossil</u> <u>index</u>.

G That's <u>going</u> <u>over</u> <u>my</u> <u>head</u>. What's a <u>fossil</u> <u>index</u>?

B Smith was helping <u>build</u> a <u>canal</u>, and he noticed that different fossils were found in <u>different</u> <u>layers</u> of rock, but the same fossils always appeared in the same layers.

G Wait. Let me <u>surmise</u> <u>the</u> <u>rest</u>. So because each layer had the same fossils in different areas, this was an <u>indication</u> <u>of</u> <u>the</u> <u>ages</u> of the rock layers and the fossils.

B You hit the nail right on the head. I guess it didn't all <u>go</u> <u>over</u> <u>your</u> <u>head</u> after all.

▶ the British Isles 영국 제도(Great Britain, Ireland 및 주변의 섬들로 구성)　formation 계층, 층　go over one's head ~로서는 이해하기 어렵다　fossil index 표준 화석　canal 운하, 수로　surmise 추측[추정]하다

여 넌 항상 책에 코를 박고 있구나. 지금 뭐 읽고 있니?

남 유명한 지질학자인 윌리엄 스미스에 관한 책이야.

여 들어 본 적 없는데. 왜 그 사람이 그렇게 유명하지?

남 그는 영국 지질학의 아버지라고도 불려. 그는 19세기 초에 영국 제도 전역의 토지 배지를 보여주는 영국 지질학 지도를 만들었어.

여 토지의 여러 가지 유형, 암석 계층, 광물, 그런 것들을 보여줬다는 거야?

남 그래, 그게 그가 유명해진 이유야. 그는 또 표준 화석이라고 불리는 것을 만들었어.

여 잘 이해가 안 돼. 표준 화석이 뭐야?

남 스미스는 운하를 짓는 것을 돕고 있던 중에 육지의 다양한 암석 층에서 여러 가지 화석이 발견되는 것을 알게 됐어. 하지만 같은 층에서는 항상 같은 화석이 나타났지.

여 잠깐. 내가 그 나머지를 추측해 볼게. 그래서 여러 지역의 각 층에서 같은 화석이 발견되었기 때문에 그건 암석층과 화석의 나이를 나타낸다는 거지.

남 바로 그거야. 이해를 전혀 못할 정도는 아니었네.

7 What is William Smith famous for?
윌리엄 스미스는 무엇으로 유명한가?

(a) Building canals all over England
영국 전역에 운하를 지은 것으로

(b) Discovering different layers of soil
토양의 여러 층을 발견한 것으로

(c) Creating a geological map of England
영국의 지질학 지도를 만든 것으로

(d) Finding many new types of fossils
새로운 종류의 화석을 많이 발견한 것으로

(e) Being the father of English geography
영국 지질학의 아버지로서

8 Level up

W The Northern Hemisphere has a great many more lakes than the Southern Hemisphere, <u>mostly</u> <u>due</u> <u>to</u> <u>glacial</u> <u>activity</u>. As the great <u>ice</u> <u>sheets</u> <u>advanced</u> during the last ice age, they cut away the land and <u>scooped</u> <u>out</u> <u>depressions</u> by the tens of thousands. As the ice sheets <u>retreated</u> and <u>melted,</u> these depressions were filled with the <u>newly</u> <u>released</u> <u>fresh</u> <u>water</u>. Examples of glacial lakes include the five Great Lakes in North America, the largest examples of glacial lakes in the world. A lake can be <u>identified</u> <u>as</u> a <u>glacial</u> <u>lake</u> by certain <u>geological</u> <u>features</u> that are located nearby. For example, small <u>rounded</u> <u>hills</u> <u>called</u> <u>drumlins</u> are often associated with glacial activity. The <u>point</u> <u>at</u> <u>which</u> the glacier stopped its movement usually has a <u>terminal</u> moraine, a long low hill that was created by the <u>glacier</u> <u>pushing</u> <u>soil</u> and rock in front of it. These are both signs that a glacier was nearby and that the lake was most likely created by the <u>glacial</u> <u>activity</u>.

▶ Northern Hemisphere 북반구　Southern Hemisphere 남반구　ice sheet 대륙 빙하, 대빙원; 빙상　cut away 베어 버리다　scoop out 파다　depression (땅의) 함몰; 움푹한 땅　tens of thousands 수만　retreat 후퇴하다; 물러서다　release 방출하다　feature 지세, 지형; 특징　drumlin 빙퇴구(氷堆丘)　terminal moraine 말단 퇴석(堆石), 종퇴석

여 북반구에는 주로 빙하 활동 때문에 남반구보다 훨씬 호수가 많습니다. 거대한 대륙 빙하가 마지막 빙하기 동안 발달되면서 육지를 잘라내고 수만 군데의 땅을 움푹하게 파냈습니다. 대륙 빙하가 없어지고 녹으면서 이 움푹한 땅은 새롭게 방출된 담수로 채워졌습니다. 빙하호의 예로는 세계에서 가장 큰 빙하호라 할 수 있는 미국의 5대호가 있습니다. 호수는 주변의 특정한 지질학적 지형에 따라 빙하호인지 아닌지 식별할 수 있습니다. 예를 들면 빙퇴구라고 불리는 작고 둥근 언덕은 빙하 활동과 관련이 있는 경우가 많습니다. 빙하가 활동을 멈추는 순간에는 대개 빙하가 앞에 있는 토양과 바위를 밀어냄으로써 생긴 길고 낮은 언덕인 말단 퇴석이 생깁니다. 이 사실들은 빙하가 가까이에 있었다는 것과, 그 호수가 빙하 활동에 의해 생겨났을 가능성이 높다는 것을 암시합니다.

8 What is the talk mainly about?
담화는 주로 무엇에 관한 내용인가?

(a) Why glacial lakes are common in northern areas
왜 빙하호가 북부 지역에서 흔한가

(b) Why the Great Lakes are the largest glacial lakes
왜 5대호가 가장 큰 빙하호인가

(c) How glacial lakes are created and can be identified
어떻게 빙하호가 생기고 식별되는가

(d) What the terrain surrounding a glacial lake is like
빙하호의 주변 지대가 어떻게 생겼는가

(e) Which lakes are glacial lakes and which are not
어떤 호수가 빙하호이고 어떤 호수가 빙하호가 아닌가

9

W An <u>urban</u> heat island is a city area that is hotter than the surrounding countryside. Often, this <u>temperature</u> <u>difference</u> may be <u>as</u> <u>high</u> <u>as</u> five <u>degrees</u> <u>Celsius</u>. With plenty of concrete and asphalt, plus tall buildings which have a larger surface area than houses and smaller buildings, <u>urban</u> <u>areas</u> <u>absorb</u> more sunlight and heat during the day. This <u>absorbed</u> <u>heat</u> is <u>released</u> very slowly at night, making city areas hotter than <u>rural</u> <u>areas</u> in the <u>nighttime</u>. Another problem is that tall buildings <u>block</u> <u>wind</u> which could <u>dissipate</u> <u>the</u> <u>heat</u> more quickly. Heat from cars, factories, air conditioning systems, and other sources contributes to the higher temperatures in cities. The biggest <u>impact</u> the <u>urban</u> <u>heat</u> <u>island</u> <u>effect</u> has is to contribute to the <u>death</u> <u>toll</u> during heat waves. In addition, there are some experts who believe the urban heat island effect is contributing to <u>changing</u> <u>weather</u> <u>patterns</u> and possibly to global warming. However, not all cities and not all city areas have these problems. Cities with a great many parks and <u>trees</u> <u>lining</u> <u>their</u> <u>streets</u> have less of an urban heat island problem because <u>vegetation</u> has a <u>cooling</u> <u>effect</u>. Some cities even have plans to build <u>rooftop</u> <u>gardens</u> to reduce the urban heat island effect. Also, by using light-colored materials and <u>reflective</u> <u>materials</u> to cover new buildings, the amount of heat absorbed during the daytime is <u>significantly</u> <u>reduced</u>.

▶ urban heat island 도시열섬　concrete 콘크리트, 콘크리트 포장면　dissipate 흩뜨리다; (열 등이) 방산(放散)하다　contribute to ~에 기여하다　heat wave 폭염　cooling effect 냉각 효과　rooftop garden 옥상 정원

여 도시열섬은 주변 시골 지역보다 더 더운 도시 지역입니다. 온도 차이는 종종 섭씨 5도까지 날 수 있습니다. 많은 콘크리트와 아스팔트와 더불어, 집과 작은 건물보다 더 큰 면적을 차지하는 고층 빌딩 때문에 도시 지역은 낮 동안 더 많은 햇빛과 열을 흡수하게 됩니다. 이렇게 흡수된 열은 밤에 매우 천천히 방출되어 밤에 시골지역보다 도시 지역이 더 더워집니다. 또 하나의 문제는 고층빌딩이 열을 더 빨리 방산(放散)시킬 수 있는 바람을 막는다는 것입니다. 차, 공장, 에어컨, 그리고 다른 원인들이 도시의 기온이 높아지는 데 기여합니다. 도시열섬 효과의 가장 큰 영향은 폭염기 사망률의 원인이 된다는 것입니다. 게다가 일부 전문가들은 도시열섬 효과가 날씨 패턴의 변화와, 어쩌면 지구 온난화에도 기여한다고 믿고 있습니다. 하지만 모든 도시와 도시 지역에 이러한 문제가 있는 것은 아닙니다. 초목은 냉각 효과가 있기 때문에, 공원이 매우 많고 거리에 나무들이 늘어서 있는 도시들에는 도시열섬 문제가 보다 적습니다. 어떤 도시들은 옥상 정원을 지어서 도시열섬 효과를 감소시키려는 계획도 가지고 있습니다. 또한 새 건물에 옅은 색 자재와 반사 자재를 사용함으로써 낮 동안에 흡수되는 열의 양을 현저하게 줄입니다.

9 담화에 따르면 다음 중 사실이 <u>아닌</u> 것은?

(a) 도시열섬 효과는 고층 빌딩에 의해 악화된다.
(b) 콘크리트와 아스팔트는 초목보다 더 많은 열을 흡수하는 경향이 있다.
(c) 어두운 색깔의 빌딩은 도시열섬 문제에 기여한다.
(d) 도시열섬 효과는 도시 지역 밖에서는 영향력이 거의 없다.
(e) 도시열섬 효과 때문에 폭염기간 동안의 사망이 늘어난다.

10

W Welcome to *Science Project*. Our guest today is Dr. Peter Beckman, an <u>expert</u> <u>on</u> <u>seismology</u>. What is <u>seismology</u>, Dr. Beckman?

M It's the study of earthquakes.

W Great. We have an e-mail question here about earthquakes. Becky Johansson of Smith Falls wants to know how earthquakes are <u>measured</u>.

M Well, Becky, and all of you other kids out there watching, we measure earthquakes using a scale of measurement called the Richter scale.

W I think most of us have heard of the Richter scale. How does it work?

M It's kind of complex, but basically, we take measurements of the earthquake using instruments and then apply formulas to get an intensity reading. We use a scale from 1 to 10.

W So 1 is good, and 10 is bad?

M Simply put, yes. Earthquakes measuring less than 2 on the Richter scale are not even felt by people, and they're the most frequent. There are about 8,000 of them per day around the world.

W Eight thousand a day! I'm glad they aren't felt. At what intensity do people feel the earth shake?

M Between 2 and 4 on the scale, but this occurs less frequently—around 49,000 times per year.

W That seems like more... Oh, you said per year, not day.

M Yes. Next, an earthquake between 4 and 6 on the scale causes noticeable shaking and usually minor—but sometimes a great deal of—damage. We have around 800 of these per year. After that, above 6 on the scale, the destruction can be very intense, and there will be many casualties. Thankfully, these powerful earthquakes are rare, with only about 18 occurring per year, and sometimes they are not near populated areas.

▶ seismology 지진학 Richter scale 리히터 스케일(지진의 척도. 1-10까지 있음) intensity 세기, 강도, 효력 formula (수학, 화학) 공식, 식(式) reading (청우계, 온도계 등의) 표시 도수, 기록 Simply put 간단히 말하면 minor 작은 편의; casualties (사고로 인한) 사상자 thankfully 다행히도; 고맙게도

여 〈사이언스 프로젝트〉를 시청해 주셔서 감사합니다. 오늘 초대 손님은 지진학 전문가 피터 벡크먼 박사이십니다. 지진학이 뭐지요, 베크만 박사님?

남 지진을 연구하는 것이지요.

여 좋습니다. 여기 지진에 관한 이메일 질문이 있는데요. 스미스 폴스에서 베키 요한슨 어린이가 지진이 어떻게 측정되는지를 알고 싶어 합니다.

남 음, 베키, 그리고 시청하고 있는 다른 모든 어린이 여러분, 우리는 리히터 지진계라는 측정 장치로 지진을 측정한답니다.

여 대부분 리히터 지진계에 대해서는 들어봤을 텐데요. 그건 어떻게 작동됩니까?

남 좀 복잡하지만 기본적으로 정밀 기계를 이용해 지진 측정을 하고나서 강도를 얻기 위해 공식을 석봉합니다. 적도는 1에서 10까지 있지요.

여 그럼 1은 좋고 10은 나쁜 건가요?

남 간단히 말하면 그렇습니다. 리히터 지진계로 2보다 약한 지진은 사람이 느끼지도 못합니다. 이런 지진이 가장 자주 일어나지요. 전 세계적으로 하루에 약 8천 건 발생하니까요.

여 하루에 8천 건이라고요! 느껴지지 않는 게 다행이네요. 사람은 어느 정도의 강도에서 땅이 움직인다고 느끼나요?

남 지진계로 2에서 4정도에서요. 하지만 그런 정도의 지진은 덜 자주 발생하지요. 일 년에 약 49,000건 정도로요.

여 더 많이 발생되는 것 같은데… 오, 일 년이라고 하셨지요, 하루가 아니라.

남 예. 다음으로 지진계 4와 6 사이의 지진은 뚜렷이 느껴지는 진동을 일으키는데, 대개 경미하지만 때로는 엄청난 피해를 일으킵니다. 이러한 지진은 일 년에 약 800건 정도 발생합니다. 그 다음으로 지진계 6 이상의 지진은 파괴 정도가 매우 심할 수 있어 많은 사상자가 발생할 것입니다. 다행히도 이러한 강력한 지진은 일 년에 약 18건 정도만 발생해 드문 편이고, 인구가 많은 지역 인근에서는 일어나지 않을 때도 있습니다.

---

10 일 년에 발생되는 각 강도의 지진 횟수로 표를 완성하시오.

리히터 지진계 상의 강도	연간 지진의 횟수
2 이하	2,920,000
2에서 4	49,000
4에서 6	800
6 이상	18

11-12 Level up

M A cave is a hole in the ground, in a cliff, or in a mountain, but that is a rather simple explanation. There are a variety of caves, and they are chiefly distinguished by how they were created and their physical characteristics. There are four main types of caves: solutional, sea, erosional, and glacier. Solutional caves form where there are large deposits of limestone or other soft rocks which are worn away by the acidic content of water over a long period of time. These caves can be very extensive, with some dozens of kilometers long, and they offer some of the most spectacular underground formations in the guise of large stalactites and stalagmites. The second type of cave is called a sea cave. Sea caves form along ocean coastlines and are created by wave action that wears away softer rock. These caves are usually not very large compared to other types of caves, with one that is 300 meters deep being the largest yet found. The third type of cave I mentioned is erosional. These caves can form almost anywhere and are created by the actions of water or wind wearing away the rock over many years. In deserts, the wind carries sand particles which act as a sandblaster and wear away rock to create erosional caves. The final type of cave I want to talk about is glacial caves. These are created in large ice formations—typically glaciers—and are made by melting, running water. Glacial caves are not very stable and can move and collapse as the glacier moves or melts. Exploration of any type of cave is dangerous and should only be done in a group that includes an expert.

▶ a variety of 다양한, 여러 가지의 chiefly 주로; 대개, 거의 distinguish 식별하다, 구분하다, 분류하다 solutional cave 석회암동굴 sea cave 해식동굴 erosional cave 침식동굴 glacier 빙하 limestone 석회암, 석회석 acidic content 산성 내용물 dozens of 수십의, 많은 guise 외관, 겉모양 stalactite 종유석 stalagmite 석순 sandblaster 모래 분사기

남 동굴이란 땅, 절벽 또는 산에 있는 구멍입니다. 하지만 이것은 꽤 단순한 설명입니다. 동굴에는 여러 가지가 있고, 그 동굴들은 주로 만들어진 방법과 생김새에 따라 구분됩니다. 동굴에는 석회암동굴, 침식동물, 해식동굴, 빙하 동굴, 이렇게 네 가지의 주요 유형이 있습니다. 석회암동굴은 오랜 시간 동안 물에 함유된 산성 물질에 의해 마모되는 석회암이나 다른 부드러운 바위의 퇴적물이 있는 곳에서 형성됩니다. 이 동굴은 수십 킬로미터로 규모가 매우 클 수 있으며, 큰 종유석과 석순 모양으로 가장 멋진 지하 형성물을 선사합니다. 두 번째 종류의 동굴은 해식동굴이라고 불립니다. 해식동굴은 해안선을 따라 형성되며, 더 부드러운 바위를 닳게 하는 파도의 작용에 의해 만들어집니다. 이 동굴들은 대개 다른 종류의 동굴들과 비교하면 그다지 크지 않은데, 이제껏 발견된 해식동굴 중에서 가장 큰 동굴은 깊이가 300미터가 되죠. 내가 언급한 동굴의 세 번째 종류로는 침식동굴이 있습니다. 이 동굴은 거의 모든 곳에서 형성되며 많은 세월 동안 암석을 닳게 하는 물이나 바람의 작용에 의해 만들어집니다. 사막에서는 바람이 모래입자를 운반하여 모래분사기 역할을 하게 해 암석을 마모시켜 침식동굴을 만듭니다.

내가 말하고자 하는 마지막 종류의 동굴은 빙하동굴입니다. 이것은 커다란 얼음 구성물, 즉 보통 빙하 안에서 생기는데, 녹아 흐르는 물에 의해 만들어집니다. 빙하동굴은 그다지 안정적이지 않아서 빙하가 움직이거나 녹으면 움직이고 무너질 수 있습니다. 어떠한 종류의 동굴 탐험도 위험하기 때문에 반드시 전문가가 포함된 단체에 속해서 해야 합니다.

11 왜 석회암이 동굴을 형성하는 데 이상적인 암석인가?
(a) 석회암은 닳으면서 종유석과 석순을 남긴다.
(b) 석회암으로 만들어진 동굴은 다른 동굴보다 더 깊고 길다.
(c) 석회암은 전 세계적으로 널리 분포되어 있어서 석회암으로 만들어진 동굴이 많다.
(d) 석회암은 다른 암석들보다 더 쉽게 닳는 부드러운 암석이다.
(e) 석회암은 다른 암석들보다 더 안정적이고 영구적인 동굴을 만든다.

12 다음 중 내용을 가장 잘 요약한 것을 고르시오.
(a) 동굴은 만들어진 방법, 구성물, 크기에 따라 많이 다르기에 길이가 수십 킬로미터까지 다양할 수 있다.
(b) 동굴은 대부분이 오랜 세월 동안 암석과 얼음을 부식시켜 영구적인 지하 조각물을 만드는 물의 작용을 통해 만들어진다.
(c) 동굴들은 여러 가지 방법으로 만들어지지만, 어떤 동굴에서든 탐험할 때는 주의해야 한다.

Practice Test
p. 128~p. 129

| 1 (d) | 2 (b) | 3 (a) | 4 (b) | 5 (c) | 6 (b) | 7 (d) |
| 8 해설 참조 | 9 (b) | 10 (a) | | | | |

1

W In southern Florida, there is a vast swamp in Everglades National Park, which is usually just called the Everglades. This area is mostly made up of water and grass as well as numerous types of trees. The underlying rock is mostly limestone, which allows the Everglades to absorb a great amount of water. Most of this water comes from rainfall and two major rivers that flow into the swamp. Much of the water in the Everglades is drained away for the use of local metropolitan areas. Within the Everglades swamp, there are several different types of land which support many ecosystems. Much of the area is grass-covered shallow water, with some oak tree-covered hummocks of land, much like small islands, protruding from the swamp. In addition to oak trees, pine, mangrove, and cypress trees abound in the Everglades. All support diverse wildlife, including over 300 species of birds, many of which use the Everglades as a place of migration. The Everglades swamp is also famous for its alligators and crocodiles, with tens of thousands of these creatures living in the swamp. The conservation of the ecosystems in the swamp is a big priority as human encroachment is endangering some species. For over a hundred years, developers have tried to drain the swamp and reclaim the land for human use. In addition, the Everglades is still in danger, despite its status as a national park, as demands from neighboring cities for its supply of fresh water grow year after year.

▶ **Everglades National Park** 에버글레이즈 국립공원 **swamp** 늪, 습지

underlying 밑에 있는 local metropolitan area 지방 대도시 지역 drain away (물이) 빠지다 ecosystem 생태계 oak 오크(떡갈나무. 졸참나무류의 낙엽 활엽수) hummock 작은 언덕; (부근의 늪지보다 높은) 수림지대 protrude 튀어나오다, 비어져 나오다 mangrove 홍수림 cypress 사이프러스 (편백나뭇과의 상록 침엽수) abound 풍부하다; 많이 있다 wildlife 야생 생물 migration 철따라 이주함 encroachment 침해, 침략; 잠식 endanger 위험에 빠뜨리다. 위태롭게 하다 drain 배수(방수)하다 reclaim 개간하다; 간척하다

여 플로리다 남부의 에버글레이즈 국립공원에는 흔히 그냥 에버글레이즈라고 부르는 거대한 습지가 있는데, 이 지역은 대부분 물과 풀, 그리고 수많은 종류의 나무로 이루어져 있습니다. 밑에 있는 암석은 대부분이 석회암이어서 에버글레이즈가 엄청난 양의 물을 흡수하도록 해줍니다. 이 물의 대부분은 빗물과 습지로 흐르는 두 개의 큰 강에서 나옵니다. 에버글레이즈의 많은 물은 지방 대도시 지역에서 사용되기 위해 빠져 나갑니다. 에버글레이즈 습지에는 많은 생태계를 유지하는 여러 형태의 땅이 있습니다. 그 지역의 상당 부분은 습지에서 튀어나온 작은 섬처럼 생긴, 오크 나무로 덮인 수림지대 땅과 함께 풀로 뒤덮인 얕은 물로 이루어져 있습니다. 에버글레이즈에는 오크 나무와 더불어 소나무, 홍수림, 사이프러스 나무가 풍부합니다. 이 모든 것은 300종이 넘는 새들을 포함한 다양한 야생생물이 살아가도록 해주는데, 이 새들 가운데 많은 종이 철마다 에버글레이즈를 이주지로 사용합니다. 에버글레이즈 습지는 또한 악어와 크로커다일로 유명합니다. 수만 마리가 그 습지에 서식하죠. 습지의 생태계 보존은 최우선 과제인데, 인간의 침해가 일부 종의 생존을 위태롭게 하기 때문입니다. 개발자들은 100년 넘게 습지의 물을 빼고 인간이 사용할 수 있도록 땅을 개간하기 위해 노력해왔습니다. 또한 에버글레이즈는 국립공원의 위상에도 불구하고 아직도 위험에 처해 있습니다. 이웃 도시들의 담수 수요가 해마다 늘기 때문이죠.

1 담화에 따르면 다음 중 사실이 <u>아닌</u> 것은?
(a) 나무들로 덮인 작은 섬들은 에버글레이즈 습지에 여기저기 흩어져 있다.
(b) 악어와 크로코다일은 에버글레이즈 습지에서 공생한다.
(c) 에버글레이즈 습지는 비와 하천계에서 물을 취한다.
(d) 에버글레이즈 습지의 배수는 꽤 최근에 일어나고 있는 일이다.
(e) 인간의 에버글레이즈 습지 물 사용은 해마다 늘고 있다.

2-3

M I'm going to be traveling in the Far East for about a week on business.

G Really, Dad? What countries are you going to?

M Just one: Korea. I have to go to a conference in Seoul, and I'll have a few days off to do some sightseeing.

G Do you know anything about Korea?

M I know a bit—what I need to know for my business.

G No, Dad, I mean the people and the country.

M Well, why don't you do some research and tell me all about it? I'm beat after a long day at the office.

G I'll get right on it. I'll just type in Korea... And here's a website. *Facts about Korea*. It's a peninsula. What's a peninsula?

M It's land that has water on three sides.

G Okay, I can see that on the map. Wait. They call the Sea of Japan the East Sea on this website.

M That's right. One of my colleagues told me that the Koreans call it the East Sea, and they are very sensitive about the issue.

G Okay. Oh, the country has a lot of mountains, especially on the east coast. The west is flatter and includes most of the country's farmland. The large cities are also mostly in the western part of the country.

M What about islands and beaches?

G The beaches on the east coast are the best. On the west coast, the waters are muddier. There are also hundreds of islands. The biggest is Jeju Island in the south. It's a volcanic island and it is almost tropical. So where will you go?

M ____

▶ conference 회의, 협의회 I'm beat. 난 너무 피곤해. get right on it 바로 일에 착수하다 peninsula 반도 farmland 농토, 농지, 경지 muddy 질퍽한, 진흙의; 선명치 않은, 탁한 tropical 열대성의, 열대의

남 아빠는 업무차 약 일주일 동안 극동지역으로 여행할 거야.

여 정말요, 아빠? 어느 나라들로 가시는데요?

남 한 나라만 가. 한국. 서울에서 열리는 회의에 가야 해. 그리고 며칠 휴가 내서 관광을 할 거야.

여 한국에 대해 아시는 것 있어요?

남 조금 알지. 내 업무로 알아야 할 부분 말이야.

여 아니요, 아빠. 사람들이나 나라에 관한 거 말이에요.

남 음, 네가 좀 조사해서 나에게 모두 알려주는 게 어떠니? 난 사무실에서 오랫동안 업무에 시달려서 너무 피곤하구나.

여 바로 할게요. 한국이라고만 자판에 쳐볼게요… 여기 웹사이트가 있네요. 〈한국에 대한 사실〉. 한국이 반도래요. 반도가 뭐예요?

남 3면에 바다가 있는 육지를 뜻해.

여 네, 지도를 보니 알겠네요. 잠깐만요. 이 웹사이트에서는 일본해를 동해라고 부르고 있네요.

남 맞아. 내 회사 동료 한 명이 한국인들은 그것을 동해라고 부르고, 그 문제에 매우 민감하다고 하더구나.

여 알겠어요. 오, 한국에는 산이 많네요, 특히 동해안쪽으로요. 서쪽은 더 평탄하고 전국의 농지가 대부분 여기 있어요. 그리고 대도시 또한 대부분 서쪽에 있고요.

남 섬과 해변은 어떠니?

여 동해안 해변이 최고에요. 서해안은 바다에 진흙이 많아요. 그리고 수백 개의 섬도 있어요. 가장 큰 섬은 남쪽에 있는 제주도예요. 화산섬이고 대체로 열대기후네요. 음, 어디 가실 거예요?

남 ____

2 대화에 따르면 다음 중 사실이 <u>아닌</u> 것은?
  (a) 남자의 딸은 반도가 무엇인지 알지 못했다.
  (b) 남자는 한국과 한국인에 대해 풍부한 지식을 가지고 있다.
  (c) 남자는 회사에서 일하느라 매우 피곤한 하루를 보냈다.
  (d) 남자는 한국에 있는 동안 회의에 참석할 것이다.
  (e) 남자의 회사 동료 중 한 명이 동해에 관련된 문제에 대해 얘기해 주었다.

3 딸의 마지막 말 다음에 아버지는 뭐라고 말하겠는가?
  (a) 모르겠어. 거기 가서 결정하지 뭐.
  (b) 서부에 있는 일본해나 가볼까 생각중이야.
  (c) 아무데도 안 가. 한국에서 자유시간이 전혀 없거든.
  (d) 난 수영하는 걸 좋아하니 서해안이 좋겠구나.
  (e) 제주도로 날아가서 여행 동안 계속 거기에 있을 거야.

4-5

W Around the world, there are areas of extremely flat grasslands. These grasslands go by various names, such as prairies in North America, steppes in Eurasia, savannas in Africa, and pampas in Argentina. All have similar characteristics. They are typically semiarid regions that get moderate rainfall. Trees are scarce, and most vegetation consists of grasses of various types, shrubs, and other small plants. There are few hills and no mountains, although nearby mountains can form what is called a rain shadow. The clouds drop their moisture on the mountains rather than the nearby land, which therefore creates the grasslands by preventing enough water from falling to enable the growth of trees. These grasslands are usually flat, and visibility extends for long distances. Agriculture in these regions can be productive if enough rain falls or there is a source of irrigation. However, in extended periods of drought, the grass and crops die, the topsoil is blown away, and agriculture is devastated. An extended period of drought in the 1930s in the North American prairies produced the disaster known as the Dust Bowl, in which millions of acres of land turned to dust. Even the use of grasslands for raising livestock can result in problems as the livestock grazing on the grasses can deplete them and reduce their soil-holding capacity. Australia's small area of grasslands experienced such a problem with both unwanted rabbits and sheep herds.

▶ grassland 목초지, 초원 prairie (미시시피 강 유역의) 대초원, 프레리 the Steppes (유럽 남동부, 아시아 남서부 등의) 대초원 지대, 스텝 savanna 사바나 (열대 지방 등의 나무 없는 대평원) pampas (남미, 특히 아르헨티나의 나무 없는) 대초원, 팜파스 semiarid 반건조한, 비가 매우 적은 (지대, 기후) moderate 적당한, 알맞은 scarce 적은, 모자라는 shrub 관목 rain shadow 비그늘, 산으로 막혀 강수량이 적은 지역 visibility 시야; 가시도 irrigation 관개, 물을 끌어들임 productive 생산적인, 생산력을 가진 drought 가뭄 devastate 황폐시키다; 철저하게 파괴하다 Dust Bowl (1930년대 황진 피해를 입은) 미국 중남부의 건조 평원 지대; 〈소문자로 시작하면〉 (모래 폭풍이 부는) 황진 지대 graze (가축이) 풀이 뜯어 먹다, 목장에서 풀을 먹다 deplete 고갈시키다; 격감시키다 sheep herd 양떼

여 전 세계에는 아주 평평한 초원지역이 있습니다. 초원은 북미의 프레리, 유라시아의 스텝스, 아프리카의 사바나, 아르헨티나의 팜파스와 같이 여러 가지 이름으로 불립니다. 모든 대초원은 비슷한 특징을 가지고 있습니다. 대초원들은 대개 적당한 비가 내리는 반건조한 지대입니다. 나무는 드물고 대부분의 초목은 다양한 종류의 풀, 관목, 그리고 다른 작은 식물들로 이루어져 있습니다. 비록 근처 산들이 비그늘이라고 불리는 것을 형성할 수는 있지만 언덕이 거의 없고 산도 없습니다. 구름은 그 근처 땅보다는 산에 비를 내리기 때문에 나무가 클 수 있을 정도의 비가 땅에 내리지 못해 초원이 형성됩니다. 이 초원은 대개 평평해서 먼 거리까지 볼 수 있습니다. 만약 충분한 비가 내리거나 관개를 할 수 있는 수원(水原)이 있다면 이 지역의 농사는 생산적일 수 있습니다. 하지만 가뭄이 오래 지속되는 기간에는 풀과 농작물이 죽고 표토가 날아가서 농사를 완전히 망치게 됩니다. 1930년대 북미 프레리의 오랜 가뭄은 수백 만 에이커의 땅을 먼지로 만든 '더스트 보울'이라고 알려진 재해를 일으켰습니다. 초원을 가축 기르는 용도로 사용하는 것도 문제를 일으킬 수 있는데, 이는 가축이 풀을 뜯어 먹어 풀이 고갈되므로 풀의 토양 수용 용량도 감소하기 때문입니다. 호주의 작은 초원에서 원치 않는 토끼와 양 떼로 그러한 문제가 일어난 적이 있습니다.

4 왜 초원 지역에서 농사를 지으면 생계가 불확실하겠는가?
  (a) 가축이 풀을 너무 많이 뜯어 먹어 표토가 파괴될 수 있어서
  (b) 매년 물 공급량이 매우 불확실하기 때문에
  (c) 폭풍에서 비롯된 바람이 매우 중요한 표토를 많이 날려버리기 때문에
  (d) 산 때문에 과수가 큰 나무로 자라지 못할 수 있기 때문에
  (e) 땅이 너무 평평해서 침식으로부터 농작물을 보호할 수 없기 때문에

5 담화에서 유추할 수 있는 것은?
  (a) 평평한 초원이 생기려면 근처에 산이 있어야 한다.
  (b) 호주 사람들은 가축떼처럼 토끼를 키우고 있었다.
  (c) 초원 지역에서 땔감을 찾기는 어려울 것이다.
  (d) 황진 지대는 너무 많은 땅이 경작된 것에서 비롯되었다.
  (e) 초원에는 대개 가장 생산적인 농지가 있다.

G Here's a fun quiz. When I say the word "desert," what do you think of?

B Sand dunes.

G Good answer. "Sand dunes" is the most common answer. Okay, smart guy, let's see if you can guess which type of sand dune I am talking about.

B Hit me with your best shot.

G This type of sand dune is from 2 meters to 40 meters high and is up to 400 meters long.

B A lot of them are very high and are very long.

G Okay, it has one side that is gentle and sloping and faces the wind, while the other side is steep and faces away from the wind.

B No, that could be a couple of types. What's the next clue?

G It's crescent-shaped.

B I got it. It's a barchan dune.

G That's right!

B I bet the next clue is that it has extended features that look like horns on an animal. And then, it says like all sand dunes, barchan dunes move with the wind and what was there one day may be gone the next.

G That's also right!

B I know. I took the quiz before!

▶ sand dune 사구(砂丘), 모래 언덕   gentle (경사, 흐름 등이) 완만한   slope 비탈, 사면; 경사   steep 가파른, 경사가 급한   crescent 초승달   barchan dune 바르한 모래 언덕   extended 쭉 뻗은, 내민   feature 용모, 얼굴 생김새

여 여기 재미있는 퀴즈가 있어. 내가 '사막'이라는 단어를 말하면, 너는 뭐가 생각나니?

남 모래 언덕.

여 좋은 답이야. '모래 언덕'이 가장 흔한 답이지. 좋아, 똑똑한 친구, 내가 어떤 종류의 모래 언덕에 대해 말하는지 알아맞힐 수 있나 보자.

남 한번 해봐.

여 이 종류의 모래 언덕은 높이가 2미터에서 40미터이고 길이가 400미터에 달하지.

남 많은 모래 언덕들이 다 크고 길어.

여 알았어, 한 쪽은 완만한 비탈이고 바람을 받는 쪽인 반면, 다른 한 쪽은 경사가 급하고 바람을 받지 않아.

남 안 돼, 그런 종류가 두 서너 개 있을 수 있어. 다음 단서는 뭐야?

여 초승달 모양이지.

남 알겠다. 그건 바르한 모래 언덕이야.

여 맞았어!

남 다음 단서는 동물의 뿔 같이 보이는 쭉 뻗은 생김새를 가지고 있다는 거였겠지. 그리고 모든 모래 언덕과 같이 바르한 모래 언덕도 바람과 함께 움직여서 어느 날에는 있었던 것이 그 다음 날에는 없어진다고 하지.

여 그것도 맞아!

남 알아. 그 문제 전에 풀었었어!

6 What distinguishes a barchan sand dune from other sand dunes?   바르한 모래 언덕은 다른 모래 언덕과 어떻게 구별되는가?

(a) Its gentle rising slope facing the wind
바람을 받는 쪽의 완만히 상승하는 경사

(b) Its extended features that are called horns
뿔이라 불리는 쭉 뻗은 생김새

(c) Its steep side facing away from the wind
바람을 받지 않는 쪽의 가파른 면

(d) Its height, which can be up to 40 meters
40미터에 이를 수 있는 높이

(e) Its movement across the desert with the wind
바람과 함께 사막을 가로지르는 움직임

M A fjord is a deep inlet of the sea that can extend hundreds of kilometers inland and has very steep sides. They are typically found in the extreme northern and southern latitudes. Scandinavia, Greenland, the Labrador coast of Canada, the many Arctic islands, the Kola Peninsula in Russia, Alaska, Chile, and New Zealand all have fjords. The longest fjord is in Greenland and is 320 kilometers long. Fjords were formed by glacial activity, with most of the present-day fjords having been formed in the last ice age. As the glaciers pushed through the hard rock, they left steep sides and deep channels. At the end of the glacier, rocky debris built up, which has resulted in a shallower depth where the fjord meets the open ocean. This shallow depth at the mouth of the fjord results in very strong currents as the tides change twice daily. While most fjords are navigable for most of their length, these strong currents call for caution.

▶ fjord 피오르드(높은 절벽 사이에 깊숙이 들어간 협만)   inlet 후미: 입구, 들이는 곳   latitude 위도   Labrador 래브라도 반도[지방](북미 허드슨 만과 대서양 사이에 있는 반도)   Arctic 북극의   push through 뚫고 나가다   rocky debris 암석 부스러기   current 해류; 기류, 조류   navigable 선박이 지나갈 수 있는, (하천, 바다 등이) 항행할 수 있는   call for action 조치가 필요하다

남 피오르드는 내륙으로 향한 수백 킬로미터에 달하는 바다의 깊은 입구로 매우 가파른 면을 지니고 있습니다. 피오르드는 대개 최북단과 최남단 위도에서 발견됩니다. 스칸디나비아, 그린란드, 캐나다 래브라도 해안, 많은 북극 섬들, 러시아의 콜라 반도, 알라스카, 칠레, 뉴질랜드에 모두 피오르드가 있습니다. 가장 긴 피오르드는 그린란드에 있으며 길이가 320킬로미터입니다. 피오르드는 빙하 활동에 의해 형성되었으며 오늘날의 피오르드 대부분은 마지막 빙하시대에 형성되었습니다. 빙하는 딱딱한 암석을 뚫고 나가면서 가파른 면과 깊은 해협을 남겼습니다. 빙하의 끝에는 암석 부스러기가 쌓여 피오르드가 트인 바다와 만나는 곳의 깊이를 얕게 만들었습니다. 피오르드 입구의 이 얕은 깊이는 조수가 하루에 두 번 바뀔 때 매우 강한 해류를 생성합니다. 대부분의 피오르드에서 선박이 지나갈 수 있는 반면, 이 강한 해류는 주의를 요합니다.

7 What is true according to the talk?
담화에 따르면 다음 중 사실인 것은?

(a) Fjords were formed when the Earth was first created.
피오르드는 지구가 처음 생성되었을 때 형성되었다.

(b) There are no dangers to ships navigating a fjord.
선박들이 피오르드를 지나가는 데는 위험이 없다.

(c) The longest fjord is found in northern Scandinavia.
가장 긴 피오르드는 스칸디나비아 북부에 있다.

(d) Fjords formed in the Northern and Southern hemispheres.
피오르드는 북반구와 남반구에서 형성되었다.

(e) Most fjords tend to be shallow with gently sloping sides.
대부분의 피오르드는 완만한 경사면에서 얕은 경향이 있다.

8

W Without the atmosphere that surrounds the Earth, life would not be possible. Not only do humans and many other life forms breathe the oxygen in the atmosphere, but they are also protected from deadly ultraviolet rays of the sun by the atmosphere. The atmosphere also helps to keep the Earth warm by maintaining the heat that the planet receives from the sun. The atmosphere has five main layers. They are, from near the surface to outer space, the troposphere, the stratosphere, the mesosphere, the thermosphere, and the exosphere. The troposphere is the lowest level. It starts from the surface of the Earth and rises to about 7 to 20 kilometers. It is thinner at the poles and thicker at the Equator. The stratosphere extends from the troposphere to about 50 kilometers above the Earth's surface. This region is vital since it contains the bulk of the ozone layer that protects the Earth from ultraviolet radiation. Next is the mesosphere, which extends to about 85 kilometers above the Earth's surface. Extreme cold can be felt in this layer since the temperature can be as low as minus 100 degrees Celsius. After this layer is the thermosphere, which is about 600 kilometers thick. Temperatures rise dramatically in the thermosphere since there is very little of the atmosphere left to block the sun's radiation and heat. Finally, there is the exosphere, which extends from the end of the thermosphere out to about 10,000 kilometers from the surface of the Earth. There is nothing remaining of the atmosphere at this point.

▶ atmosphere 대기; 공기 ultraviolet ray 자외선 outer space (대기권 외) 우주 공간 troposphere 대류권 stratosphere 성층권 mesosphere 중간층(권) thermosphere 열권, 온도권 exosphere 외기권 pole 극, 극지 equator 적도 radiation 방사, 복사; 방열(放熱); 복사 에너지

여 지구 주위를 둘러싸는 대기가 없다면 생명체는 존재할 수 없습니다. 인간과 많은 다른 생명체들은 대기에 있는 산소로 호흡할 뿐만 아니라 대기 덕분에 태양에서 나오는 치명적인 자외선으로부터 보호받습니다. 대기는 또한 태양으로부터 행성이 받는 열을 유지함으로써 지구를 따뜻하게 유지하는 데 도움을 줍니다. 대기에는 5개의 주요 층이 있습니다. 5개의 주요 층에는 지구 표면에서부터 우주 공간까지 대류권, 성층권, 중간권, 열권, 외기권이 있습니다. 대류권은 가장 낮은 층입니다. 대류권은 지구 표면에서부터 약 7에서 20킬로미터까지 올라갑니다. 대류권은 극지에서는 더 얇고 적도에서는 더 두껍습니다. 성층권은 대류권에서 지구 표면 위로 약 50킬로미터까지 이릅니다. 이 지대는 지구를 자외선 방사로부터 보호하는 오존층을 함유하고 있기 때문에 매우 중요합니다. 다음은 중간권입니다. 지구 표면 위로 약 85킬로미터까지 미칩니다. 이 층에서는 온도가 영하 100도까지 내려갈 수 있기 때문에 극한의 추위를 느낄 수 있습니다. 이 층 다음에는 열권이 있습니다. 약 600킬로미터 두께죠. 열권에는 태양의 방열을 막을 대기가 거의 없기 때문에 온도가 엄청나게 올라갑니다. 마지막으로 외기권이 있는데, 열권 말단에서 지구표면으로부터 약 1만 킬로미터까지 미칩니다. 이 지점에는 대기가 전혀 남아 있지 않습니다.

8 지구 대기층에 대한 정보로 표를 완성하시오.

층	시작	끝
대류권	0 km / Earth's surface (지구 표면)	7~20킬로미터
성층권	7~20 km	50킬로미터
중간권	50 km	85 km
열권	85킬로미터	685 km
외기권	685킬로미터	10,000 km

Reading

▶ cartography 지도 제작(법) layout 레이아웃; 배치(도), 설계(법) geography 지리, 지형, 지세 Mercator projection 메르카토르(식 투영) 도법 cartographer 지도 제작자 two dimensions 평면, 2차원 mathematical formula 수학 공식 latitude 위도 longitude 경도 unrolled cylinder 펴진 원통 sphere 구(球); 구형 distortion 왜곡, 곡해 correspondingly 상응하게, 유사하게

지도 제작법은 대개 평평한 표면에 지구의 특징을 나타내는 지도를 만드는 기술입니다. 많은 종류의 지도가 있지만 가장 보편적인 종류는 자치시나 도시의 배치, 지역이나 나라의 지형 또는 세계의 대륙과 섬의 위치를 보여주는 것입니다. 보편적인 세계 지도를 메르카토르 도법이라고 부릅니다. 네덜란드 지도 제작자 헤르하르뒤스 메르카토르가 1569년에 이 지도를 만들었습니다. 메르카도르 지도와 다른 많은 지도의 문제점은 지구를 정사각형이나 직사각형 종이에 평면적으로 보여주려 한다는 것입니다. 하지만 지구는 굴곡이 있고 극지에서는 좁아지므로 평평하지 않습니다. 이 문제를 해결하기 위해 메르카토르는 직사각형 종이에 지도를 맞추고 동시에 친숙한 작은 땅 형태를 유지하면서 지도에 위도와 경도선을 줄 수 있도록 수학 공식을 사용했습니다. 아쉽게도 이 지도는 판판하게 펴져 있기 때문에 전 세계가 구형이 아니고 펴진 원통형과 같아 약간의 왜곡이 있습니다. 특히 북반구는 실제보다 더 크게 보여서 그에 상응해 남아메리카, 아프리카, 호주 같은 대륙은 실제보다 더 작게 보입니다.

M Okay, everyone, let's look at this Mercator projection map I have up here on the screen. Notice the way that the Northern Hemisphere seems larger than the Southern Hemisphere? This is a distortion and is typical of Mercator projection maps, although they are not alone in this regard. Mercator projection maps have been in use for over 400 years since their creation by Dutchman Gerardus Mercator in 1569. So why hasn't anyone come up with something better? First, Mercator projection maps were popular because of the straight lines on them, which sea navigators preferred. Second, the distortions are mainly above 70 degrees north latitude and below 70 degrees south latitude. Since few people live in these regions and they are rarely traveled, there was little incentive to change the map. Nowadays, however, one of the big complaints about the Mercator projection is that it shows the northern continents and land masses as being bigger than the southern ones. For example, look at Greenland. It seems bigger than South America and Africa, but, of course, it isn't. Africa is ten times bigger and is the second largest continent while South America is six times bigger than Greenland. But you wouldn't know that just by looking at a Mercator projection map, would you? Some people have taken exception to these distortions since they seem to imply that the southern continents are not as significant as the northern ones. They claim a more suitable map is a sinusoidal projection. Here... this type of map has a more spherical shape, is pointed at the two poles, and is more rounded at the Equator. You can see the proportions of the continents more closely resemble the reality of the world's geography.

▶ in this regard 이 점에 관해서는 come up with 생각나다, 떠오르다; 발견하다 sea navigator 해양 항해자 incentive 동기, 자극 imply 함축하다; 의미하다 take exception 이의를 제기하다 sinusoidal projection 상송 도법, 정현(正弦) 곡선 도법 spherical shape 구형(球形) pointed 뾰족한 proportion 비율, 비

남 좋습니다, 여러분, 내가 여기 스크린에 올려놓은 메르카토르 도법 지도를 보십시오. 북반구가 남반부보다 커 보이는 것을 눈치챘나요? 이것이 왜곡이고, 메르카

토르 도법의 전형적인 문제입니다. 비록 이 점에 있어서는 이 지도들만 그런 건 아니지만 말이죠. 메르카토르 도법 지도는 네덜란드인 헤르하르뒤스 메르카토르에 의해 1569년에 만들어진 이래로 400년 넘게 사용되고 있습니다. 그런데 왜 다른 사람이 더 나은 것을 만들어내지 않았을까요? 첫 번째 이유는 메르카토르 도법 지도는 직선이 있기 때문에 유명했는데, 그래서 해양 항해사들이 선호했지요. 두 번째로는 왜곡이 주로 북위 70도 위와 남위 70도 아래에 있기 때문입니다. 이 지역에는 사람들이 거의 살지 않고 그곳을 다닐 일도 드물었기 때문에 지도를 변경할 필요성이 별로 없었습니다. 하지만 요즘에는 메르카토르 도법에 대한 가장 큰 불만 중의 하나가 북부 대륙과 토지가 남부의 것들보다 크게 보인다는 것입니다. 예를 들면, 그린란드를 보세요. 남미와 아프리카보다 더 커보이죠. 하지만 물론 그렇진 않습니다. 아프리카가 10배 더 큰 데다가 두 번째로 큰 대륙인 한편, 남아메리카는 그린란드보다 6배 더 큽니다. 하지만 메르카토르 도법 지도만 봐서는 그걸 알 수 없죠, 그렇죠? 어떤 사람들은 남쪽 대륙이 북쪽 대륙만큼 중요하지 않다고 암시하는 것 같아 이 왜곡에 이의를 제기합니다. 그들은 더 적합한 지도가 상송 도법이라고 주장합니다. 여기 이런 종류의 지도는 좀 더 구형(球形)이고 양극이 뾰족하고 적도에서 좀 더 둥글어집니다. 대륙들의 비율이 실제 세계 지형과 더 닮았다는 것을 볼 수 있죠.

9 읽기와 듣기 지문에 따르면 다음 중 사실이 <u>아닌</u> 것은?
(a) 메르카토르 도법 지도는 한때 해양 항해자에게 인기가 있었다.
(b) 메르카토르 도법 지도는 17세기에 처음 만들어졌다.
(c) 메르카토르 도법보다 더 실제와 비슷한 지도들이 있다.
(d) 모든 사람이 메르카토르 도법 지도 사용에 찬성하는 것은 아니다.
(e) 메르카토르 도법 지도에서는 극북과 극남 지역이 더 커보인다.

10 읽기와 듣기 지문에서 유추할 수 있는 것은?
(a) 메르카토르 도법 지도만이 왜곡을 보이는 유일한 지도는 아니다.
(b) 네덜란드 사람들은 메르카토르 생전에 항해술로 유명했다.
(c) 남아메리카 사람들은 그린란드가 더 작은 땅이라고 불평했다.
(d) 항해사들은 더 이상 항해에 메르카토르 도법 지도를 사용하지 않는다.
(e) 메르카토르 도법 지도는 전부 상송 지도로 교체되었다.

*Dictation 정답: Exercise 스크립트 밑줄 참조

UNIT 10 International Relations

Preparation
p. 135

Vocabulary Preview

A

1 **brinkmanship**: 유리한 입장에 서기 위해 상대방을 위협하는 기술
2 **deterrence**: 종종 무기나 처벌로 위협함으로써 어떤 일을 방지하는 것
3 **petition**: 권한이 있는 사람에게 공식적으로 요청하다
4 **exacerbate**: 어떤 것을 이전보다 더 나쁜 상태로 만들다
5 **isolationism**: 국가에 직접적으로 영향을 미치지 않는 외교 문제에 관해서 관여하지 않는 정책

B

1 **negotiation** / 양측의 완고한 입장 때문에 평화 조약 협상은 어려움에 빠졌다.
2 **retaliation** / 대개의 경우 보복에 대한 두려움 때문에 한 국가가 다른 국가를 공격하지 않을 것이다.
3 **In hindsight** / 지나고 보니 제2차 세계대전이 일어나기 전에 영국과 프랑스가 히틀러를 저지할 수 있었다는 것이 분명히 드러난다.

4 **conflict** / 역사상 가장 큰 싸움은 제2차 세계대전이었으며 그 기간 동안 6천만 명 이상이 죽었다.
5 **occupation** / 일본의 한국 점령은 양국 관계에서 여전히 민감한 사항이다.
6 **neutral** / 스위스와 스웨덴을 포함한 몇몇 유럽 국가들은 제1, 2차 세계대전 동안 중립을 택해 양측 어디에도 가담하지 않았다.
7 **treaty** / 몇 주 후에 조약이 협상되고 교전국들이 서명했다.

Expressions and Meanings

1 바로 그거야.
2 그게 어때서 야단인지 모르겠네.
3 그 생각만 하면 화가 치밀어.
4 좀 자세히 말해줄래?
5 누구도 그를 저지할 만한 배짱은 없었다.
6 너 헛수고 하고 있어.
7 그건 자존심이 걸린 문제야.

ⓓ 맞아.
ⓖ 그게 왜 문제라는 거지?
ⓐ 그것 때문에 정말 화가 나.
ⓕ 그것에 대해 좀 더 말해줘.
ⓑ 누구도 그를 저지하기 위해 뭔가를 할 만한 용기는 없었다.
ⓒ 그건 시간 낭비일 뿐이야.
ⓔ 그건 내 자긍심을 위해 중요해.

Listening Drill 1
p. 136~p. 137

Monolog

O (1) 1918 (2) assassination (3) heir (4) throne (5) investigators (6) treaties (7) Russia (8) France (9) Britain (10) Russia (11) Germany (12) neutral (13) Britain
G 1 (b) 2 (a)
S (1) T (2) F (3) F (4) T

M World War I started in 1914, mainly as the result of an assassination that unleashed the intricacies of a system of treaties. In 1914, Europe was a powder keg of tensions and was ready to explode at the first sign of trouble. That spark came on June 28, 1914, when the heir to the Austro-Hungarian throne, Franz Ferdinand, was assassinated in Sarajevo. The Austro-Hungarians blamed Serbia for supporting the attackers and demanded that Austro-Hungarian investigators be allowed into Serbia to conduct their own investigation. The Serbs refused and turned to Russia for support in case of war. Then, a series of treaties came into effect. The Austro-Hungarians had a treaty with Germany, and the Russians had a treaty with France. These treaties stated that all of the parties agreed to help the other in case of war. In addition, Britain had an understanding with France and Russia to support them in case of war. As events began to unfold, the German military plan called for the German army to strike first and to strike fast, before France and Russia could mobilize their armies. Germany felt it could not change this plan and had to unleash its war machine on France first. But to do so, its armies had to march through neutral Belgium. This enraged the British, so they declared war on Germany. By August 4, all of the major powers were at war, and the fighting did not end until November 11, 1918.

▶ **assassination** 암살 **unleash** 자유롭게 하다, (감정 따위를) 폭발시키다

intricacy 복잡함, 복잡하게 얽힌 일 treaty 조약 powder keg 화약통 heir 후계자, 계승자; 상속인 *cf.* an heir to the throne 왕위 계승자 investigator 조사관; 수사관 come into effect 효력을 나타내다; 실시되다 understanding 협정, 합의 unfold 전개되다 mobilize 동원하다; 결집하다 war machine 군수 neutral 중립(국)의 enrage 격분하게 하다

남 제1차 세계대전은 복잡하게 얽힌 조약 체제를 뒤흔든 한 건의 암살 사건 때문에 1914년에 일어났습니다. 1914년, 유럽은 긴장으로 가득 찬 화약고였으며 문제의 징후가 보이기만 하면 폭발할 준비가 되어 있었죠. 1914년 6월 28일 오스트리아 – 헝가리 제국의 왕위 계승자인 프란츠 페르디난드가 사라예보에서 암살된 사건이 그 발단이 되었습니다. 오스트리아 – 헝가리 제국은 세르비아가 그 암살자들을 도왔다고 비난하면서 자체 조사를 할 수 있게 오스트리아 – 헝가리 제국 조사단의 세르비아 입국을 허용해줄 것을 요구했습니다. 세르비아는 이를 거절하고 전쟁이 일어날 경우를 대비해 러시아에 지원을 요청했습니다. 그러자 일련의 조약들이 발효되었습니다. 오스트리아 – 헝가리 제국은 독일과, 러시아는 프랑스와 조약을 맺고 있었습니다. 이 조약들에는 전쟁이 날 경우 모든 동맹국이 다른 동맹국을 돕기로 합의한 내용이 담겨 있었습니다. 게다가 전쟁이 나면 영국은 프랑스와 러시아를 돕기로 협약되어 있었죠. 개전되자 독일군은 프랑스와 러시아가 군대를 동원하기 전에 선제공격을 가하면서 재빠르게 공격하기로 했습니다. 이 계획은 수정할 수 없는 것이었기에 독일군은 먼저 프랑스를 공격해야만 했습니다. 하지만 그러려면 독일군은 중립국인 벨기에를 통과해야 했죠. 이에 격분한 영국은 독일에 선전포고를 했습니다. 8월 4일까지 주요 열강은 모두 전쟁에 휘말렸고 전투는 1918년 11월 11일에야 비로소 끝이 났습니다.

General Questions

1 담화의 주목적은 무엇인가?

(a) 제1차 세계대전의 초기 전투에 관해 묘사하려고
(b) 제1차 세계대전 배후에 있는 여러 요인에 관해 알아보려고
(c) 프란츠 페르디난드의 암살에 관해 이야기하려고
(d) 독일군의 전략에 대해 살펴보려고

2 다음 중 가장 잘 요약된 것을 고르시오.

(a) 유럽의 강대국들은 1914년 전쟁으로 이어진 일련의 사건들을 촉발시킨 한 건의 암살 사건으로 인해 전쟁에 뛰어들게 되었다.
(b) 프란츠 페르디난드의 암살은 1914년 여러 나라를 전쟁에 돌입하게 만든 단 하나의 원인이다.

Specific Questions

다시 듣고 옳은 문장에는 T, 틀린 문장에는 F를 쓰시오.

(1) 프란츠 페르디난드는 오스트리아 – 헝가리 제국의 왕위 계승자였다.
(2) 독일은 오스트리아 – 헝가리 제국이 러시아와 싸우는 것을 돕기를 거부했다.
(3) 러시아와 영국은 강력한 상호 방위 조약을 맺고 있었다.
(4) 벨기에의 중립성이 침해되자 영국은 전쟁에 참여하게 되었다.

Dialog

Ⓝ (1) islets (2) oil (3) gas (4) fish (5) Korea (6) police
(7) scientific groups (8) Japan (9) Koreans
Ⓖ 1 (c) 2 (a)
Ⓢ (1) F (2) F (3) T (4) T

B What's all this I heard about Dokdo Island?

G What do you know already?

B Just that there are two small islets in the East Sea that are disputed by Japan and Korea.

G That about sums it up. The island belongs to Korea, but the Japanese are making a claim for it based on the time when they occupied Korea.

B I don't understand what all the fuss is about. I mean, they are just two small rocky islets not worth very much.

G That's where you're wrong. They may have valuable oil and gas reserves underneath them. There are also plenty of fish in the sea nearby the island, so it is important.

B Does anyone live there?

G Currently, there is one Korean fisherman and his wife there as well as plenty of Korean police, military, and some scientific groups.

B So Korea owns the island now?

G Yes. But the Japanese keep saying it is theirs when it is not. There is a lot of pride at stake in this issue, you know.

B I can understand it is because of the past Japanese occupation of Korea.

G That's right. We Koreans have some very strong feelings about that issue. We have tried to make friends with the Japanese, but they are very stubborn and won't admit they made mistakes. Now this Dokdo Island issue just makes my blood boil.

▶ islet 작은 섬 That about sums it up. 요약하면 그래. 그거야. fuss 야단법석, 언쟁, 싸움 reserve 매장량 at stake 걸린, 관련이 된 occupation 점령 stubborn 완고한, 고집이 센 make someone's blood boil 격분시키다

남 도대체 내가 들은 독도 문제라는 게 다 뭐야?

여 네가 이미 알고 있는 건 뭔데?

남 동해에 있는 작은 섬 두 개를 두고 일본과 한국이 다투고 있다는 정도?

여 그거야. 그 섬은 한국 영토인데 일본이 한때 한국을 점령했던 때를 근거로 자기네 거라고 주장하고 있는 거지.

남 뭣 때문에 이 난리법석인지 이해가 안 돼. 내 말은, 그냥 별 가치도 없는 두 개의 작은 돌투성이 섬일 뿐이잖아.

여 그게 네가 잘못 알고 있는 거야. 섬 밑에 귀중한 석유와 천연가스가 매장되어 있을지도 모르거든. 또 그 부근 바닷속에는 물고기도 풍부하기 때문에 그 섬이 중요한 거야.

남 거기에 누가 사니?

여 현재는 어부 한 사람과 그의 아내가 있어. 그뿐만 아니라 많은 한국 경찰과 군인도 있고 과학자들도 몇 명 있지.

남 그러니까 지금은 한국이 그 섬을 소유하고 있다는 거지?

여 응. 하지만 일본인들은 그렇지 않은데도 자꾸 자기네 거라고 하고 있어. 너도 알다시피 이건 엄청난 자존심이 걸린 문제야.

남 그건 옛날에 일본이 한국을 점령했었기 때문에 그런 것 같아.

여 맞아. 우리 한국 사람들은 그 문제에 관해선 격렬한 감정을 가지고 있어. 우린 일본인과 친구가 되기 위해 노력하는데 그들은 정말 완고한 데다 자기들이 잘못했다는 것을 인정하려 하질 않아. 독도 문제 때문에 진짜 열 받는다니깐.

General Questions

1 대화의 주제는 무엇인가?

(a) 독도의 천연자원
(b) 독도가 한국 영토인 몇 가지 이유
(c) 한국과 일본 간의 영토 분쟁
(d) 독도 거주민들과 그들의 직업

2 다음 중 가장 잘 요약된 것을 고르시오.

(a) 독도에 대한 한국의 실질적인 영유권에도 불구하고 일본은 아직도 그 섬에 대한 영유권을 주장하고 있는데 그것이 한국인들을 화나게 하고 있다.
(b) 독도 영유권에 관한 문제는 과거 일본의 한국 강점과 얽혀 국가적 자존심과 관련된 문제이다.

Specific Questions

다시 듣고 옳은 문장에는 T, 틀린 문장에는 F를 쓰시오.
(1) 독도 부근에는 가스와 석유자원이 있을 수 있다.
(2) 독도에는 공무원들만 산다.
(3) 일본은 그들의 주장을 철회하기를 완강하게 거부하고 있다.
(4) 소년은 처음에는 독도가 아무 가치도 없다고 생각한다.

Listening Drill 2　　　　p. 138~p. 139

Long Lecture

(1) democracy　(2) communism　(3) 1991　(4) power vacuum　(5) strongest　(6) weakened　(7) buffer zone　(8) Eastern　(9) western　(10) eastern　(11) flash points　(12) nuclear arsenals　(13) economically

1 (a)　　**2** (a)　　**3** (1) T　(2) F　(3) T　(4) T　　**4** (b)

Dictation 정답: 스크립트 밑줄 참조

W　The Cold War was a long <u>struggle</u> between the <u>ideology</u> <u>of</u> <u>democracy</u> and the <u>ideology</u> <u>of</u> <u>communism</u> that lasted from 1946 until 1991. At the <u>center</u> <u>of</u> the Cold War was the ever-present <u>tension</u> between the United States on the side of democracy and the Soviet Union on the side of communism. The Cold War began as World War II <u>was</u> <u>ending</u>. Following the war, a <u>power</u> <u>vacuum</u> <u>existed</u> in Europe, and the <u>strongest</u> <u>nations</u> were the United States and the Soviet Union. France and Britain <u>were</u> <u>weakened</u> by the war, and Germany and Italy <u>were</u> <u>defeated</u> and <u>occupied</u>. Germany <u>was</u> <u>divided</u> <u>by</u> the <u>victorious</u> Allies at the end of the war, and the <u>four</u> <u>main</u> <u>victors</u>—America, Britain, France, and the Soviet Union—each occupied a section of the country. During the war, the Soviets had <u>suffered</u> <u>great</u> <u>devastation</u> and <u>loss</u> <u>of</u> <u>life</u>. To prevent this from happening again in the future, they <u>built</u> a <u>buffer</u> <u>zone</u> of <u>communist</u> <u>states</u> in Eastern Europe. In addition, in their zone of Germany, the Soviets <u>set</u> <u>up</u> a <u>communist</u> <u>government</u>. Soon, Europe was divided into the <u>democratic</u> <u>western</u> <u>states</u> supported by America, and the communist eastern states supported by the Soviet Union. From this beginning, the Cold War <u>grew</u> <u>and</u> <u>spread</u> around the world. <u>Flash</u> <u>points</u> were the city of Berlin, China, Korea, Vietnam, Afghanistan, and many smaller places. Each side built <u>massive</u> <u>nuclear</u> <u>arsenals</u> and <u>huge</u> <u>military</u> <u>forces</u> that had the potential to go to war in a very short time. In the end, the Soviets could not <u>compete</u> <u>economically</u>, and the whole communist system came to an end by 1991.

▶ ever-present 항상 존재하는　power vacuum 권력 부재, 힘의 공백　victorious 승리를 거둔, 승리의　ally 동맹국 *cf.* the Allies 세계대전 중의 연합국　devastation 유린, 황폐　buffer zone 완충 지대　flash point 일촉즉발의 위기 (지역); 발화점　arsenal 무기고　military force 병력, 군력

여　냉전은 1946년에 시작해 1991년까지 지속된 민주주의와 공산주의 이념 간의 오랜 투쟁이었습니다. 민주주의 진영의 미국과 공산주의 진영의 소련 간에 늘상 존재했던 긴장이 냉전의 중심에 있었습니다. 냉전은 제2차 세계대전이 끝나면서 시작되었습니다. 전쟁이 끝난 뒤 유럽에는 권력의 공백이 생겼고, 가장 강한 국가는 미국과 소련이었습니다. 프랑스와 영국은 전쟁으로 약해졌고 독일과 이탈리아는 전쟁에 패해 점령당했습니다. 독일은 종전 후 승리한 연합국에 의해 분할되었고, 주요 4개 전승국인 미국, 영국, 프랑스, 소련이 각각 한 구역씩 차지했습니다. 전쟁 중에 소련은 거의 초토화되었으며 엄청난 인명 손실을 입었죠. 미래에 이런 일이 또다시 일어나는 것을 방지하기 위해 소련은 동유럽에 공산국가들로 완충 지대를 만들었습니다. 소련은 아울러 자신들이 점령한 독일 지역에 공산 정권을 세웠습니다. 머지않아 유럽은 미국이 지원하는 민주주의 서유럽 국가와 소련이 지원하는 공산주의 동유럽 국가들로 나뉘게 되었습니다. 이를 시작으로 냉전이 무르익으면서 전 세계로 퍼져나갔습니다. 첨예하게 위기감이 감돌았던 곳은 베를린과 중국, 한국, 베트남, 아프가니스탄, 그리고 그보다 작은 여러 지역이었습니다. 각 진영은 대규모의 핵무기고와 단시간 내에 전쟁에 투입할 수 있는 대규모 병력을 구축했습니다. 마침내 소련이 경제적으로 경쟁할 수 없게 되자 1991년 공산주의 체제는 모두 종말을 맞게 되었습니다.

1 강의의 목적은 무엇인가?
　(a) 국제적인 긴장이 감돌았던 시기를 설명하려고
　(b) 냉전의 원인을 살펴보려고
　(c) 공산주의가 냉전에서 민주주의에게 왜 패했는지 설명하려고
　(d) 두 이념 간의 차이를 설명하려고

2 다음 중 가장 잘 요약된 것을 고르시오.
　(a) 1991년 공산주의가 붕괴되면서 종식된 냉전은 미국과 소련 간에 발생해 전 세계로 퍼졌던 긴장의 시기였다.
　(b) 냉전은 공산주의와 민주주의 간에 있었던 일련의 분쟁으로, 그 결과는 전쟁터가 아닌 다른 곳에서 결정되었다.

3 옳은 문장에는 T, 틀린 문장에는 F를 쓰시오.
　(1) 냉전은 부분적으로 제2차 세계대전의 결과에서 야기되었다.
　(2) 소련은 서유럽에 완충 지대를 구축하기로 결정했다.
　(3) 냉전은 각 진영의 경제력에 의해 판가름 났다.
　(4) 양 진영은 군대와 핵무기를 많이 차지하려고 경쟁했다.

4 제2차 세계대전 이후 유럽에 권력의 공백이 생긴 이유는 무엇인가?
　(a) 소련과 미국이 유럽 열강의 자리를 차지했다.
　(b) 이전의 주요 강대국들이 패전국이 되었거나 전쟁으로 인해 약해졌다.
　(c) 전쟁으로 전 유럽 대륙이 초토화되어 힘이 약해졌다.
　(d) 유럽 국가들에게는 자국을 복구할 수 있는 자원이 남아 있지 않았다.

Exercise　　　　p. 140~p. 141

1 (b)　　**2** 해설 참조　　**3** (a)　　**4** (c)　　**5** (d)　　**6** (b)　　**7** (c)　　**8** (d)　　**9** (b)　　**10** 해설 참조　　**11** (a)　　**12** (c)

1

W　In 1962, the world almost <u>came</u> <u>to</u> <u>an</u> <u>end</u> in a nuclear holocaust. In October of that year, American spy planes <u>spotted</u> <u>nuclear</u> <u>missiles</u> on the island of Cuba, only 145 kilometers from <u>American</u> <u>soil</u>. The Soviets had placed the missiles there <u>with</u> <u>the</u> <u>agreement</u> <u>of</u> Cuba's communist leader, Fidel Castro. For thirteen days, a <u>terrible</u> <u>tension</u> <u>gripped</u> the world as the Americans and Soviets <u>stood</u> <u>eyeball</u> <u>to</u> <u>eyeball</u> over the missiles. The Soviets said the missiles were <u>defensive</u> <u>in</u> <u>nature</u> and were a response to American nuclear missiles in Turkey, which were <u>positioned</u> close to the Soviet homeland. The Americans wanted the missiles removed and threatened to invade Cuba unless they were <u>taken</u> <u>away</u>. At the center of this crisis were American President John F. Kennedy and Soviet leader Nikita Khrushchev. Kennedy was younger and <u>less experienced</u>, but <u>showed</u> <u>his</u> <u>skill</u> at this game of <u>brinkmanship</u>. Khrushchev realized too late that he had made a mistake and that to remove the missiles would be a <u>severe</u> <u>blow</u> <u>to</u> Soviet <u>pride</u>. Fortunately, <u>cooler</u> <u>heads</u> <u>prevailed</u>, and the two sides <u>reached</u> <u>an</u> <u>agreement</u> for the Americans to remove the missiles from Turkey and the Soviets to do the same in Cuba. Publicly, however, it was great <u>diplomatic</u> <u>victory</u> for Kennedy, as the Soviets appeared to have given up and <u>backed</u> <u>down</u> <u>against</u> American pressure. For Khrushchev, it was a <u>fatal</u> <u>mistake</u>, as the Cuban Missile Crisis failure was key to his <u>removal</u> <u>from</u> <u>power</u> two years later.

▶ nuclear holocaust 핵무기에 의한 대참사 spy plane 정찰기 spot 발견하다
soil 국토, 나라 eyeball to eyeball 얼굴을 맞대고; 서로 노려보며 in nature 사실상,
현실적으로 brinkmanship 벼랑 끝 전술 blow 타격 prevail 지배하다. 우세하다
back down (의견ㆍ주장 등을) 굽히다. 철회하다

여 1962년 세계는 핵무기에 의한 대참사로 거의 종말을 맞을 뻔했습니다. 그해 10월 미국의 정찰기가 미국 본토로부터 겨우 145킬로미터 떨어진 쿠바의 한 섬에서 핵미사일을 발견했습니다. 소련이 쿠바의 공산주의 지도자인 피델 카스트로의 동의하에 그곳에 미사일을 배치한 것이었죠. 미국과 소련이 미사일을 놓고 신경전을 벌이던 13일 동안 끔찍한 긴장감이 전 세계를 사로잡았습니다. 소련은 그 미사일이 사실상 방어용이며 소련 본토와 가까운 터키에 배치된 미국의 핵미사일에 대한 대응이라고 말했습니다. 미국은 미사일이 철수되길 원했고, 그렇게 하지 않으면 쿠바를 침공하겠다고 위협했죠. 이 같은 위기의 한가운데에는 미국의 대통령 존 F. 케네디와 소련의 지도자 니키타 흐루시초프가 있었습니다. 케네디는 더 젊고 경험이 적었으나, 이 벼랑 끝 전술 게임에서 그의 역량을 보여주었습니다. 흐루시초프는 자신이 실수했으며 미사일을 철수하면 소련의 자존심에 심각한 타격을 입게 될 것이라는 사실을 너무 늦게 깨달았습니다. 다행히 냉정한 이성이 우세하여 양측은 미국이 터키에서 미사일을 철수하고 소련 역시 쿠바에서 그렇게 하기로 합의를 보았습니다. 그러나 그것은 소련이 미국의 압력에 굴복해 물러서는 것처럼 보였기 때문에 공식적으로는 케네디의 외교적 승리였습니다. 흐루시초프에게 그것은 치명적인 실수였는데요, 왜냐하면 2년 뒤 그의 실각에 쿠바 미사일 위기의 실패가 결정적인 역할을 했기 때문입니다.

1 담화의 주제는 무엇인가?
(a) 케네디와 흐루시초프의 관계
(b) 1962년 쿠바 미사일 위기를 둘러싼 사건들
(c) 쿠바가 소련의 미사일을 자국의 영토에 배치하도록 허용한 이유
(d) 존 F. 케네디의 국제적인 협상 기술
(e) 1962년 쿠바 미사일 위기를 종식시킨 거래

2

M North Korea just <u>set</u> <u>off</u> another <u>nuclear</u> <u>weapon</u>. That's two tests since 2006.

W Should we be worried about North Korea attacking someone?

M I'm not worried. They don't have that many <u>nuclear</u> <u>weapons</u>. Some experts think they only have enough <u>material</u> to <u>build</u> <u>a</u> <u>few</u> <u>bombs</u>.

W One would be <u>one</u> <u>too</u> <u>many</u>. Which countries have <u>nuclear</u> <u>weapons</u>? I know America and Russia have them.

M Russia has the most. It has around 15,000, and America has around 10,000. The United States was the first country to get nuclear weapons in 1945, and it was <u>followed</u> <u>by</u> Russia in 1949.

W What about China? The Chinese <u>must</u> <u>have</u> <u>gotten</u> nuclear weapons a long time ago, too.

M Actually, China was the <u>fifth</u> <u>country</u>. The British were the third in 1952 and they were followed by the French in 1960 and the Chinese in 1964. All have <u>small</u> <u>arsenals</u>. France has about 350 weapons, and the British and Chinese have around 200 each.

W So, that's everyone? I mean, it's still too many, but at least there is <u>less</u> <u>tension</u> now that the <u>Cold</u> <u>War</u> <u>is</u> <u>over</u>.

M Hold on. We forgot about India and Pakistan, and those two are <u>enemies</u>. India <u>exploded</u> its first <u>atomic</u> <u>weapon</u> in 1970, and Pakistan did the same in 1998. Each country has about 60 <u>nukes</u>. And then there is Israel, which many people <u>believe</u> <u>acquired</u> <u>nuclear</u> <u>weapons</u> in 1967 and has about 80 weapons, but the Israelis have never <u>confirmed</u> this.

W I wish they would just <u>get</u> <u>rid</u> <u>of</u> all of them to make the world safe.

▶ set off 폭발시키다 one too many 도가 지나친, 불필요한
atomic weapon 핵무기, 원자 무기 nuke 핵무기 confirm 확인하다

남 북한이 또 다른 핵무기 폭발 실험을 했어. 2006년 이후 두 번째야.
여 북한이 누군가를 공격할 것에 대해 걱정해야 할까?
남 난 걱정 안 해. 북한은 그렇게 많은 핵무기를 갖고 있지 않거든. 일부 전문가들은 북한이 폭탄 몇 개 만들 수 있을 정도의 원료만 갖고 있다고 생각해.
여 하나라도 많은 거지. 어떤 나라들이 핵무기를 갖고 있지? 미국과 러시아가 갖고 있다는 건 알고 있는데.
남 러시아가 제일 많이 갖고 있어. 러시아에는 약 1만 5천 기 정도 있고 미국이 1만 기 정도지. 미국은 1945년에 최초로 핵무기를 보유한 나라였고 그 다음이 러시아로 1949년이었어.
여 중국은 어때? 중국도 틀림없이 오래 전에 핵무기를 가졌을 것 같은데.
남 사실 중국은 다섯 번째 나라야. 영국이 1952년으로 세 번째였고, 그 다음이 프랑스로 1960년, 중국은 1964년이었어. 모두 보유량은 적어. 프랑스는 350기 정도이고, 영국과 중국은 각각 약 200기 정도지.
여 그 나라들이 다야? 내 말은 그래도 너무 많다는 거지. 하지만 지금은 적어도 냉전이 끝나서 긴장도 덜하잖아.
남 잠깐만. 인도와 파키스탄을 깜빡했네. 그 두 나라는 서로 적이야. 인도는 1970년에 처음으로 핵무기를 실험했고, 파키스탄은 1998년에 했어. 두 나라는 각각 약 60기 정도의 핵무기를 보유하고 있어. 그리고 이스라엘도 있는데, 많은 사람들은 이스라엘이 1967년에 핵무기를 손에 넣어 약 80기 정도 갖고 있다고 믿고 있지만 이스라엘은 한 번도 이에 대해 확인해주지 않았어.
여 세상을 안전하게 만들기 위해 모든 나라가 핵무기를 다 없애버렸으면 좋겠어.

2 빈칸에 정보를 채워 표를 완성하시오.

국가	획득 연도	핵무기 수
미국	1945	10,000
러시아	1949	15,000
Britain (영국)	1952	200
프랑스	1960	350
China (중국)	1964	200
이스라엘	1967	아마도 80
인도	1970	60
파키스탄	1998	60

M In any kind of strategy, whether it is in <u>international</u> <u>diplomacy</u>, <u>warfare</u>, business, or even a common everyday situation, <u>deterrence</u> may <u>come</u> <u>into</u> <u>effect</u>. <u>Deterrence</u> is based on the idea that someone can be stopped from doing something because he or she does not want to <u>suffer</u> <u>any</u> <u>possible</u> <u>consequences</u>. For example, a nation wants another nation's oil. It can <u>negotiate</u> and buy the oil, or it could <u>attack</u> and take the oil. However, the first nation knows that the nation with the oil has a <u>strong</u> <u>military</u>, so it decides to negotiate for the oil. The <u>strong</u> <u>military</u> <u>force</u> of the nation with the oil acts as a <u>deterrent</u> to the first nation. The first nation <u>surmised</u> that the <u>consequences</u> <u>of</u> <u>attacking</u> are too great, and, therefore, the first nation is <u>deterred</u> from attacking. Unfortunately, <u>deterrence</u> has not always worked, and nations <u>have</u> <u>gone</u> <u>to</u> <u>war</u> even when they know the other side is strong. This is mainly because they believe they can <u>surprise</u> and <u>defeat</u> the other nation quickly. However, since the <u>advent</u> of <u>nuclear</u> <u>weapons</u>, a new kind of deterrence has <u>come</u> <u>into</u> <u>play</u>. Surprise and speed in an attack <u>no</u> <u>longer</u> <u>matter</u> when the enemy nation can <u>launch</u> nuclear missiles in a matter of seconds and <u>destroy</u> <u>entire</u> <u>cities</u>. During the Cold War, the Russians and the Americans knew they would just <u>end</u> <u>up</u> <u>destroying</u> each other and the world, so their nuclear weapons acted as a <u>deterrent</u>.

▶ diplomacy 외교 warfare 전쟁 deterrence (전쟁) 억지(력) negotiate 협상하다, 교섭하다 deterrent 억지물, 억지력 deter 단념시키다, 막다 surmise 짐작하다, 추측하다 surprise 기습하다; 기습 (공격) advent 출현, 도래 come into play 작동하기 시작하다 a matter of 대충; 약; ~의 문제 launch 발사하다

남 어떤 종류의 전략에서든, 그것이 국제 외교든 전쟁이나 사업, 심지어 흔한 일상적인 상황에서든, 억지력이 작용합니다. 억지력은 누군가 어떤 일을 함으로써 그로 인해 일어날지도 모를 결과를 겪고 싶지 않기 때문에 그 일을 하지 않게 될 것이라는 생각에 근거합니다. 예를 들어 어떤 나라가 다른 나라의 석유를 원한다고 칩시다. 그 나라는 협상을 해서 석유를 살 수도 있고, 침공해서 빼앗을 수도 있습니다. 하지만 첫 번째 나라는 석유를 갖고 있는 나라가 강한 군사력을 보유하고 있다는 것을 알기 때문에 석유를 얻기 위해 협상을 하기로 결정합니다. 석유를 갖고 있는 나라의 강한 군사력이 첫 번째 나라에 억지물로 작용하는 것이죠. 침공의 결과가 너무 클 것이라고 짐작했기에 첫 번째 나라의 침공이 억지되는 것입니다. 불행히도 억지력이 항상 작용하는 것은 아니라서 많은 나라들이 상대가 강하다는 것을 알면서도 전쟁을 벌입니다. 이는 주로 자신들이 다른 나라를 기습해서 신속하게 패배시킬 수 있다고 믿기 때문입니다. 그러나 핵무기의 출현으로 새로운 종류의 억지력이 작용하게 되었습니다. 적국이 핵 미사일을 몇 초 안에 발사해 모든 도시를 파괴할 수 있다면 기습 공격과 빠른 기동성은 더 이상 중요하지 않게 됩니다. 냉전 기간 중에 러시아와 미국은 자신들이 서로와 전 세계를 결국 파괴하고 말 것임을 알았기에 그들의 핵무기가 억지력으로 작용했습니다.

3 억지력은 러시아와 미국의 핵전쟁을 방지하는 데 어떻게 도움이 되었는가?
(a) 양측은 상대편이 먼저 파괴된다 해도 그들이 자신들을 파괴시킬 수 있다는 것을 알고 있었다.
(b) 양측은 상대편이 절박한 처지가 아닌 이상 보복하지 않으리라는 것을 알고 있었다.
(c) 양측은 상대편에 대한 우위를 확보하고 싶어했지만 핵무기 때문에 그럴 수 없었다.
(d) 양측은 서로 상대편을 기습할 수 없었기 때문에 개전을 주저했다.
(e) 양측은 상대편의 영토를 차지하고 싶어했기 때문에 핵무기 사용은 고려 대상이 아니었다.

4 담화에서 유추할 수 있는 것은 무엇인가?
(a) 억지력은 미국의 주된 전략이다.
(b) 억지력은 지금까지 대부분 실패했다.
(c) 억지력은 전쟁뿐 아니라 다양한 인간 활동에 적용된다.
(d) 억지력은 핵무기에만 효과가 있다.
(e) 억지력은 어떤 나라를 침략하는 데 효과적인 방식이다.

M So, Janice, what would you like to write your <u>history</u> <u>report</u> <u>on</u>?

G I was thinking about doing it on the United Nations.

M Well, another student is already doing that. How about doing yours on the League of Nations?

G I don't know much about it. What is it?

M The League of Nations came about after World War I. It was <u>formed</u> <u>to</u> <u>have</u> <u>a</u> <u>place</u> where nations could take their problems and try to <u>find</u> <u>a</u> <u>solution</u> rather than <u>going</u> <u>to</u> <u>war</u>.

G <u>That's</u> <u>sort</u> <u>of</u> like the United Nations now, isn't it?

M Yes, they <u>were</u> <u>both</u> <u>based</u> <u>on</u> the same idea of having a place where nations could <u>discuss</u> <u>their</u> <u>differences</u>. Unfortunately, the League of Nations was a <u>failure</u>.

G Really? Why was it a <u>failure</u>? Could you <u>fill</u> <u>in</u> <u>the</u> <u>blanks</u> for me?

M Sure. First, the United States never <u>became</u> <u>a</u> <u>member</u>.

G Really? Why not?

M Well, US President Woodrow Wilson wanted to join, but the American Congress and many Americans did not want to <u>take</u> <u>part</u> <u>in</u> the League of Nations. They wanted <u>nothing</u> <u>to</u> <u>do</u> <u>with</u> Europe after the war ended.

G So what happened to the League of Nations?

M It proved to be <u>ineffective</u>. The Japanese <u>walked</u> <u>out</u> <u>of</u> the league after it condemned Japan's invasion of China in 1931. In 1935, Italy invaded Ethiopia, but the league could do nothing because it had no <u>military</u> <u>forces</u>. After that, no one <u>paid</u> <u>any</u> <u>attention</u> <u>to</u> it.

G And no one had the <u>guts</u> to stop Hitler when he <u>became</u> <u>aggressive</u> in the late 1930s, right?

M Exactly. The Second World War started, but the League of Nations could do nothing to prevent it. It was finally <u>disbanded</u> in 1945 when the UN was created.

▶ come about 생기다 Could you fill in the blanks for me? 좀 더 자세히 설명해 주시겠어요? ineffective 쓸모가 없는, 무력한 walk out 떠나다, 퇴장하다 condemn 비난하다 gut 용기, 배짱 aggressive 침략적인, 공격적인 disband 해산하다

남 그래, 재니스, 넌 역사 과제로 무엇에 대해 쓰고 싶니?
여 국제연합에 대해 써볼까 생각하고 있었어요.
남 음. 그건 이미 다른 학생이 하고 있단다. 국제연맹에 대해 써보면 어떻겠니?
여 거기에 대해서는 잘 모르는데요. 그건 뭐죠?
남 국제연맹은 제1차 세계대전 이후에 생겼단다. 전쟁을 하기보다는 각 나라가 문제를 들고 와서 해결책을 찾아볼 수 있는 장소를 마련하기 위해 만들어졌지.
여 지금의 국제연합 같은 거군요, 그렇죠?

남 맞아. 둘 다 여러 나라들이 서로의 의견 차이를 논의할 수 있는 곳을 마련한다는
 같은 생각을 바탕으로 하고 있어. 안타깝게도 국제연맹은 실패작이었지만 말이다.

여 정말요? 왜 실패작이었죠? 좀 더 자세히 설명해주실 수 있나요?

남 물론이지. 먼저, 미국이 회원국이 되지 않았단다.

여 그래요? 왜요?

남 음, 우드로 윌슨 미국 대통령은 참가하고 싶어했지만 미국 의회와 많은 미국인들
 은 국제연맹에 가입하고 싶어하지 않았어. 제1차 세계대전이 끝나자 유럽과 관
 계를 맺지 않으려 했거든.

여 그래서 국제연맹은 어떻게 되었죠?

남 아무 힘도 없게 되었지. 국제연맹이 1931년 일본의 중국 침략을 비난하자 일본
 은 연맹을 탈퇴해버렸어. 1935년에는 이탈리아가 에티오피아를 침략했지만 연
 맹에는 병력이 없었기 때문에 아무것도 할 수 없었단다. 그 후로는 아무도 연맹
 에 신경을 쓰지 않았지.

여 그래서 1930년대 말에 히틀러가 호전적으로 변했을 때 아무도 말릴 배짱이 없
 었던 거군요, 그렇죠?

남 그렇지. 제2차 세계대전이 시작되었지만 국제연맹은 전쟁을 막기 위해 할 수 있
 는 게 아무것도 없었단다. 결국 국제연합이 창설된 1945년에 해체되고 말았지.

5 국제연맹의 주목적은 무엇이었는가?

(a) 제1차 세계대전 이후 남겨진 문제들을 논의하는 곳이었다.

(b) 군사력을 사용하여 전쟁을 막기 위한 조직이었다.

(c) 국제연합을 창설하기 위해 시험적으로 운영되었다.

(d) 국가들이 서로 간의 의견 차이에 관해 대화할 수 있는 기구였다.

(e) 평화에 헌신하는 국가들의 조직이었다.

6 다음 중 내용을 가장 잘 요약한 것을 고르시오.

(a) 국제연맹은 다국적군을 창설하기 위한 시도였으나 누구도 군대를 제
 공하지 않자 실패로 돌아갔다.

(b) 국제연맹은 국제연합의 선구였지만 태생적인 약점 때문에 결국 실패
 하고 말았다.

(c) 국제연맹은 미국이 가입을 거부했기 때문에 처음부터 실패작이었다.

---

7 Level up

B It's been over 60 years since the Americans used the A-bomb on Japan.

G Why did they have to do that? I mean, in our history class, the teacher said that Japan was already <u>defeated</u> and was <u>trying to surrender</u>.

B Not everyone wanted to <u>surrender</u>. There was <u>division</u> in the Japanese government and military. Japan still had millions of men in the army in Japan and China in 1945.

G But its <u>navy was defeated</u>, and its <u>merchant fleet</u> was destroyed.

B True, yet the Americans believed the Japanese would <u>fight fanatically</u> if they invaded Japan. Using the <u>atomic bomb</u> was a way to get them to surrender with <u>as few deaths as possible</u>.

G But almost 200,000 people died at Hiroshima and Nagasaki.

B Yes, but if there had been an invasion, millions of people would have died. It seems <u>cruel</u>, but those were the <u>cold hard facts of war</u> in those days. <u>In hindsight</u>, many think the atomic bomb helped save lives.

G I understand, but I still think the Americans <u>should have at least tried</u> harder to negotiate for Japan's surrender.

▶ A-bomb 원자탄 division (의견) 차이, 불일치 navy 해군; 함대
 merchant fleet (한 나라의) 전체 상선 fanatically 광적으로
 cold hard fact 매정하고 냉정한 사실 in hindsight 지나고 나서 보니까

남 미국이 일본에 원자탄을 투하한 지 60년이 넘었어.

여 왜 그래야만 했던 거지? 역사 시간에 선생님께서 일본은 이미 전쟁에 져서 항복
 하려 했다고 말씀하셨거든.

남 모두가 다 항복하려 했던 건 아니었어. 일본 정부와 군부 사이에는 의견 차이가
 있었거든. 1945년에 일본은 여전히 일본과 중국에 수백만 명의 육군을 보유하
 고 있었어.

여 하지만 일본 해군은 패했고 상선(商船)도 파괴되었잖아.

남 맞아. 하지만 미국은 만약 일본을 공격한다면 그들이 미친 듯이 싸울 거라고 생
 각했어. 원자탄을 이용하는 것이 가능한 한 적은 사망자를 내며 일본을 항복시키
 는 방법이었지.

여 하지만 거의 20만 명의 사람들이 히로시마와 나가사키에서 죽었잖아.

남 그래, 하지만 만약 일본 본토를 공격했다면 수백만 명의 사람들이 죽었을 거야.
 잔인한 것 같지만 당시로서는 그게 전쟁의 냉혹한 현실이었어. 지나고 나서 보니
 원자탄이 사람들의 목숨을 구하는 데 도움이 되었다고 많이들 생각하지.

여 이해는 가. 그래도 난 미국이 적어도 일본의 항복을 이끌어내기 위해 협상하는
 데 더 노력을 기울였어야 했다고 생각해.

7 What is the main reason the Americans used the atomic bomb on Japan in 1945?

1945년에 미국이 일본에 원자탄을 사용한 주원인은?

(a) To damage Japan before an invasion
 일본을 침공하기 전에 피해를 입히려고

(b) To test the bomb they had produced
 자신들이 만든 원자탄을 시험해보려고

(c) To avoid a costly invasion of Japan
 일본을 공격하는 데 따른 엄청난 희생을 피하려고

(d) To end the split in Japan's leadership
 일본 지도부 내의 분열을 끝내려고

(e) To destroy Japan's large army
 일본의 대규모 육군을 섬멸하려고

---

8 Level up

M <u>Diplomacy</u> is the art of negotiating with other countries to <u>achieve</u> <u>one's</u> <u>political</u> <u>aims</u>. These aims are often related to getting what you want by giving up <u>as little as possible</u>. In some cases, <u>misunderstandings</u> can result as one side <u>misinterprets the intentions</u> of the other, and this can lead to a <u>failure of diplomacy</u>. In a <u>classic example</u>, Saddam Hussein, the leader of Iraq for many years, misunderstood the intentions of the United States prior to his invasion of Kuwait in August 1990. He <u>had an interview</u> with the American <u>ambassador</u> to Iraq a short time before the invasion, and Hussein believed that the Americans <u>had no interest in</u> Kuwait and would not <u>oppose</u> an Iraqi invasion. However, he couldn't have been more wrong. When his forces invaded and occupied Kuwait, the Americans were <u>among the first</u> to condemn the actions, and they later <u>led a coalition</u> that defeated the Iraqi army and <u>liberated</u> Kuwait.

▶ misunderstanding 오해, 잘못 생각함 diplomacy 외교 misinterpret 오해하다
 ambassador 대사 oppose ~에 반대하다 coalition 연합, 합동 cf. coalition
 forces 연합군, 다목적군 liberate 해방하다

남 외교란 자국의 정치적 목적을 달성하기 위해 다른 국가와 협상하는 기술입니다.
 이런 목적은 보통 가능한 한 적게 포기하면서 원하는 것을 얻어내는 것과 관련되
 어 있습니다. 어떤 경우에는 한쪽이 다른 쪽의 의도를 잘못 이해해서 오해가 생
 길 수 있는데, 이는 외교 실패로 이어질 수 있습니다. 대표적인 예로, 오랫동안

이라크의 지도자였던 사담 후세인은 1990년 8월에 쿠웨이트를 침공하기에 앞서 미국의 의도를 오해했습니다. 그는 침공 전에 이라크 주재 미국 대사와 잠시 면담을 가졌는데, 후세인은 미국이 쿠웨이트에는 관심이 없으며 이라크의 침공에도 반대하지 않을 것이라고 믿었죠. 그러나 이것은 그가 완전히 잘못 생각한 것이었습니다. 이라크 군이 쿠웨이트를 침공해 점령하자 미국은 가장 먼저 그 행위를 비난한 쪽에 속했으며, 나중에는 다국적 군을 이끌고 이라크 군을 물리쳐 쿠웨이트를 해방시켰습니다.

8 What is the main topic of the talk? 담화의 주제는 무엇인가?

(a) The purpose of the Iraqi invasion of Kuwait in 1990
1990년에 이라크가 쿠웨이트를 침공한 목적

(b) A diplomatic mistake made by a U.S. ambassador
미국 대사가 저지른 외교적 실수

(c) Saddam Hussein's misinterpretation of America's warning
미국의 경고에 대한 사담 후세인의 잘못된 해석

(d) A diplomatic misunderstanding that led to a war
전쟁으로 이어진 외교적 오해

(e) A false impression that caused diplomatic difficulties
외교 문제를 일으킨 잘못된 인상

9

W Appeasement is a <u>diplomatic</u> <u>tactic</u> used to give one side what it wants in order to avoid a more <u>aggressive</u> <u>response</u> from that side. As a <u>negotiating</u> <u>tool</u>, it has proven useful <u>at</u> <u>avoiding</u> <u>wars</u>, but it also has a lot of <u>negativity</u> attached to it since <u>appeasement</u> is often <u>associated</u> <u>with</u> the Munich Agreement of 1938. At that time, Adolf Hitler was <u>making</u> <u>aggressive</u> <u>moves</u> toward Czechoslovakia by claiming that parts of that nation, called the Sudetenland, really <u>belonged</u> <u>to</u> Germany. A <u>conference</u> <u>was</u> <u>held</u> in Munich between Hitler, Benito Mussolini of Italy, British Prime Minister Neville Chamberlain, and French Premier Edourad Daladier. <u>Over</u> <u>the</u> <u>course</u> <u>of</u> discussions, it was agreed that the Germans would be given the Sudetenland. The Czechs <u>had</u> <u>been</u> <u>prepared</u> <u>to</u> <u>fight</u>, but they gave up after Britain and France failed to support them. This act of <u>appeasement</u> of Hitler was <u>hailed</u> at the time for avoiding war, but, <u>in</u> <u>hindsight</u>, it is now seen as a <u>crucial</u> <u>mistake</u>. Hitler could not be <u>appeased</u>, and, in early 1939, Germany <u>annexed</u> the rest of Czechoslovakia and then <u>turned</u> <u>its</u> <u>eyes</u> toward Poland. When Germany attacked Poland in September 1939, it was clear to all that Hitler could not be stopped <u>short</u> <u>of</u> <u>war</u>. Britain and France <u>declared</u> <u>war</u> <u>on</u> Germany in support of Poland, and World War II began. Ever since, the word <u>appeasement</u> has been associated with <u>weakness</u> <u>in</u> <u>negotiating</u>.

▶ appeasement 유화정책 tactic 전술, 작전 negativity 부정성
be associated with ~이 연상되다; ~와 관련되다 hail 환영하다 annex 합병하다
short of ~을 제외하고, ~을 제쳐놓고

여 유화정책이란 상대방의 보다 공격적인 반응을 피하기 위해 그들이 원하는 것을 내주는 외교 전술입니다. 하나의 협상 도구로서 유화정책은 전쟁을 피하는 데 유용한 것으로 판명되었지만 종종 1938년 뮌헨 협정을 연상시키기 때문에 부정적인 측면도 많습니다. 그 당시 아돌프 히틀러는 체코슬로바키아의 주데텐란트라는 지역이 사실은 독일 소유라고 주장하면서 체코슬로바키아에게 공격적인 행동을 취하고 있었습니다. 히틀러와 이탈리아의 베니토 무솔리니, 네빌 챔벌린 영국 수상, 에두아르 달라디에 프랑스 총리가 참석한 가운데 뮌헨에서 회담이 열렸습니다. 회담에서는 논의를 거쳐 독일에게 주데텐란트를 내주기로 합의했습니다.

체코슬로바키아는 전쟁할 준비가 되어 있었지만 영국과 프랑스가 자신들을 지지하지 않자 전쟁을 포기했습니다. 히틀러에 대한 이 유화정책 조치는 당시에는 전쟁을 피했기 때문에 환영받았지만 시간이 지난 지금에 와서는 결정적인 실수로 간주되고 있습니다. 히틀러는 유화될 수 없는 인물이었고, 1939년 초 독일은 체코슬로바키아의 나머지 지역을 합병한 뒤 폴란드로 눈을 돌렸습니다. 1939년 9월, 독일이 폴란드를 침공하자 히틀러를 전쟁 없이는 멈출 수 없을 것이라는 사실이 모두에게 분명해졌습니다. 영국과 프랑스가 폴란드 편에 서서 독일에 선전포고를 했고, 제2차 세계대전이 시작되었습니다. 그 후로 유화정책이라는 말은 협상에서 유약함과 결부됩니다.

9 담화에 따르면 사실이 <u>아닌</u> 것은?

(a) 네 명의 지도자가 뮌헨 회담에서 만났다.
(b) 주데텐란트는 독일 영토였다.
(c) 히틀러는 체코슬로바키아를 모두 차지하려는 야욕이 있었다.
(d) 뮌헨 협정은 처음에는 효과적인 것처럼 보였다.
(e) 영국과 프랑스는 1939년 폴란드를 지지했다.

10

B I just got our assignment from the teacher. We have to do a presentation on UN <u>peacekeeping</u>.

G That sounds like it's going to be tough.

B I've already found a few websites. Let's have a look. First, what's the <u>definition</u> of <u>peacekeeping</u>?

G It says here that <u>peacekeeping</u> is the use of <u>neutral</u> <u>armed</u> <u>forces</u> to separate warring parties and to act as <u>observers</u> to ensure that the <u>terms</u> of a <u>peace</u> <u>settlement</u> are <u>carried</u> <u>out</u>.

B Sounds good. How many <u>peacekeeping</u> <u>missions</u> are there currently?

G Right now, there are 19 peacekeeping missions worldwide. The longest <u>ongoing</u> one is in the Middle East. It started in 1948 during the first Arab-Israeli war.

B Okay, let me <u>write</u> that <u>down</u>. Oh, and here it shows the number of <u>troops</u> involved and where they're from. There are 83,326 <u>military</u> and <u>police</u> <u>forces</u> involved in UN peacekeeping missions. They come from 117 different countries. There are also around 15,000 <u>civilians</u> used for <u>support</u>.

G Have any of them been hurt while on peacekeeping missions?

B Since 1948, 2,386 people have been killed while doing peacekeeping missions.

G Wow, that's a lot. I didn't expect the number to be so high. How did they get killed? I mean they <u>are</u> <u>supposed</u> <u>to</u> <u>be</u> at <u>peace</u>.

B They are supposed to be, but sometimes they're not. Some were killed by <u>landmines</u> and bombs, and others were killed by <u>gunfire</u>. Still others were <u>kidnapped</u> and <u>deliberately</u> <u>murdered</u>.

G That's awful. Why should countries send troops if that is what is going to happen to them?

B I guess if the UN and its member countries did nothing, these <u>conflict</u> <u>situations</u> could be a lot worse.

▶ peacekeeping 평화의 유지; 평화를 유지하는 warring 투쟁(중)의, 교전중의
peace settlement 평화협정, 강화 carry out 수행하다, 실행하다

observer 감시자, 관찰자 ongoing 진행 중의 civilian 민간인, 일반 시민
landmine 지뢰 gunfire 총격 kidnap 유괴하다, 납치하다 deliberately 고의로,
일부러 awful 끔찍한, 아주 심한 conflict 분쟁

남 방금 선생님이 우리에게 내주신 과제를 받았어. 우리는 유엔의 평화유지에 대해
발표해야 해.

여 어려울 것 같네.

남 내가 벌써 웹사이트를 몇 개 찾아놨어. 한번 보자. 먼저 평화유지의 정의는?

여 여기에는 평화유지란 중립적인 무장 병력을 이용해 교전국들을 떼어놓고 강화
조건이 제대로 실행되도록 감시자 역할을 하는 것이라고 나와 있어.

남 멋진데. 현재 얼마나 많은 평화유지 임무가 수행되고 있지?

여 현재 전 세계적으로 19건의 평화유지 임무가 가동 중이야. 제일 오랫동안 진행
되고 있는 건 중동에서고. 1948년 제1차 중동전쟁 때 시작되었지.

남 알겠어. 적어놓을게. 아, 그리고 참여한 군대의 숫자와 파견국도 여기 나와 있어.
유엔 평화유지 임무에는 83,326명의 군인과 경찰 병력이 참여하고 있는데, 그들은
117개국에서 파견되었대. 약 1만 5천 명의 민간인도 지원 부대로 활용되고 있네.

여 그들 가운데 평화유지 임무 중에 부상당한 사람이 있대?

남 1948년 이후 2,386명이 평화유지 임무를 수행하다 사망했어.

여 와, 정말 많다. 그렇게 많을 줄은 몰랐어. 어떻게 하다 죽었지? 내 말은, 그들은
평화롭게 지낼 거 아니야?

남 원래는 그렇지만 안 그럴 때도 있어. 지뢰와 폭탄에 목숨을 잃은 사람도 있고 총
격으로 사망한 사람도 있어. 게다가 납치당해 고의적으로 살해되기도 했지.

여 끔찍해. 평화유지군에게 그런 일들이 일어나는데 왜 여러 나라에서 군대를 보내
야 하는 거지?

남 내 생각에는 유엔과 회원국들이 아무 조치도 취하지 않는다면 이런 분쟁 상황들
이 훨씬 더 악화될 수 있기 때문인 것 같아.

10 빈칸에 정보를 채워 표를 완성하시오.

현재의 임무 건수	19
가장 오랫동안 진행중인 임무	in the Middle East since 1948 (1948년 이후 중동)
현재 임무 수행 중인 군인과 경찰의 수	83,326
민간인 지원자	15,000
임무 중 사망자의 수	2,386

11-12   Level up

W Isolationism was an American <u>foreign</u> <u>policy</u> during the period between World War I and World War II. During this time, America tried to <u>remain</u> <u>isolated</u> from <u>world</u> <u>affairs</u>. Prior to the 20th century, the United States had a long history of <u>staying</u> <u>out</u> <u>of</u> <u>world</u> <u>affairs</u>. When World War I started in 1914, America stayed out of the war until forced to <u>declare</u> <u>war</u> <u>on</u> Germany in 1917 after German <u>submarines</u> began sinking American ships that were carrying cargo to Britain and France. After the war, many Americans felt they had been <u>tricked</u> <u>into</u> <u>declaring</u> war by the British, the French, and the <u>industrialists</u> who made money by <u>supplying</u> <u>war</u> <u>materials</u>. There were calls for a return to isolationism. During the 1930s, <u>a</u> <u>series</u> <u>of</u> aggressive actions on the world stage by Japan, Italy, and Germany <u>remained</u> <u>unchecked,</u> <u>in</u> <u>part</u> due to American <u>isolationism.</u> Britain and France were the world's <u>great</u> <u>powers</u> at that time, but they were <u>reluctant</u> to <u>take</u> <u>on</u> any enemy without American help. They knew they <u>had</u> <u>barely</u> <u>won</u> World War I with American help, and they were afraid of defeat and of millions more dead in a new war. When the Japanese attacked China, Italy attacked Ethiopia, and Germany <u>gobbled</u> <u>up</u> Austria and Czechoslovakia, <u>nobody</u> <u>lifted</u> <u>a</u> <u>finger</u> to stop them.

American President Franklin Roosevelt wanted to break America's <u>isolationism</u>, but <u>domestic</u> <u>political</u> <u>concerns</u> prevented him from doing so. When World War II <u>broke</u> <u>out</u> in 1939 in Europe, America was once again a <u>nonparticipant</u> and did not join the war until December 7, 1941, when the Japanese attacked Pearl Harbor in Hawaii and <u>left</u> America <u>no</u> <u>choice</u> but to enter the war.

▶ isolationism 고립주의 foreign policy 외교 정책 world affair 세계 정세
stay out of 간섭하지 않다; 피하다 cargo 화물, 짐 submarine 잠수함
trick into 속여서 ~하게 하다 industrialist 제조업자, 기업가
war materials 군수〔군용〕물자, 군수품 take on 대결하다 gobble 게걸스럽게
먹다 not lift a finger 손가락 하나 까딱하지 않다, 노력하지 않다 domestic 국내의

여 고립주의는 제1차 세계대전과 제2차 세계대전 사이의 기간 동안 미국이 취한 외
교 정책이었습니다. 이 기간 동안 미국은 세계 정세에서 떨어져 있으려고 노력했
습니다. 20세기 이전에, 미국은 세계 정세에서 한 발 물러나 있었던 오랜 전력이
있었죠. 1914년에 제1차 세계대전이 일어났을 때, 영국과 프랑스로 향하는 화물
을 실어나르던 미국 선박들을 독일 잠수함이 침몰시키기 시작한 후 마지못해 독
일에 선전포고를 하게 된 1917년까지 미국은 전쟁을 방관하고 있었습니다. 제1
차 세계대전이 끝난 뒤 많은 미국인들은 자신들이 영국과 프랑스, 그리고 군수품
을 공급해 돈을 번 기업가들에게 속아서 선전포고를 했다고 느꼈습니다. 고립주
의로 되돌아가야 한다는 여론이 일었죠. 1930년대에 일본, 이탈리아, 독일이 세
계 무대에서 취한 일련의 공격적인 행동은 부분적으로는 미국의 고립주의 때문
에 방치된 것이었습니다. 당시 영국과 프랑스는 강대국이었지만 미국의 도움 없
이는 그 어떤 적과도 맞서길 꺼려했습니다. 그들은 자신들이 미국의 도움으로 제
1차 세계대전에서 간신히 승리했다는 것을 알고 있었으며, 새로운 전쟁이 터져
수백만 명이 죽고 패배할까 봐 두려웠습니다. 일본이 중국을 공격하고, 이탈리
아가 에티오피아를 공격하고, 독일이 오스트리아와 체코슬로바키아를 집어삼켰
을 때, 아무도 그들을 막기 위해 손가락 하나 까딱하지 않았습니다. 프랭클린 루
즈벨트 미국 대통령은 미국의 고립주의를 깨고 싶어했지만 국내의 정치적 우려
때문에 그럴 수가 없었습니다. 1939년 유럽에서 제2차 세계대전이 일어났을 때
미국은 또다시 방관자였고, 1941년 12월 7일 일본이 하와이의 진주만을 공격해
선택의 여지가 없어지자 비로소 참전하게 되었습니다.

11 미국의 대중은 왜 제1차 세계대전 후에 고립주의로 돌아가길 원했는가?
(a) 그들은 속아서 전쟁에 참여하게 되었다고 느꼈다.
(b) 그들은 이탈리아, 독일, 일본의 행위를 지지했다.
(c) 그들은 피비린내 나는 새 전쟁에 뛰어드는 것이 내키지 않았다.
(d) 그들은 미국이 전쟁에 질 거라고 생각했다.
(e) 그들은 영국과 프랑스의 정책을 지지하지 않았다.

12 다음 중 내용을 가장 잘 요약한 것을 고르시오.
(a) 고립주의는 하나의 외교 정책으로서 미국에 유익하게 기여했지만,
미국은 공격을 받자 두 번이나 전쟁에 휘말렸다.
(b) 미국은 제2차 세계대전 이전에 고립주의 정책을 유지했는데 이는 일
본이나 이탈리아, 독일과 맞서서 이길 수 없다고 느꼈기 때문이다.
(c) 미국의 고립주의는 처음에는 전쟁을 피할 수 있게 해주었지만 결국
미국이 전쟁에 휘말려드는 것을 막지는 못했다.

Practice Test p. 142~p. 143

1 (a)   **2** (d)   **3** (c)   **4** (e)   **5** (c)   **6** (b)   **7** (d)
8 해설 참조   **9** (c)   **10** (b)

1

M The creation of Israel in 1948 started a long series of conflicts in the Middle East that has not ended to this day. The land where Israel is now located was once called Palestine and was also once the Biblical homeland of the Jewish people. For centuries, Palestine belonged to Turkey, but then it became a British colony after World War I. Its population consisted of both Arabs and Jews. After World War II, and the Holocaust in Europe, many Jewish survivors sought a new land in Palestine. They petitioned the British and the United Nations to allow them to create a Jewish state called Israel. In 1948, their desire was granted. The surrounding Arab states had sworn to destroy any Jewish state, and warfare broke out immediately. Since then, there have been four major wars in 1948-49, 1956, 1967, and 1973, in addition to many smaller conflicts and terrorist actions. The Israelis have been victorious in all of these wars. As a result, most of the Arab states have signed peace treaties with Israel or have reluctantly given up open armed conflict. However, terrorism is still a fact of life in Israel, and there are many problems with the former Palestinian Arabs who now have their own small territories. The tensions here are exacerbated by the presence of oil in many Arab states and by the religious aspects of the conflict. For now, there is a somewhat shaky peace, but it could erupt into war again at any time.

▶ **Biblical** 성서의, 성서에서 나온 **petition** 청원하다, 탄원하다 **grant** 승인하다, 허가하다 **swear** 맹세하다, 선언하다 *cf.* sworn은 swear의 과거분사형
peace treaty 평화 조약 **open** 공공연한 **armed conflict** 무력 대립
territory 영토, 지역 **exacerbate** 악화시키다 **shaky** 위태로운, 불안정한

남 1948년 이스라엘의 건국으로 중동에서는 오늘날까지 끝이 나고 있지 않는 일련의 길고 긴 분쟁이 시작되었습니다. 현재 이스라엘이 위치한 땅은 한때 팔레스타인으로 불렸으며, 성서에서 언급된 유대 민족의 조국이기도 했습니다. 팔레스타인은 수세기 동안 터키령이었지만, 제1차 세계대전 이후에 영국 식민지가 되었습니다. 팔레스타인의 인구는 아랍인과 유대인으로 구성되어 있었습니다. 유럽에서 제2차 세계대전과 유대인 대학살이 끝난 뒤 많은 유대인 생존자들은 팔레스타인에 새로운 나라를 세우려고 했습니다. 그들은 이스라엘이라는 유대인 국가를 세울 수 있게 해달라고 영국과 국제연합에 청원했습니다. 1948년에 그들의 요구가 받아들여졌습니다. 주변의 아랍 국가들은 어떠한 유대인 국가든 파괴할 것이라고 선언했으며 곧바로 전쟁이 일어났습니다. 그 이후로 1948~1949년, 1956년, 1967년, 1973년에 네 차례의 대규모 전쟁이 일어났고 그 밖에도 수많은 소규모 분쟁과 테러 행위가 있었습니다. 이스라엘은 이 모든 전쟁에서 승리를 거두었습니다. 그 결과 대부분의 아랍 국가들은 이스라엘과 평화 조약을 맺거나 마지못해 공공연한 무력 대립을 포기했습니다. 그러나 이스라엘에서 테러 행위는 여전히 발생하는 현실이며, 현재 자신들의 작은 국가를 갖고 있는 예전 팔레스타인 아랍인들과는 많은 문제가 있습니다. 이 지역의 긴장은 많은 아랍 국가들에 매장되어 있는 석유의 존재와 분쟁의 종교적인 측면 때문에 악화되었습니다. 지금 당장은 다소 불안정한 평화 상태지만 언제라도 전쟁이 다시 일어날 수 있습니다.

1 일부 아랍 국가들이 이스라엘과 평화 상태를 유지하는 이유는 무엇인가?
(a) 이스라엘을 공격했을 때마다 패했다.
(b) 이스라엘이 자신들의 유전을 공격할까 봐 염려했다.
(c) 팔레스타인 아랍인들에게는 현재 자기 나라가 있다.
(d) 영국과 유엔이 평화 조약을 체결했다.
(e) 이스라엘과 더 이상 아무런 문제가 없다.

2-3

W What's this rally about anyways?
M It's about the war in Iraq.

W Wait. I don't think I want to support war, especially not the one in Iraq.
M Come on. We need to show our support for the troops over there.
W Do you really think that we should support a war that is wrong?
M I don't think it's wrong. Our soldiers are there to stop terrorism and to protect the Iraqi people.
W And what a great job we've been doing. You know, they estimate that more than 100,000 Iraqis have died since we invaded Iraq in 2003. And don't forget the more than 4,000 Americans who have died, too.
M I haven't forgotten. That's why I'm going to the rally. I don't care why we are in the war, I just know we are and that those soldiers need the support of the homeland so that they can get through this.
W The war is wrong. Admit it. They went there to find nuclear and biological weapons but found nothing.
M Maybe the initial reasons to go there were wrong, and maybe we should leave, but those soldiers have got no choice. They are ordered to go, so they go even if they don't believe in what they are fighting for.
W I see your point, but I'm still not going to the rally. War, any war, is just wrong.
M There's no use in flogging a dead horse. Your mind is made up, so don't go. But I'm still going.
W ___________________________________

▶ **rally** 집회 **get through** 극복하다, 완수하다 **biological weapon** 생물학(생화학) 무기 **flog a dead horse** 헛수고를 하다

여 그런데 이 집회는 뭐에 관한 거야?
남 이라크 전쟁에 대한 거야.
여 잠깐. 난 전쟁을 지지하고 싶지는 않아. 특히 이라크 전쟁은 말이야.
남 이봐. 우린 그곳에 파견된 군대에게 우리의 지지를 보여줄 필요가 있어.
여 넌 정말 우리가 잘못된 전쟁을 지지해야 한다고 생각하니?
남 난 잘못됐다고 생각하지 않아. 우리 군인들은 테러 행위를 막고 이라크인을 보호하기 위해 거기에 가 있는 거라고.
여 우리가 하고 있는 그 잘난 일 말이지. 너도 알다시피 2003년에 우리가 이라크를 침공한 이후 10만 명이 넘는 이라크인이 죽은 것으로 추정되고 있어. 또 4,000명 이상의 미국인이 죽은 것도 잊지 말라고.
남 기억하고 있어. 그게 바로 내가 집회에 나가려고 하는 이유야. 나는 우리가 왜 전쟁을 하고 있는지는 관심 없어. 난 단지 우리가 전쟁을 하고 있고, 또 그곳에 있는 군인들이 이 상황을 극복하려면 고국의 지지가 필요하다는 사실을 알고 있을 뿐이지.
여 이 전쟁은 잘못된 거야. 그 사실을 인정하라고. 미군은 핵무기와 생화학 무기를 찾으러 거기에 갔지만 아무것도 발견하지 못했잖아.
남 처음 그곳에 간 이유는 잘못됐을 수도 있어. 그리고 어쩌면 우린 철수해야 하는 건지도 몰라. 하지만 그곳에 있는 군인들에겐 선택의 여지가 없어. 그들은 비록 자신들이 싸우는 이유에 동의하지 않는다 해도 그곳에 가라는 명령을 받아서 가는 거야.
여 무슨 말인지 알겠는데 난 그래도 집회에는 안 갈 거야. 전쟁은 어떤 전쟁이든 다 나쁜 거니까.
남 헛수고 해봐야 소용 없지 뭐. 네 마음이 그리 정해졌으니 가지 마. 하지만 난 갈 거야.
여 ___________________________________

2 대화에서 유추할 수 있는 것은 무엇인가?

(a) 여자의 친척이 이라크에서 싸우고 있다.

(b) 남자는 군대에 있을 때 이라크에 다녀왔다.

(c) 집회는 평화 단체에 의해 저지되고 있다.

(d) 남자와 여자는 모두 미국인이다.

(e) 남자가 아는 사람이 이라크에 있다.

3 여자는 남자의 마지막 말 다음에 뭐라고 말하겠는가?

(a) 넌 전쟁광이라 모든 전쟁을 그저 재미있는 게임이라고 생각하는구나.

(b) 네가 왜 이러는지 이해가 안 돼. 전쟁은 모두 나쁜 거라고!

(c) 네가 왜 그러는지 이해하지만 난 이 전쟁을 지지할 수 없어.

(d) 정부는 군인들을 집으로 돌려보내고 전쟁을 끝내야 해.

(e) 그곳에 있는 군대를 지지하는 집회는 좋은 생각이지만 난 너무 바빠.

4-5

W The Vietnam War lasted from 1945 to 1975. During that period, the Vietnamese initially fought a war of liberation from their French colonial masters from 1945 to 1954. After they successfully defeated the French, the subsequent peace treaty left Vietnam divided into North and South Vietnam. The next round of battle was fought for the unification of the country. North Vietnam was communist and was supported by the Soviet Union and China, while South Vietnam was democratic and was supported by the United States. Starting soon after the French left, the Americans began sending military advisors to South Vietnam, and then they began sending larger and larger numbers of special forces. Despite the skills of these soldiers, they were too few to stop the North Vietnamese from supporting a rebellion in South Vietnam. In 1964, a small naval battle between North Vietnamese and American forces in the Gulf of Tonkin near North Vietnam was the pretext for the Americans to begin bombing North Vietnam. Soon, large numbers of American combat troops entered South Vietnam. For the next eight years, the two sides engaged in deadly battle. By the time the Americans left in 1973, 58,000 Americans had died, and hundreds of thousands of Vietnamese had perished. The war had divided America into those who supported the war and those who were against it, and it had alienated the youth of America against its leadership. In the end, it was all for nothing as, by 1975, the North Vietnamese had soundly defeated the South Vietnamese and united the nation.

▶ **liberation** 해방 **subsequent** 다음의, 그 후의 **unification** 통일 **rebellion** 반란, 폭동 **pretext** 구실, 명목 **combat troop** 전투 부대; 전투병 **engage in battle** 싸우다, 교전하다 **perish** 죽다, 사라지다 **alienate** 멀리하다, 불화하게 하다 **soundly** 확실하게, 전적으로

여 베트남전은 1945년부터 1975년까지 지속되었습니다. 그 기간 중 1945년부터 1954년까지 베트남은 처음에는 프랑스의 식민 지배에서 벗어나기 위한 해방 전쟁을 치뤘습니다. 성공적으로 프랑스를 물리친 뒤 곧이어 맺어진 평화 조약은 베트남을 남과 북으로 갈라놓았습니다. 두 번째 전쟁은 통일을 위한 전쟁이었습니다. 북베트남은 공산주의로 소련과 중국의 지지를 받았던 반면 남베트남은 민주주의로 미국의 지지를 받았습니다. 프랑스가 철수하자 미국은 곧 남베트남에 군사 고문단을 파견하기 시작했고 그 뒤 점점 더 많은 특수 부대를 보내기 시작했습니다. 파견된 군인들의 실력에도 불구하고 남베트남의 폭동을 지원하는 북베트남을 저지하기에는 그 수가 너무 적었습니다. 1964년, 북베트남 인근의 통킹

만에서 북베트남군과 미군 간에 일어난 소규모 해상 전투를 구실로 미국은 북베트남을 폭격하기 시작했습니다. 곧 대규모의 미국 전투 부대가 남베트남에 상륙했습니다. 이후 8년 동안 양측은 치열한 전투를 벌였습니다. 1973년 미국이 철수할 때까지 5만 8천 명의 미국인과 수십만 명의 베트남인이 사망했습니다. 베트남전으로 미국은 전쟁에 찬성하는 쪽과 반대하는 쪽으로 분열되었고 미국 젊은이들은 지도부와 멀어졌습니다. 결국 1975년, 북베트남이 남베트남을 완전히 꺾고 나라를 통일하면서 전쟁은 허사로 돌아갔습니다.

4 미국은 왜 북베트남을 폭격하기 시작했는가?

(a) 프랑스군을 지원하기 위해서였다.

(b) 북베트남 침공을 위한 사전 준비였다.

(c) 북베트남을 위협해서 항복을 받아내기 위한 것이었다.

(d) 특수 부대 고문단의 조언에 따라 이루어진 것이었다.

(e) 통킹 만에서 벌어진 해상 전투에 대한 대응이었다.

5 담화에서 유추할 수 있는 것은 무엇인가?

(a) 프랑스는 많은 전투에서 이겼지만 결국은 베트남과의 전쟁에서 졌다.

(b) 미국의 개입 없이 남베트남은 북베트남으로부터 쉽게 나라를 지켰다.

(c) 북베트남은 1954년 자신들의 나라가 분단되는 것에 찬성하지 않았다.

(d) 미국은 북베트남이 졌다는 것을 확신한 뒤에 전쟁 지역을 떠났다.

(e) 미국은 나라를 통일하려는 북베트남의 시도에 찬성했다.

6 Level up

W Sorry I'm late. There was this parade in downtown Seoul today. Do you have any idea why they are having a parade?

M It's the anniversary of the start of the Korean War. It began on June 25, 1950.

W When did it end?

M It hasn't really ended. An armistice was signed by all participants, and the fighting came to an end on July 27, 1953, but they are still technically at war since there was no final peace treaty.

W That sounds a bit ridiculous. Why can't they just sit down and end the whole thing?

M It's not as easy as you'd think. Even during the war, the negotiations dragged on and on, while many people died.

W I guess they had a lot of important things they couldn't agree on.

M Some things, yes, like where the final border would be and how to exchange prisoners of war. But a lot of disagreements were silly. These included the shape of the negotiation table and the size of the flags in the room.

W It's a wonder they ever managed to end the fighting.

▶ **armistice** 휴전, 휴전 조약 **technically** 전문적으로 **ridiculous** 우스운, 어리석은 **drag on** 질질 끌다

여 늦어서 미안. 오늘 서울 시내에서 거리 행진이 있었거든. 왜 거리 행진을 하는지 뭐 아는 거 있니?

남 한국전쟁 발발 기념일이야. 1950년 6월 25일에 일어났지.

여 언제 끝났는데?

남 진짜로 끝나지는 않았어. 모든 참전국이 휴전 협정을 맺어서 1953년 7월 27일에 전투는 끝났지만, 엄밀히 말해 아직 전쟁 중이야. 최종적인 평화 조약을 맺지 않았거든.

여 좀 웃기는 것 같아. 왜 매듭을 짓지 못하는 거지?

남 네가 생각하는 것처럼 그렇게 쉬운 게 아니야. 심지어 전쟁 중에 많은 사람들이
　죽어나가는데도 협상을 질질 끌었다고.

여 합의하기 힘든 중요한 사항이 많이 있었나 보네.

남 그런 사항도 있었지. 최종적인 국경선을 어디로 하느냐와 전쟁 포로를 어떻게 교환
　하느냐 같은 것 말이야. 하지만 의견 차이가 난 많은 부분은 어처구니 없는 것들이
　었어. 협상 테이블의 모양과 회담 장소에 걸리는 국기의 크기 같은 것도 포함되어
　있었거든.

여 전쟁을 끝내긴 했다는 게 놀랍네.

6　What is NOT mentioned in the dialog?
대화에서 언급되지 <u>않은</u> 것은?

(a) The date that the Korean War started　한국전쟁이 일어난 날짜

(b) The details on prisoner of war exchanges
　　전쟁 포로 교환에 관한 세부 사항

(c) The disagreements the negotiators had
　　협상자들 간의 의견 차이

(d) The reason why the woman is late　여자가 늦은 이유

(e) The date the armistice was signed　휴전 협정이 맺어진 날짜

M Terrorism is the use of violent acts to gain political goals. Some examples of terrorism tactics include bombings, the hijacking of aircraft and ships, the kidnapping of important officials, the hostage taking of civilians, and the assassination of public officials. Terrorism is often used by small groups that are too weak to face the police and military forces of their target country. Terrorists hope to spread fear and panic by making random attacks against the civilian population. In doing so, they hope to weaken the government's position and to bring about a change in government. Terrorist groups often spring up in countries where there is severe repression. Most of the time, these groups are a minority or are disadvantaged in some way. Refugees are another source of terrorists. The millions of Palestinian refugees have been a prime source of terrorists since the 1960s. The policy of most world governments is to classify terrorists as criminals and not to negotiate with them.

▶ hijack (선박, 항공기를) 납치하다　hostage 인질　panic 공포, 공황
bring about 야기하다, 초래하다　spring up 싹이 트다　repression 억압
disadvantaged 불리한, 혜택받지 못한　refugee 난민, 망명자　classify 분류하다

남 테러란 정치적인 목적을 달성하기 위해 폭력 행위를 이용하는 것입니다. 테러 전
술의 예로는 폭탄 투하, 항공기 및 선박 납치, 요인 납치, 민간인 대상의 인질극,
공무원 암살이 있습니다. 테러는 보통 자신들이 목표로 삼는 나라의 경찰 및 군
병력과 정면으로 맞서기에는 힘이 약한 소규모 단체에 의해 저질러집니다. 테러
리스트는 민간인을 대상으로 무작위 공격을 함으로써 두려움과 공포를 퍼뜨리려
고 합니다. 그렇게 해서 그들은 그 정부의 입장을 약화시키고 정부를 변화시킬 수
있기를 바라죠. 테러 단체는 흔히 억압이 심한 나라에서 생기는데, 대개는 소수파
이거나 몇 가지 면에서 불리한 입장의 사람들인 경우가 많습니다. 난민은 테러리
스트의 또 다른 공급원입니다. 수백만 명의 팔레스타인 난민들은 1960년대 이후
테러리스트들의 주 공급원이 되어 왔습니다. 세계 대부분의 정부들은 테러리스트를
범죄자로 분류하고 그들과는 협상하지 않는다는 정책을 갖고 있습니다.

7　What is the main purpose of the talk?
담화의 주목적은 무엇인가?

(a) To discuss why people become terrorists
　　사람들이 왜 테러리스트가 되는지 이야기하려고

(b) To examine the goals of terrorists
　　테러리스트의 목적에 대해 살펴보려고

(c) To show people's reaction to terrorism
　　테러에 대한 사람들의 반응을 보여주려고

(d) To give an overall view of terrorism
　　테러에 대해 전반적으로 고찰하려고

(e) To prove that terrorism can be effective
　　테러가 효과적일 수도 있다는 것을 증명하려고

8

W The military forces of the world number in the tens of millions, and they are being supplied with the most sophisticated weapons in history. Military forces are often divided into active troops—those currently in uniform—and reserve troops—those that have some military training and can be called up from civilian life in a short time. Currently, China has the largest military forces in the world. It has 2.3 million active troops and 800,000 reserves. In second place is the United States with 1.5 million active soldiers and 1 million in reserve. While North Korea has fewer active troops, at 1.1 million, it has the potential to field 4.7 million reserve soldiers. Russia is in a similar position. It has 1 million active soldiers and a potential 20 million in reserve. As far as weapons go, the Russians have the most tanks with 22,000. They are followed by the United States with 7,600, China with 7,500, and North Korea with 3,500. None of the other nations approaches the United States in the size and the quality of their navy or aircraft. America has 12 aircraft carrier battle groups while Russia has one, and China and North Korea have none. America has over 3,000 first-line tactical fighter and bomber aircraft and thousands more in reserve. China comes in a close second with 2,500 aircraft while the Russians have 1,500, and North Korea comes in last with a little more than 500 aircraft.

▶ number (총수가) ~에 달하다　sophisticated 매우 복잡한, 정교한
active troop 현역군　reserve troop 예비군　call up 소집하다
field 전선에 배치하다　as far as ~ go ~에 관해서라면　aircraft carrier 항공모함
battle group 전투군　first-line 일선의　approach ~에 이르다, 필적하다

여 전 세계의 군인은 수천만 명에 이르며 그들은 역사상 가장 정교한 무기로 무장하
고 있습니다. 군인은 보통 지금 현재 군복을 입고 있는 현역군과 약간의 군사 훈
련을 받고 민간인으로 생활하다 단시간에 소집될 수 있는 예비군으로 분류됩니다.
현재 중국이 세계에서 가장 많은 병력을 보유하고 있습니다. 230만 명의 현역군
과 80만 명의 예비군이 있죠. 두 번째는 미국으로 150만 명의 현역군과 100만
명의 예비군을 보유하고 있습니다. 북한은 현역군의 수가 110만 명으로 중국과
미국보다는 적지만 전쟁에 투입할 수 있는 470만 명의 예비군을 보유하고 있습
니다. 러시아는 비슷합니다. 100만 명의 현역군과 2,000만 명의 예비군을 보유
하고 있죠. 무기에 관해서라면 러시아가 22,000대로 가장 많은 전차를 보유하고
있습니다. 미국이 그 다음으로 7,600대, 중국이 7,500대, 그리고 북한이 3,500
대를 보유하고 있습니다. 해군이나 공군의 규모와 질적인 측면에서는 그 어떤 나
라도 미국을 따라올 수 없습니다. 미국은 12개의 항공모함 전투단을 보유하고
있는 반면 러시아는 1개를 보유하고 있으며 중국과 북한은 없습니다. 미국은 일
선에 배치된 3,000대 이상의 전술 전투기와 폭격기를 보유하고 있으며 수천 대
이상의 항공기를 예비로 갖고 있습니다. 중국이 2,500대로 두 번째를 차지하면
서 그 뒤를 바짝 쫓고 있으며 러시아는 1,500대, 마지막으로 북한은 500대 조금
넘는 항공기를 보유하고 있습니다.

8 표에 나라 이름과 빠진 정보를 채워 넣으시오.

국가	현역군 (백만)	예비군 (백만)	항공기	항공모함
중국	2.3	0.8	2,500	0
미국	1.5	1	3,000 이상	12
Russia	1	20	1,500	1
North Korea	1.1	4.7	500 이상	0

9-10 **Integrated Questions**

Reading

▶ make peace 화해하다, 평화 조약을 맺다 Central Powers 제1차 세계대전 중에 연합군과 싸운 독일·오스트리아 등의 동맹제국 controversial 논쟁의 여지가 있는, 쟁점이 되는 humiliation 굴욕, 창피 revenge 복수; 설욕의 기회 stand out 두드러지다, 눈에 띄다 in the first place 우선, 애당초 clause 절; 조항 infuriate 격분시키다 stab someone in the back 배신하다, 등을 치다 interwar 제1·2차 대전 사이의

1918년 11월 11일 제1차 세계대전이 끝난 뒤 승전국 지도자들은 강화 조약을 맺기 위해 파리에 모였다. 몇 달 뒤 그들은 전쟁에 패한 동맹국들에게 5개의 조약을 제시하고 강제로 거기에 서명하도록 했다. 이들 조약 가운데 가장 논란의 여지가 많았던 것은 1919년 6월 28일 독일이 서명한 베르사유 조약이었다. 베르사유 조약은 흔히 제2차 세계대전의 원인을 제공했다는 이유로 비난받고 있다. 그 조약은 독일인에게는 굴욕적인 것이어서 많은 이들에게 자신들의 패배를 설욕해야 한다는 생각을 갖게 만들었다. 다른 무엇보다도 네 가지 조항이 두드러졌다. 첫째, 독일이 그 전쟁을 먼저 일으켰다는 비난을 받았다. 이른바 '전쟁 책임 조항'이라는 이 조항은 독일을 격분시켰는데 이는 결코 사실이 아니었다. 둘째, 독일은 자신들이 공격으로 인해 발생한 자신 파괴를 배상해야만 했다. 셋째, 독일의 군 병력은 겨우 10만 명으로 감축되었으며 전차나 항공기, 잠수함 보유는 허용되지 않았다. 끝으로, 독일은 동부와 서부 영토의 상당 부분을 잃게 되었다. 독일 정치인들은 선택의 여지 없이 그 조약에 서명할 수밖에 없었다. 아돌프 히틀러는 이후, 독일이 믿는 도끼에 발등이 찍힌 거라고 주장하며 이 같은 사실을 양차 대전 사이의 기간 동안 나치당에 대한 지지를 구축하는 데 이용했다.

M It has been common to blame the Treaty of Versailles of 1919 for the rise of Adolf Hitler to power and eventually the start of World War II. When he came to power in 1933, Hitler set about to undo the Treaty of Versailles by rebuilding the military and regaining Germany's lost lands. So, there is no doubt that the shabby treatment of Germany by the Allies at the end of the World War I helped sow the seeds of World War II. However, while Hitler used the humiliating treaty to rally the Germans behind him, the Treaty of Versailles was not the only reason Hitler came to power in 1933. In fact, he never received the full political support of the German people. His rise to leadership had a lot to do with the Great Depression. Hitler was appointed leader during a time of great economic difficulty. Germany had over six million unemployed, and many of them flocked to Hitler when he promised jobs to them. Despite this support, Hitler was never directly elected by the German people, and his Nazi Party never achieved a majority in the German legislature. But Hitler was powerful enough not to be ignored in a German coalition government. Once he was appointed chancellor in 1933, he used his new powers to become a dictator and to take complete control of Germany. From that point, he began to tear apart the Treaty of Versailles, first by rearming Germany and later by trying to regain Germany's lost territory. France's and Britain's reluctance to act, and America's isolationism allowed Hitler to rearm his military and to go on the march that led to World War II, which began in 1939.

▶ come to power 정권을 잡다, 세력을 얻다 set about 착수하다, ~하기 시작하다 undo (이미 한 일을) 원래로 되돌리다; (노력 등의) 결과를 망치다 shabby 인색한 rally 다시 불러 모으다, 규합하다 behind 뒤에서 지지하는 flock 모이다, 떼 지어 가다 coalition (정치적인) 연립, 제휴 chancellor 수상 dictator 독재자 tear apart 잡아 찢다 rearm 재무장하다[시키다]

남 1919년의 베르사유 조약으로 인해 아돌프 히틀러가 정권을 잡고 결국은 제2차 세계대전을 촉발시켰다고 보는 것이 일반적입니다. 히틀러는 1933년 정권을 잡자 군대를 재건하고 독일의 빼앗긴 영토를 수복함으로써 베르사유 조약을 무효화하기 시작했습니다. 제1차 세계대전이 끝나고 연합국들이 독일을 인색하게 대우해서 제2차 세계대전의 씨앗을 뿌리는 데 일조했다는 점에는 의심의 여지가 없죠. 그러나 히틀러가 그 굴욕적인 조약을 이용해 독일인을 결집시켜 자신을 지지하게 만들기는 했지만, 베르사유 조약이 히틀러가 1933년 정권을 장악하게 된 유일한 이유는 아니었습니다. 사실 그는 한 번도 독일인의 전폭적인 정치적 지지를 받아본 적이 없었습니다. 그가 지도자로 부상한 것은 대공황과 깊은 관계가 있습니다. 히틀러는 경제적으로 대단히 어려운 시기에 지도자로 임명되었습니다. 독일에는 6백만 명 이상의 실직자가 있었는데요, 그들 중 많은 수가 히틀러가 일자리를 약속하자 그에게 모여들었습니다. 이 같은 지지에도 불구하고 히틀러는 단 한 번도 독일 국민에게 직접적으로 선출된 적이 없으며 그가 이끄는 나치당은 독일 의회에서 결코 다수 의석을 얻지 못했습니다. 그러나 히틀러에게는 독일 연립내각이 무시할 수 없을 정도의 권력이 있었습니다. 1933년에 수상으로 임명되자 그는 자신의 새로운 권력을 이용해 독재자가 되어 독일을 완전히 장악했습니다. 그때부터 히틀러는 처음에는 독일을 재무장시키고 나중에는 독일이 빼앗긴 영토를 회복하기 위해 노력하면서 베르사유 조약을 깨기 시작했습니다. 행동에 나서기를 꺼려한 프랑스와 영국, 그리고 미국의 고립주의가 히틀러로 하여금 군대를 재무장하고 1939년에 시작된 제2차 세계대전으로 이어지는 행진을 계속할 수 있게 한 거죠.

9 읽기와 듣기 지문에 제시된 정보에 따르면 베르사유 조약과 관련된 내용 중 사실이 <u>아닌</u> 것은?
   (a) 독일 국민에게 굴욕적인 조약이었다.
   (b) 제2차 세계대전을 일으킨 원인으로 지목된다.
   (c) 독일에서 군대를 완전히 없앴다.
   (d) 히틀러가 자신의 명분을 위해 사람들을 규합하는 데 이용되었다.
   (e) 독일은 위협에 의해 그 조약에 서명했다.

10 히틀러는 1933년 어떻게 독일의 지도자가 되었는가?
   (a) 그는 독일 국민에 의해 직접 선출되었다.
   (b) 그는 많은 추종자를 거느리고 있었기 때문에 지도자로 임명되었다.
   (c) 그가 이끄는 나치당이 의회에서 가장 많은 의석을 차지했다.
   (d) 그는 지지를 얻기 위해 베르사유 조약을 조약을 파기했다.
   (e) 그는 프랑스와 영국, 미국에게 두려움의 대상이었다.

***Dictation 정답**: Exercise 스크립트 밑줄 참조

Vocabulary Preview

A

1 disintegrate: 굉장히 작은 조각으로 부서지다
2 hoax: 사람을 속여서 사실이 아닌 것을 사실인 것마냥 믿게 하는 계획
3 propaganda: 상대방의 명성을 떨어뜨리거나 자신의 입지를 강화하기 위해 사용되는 방법이나 정보
4 consortium: 공동의 목적을 위해 설립된 기관들의 연합
5 extraterrestrial: 지구 밖에서 비롯되거나 일어나는

1 From that point on / 미·소 우주 경쟁은 1975년에 끝났다. 그때부터 그 두 나라는 우주 탐사에 제한적으로 협력하기 시작했다.

2 fill in the blanks / 우주 비행의 역사에는 누락된 세부 사항이 존재하기 때문에 역사가들은 그 공백을 메우기 위해 노력하고 있다.

3 cosmonaut / 러시아 우주 계획에서 우주 여행자를 가리켜 사용되는 공통 용어는 '코스모넛'이다.

4 one step ahead / 우주 경쟁에서 미국은 항상 소련보다 한 발 앞서 있었다.

5 out of control / 로켓은 불안정해서 발사 몇 초 후에 통제 불능이 되었다.

6 gullible / 달 착륙이 미국 정부에 의해 조작되었다고 믿는 걸 보면 사람들이 얼마나 잘 속는지 알 수 있다.

7 docking / 그 우주 왕복선은 현재 국제 우주 정거장에 도킹 중이다.

Expressions and Meanings

1 김 새게 해서 미안해.

2 그건 좀 민감한 주제야.

3 나 그거 할래.

4 그건 꿈 같은 얘기야.

5 어찌 해야 할지 잘 모르겠어.

6 구체적인 건 잘 모르겠어.

7 마음대로 해.

g 너 맥 빠지게 하려던 건 아니었는데.

e 그 얘긴 하고 싶지 않은데.

d 나 그거 하고 싶어.

a 그건 이루는 게 불가능해 보이는 소망이야.

b 어떻게 해야 할지 모르겠어.

c 나에게 모든 정보가 다 있는 건 아니야.

f 네가 원하는 대로 해.

Listening Drill 1
p. 150~p. 151

Monolog

O (1) Dutch (2) 1608 (3) Reflecting (4) directly (5) lens (6) mirror (7) distortions (8) one-meter (9) size limits (10) 9.8 (11) atmosphere

G 1 (b) 2 (b)

S (1) T (2) F (3) T (4) T

W The telescope is one of mankind's more fascinating inventions. With it, we as humans have observed the distant planets, stars, and galaxies and have learned much about the universe around us. Many people believe the Italian scientist Galileo Galilei invented the first telescope, but the credit should really go to three Dutch inventors: Hans Lippershey, Jacob Metius, and Zacharias Janssen, who made the first telescope in 1608. The next year, Galileo improved on their design and began to make observations using his telescope. The operation of a telescope is quite simple. It works by gathering light to make distant objects appear closer. There are two main types of telescopes: reflecting and refracting telescopes. Reflecting telescopes operate by gathering light and bouncing it onto a mirror where the observer sees the image. With refracting telescopes, the observer looks directly through a lens and sees the image directly. Astronomers measure the size of a telescope by the size of its light-gathering component, which is a mirror or a lens. With bigger light-gathering devices, more distant and fainter objects can be seen. Refracting telescopes have size limits. A one-meter lens is the maximum possible size that will not cause

distortion of the image. Reflecting telescopes have no practical limit to their size. The largest yet built is 9.8 meters in diameter and is located on Mauna Kea in Hawaii. Like the lens, the Earth's atmosphere also distorts images, so the best telescope images currently come from the Hubble Space Telescope, despite it being smaller than the largest ones on Earth.

▶ reflecting telescope 반사망원경 refracting telescope 굴절망원경 bounce (소리·빛이) 반사하다 distortion 왜곡 in diameter 지름[직경]이 얼마인

여 망원경은 인류의 아주 멋진 발명품 중 하나입니다. 인간은 망원경으로 먼 곳에 있는 행성, 별, 은하를 관찰하고 인간을 둘러싼 우주에 대해 많은 것을 배웠습니다. 이탈리아의 과학자 갈릴레오 갈릴레이가 최초로 망원경을 발명했다고 생각하는 사람들이 많지만, 사실 그 공은 네덜란드의 세 발명가 한스 리퍼쉬, 제이콥 메티우스, 자카리아스 얀센에게 돌려져야 합니다. 1608년에 처음으로 망원경을 만들었죠. 그 다음 해, 갈릴레오는 그들의 설계를 개선해서 만든 자신의 망원경으로 관측을 시작했습니다. 망원경의 작동 원리는 꽤 단순합니다. 멀리 있는 물체가 더 가까이 보이도록 빛을 모으는 것이죠. 망원경에는 크게 반사망원경과 굴절망원경의 두 가지 유형이 있습니다. 반사망원경이 빛을 모아서 거울에 반사시키면 관측자는 거울에서 상(像)을 보게 되는 방식입니다. 굴절망원경으로 관측자는 렌즈를 통해 형상을 직접 보게 됩니다. 천문학자는 망원경의 크기를 빛을 모으는 부속품, 즉 거울이나 렌즈의 크기로 잽니다. 빛을 모으는 장치가 클수록 더 멀리 있고 희미한 물체를 볼 수 있습니다. 굴절망원경에는 크기 제약이 있습니다. 지름 1미터 렌즈가 상의 왜곡을 일으키지 않는 최대 크기입니다. 반사망원경은 크기에 실질적인 제약이 없습니다. 지금까지 만들어진 가장 큰 반사망원경은 직경 9.8미터로 하와이의 마우나케아에 있습니다. 지구의 대기도 렌즈처럼 상을 왜곡시키기 때문에 현재 가장 좋은 상은 허블 우주 망원경에서 보입니다. 비록 지구 상의 가장 큰 망원경들보다는 크기가 작지만요.

General Questions

1 담화의 목적은 무엇인가?

(a) 망원경의 설계 유형과 크기 제약에 대해 이야기하려고

(b) 망원경의 발명과 두 가지 주요 유형에 대해 설명하려고

(c) 거울 망원경이 더 좋은 이유를 살펴보려고

(d) 갈릴레오가 최초의 망원경을 발명하지 않았다는 것을 증명하려고

2 다음 중 가장 잘 요약된 것을 고르시오.

(a) 망원경은 크게 두 종류가 있는데 각각 기능과 크기가 매우 다르며, 이러한 차이는 인간의 우주 탐사 능력에 영향을 미쳤다.

(b) 크기나 멀리 떨어진 물체를 관측할 수 있는 능력과 같은 제약이 있긴 하지만 두 가지 유형의 망원경의 발명으로 우주에 대한 인간의 지식은 매우 증대되었다.

Specific Questions

다시 듣고 옳은 문장에는 T, 틀린 문장에는 F를 쓰시오.

(1) 망원경은 17세기 초에 유럽에서 발명되었다.

(2) 굴절망원경은 사람들이 더 큰 렌즈를 만들 수 없기 때문에 크기 제약이 있다.

(3) 대기가 없기 때문에 우주에 있는 망원경에는 더 좋은 상이 맺힌다.

(4) 가장 큰 반사망원경은 미국에 있다.

Dialog

N (1) science elective (2) everyone (3) astronomy / she decides to take it (4) astronomy (5) assignments (6) easy (7) telescopes (8) physics (9) in a group / doesn't expect much

G 1 (b) 2 (a)

S (1) F (2) F (3) T (4) F

W I have to pick some more classes for my first term at my new university. Can you give me some advice?

M What haven't you picked yet?

W I still need to decide on a science elective. Everyone has to take at least one science course.

M How about astronomy? I took it last year. The professor is really cool, and it was a very interesting class.

W Oh, astronomy is just so boring. All you do is look at the stars. It won't help me get ahead in life anyway.

M Suit yourself, but I'm telling you it was fun, and the assignments and exams were really easy.

W Yeah? So, well, what did you study in astronomy last year?

M We studied the formation of the universe, star classification, how galaxies are formed, black holes, dwarf stars, the solar system, the Space Race, types of telescopes, and lots of other cool things.

W Did you get to use any telescopes?

M Sure, several times. I even saw the Space Shuttle once when it was on a mission.

W No way! Is there any science involved? I mean, like equations and formulas and stuff?

M There's some physics, and it is a little tricky. But you do assignments in a group, and there's always at least one math or physics major in your group, so don't worry about it. Besides, the professor doesn't expect much from first-year students who are not astronomy majors. He knows most people take his class to cover the science elective.

W Sounds good. Sign me up for astronomy.

▶ elective 선택 과목 get ahead 출세하다, 성공하다 Suit yourself. 네 마음대로 해.
dwarf star 왜성 equation 방정식 formula 공식 tricky 다루기 힘든, 까다로운
Sign up for~ 나는 ~을 하고 싶다.

여 대학 첫 학기 수업을 선택해야 하는데 조언 좀 해줄래?
남 아직 선택하지 않은 게 뭔데?
여 과학 선택 과목을 정해야 해. 모든 신입생들은 과학 강좌에서 최소 한 과목은 수강해야 하거든.
남 천문학 어때? 내가 작년에 들었는데 교수님이 정말 멋지고 수업도 아주 재미있었어.
여 으, 천문학은 너무 지루해. 별 쳐다보는 게 전부잖아. 어쨌든 인생에서 성공하는 데는 별 도움이 안 될 거라고.
남 마음대로 해. 하지만 그 수업은 재미있었고, 과제와 시험이 정말 쉬웠어.
여 그래? 그럼, 작년 천문학 수업에서는 뭘 배웠어?
남 우주의 형성, 별의 분류, 은하가 어떻게 형성되었는지, 블랙홀, 왜성, 태양계, 우주 경쟁, 망원경의 종류, 그리고 그밖의 많은 멋진 것들을 공부했지.
여 망원경도 사용해봤어?
남 물론이지, 여러 번 썼어. 한번은 임무 수행 중인 우주선도 봤지.
여 그럴리가! 과학도 연관이 돼? 내 말은, 방정식이랑 공식 같은 것을 말이야.
남 물리학이 조금 나오는데 그건 좀 까다롭기. 하지만 그룹으로 과제를 하는 데다 그룹 안에 수학이나 물리학 전공자가 최소한 한 사람은 항상 있으니까 걱정하지 마. 게다가 교수님도 천문학 전공이 아닌 새내기 학생들에게 많은 걸 기대하지 않으셔. 학생들 대부분이 과학 선택 과목을 이수하기 위해 그 수업을 수강한다는 걸 교수님도 아시거든.
여 괜찮겠는걸. 나 천문학 수업 들을래.

1 여자가 남자에게 얘기를 하는 주된 이유는 무엇인가?
(a) 그가 그녀에게 뭔가 를 하게끔 납득시켜 주기를 원해서
(b) 강의를 선택하는 데 그의 조언이 필요해서
(c) 그녀의 교수가 어떤 사람인지 알고 싶어서
(d) 어떤 수업에서 그가 그녀를 좀 도와줬으면 해서

2 다음 중 가장 잘 요약된 것을 고르시오.
(a) 여자는 어떤 대학 수업에 대해 그 수업을 이전에 수강했던 사람과 이야기를 나눈 후 그 수업에 등록하기로 결정한다.
(b) 여자는 어떤 과목을 수강해야 할지 결정을 못 내려서 어느 과목이 가장 좋은지 알아보기 위해 물어보고 다닌다.

다시 듣고 옳은 문장에는 T, 틀린 문장에는 F를 쓰시오.
(1) 여자는 이미 최소 일 년은 대학에 다녔다.
(2) 그 대학의 새내기들은 과학 선택 과목을 수강하지 않기로 결정할 수 있다.
(3) 천문학 수업 학생들은 수업 과제를 할 때 그룹으로 한다.
(4) 남자는 천문학 수업에서 망원경을 사용했지만, 다소 지루한 경험이었다.

Listening Drill 2   p. 152~p. 153

Long Lecture

○ (1) dwarf planet (2) dwarf planets (3) comets
   (4) asteroids (5) satellites (6) separate (7) regular
   (8) satellite (9) elliptical (10) closer (11) moon
   (12) dwarf planet

1 (d)   2 (b)   3 (1) T (2) T (3) F (4) T   4 (d)
Dictation 정답: 스크립트 밑줄 참조

M Today, I'd like to talk about Pluto, which is no longer a planet. Well, actually, this is old news since it hasn't been considered a planet since 2006. From 1930, when it was first discovered, until 2006, Pluto was classed as one of the nine planets. Now there are only eight of what are now called "classical planets." Pluto has been downgraded to dwarf planet status. All of this was decided at a conference of the International Astronomical Union, or IAU, in 2006. The members decided on a new classification system for the solar system and made three groups: classical planets, consisting of the eight remaining planets, dwarf planets, consisting of Pluto and two others, and small solar system bodies, consisting of comets, asteroids, and other small objects. Objects that orbit the classical planets are considered separate and are called satellites, despite some being larger than classical planets and dwarf planets. For example, Titan, which orbits Saturn, is bigger than Mercury. The IAU states that a classical planet must have an independent, regular orbit around the sun. It also must not have any bodies—such as asteroids—surrounding it, other than satellites. Pluto fails to qualify since its orbit is rather elliptical, and, at times, Pluto is even closer to the sun than Neptune. In addition, Pluto's moon Charon is so large it may actually qualify as a dwarf planet. There were some

<u>protests</u> about this <u>status</u> <u>change</u> for Pluto, but, for the most part, the <u>participants</u> at the conference agreed that the change was <u>necessary</u>. Now we just have to <u>get</u> <u>used</u> <u>to</u> saying there are eight planets, rather than nine.

▶ Pluto 명왕성   class ~에 속하다, 분류되다   dwarf planet 왜행성   comet 혜성
asteroid 소행성   orbit 주위를 궤도를 그리며 돌다; 궤도   Saturn 토성
Mercury 수성   other than ~을 제외하고   elliptical 타원형의   at times 때때로
Neptune 해왕성

남 오늘은 더 이상 행성이 아닌 명왕성에 대해 이야기해보도록 하겠습니다. 음, 사실, 명왕성은 2006년부터 행성이 아닌 걸로 간주되었으니 오래된 소식이긴 하네요. 처음 발견된 1930년부터 2006년까지 명왕성은 9개 행성 가운데 하나로 분류 됐는데요. 이제는 '고전 행성'이라고 불리는 8개의 행성만이 있습니다. 명왕성은 왜행성 지위로 강등되었죠. 이 모두는 국제천문연맹, 즉 IAU의 2006년 총회에 서 결정되었습니다. 위원들은 태양계의 분류 체계를 새로 정하고 세 분류로 나누 었습니다. 남아 있는 8개 행성으로 구성된 고전 행성, 명왕성과 다른 두 별로 구 성된 왜행성, 그리고 혜성·소행성·다른 작은 천체들로 구성된 태양계 소천체 로 말이죠. 고전 행성 주위를 궤도를 그리며 도는 천체에는 고전 행성과 왜행성 보다 더 큰 것도 있지만 별개의 것으로 간주해서 위성이라 부릅니다. 예를 들어 토성의 둘레를 도는 타이탄은 수성보다 크죠. 고전 행성은 태양 주위를 독 립적이고, 일정한 궤도로 돌아야 한다고 IAU는 명시하고 있습니다. 고전 행성은 또한 위성 외에는 주위에 소행성 같은 어떤 천체도 가지고 있어서는 안 됩니다. 명왕성은 궤도가 약간 타원형이어서 해왕성보다 태양에 더 가까이 접근할 때도 있기 때문에 자격이 안 되죠. 게다가 명왕성의 위성인 카론은 너무 커서, 사실상 왜행성 자격이 된다고 볼 수도 있습니다. 명왕성의 이러한 지위 변화에 대한 약 간의 반대도 있긴 했지만 총회 참석자 대부분은 그 변화가 필요하다는 데 동의 했습니다. 이제 우리는 행성이 9개가 아니라 8개라고 말하는 데 익숙해져야겠죠.

1 강의의 주목적은 무엇인가?
(a) 새로운 행성 분류 체계에 대해 이야기하려고
(b) 여러 행성들의 궤도를 살펴보려고
(c) 몇몇 행성이 왜 왜행성이라고 불리는지 설명하려고
(d) 한 행성의 지위가 왜 바뀌었는지 설명하려고

2 다음 중 가장 잘 요약된 것을 고르시오.
(a) 한 국제 총회에서 새로운 행성 분류 체계가 만들어졌는데, 그에 따라 익히 알려진 9개 행성이 8개로 사실상 줄었다.
(b) 국제 총회의 결정 때문에 명왕성은 여러 가지 이유로 왜행성 등급으 로 강등되었다.

3 옳은 문장에는 T, 틀린 문장에는 F를 쓰시오.
(1) 고전 행성은 궤도가 일정해야 하고 위성 외에는 궤도에 다른 천체가 없어야 한다.
(2) 명왕성의 위성인 카론은 언젠가는 위성이 아닌 것으로 분류될 수도 있다.
(3) 태양 주위를 도는 명왕성의 궤도는 8개의 고전 행성의 궤도와 유사하 다.
(4) 고전 행성이나 왜행성 혹은 위성 자격을 갖추지 못한 천체를 위해 새 로운 등급이 신설되었다.

4 위성이 고전 행성으로 간주되지 않는 이유는?
(a) 행성의 자격을 갖출 만큼 충분히 크지 않다.
(b) 둘레를 도는 위성이 없다.
(c) 궤도가 일정하지 않고 타원형이다.
(d) 자체적으로 태양 주위를 궤도를 그리며 돌지는 않는다.

---

1 (c)　**2** 해설 참조　**3** (e)　**4** (d)　**5** (b)　**6** (c)　**7** (a)　**8** (d)
9 (b)　**10** (d)　**11** (d)　**12** (a)

1

W Galaxies are large <u>clusters</u> <u>of</u> <u>stars</u> that form the basic units of the universe. It is estimated that there are millions upon millions of galaxies in the universe. They <u>vary</u> <u>in</u> <u>shape</u> and <u>size</u>, but all formed in the <u>same</u> <u>fashion</u>. Astronomers generally agree that the <u>universe</u> <u>started</u> <u>with</u> the Big Bang about <u>14</u> <u>billion</u> years ago. At this time, there were only <u>dark</u> <u>matter</u>, helium, and hydrogen in the universe. Gradually, over the course of some <u>500</u> <u>million</u> <u>years</u>, clumps of dark matter <u>collided</u> and gathered together to <u>form</u> <u>larger</u> <u>bodies</u>. Eventually, they had enough mass to <u>have</u> <u>gravity</u>, which <u>attracted</u> more dark matter, helium, and hydrogen. This early form of a galaxy is called a <u>protogalaxy</u>. The shape of the galaxy now <u>formed</u> <u>over</u> another billion years. The helium and hydrogen moved toward the <u>inner</u> <u>area</u> of the galaxy, called the <u>core</u>, while the dark matter <u>stayed</u> <u>on</u> the <u>outside</u> <u>edge</u>, which is called the halo. In the core, the helium and hydrogen <u>collided</u> and began to create the first stars. Also, in the center of the core an <u>inner</u> <u>black</u> <u>hole</u> formed, which <u>prevented</u> the galaxy <u>from</u> <u>becoming</u> too large by <u>drawing</u> <u>matter</u> <u>toward</u> its center during the early period of the galaxy's formation. Without this black hole, astronomers believe there would be <u>no</u> <u>limit</u> <u>to</u> how large a <u>galaxy</u> <u>could</u> <u>grow</u>.

▶ cluster 성단(星團)   millions upon millions of 무수히 많은   hydrogen 수소
clump 덩어리   collide 충돌하다   mass 질량, 부피   gravity 중력
protogalaxy 원시 은하(계)

여 은하는 우주의 기본 단위를 형성하는 거대한 성단입니다. 우주에는 무수히 많은 은하가 있는 것으로 추정됩니다. 은하는 모양과 크기는 모두 다르지만 형성되는 방식은 같습니다. 천문학자들은 우주가 약 140억 년 전에 빅뱅과 함께 생성되었 다는 데 일반적으로 의견을 같이합니다. 그 당시 우주에는 암흑 물질과 헬륨, 수 소밖에 없었습니다. 암흑 물질 덩어리는 약 5억 년에 걸쳐 서서히 서로 충돌하 고 합쳐져 더 큰 천체를 형성했습니다. 마침내 중력이 생길 정도로 충분한 질량 을 갖추게 되자 더 많은 암흑 물질과 헬륨, 수소를 끌어당겼죠. 이러한 초기 형태 의 은하를 원시 은하라고 합니다. 지금의 은하 모양은 거기서 10억 년 이상이 더 지나 만들어졌습니다. 헬륨과 수소는 은하 내부의 핵으로 이동하고, 암흑 물질은 헤일로라는 바깥 가장자리에 있게 되었습니다. 핵에 있던 헬륨과 수소는 충돌하 여 최초의 별을 만들어내기 시작했습니다. 또한 핵 중심부에 내부 블랙홀이 형성 되어 은하가 형성되던 초기에 블랙홀의 중심으로 물질을 빨아들임으로써 은하가 너무 커지지 않을 수 있었죠. 이 블랙홀이 없었다면 은하는 무한대로 커졌을 거 라고 천문학자들은 생각합니다.

1 담화의 주목적은 무엇인가?
(a) 우주의 나이에 대해 논하려고
(b) 은하에 대한 몇 가지 기본적인 사실을 제공하려고
(c) 은하가 어떻게 형성되는지 설명하려고
(d) 은하의 구성을 묘사하려고
(e) 은하에 왜 크기 제약이 있는지 보여주려고

W The Earth is our home, yet a lot of people know very little about it. Today, I am <u>interviewing</u> <u>astronomer</u> Bruce Campbell, who is going to <u>fill</u> <u>in</u> some of the <u>blanks</u> for us.

M Thanks, Wendy. Well, I'm at a bit of a loss. Where should I start?

W How about with a few basic facts about the Earth?

M Certainly. In <u>our</u> <u>solar</u> <u>system</u>, Earth is the third planet from the sun. It is, <u>on</u> <u>average</u>, <u>150</u> <u>million</u> kilometers away from the sun, but it's sometimes a bit closer and sometimes a bit <u>farther</u> <u>away</u>.

W But not too close, I hope!

M No, no, just a few million extra kilometers. The Earth's <u>period</u> <u>of</u> <u>revolution</u> around the sun is <u>365.256 Earth</u> <u>days</u>.

W I've always thought it was 365 exactly. Is that why we <u>have</u> <u>leap</u> <u>years</u>?

M Yes, because the <u>rotation</u> is not exactly 365 days, every four years we must add a day to our calendars to make up for the difference. Now you should also know that the day itself is not exactly 24 hours. It is 23 hours, 56 minutes, and 4.2 seconds long. This is the time it takes the Earth to <u>rotate</u> <u>on</u> <u>its</u> <u>axis</u>.

W Okay, what about some of the <u>physical</u> <u>characteristics</u> of the Earth?

M The Earth is about <u>12,740</u> kilometers in <u>diameter</u> at the <u>Equator</u>, but, again, this is not the same in every direction as the Earth isn't a <u>perfect</u> <u>sphere</u>. Finally, I guess I should mention the <u>average</u> <u>temperature</u> of the Earth's surface is <u>15</u> <u>degrees</u> <u>Celsius</u>, which is what makes life possible here.

▶ fill in the blanks 공백을 메우다　at a loss 어찌할 바를 몰라　revolution 공전　leap year 윤년　rotation (지구의) 자전　axis 축　the equator 적도

여 지구는 우리가 살고 있는 곳인데도 많은 사람들이 지구에 대해 잘 모르고 있죠. 오늘은 천문학자 브루스 캠벨 씨를 모시고 같이 이야기를 나누며 우리가 몰랐던 것들에 대한 설명을 들어보도록 하겠습니다.

남 고마워요, 웬디. 음, 어떡할까요. 어디서부터 시작하죠?

여 지구에 관한 몇 가지 기본적인 내용부터 시작하면 어떨까요?

남 좋습니다. 우리가 속해 있는 태양계에서 지구는 태양으로부터 세 번째 행성입니다. 태양에서 평균 1억 5천만 킬로미터의 거리에 있는데, 그보다 좀 더 가까울 때도 있고 좀 더 멀어질 때도 있습니다.

여 하지만 아주 가까운 건 아니겠죠!

남 아뇨, 아뇨, 불과 몇 백만 킬로미터인걸요. 지구가 태양 주위를 공전하는 주기는 지구 날짜로 365.256일입니다.

여 전 딱 365일인 줄 알았어요. 그래서 윤년이 있는 건가요?

남 예, 자전이 정확하게 365일인 건 아니라서 그 간극을 메꾸기 위해 4년마다 달력에 하루를 보태야 하죠. 그런데 하루가 딱 24시간은 아니라는 것도 아셔야겠네요. 23시간 56분 4.2초예요. 지구가 축을 중심으로 자전하는 데 걸리는 시간이죠.

여 그렇군요. 지구의 물리적 특성은 어떻게 되나요?

남 지구의 적도 지름은 약 12,740킬로미터인데 지구가 완전한 구체는 아니기 때문에 이 역시 모든 방향에서 똑같지는 않습니다. 마지막으로 지구의 평균 지표면 온도는 섭씨 15도라는 점을 말씀드려야 할 것 같군요. 그래서 지구에서 생명이 존재할 수 있는 거죠.

2　지구에 대한 정보로 표를 완성하시오.

태양으로부터의 평균 거리	150 million kilometers (1억 5천만 킬로미터)
공전 주기	365.256 Earth days (지구 날짜로 365.256일)
자전 주기	23 h 56 m 4.2 s (23시간 56분 4.2초)
적도 지름	12,740 kilometers (12,740 킬로미터)
평균 지표면 온도	15 degrees Celsius (섭씨 15도)

3-4

W The exploration of space has <u>come</u> <u>with</u> <u>a</u> <u>price</u>, not just <u>in</u> <u>terms</u> <u>of</u> money but also in human lives. Since the Space Age began in 1957, many people have died in accidents on the ground, and 18 people have lost their lives in <u>spaceship</u> <u>flights</u>. Four of the dead were Russian <u>cosmonauts</u>, who died in <u>two</u> <u>separate</u> <u>accidents</u> during their return to Earth. In one accident in 1967, the spacecraft's <u>parachutes</u> <u>failed</u> <u>to</u> <u>open</u> properly, and the lone cosmonaut <u>died</u> <u>on</u> <u>impact</u> <u>with</u> the Earth. In the second incident in 1971, three cosmonauts died from depressurization. A <u>hatch</u> had <u>failed</u> <u>to</u> <u>close</u> properly when they were preparing to return to Earth after <u>docking</u> <u>with</u> a <u>space</u> <u>station</u>. The <u>remaining</u> 14 people died in the two American Space Shuttle disasters. The first <u>occurred</u> <u>on</u> January 28, 1986, when the shuttle *Challenger* <u>exploded</u> <u>during</u> <u>takeoff</u>, killing its seven occupants. A <u>full</u> <u>investigation</u> revealed that <u>fuel</u> <u>leaks</u> from one of the <u>two</u> <u>booster</u> <u>rockets</u> had <u>ignited</u> the main fuel tank. The second Space Shuttle disaster involved the <u>disintegration</u> of the *Columbia* on reentry on February 16, 2003. It was later determined that, <u>during takeoff</u>, a piece of <u>foam</u> protecting the fuel tank had <u>broken off</u>, struck the <u>leading edge</u> of the left wing, and made a hole in the left wing. This was unknown to all, and, <u>on reentry</u>, the wing began to disintegrate, causing the shuttle to <u>tumble</u> <u>out</u> <u>of</u> <u>control</u> and also to disintegrate, killing all seven astronauts <u>on</u> <u>board</u>.

▶ lone 혼자의, 고독한; 고립된　cosmonaut 러시아 우주 비행사　depressurization 감압　hatch 승강구, 출입구　dock 도킹하다, (우주선끼리) 결합하다　space shuttle 우주 왕복선　occupant 탑승자　booster rocket 보조 추진 로켓　ignite ~에 불을 붙이다, 점화하다　disintegration 붕괴, 분해　reentry 재진입, 귀환　foam 발포체　break off 부러지다, 갈라지다　leading edge (프로펠러, 날개의) 앞쪽 언저리[끝]　disintegrate 산산조각이 나다　tumble 굴러 떨어지다　out of control 통제가 안 되는

여 우주 탐사에는 으레 대가가 따릅니다. 돈뿐만이 아니라 인간의 생명까지도요. 1957년에 우주 시대가 시작된 이래 많은 사람들이 지상에서 사고로 죽었으며 18명이 우주 비행 중에 목숨을 잃었습니다. 그들 중 네 명은 지구로 귀환하던 중 서로 다른 두 건의 사고로 죽은 러시아 우주 비행사들이었습니다. 1967년에 있었던 한 사고에서는 우주선의 낙하산이 제대로 펴지지 않아 러시아 우주 비행사 한 명이 땅에 떨어져 숨졌습니다. 1971년에 있었던 두 번째 사고에서는 세 명의 러시아 우주 비행사가 압력 강하로 사망했는데요. 우주 정거장과 도킹한 후 지구로 귀환할 준비를 하고 있을 때 승강구가 제대로 닫히지 않았던 거죠. 나머지 14명은 2건의 미국 우주 왕복선 참사로 사망했습니다. 첫 번째 사고는 1986년 1월 28일에 일어났는데, 우주 왕복선 챌린저 호가 이륙 도중에 폭발하여 탑승자 7명이 숨졌습니다. 전면적인 조사를 통해 두 개의 보조 추진 로켓 중 하나에서 연료가 새어나와 본체 연료 탱크가 점화된 것으로 밝혀졌습니다. 두 번째 우주 왕복선 참사는 2003년 2월 16일 콜럼비아 호가 지구 대기권으로 귀환하다가 해체되면서 일어났습니다. 나중에 규명된 바에 따르면 이륙할 때 연료 탱크를 보호하는 발포체 하나가 떨어져나가 왼쪽 날개의 앞쪽 언저리에 부딪혀 왼쪽 날개에 구멍이 난 것이었죠. 이 사실을 아무도 모르고 있다가 대기권 재진입 시 왼쪽 날개가

부서지기 시작했고 이로 인해 왕복선은 통제 불능 상태에 빠져 역시 분해되고 말았습니다. 탑승하고 있던 7명의 우주 비행사 모두 사망했죠.

3 러시아의 네 우주 비행사가 사망한 주원인은 무엇이었는가?

(a) 복잡한 우주선 작동에 서툴러서

(b) 곤경에 처한 우주 비행사들을 구출해지 못해서

(c) 시험도 거치지 않고 서둘러 우주선을 비행시켜서

(d) 우주 정거장을 제대로 만들지 않아서

(e) 우주선 주요 부분의 기계적 결함으로

4 콜럼비아 호 우주 왕복선 참사에 대해 담화로부터 유추할 수 있는 것은?

(a) 우주 비행사들은 날개에 구멍이 나 있다는 것을 알고 있었지만 일단 착륙하기로 결정했다.

(b) 콜럼비아 호의 연료와 산소가 떨어져가고 있었기 때문에 승무원들은 착륙을 위해 노력해야 했다.

(c) 지상 관제소에서는 날개 손상을 알고 있었지만 승무원들에게는 이 사실을 알리지 않았다.

(d) 비행 중 우주선 외부의 손상을 살펴볼 방법이 마련되어 있지 않았다.

(e) 시험을 해보았던 지상의 전문가들은 발포체가 왕복선 날개에 손상을 줄 수 있으리라고 생각하지 않았다.

5-6 Level up

G So, what did you <u>learn</u> <u>about</u> <u>stars</u> for our project?

B One of the more <u>interesting</u> <u>aspects</u> <u>of</u> stars is that they have <u>life</u> <u>cycles</u> like <u>living</u> <u>organisms</u>.

G But they aren't living things, are they? Stars are just <u>collections</u> <u>of</u> <u>matter</u> that come from <u>collapsing</u> <u>giant</u> <u>molecular</u> <u>clouds</u>.

B Right. And these <u>giant</u> <u>clouds</u> <u>of</u> <u>matter</u> were mostly composed of helium and hydrogen. They collapsed, and <u>fragments</u> <u>condensed</u> into <u>swirling</u> <u>masses</u>, which formed the beginnings of stars, called <u>protostars</u>.

G So, a <u>protostar</u> is the <u>first</u> <u>stage</u> <u>of</u> a star?

B Yes. Eventually, most <u>protostars</u> <u>change</u> <u>into</u> stars by the fusion of hydrogen into helium.

G Just like in a <u>nuclear</u> <u>reactor</u>.

B Yes, but on a much more <u>massive</u> <u>scale</u>. The size and life of the star <u>depend</u> <u>on</u> the masses involved and the ability of the star to <u>convert</u> hydrogen into helium.

G What did you find out about our sun?

B It's a medium-sized star that <u>burns</u> <u>brightly</u>, but, thankfully, it'll never <u>achieve</u> great mass. Our sun is currently about <u>four</u> <u>and</u> <u>a</u> <u>half</u> <u>billion</u> years old.

G When will it die?

B One website said that by the time it is nine to ten billion years old, its <u>hydrogen</u> <u>supply</u> will be <u>exhausted</u>. Then, the sun will <u>expand</u> <u>into</u> a massive <u>red</u> <u>giant</u> and will eventually explode and become a <u>planetary</u> <u>nebula</u>.

G Right. That is a glowing cloud of <u>gas</u> <u>and</u> <u>plasma</u> that eventually disappears. Is that the final stage of a star's life?

B No. What will remain is the collapsed <u>inner</u> <u>core</u> of the sun, which will be about the size of the Earth. This is called a <u>white</u> <u>dwarf</u>. This remnant will continue to <u>give</u> <u>off</u> <u>heat</u> for many millions of years and will finally just become a black rock, which is the final stage of star death.

▶ life cycle 생활 주기; 생활사 molecular 분자의 fragment 조각, 파편 condense 압축되다 swirling 소용돌이치는 protostar 원시별 nuclear reactor 원자로 exhaust 다 써버리다, 소진시키다 planetary nebula 행성 모양의 성운 glowing 빨갛게 달아오른 remnant 잔여물

여 그래, 별에 대한 우리 과제에 쓸 별에 관한 사실을 뭐 좀 알아냈니?

남 별이 가지고 있는 꽤 흥미로운 점 중 하나는 살아 있는 유기체처럼 생활 주기가 있다는 거야.

여 하지만 별은 살아 있는 게 아니잖아? 별은 그냥 붕괴하는 거대 분자 구름에서 나오는 물질의 집합체야.

남 맞아. 그리고 그 거대한 물질 구름은 대부분 헬륨과 수소로 구성되었어. 구름이 붕괴하면서 그 조각들이 소용돌이치는 덩어리로 압축되어 원시별이라고 하는 초기 별이 만들어졌지.

여 그럼 원시별이 별의 첫 단계야?

남 응. 결국 대부분의 원시별은 수소가 헬륨으로 핵융합되면서 별이 돼.

여 원자로 속에서처럼 말이지.

남 응, 하지만 훨씬 더 어마어마한 규모로. 별의 크기와 수명은 질량에 따라, 수소를 헬륨으로 변환하는 별의 능력에 따라 달라.

여 우리 태양계의 태양에 대해서는 뭐 알아냈어?

남 우리 태양은 밝게 불타는 중간 크기의 별인데 다행히도 질량이 많이 늘지는 않을 거야. 우리 태양은 현재 약 45억 년 정도 됐어.

여 태양은 언제 없어질까?

남 한 웹사이트에는 90에서 100억 년쯤 되면 수소 공급이 바닥날 거라고 나와 있어. 그럼 태양은 엄청난 질량의 적색 거성으로 팽창해 결국 폭발해서 행성상 성운이 되겠지.

여 맞아. 그건 빨갛게 타오르는 가스와 플라즈마 구름인데 결국 사라지지. 그게 별의 마지막 단계인가?

남 아니. 태양의 붕괴된 내부 핵이 지구 크기만하게 남게 될 거야. 백색 왜성이라는 건데. 이 잔여물이 수백만 년 동안 열을 계속 방출하다가 마침내 검은 돌이 되는데 그것이 별이 소멸하는 마지막 단계야.

5 별의 크기와 수명에서 중요한 요소는 무엇인가?

(a) 헬륨을 수소로 전환하는 능력과 포함하고 있는 질량

(b) 원시별을 형성하는 초기 물질의 구성과 질량

(c) 적색 거성에서 행성상 성운으로, 그리고 다시 백색 왜성으로 이행하는 것

(d) 원시별이 만들어진 거대 분자 구름의 크기

(e) 별이 백색 왜성이 되기 전 내부 핵의 크기

6 다음 중 내용을 가장 잘 요약한 것을 고르시오.

(a) 별은 다른 살아 있는 유기체처럼 생활 주기가 있어서 수소와 헬륨 공급이 소진되면 결국 사멸된다.

(b) 별은 내부의 검은 핵으로 변하기 전에 잠깐 동안 밝게 빛나면서 생명의 몇 가지 단계를 거치며 진화한다.

(c) 별은 수소를 헬륨으로 변환하는 능력과 질량에 따라 조금씩 다르게 생명의 여러 단계를 거친다.

---

7 Level up

W I heard that a Korean woman has <u>joined</u> <u>the</u> <u>ranks</u> <u>of</u> astronauts. You must be proud of her and of your country.

M Yes, we are all very proud. Yi So-Yeon went into space in 2008 aboard a Russian spaceship. The ship <u>docked</u> <u>with</u> the International <u>Space</u> <u>Station</u>, and she spent around ten days there.

W That's amazing. What did she do while she was <u>on</u> <u>board</u> the space station?

M I'm not sure. I recall that she was <u>conducting</u> some <u>scientific</u> <u>experiments</u>, something to do with <u>fruit</u> <u>flies</u>, and, maybe, I think, she observed Chinese <u>dust</u> <u>storms</u>

blowing into Korea. But don't <u>quote</u> me on that.

W Wasn't a man <u>selected</u> as the first Korean to <u>go into</u> <u>space</u>, but his flight was cancelled?

M Ah, not exactly. He was replaced. This is a little embarrassing and is <u>kind of</u> a <u>touchy topic</u>.

W Oh, I'm sorry.

M It's okay. The reason they <u>made the switch</u> was that the Russians think he <u>broke some rules</u> while he was training in Russia. The details are <u>sketchy</u>, so it's best not to say much about it.

W I understand.

▶ fruit fly 초파리 dust storm 황진, 흙먼지 폭풍 Don't quote me on that 그 점에 대해 나를 인용하지 마라, 즉 정확한 사실이라고 확신할 수는 없다는 의미 embarrassing 난처한, 곤란한 touchy 조심스러운, 예민한 switch 변경 sketchy 대강의, 개략적인

여 한국인 여성이 우주 비행사의 반열에 올랐다던데. 그 사람과 너희 나라가 정말 자랑스럽겠다.

남 응, 모두들 아주 자랑스러워하지. 이소연 씨는 러시아 우주선을 타고 2008년에 우주에 갔어. 우주선이 국제 우주 정거장에 도킹하고나서 거기서 열흘 가량을 보냈지.

여 굉장하다. 우주 정거장에 있는 동안 그녀는 뭘 했어?

남 확실히는 몰라. 내 기억으로는 초파리와 관련된 어떤 과학 실험들을 하고 아마 한국으로 불어오는 중국의 황사도 관측했던 것 같아. 확실한 건 아냐.

여 우주에 갈 최초의 한국인으로 남자가 뽑혔다가 취소되지 않았나?

남 아, 꼭 그런 것만도 아냐. 교체된 거지. 조금 당혹스럽고 말하기 거북한 건데.

여 아, 미안해.

남 괜찮아. 교체된 이유는 러시아 사람들이 그 남자가 러시아에서 훈련받는 동안 몇 가지 규칙을 어겼다고 생각해서야. 구체적인 건 잘 모르겠어. 그래서 거기에 대해서는 여러 말 안 하는 게 상책이지.

여 무슨 말인지 알겠어.

7 Why does the man say, "Don't quote me on that," when discussing Yi So-Yeon's space trip?
이소연의 우주 여행에 대해 이야기하면서 남자는 왜 "Don't quote me on that"이라고 말하는가?

(a) He is a little uncertain of the facts of her space trip.
그는 그녀의 우주 여행에 대해 확실히는 모른다.

(b) He is embarrassed because he knows so little.
그는 자신이 아는 게 너무 없어서 창피하다.

(c) He feels that the trip is not important enough to discuss.
그는 그 여행이 이야기할 만큼 중요하지는 않다고 생각한다.

(d) He is careful not to talk about it in too much detail. 그는 그에 대해 너무 구체적으로 이야기하지 않으려고 주의하고 있다.

(e) He says that the details of what happened are too sketchy to discuss. 일어났던 일에 대한 구체적인 내용이 별로 알려진 게 없어서 이야기하기가 어렵다는 말이다.

8 Level up

W Approximately 50 <u>astronomical units</u> from the sun, or fifty times the distance from the Earth to the sun, lies the Kuiper Belt. Astronomers believe this donut-shaped region is where all of the <u>comets that orbit</u> the sun <u>on regular paths</u> come from. <u>Comets</u> are not the only objects in the Kuiper Belt. Astronomers estimate there are <u>over 70,000 objects</u> in this region. Some are <u>comets</u>, some are <u>asteroids</u>, others are <u>icy balls of matter</u>, and many others have yet to be examined. Most of the objects examined are over 96 kilometers <u>in diameter</u>, and six of them are larger than 800 kilometers <u>in diameter</u>. Pluto is considered to be in the Kuiper Belt due to its distance from the sun. Astronomers are <u>keeping an eye on</u> this region and are <u>tracking</u> many of the <u>larger objects</u> because some objects that could <u>potentially collide with</u> the Earth in the future may come from the Kuiper Belt.

▶ astronomical unit 천문 단위 track 추적하다, 자국을 쫓다

여 태양으로부터 약 50천문 단위, 즉 지구에서 태양까지의 거리의 50배 되는 지점에 카이퍼 벨트가 있습니다. 천문학자들은 이 도넛 모양의 구역에서 규칙적인 궤도로 태양 주위를 공전하는 혜성이 온다고 생각합니다. 카이퍼 벨트에는 혜성만 있는 것은 아닙니다. 천문학자들은 그 구역에 7만 개 이상의 행성이 있을 거라고 추정합니다. 그 중에는 혜성도 있고, 소행성도 있으며, 얼음 덩어리로 된 물질과 아직 조사하지 못한 다른 많은 것들이 있죠. 밝혀진 행성들 중 대부분은 지름이 96킬로미터 이상이고 그 중 6개는 지름이 800킬로미터보다 더 큽니다. 명왕성은 태양과의 거리 때문에 카이퍼 벨트에 있는 것으로 간주됩니다. 천문학자들은 이 구역을 계속 주시하며 크기가 큰 편에 속하는 여러 행성들의 경로를 추적하고 있습니다. 미래에 지구와 충돌할 가능성이 있는 몇몇 행성이 카이퍼 벨트에서 올 수도 있으니까요.

8 What is the purpose of the talk? 담화의 목적은 무엇인가?

(a) To explain where comets are first created
혜성이 처음에 어디서 만들어지는지 설명하려고

(b) To demonstrate how space distances are measured
우주의 거리 측정이 어떻게 이루어지는지 실증하려고

(c) To show how objects are tracked in space
우주에서 행성의 경로를 어떻게 추적하는지 보여주려고

(d) To discuss a region of space with many objects
행성이 많이 있는 우주의 한 구역에 대해 이야기 하려고

(e) To prove that the Earth is in danger of collisions
지구가 충돌 위험에 있다는 것을 증명하려고

9

M There are two main types of eclipses—solar and lunar. Both types <u>occur rarely</u> and only when there is a <u>unique alignment of</u> the Earth, sun, and moon. During a solar eclipse, the moon covers the sun, but during a lunar eclipse, the Earth is between the moon and the sun and <u>blocks the sunlight</u>. Lunar eclipses can be seen over a large part of the world and can last for <u>more than an hour</u>, but solar eclipses can only be <u>observed along a narrow path</u> several hundred kilometers wide and do not last for a long time—often <u>less than five</u> minutes. Solar eclipses can be either partial or total. During a <u>partial eclipse</u>, only part of the sun may be covered by the moon's alignment with it. During a <u>total eclipse</u>, the entire sun is covered by the moon. The <u>reason this occurs</u> is that, because of the distance the Earth is from the sun and the moon, both the sun and the moon appear to be the same size to an observer on Earth. <u>Observers of</u> a total solar eclipse need to <u>take care of their eyes</u>. During a solar eclipse, people can <u>suddenly be blinded</u> by the <u>intensity of</u> the sun's light when the eclipse <u>begins to end</u>. Using a viewer designed to observe solar eclipses is the best way to avoid this danger. With lunar eclipses, there is no such danger.

▶ eclipse 식(蝕)   alignment 정렬   intensity 강렬함

남 식(蝕)에는 크게 두 가지 종류가 있는데요. 바로 일식과 월식입니다. 둘 다 잘 일어나지 않고 지구와 태양, 달이 특수하게 정렬될 때만 일어납니다. 일식 때는 달이 태양을 가리지만, 월식 때는 지구가 달과 태양 사이에 위치해 태양 빛을 가립니다. 월식은 세계 대부분의 지역에서 볼 수 있고 한 시간 넘게 지속되기도 하지만, 일식은 몇 백 킬로미터 넓이의 좁은 경로를 따라서만 관측될 수 있으며 지속되는 시간도 짧습니다. 5분이 안 될 때도 많죠. 일식은 부분 일식이거나 개기 일식일 수도 있는데요. 부분 일식 때는 달과 태양의 정렬로 태양의 일부분만이 가려집니다. 개기 일식 때는 태양이 달에 의해 완전히 가려지죠. 이런 현상이 일어나는 이유는 지구와 태양 및 달의 거리로 인해 태양과 달이 지구에 있는 관찰자에게는 같은 크기로 보이기 때문입니다. 개기 일식을 관찰할 때는 눈을 조심해야 합니다. 일식 때는 태양 빛이 너무 강해서 일식이 끝나기 시작하면 갑자기 눈이 안 보이게 될 수 있습니다. 일식을 관찰할 수 있도록 설계된 관측기를 사용하는 것이 이러한 위험을 피하는 가장 좋은 방법이죠. 월식에는 그런 위험이 없습니다.

9 담화에 따르면 다음 중 사실이 <u>아닌</u> 것은?
(a) 일식은 수명이 그다지 길지 않다.
(b) 월식 때는 태양이 달을 가린다.
(c) 월식 때는 지구가 달의 태양 빛을 가린다.
(d) 월식 때는 눈을 보호할 필요가 없다.
(e) 일식 때는 달이 태양을 가린다.

10

G   Dad, what's a light year?

M   Where did you hear that term?

G   From this science fiction show. It said a planet was only a few hundred light years away, and then the spaceship was there <u>in a few seconds</u>. That's not possible, right?

M   <u>Not nowadays</u>, that's for sure. It's not possible without a faster-than-light-speed ship. A light year? <u>To put it as easily as</u> I can, imagine the light from a flashlight. Now, if you took that light and <u>pointed it at</u> the sky, the distance that the light <u>travels in one Earth year</u> is a light year.

G   What's the speed of light?

M   I don't know exactly. I guess we can <u>look it</u> up.

G   I'll do it. Hmm... This astronomy book says the speed of light is approximately <u>300,000 kilometers</u> per second, which is about <u>180,000 miles</u> per second.

M   Let's do an experiment. How long would it <u>take to get to</u>, say, the sun, from Earth, at the speed of light?

G   You want me to <u>figure it out</u>?

M   Sure, why not? How far is the sun from the Earth?

G   That's an easy one because we did that in science class this term. I think it was <u>93 million</u> miles.

M   Right. Now, if your spaceship had a <u>light-speed drive</u>, how long would it take to reach the sun?

G   I need a calculator first. Let's see. Just one second... Ah, I've got it.

▶ flashlight 손전등   Earth year 지구년, 지구의 1년   say 말하자면, 이를테면

여 아빠, 광년이 뭐예요?

남 그 말은 어디서 들었니?

여 여기 공상 과학 프로그램에서요. 어떤 행성이 겨우 몇 백 광년밖에 떨어져 있지 않아서 우주선이 몇 초만에 간다고 나오던데요. 불가능한 일이죠, 그렇죠?

남 확실히 지금은 가능하지 않지. 빛의 속도보다 빠른 우주선이 없이는 불가능해.

광년이라고 했니? 최대한 쉽게 설명하자면 손전등의 불빛을 생각해보렴. 자, 네가 그 불빛을 하늘에 비추었다고 가정했을 때 그 빛이 1지구년 동안 이동하는 거리가 1광년이란다.

여 빛의 속도는 어떻게 되는데요?

남 정확히는 나도 모르겠구나. 찾아봐야겠다.

여 제가 찾아볼게요. 흠… 이 천문학 책에는 빛의 속도가 초당 약 30만 킬로미터라고 나와 있는데요. 초속 18만 마일쯤 된대요.

남 실험을 하나 해보자꾸나. 이를테면 지구에서 태양까지는 빛의 속도로 얼마나 걸릴까?

여 저더러 계산하라고요?

남 그래, 못할 게 뭐니? 태양은 지구로부터 얼마나 떨어져 있지?

여 그거야 쉽죠. 이번 학기 과학 시간에 했었거든요. 9,300만 마일이었던 것 같아요.

남 맞았다. 이제 네 우주선이 광속으로 움직인다고 가정하면 태양에 도착하는 데는 얼마나 걸릴까?

여 일단 계산기가 있어야 해요. 어디 보자. 1초에… 아, 알았어요.

10 광속으로 움직이는 우주선은 지구에서 태양에 도착하기까지 얼마나 걸리겠는가?
(a) 51분 6초   (b) 310초
(c) 9분 3초   (d) 8분 6초
(e) 1초

11-12   Level up

W   Why is there life on Earth but not on Mars or Venus? It is because of <u>our location</u>. Earth is in a unique position among the planets in that it is not too close to the sun so that <u>it fries us</u>, nor is it so far away that we're in a <u>state of perpetual</u> winter. With an <u>average temperature of 15 degrees Celsius</u>, Earth is ideal for life. If the temperature were just a few degrees colder or hotter, our ecosystems on Earth would be <u>so disrupted</u> that life might not survive. Imagine if <u>Earth's orbit</u> somehow changed to make us closer to or <u>farther away from</u> the sun, yet the change was so slight that life was still <u>somehow possible</u>. There would be <u>drastic changes</u> in where people live. If the Earth moved closer to the sun, then the <u>equatorial regions</u> would become <u>unbearably hot</u>, and people, animals, and plants could not survive there. There would be <u>mass migrations</u> north and south, with most people going north due to its <u>larger landmass</u>. <u>Unsettled regions</u> of the Northern Hemisphere, such as Canada, Alaska, and Russia would become <u>prime real estate</u> on an Earth that moved closer to the sun. Of course, things might get too unbearable if one moved too far north or south, since the <u>polar regions</u> get almost <u>continuous sunlight</u> for part of the year. Also, the <u>polar regions</u> would most likely <u>lose their icecaps</u>, <u>leading to</u> a rise in the world's ocean levels, which would cause even more people to migrate. The opposite would occur <u>during a move</u> away from the sun. The <u>northernmost</u> and <u>southernmost</u> regions of the planet would be too cold to support life while the <u>equatorial regions</u> would be <u>overrun</u> by those escaping the cold.

▶ perpetual 영구의, 계속 반복되는   equatorial 적도의   landmass 광대한 땅, 대륙   the Northern Hemisphere 북반구   polar 극지의   icecap 만년설   northernmost 가장 북쪽의   southernmost 가장 남쪽의   overrun 들끓다, 범람하다

여 화성이나 금성이 아닌 지구에 생명이 존재하는 이유는 무엇일까요? 그것은 우리

의 위치 때문입니다. 지구는 튀겨질 정도로 태양에 너무 가깝지도 않고, 끝없이 겨울이 계속될 정도로 너무 멀리 떨어져 있지도 않다는 점에서 행성들 사이의 독특한 위치에 있죠. 지구는 평균 기온이 섭씨 15도로 생명체에 이상적입니다. 기온이 몇 도만 더 춥거나 더웠어도 지구의 우리 생태계는 상당히 망가져서 생명이 살아남지 못했을지도 모르죠. 지구의 궤도가 어쩌다 바뀌어서 우리가 태양에 더 가까워지거나 더 멀어졌다고 상상해보세요. 아직은 그 변화가 미미해서 생명체는 어떻게든 여전히 존재할 겁니다. 사람들이 사는 곳에는 급격한 변화가 생기겠죠. 지구가 태양에 더 가까워지면 적도 지역은 견딜 수 없을 정도로 뜨거워져서 사람과 동물, 식물이 그곳에 살 수 없을 거예요. 북쪽과 남쪽으로 대이주가 일어날 텐데, 북쪽 대륙이 더 크기 때문에 대부분의 사람들이 북쪽으로 이동할 것입니다. 캐나다, 알래스카, 러시아 같이 북반구의 정착민이 없었던 지역이 태양에 가까워진 지구에서는 주요 부동산이 될 거예요. 물론 북쪽이나 남쪽으로 너무 멀리 가면 극지에는 연중 얼마간은 거의 계속해서 햇빛이 내리쬐기 때문에 너무 견디기 힘들 수도 있습니다. 또한 극지방의 만년설이 대부분 녹아 전 세계의 해수면이 상승하게 되어 훨씬 더 많은 사람들이 이주하게 될 겁니다. 태양에서 멀어질 때는 정반대의 상황이 벌어지겠죠. 지구의 최북단과 최남단 지역은 너무 추워서 생명을 유지할 수 없고, 적도 지역은 추위를 피해 온 사람들로 북새통을 이룰 것입니다.

11 강의에 따르면 지구가 태양에 더 가까워질 경우 북반구에 사람들이 더 많아지게 되는 주된 이유는 무엇인가?

   (a) 일 년 중 얼마간은 계속해서 햇빛이 내리쬘 테니까
   (b) 산이 아주 많아서 만년설이 녹아도 홍수가 나지 않을 테니까
   (c) 극지방의 만년설이 녹아 더 많은 물을 제공할 테니까
   (d) 남반구보다 공간이 더 많으니까
   (e) 눈과 얼음이 더 많아서 계속 서늘할 테니까

12 다음 중 내용을 가장 잘 요약한 것을 고르시오.

   (a) 지구에 생명이 유지될 수 있는 것은 지구의 우주 내 위치 덕분이라서 이 위치가 조금만 바뀌어도 대이주가 일어날 것이다.
   (b) 지구는 너무 뜨겁지도 춥지도 않은 위치 때문에 태양계에서 생명이 존재하는 유일한 장소이다.
   (c) 지구는 우주에서 생명이 존재할 수 있는 위치에 있지만 이 위치가 조금만 바뀌어도 지구상의 모든 생명은 종말을 맞게 된다.

Practice Test

p. 156~p. 157

1 (d)	2 (b)	3 (d)	4 (b)	5 (b)	6 (c)	7 (d)
8 해설 참조		9 (c)	10 (d)			

1

M Dark spots on the surface of the sun are called sunspots, and they are important because they may be responsible for changes in Earth's temperature and can interfere with radio, electrical, and magnetic fields on Earth. Sunspots are up to tens of thousands of kilometers in diameter. They are cooler than the surrounding surface and are the result of intense magnetic activity in the sun, which reduces internal convection. This makes the area appear to be darker than the surrounding surface of the sun. Sunspots have two distinct parts: the inner umbra, which is darker, and the outer penumbra, which is lighter in color. Strangely, these dark, cool sunspots cause the sun to appear brighter and to become hotter. The edges of sunspots have a higher degree of intense solar activity, which produces slightly more solar radiation during times of intense sunspot activity. Sunspots have been observed since ancient times, and astronomers

have been recording sunspots since the 17th century. Sunspots come in cycles and reach a minimum of activity every 11.3 years. Maximum activity occurs irregularly between the periods of minimum activity. Sometimes there have been longer periods of less activity. A low point in sunspot activity during the 17th century resulted in lower temperatures on Earth, and caused problems in crop yields and food supplies.

▶ sunspot 흑점 interfere with 방해하다, 간섭하다 magnetic field 자기장 convection (열의) 전달, 대류 umbra 본영, 암부 penumbra 반영, 반암부 radiation 복사, 방사 yield 생산량

남 태양의 표면에 있는 검은 점들을 흑점이라고 하는데 흑점은 지구 기온 변화의 원인이 되고 지구의 무선 통신, 전기, 자기장을 교란할 수도 있기 때문에 중요합니다. 흑점은 지름이 몇 만 킬로미터에 달합니다. 흑점은 주위 표면보다 온도가 낮으며, 태양 내 강력한 자기 활동의 결과로서 그로 인해 내부 대류가 감소합니다. 그래서 태양의 주위 표면보다 흑점이 더 어둡게 보이죠. 흑점에는 두 개의 두드러진 부분이 있는데 내부의 어두운 부분인 본영과 외부의 좀 더 밝은 부분인 반영입니다. 기이하게도 이 어둡고 온도가 낮은 흑점들로 인해 태양은 더 밝아 보이고, 더 뜨거워집니다. 흑점 가장자리에서는 보다 강도 높은 수준의 태양 활동이 일어나서 흑점 활동이 격렬히 일어나는 동안에는 조금 더 많은 태양 복사가 발생합니다. 흑점은 고대부터 관측되었으며 천문학자들은 17세기 이래로 흑점에 대해 기록해오고 있습니다. 흑점은 주기적으로 나타나는데 11.3년에 한 번씩 최소 활동 상태에 도달합니다. 최대 활동은 최소 활동기 사이에 불규칙적으로 나타납니다. 활동이 적은 시기가 더 오랫동안 지속되기도 했고요. 17세기에 흑점 활동이 낮았을 때는 지구의 기온이 떨어져서 작물 수확량과 식량 공급에 문제가 생겼습니다.

1 다음 중 흑점에 대해 옳은 것은?

   (a) 암부는 흑점의 바깥 부분이다.
   (b) 최대 흑점 주기는 11.3년이다.
   (c) 흑점은 최근에 발견되었다.
   (d) 흑점은 지구의 기후에 영향을 미칠 수도 있다.
   (e) 흑점 활동으로 복사가 적게 일어난다.

2-3

B I'd like to live on the moon someday.

G That's a pie-in-the-sky dream if I've ever heard one. There's no way humans could live on the moon.

B Why not? We've been to the moon, and people have lived in space for months at a time. Why should the moon be any different?

G First off, there is the expense involved. What government is going to pay to put buildings on the moon? And imagine how difficult it would be to build if the workers all had to wear those bulky spacesuits?

B Maybe, but they are building a space station now, and over a dozen countries are cooperating with one another. Perhaps the same could happen on the moon, or maybe a consortium of wealthy companies might do it. They could have a hotel, and people could pay to fly there on a regular shuttle once a week.

G It'll never be built by any company if there is no chance of making a profit. And no government would sponsor a moon hotel. What would be the purpose of this moon hotel anyway? Just so some rich tourists can go play golf in zero gravity?

B Actually, the moon has one sixth of Earth's gravity. It's not in zero gravity. Anyway, they could do scientific experiments or make plans for the permanent settlement of other planets.

G Maybe, but isn't that what the space station is for?

B Yeah. Maybe you're right. I guess there's no chance for it at all. At least not in our lifetimes.

G Sorry to take the wind out of your sails. Perhaps _______________________________________.

▶ pie-in-the-sky 실현 가능성이 적은 at a time 한 번에 first off 우선, 첫째로 bulky 부피가 큰, 거대한 consortium 합작 기업, 합작단 just so 바로 그대로 zero gravity 무중력 (상태) take the wind out of sb.'s sails 김 새게 하다, 맥 빠지게 하다

남 난 언젠가는 달에서 살고 싶어.
여 그건 내가 지금껏 들어본 것 중 가장 꿈 같은 얘기네. 인간이 달에 살 수는 없어.
남 왜 못 살아? 달에도 갔다 왔고 한 번에 여러 달씩 우주에서 산 사람들도 있잖아. 달이라고 다를 이유가 있겠어?
여 먼저 들어가는 비용이 있어. 어떤 정부가 달에 건물을 짓는다고 돈을 쓰겠어? 일꾼들 모두가 그 커다란 우주복을 입어야 한다면 건물 짓기가 얼마나 힘들지 상상해봐.
남 그럴 수도 있겠네. 하지만 지금 우주 정거장도 짓고 있고 12개국 이상이 서로 협력하고 있잖아. 아마 달에서도 그렇게 할 수 있을 거야. 아니면 돈 많은 기업들이 합작해서 할 수도 있지. 그들은 호텔을 갖게 될 수도 있을테니, 사람들은 돈을 내고 일주일에 한 번 정기적으로 운행하는 왕복선을 타고 거기 갈 수도 있겠지.
여 이윤이 남을 가능성이 없다면 어떤 기업도 호텔을 짓지 않을 거야. 그리고 달에 있는 호텔을 후원해줄 정부도 없을 테고. 결국 이 달 호텔의 목적이 뭔데? 몇몇 부유한 관광객들이 무중력 상태에서 골프 치러 가는 거?
남 사실 달은 지구 중력의 1/6이야. 무중력 상태가 아니지. 아무튼 과학 실험을 하거나 다른 행성에 영구 정착하는 계획을 세울 수도 있잖아.
여 그럴 수도 있겠지. 하지만 그래서 우주 정거장이 있는 거 아니니?
남 그래. 어쩌면 네 말이 맞을 수도 있어. 가능성이 전혀 없는 것 같네. 최소한 내 평생에는 안 되겠어.
여 김 새게 해서 미안해. 아마 _______________________________________.

2 소년의 기분은 대화 초반 때와 끝날 때 어떻게 비교되는가?
　　(a) 희망적인 생각 – 더없는 슬픔
　　(b) 희망찬 바람 – 마지못한 수긍
　　(c) 암울한 낙담 – 갑작스러운 희망
　　(d) 완전한 무관심 – 애처로운 우울함
　　(e) 끝없는 낙관주의 – 철저한 무관심

3 소년의 말 다음에 소녀는 뭐라고 말하겠는가?
　　(a) 그걸 위해 네가 기금 마련 캠페인을 시작할 수도 있겠네.
　　(b) 그냥 네가 부자가 되도록 노력해서 직접 지을 수도 있겠다.
　　(c) 우리가 간절히 바라면 지금으로부터 몇 년 뒤에는 이루어질 거야.
　　(d) 언젠가 네 꿈이 이뤄지는 걸 네 손주들은 볼 거야.
　　(e) 그 일을 해달라고 요청하는 편지를 우리가 정부에 보낼 수 있겠지.

4-5

M The Space Race was a massive scientific and technological effort by the United States and the Soviet Union to be the first to put a man into space and eventually on to the moon. Both nations used the Space Race as propaganda to prove the soundness of their competing economic and political systems—democracy and communism. At the end of World War II, both nations had captured German rocket specialists that had worked on German ballistic missiles during the war. These rocket specialists were put to work creating rockets to reach the stars. In October 1957, the Soviets were first off the mark when they launched a small satellite, called *Sputnik*, into Earth's orbit. This caused great consternation in America, and the Americans quickly launched their own satellite and increased their space program's funding. However, the Soviets were still one step ahead of them and triumphed at the next stage by placing a man into space. Yuri Gagarin was launched into Earth's orbit on April 12, 1961, just a few weeks before Alan Shepard made the first American space flight. The new American president, John F. Kennedy, vowed to place a man on the moon by the end of the 1960s. Despite their earlier victories, the Soviets stalled in their effort to reach the moon, and the Americans beat them to it on July 20, 1969. By the 1970s, an era of friendship in space had begun between America and the Soviet Union. From that point on, space missions became more about cooperation than competition. Today, the manufacture of the International Space Station is a symbol of this cooperative effort to explore space.

▶ propaganda 선전 ballistic missile 탄도 미사일 off the mark 스타트를 끊어 consternation 경악 one step ahead 한 발 앞선 vow 맹세하다, 단언하다 stall 꼼짝 못하다, 멎다 from that point on 그때부터

남 우주 경쟁은 최초로 인간을 우주에 보내고 최종적으로는 달에 착륙시키기 위해 미국과 소련이 쏟아부은 대규모의 과학적, 기술적 노력이었습니다. 두 나라는 민주주의와 공산주의라는, 서로 경쟁하고 있는 자신들의 경제 및 정치 체제가 건전하다는 점을 증명하기 위해 우주 경쟁을 선전 도구로 이용했습니다. 제2차 세계 대전이 끝나자 양국은 전쟁 동안 독일의 탄도 미사일을 만들었던 독일 로켓 전문가들을 체포했습니다. 이 로켓 전문가들은 별에 도착하는 로켓 만드는 일에 투입되었죠. 1957년 10월, 지구 궤도에 스푸트니크라는 작은 인공위성을 쏘아올리면서 소련이 먼저 테이프를 끊었습니다. 이에 깜짝 놀란 미국은 서둘러 자신들의 인공위성을 쏘아올리고 우주 계획 자금을 늘렸습니다. 그러나 여전히 미국보다 한 발 앞서 있던 소련은 우주에 인간을 보냄으로써 다음 단계에서도 승리를 차지했습니다. 유리 가가린은 1961년 4월 12일 지구 궤도에 올라갔습니다. 앨런 셰퍼드가 미국인으로서는 최초로 우주 비행을 하기 불과 몇 주 전이었죠. 새 미국 대통령 존 F. 케네디는 1960년대 말까지 달에 인간을 착륙시키겠다고 약속했습니다. 초반의 승리에도 불구하고 달에 가기 위한 소련의 노력이 정체를 겪으며 1969년 7월 20일 미국이 소련을 추월했습니다. 1970년대에 미국과 소련 사이에 우주에서의 우호의 시대가 시작되었습니다. 그때부터 우주 작전은 경쟁보다는 협력에 가까워졌습니다. 오늘날 국제 우주 정거장의 건설은 우주를 탐사하기 위한 이러한 협력적인 노력의 상징입니다.

4 강의에 따르면 사실이 <u>아닌</u> 것은?
　　(a) 소련과 미국 모두 우주 계획에 체포한 독일 과학자들을 이용했다.
　　(b) 미국은 지구 주변을 도는 궤도로 첫 인공위성을 쏘아올렸다.
　　(c) 소련은 미국이 하기 바로 직전에 인간을 우주에 쏘아올렸다.
　　(d) 소련보다 먼저 달에 도착하는 것은 케네디 행정부의 최우선 사항 중 하나가 되었다.
　　(e) 우주 경쟁은 소련과 미국의 관계에 변화가 생긴 후 1970년대에 끝났다.

5 강의에 따르면 우주 경쟁은 소련과 미국에게 왜 그렇게 중요했는가?
　　(a) 그들의 경제적, 기술적 힘을 나타내는 표시였다.
　　(b) 그들의 경쟁하는 생활 방식의 가치를 상징했다.
　　(c) 우주조차 그들의 지배하에 있음을 보여주었다.
　　(d) 그들이 세계에서 최고의 국가임을 증명했다.
　　(e) 서로의 차이로 전쟁하는 것 대신이었다.

W What's your star sign?

M Sorry. I'm from China. Please explain what you mean.

W Star sign? It's the time of year you were born which corresponds with one of the twelve constellations of the zodiac. I was born in early July, so I am a Cancer.

M Isn't cancer a disease?

W Yes, but it is also the name of one of the constellations, which is shaped like a crab. Constellations are star groups that seem to have familiar shapes in the night sky. You've heard of the Big Dipper and Little Dipper, right?

M Yes, I have learned about those stars before. They are shaped like a ladle for getting water, and one of them has the North Star.

W Right. So, there are 88 major constellations—counting both the Northern and Southern hemispheres—but 12 main constellations make up the zodiac. Understand?

M Yes, but why are Americans so interested in star signs?

W We use them to determine someone's personality and to find out who is good match for you. We also call them horoscopes.

M Ah, in China, we have something similar, but it is based on the year you were born.

▶ star sign 〈점성술〉 별자리 correspond with 해당하다, 상응하다 constellation 〈천문〉 별자리, 성좌 zodiac 12궁도 Cancer 게자리 familiar 낯익은, 잘 알려진 Big Dipper 북두칠성 Little Dipper 소북두칠성, 작은곰자리 ladle 국자 horoscope 별점, 점성술

여 당신은 별자리가 뭐죠?

남 죄송합니다. 제가 중국에서 왔거든요. 무슨 뜻인지 설명 좀 해주세요.

여 별자리요? 1년 중 당신이 태어난 때와 일치하는 12궁도에 있는 12개의 성좌 중 하나예요. 저는 7월 초에 태어나서 캔서죠.

남 캔서는 병 아닌가요?

여 맞아요, 하지만 성좌 중 하나의 이름이기도 해요. 캔서는 모양이 게처럼 생겼거든요. 성좌는 밤하늘에 낯익은 모양을 하고 있는 것처럼 보이는 별의 무리예요. 북두칠성과 소북두칠성은 들어보셨을 거예요, 그렇죠?

남 예, 전에 그 별들에 대해 배운 적이 있어요. 물을 뜨는 국자 같은 모양이죠. 그리고 그 중에 북극성이 있잖아요.

여 맞아요. 그러니까 북반구와 남반구 모두 합해서 88개의 주요 성좌가 있지만 12개의 핵심 성좌가 12궁도를 이루죠. 이해하겠어요?

남 예, 하지만 왜 미국인들은 별자리에 그렇게 관심이 있는 거죠?

여 누군가의 성격을 판단하고 누가 당신에게 잘 어울리는지 알아내기 위해 별자리를 이용하는 거예요. 별점이라고도 부르죠.

남 아, 중국에도 비슷한 게 있는데 그건 태어난 해를 기준으로 해요.

6 What is NOT true according to the dialog?

대화에 따르면 사실이 <u>아닌</u> 것은?

(a) Constellations are well-known patterns observed among the stars. 별자리는 별들에서 볼 수 있는 잘 알려진 모양이다.

(b) People use constellations to try to figure out someone's character.
사람들은 누군가의 성격을 알아내기 위해 별자리를 이용한다.

(c) There are 88 major constellations found in the Northern Hemisphere. 88개의 주요 별자리는 북반구에서 발견된다.

(d) Star sign and horoscope are terms used to talk about constellations.
별자리와 별점은 성좌에 대해 이야기할 때 쓰이는 용어이다.

(e) The North Star is contained in the pattern of a familiar constellation. 북극성은 잘 알려진 성좌 모양에 들어 있다.

M There are chunks of material in space—sometimes rock and sometimes ice—that sometimes enter the Earth's atmosphere and sometimes land on Earth. While these chunks of rock and ice are still in space, we call them meteoroids. When they burn up in the atmosphere in a fiery streak of light, we call them meteors. And when they land on Earth, they are called meteorites. Scientists classify meteorites into three categories, which depend on their composition. Iron meteorites are composed mostly of iron but have some nickel and other metals. Stone meteorites contain mostly silicates. Finally, stony iron meteorites contain high levels of both iron and stone. Historically, large meteorites striking the Earth may have been responsible for some major events, such as the demise of the dinosaurs. There is evidence of large meteorite strikes in South Africa, in Quebec and Ontario in Canada, in Arizona in the United States, and in northwest Australia. A mysterious explosion which felled tens of thousands of trees in Siberia in Russia in 1908 has often been blamed on a meteorite that exploded in mid air.

▶ chunk 큰 덩어리 meteoroid 유성체 fiery 불 같은, 타는 듯한 meteor 유성 meteorite 운석 silicate 규산염 demise 소멸 fell 쓰러뜨리다, 죽이다 in mid air 공중에

남 우주에는 물질 덩어리들이 있습니다. 돌인 경우도 있고 얼음인 경우도 있죠. 그것들이 때때로 지구의 대기권으로 들어와 어떤 때는 지구에 떨어지죠. 이런 돌과 얼음 덩어리들이 아직도 우주에 있을 때는 유성체라고 합니다. 유성체가 대기권에서 불 같은 빛줄기로 대기권에서 타오를 때는 유성이라고 하고요. 그리고 그것이 지구에 떨어지면 운석이라고 부릅니다. 과학자들은 운석을 구성 성분에 따라 세 가지로 분류합니다. 철질운석은 대부분 철로 구성되어 있지만 약간의 니켈과 다른 물질도 들어 있습니다. 석질운석은 대부분 규산염으로 이루어져 있습니다. 마지막으로 석철운석은 철과 암석 모두 다량 함유되어 있습니다. 역사상, 지구에 떨어지는 커다란 운석은 공룡의 멸종 같은 몇몇 주요 사건의 원인이었을 수도 있습니다. 남아프리카, 캐나다의 퀘벡과 온타리오, 미국의 애리조나, 북서오스트레일리아에 거대한 운석이 떨어진 증거가 있습니다. 1908년 러시아의 시베리아에 있는 수만 그루의 나무를 쓰러뜨린 수수께끼의 폭발은 공중에서 폭발한 운석 때문이라는 설이 많습니다.

7 What is correct according to the talk?

담화에 따르면 맞는 것은 무엇인가?

(a) Iron and ice are the main components of meteorites.
철과 얼음이 운석의 주요 구성 성분이다.

(b) Meteorites burn up in the Earth's atmosphere.
운석은 지구의 대기권에서 타버린다.

(c) The explosion in the Siberian forest was manmade.
시베리아 산림에서 일어난 폭발은 인재였다.

(d) Meteorites are meteoroids that survive Earth entry.
운석은 지구 진입에서 살아남은 유성체이다.

(e) Stone meteorites are composed of various rocks.
석질운석은 다양한 암석으로 구성되어 있다.

W Based on the Harvard University classification system for stars, most astronomers use a system of letters to distinguish star types. From largest to smallest they are O, B, A, F, G, K, and M. The largest and rarest stars are the "O" stars, often called super giants. They are blue and are more then 30,000 times brighter than our sun. The surface temperature of "O" stars is between 30,000 and 60,000 degrees Kelvin. Kelvin is a measure of temperature in which zero Kelvin is equal to minus 273 degrees Celsius. "B" stars are the next rarest and largest, have temperatures from 10,000 to 30,000 degrees Kelvin, are 25,000 to 30,000 times brighter than the sun, and are bluish white in color. "A" stars are 5 to 25 times brighter than our sun, appear to be white, and register between 7,000 and 10,000 degrees Kelvin. Moving on to "F" stars, they are yellowish white, are one and a half to five times brighter than the sun, and have temperatures from 6,000 to 7,000 degrees Kelvin. Our sun is a "G" star and is yellow in color. Most G stars average 5,000 to 6,000 degrees Kelvin and have 0.6 to 1.5 times the sun's brightness. Finally, the "K" and "M" stars are the smallest and coldest. "K" stars are orange, are about a thousand degrees cooler than "G" stars, and have a brightness between 0.08 and 0.6 that of the sun. "M" stars are red, have less than 0.08 brightness of the sun, and are between 2,000 and 4,000 degrees Kelvin.

▶ **super giant** 초거성 **bluish** 푸르스름한 **register** (온도계 따위가) ~도를 가리키다: 등록하다

여 하버드 대학의 별 분류 체계를 토대로, 대부분의 천문학자들은 별의 종류를 구분하는 데 문자 체계를 사용합니다. 가장 큰 별부터 가장 작은 별 순서로 O, B, A, F, G, K, M이라고 합니다. 가장 크고 희귀한 별은 O별인데 흔히 초거성이라고도 합니다. 초거성은 푸른색으로 우리 태양보다 30,000배 더 밝습니다. O별의 표면 온도는 30,000에서 60,000 켈빈 온도입니다. 켈빈은 온도 측정 단위인데 0 켈빈은 섭씨 영하 273도와 같죠. B별은 그 다음으로 희귀하고 큰 별로, 온도는 10,000에서 30,000 켈빈 온도이며, 태양보다 25,000에서 30,000배 밝고, 색깔은 푸르스름한 흰색입니다. A별은 우리 태양보다 5에서 25배 밝고, 흰색으로 보이며, 7,000과 10,000 켈빈 온도 사이입니다. 다음으로 F별로 넘어가 보면, 이것은 누르스름한 흰색으로 태양보다 1.5에서 5배 더 밝고 온도는 6,000에서 7,000 켈빈 온도입니다. 우리 태양은 G별이며 색깔은 노란색입니다. 대부분의 G별은 평균 5,000에서 6,000 켈빈 온도로 태양의 0.6에서 1.5배 밝기입니다. 마지막으로 K와 M별은 가장 작고 가장 온도가 낮습니다. K별은 오렌지색으로 G별보다 1,000도 정도 온도가 낮으며 태양의 0.08에서 0.6 사이의 밝기를 갖고 있습니다. M별은 빨간색으로 태양의 0.08배 밝기보다 어두우며, 2,000에서 4,000 사이의 켈빈 온도입니다.

8 빠진 별 분류 정보를 넣어 표를 완성하시오.

별의 종류 (가장 큰 별부터 가장 작은 별 순서)	색상	대략적인 온도 (켈빈)	밝기 (1 = 태양의 밝기)
O	푸른색	30,000~60,000	30,000 이상
B	푸르스름한 흰색	10,000~30,000	25,000~30,000
A	white (흰색)	7,000~10,000	5~25
F	누르스름한 흰색	6,000~7,000	1.5~5
G	노란색	5,000~6,000	0.6~1.5
K	오렌지색	4,000~5,000	0.08~0.6
M	red (빨간색)	2,000~4,000	0.08 이하

Reading

▶ **raise** (질문 등을) 제기하다 **probe** 무인 우주 탐사선, 우주 탐사 로켓 **flyby** 저공 비행, 접근 비행 **trillion** 1조 **spot** 발견하다 **sighting** 관찰, 목격 **abduct** 납치하다, 유괴하다 **weather balloon** 기상 관측 기구 **hoax** 조작, 장난 **abductee** 납치된 사람

많은 사람들이 자주 제기하는 질문은 지구 바깥에 생명이 존재하느냐이다. 지금까지 그 대답은 '아니다, 존재하지 않는다' 였다. 과학 탐사용 로켓의 화성 착륙과 다른 행성들에 대한 저공 비행 관찰 결과 어떤 생명의 흔적도 발견되지 않았다. 이것이 우주의 다른 어느 곳에도 생명이 존재하지 않는다는 것을 의미하지는 않는다. 논리적으로 수백만 개의 은하와 수조 개의 별, 그리고 태양계와 지구처럼 생긴 행성들이 무수히 많을 가능성을 감안하면 생명체에 적합한 조건이 어딘가에는 틀림없이 존재할 것이다. 우리가 생명체를 발견하지 못한 주된 이유는 엄청난 거리와 관련이 있다. 과학 탐사선을 태양계의 먼 곳으로 보내는 것조차 성공하기까지는 수십 년이 걸렸다. 게다가 가장 성능 좋은 망원경으로도 다른 어딘가에 생명이 존재한다는 사실을 증명할 만한 것을 아무것도 발견하지 못했다. 그럼 그 모든 UFO 목격 사례와 외계인에게 납치되었었다는 사람들의 주장은 어찌 된 걸까? 이것이 지구 바깥 우주에 생명이 있다는 증거가 아닐까? UFO를 목격했다는 대부분의 주장은 면밀히 살펴보면 논리적으로 설명된다. 어떤 것은 군용기였고 어떤 것은 기상 관측 기구였으며 또 어떤 것은 새였고 잘 꾸며진 조작인 경우도 있었다. 사람들은 외계인에게 납치되었던 걸까? 증거란 것이 전적으로 납치된 사람들의 이야기만을 근거로 하고 있고 어떤 독립적인 증거물도 없으므로 그러한 주장이 사실인지 아닌지에 대해 동의하기는 어렵다.

M The idea that there are aliens flying around in UFOs has been so firmly planted in the minds of many people around the world that they believe there is a massive conspiracy to keep the human race from finding out that extraterrestrial beings exist. The major advocates of this theory believe that governments are hiding crashed alien ships and dead alien bodies and are dismissing claims of UFOs with investigations that "prove" they are hoaxes or can be reasonably be explained. For example, in America, there is the infamous Area 51 in the Nevada desert. It is supposedly a secret base where alien research is conducted. Of course, when these conspiracy advocates are asked to offer proof that aliens exist, most of what they provide is mere coincidence or else it is impossible to prove the truth of it. For example, the idea that aliens helped build some ancient civilizations is based on a few ancient engravings. These seem to show spacemen inside spaceships. Also, there are lines in the desert in Peru that are supposed to be ancient airports for spaceships. In addition, there are stories of crashed alien ships, such as the famous one at Roswell, New Mexico, in 1947, which are based on accounts that cannot be proven one way or another. Finally, the people who say that aliens captured them, took them aboard their spaceships, and conducted experiments on them have no proof and may in fact just be attention seekers.

▶ **fly around** 바삐 돌아다니다 **conspiracy** 음모 **extraterrestrial** 지구 밖의, 외계의 **advocate** 옹호자, 지지자 **dismiss** 간단히 처리해버리다, 기각하다 **infamous** 악명 높은, 평판이 나쁜 **supposedly** 짐작컨대, 아마도 **coincidence** 우연의 일치 **engraving** 조각, 조판 **one way or another** 어떻게든 **account** 이야기, 설명

남 UFO를 타고 돌아다니는 외계인이 존재한다는 생각이 전 세계 많은 사람들의 머릿속에 너무나 확고히 심어져 있어서, 많은 이들은 외계 생명체가 존재한다는 것을 사람들이 알아내지 못하게 하려는 거대한 음모가 있다고 믿습니다. 이 이론의 지지자들 대부분은 정부가 부서진 외계 비행선과 외계인의 시체를 숨기고 있

으며, 그런 것들이 속임수이거나 합리적으로 설명 가능하다는 것을 '증명하는' 조사로 UFO에 대한 주장을 간단히 처리해 버리고 있다고 생각합니다. 예를 들어 미국 네바다 사막에는 악명 높은 51구역이 있죠. 외계인 연구가 수행되는 비밀 기지로 짐작되는 곳입니다. 물론 이러한 음모 지지자들에게 외계인이 존재한다는 증거를 대보라고 요청할 때 그들이 제시하는 대부분의 증거는 우연의 일치이거나 사실인지 아닌지 증명하기 불가능한 것입니다. 예를 들면 외계인이 몇몇 고대 문명의 건설을 도왔다는 생각은 일부 고대 조각들을 기초로 하고 있죠. 이것들이 우주선 안에 있는 우주인을 나타내는 것처럼 보인다는 것이죠. 또한 페루의 사막에는 우주선용 고대 비행장이었을 것 같은 선이 그려져 있습니다. 게다가 1947년 뉴멕시코의 로즈웰에서 있었던 유명한 사건처럼 어떻게도 입증될 수 없는 설명을 바탕으로 한 부서진 외계 우주선 이야기들이 있습니다. 마지막으로 외계인이 자신을 납치해서 우주선에 태워 자기에게 실험을 했다고 말하는 사람들은 아무런 증거도 가지고 있지 않으며, 사실상 단지 주목을 끌고 싶어하는 사람들일 수도 있습니다.

9 지구 밖 우주에 생명이 존재한다는 것이 왜 논리적으로 가능한가?
(a) 외계인에게 납치됐었다고 말하는 사람들이 있다.
(b) 망원경으로 다른 행성에서 생명체처럼 보이는 것을 발견했다.
(c) 엄청난 수의 별은 지구 같은 다른 행성이 존재할 수 있음을 의미한다.
(d) UFO 보도의 절대적인 숫자는 일부는 사실임에 틀림없음을 의미한다.
(e) 태양계 구석구석에 보낸 우주 탐사선이 생명의 증거를 발견했다.

10 UFO 목격과 외계인 납치 주장에 대해 읽기와 듣기 지문으로부터 유추할 수 있는 것은 무엇인가?
(a) 그런 사건을 모두 은폐하려는 정부 계획이 있다.
(b) 과거에 외계 생명체가 지구에 왔었다는 증거가 있다.
(c) 지구를 방문하거나 지구에 추락한 우주선은 없었다.
(d) 그 이야기들 중 일부가 사실인지 아닌지 우리는 결코 알지 못할 수도 있다.
(e) 그것은 모두 전 세계 사람들을 속이려는 정교한 조작이다.

*Dictation 정답: Exercise 스크립트 밑줄 참조

UNIT
12 **Human Health**

Preparation
p. 103

Vocabulary Preview

A
1 **quarantine**: 전염병이 있는 사람을 격리하다
2 **incubation**: 병이 숙주 안에서 자라고 있지만 증상은 없는 기간
3 **temptation**: 무엇에 대한 욕구나 갈망
4 **inconclusive**: 불확실한; 명확하지 않은; 설득력이 없는
5 **circadian**: 생명체의 일일 주기와 관련된

B
1 **overwhelmed** / 나는 일에 파묻혀 있어. 할 일은 너무 많은데 할 시간은 없다고.
2 **alleviate** / 약은 여러 일반적인 질병의 증상을 완화시킬 수 있다.
3 **relapse** / 담배를 끊은 많은 사람들이 다시 흡연을 시작한다.
4 **waste away** / 어떤 질병들은 사람이 죽음에 이를 때까지 약하고 무기력하게 만들어 몸을 쇠약하게 한다.
5 **on edge** / 미안하지만, 내 시험 결과가 걱정되어서 좀 초조하네.
6 **nausea** / 그 약은 메스꺼움과 설사를 일으킬 수 있으니 난 안 먹겠어요.

7 **worse comes to worst** / 난 최악의 경우에는 병을 고치기 위해 수술 받아야 할 거야.

Expressions and Meanings

1 나는 최선을 다할 거야.　　　ⓔ 나는 최선을 다 할 거야.
2 그들이 그애 버릇을 망쳐.　　　ⓐ 그들은 걔가 원하는 것은 무엇이든 줘.
3 이 프로젝트들을 최대한 빨리 처리해.　　　ⓖ 이 일들을 최대한 빨리 처리해.
4 이것은 장벽이 되었어.　　　ⓑ 이것은 장애물이야.
5 물론이지, 어서 말해봐.　　　ⓕ 좋아, 말해봐.
6 넌 뭔가를 그만둘 수도 있겠지.　　　ⓒ 네가 관련된 뭔가를 포기해.
7 그것이 또 한 번 고개를 쳐들었어　　　ⓓ 나쁜 일이 다시 일어났어.

Listening Drill 1 p. 164~p. 165

Monolog

Ⓞ (1) northeast Asia　(2) fleshy root　(3) energy　(4) blood circulation　(5) stress　(6) cancer　(7) antibiotic　(8) infections　(9) sleeplessness　(10) headaches　(11) inconclusive
Ⓖ 1 (a)　2 (b)
Ⓢ (1) F　(2) T　(3) T　(4) T

W Ginseng is a plant found in northeastern Asia that has some healthy benefits for the people that consume it. The plant has a fleshy root that is often fork-shaped and which is the part that people eat. Ginseng roots are either consumed raw or used in cooking, and their extracts are taken in pill form or as an additive in drinks. Reported health benefits include increased energy, improved blood circulation, reduced stress, and reduced risks of getting cancer. The roots have also been used in alternative treatments for certain types of diabetes. Some possible side effects of ginseng consumption include sleeplessness, headaches, nausea, and diarrhea. Many studies have been done on different types of ginseng in order to gauge their medicinal properties. While some studies have been inconclusive, others have shown some interesting results. In particular, studies of Korean red ginseng have shown that it has properties which have been effective at preventing stomach cancer and breast cancer relapses. Red ginseng is also reported to have an antibiotic effect on infections. Although much about ginseng is still unknown and needs to be studied further, in Asia it is widely regarded as a healthy food and can be found in many dishes, such as samgyetang, or chicken stew, in Korea.

▶ **healthy benefit** 건강상의 이로움　**consume** 소비하다, 소모하다　**fleshy** 살집이 좋은, 꽤 살찐　**extract** 추출물; 달여낸 즙, 정제　**addictive** (약이) 습관(중독)성의　**blood circulation** 혈액순환　**alternative treatment** 대체치료　**diabetes** 당뇨병　**gauge** 판단하다; 평가하다　**medicinal** 약(용)의; 약효 있는 *cf.* medicinal property 약효 성분　**inconclusive** 결론에 이르지 못하는, 결정(확정)적이 아닌　**relapse** 병이 도지다, 재발하다　**be reported to** ~라고 보고되다　**antibiotic** 항생의　**infection** 감염; 병균 감염　**be regarded as** ~로 간주되다

여 인삼은 동북아시아에서 발견되는 식물로, 먹는 사람에게 건강상의 이로움을 줍니다. 이 식물은 통통한 뿌리가 있고 흔히 갈퀴 같은 모양으로, 사람들은 이 뿌리 부분을 먹죠. 인삼 뿌리는 날로도 먹고 익혀서도 먹으며, 추출액은 정제 형태로 또는 음료의 첨가물로 섭취됩니다. 세간에 보고된 건강상 이점으로는 원기 증강, 혈액순환 향상, 스트레스 감소, 암 발생 위험 감소 등이 있고요. 뿌리는 특정 유형 당뇨병의 대체치료에 쓰이기도 합니다. 인삼을 먹음으로써 일어날 수 있는 부작용으로는 불면증, 두통, 메스꺼움, 설사 등이 있습니다. 인삼의 의학적 특성을 가늠하기 위해 여러 종류의 인삼에 대해 많은 연구가 이루어져 왔습니다. 일부 연구에서는 결론이 나지 않았지만, 다른 연구에서는 흥미로운 결과들을 볼 수 있는데요. 특히 한국의 홍삼에 대한 연구에서 홍삼이 위암과 유방암 재발을 막는 데 효과적인 특성이 있다는 것이 나타났습니다. 홍삼은 또한 감염에 항생 효과가 있는 것으로 보고되어 있습니다. 아직은 인삼에 대해 많이 알려지지 않았고 연구를 더 해야 하지만, 아시아에서는 건강식품으로 널리 인식되어 있으며 한국에서는 삼계탕과 같은 여러 요리에서 접할 수 있습니다.

General Questions

1 담화의 목적은 무엇인가?

   (a) 인삼의 건강상 특성을 살펴보는 것

   (b) 인삼을 먹는 방법들에 대해 설명하는 것

   (c) 인삼이 건강상 이점이 있다는 것을 증명하는 것

   (d) 의학 연구에 결론이 안 날 수도 있다는 것을 보여주는 것

2 다음 중 가장 잘 요약된 것을 고르시오.

   (a) 수년간의 연구에도 불구하고 인삼의 약효는 아직 사실로 증명되지는 않고 있다.

   (b) 인삼의 몇몇 건강상 이점이 사실이라고 증명되기는 했지만 아직도 더 많은 연구가 필요하다.

Specific Questions

다시 듣고 옳은 문장에는 T, 틀린 문장에는 F를 쓰시오.

(1) 인삼을 먹는 사람들은 뚜렷한 부작용을 보이지 않았다.

(2) 인삼은 일부 암의 재발을 막는 데 도움을 준다.

(3) 인삼에 약이 되는 이점이 있다는 것을 모든 연구가 증명하지는 않는다.

(4) 인삼은 감염을 치료하는 데 이로운 것으로 보인다.

Dialog

N (1) bigger   (2) healthy   (3) junk food   (4) special occasions   (5) birthday   (6) whatever he wants   (7) video games   (8) cook   (9) fast food / dislikes

G 1 (d)   2 (b)

S (1) T   (2) F   (3) T   (4) F

B I hate to say this, but your little brother is getting fat.

G I know. It's embarrassing. He's only 10 years old, but he is already bigger than me.

B Your parents should put him on a diet or make him do more exercise or something. It's not healthy.

G It's their fault he's so big. They spoil him rotten. They let him eat whatever he wants and then let him watch cartoons and play video games rather than exercise or play outdoors.

B That would never happen in my house. My mother never buys junk food like soda, chips, or cookies. We only get ice cream once in a while, like on a special day, such as my birthday. And my mom yells at me if I spend too much time watching TV.

G That's the way it should be. My parents both work, and my mom often comes home late, so we eat a lot of fast food. Sometimes, she just orders pizza because she is too tired to cook. My brother loves it, but I get so disgusted I can't eat sometimes.

B I have noticed a lot of young kids in Korea are getting overweight these days. It's becoming a serious problem.

G There are too many temptations. Everywhere you go, there are snack foods, ice cream, hamburgers, and lots of other kinds of junk food. What can I do to help my brother?

B I don't know for sure, but he needs help before he has serious health issues in the future.

▶ I hate to say this, but 이런 말하고 싶지 않지만 embarrassing 당황케 하는; 난처한 be on a diet 다이어트 중이다 spoil 못되게[버릇없게] 만들다 rotten 버릇없는, 무례한 once in a while 이따금, 때때로 disgusted 싫증난, 메스꺼운 overweight 과체중의, 너무 살찐 temptation 유혹(물) everywhere you go 어디서나 junk food 인스턴트 식품

남 이런 말은 하고 싶지 않지만 네 남동생 갈수록 살이 찌네.

여 알아. 창피한 일이야. 열 살 밖에 안 됐는데 이미 나보다 덩치가 더 커.

남 너희 부모님이 네 동생에게 다이어트를 시키거나 운동이라도 더 하게 하든가 뭔가 해야 할 것 같아. 건강에 안 좋잖아.

여 걔가 그렇게 덩치가 큰 건 부모님 탓이야. 부모님이 애 버릇을 망치고 계셔. 걔가 원하는 건 무엇이든 먹게 허락하시고, 운동을 하거나 밖에서 놀기보다는 만화 보고 비디오 게임 하게 그냥 내버려 두시거든.

남 우리 집에서는 절대 있을 수 없는 일이군. 우리 엄마는 청량음료나 감자튀김, 과자 같은 인스턴트 식품은 아예 사지 않으셔. 내 생일날 같은 특별한 날에나 어쩌다 아이스크림을 먹을 수 있을 뿐이지. 게다가 내가 너무 오래 TV를 보고 있으면 호통을 치셔.

여 원래 그렇게 해야 해. 우리 부모님은 두 분 다 일을 하시고, 엄마가 종종 집에 늦게 오셔서 우리는 패스트푸드를 많이 먹어. 엄마가 너무 피곤해서 요리를 못 할 때는 그냥 피자를 주문하시기도 하고. 남동생은 좋아하지만 난 질려서 어떨 땐 못 먹겠더라고.

남 난 요즘 한국의 많은 어린이들이 과체중이 되고 있다는 것을 알게 됐어. 점점 심각한 문제가 되고 있지.

여 유혹이 너무 많아. 어딜 가든 간식거리에, 아이스크림, 햄버거, 그리고 여러 종류의 많은 인스턴트식품이 있어. 동생을 돕기 위해 내가 뭘 해야 할까?

남 확실히는 모르겠지만, 네 동생은 나중에 건강에 심각한 문제가 생기기 전에 도움을 받아야 해.

General Questions

1 대화의 요지는 무엇인가?

   (a) 건강한 식사와 생활은 어린 시절에 시작해야 한다.

   (b) 부모님은 아이의 체중 문제에 책임이 있다.

   (c) 간식은 피해야 할 유혹이다.

   (d) 체중 증가는 대개 건강하지 못한 생활방식의 결과이다.

2 다음 중 가장 잘 요약된 것을 고르시오.

   (a) 소녀는 체중과 관련이 있는 남동생의 건강 문제에 부모님이 충분한 관심을 보이지 않아서 안타까워한다.

   (b) 소녀는 남동생의 체중 문제가 가족의 생활양식뿐만 아니라 부모님이 그를 대하는 방식과 어떻게 관련이 있는지를 설명한다.

Specific Questions

다시 듣고 옳은 문장에는 T, 틀린 문장에는 F를 쓰시오.

(1) 소년은 소녀의 남동생이 체중이 늘었다는 것을 알아챘다.

(2) 소년의 가족은 소녀의 가족과 생활방식이 비슷하다.
(3) 소녀의 부모님은 식사를 준비할 시간이 넉넉하지 않다.
(4) 소녀와 남동생은 식성이 같다.

Listing Drill 2

p. 166~p. 167

Long Lecture

○ (1) genes (2) resistant (3) viruses (4) edible (5) ripen
(6) shelf life (7) pigs (8) salmon (9) surviving
(10) grown (11) side effects (12) Europe
(13) North America (14) patented

1 (c) **2** (a) **3** (1) T (2) T (3) F (4) F **4** (b)

Dictation 정답: 스크립트 밑줄 참조

M Genetically modified food is any food that has had
its genes altered in some way. Genetic modification is
almost always done with plants although there have
been some alterations made to some livestock. The
main reasons for doing genetic alterations are to make
the plants more resistant to insects or viruses, to make
them less edible to herbivore, and to allow them to
ripen more slowly and thus have longer shelf lives. By
making plants more resistant to the things that would
have normally killed them, they have a greater chance
of surviving and can be grown in more areas than
possible prior to undergoing genetic modifications.
Currently, the most common genetically modified
plants are soybeans, corn, rice, canola, potatoes,
sugarcane, and cotton. There are also some attempts
underway to genetically modify pigs and salmon.
Genetically modified food has generated a controversy
over whether it is safe for humans. There are fears that
people may suffer as-yet-unknown side effects from
eating genetically modified food. To alleviate these
concerns, in Europe, Japan, and several other countries,
food must be labeled to tell consumers if it is genetically
modified. In North America, however, manufacturers
do not have to label genetically modified food as such.
There are some suggestions that genetically modified
food will alleviate the world's hunger problems because
it can be grown in more areas and the crops can resist
more dangers. However, genetically modified plants
are patented by the designers, and farmers have to pay
for the right to use the seeds. For many poor farmers
in the developing world, this constitutes a barrier to
them affording and possibly enjoying any benefits from
genetically modified crops.

▶ genetically modified 유전자 조작의 gene 유전자, 유전 인자 alter 개조하다,
변경하다 modification 변경, 변형 almost always 대개 livestock 가축
alteration 변경, 개조 be resistant to ~에 저항력이 있는, 내성이 있는
herbivore 초식동물 edible 먹을 수 있는, 식용에 알맞은 shelf life 저장수명:
유통기한 undergo 받다: 겪다 underway 진행 중인 controversy 논쟁: 언쟁
label 라벨[표]을 붙이다 as such 그것 나름으로: 그것만으로 patent ~의 특허
를 얻다: 특허권을 주다

남 유전자 조작 식품은 어떤 방식으로든 유전자를 조작한 모든 식품입니다. 유전자
조작은 가축에게도 행해지지만 대개 식물에서 이루어집니다. 유전자 조작을 하는
주요한 이유는 식물들이 곤충이나 바이러스에 대한 저항력을 더 갖추게 하거나

초식동물에게 덜 먹히게 하거나 좀 더 천천히 익게 해서 더 오래 저장할 수 있도
록 하기 위해서죠. 식물을 죽게 만드는 것들에 대해 더 저항력을 가지게 함으로
써 생존할 기회가 더 많아지고, 유전자 조작을 받기 전보다 더 많은 지역에서 자
랄 수 있게 됩니다. 현재, 가장 흔한 유전자 조작 식물은 콩, 옥수수, 쌀, 캐놀라,
감자, 사탕수수, 면입니다. 또한 돼지와 연어를 유전적으로 조작하려는 시도도
진행 중이죠. 유전자 조작 식품이 인간에게 안전한지 여부에 대해서는 논란이 있
습니다. 사람이 유전자 조작 식품을 먹으면 아직 알려지지 않은 부작용을 겪을
거라는 두려움이 있는 것이죠. 이러한 걱정을 덜기 위해서 유럽, 일본 그리고 다
른 몇몇 나라들에서는 소비자들이 유전자 조작이 되었는지 알 수 있도록 식품에
반드시 라벨을 붙여야 합니다. 하지만 북미에서는 제조업자들이 유전자 조작 식
품에 라벨을 붙이지 않아도 됩니다. 유전자 조작 식품은 더 많은 지역에서 자랄
수 있고 농작물이 더 많은 위험을 견뎌낼 수 있으므로 세계의 기근 문제를 완화
해 줄 것이라는 의견이 있습니다. 하지만 유전자 조작 식물은 설계자에게 특허권
이 있어서 농부들이 씨앗을 사용하는 권한에 대한 비용을 지불해야 합니다. 이것
은 개발도상국의 많은 가난한 농부들이 유전자 조작 농작물에서 얻을 수 있는 혜
택을 누리기 힘들게 만드는 장애물입니다.

1 강의에 따르면 다음 중 유전자 조작 농작물의 목적이 아닌 것은?
(a) 거의 모든 장소에서 재배하는 것
(b) 전 세계의 기근 문제를 해결하는 것
(c) 더 쉽게 수확하는 것
(d) 신선함을 더 오래 유지시키는 것

2 다음 중 가장 잘 요약된 것을 고르시오.
(a) 유전자 조작 식품이 더 많은 지역에서 자랄 수 있고 더 강한 생존력
을 보증하는 반면 혹시 일어날 수 있는 건강문제와 이용가능성에 대
한 문제로 논란이 되고 있다.
(b) 비록 유전자 조작 식품이 거의 모든 장소에서 살아남을 수 있지만 많
은 가난한 농부들은 씨앗을 살 여유가 없어서 유전자 조작 식품이 빈
곤국에 널리 퍼지지 못한다.

3 옳은 문장에는 T, 틀린 문장에는 F를 쓰시오.
(1) 유전자 조작 식물은 수확이 더 잘 된다.
(2) 유럽에서는 식품 라벨에 유전자 조작 식품에 대한 정보를 명시해야 한다.
(3) 유전자 조작 식품은 경제적으로 어려운 지역에서 꽤 흔하다.
(4) 유전자 조작 음식에 건강상 문제가 있다는 것이 증명되었다.

4 유전자 조작 식물이 가난한 지역으로 널리 퍼지지 못하는 주요 장애요인
은?
(a) 이 식물들을 섭취함으로써 일어날 수 있는 부작용에 대한 건강상 우려
(b) 이 식물들의 구입과 관련된 경제적 문제
(c) 이 식물들이 다른 지역에 적응하는 것과 관련된 문제
(d) 이 새로운 식물들에 대한 특허권과 관련된 어려움

Exercise

p. 168~p. 169

1 (b) **2** 해설 참조 **3** (b) **4** (c) **5** (e) **6** (c) **7** (b)
8 (a) **9** (c) **10** 해설 참조 **11** (c) **12** (c)

1

M Okay, everyone, I'm sure you've heard about mad
cow disease, or Creutzfeldt-Jakob disease. It is a
disease that wastes away the brain cells and eventually
leads to death. There is no known cure. It is passed
to humans from animals, usually cattle, which are
infected. Humans can contract the disease through the
consumption of beef. People who are afflicted with
mad cow disease gradually lose control of all of their

bodily <u>functions</u> until death occurs. The <u>outbreak</u> of many cases in Britain in the 1980s <u>caused</u> a <u>panic</u> that <u>resulted in</u> over four million British <u>cattle being destroyed</u>, and many people <u>changed their eating habits</u>. In America and Canada, a few cases of the <u>animal form</u> of the disease in beef cattle <u>caused widespread disruption</u> of the beef industry in both nations. <u>Despite the panic</u> over mad cow disease, only <u>206 people</u>, most of them in Britain, <u>have died</u> of it so far. However, many more people <u>may be infected</u> because the disease has a <u>long incubation period</u>— from many months to a few <u>decades</u>. In response to <u>widespread media coverage</u> of the disease, many people have <u>refused to eat</u> beef because of <u>fears of catching</u> mad cow disease. The <u>overconsumption</u> of beef has long been <u>accused of</u> causing heart and <u>gastric diseases</u>, which kill millions of people worldwide every year. <u>Ironically</u>, it took a disease that has killed very few to <u>make people decide</u> that beef is an <u>unhealthy</u> food choice.

▶ waste ~을 소모[마모]시키다 contract the disease 병에 걸리다
be afflicted with ~에 걸리다, ~을 앓다 bodily function 신체의 기능
outbreak 발생, 발발 case 병상(病狀): 사례: 환자 eating habit 식습관
widespread 광범위한, 일반적인 disruption 붕괴; 혼란
incubation period 잠복기 (in) response to ~에 부응하여
media coverage 언론 보도 be accused of (~점에서) 비난 받고 있다
gastric 위의 ironically 얄궂게도

남 좋아요, 여러분, 광우병이나 크로이츠펠트야콥병에 대해선 모두 들어 봤을 겁니다. 광우병은 뇌세포를 마모시켜 결국에는 죽음에 이르게 하는 병이죠. 알려진 치료법은 없습니다. 광우병은 동물, 대개 감염된 소에서 인간에게 옮겨집니다. 인간은 쇠고기를 섭취함으로써 이 병에 걸릴 수 있습니다. 광우병에 걸린 사람은 차츰 모든 신체기능 제어 능력을 잃고 죽음에 이르게 되죠. 1980년대 영국에서는 이 질병이 여러 건 발생해 4백만 마리의 영국 소들이 도살되는 공황상태가 야기되었고, 많은 사람들은 식습관을 바꾸었습니다. 미국과 캐나다에서는 이 질병의 동물적 형태가 소에 나타난 사례가 몇 건 발생해 두 나라 쇠고기 산업에 엄청난 파장이 일어났죠. 광우병에 대한 공포에도 불구하고 지금까지 단 206명만이 대부분 영국에서 광우병으로 사망하였습니다. 하지만 그 병의 잠복기는 수개월에서 수십 년에 이를 정도로 길기 때문에 더 많은 사람들이 감염되어 있을지도 모릅니다. 광범위한 언론 보도로, 많은 사람들은 광우병에 걸릴 거라는 두려움 때문에 쇠고기를 먹지 않으려 하죠. 쇠고기의 지나친 섭취는 매년 전 세계적으로 수백만 명을 사망케 하는 심장병과 위장병을 일으킨다고 오랫동안 비난받아오고 있습니다. 아이러니하게도, 사람을 거의 죽게 만들지 않은 질병이 사람들로 하여금 쇠고기가 건강에 유해한 음식이라고 단정하게 만든 것이죠.

1 강의의 주요 목적은 무엇인가?
(a) 질병이 동물에게서 사람에게 전염되는 방식을 설명하려고
(b) 질병 때문에 사람들이 어떻게 식습관을 바꾸었는지 논하려고
(c) 특정 산업에서 발생되는 질병의 악영향을 설명하려고
(d) 질병에 대한 공포심을 일으키는 언론의 역할을 살펴보려고
(e) 어떤 질병은 많은 사람들이 생각하는 것만큼 치명적이지 않다는 것을 증명하려고

2

W So, Mr. Davis, it seems your <u>blood pressure</u> is a <u>little bit high</u>.

M Oh, how high was it?

W Normal blood pressure is <u>90 to 120</u> over 60 to 80. <u>Higher or lower</u> than this, we have a problem. Yours was a little high at <u>130</u> over <u>90</u>.

M Ah, I really <u>don't understand</u> what you just said.

W We <u>measure blood pressure</u> with millimeters of mercury <u>based on</u> the old <u>mercury pressure gauge</u> that we used to use.

M Okay, I think I understand so far.

W Good. There are <u>two types of</u> blood pressure: systolic, which is the <u>highest amount of pressure</u> in the arteries, and diastolic, which is the lowest amount of pressure. <u>Normal systolic pressure</u> is 90 to <u>120 millimeters</u> of mercury. Normal diastolic pressure is 60 to 80.

M So my systolic was 130, and <u>my diastolic was</u> 90?

W Yes. Let's <u>take another reading</u>. Some people <u>get nervous</u> when visiting a doctor. Try to <u>calm yourself</u>. Think of a <u>peaceful place</u>.

M Ah, okay, I'm thinking... Okay, I'm there.

W Just a moment... and there. Now it's <u>125</u> over <u>80</u>. It's still a bit high on the systolic.

M What should I do?

W Lose a bit of weight, <u>exercise more</u>, eat <u>less meat</u>, and <u>drink less alcohol</u>.

M What happens if I can't get my <u>blood pressure down</u>?

W You could have a <u>heart attack</u> or a <u>stroke</u>. If <u>worse comes to worst</u>, we can always <u>start you on medication</u>.

M I'll certainly <u>do my best</u> to <u>reduce</u> my blood pressure.

▶ blood pressure 혈압 mercury 수은: (the —) 수은주 gauge 계량기, 계기
systolic pressure 최고 혈압 artery 동맥 diastolic pressure 확장기 혈압, 최저 혈압 heart attack 심장마비 stroke (뇌졸중 등의) 발작

여 데이비스 씨, 혈압이 조금 높으시네요.
남 아, 얼마나 높은데요?
여 정상 혈압은 90에서 120, 60에서 80입니다. 이보다 높거나 낮으면 문제가 있는 거지요. 데이비스 씨의 혈압은 130에 90으로 조금 높습니다.
남 아, 방금 하신 말씀이 잘 이해가 안 가네요.
여 우리는 예전에 사용했던 기존의 수은 혈압 측정기를 기초로 수은의 밀리미터로 혈압을 측정한답니다.
남 네, 지금까진 알겠어요.
여 좋습니다. 혈압에는 두 가지 유형이 있어요. 동맥에서 가장 높은 압력양인 최고 혈압, 그리고 가장 낮은 압력양인 최저 혈압이죠. 정상적인 최고 혈압은 수은 90에서 120밀리미터이고 정상 최저 혈압은 60에서 80입니다.
남 그러니까 제 최고 혈압은 130이고 최저 혈압은 90이라고요?
여 맞아요. 다시 한 번 측정해 보지요. 어떤 분들은 병원에 오시면 긴장하시거든요. 마음을 가라앉히시고, 평화로운 곳을 생각해 보세요.
남 아, 알겠어요, 생각하고 있어요… 됐어요, 생각했어요.
여 잠시만요… 보세요. 지금은 125에 80이네요. 최고 혈압이 아직 조금 높네요.
남 어떻게 해야 하죠?
여 체중을 좀 줄이시고 운동을 더 하시고, 고기와 술을 적게 드세요.
남 만약 제 혈압이 낮아지지 않으면 어떻게 되나요?
여 심장마비나 발작이 올 수 있습니다. 더 나빠지면 약 복용부터 시작할 수 있지요.
남 혈압을 줄이도록 최선을 다할게요.

2 대화문의 혈압에 대한 자료로 다음 표를 완성하시오

혈압 유형	고혈압	저혈압
정상	90~120	60~80
높음	over 120 (120 초과)	over 80 (80 초과)
낮음	under 90 (90 미만)	under 60 (60 미만)
데이비스 씨, 첫 번째 측정	130	90
데이비스 씨, 두 번째 측정	125	80

3-4

W   I would now like to <u>discuss pathogens</u>, which <u>include</u> <u>bacteria</u>, <u>fungi</u>, viruses, and prions. <u>Simply put</u>, a pathogen is any kind of <u>biological agent</u> that can introduce a disease into a host. Pathogens are <u>related to</u> the <u>transmission of diseases</u> in humans and animals. This transmission is usually the <u>result of</u> the <u>consumption</u> of water or food that is <u>contaminated with</u> the pathogen. Once one animal or human is <u>infected</u>, then the pathogen can <u>spread to others</u>. Some pathogens <u>reside in animals</u> for a long time and <u>do not harm</u> the animals but can still be <u>deadly to humans</u>. An example of this is the many types of <u>infections found in bats</u>. These infections are <u>not damaging</u> to the bats but can <u>harm humans</u> or other animals if they <u>are bitten</u> by the bat. Sometimes, the pathogen is <u>equally deadly</u> in animals and humans, such as with <u>mad cow disease</u>, which is <u>caused by</u> prions. Humans and animals have <u>immune systems</u> that can <u>defend</u> the body <u>against infections</u> by pathogens, but sometimes this immune system is <u>compromised</u>. For example, a person <u>undergoing radiation treatment</u> for cancer may have a <u>weakened immune system</u> that can allow a pathogen to <u>more easily infect</u> the person. Fortunately, many pathogens cannot survive <u>outside of</u> a host body for long, so <u>they die</u>. However, some, such as <u>smallpox</u>, can survive for a few years outside of a host body.

▶ pathogen 병원균, 병원체   fungi fungus(진균류, 효모균, 균)의 복수형
prion 프라이온(광우병을 일으킨다고 생각되는 감염성 단백질 입자)
simply put 간단히 말하면   agent 병원체   be contaminated with ~에 오염이
되다   reside (장기간) 거주하다; 있다   infection 전염병; 병균 감염
immune system 면역 체계   compromised 면역 반응 따위가 제대로 발휘되지
못하는   radiation treatment 방사선 치료   smallpox 천연두

여   이제 박테리아, 진균류, 바이러스, 프라이온을 포함한 병원균에 대해 논의해 보
겠습니다. 쉽게 말해 병원균은 숙주에 질병을 들여올 수 있는 온갖 종류의 생물
학적 병원체입니다. 병원균은 인간과 동물의 질병 전염과 연관이 있죠. 이 전염
은 대개 병원균에 오염된 물이나 음식 섭취로 일어납니다. 한 동물이나 인간이
감염되면 병원균은 다른 동물이나 인간에게 퍼질 수 있습니다. 어떤 병원균들은
오랫동안 동물 몸 안에 살면서 그 동물에게는 해를 주지 않지만 인간에게는 치
명적일 수 있습니다. 예를 들어 박쥐에게서 발견된 여러 종류의 전염병이 있죠.
이 전염병은 박쥐에게는 해를 입히지 않지만 박쥐에게 물린 인간이나 다른 동물
에게 해를 끼칠 수 있습니다. 프라이온에 의해 발생되는 광우병과 같은 경우처럼
병원균이 동물과 인간에게 똑같이 치명적일 때도 있지요. 인간과 동물은 병원체
에 의한 전염병에 대항하여 몸을 방어하는 면역 체계를 가지고 있지만 때때로 이
면역 체계가 제대로 기능하지 못하기도 합니다. 예를 들면 암으로 방사선 치료를
받는 사람은 면역 체계가 약화되어 병원균에 더 쉽게 감염될 수 있죠. 다행히 여
러 병원균은 숙주 밖에서는 오랫동안 살아남을 수 없어 죽게 됩니다. 하지만 천
연두와 같은 몇몇 병원균은 숙주 몸 밖에서도 몇 년 동안 살아남을 수 있습니다.

3 담화에 따르면, 병원균의 가장 큰 약점은 무엇인가?
(a) 사람을 병에 걸리게 한 다음에는 살아남을 수 없다.
(b) 장기 생존을 위해 숙주에 의존한다.
(c) 사람에게서 동물로 전염될 수 없다.
(d) 식수원과 음식원에서만 살아남을 수 있다.
(e) 많은 양의 방사선에 의해 파괴된다.

4 담화에서 유추할 수 있는 내용은?
(a) 바이러스는 언급된 병원균 중에서 가장 치명적인 형태이다.
(b) 많은 암 환자들이 방사선 치료 후에 감염이 된다.
(c) 박쥐는 여러 질병에 매우 강한 면역성을 가지고 있다.
(d) 천연두 바이러스는 오랫동안 생존하기 위해 살아 있는 숙주가 필요하다.
(e) 프라이온은 다른 형태의 병원균보다 더 많은 질병을 일으킨다.

5-6   Level up

B   What's the matter? You <u>seem restless</u> and <u>on edge</u> lately.

G   There just never seems to be <u>enough time to do</u> all of the things I have to do. I <u>feel overwhelmed</u>.

B   I think you <u>have too much stress</u> in your life. You <u>need to relax</u> more.

G   I wish I knew how. I've <u>got to prepare</u> for the <u>college entrance exam</u>, I have two projects and two papers <u>due</u> in the next month, I'm <u>on the volleyball</u> team, and I'm involved in student government.

B   Maybe you could <u>drop something</u> to <u>make things easier</u> on yourself.

G   No, I am <u>too deeply involved</u> in everything. I can't <u>give anything up</u>. Not now.

B   Then you need to <u>find a way to manage</u> your stress. Are you getting enough sleep?

G   About six hours a night.

B   That's not enough. You need <u>at least eight hours</u> of good sleep.

G   I'll try. What else can I do?

B   <u>Take a hot shower</u> in the evening. <u>Even better</u> would be a bath. Don't drink coffee or <u>anything with caffeine</u> in it. And <u>deal with</u> these projects ASAP. Get one of them <u>done this week</u>. And do a little bit on the others each day. By <u>taking care of</u> these problems, then you will <u>have less</u> stress.

G   Got it.

B   And there's one more thing. Don't try to do so much at the same time. <u>Give yourself a break</u>.

G   I <u>find it hard</u> to say no to people when they ask me to do stuff.

B   <u>You'd better learn</u> how to say no, or all of this stress is going to make your head <u>explode</u> some day.

▶ restless 불안한; 침착하지 못한   on edge 불안하여, 초조하여   overwhelm 압도하다,
질리게 하다; 당황하게 하다   relax 정신적 긴장을 풀다   due 지불 기일이 된, 당연히
치러야 할   student government 학생회, 학생 자치회   manage 잘 다루다; 잘 해
가다   at least 적어도   at the same time 동시에   stuff 일; 물건

남   무슨 일 있니? 너 요즘 불안하고 초조해 보여.
여   해야 할 일은 많은데 시간이 너무 없어. 무얼 어떻게 해야 할지 모르겠어.
남   네가 스트레스를 너무 많이 받고 있는 것 같구나. 긴장을 좀 풀어야겠다.

여 그럴 방법을 알면 좋겠어. 난 대학입시를 준비해야 하고 다음 달까지 내야 할 프로젝트와 리포트가 각각 두 개씩 있어. 게다가 난 배구팀이고 학생회 소속이기도 해.

남 좀 편해지려면 그 중 어떤 일은 그만두어야겠네.

여 안 돼, 난 그 일들 모두에 아주 깊이 관여하고 있다고. 그 어떤 것도 포기할 수 없어. 지금은 안 돼.

남 그렇다면 네 스트레스를 관리할 방법을 찾아야 해. 잠은 잘 자고 있니?

여 밤에 한 6시간 정도.

남 그 정도로는 충분치 않아. 적어도 8시간의 숙면이 필요해.

여 노력해 볼게. 그 외에 뭘 해야 할까?

남 저녁에 뜨거운 물로 샤워를 하도록 해. 목욕이라면 훨씬 좋겠지. 커피나 카페인이 들어 있는 것들은 마시지 마. 그리고 그 프로젝트들을 되도록 빨리 끝내도록 해. 그 중 한 개는 이번 주에 끝내도록 하고. 다른 것들도 매일 조금씩 해. 이 문제들을 처리하면 스트레스를 덜 받게 될 거야.

여 알았어.

남 그리고 하나 더. 동시에 너무 많은 일을 하려고 하지 마. 쉴 틈을 좀 가져.

여 사람들이 나에게 일을 부탁할 때 안 된다고 말하기가 힘들어.

남 넌 거절하는 법을 배워야 해. 그렇지 않으면 이 모든 스트레스로 언젠가는 네 머리가 폭발할 거라고.

5 왜 소녀는 하고 있는 일들을 하나도 포기하지 않으려 하는가?
  (a) 하고 있는 모든 일을 너무 좋아해서 그만두고 싶어하지 않는다.
  (b) 하고 있는 모든 일을 싫어하지만 그만둘 방법을 찾지 못했다.
  (c) 어떤 일들은 해야 하는 것들이고 그 외의 것들은 좋아하는 취미이다.
  (d) 사람들에게 거절하는 게 힘들어서 그만두지 않는 편이 더 쉽다.
  (e) 자신이 지금 모든 것에 너무 깊이 관여하고 있어서 그만둘 수 없다고 생각한다.

6 다음 중 내용을 가장 잘 요약한 것을 고르시오.
  (a) 소년은 소녀에게 스트레스를 줄이는 가장 좋은 방법은 매일 학교 프로젝트를 맨 먼저 하는 거라고 말한다.
  (b) 소년은 소녀에게 현재 받고 있는 스트레스를 줄이기 위해 더 빨리 일하라고 충고한다.
  (c) 소년은 소녀에게 스트레스 줄이는 요령을 알려주고, 일을 덜하고 사람들에게 좀 더 자주 거절하라고 충고한다.

W <u>Welcome</u> <u>to</u> the Silver Sun Health Club, Mr. Watson.

M Hi. It's <u>my</u> <u>first</u> <u>time</u> in a health club, and I really <u>have</u> <u>no</u> <u>idea</u> where to start. What kind of <u>exercise</u> <u>do</u> <u>you</u> <u>recommend</u> I do?

W You should do a <u>combination</u> of <u>stretching</u>, <u>aerobic</u>, and anaerobic exercises.

M Sorry, but could you <u>explain</u> <u>further</u>?

W There are two <u>main</u> <u>types</u> of exercise: aerobic and anaerobic. Aerobic exercise <u>benefits</u> your <u>heart</u> <u>and</u> <u>lungs</u> and increases your <u>endurance</u>. It's a lower-intensity exercise that is done for a long time.

M Ah, like when you <u>run</u> or <u>play</u> <u>sports</u>? That kind of thing?

W Yes, running is <u>one</u> <u>of</u> the main <u>aerobic</u> exercises. Now, anaerobic exercise is for <u>strength</u> <u>and</u> <u>conditioning</u>. It's an <u>intense</u> <u>activity</u> that is done for shorter periods. <u>Weight</u> <u>training</u> is the <u>main</u> <u>form</u> of anaerobic exercise. You <u>train</u> and <u>condition</u> <u>individual</u> <u>muscles</u> by doing different exercises. <u>Resistance</u> <u>to</u> the weights helps <u>build</u> <u>up</u> <u>muscle</u> <u>mass</u>.

M What is the <u>main</u> <u>benefit</u> of muscle mass?

W First, it makes your body <u>look</u> <u>better</u>. But, most importantly, increased muscle mass <u>improves</u> your body's <u>ability</u> <u>to</u> <u>burn</u> fat and to maintain a healthy body.

▶ aerobic 유산소의   anaerobic 무산소의   a combination of ~의 배합
benefit ~에게 이롭다   endurance 지구력; 인내   intensity 강도, 세기
conditioning (심신의) 조절; 컨디션 조절   intense 격렬한, 심한
resistance 저항(력)   mass 크기, 양, 부피   most importantly 가장 중요한 것은

여 실버 선 헬스클럽에 오신 것을 환영합니다, 왓슨 씨.

남 안녕하세요. 헬스클럽에 처음 온 거라 어디서부터 시작해야 할지 정말 모르겠네요. 저한테 추천할 만한 운동이 있나요?

여 회원님은 스트레칭, 유산소, 무산소 운동을 병행하셔야 합니다.

남 미안하지만 더 자세히 설명해 주시겠어요?

여 운동에는 두 가지 주요 유형이 있는데요. 바로 유산소와 무산소죠. 유산소 운동은 심장, 폐에 좋고 지구력을 늘려 줍니다. 오랜 시간 동안 하는, 강도가 더 낮은 운동이고요.

남 아, 뛰거나 스포츠를 할 때처럼 말이죠? 그런 것들 말인가요?

여 예, 달리기는 주요 유산소 운동 중 하나입니다. 자, 무산소 운동은 힘과 조절을 위한 운동입니다. 짧은 시간 동안 하는 격렬한 운동이죠. 웨이트 트레이닝은 무산소 운동의 주 형태입니다. 여러 가지 운동을 함으로써 각각의 근육을 훈련시키고 조절하게 되죠. 무게에 대한 저항은 근육을 늘려 주는 데 도움이 되고요.

남 근육의 주요 이점은 무엇인가요?

여 우선, 근육은 몸을 더 멋져 보이게 합니다. 하지만, 가장 중요한 것은 근육이 많아지면 지방을 연소시키고 건강한 몸을 유지하게 해서 신체능력을 향상시켜 준다는 것이죠.

7 What is the difference between aerobic and anaerobic exercise? 유산소 운동과 무산소 운동의 차이점은 무엇인가?
  (a) Aerobic exercise is for endurance, and anaerobic exercise is for stretching. 유산소 운동은 지구력을 위한 것이고 무산소 운동은 스트레칭을 위한 것이다.
  (b) Anaerobic exercise builds muscles while aerobic exercise builds endurance. 유산소 운동은 지구력을 키워 주는 반면 무산소 운동은 근육을 키워 준다.
  (c) Aerobic exercise reduces weight, but anaerobic exercise makes the body gain weight. 유산소 운동은 체중을 줄여 주지만 무산소 운동은 체중을 늘게 만든다.
  (d) Anaerobic exercise builds endurance, and aerobic exercise builds strength.
    무산소 운동은 지구력을 키워 주고 유산소 운동은 힘을 키워 준다.
  (e) Aerobic exercise is for stretching while anaerobic exercise builds muscles. 무산소 운동은 근육을 키워 주는 반면 유산소 운동은 스트레칭을 위한 것이다.

W Since <u>ancient</u> <u>times</u>, it has been known that <u>certain</u> <u>foods</u> have the <u>ability</u> <u>to</u> <u>improve</u> the health of the human body while a <u>lack</u> <u>of</u> <u>those</u> <u>foods</u> can cause problems. It <u>wasn't</u> <u>until</u> the <u>early</u> <u>20th</u> <u>century</u> that <u>researchers</u> <u>discovered</u> that certain elements in food, which we <u>now</u> <u>call</u> <u>vitamins</u>, were the reason for this. There are two main types of vitamins: <u>water-soluble</u> and <u>fat-soluble</u> <u>vitamins</u>. Water-soluble vitamins are <u>absorbed</u> by the body <u>through</u> <u>water</u> and therefore <u>pass</u> <u>out</u> of the body <u>quite</u> <u>easily</u> <u>through</u> <u>urine</u>. These types of vitamins <u>include</u> vitamin B and C and <u>must</u> <u>be</u> <u>replaced</u> daily through food or <u>supplements</u>. The second type is fat-soluble vitamins. They are absorbed by <u>fat</u> <u>cells</u> in the <u>intestine</u>. As such, they can <u>be</u> <u>stored</u> in the body for a long time and do not need to <u>be</u> <u>replaced</u> on a <u>daily</u> <u>basis</u>. This group includes vitamin A, D, E, and K. Unfortunately, people sometimes <u>take</u> <u>too</u> <u>many</u> of these vitamins, so their bodies may have <u>negative reactions</u>, such as <u>heart</u> <u>problems</u>.

▶ soluble 녹는, 용해할 수 있는 absorb 흡수하다 replace 대체하다, 바꾸다 supplement 보조제 urine 소변 on a daily basis 매일 negative reaction 부정적인 반응

여 고대부터 특정 식품이 인간의 건강을 향상시켜 주는 한편 이 식품이 부족하면 병이 생긴다고 알려져 왔습니다. 20세기 초가 되어서야 학자들은 지금 비타민이라고 불리는 식품의 특정요소가 바로 그 원인임을 발견했습니다. 비타민에는 크게 2가지 종류가 있습니다. 수용성 비타민과 지용성 비타민이죠. 수용성 비타민은 물을 통해 몸에 흡수되기 때문에 소변을 통해 매우 쉽게 몸 밖으로 나가버립니다. 이러한 유형의 비타민에는 비타민 B와 C가 있으며 음식이나 보조제를 통해 매일 섭취해야 하죠. 두 번째 유형은 지용성 비타민입니다. 지용성 비타민은 창자에 있는 지방 세포에 의해 흡수됩니다. 그렇기 때문에 지용성 비타민은 오랫동안 몸에 축적될 수 있어 매일 섭취할 필요는 없죠. 여기에는 비타민 A, D, E, K가 있습니다. 안타깝게도 이러한 비타민을 너무 많이 섭취하여 몸에서 심장병 같은 부정적인 반응을 나타내는 경우도 있습니다.

8 What is the main purpose of the talk?
담화의 목적은 무엇인가?

(a) To describe the differences in two main types of vitamins
비타민의 두 가지 종류의 차이점을 설명하려고

(b) To examine the health benefits of two types of vitamins
두 가지 종류의 비타민의 건강상 이점을 조사하려고

(c) To discuss the historical research done on vitamins
비타민에 대한 역사적인 연구에 대해 논하려고

(d) To analyze why vitamins can cause negative reactions
왜 비타민이 역효과를 일으키는지 분석하려고

(e) To show that not all vitamins react in the same way
모든 비타민이 같은 방식으로 반응하는 것은 아님을 보여 주려고

9

M The <u>life</u> <u>expectancy</u> of Koreans is <u>73</u> <u>years</u> <u>for</u> <u>males</u> and 80 years for females. <u>Approximately</u> 275,000 people die in Korea each year. In 2008, the leading <u>causes</u> of death were <u>cancer</u>, followed by cerebrovascular disease and <u>heart</u> <u>disease</u>. The leading <u>types</u> of <u>cancer</u> in Korea are those that <u>affect</u> <u>the</u> <u>respiratory</u> <u>system</u>, the stomach, and the <u>liver</u>. Cerebrovascular diseases are those <u>related</u> <u>to</u> <u>the</u> <u>blood</u> <u>vessels</u> that <u>supply</u> <u>blood</u> to the brain. Sometimes, there is <u>blockade</u> of these blood vessels. This is called a <u>stroke</u>, and it can lead to death or <u>disability</u>. Deaths for heart diseases can be <u>broken</u> <u>down</u> into two types: <u>cardiovascular</u> <u>problems</u> and ischaemic heart problems. Cardiovascular problems are related to the <u>blockage of blood vessels</u> while ischaemic heart problems <u>result</u> <u>in</u> <u>less</u> <u>blood</u> <u>flowing</u> in and out of the heart. <u>Undoubtedly</u>, some of these health problems are <u>closely</u> <u>associated</u> <u>with</u> the lifestyles of Koreans. In particular, high stress <u>from</u> <u>work</u> and <u>family</u> <u>pressures</u> <u>contributes</u> <u>to</u> cerebrovascular and heart disease. Cancer of the lungs and other parts of the <u>respiratory</u> <u>system</u> is a result of the <u>high</u> <u>incidence</u> <u>of</u> <u>smoking</u> while liver problems are <u>linked</u> <u>with</u> the

<u>overconsumption</u> of alcohol. Finally, the high incidence of stomach cancer may or may not be the <u>result</u> <u>of</u> the <u>spicy</u> <u>diet</u> Koreans enjoy. While some studies <u>suggest</u> that the overconsumption of <u>red</u> <u>peppers</u>, in particular spicy kimchi, is the <u>cause</u> <u>of</u> <u>stomach</u> <u>cancer</u>, other studies suggest kimchi has <u>medicinal</u> <u>benefits</u>.

▶ life expectancy 평균 수명 leading cause 주요 원인 followed by 뒤이어, 잇달아 cerebrovascular disease 뇌혈관 질환 affect 작용하다: 침범하다 respiratory system 호흡기 liver 간 blood vessel 혈관 blockade 봉쇄, 폐쇄 stroke 뇌졸중 disability 장애 ischaemic heart problem 허혈성 심장 문제 be associated with ~와 관련되다; ~이 연상되다 contribute to ~의 원인이 되다 incidence 빈도, 발생률 be linked with ~와 연결되다 overconsumption 과소비 spicy diet 매운 음식

남 한국인의 평균 수명은 남성은 73세이고 여성은 80세입니다. 대략 27만 5천 명이 매년 한국에서 사망하죠. 2008년에는 사망의 주요 원인이 암이었고 그 다음이 뇌혈관 질환과 심장 질환이었습니다. 한국에서 주요 암의 종류는 호흡기, 위, 간에 침범하는 것들이었습니다. 뇌혈관 질환은 혈액을 뇌에 공급하는 혈관과 관련된 것입니다. 때때로 이 혈관들이 막히기도 하죠. 이것을 뇌졸중이라고 하며 이로 인해 죽음이나 장애에 이를 수 있습니다. 심장 질환에 의한 죽음은 뇌혈관 문제로 인한 것과 허혈성 심장병으로 인한 것, 이렇게 두 가지 유형으로 나뉠 수 있습니다. 뇌혈관 문제는 혈관 막힘과 관련이 있는 반면, 허혈성 심장병은 심장 안팎으로 혈액이 덜 순환하여 일어나는 것입니다. 의심할 여지없이, 이 심장병 중 일부는 한국인들의 생활양식과 밀접한 관련이 있습니다. 특히 직장에서의 많은 스트레스와 가족의 압력이 뇌혈관 질환과 심장 질환의 원인이 되죠. 폐와 기타 호흡기의 암은 잦은 흡연의 결과이며 간 문제는 과음과 연결되어 있습니다. 마지막으로 위암이 많이 발병하는 것은 한국인들이 즐기는 매운 음식이 원인일 수도, 아닐 수도 있습니다. 어떤 연구에서는 빨간 고추의 과용, 특히 매운 김치는 위암의 원인이 된다고 하는 반면, 다른 연구들은 김치에 약효가 있다고 합니다.

9 담화에 따르면 다음 중 사실이 <u>아닌</u> 것은?

(a) 한국 여성들은 남자들보다 평균 수명이 더 길다.
(b) 뇌졸중은 매우 스트레스가 많은 생활양식에서 기인할 수 있다.
(c) 심장질환은 현재 한국에서 주요 사망 원인이다.
(d) 김치가 위암을 일으키는지 아닌지는 불분명하다.
(e) 간질환은 음주와 직접적으로 관련이 있다.

10

W James, that's the <u>fifth</u> <u>time</u> this month you have <u>fallen</u> <u>asleep</u> in my class. I want to know <u>what's</u> <u>going</u> <u>on</u> in your life that is <u>making</u> <u>you</u> <u>so</u> <u>tired</u>.

B I'm sorry, Ms. Roberts, but your class <u>starts</u> <u>at</u> 8:30 AM. It's just <u>too</u> <u>early</u> for me.

W What time do you go to sleep?

B About 1 or 2 AM. I know I should <u>go</u> <u>to</u> <u>bed</u> <u>earlier</u>. I tried that, but I <u>can't</u> <u>fall</u> <u>asleep</u> before then.

W Well, it's not really <u>your</u> <u>fault</u>. It's the <u>circadian</u> <u>rhythms</u> of teenagers.

B The what?

W Circadian rhythms. They are what <u>regulate</u> your body's <u>sleeping</u> <u>patterns</u>. For example, <u>adults</u> <u>sleep</u> seven or eight hours a night. They usually go to bed <u>between</u> 10 PM and midnight <u>while</u> <u>babies</u> will sleep from <u>14</u> <u>to</u> <u>18</u> hours a day at any time of the day or night. <u>As</u> <u>we</u> <u>get</u> <u>older</u>, the need for sleep <u>lessens</u>, and the time we sleep changes. Children over five can sleep eight to ten hours and usually go to bed between 8 and 10 PM.

B　What about teenagers?

W　Teenagers sleep eight to ten hours a day also, but many sleep less than seven hours. Their circadian rhythms make them more alert in the late evening than in the morning. Teens tend to go to sleep between 10 PM and midnight. However, many teens stay up later because of schoolwork or Internet usage, or they watch TV or movies.

B　That's about right. Then we have to get up and take these early classes.

W　You are just sleep-deprived. Your body needs more sleep than you are getting. At least try to go to bed before midnight.

B　I'll give it my best shot.

▶ circadian rhythms 24시간 주기 리듬 regulate 조절(조정)하다 lessen 줄어들다
alert 눈을 부릅뜬; 기민한, 민활한 tend to ~하는 경향이 있다
sleep-deprived 수면 부족인

여　제임스, 내 수업시간에 존 게 이번 달만 벌써 다섯 번째야. 네 생활이 어떻기에 그렇게 피곤해하는지 알고 싶구나.

남　죄송해요, 로버츠 선생님. 하지만 선생님 수업은 아침 8시 30분에 시작되잖아요. 그건 저한테 너무 이르다고요.

여　몇 시에 자니?

남　한 새벽 1, 2시쯤이요. 더 일찍 자야 된다는 건 알아요. 노력해 봤지만 그 전엔 잠이 안 와요.

여　음, 네 잘못은 아니야. 십대의 24시간 주기 리듬 때문이지.

남　뭐라고 하셨어요?

여　24시간 주기 리듬 말이야. 그건 네 신체의 수면 패턴을 조절한단다. 예를 들면, 성인들은 밤에 7, 8시간을 자지. 성인들은 대개 밤 10시에서 자정 사이에 잠자리에 들지. 반면에 아기들은 낮밤 상관없이 언제든 하루에 14시간에서 18시간을 자고. 나이가 들면서 수면의 필요성이 줄어들고 잠자는 시간이 바뀌게 돼. 5세 이상의 아이들은 8시간에서 10시간을 자는데 대개 저녁 8시에서 10시 사이에 자게 되지.

남　십대들은요?

여　십대들도 8시간에서 10시간을 자지만 많은 십대들이 7시간을 못 자지. 24시간 주기 리듬이 아침보다는 늦은 저녁에 십대들을 더 활발하게 만든다. 십대들은 저녁 10시에서 자정 사이에 자는 편이야. 하지만 많은 십대들이 학업이나 인터넷 때문에 더 늦게까지 깨어있다. TV나 영화를 보기도 하고.

남　맞아요. 그러고 나서 우리는 일찍 일어나서 이렇게 이른 수업을 들어야 하잖아요.

여　넌 수면 부족일 뿐이야. 네 몸은 네가 자는 시간보다 더 많은 잠이 필요해. 적어도 자정 전에는 자도록 해봐.

남　최선을 다해 볼게요.

10 여러 나이집단의 수면 습관에 대한 자료를 완성하시오.

나이집단	하루 평균 수면시간	잠드는 시간
아기들	14-18 hours (14~18 시간)	언제든지
어린이들	8-10 hours (8~10 시간)	8-10 PM (저녁 8~10시)
십대들	8~10시간	10 PM to midnight (저녁 10시~ 자정)
성인들	7-8 hours (7~8 시간)	10 PM to midnight (저녁 10시~ 자정)

11-12　Level up

W　There is a rare but terrible genetically inherited disease, called ALD, which afflicts young boys. ALD symptoms usually occur when the boy is between four and ten years of age, and the patient dies about one to two years later. The disease destroys myelin, which is the protective covering on nerves, and this destruction prevents the nerves from sending signals to parts of the body. The body gradually shuts down, and the child loses the ability to walk, speak, see, and talk until death occurs. There was no known treatment until an American couple found one for their ailing son in the 1980s. In 1984, five-year-old Lorenzo Odone was diagnosed with ALD, and his parents searched for a cure. Eventually, they came up with a mixture of different oils found in certain foods, which they named Lorenzo's Oil. The oil slowed Lorenzo Odone's disease until he died in 2008 at the age of 30. Other sufferers of ALD have had similar results, with some slowing and stopping the progression of the destruction of the myelin nerve coverings. However, the oil is not a cure but rather a treatment that prevents the myelin covers from being destroyed. It is unknown if the oil prevents the outbreak of ALD. Currently, boys who test for the genetic problem causing ALD take the oil before there are signs of the disease. However, not all boys with the genetic problem develop ALD. Therefore, if boys who are put on Lorenzo's Oil don't get the disease, it is not certain if it was the oil that prevented the disease from occurring. In spite of that, for those parents whose sons have the genetic mutation and have not been afflicted yet, Lorenzo's Oil is a miracle cure.

▶ genetically inherited disease 유전병 afflict 괴롭히다 myelin 미엘린 (수초를 이루는 물질) protective covering 보호 덮개 shut down 닫다, 내리다
treatment 치료제 ailing 병든 be diagnosed with ~로 진단받다
come up with 찾아내다 mixture 혼합물 sufferer 환자 sign 징후, 전조, 조짐
mutation 돌연변이

여　희귀하지만 지독한 유전병으로 ALD라는 것이 있는데요, ALD는 어린 소년들을 괴롭히죠. ALD 증상은 대개 4세에서 10세 사이에 나타나며 환자는 약 1년에서 2년 후에 사망하게 됩니다. ALD는 신경을 보호하는 덮개인 미엘린을 파괴하여 신경이 신체 부위에 신호를 보내는 것을 막습니다. 신체는 점차 기능을 상실하고, 아이는 걷고 말하고 보고 이야기하는 능력을 잃고 사망하게 됩니다. 1980년대에 한 미국인 부부가 병든 아들을 위해 치료제를 발견하기 전까지는 알려진 치료제가 없었죠. 1984년에 다섯 살의 로렌조 오돈은 ALD 진단을 받았고 그 부모는 치료법을 찾기 시작했습니다. 마침내 그들은 특정 식품들에서 나오는 여러 기름의 혼합물을 발견해냈고 그것을 로렌조 오일이라고 이름지었죠. 그 기름은 로렌조 오돈이 2008년 30세의 나이로 세상을 떠날 때까지 병의 진행을 늦추었습니다. 다른 ALD 환자들도 미엘린 신경 덮개 파괴의 진행이 늦춰지거나 멈추는 비슷한 결과를 얻었습니다. 하지만, 그 기름은 치유법은 아니고 미엘린 덮개가 파괴되는 것을 막는 치료제에 가깝습니다. 그 기름이 ALD 발병을 막는지는 알려지지 않았죠. 현재 ALD를 일으키는 유전적 문제로 검사를 받은 소년은 병의 기미가 있기 전에 그 기름을 섭취합니다. 하지만 유전적 문제가 있는 모든 소년들이 ALD에 걸리는 것은 아닙니다. 따라서 로렌조 오일을 복용한 소년들이 병에 걸리지 않는다고 해서 그 기름이 병의 발생을 막은 건지 아닌지는 확실하지 않습니다. 그럼에도 불구하고 유전적 돌연변이를 가지고 있지만 아직 병으로 고통 받지 않은 아들을 가진 부모에게는 로렌조 오일은 기적의 치료법입니다.

11 강의에서 유추할 수 있는 것은?

(a) 오돈 가족은 로렌조 오일을 제조할 수 있는 오일을 발견하기 위해 많은 돈을 썼다.

(b) ALD가 보통 소년들에게 발병되지만 소녀들이 ALD에 걸리는 사례들도 있었다.

(c) 특정 식품의 기름 부족은 ALD로 인해 미엘린 신경 덮개가 파괴되는 데 일조할 수 있다.

(d) 소년이 ALD를 일으키는 유전적 돌연변이를 가지고 있는지 알아낼

방법이 아직 없다.

(e) 오돈 가족은 로렌조 오일에 대한 특허권을 가지고 있어 상당한 보상을 받았다.

12 다음 중 내용을 가장 잘 요약한 것을 고르시오.

(a) 치명적인 질병인 ALD는 로렌조 오돈의 이름을 딴 기름을 만든 그 부모의 노력으로 대부분 치료가 되었다.

(b) 로렌조 오일은 ALD의 치유법은 아니고 실제 효과가 확실하지 않은 치료제이다. 왜냐하면 그 기름을 먹은 모든 소년들이 병의 징후를 가지고 있는 것은 아니기 때문이다.

(c) 로렌조 오돈의 부모가 1980년대에 치료제를 발견하기까지 유전병인 ALD는 로렌조 오돈과 다른 소년들에게는 사형선고였다.

Practice Test
p. 170~p. 171

1 (d)　**2** (b)　**3** (e)　**4** (c)　**5** (e)　**6** (b)　**7** (a)
8 해설 참조　**9** (d)　**10** (b)

1

M　The health risks of smoking, including the effects of secondhand smoke, have long been known. But a new term is now coming into use: third-hand smoke. What is third-hand smoke? It is the remains, or residue, of the use of tobacco products that stay on the surface of walls, furniture, cupboards, and just about any other indoor surface. It also remains in your clothing. Have you ever been around a smoker, and then, later on, your clothes smelled like cigarette smoke? That's third-hand smoke. The reason this is becoming an issue now is that health concerns over third-hand smoke are growing. The human body can absorb the nicotine of smoking residue through the skin. This can be harmful for anyone, but it is especially a concern for infants and children. Many governments have banned smoking in public places like bars and restaurants. But many people still smoke at home. Even if these smokers sit near a window or go out to a balcony or front porch, the residue of the smoke remains on the surrounding surfaces. Not much can be done about a person's right to smoke in his or her home, but there needs to be more awareness of third-hand smoke, especially for smokers who have children.

▶ **come into use** 사용하게 되다　**remains** 나머지, 남은 것　**residue** 찌꺼기, 잔류물　**ban** 금지하다　**awareness** 자각, 인식

남　간접흡연의 영향을 포함하여 흡연의 건강상 위험은 오랫동안 알려져 왔습니다. 하지만 이제는 새로운 용어가 사용되기 시작하고 있습니다. 바로 3차 흡연이죠. 3차 흡연은 무엇일까요? 3차 흡연은 벽면, 가구, 찬장, 그리고 실내 표면에 남아 있는 담배 제품의 잔존물 또는 찌꺼기입니다. 그것은 옷에도 남습니다. 흡연자 주위에 있다가 나중에 옷에서 담배 냄새가 난 적이 있나요? 그것이 3차 흡연입니다. 이것이 지금 이슈가 되고 있는 이유는 3차 흡연에 대한 건강상 우려가 커지고 있기 때문입니다. 인간의 몸은 피부를 통해 흡연 잔류물의 니코틴을 흡수할 수 있습니다. 이것은 누구에게든 해로울 수 있지만 특히 갓난아기와 어린이들이 걱정이죠. 여러 정부에서 술집과 레스토랑과 같은 공공장소에서의 흡연을 금지했습니다. 하지만 많은 사람들은 여전히 집에서 담배를 피웁니다. 이 흡연자들이 창문 가까이에 앉거나 발코니나 현관으로 나간다 할지라도 흡연 잔류물은 주위 표면에 남아 있습니다. 자기 집에서 흡연하는 사람의 권리에 대해서까지 뭐라 할 수는 없지만 특히 자녀가 있는 흡연자들은 3차 흡연에 대해 더 많이 자각해야 합니다.

1 왜 3차 흡연이 건강상 문제로 여겨지는가?

(a) 사람들의 옷에 남아 피부 트러블을 일으킬 수 있다.

(b) 사람들이 흡연하는 집에 갓난아기들과 어린이들이 산다.

(c) 담배 연기를 들이마시는 비흡연자들의 건강에 해를 끼친다.

(d) 담배 제품에서 나오는 잔류물은 피부를 통해 흡수될 수 있다.

(e) 실내에서 흡연을 하는 사람들의 건강에 부정적인 영향을 미친다.

2-3

M　Hello, Candice. How are you today?

G　Nervous. I don't like coming to the dentist's.

M　Well, don't worry. Today, I am just doing a checkup. First, I'd like to ask you some questions about your dental health care habits, okay?

G　Sure, fire away.

M　Good. Now, how often do you brush your teeth?

G　Ah, let's see, in the morning before school and before I go to bed. Oh, and usually after dinner, but sometimes I forget.

M　So, I would say three times a day. That's good, but you should also brush after lunch. Brushing after each meal is important because it removes residual food particles from your teeth.

G　I know, but no one brushes after lunch at school.

M　It's a problem for many teenagers. Now, do you also floss your teeth?

G　Ah, not really. Should I?

M　Yes, flossing between the teeth is important to remove any difficult-to-reach food particles. Also, after some time, there can be a buildup of food that contributes to tooth decay. Now, what about your diet? Do you eat a lot of chocolate and candy and drink soda?

G　Sure. Everyone my age does. It's no big deal.

M　It is for your teeth. These foods are high in sugar content, which is the biggest destroyer of teeth. I think you need to consider replacing these foods with more fruit and drink less or no soda.

G　Okay, I'll try. So is that it? Can I go?

M　_______________________________________

▶ **fire away** (질문·일 등을) 서슴없이 시작하다　**residual** 남은: 잔여의　**floss** 치실로 치간을 청소하다; 치실　**food particle** 음식물 찌꺼기　**buildup** 축적　**sugar content** 당도

남　안녕, 캔디스. 오늘 기분이 어떠니?

여　긴장돼요. 전 치과 오는 거 싫어요.

남　음, 걱정 마라. 오늘은 검진을 하는 것뿐이니까. 우선, 네 치아건강 습관에 대해 좀 물어볼게, 알겠지?

여　네, 그러세요.

남　좋아. 자, 얼마나 자주 이를 닦니?

여　음, 보자, 아침, 등교 전, 잠자기 전에요. 오, 그리고 보통 저녁식사 후에요. 하지만 어떤 때는 이 닦는 것을 잊어 버려요.

남　그럼, 하루에 3번이라고 해도 되겠네. 그건 좋다만 점심식사 후에도 이를 닦아야 해. 이에서 음식물 찌꺼기를 제거해야 하기 때문에 매 식사 후에 이를 닦는 것이 중요해.

여　알지만 학교에서 점심 먹고 이를 닦는 애들은 아무도 없어요.

남　그게 많은 십대들의 문제지. 음, 치실도 사용하니?

여　음, 아니오. 해야 하나요?

남 그럼, 치아 사이를 치실로 청소하는 것은 칫솔이 닿기 힘든 곳에 있는 음식물 찌꺼기를 없애는 데 중요하지. 또, 시간이 지나면 음식 찌꺼기가 쌓여서 충치를 일으킬 수 있어. 자, 먹는 음식은 어때? 초콜릿과 사탕을 많이 먹고 청량음료도 마시니?

여 물론이죠. 우리 나이 또래들은 다 그래요. 별로 대수로운 일은 아닌걸요.

남 네 치아에는 대단한 일이지. 그런 음식들은 당도가 높잖아. 그건 치아의 가장 무서운 파괴자야. 이러한 음식들 대신 과일을 더 먹고, 청량음료를 거의 마시지 않거나 아예 안 마셔야 한단다.

여 좋아요, 노력해 볼게요. 다 끝난 건가요? 가도 돼요?

남 ____

2 대화에서 유추할 수 있는 것은?

(a) 치실로 청소하는 것은 어린이들이나 십대들에게는 그다지 필요하지 않다.

(b) 소녀의 학교에서는 점심식사 후에 이 닦기를 강요하지 않는다.

(c) 소녀의 부모님은 소녀의 치아 건강에 신경을 쓰지 않는다.

(d) 하루에 4번의 이 닦기는 좋은 치아 위생을 보장한다.

(e) 대부분의 사람들은 치과에 갈 때 긴장한다.

3 치과의사는 다음에 소녀에게 무엇이라고 말하겠는가?

(a) 물론이지. 이 컵에 침을 뱉고나면 가도 돼.

(b) 아니, 이제 그 충치들을 뽑아야 해.

(c) 아직은 안 돼. 넌 솔직하지 않았어.

(d) 내가 너의 나쁜 습관을 네 부모님에게 말한 다음에.

(e) 아, 안 돼. 이제 입 안을 봐야지. 입 크게 벌려.

4-5

M Green tea is a very popular drink in East Asian countries, particularly Korea, China, and Japan. This is the rawest form of tea as the tea leaves undergo almost no processing. What is remarkable about green tea is that it may in fact have the ability to prevent cancer. Studies done in China and Japan with groups of people who consumed at least one cup of green tea a week over many years showed that these people had lower rates of cancer in their digestive tracts than those who did not consume green tea. Researchers have also done studies which show that women who consume green tea regularly have a smaller chance of getting breast cancer. Reduced blood pressure, lower cholesterol, and a reduced incidence of heart disease have also been associated with the regular drinking of green tea. Other studies have shown that green tea may alleviate symptoms from other such brain and nervous system disorders as Alzheimer's and Parkinson's disease. While these healthy benefits of green tea consumption have been proven in some clinical trials, as of yet, the medical community is not making claims for any miraculous properties for green tea. Researchers need to make further investigations into green tea before they have conclusive proof that green tea has healing powers.

▶ remarkable 주목할 만한; 뛰어난 the digestive tract 소화관 nervous system disorder 신경계 장애 clinical trial 임상 실험 as of yet 현재로서는, 지금까지 medical community 의료계 claim 주장, 단언 investigation 조사, 연구 conclusive proof 결정적인 증거, 확증 healing power 치유력

남 녹차는 동아시아 국가들, 특히 한국, 중국, 일본에서 매우 인기있는 음료입니다. 녹차는 찻잎이 거치는 처리과정이 거의 없기 때문에 가장 가공되지 않은 형태

의 차입니다. 녹차에 대해 주목할 만한 것은 실제로 녹차에 암을 예방하는 효능이 있다는 것이죠. 중국과 일본에서 수년간 일주일에 적어도 한 잔의 녹차를 마신 사람들과 함께 진행된 연구에서는 이들이 녹차를 마시지 않는 사람들보다 소화관 계통의 암 발생 비율이 낮다는 것이 밝혀졌습니다. 학자들은 또한 녹차를 정기적으로 마시는 여성들은 유방암에 걸릴 확률이 적다는 것을 보여주는 연구도 수행했습니다. 혈압이 낮아지고 콜레스테롤이 줄고 심장병 발병율이 줄어드는 것 또한 규칙적인 녹차 음용과 관련이 있죠. 다른 연구는 녹차가 알츠하이머와 파킨슨병과 같은 뇌 및 신경 질환 증상을 경감시킬 수도 있음을 보여줍니다. 녹차 섭취의 이러한 건강상 이점이 몇몇 임상 실험에서 증명되고 있는 반면, 의학계에서는 지금까지 녹차의 기적적인 특성에 대해 목소리를 내지 않습니다. 학자들은 녹차에 치유력이 있다는 결정적인 증거를 잡게 될 때까지 녹차에 대해 더 깊게 연구해야 합니다.

4 녹차와 관련되지 <u>않은</u> 건강 문제는?

(a) 파킨슨병과 알츠하이머병의 악영향 감소

(b) 여성 유방암 발병률의 감소

(c) 중국인과 일본인의 폐암 감소

(d) 혈압이 낮아지고 심장병 발병 확률이 감소

(e) 위암과 장암 발생률 감소

5 담화를 통해 추론할 수 있는 것은?

(a) 녹차는 매일 마셔야만 이롭다.

(b) 다른 형태의 차에도 녹차와 비슷한 건강상 이점이 있다.

(c) 녹차는 여러 종류의 암을 치료하는 데 이롭다.

(d) 녹차 소비는 아시아 밖에서도 일반적이다.

(e) 녹차의 건강상 이점에 대한 연구는 진행 중이다.

6   Level up

M So, doctor, what's the news?

W I'm afraid it's not good. You are at serious risk of contracting diabetes, Mr. Caldwell.

M Oh, what can I do about it?

W First, you need to start an exercise program. With your sedentary lifestyle, your weight is going to cause complications. You need to lose about ten kilograms.

M Okay, I'll do my best. What about my diet?

W Start by eating more fruits and vegetables, and cut down on anything with sugar in it. There are several types of diabetes and causes, but it is always associated with the body's problems with sugar levels.

M So no candies, chocolates, sugary cereals, or sugar in tea or coffee.

W That's a start. But be careful of foods with starch in them, such as pasta and bread. They also contribute to weight gain.

M Is there really a chance I could get diabetes?

W It's in your family, and, with your lifestyle, I'd say you are a prime candidate for it.

M I think I'll start exercising right now with a nice walk home.

▶ at risk of ~의 위험에 놓여있다 contract (병에) 걸리다 diabetes 당뇨병 sedentary 앉아 있는; 잘 앉는 complications 합병증; 귀찮은 문제 sugar level 혈당 수치 starch 전분, 녹말 prime 제1의, 주요한

남 자, 의사 선생님, 결과가 어떤가요?

여 별로 좋지 않습니다. 콜드웰 씨, 환자분은 당뇨병에 걸릴 위험이 매우 높습니다.

남 아, 제가 어떻게 해야 하죠?

여 우선, 운동 프로그램을 시작하셔야 합니다. 앉아서만 생활하는 습관에다가 체중 때문에 합병증이 생길 거예요. 한 10킬로그램은 감량하셔야 합니다.

남 알겠습니다, 최선을 다하죠. 식이요법은요?

여 과일과 채소를 더 많이 드시는 것부터 시작해서 설탕이 들어 있는 음식은 전부 줄이도록 하세요. 당뇨병의 원인과 유형은 여러 가지가 있지만 항상 혈당 수치로 인한 신체적 질환과 연관되어 있죠.

남 그럼 사탕, 초콜릿, 달콤한 시리얼이나, 차나 커피의 설탕은 안 되는군요.

여 거기서부터 시작하세요. 하지만 파스타나 빵과 같은 전분이 있는 음식도 조심하시고요. 그것도 체중 증가에 일조하거든요.

남 제가 당뇨병에 걸릴 가능성이 정말 있는 건가요?

여 가족력도 있으시고 생활방식도 그렇고, 최고 위험군에 속하신다고 할 수 있습니다.

남 집에 걸어가는 걸로 지금 당장 운동을 시작해야겠네요.

6 What is NOT true about diabetes according to the dialog?
대화에 따르면 다음 중 당뇨병에 대한 사실이 <u>아닌</u> 것은?

  (a) It is associated with a person's lifestyle.
  당뇨병은 생활양식과 관련이 있다.

  (b) It causes people to eat much and to gain weight.
  당뇨병으로 인해 더 많이 먹게 되고 체중이 늘게 된다.

  (c) It is preventable by exercise and a proper diet.
  당뇨병은 운동과 적절한 식이요법으로 예방할 수 있다.

  (d) It can be genetically inherited from one's parents.
  당뇨병은 부모로부터 유전될 수 있다.

  (e) It is related to the amount of sugar in the body.
  당뇨병은 체내 당의 양과 관련이 있다.

w The human eye is the only body part that stays the same size from birth to death. Unfortunately, the eye can suffer many other changes. As people grow older, they have vision problems, two of which are cataracts and glaucoma. Cataracts appear as whitish, cloudy spots on the lens of the eye. They can be slightly cloudy or completely opaque. They block light from reaching the eye, which results in complete vision loss. The most common treatment is the surgical removal of the lens to replace it with an artificial lens. Glaucoma is a disease of the optic nerve which connects the eye to the brain and is often the result of increased pressure inside the eye. There are several different types and various causes of glaucoma, but all can eventually lead to a partial loss of vision and even blindness. Glaucoma can come on suddenly and painfully, or it can come on slowly and painlessly, which makes it unknown to the person, who suffers from a progressive loss of vision that cannot be restored. However, there are some successful treatments, including both surgery and drugs.

▶ cataract 백내장 glaucoma 녹내장 lens 수정체 opaque 불투명한
surgical 수술상의; 외과적인 artificial 인공적인 progressive 점진적인; 진행성의

여 인간의 눈은 출생에서 사망까지 같은 크기를 유지하는 유일한 신체 부위입니다. 불행하게도 눈은 그 외의 많은 변화를 겪을 수 있습니다. 사람들은 나이가 들수록 시력에 문제가 생기게 되죠. 그 중 두 가지가 백내장과 녹내장입니다. 백내장은 눈의 수정체에 희끄무레하고 흐릿한 점처럼 나타납니다. 백내장은 약간 흐릿할 수도 있고 완전히 불투명할 수도 있지요. 백내장은 빛이 눈에 닿는 것을 막아 시력이 완전히 상실될 수 있죠. 가장 보편적인 치료법은 수술로 수정체를 제거하고 인공 수정체로 대체하는 것입니다. 녹내장은 눈에서 뇌로 연결되는 시신경에 발생하는 병으로, 종종 눈 안쪽의 안압이 증가되어 생깁니다. 녹내장에는 여러

종류와 원인이 있지만 모든 녹내장은 결국 시력의 일부 상실 내지는 실명까지 일으킵니다. 녹내장은 갑자기 고통스럽게 오거나 천천히 고통 없이 올 수도 있습니다. 천천히 고통 없이 오기 때문에 환자는 자신의 병을 인지하지 못하고, 점진적으로 시력을 잃어 회복할 수 없게 됩니다. 하지만 수술과 약물 두 가지를 포함하는 성공적인 치료법이 몇가지 있기도 합니다.

7 Which statement is true according to the talk?
담화에 따르면 다음 중 사실인 것은?

  (a) Glaucoma may remain undetected for a long time.
  녹내장은 오랫동안 발견이 되지 않을 수도 있다.

  (b) The human eye changes shape as the body grows.
  인간의 눈은 몸이 자라면서 모양도 변한다.

  (c) Cataracts hardly ever result in blindness.
  백내장은 거의 실명에 이르지 않는다.

  (d) Black spots on the eye are a sign of cataracts.
  눈에 있는 검은 점들은 백내장의 징조이다.

  (e) Glaucoma is related to a problem with the lens.
  녹내장은 수정체 문제와 관련이 있다.

w One of the deadliest diseases ever to affect humans is Ebola, which is named after the virus that causes the disease. Ebola was first detected in 1976 in a 44-year-old school teacher near the Ebola River in the Democratic Republic of the Congo in central Africa. The disease is classed as a hemorrhagic fever, so it is a disease that results in excessive bleeding. The cause of death from Ebola is often due to organ failure, shock, or uncontrolled bleeding from the internal organs and from the body's openings. There have been six severe outbreaks of Ebola in the Congo. In each case, the number of deaths exceeded 50 percent of those infected. In 1976, 318 people contracted the disease, and 280 victims died. The next outbreak occurred in 1994, when 29 of 49 victims died from the disease. A deadlier outbreak of Ebola occurred in 1995, when 315 people became ill, and 256 of them died as a result. The next year, the deadly virus struck again, and although it was less widespread, 68 of 93 sufferers died. For a few years, the virus claimed no human victims, but it once more reared its ugly head from 2001 to 2002. Out of the 122 people who contracted Ebola, 97 of them died. The most recent outbreak was in 2003. There was a death toll of 128 people out of 142 who contracted the disease, which was the highest percentage of deaths ever of those infected.

▶ be classed as ~으로 분류되다 hemorrhagic fever 출혈열 excessive 과도한
organ 장기 uncontrolled 억제되지 않은 internal 내부의 struck strike (병, 죽음이 갑자기 덮치다)의 과거형 death toll 사망자 수

여 인간에게 영향을 미친 가장 치명적이었던 질병 중 하나는 에볼라입니다. 에볼라는 질병을 일으키는 바이러스 이름을 따서 명명되었는데요. 에볼라는 1976년 중앙아프리카의 콩고 공화국에 있는 에볼라강 인근의 44세 학교 교사에게서 처음 발견되었죠. 에볼라는 출혈열로 분류됩니다. 따라서 에볼라는 과도한 출혈을 일으키는 질병이죠. 에볼라에 의한 사망 원인은 종종 장기 기능 부전, 쇼크, 또는 내부 장기와 몸에 있는 구멍에서 멈추어지지 않는 출혈 때문입니다. 콩고에는 심각한 에볼라 발병이 6차례 있었습니다. 각각의 경우 사망자 수가 감염자의 50%를 넘었죠. 1976년에는 318명이 에볼라에 걸렸고 280명의 희생자가 사망했습니다. 그 다음 발병은 1994년에 일어나 49명 가운데 29명이 숨졌습니다. 더 치

명적인 에볼라 발병은 1995년이었는데, 315명이 병에 걸리고 256명이 사망했습니다. 그 다음해에 그 치명적인 바이러스가 다시 덮쳤는데, 조금 덜 퍼지긴 했지만 환자 93명 중 68명이 목숨을 잃었습니다. 몇 년 동안 그 바이러스가 인명을 앗아가지는 않았지만 2001년부터 2002년까지 다시 기승을 부리기 시작했죠. 에볼라에 감염된 122명 가운데 97명이 사망했습니다. 가장 최근의 발병은 2003년에 있었습니다. 에볼라에 감염된 142명 중 128명의 사망자가 있었으니 감염자 사망률이 가장 높은 경우였습니다.

8 언급된 해에 에볼라에 걸린 사람들 중에 생존한 사람들의 숫자를 보여주는 그래프를 완성하시오.

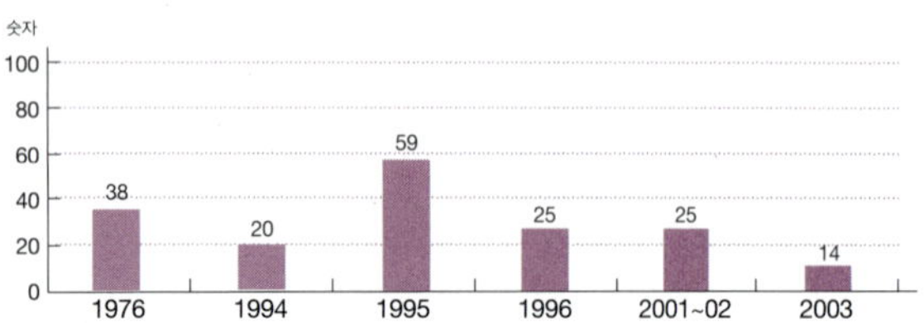

9-10 **Integrated Questions**

Reading

▶ pandemic 전국〔세계〕적 유행병 Black Death 흑사병, 페스트 catastrophic 파멸의; 큰 재앙의 bubonic plague 선(腺)페스트 originate 시작하다; 비롯하다 more recently 보다 최근에는 strike down 죽이다; (병이) 들다 army camp 군대 캠프 quarantine measures 검역 조치 rapid rate 급속도 justify 옳다고 하다; 정당화하다 in a short time 단시일에 visible 명백한, 보아 알 수 있는 swine 돼지 estimated 견적의, 추측의

세계적인 유행병이란 널리 퍼져서 매우 많은 사람들을 죽게 만드는 치명적인 질병이 발생하는 것을 가리킨다. 역사상 여러 건의 대형 유행병이 있었지만 흑사병만큼 비극적인 것은 없었다. 요즘은 선페스트라고 알려져 있는 흑사병은 아시아나 중동 어디에선가 처음 시작되었을 것이다. 이 역병은 1347년 유럽에 처음 나타났고, 6년 후 유럽에서는 3천만 명이 사망한 한편 다른 국가들에서는 그보다 더 많은 4천 5백만 명이 목숨을 잃었다. 보다 최근인 1918년부터 1920년 사이에 한 유형의 독감이 전 세계적으로 약 5천만 명을 공격했다. 이 질병은 미국이나 유럽의 군부대에서 시작되었을지도 모른다. 아마 돼지나 양 등의 동물들로부터 인간에게 전염된 것으로도 여겨진다. 이 질병으로 대부분 젊은 사람들이 죽었고 너무나 빠르게 퍼져서 방역 조치들은 거의 효과가 없었다. 요즘 시대에 이러한 세계적 유행병의 발병을 우려하는 것은 너무나 당연하다. 비행기로 여행을 하는 현대에는 질병이 짧은 시간 안에 전 세계에 퍼질 수 있다. 어떤 유행병들은 수년이 지난 후에야 유행병임이 드러날 수도 있는데, 아프리카에서 시작해 전 세계로 퍼져 1980년 이래로 약 2천 2백 만 명의 목숨을 앗아간 에이즈가 하나의 예다. 요즘 발발한 H1N1 신종플루가 1918년의 발병과 같은 수준에는 아직 이르지 않았지만 그 전염 경로를 막지 못한다면 쉽사리 그렇게 될 수 있을 것이다.

M The chances of a pandemic occurring in the future are just as strong as they were in the past, but certain measures have been taken to lessen the chance of a widespread, devastating pandemic like those which happened in the past. The Black Death of the 14th century took many years to reach some areas that became infected. This was partially the result of the slow methods of travel used in that period. But the Black Death spread and killed millions because of several other factors, including a lack of mass communication, a lack of quarantine procedures, and a lack of international organizations to help prevent the spread of disease. These factors also played a role in a more recent pandemic: the influenza outbreak of 1918 to 1920. It was a rapid-spreading disease that experts now estimate reached every part of the globe within about nine months and may have infected one

third of the world's population. This was due to the increased speed of travel, such as by coal and oil-fired steamships and by trains. As with the Black Death, there were few international measures taken to ensure that the disease did not spread. If such an outbreak occurred today, it may not spread as rapidly. Even though airline travel makes the speed of transmission faster, the world is more organized and prepared for such a pandemic. Airports and seaports around the world are on the lookout for infected passengers and use modern sophisticated cameras to gauge the body temperature of people as they arrive. If anyone displays an unusually high temperature, that person is immediately quarantined.

▶ devastating 파괴적인; 지독한 reach 퍼지다, 미치다 mass communication 대중 매체, 매스컴 play a role in ~의 역할을 하다 estimate 추정하다 oil-fired 기름〔석유〕을 연료로 쓰는 steamship (대형) 기선, 상선 as with ~와 마찬가지로 ensure 보증하다; 지키다 transmission 전염; 전달 organized 조직된; 계획된 seaport 항구 be on the lookout for 감시하다 sophisticated 정교한, 매우 복잡한 unusually 현저하게; 이상하게 quarantine 격리하다

남 앞으로 세계적인 유행병이 일어날 확률은 과거와 마찬가지로 높지만, 과거에 발생되었던 것처럼 널리 퍼지고 파괴적인 세계적 유행병이 발생할 가능성을 줄이기 위해 특정 조치가 취해져 왔습니다. 14세기의 흑사병은 감염 지역으로 퍼지는 데 수년이 걸렸죠. 이는 부분적으로는 그 시기에 여행 방식이 느렸기 때문입니다. 하지만 대중 매체 및 검역 절차의 결여, 병의 확산 방지를 돕는 국제기구의 부재를 포함한 다른 여러 요소 때문에 흑사병이 수백만 명에게 퍼져 목숨을 앗아갔습니다. 이러한 요소는 1918년에서 1920년 사이의 독감 발생과 같은 보다 최근의 세계적인 유행병에도 한몫을 했는데요. 그 독감은 빨리 퍼졌는데, 현재 전문가들은 약 9개월 안에 지구의 곳곳에 퍼져 세계 인구의 3분의 1이 감염되었을 것이라고 추정하고 있습니다. 이는 석탄과 석유를 연료로 쓰는 기선과 기차로 빨라진 여행 속도 때문이었죠. 흑사병 때처럼 병이 퍼지지 않도록 관리하는 국제적인 조치도 거의 없었습니다. 그런 병이 오늘날 발생한다면 그렇게 빨리 퍼지지는 못할 것입니다. 비행기 여행이 전염 속도를 더 빠르게 하지만 세계는 보다 조직화되어 그러한 세계적 유행병에 준비가 되어 있습니다. 전 세계의 공항과 항구는 전염된 여행객들에 대한 감시를 하고 있고 여행객이 도착하면 체온을 측정하기 위해 정교한 현대식 카메라를 사용합니다. 어떤 사람의 체온이 현저히 높게 나타나면 그 사람은 바로 격리되죠.

9 읽기와 듣기 지문에 따르면 다음 중 유행병에 대해 옳지 <u>않은</u> 것은?
 (a) 유행병은 빠르게 발생되거나, 세계적 유행병이 되는 데 시간이 오래 걸린다.
 (b) 유행병은 엄격한 검역 조치를 통해 통제될 수 있다.
 (c) 유행병은 국제 운송수단의 사용을 통해 퍼질 수 있다.
 (d) 유행병은 한 차례 발생되며 같은 장소에 다시 발생하지 않는다.
 (e) 유행병은 과거보다 현대에 더 잘 통제된다.

10 읽기 지문과 듣기에서 추론할 수 있는 것은?
 (a) 흑사병은 전 세계적으로 근절되었다.
 (b) 어떤 유행병은 오랜 잠복기간을 가진다.
 (c) 현재의 H1N1 플루는 1918년 독감과 비슷하다.
 (d) 모든 공항에는 체온 감지 카메라가 있다.
 (e) 1918년 세계 인구의 3분의 1이 독감으로 죽었다.

***Dictation 정답**: Exercise 스크립트 밑줄 참조

MEMO

MEMO

MEMO